This facsimile of the first edition
of "A History of the Pioneer
Families of Missouri" is reproduced from a copy obtained from
the original publisher.

The introduction and index prepared by W. W. Elwang and
published by Lucas Brothers,
Columbia, Missouri.

1935

HON. J. F. JONES
CALLAWAY CO.

MRS. SAM. MILLER

THE FIRST METHODIST
OF CALLAWAY CO.

MAJOR BAUGHMAN
THE
MONTGOMERY CO. HERMIT.

COL. NATHAN BOONE

DANIEL BOONE

Hon. IRVIN O. HOCKADAY
CALLAWAY CO.

LOUIS HOWELL.

FRANCIS SKINNER

MRS. REBECCA HEALD.

MRS. THOMAS HOWELL.

CHAS. JUEHNE.LITH. ST. LOUIS,

A HISTORY

OF THE

PIONEER FAMILIES

OF

MISSOURI,

WITH NUMEROUS SKETCHES, ANECDOTES, ADVENTURES, ETC., RELATING TO

EARLY DAYS IN MISSOURI.

ALSO THE LIVES OF

DANIEL BOONE

AND THE CELEBRATED INDIAN CHIEF

BLACK HAWK,

WITH NUMEROUS BIOGRAPHIES AND HISTORIES OF PRIMITIVE INSTITUTIONS.

BY WM. S. BRYAN AND ROBERT ROSE.

GENEALOGICAL PUBLISHING CO., INC.
Baltimore 1984

Originally published: St. Louis, 1876.
Facsimile edition, with added Introduction
and Index, published: Columbia, Missouri, 1935.
Reprinted by Genealogical Publishing Co., Inc.
Baltimore, 1977, 1984 (a reprint of the 1935 edition).
Library of Congress Catalogue Card Number 76-55479
International Standard Book Number 0-8063-0753-6
Made in the United States of America

PREFACE.

THIS book has been written in the midst of tribulation. When the authors began their work, two years ago, they had no adequate idea of the magnitude of the task which lay before them; but they know very well now: The histories of more than eight hundred pioneer families of the five counties embraced in this work are given, with the names of their children, and other matters of interest. We have endeavored to have every name and incident correct, but of course there are some errors. There are many obstacles in the way of obtaining information of this kind, members of the same family frequently giving entirely different accounts of important events in their history. Mr. Rose has personally visited one or more members of each family whose history is given, and from his notes thus obtained the histories have been written. Where differences occurred in the statements of different members of the same family, we have carefully compared them and endeavored to sift the facts from each; and we feel confident that this book is as near correct as it is possible for any work of the kind to be.

The delay in issuing the book has been unavoidable; first owing to the time spent in gathering the materials, and then to numerous unavoidable delays in the printing office. But the matter is just as fresh and entertaining as though it had been issued a year ago.

We do not expect the reader to believe all the remarkable yarns related under "Anecdotes and Adventures." Some of them were given to us merely as caricatures of early times, and they can easily be distinguished from the real adventures.

INDEX.

BY WAY OF INTRODUCTION

"I AM AFRAID our democracy is only skin deep," said a Federal judge from the bench not long ago as he sentenced a genealogical racketeer to a prolonged vacation behind the walls of a penitentiary. The evidence in the case has disclosed the interesting fact that the American people were fairly clamoring for family trees, coats-of-arms, and other heraldic devices, and to obtain them had paid this crook over $100,000 for genealogies and armorial designs that were nothing more than the ingenious fancies of an embezzler's brain. He had for some time received between 300 and 400 letters a day in response to his seductive advertisements.

* * * *

Now, the motives underlying this widespread desire for a long and worthy ancestry are, of course. quite varied. Too often it is the result of sheer vanity. But it is also true that an honest and wholesome, even though somewhat prideful. wish to treasure up the lineage and achievements of forebears is the basic motive of many of those who covet the distinction of belonging to old even though not distinguished families. With sincerity to serve this class is certainly a worthy purpose. Hence the re-issue. in this *de luxe* edition, of "Pioneer Families of Missouri." Copies of the original and only edition in 1876 have become very, very scarce, and correspondingly quite expensive, thus putting them entirely beyond the reach of most of those who might be interested in their contents.

* * * *

"Pioneer Families of Missouri" is a unique and invaluable work of its kind. Although three of the five "parts" into which it is divided are comparatively of little interest and less historical value, being composed almost entirely of matter quite extraneous to genealogy, parts I and III are a veritable treasure trove. This is true of Part I because it contains a "Life of Daniel Boone" with important authoritative genealogical and historical data about the Boone and Bryan families by an ardent admirer of the great frontiersman. But it is true pre-eminently of Part III which, within the compass of less than 275 pages, contains the more or less complete genealogical histories of more than 800

(v)

families, of the families which, in the five contiguous counties
of St. Charles, Montgomery, Warren, Audrain, and Callaway,
laid the foundations upon which Missouri, the mother-state of
the Great West, was builded.

*   *   *   *

Until quite recently the writer's interest in genealogical lore
was meager enough. A confirmed democrat and proletarian, I
have held to the conviction that what a man does here and now
is of more commanding importance than what his ancestors were
and did in the distant past, perhaps as "robber barons" on land
or "pirates bold" on the seven seas. I have never, therefore,
made any attempt to trace even my own ancestry, but chiefly,
perhaps, because I feared to stumble upon too many bars-sinister
to explain if not to excuse my own lack of achievement. However, when I became associated some years ago with the Missouri
Store Company, in Columbia, Missouri, as manager of its Fine
and Rare Book Department, my attention was quickly attracted
to an extensive and persistent demand from all over the country
for books of genealogy and, in Missouri, my native state, especially for copies of "Pioneer Families." And when in the
routine of business I sought to supply the demands of patrons
for this latter work, my surprise was great to learn that it was
an almost impossible task to find a single copy. The book was
a "rare" one indeed, and the price for the very few specimens
that came out of hiding from time to time was quite high. My
interest gradually increased and I began, almost sub-consciously,
to speculate about the origin of this mysterious book, about its
authors, where and when they were born, married, and when
they had died, as well as about what else they might have done
in the making of books or other things. When, at a later date,
the plans for this reproduction of the book in facsimile began to
take shape, it became imperative to translate this hitherto rather
vague interest into verifiable biographical and historical data.

*   *   *   *

Here again my astonishment was great. Like most of the
copies of their book, the authors themselves seemed to have
entirely disappeared from human ken. Those from whom information was sought, such as old newspaper men, county and
other historians, collectors of Missouriana, historical societies,
knew nothing about these men. But gradually by means of diligent correspondence, for much of which I am deeply indebted
to my good friend, Mr. Floyd C. Shoemaker, the able Secretary

of the State Historical Society, slight clues were picked up here and there and pieced together, until finally we were led to Nevada, Missouri, there to find, to our great astonishment and greater gratification, Mr. William S. Bryan himself, one of the co-authors of "Pioneers" and its financial sponsor and publisher. He is in his 89th year, but hale and hearty and still deeply immersed in literary labors. Our problem was solved!

* * * *

Mr. Bryan says that Robert Rose was responsible for the germinal idea of "Pioneer Families," but adds that the idea appealed to him also. Rose seems to have been a good-natured fellow with a roving disposition. He had a habit of riding about the countryside on horseback, with a pair of saddlebags as his only impedimenta, and subsisting mainly upon the generous hospitality of the people. During these perambulations he took great delight in quizzing as many persons as possible, particularly the "old timers," about their early days in Missouri, their ancestry, and the customs and adventures of those rugged and often dangerous days. The gleanings from these more or less fortuitous interviews he jotted down briefly on scraps of paper, which he then thrust higgledy-piggledy into the saddlebags. When he had accumulated a large quantity of such notes the brilliant idea occurred to him to make a book of them. As Mr. Bryan jestingly puts it, "by some unfortunate accident he located" and laid the proposition before him. Mr. Bryan was favorably impressed and agreed to furnish the necessary funds; while Rose continued his itineraries and supplied sufficient "copy" for a book, in the meanwhile cherishing a secret, but as it proved, a forlorn hope that the sale of the book would make both himself and his partner in the enterprise rich. The more or less inchoate matter which he collected and hoarded in the saddlebags was at intervals turned over to Mr. Bryan to be sifted, arranged, written up, and finally printed and published. The first and only edition numbered 500 copies, and fell still-born from the press. About 200 copies were bound and either sold at $2.50 per copy or given away; the remaining sheets were disposed of as so much waste paper. But though the material reward for the two years of labor and expense which it took to bring out the book was *nil,* it is not too much to say that the result otherwise was monumental and invaluable. During 1874-1876 many "old timers," both men and women, were yet alive, fourscore years and ten and more of age, with vivid recollections of the days when forests had to be cleared and crops planted and harvested almost under the guns of hostile Indians; when log forts dotted the land, and towns were laid out in the uncharted wilderness. These old people passed away rapidly very soon afterward, and with their passing their personal experiences of the early days in Missouri would have been lost forever had not our roving Rose garnered them on scraps of paper in his saddlebags. If the task had not been undertaken precisely at that time, and in the homely manner in which it was done, the priceless data now preserved between the covers of "Pioneer Families" would never have been collected at all.

* * * *

Of Robert Rose's career before and after he "located" Mr. Bryan, very little is known. Mr. Hughes Pegram, of Montgomery County, the son of James Pegram, one of the settlers of that county who knew Rose, describes him as about six feet in height, slender, dark complexioned, with a short beard. For a few months after the publication of "Pioneers" he seems to have tried peddling it from door to door in the region which he had combed over for its contents. The result was heart-breakingly disappointing and he died soon afterward, probably in 1878, in dire poverty, at about sixty-two years of age. He lies buried somewhere in Montgomery County. Could there be a more vivid illustration of what is sometimes spoken of as the irony of history, that so little can be said about the man whose unremunerated job it was to rescue thousands of his fellows from oblivion? Happily, it is quite otherwise of Mr. Bryan, of whom a quite fairly complete genealogy and life-sketch can be set down here, the latter supplied in part by himself and the former secured from other sources.

* * * *

William Smith Bryan is a descendant of a notable family, the history of which, in America, goes back to 1615, when another William Smith Bryan landed on these shores from Ireland. It appears that he had aroused the hostility of the British government by a too ardent Irish patriotism and had been deported as a rebellious subject. At this time this Bryan was supposed to be the only living lineal descendant of Brian Borou, one of the half mythical Kings of the Emerald Isle. It is recorded that he had quite a number of children, eleven in fact, but the record of only one, Francis, has come down to us. He accompanied his father to America, and in due time himself became the father of two sons, Morgan and William S., who were born in Denmark, whither their father had fled after an unsuccessful return to Ireland to regain his hereditary title and estate. His son Morgan, by some turn of Fortune's wheel, became a standard bearer for William of Orange and was present at the battle of the Boyne. He came to Pennsylvania in 1695 and married Martha Strode, whom he had met on the ship which brought him over. Their children were Joseph, Samuel, James, John, Morgan, Eleanor, Mary, William, Thomas, and Sarah. James married Mary Austin of South-east Missouri and of the family after whom Austin, Texas, is named. Their son, Jonathan, settled on Femme Osage Creek in St. Charles County in 1800. His son Elijah married Lydia Anne McClenny and became the father of W. S. Bryan, co-author and principal sponsor of "Pioneer Families of Missouri."

* * * *

William Smith Bryan was born on a farm near Augusta, in St. Charles County, on January 8, 1846. He was educated at home by two sisters, who were school teachers. Later he graduated from Stewart's Commercial College in St. Louis. On November 25, 1875, he married Nancy Mildred North. The fruits of this union were two daughters and a son. The latter, William S., was a lieutenant of infantry in the U. S. Army during the World War, and was recently decorated for valor.

In 1865, aged nineteen, Mr. W. S. Bryan, Sr., went to Council Grove, Kansas, and learned to set type in the printing office of his brother James, who was then editing and publishing a small weekly paper. The next year he returned to his native state and established the St. Charles *News* in company with Joseph H. and William A. Pereau, whose family had settled in Missouri during the Spanish regime. Having sold the *News* in 1873 he became for a short time editor of and contributor to a literary publication in St. Joseph. During 1873-75 he was the editor and publisher of the Montgomery, Mo., *Standard*. In 1880 he established the Historical Publishing Company in St. Louis, with branches in Boston, Philadelphia, Richmond, Toronto, Chicago, and other important cities. The panic of 1893-96 put an end to this enterprise, which previously had been markedly successful. In 1898 he edited the *Mississippi Valley Democrat* in St. Louis. In 1906 he was the editor of the "United States Encyclopedia" and an assistant editor of the "Encyclopedia Americana."

Mr. Bryan is the author, among other works, of "Footprints of the World's History" (1893), "America's War for Humanity" (1898), "Our Islands and Their People" (1900). He also completed eight of the volumes of Ridpath's "History of the United States," which were left unfinished when that author was overtaken by death. In like manner he completed the last three volumes of the same historian's "Universal History." He is now busily at work on a book to be called "Episodes in the Life of Daniel Boone," which he hopes to publish in the near future.

* * * *

As was said above, "Pioneer Families" is a unique book. It is one of the most remarkable genealogical feats ever attempted. Here, indeed, the reader's disappointment will be great if he looks for "scientific" pedigree or radial charts, or expects to find evidence of learned fussing over musty town, state, or national records. There is no evidence here that the "old family Bible," or funeral sermons and historical orations had been sought for far and near and carefully conned. There is no reference to "family crests." Here we have only what is so modestly stated in the brief preface, that "Mr. Rose has personally visited one or more of each family whose history is given, and from notes thus obtained the histories have been written." These are mostly just a plain A begat B and B begat C. That there was a conscientious effort to avoid errors is evident from the further assertion that "Where differences occurred in the statements of different members of the same family, we have carefully compared them and endeavored to sift the facts from each; and we feel confident that this book is as near correct as it is possible for any work of the kind to be."

Here, furthermore, is no comparatively simple effort to trace a single lineage backward to some distant ancestor. Here is rather the much more ambitious and stupendous task to secure through personal interviews with the people chiefly concerned a reliable, even though only a skeleton record of over 800 families scattered over five counties which sprawled over an area of 2890 square miles of territory that was quite innocent of what are now considered to be traversable roads. But there can be no doubt that it was precisely this intimate intercourse throughout two or more years between Rose and the people in whom he was interested that finally gave such a human, often such a poignant human touch to these pages. The diverting anecdotes, the serious and humorous stories, the historical incidents and dramatic events that so often interrupt the otherwise dry genealogies, the hilarious illustrations, are most entertaining and instructive features. They often fairly reek of the soil and are an important contribution to the sometimes recklessly mendacious folklore of those strenuous times. The passing of them from mouth to ear around the logfires in winter or under the rustling trees in summer must often have relaxed the over-strained nerves of the pioneers.

* * * *

The "histories" are limited to those families which settled in the above named five counties, which lie almost entirely north of the Missouri River. Contemporary settlements in Pike, Boone, Howard and Cooper counties are scarcely mentioned, and then only casually. The very important French immigration (the so-called creoles, the Chouteaus, Gratiots, Cabannes, Papins, Pauls, etc.) into St. Louis and its immediate vicinity is only lightly touched upon. In his "Creoles of St. Louis" (1893) Paul Beckwith does these full justice. The equally important though much later German immigration is briefly sketched under a separate heading. The very early influx into South-east Missouri is entirely ignored. This latter omission is all the more strange because as early as 1793 a Dr. Jesse Bryan, who had been a surgeon in the Continental Army, and a rather important member of the Bryan clan, settled in what is now Ste. Genevieve County, where he died in 1843. Furthermore, Mr. W. S. Bryan's grandfather James got his wife, Mary Austin, from that region. Lack of time and means no doubt sufficiently explain these omissions. To have tried to compass the entire State would have been a Herculean task indeed for our two amateur genealogists. Let us be grateful for what they actually accomplished. However, it is clear that the title of their book was somewhat too ambitious. "Some Pioneer Families of Missouri" would have been better. "Some American Pioneer Families of Missouri" would have defined its content yet more correctly. But, mayhap, this is carrying criticism a bit too far.

* * * *

To justify what was said above about the very early influx into south-east Missouri, we briefly indicate here a few of the families which settled in that region:

Aubuchon, Antoine, and his wife Ellen N., were natives of Ste. Genevieve County. Their son Francis was born there in 1812. He married Teressa Coleman, who bore him six children. Of these, Ferdinand married Luella Brooks. They had six children. After his first wife's death he married Annabella Brannon. His brother Peter married Eliza A. Brickley. They had eleven children. Adrian, another brother, married Paulina Rouggly.

Cissell, Joseph, and his wife Mary Ann Miles, came from Kentucky and settled in what is now Perry County in 1803. They had five children. Their son Vincent married Carolina French. Eight children were the fruits of this union. Lewis, the second son, married Sarah Mattingly, who bore him nine children. John V. married Melissa Brewer, and, after her death, Theresa Brewer. Loretta married Wilfred Brewer. Leo F. first married Katie Frazier, and, after her death, Louisa Brewer. Emanuel married Emma Mattingly. Ezekiel married Louisa Rankin. Kendrick married Alice Brewer. Jane F. married William Difani.

DeLassus, Ceran E. and his wife Elenore Beauvais were natives of Ste. Genevieve county. They had eleven children, of whom Ceran F., the oldest, married Mattie E. Walton. They had several children. Joseph L. married Josephine Stewart, who presented him with five children. Joseph R. married Elizabeth J. Shelby.

Hagan, Aquilla, and his wife Mary Tucker, came from Kentucky to Perry County in 1797. They had nine children. Of these Rebeccah Ann married John Brewer, whose family settled in Perry County in 1818. The Brewers had eight children. After Rebeccah Ann's death her husband married Cecelia Layton. She bore him ten children. Gregory, Rebeccah Ann's son, married Sarah Riney. They had nine sons and four daughters.

Kenner, Francis, settled in Ste. Genevieve County from Tennessee in 1802. He married Elizabeth Pillars in 1804. She bore him sixteen children. Their son, Housand, married Ophelia Duvall. They had six children.

Moore, James, came to Perry County in 1790. His son James J. married Cecelia Manning, who bore him ten children. Of these, Basil married Emma Burgee, and had by her six sons and a daughter.

Obuchon, Francis, was born in Ste. Genevieve County in 1791. In 1816 he married a widow Pratte. After her death he married Judith Calliot, who bore him five children. Louis, their oldest son, married Lucinda Perry. They had eight children.

Rozier (Rosier?), Ferdinand, was born in France in 1777, and settled in Ste. Genevieve about 1810. He married Constance Roy, of Illinois. in 1795. They had ten children. Firmin A. married Mary M. Vallé. Felix married Louise Vallé. Charles

C. married Emily La Grave. Francis C. married Zoe Vallé. Their son Henry L. was married twice, first to Mary A. Janis, and then to Sallie M. Carlisle. The former bore him three sons, the latter, two daughters. The Vallés were connected by marriage with the Chouteaus of St. Louis.

St. Gem, John Baptiste, a French-Canadian, settled at Kaskaskia, Illinois, during the last half of the eighteenth century. John B. Jr., and Vital, his sons, were among the earliest settlers west of the Mississippi. John B. Jr.'s son Augustus, born in Ste. Genevieve in 1791, married Felicite Desile Le Clerc in 1821, and by her had ten children. Of these, Gustavus married Elizabeth Skewes. They had three children.

Howard, Henry, settled in Cape Girardeau County in 1799. His son, Hamilton B., married Sarah Daughtery. Their son H. W. married Mary P. Shaver. After her death he married Rachel G. Horrell. They had three children.

Barks, Humteel, located in Cape Girardeau County in 1800. His son, Joseph, married Serena Parton. Their son Jonathon H. married Josephine Snider. After her death he married Narcissa Jones. George H., another son of Joseph, married Sarah Newkirk. After her death he married Mary A. Proffer.

Tucker, Peter, came to Perry County early in the nineteenth century. His son, Raymond, born in 1811, married Mary Martina Cissell. Their son Nereus married Tresa Tucker.

Tucker, Josiah, was born in Perry County in the early years of the nineteenth century. He married Sarah Miles, by whom he had eleven children. Simeon I. married Mary A. Cissell. They had five children. Leo P., another son of Josiah, married Elizabeth McBride.

Layton, Joseph, settled in Perry County in 1808. His son John B., married Elizabeth Hagan and by her had fifteen children. Three of his sons had forty-six children among them. Felix Layton married Melissa A. Layton. They had fifteen children.

Kinder, Adam, settled in Cape Girardeau County in 1800. His son, Joel, married Irene Thompson. After her death he married Sarena Thompson. By the former he had Levi J., who married Martha J. O'Neal. They had five children: Susan J., who married William J. Strong; Sarah E., who married John Hamilton; William M.; Mary, who married Daniel Lape; Martha Ann, who married Jacob Thompson.

Beauvais, Joseph, and his wife Cecilia Obuchon, were natives of Ste. Genevieve County. His ancestors came from Canada to the western territory during the first half of the eighteenth century. They had two children, Eleanora and Peter. After the death of his first wife, Joseph married a widow DeLassus. By her he had two children, Matilda and Mary. His second wife having died, Joseph married a widow Struve. His son Peter, by his first wife, was born in 1815. He was twice married, first to Elizabeth Henderson, who left him three children. His second wife was Rachel Smith. Seven children blessed this union.

McCormick, Andrew, of Scotch-Irish descent, came to America before the Revolution. In 1807 he settled in Washington County. His son, Joseph, married Jane Robinson. Of their six children, James R. married B. N. Nance, who bore him two children. Of these, Emmet C. was married twice. By his second wife, Susan E. Garner, he had one child, James E.

Oliver, Thomas, of Virginia, served in the Revolutionary war. His son, John, settled in Cape Girardeau County in 1819. He first married a Miss Cobb. After her death he married Margaret Sloan, and had four children: Louella, John F., R. B., and Henry C.

* * * *

Quite a number of what appear to be isolated individuals, both men and women, flit like ghosts across the pages of the "histories." Like Melchizedec, they have neither father nor mother. They stir the reader's curiosity. Whence came they? Whither did they go? The men folk of this transient company may have been restless, roving individuals who tarried here and there only long enough to "stake a claim" and to court and marry the women of their choice and then either moved still farther west into the unbroken wilderness, or returned to the eastward from whence they came. But that does not explain the transient women. Some of these came from Tennessee, Kentucky and Virginia to be married to men to whom they had been previously engaged, and then moved on with their new husbands. Some of them, however, must have belonged to households on the ground but which were omitted from the "histories" because they had otherwise left no trace behind them. There were numerous families that "settled" just long enough to raise a crop or two, and then sought for pastures new, always hoping to do better somewhere else.

* * * *

But that there was no pressure of subsistence upon the population of those early days is abundantly demonstrated by the enormous number of children per family frequently recorded in the "histories." Of the more than 800 families dealt with, in each of 244 there were more than ten children, or 3038 in all, which means roughly 12.05 offspring per family! No birth control then as now for, obviously, in the task of clearing the forests and sowing and reaping the crops, children were a highly desirable potential asset. But some of our pioneers seem to have been just a bit inclined to overdo the production of these assets, for no less than fifteen of the 244 families mentioned had among them a small army of 365 children, or twenty-four per family! One hardy and hearty pioneer had no less than twenty-nine sons and daughters by two wives, two in sequence, not at one time. Two each had twenty-eight by two wives. One had twenty-six by two wives. One had twenty-four by two wives. One had twenty-two by two wives. One had twenty-two by one wife. One had twenty-two by six wives. Two had twenty-one by two wives. One had twenty-one by three wives. One had twenty by one wife. One had twenty by two wives. One had twenty by three wives. Those were heroic days indeed!

* * * *

Consider the names with which some of those children were burdened or adorned. Here is a list, picked at random:

Alcana	Barsheba	Ibby	Original
Aletha	Behethler	Icham	Parthana
Amazon	Clemency	Ithiel	Penina
Appalana	Crescentia	Kittura	Pleasant
Archa	Delphi	Mahala	Rutia
Arphaxad	Devolia	Martellus	Sedreia
Arsissa	Dulcinea	Mecha	Tocal
Asap	Eglantine	Medora	Torcai
Assanith	Emmarilla	Mourning	Urila
Atha	Erretta	Ninian	Usurdus
Atossa	Feminine	Obedience	Zarina
Azal	Fortunatus	Orientha	Zelpha

And one poor girl whose surname was Money was baptized Cautious!

However, to do our pioneers full justice in this matter of nomenclature, it must be added that the great majority of the names which they gave their children were beautifully simple. They took them, for the most part, from the Bible, the book with which they were most familiar either from their own reading or because they heard it read and quoted by their missionary preachers, often sons of the soil like themselves. A family roll call sometimes sounded like a roster of the Twelve Apostles. Every biblical name from Adam, through Melchizedec, to Zachariah (except Satan!) is repeatedly met with. Elizabeth, Mary, Rebeccah, and Sarah are in the majority for the girls, while John, James, Joseph, and Samuel predominate for the boys. Outside of the Bible, Nancy and William are prime favorites.

* * * *

Just a glance at the illustrations in our volume. The two full-page plates on which are reproduced the likenesses of some of the more or less prominent pioneers, are lithographs made from old daguerreotypes and photographs which the indefatigable Rose collected during his peregrinations. The lithographing was done by Charles Juehne, a German, located at 414 Olive St., St. Louis. The picture of Daniel Boone was copied from Harding's portrait of the frontiersman. Mr. Bryan's father, who knew Boone well, used to say that it was a "speaking likeness" of the old hero, though a bit thinner than usual owing to the subject's illness just before the portrait was painted.

The crude woodcuts only too sparsely scattered here and there through the text, most of them so divertingly preposterous, were done by J. G. Harris & Co., also of St. Louis, and located at 416 North 2nd St. They are the artist's (?) quite original conception of what is supposed to be related in the context which, by the way, he can not have conned very carefully. For example, on page 508 he depicts one Skilt's adventure with wild turkeys. Notice the enormous size of the two birds, which in the text are said to be "just going into the clouds," and then compare it with that of the woman standing on the ground. His idea of Linear Perspective seems to have been exactly the reverse of the orthodox theory! Harris, the artist, claimed to be a pioneer himself and therefore quite familiar with the grotesque scenes which he reproduced. Comments Mr. Bryan to the writer: "I think he must have been" a pioneer, and "perhaps he was related to Dickens' famous Mrs. Harris in "Martin Chuzzlewit," the lady to whom Sarah Gamp appealed for confirmation of all her statements. And he adds: "I love them [the wood-cuts] so much that I dream about them at night."

* * * *

Merely to keep the record straight, attention may be drawn to one or two historical statements that do not seem to be in accord with the facts. On page 55 it is said that "eighty-one years ago there was not an American settlement west of Kentucky, and the Indians of Illinois, and all that vast territory lying to the north, west and south-west, were undisturbed in their hunting grounds." That is to say, of course, that this condition existed eighty-one years before the publication date of "Pioneer Families," which is 1876, therefore in 1795. But. as will be noted below, there were actual American settlers in what is now Missouri as early as 1787, and on the opposite side of the Mississippi, in Kaskaskia, one hundred Americans signed a contract, in 1787, with one Bartholomew Tardiveau, by which he engaged to become their lobbyist in Washington to obtain from Congress certain grants of land.

On page 58 this statement occurs: "The first American settlements in the present limits of the State of Missouri were made in 1795, on Femme Osage creek, in what is now St. Charles County." But one John Dodge had settled in what is now Ste. Genevieve County as early as 1787, and Israel Dodge soon followed him. Israel's daughter Nancy, by the way, married John Sefton, and their daughter Rebeccah married Auguste René Chouteau. John Moore came to what is now Perry County in 1790, and it is on record that a Baptist preacher ministered to the scattered Americans as early as 1794. It is a reasonable assumption that they had arrived there at least a year or two earlier. Dr. Jesse Bryan settled in Ste. Genevieve County in 1793.

* * * *

Finally, the reader's attention is called to the two very complete indexes that have been added to this edition of "Pioneer Families." They provide a long needed "open sesame" to the entire contents of the book, but more especially to the "histories of families." For the first time the seeker after the genealogical lore contained in these pages will be able, almost in a moment, to turn to practically every name that occurs in the "histories." It is needless to point out what an invaluable feature this is of the present edition. It transforms the work into a really serviceable handbook of early Missouri genealogical data.

W. W. ELWANG.

Columbia, Mo.

PART I.

LIFE OF DANIEL BOONE.

ONE of the pioneers of Missouri, who is still living, in St. Charles county, in his 79th year, and who knew Daniel Boone intimately, as a youth knows an old man, thus describes his personal appearance during the last nineteen years of his life:

"He was below the average height of men, being scarcely five feet eight inches, but was stout and heavy, and, until the last year or two of his life, inclined to corpulency. His eyes were deep blue, and very brilliant, and were always on the alert, passing quickly from object to object, a habit acquired, doubtless, during his hunting and Indian fighting experiences. His hair was gray, but had been originally light brown or flaxen, and was fine and soft. His movements were quick, active and lithe, his step soft and springy, like that of an Indian. He was nearly always humming or whistling some kind of a tune, in a low tone; another habit of his lonely days in the woods. He was never boisterous or talkative, but always cool and collected, and, though he said but little, his words carried weight with them, and were respected and heeded by his hearers. I never saw him angry or disconcerted in the least, and his manners were so kind and gentle towards every one, that all who knew him loved him. During the last year or two of his life, he became feeble and emaciated, and could no more enjoy himself at his favorite pastime of hunting; but his grand spirit never faltered or clouded, and, to the day of his death, he was the same serene, uncomplaining man he had always been."

The historian Peck, who visited Boone in 1818, two years before his death, thus speaks of him:

"In boyhood I had read of Daniel Boone, the pioneer of Kentucky, the celebrated hunter and Indian-fighter; and imagination had portrayed a rough, fierce-looking, uncouth specimen of humanity, and, of course, at this period of life, a fretful and unattractive old man. But in every respect the reverse appeared. His high, bold forehead was slightly bald, and his silvered locks were combed smooth; his countenance was ruddy and fair, and exhibited the simplicity of a child. His voice was soft and melodious. A smile frequently played over his features in conversation. At repeated interviews, an irritable expression was never heard. His clothing was the coarse, plain manufacture of the family; but everything about him denoted that kind of comfort, which was congenial to his habits and feelings, and evinced a happy old age.

"Every member of the household appeared to delight in administering to his comforts. He was sociable, communicative in replying to questions, but not in introducing incidents of his own history. He was intelligent, for he had treasured up the experiences and observations of more than fourscore years. · · · · The impression on the mind of the writer, before a personal acquaintance, that he was moody, unsocial, and desired to shun society and civilization, was entirely removed. He was the archetype of the better class of western pioneers, benevolent, kind-hearted, liberal, and a true philanthropist. That he was rigidly honest, and one of nature's noblemen, need not be here said. It is seen in his whole life. He abhorred a mean action, and delighted in honesty and truth. · · · · He was strictly moral, temperate, and chaste."

The portrait which we give as a frontispiece, is from a photograph of the painting made by Mr. Chester Harding, the distinguished artist of Boston, who came to Missouri in 1820, at the request of Revs. James E. Welch and John M. Peck, expressly to paint the picture. Boone, at that time, was at the home of his son-in-law, Mr. Flanders Callaway, near the village of Marthasville, in Warren county. He was at first very much opposed to having his portrait painted, being governed by feelings of modesty and a strong dislike to anything approaching display or public attention; but he was finally prevailed upon by friends and relatives to sit for his picture. He was quite feeble at the time, and was supported in his chair by Rev. Mr. Welch. He wore his buckskin hunting shirt, trimmed with otter's fur, and the knife that is seen in his belt, is the same that he carried with him from North Carolina on his first expedition to Kentucky.

This picture is pronounced by persons who knew Boone intimately, to be a perfect likeness, and the following certificate from Rev. James E. Welch, who is still living, at Warrensburg, Mo., may be of interest in this connection:

" I, James E. Welch, of Warrensburg, Johnson Co., Mo., hereby certify that I believe this portrait to be a correct copy of Harding's picture of Col. Daniel Boone, which was painted in the summer of 1820. I stood by and held the Colonel's head while the artist was painting it, and my impressions at the time were, that it was an *excellent likeness of the old pioneer*, which I believe was the only picture ever taken of Col. Boone.

" Given under my hand, May 16, 1876.

" JAMES E. WELCH."

Daniel Boone was born in Bucks county, Pennsylvania, October 22, 1734. His grandfather, George Boone, was a native of England, and resided at Brandwich, about eight miles from Exeter. In 1717 he emigrated to America, with his family, consisting of his wife and eleven children, two daughters and nine sons. Soon after his arrival in America he purchased a large tract of land in what is now Bucks county, Pennsylvania, settled upon it, and named it Exeter, after his native town. The township still bears that name.

The names of only three of the eleven children have come down to the present time, John, James, and Squire. The latter was the father of Daniel Boone. He had seven sons and four daughters, whose names are here given in the order of their births, from information furnished by the late Daniel Bryan, the celebrated gunsmith of Kentucky, who was a nephew of Daniel Boone: Israel, Sarah, Samuel, Jonathan, Elizabeth, DANIEL, Mary, (mother of Daniel Bryan), George, Edward, Squire, Jr., and Hannah. The maiden name of the mother of these children was Sarah Morgan.

When Daniel was a small boy, his father removed to Berks county, not far from Reading, which was then a frontier settlement, exposed to assaults from the Indians and abounding with game. Panthers, wild-cats, and other dangerous wild animals were numerous, and young Daniel, at a very early age, began to exhibit both skill and courage in hunting them.

One day, while out hunting, in company with several other boys, a loud cry was heard ringing through the woods. They all knew too well that the sound proceeded from the throat of a ferocious panther, and all except Boone fled in terror. He bravely stood his ground, and shot the panther dead just as it was in the act of springing upon him.

'This and other similar incidents soon gave him an enviable local reputation, which was a forerunner of his national celebrity at a later period.

Boone's school days were short, and his education, so far as book knowledge was concerned, imperfect. The school houses of that period (a few specimens of which are still to be seen in some of our frontier settlements) were built of rough, unhewn logs, notched together at the corners, and the spaces between them filled with mud and sticks. A large chimney, built of sticks and plastered with mud, supported at the back and sides, where the fire burned, with a wall of stones, stood at one end; a hole cut in the side, and closed with a frame of puncheons, or often with nothing more than a blanket or the skin of some wild animal, constituted the door, while a window was made on the opposite side by removing a log and covering the aperture with a puncheon, fastened to the log above with hinges of raw hide, which admitted of its being raised or lowered as the weather and light permitted. No glass was used, as it could not be had. The earth formed the floor—rough clapboards, fastened with wooden pins, or weighted down with poles and stones, the roof, and the seats were made by splitting saplings in the middle and setting them, with the flat side upward, on four pins for legs, two at each end. The only writing desk was an inclined puncheon, supported on wooden pins that were driven into the logs.

It was in such a school house as this, surrounded by a dense forest that furnished fuel for the fire, and near a spring of sparkling water that provided draughts for the thirsty, that Boone received his education, which embraced only a few easy lessons in spelling, reading, arithmetic and writing.

His school days came to a sudden and rather violent end. The teacher, a dissipated Irishman, kept his bottle of whisky hid in a thicket near the school house, and visited it frequently during the day for refreshment and consolation. The boys noticed that after these visits he was always crosser and used the rod more freely than at other times, but they did not suspect the cause. One day, young Boone, while chasing a squirrel, came accidentally upon the teacher's bottle, and at the first opportunity informed his playmates of his discovery. They decided, upon consultation, to mix an emetic with the liquor, and await the result. The emetic was procured that night, and promptly placed in the bottle next morning. A short time after school opened, the teacher retired for a few minutes, and when he came back he was very sick and very much out of humor. Daniel Boone was called up to recite his lesson in arithmetic, and upon his making a slight

DANIEL BOONE WHIPS THE SCHOOL MASTER.

mistake, the teacher began to flog him. The boy, smarting with pain, made known the secret of the whisky bottle, which so enraged the school master that he laid on harder and faster than ever. Young Boone, being stout and athletic for his age, grappled with the teacher; the children shouted and roared, and the scuffle continued until Boone knocked his antagonist down on the floor, and fled out of the room.

Of course the story spread rapidly over the neighborhood, and the teacher was dismissed in disgrace. Daniel was rebuked by his parents; and so ended his school days.

When Daniel was about eighteen years of age, his father moved his family to North Carolina, and settled on the Yadkin river, in the north-western part of the State, about eight miles from Wilkesboro. Here game was abundant, and the young hunter spent much of his time in the pursuit of his favorite amusement.

He was often accompanied on his hunting expeditions by one or more of the sons of Mr. William Bryan, a well-to-do farmer who lived near his father's, who was blessed with a number of stalwart sons and blooming daughters. Their association and mutual love of hunting soon begot a strong friendship, which lasted through life; and, being strengthened and cemented by intermarriage and continued association, was transmitted through their children to future generations, and the two families are still closely allied by ties of blood and friendship.

But it was not farmer Bryan's sons, alone, that drew Daniel Boone so often to the house. There were other attractions there in the bright eyes of a daughter named Rebecca, and it soon became whispered about that Daniel was courting her. These whisperings were at length confirmed by the announcement of the approaching wedding, which came off in due time, and was celebrated in the most approved style of the times.

Rebecca Bryan was a very attractive, if not really a handsome young woman, and the love which she inspired in the breast of young Boone never cooled or abated during their long and eventful married life. Each was devoted to the other, and the dangers and hardships through which they passed cemented their love and drew them more closely together. She was in every respect a fit companion and helpmeet for the daring pioneer.

Nine children resulted from this marriage, viz.: James, Israel, Susanna, Jemima, Lavinia, Daniel M., Rebecca, Jesse, and Nathan.

James, the eldest son, was killed by the Indians, in his 16th year, while his father was making his first attempt to move his family from North Carolina to Kentucky. The particulars of this sad event will be given elsewhere.

Israel was killed at the battle of Blue Licks, in Kentucky, August 19, 1782, in his 24th year.

Susanna married William Hayes, an Irishman, and a weaver by trade. They lived in St. Charles county, Mo., and she died in her 40th year.

Jemima married Flanders Callaway, and lived in what is now Warren county, Mo. She died in 1829, in her 67th year. While the family were living in the fort at Boonesborough, Ky., she and two young friends, Betty and Frances Callaway, daughters of Col. Richard Callaway, were captured by the Indians while gathering wild flowers on the opposite bank of the Kentucky river, which they had crossed in a canoe. They were pursued by Boone and Callaway and six other men, and recaptured the following day.

Lavinia married Joseph Scholl, and lived in Kentucky. She died in her 36th year.

Daniel M. married a Miss Lewis, of Missouri, and died July 13, 1839, in his 72d year. He settled in Darst Bottom, St. Charles county, in 1797, but moved to Montgomery county in 1816. He held several important positions under the government, and during the Indian war was appointed Colonel of the militia. He made most of the early government surveys in the present counties of St. Charles, Warren, Montgomery, and Lincoln. At the time of his death he was living in Jackson county. In personal appearance he resembled his father more than any of the other children. He was below the medium height, and stoutly built had light hair, blue eyes, fair complexion, and his voice was like a woman's.

Rebecca, the youngest of the four daughters, married Phillip Goe, and lived and died in Kentucky.

Jesse married Cloe Vanbibber, and settled in Missouri in 1819. He had received a good education, and became a prominent and influential man before his death, which occurred in 1821, at St. Louis, while serving as a member of the first Missouri Legislature. His children were, Alonzo, Albert G., James M., Van D., Harriet, Minerva, Pantha, and Emily.

Nathan Boone, the youngest child of Daniel Boone, came to Missouri in 1800. He married Olive Vanbibber, a sister of Jesse Boone's wife, and they had thirteen children, viz: James, Howard, John, Delinda, Malinda, Mary, Susan, Nancy, Jemima, Lavinia, Olive, Melcina, and Mahaley. Nathan Boone was also a surveyor, and made a number of government surveys. At the commencement of the Indian war of 1812–1815 he raised a company of rangers, and received his commission as Captain from President Madison in March, 1812. In August, 1833, he was commissioned Captain of dragoons by President Jackson, and during President Polk's administration he was promoted to Major of dragoons. In 1850 he was again promoted, and received his

commission as Lieutenant-Colonel of dragoons from President
Fillmore. He died October 16, 1856, in his 76th year; and his
wife died November 12, 1858, in her 75th year.

Nathan and Jesse Boone were tall, square-shouldered, power-
fully built men, with light hair and blue eyes, like their father.

For several years after his marriage, Boone followed the occupation of a farmer, going on an occasional hunt, when the loss of
time would not interfere with the proper cultivation of his crops.

But as the population increased, his neighborhood began to fill
up with a class of citizens who possessed considerable means, and
were somewhat aristocratic in their habits, which, of course, did
not suit Boone and his plain backwoods associates, who longed for
the wild, free life of the frontier. Several companies were, at
different times, organized and penetrated the wilderness along the
head waters of the Tennessee river, in quest of game, and, finally,
in 1764, Boone and a small party of hunters proceeded as far as
Rock Castle, a branch of the Cumberland river, and within the
present boundaries of Kentucky. This expedition was undertaken
at the solicitation of a company of land speculators, who employed
Boone to ascertain and report concerning the country in that
quarter. He was highly pleased with the country, climate, abundance of game, etc., but owing to his duties at home, he did not
make another expedition to Kentucky until 1769.

In 1767 a hunter named John Finley, accompanied by two or
three companions, proceeded as far as the Kentucky river, and
spent a season in hunting and trading with the roving bands of
Indians. To them the country seemed almost a paradise, and
upon their return to North Carolina they gave such a glowing
description of it that Boone and several of his neighbors decided
to go on an excursion there; but several months elapsed before
their arrangements could be completed.

A party of six was formed, and Boone chosen their leader. His
companions were John Finley, John Stewart, Joseph Holden, James
Moncey, and William Cool. They set out on their perilous journey
May 1, 1769, and by the 17th of June they were in the heart of the
Kentucky wilderness. They carried nothing with them except their
rifles, tomahawks, knives and ammunition. They slept in the
woods, without covering, and depended for food upon the game
they killed each day. Their dress consisted of a loose, open
frock, made of dressed deer skin, and called a hunting shirt; leggins, made of the same material, covered their lower extremities,

to which was appended a pair of moccasins for the feet. A cap, made of beaver or raccoon skin, covered their heads, and the capes of their hunting shirts and seams of their leggins were ornamented with leather fringe. Their under-clothing, when they wore any, was made of coarse cotton.

Such a suit as this would stand almost any amount of wear and tear, and it was what they needed in climbing the rocky mountains and forcing their way through the dense thickets of undergrowth and briars that lay in their course. No thorn or briar could penetrate the heavy deer skin, and they could tread upon the most venomous serpent with impunity, as its fangs could not reach their flesh.

Vast herds of buffalo roamed over the prairies and through the wilderness of Kentucky, at that time, and Boone and his companions spent the summer in hunting them, and examining the country. It is generally supposed that the scene of their summer's operations lay in what is now Morgan county, on the waters of Red river, a branch of the Kentucky.

And here we must correct an error that has existed since the earliest settlement of Kentucky, in regard to the meaning of the name. *Kain-tuck-ee* is a Shawnee word, and signifies, "at the head of the river." The repeated statement that it meant "dark and bloody ground," is a fiction.

The habits of the buffalo are peculiar. In moving from one place to another they travel in vast herds, and always go in a stampede. The cows and calves, and old and decrepid ones are placed in front, while the stout and active ones bring up the rear. Nothing will stop or turn them, and woe to any that stumble and fall, for they are immediately trampled to death by those behind. When a ravine, creek, or river comes in their way, they plunge in and swim across, the weak and timid ones being forced in by the strong. If any living thing gets in their way, death is the inevitable result.

On two occasions Boone and his companions came near being trampled to death in this way, and nothing but their presence of mind saved them. One time they sprang behind trees, and as the buffaloes passed on either side, they coolly punched them with the breeches of their guns, and laughed to see them jump and bellow. The next time, however, they were in the open prairie, with no trees to protect them. Death seemed unavoidable, for the herd was so large that it extended a mile or more on either side, and the speed of the fleetest horse could not have carried them out of danger. To run, therefore, was useless, and nothing apparently remained but to stand and meet their fate, terrible as it might be. Several of the party were unnerved by fright, and began to bewail their fate in the incoherent language of terror. But Boone remained perfectly cool. "Now, boys," said he, "don't make fools of yourselves, for I will bring you out of this scrape yet." As the herd approached, he carefully examined the flint and priming of his gun, to see that all was right. By this time the buffaloes were within thirty yards of him, when coolly raising his rifle to his shoulder, he glanced along the bright barrel, touched the trigger, and the sharp report rang out above the roar of the rushing bisons. A large bull in the front rank, plunged forward, and fell, mortally wounded and bellowing, at their very feet. As the herd came on they would snort and spring around their wounded companion, and thus a lane was opened through their ranks, and the hunters were saved.

In December they divided into two parties, for the greater convenience of hunting, and that their observations might be extended over a larger area of country. Boone and Stewart formed one party, and on the twenty-second of December they were on the banks of the main Kentucky river. In the evening of that day, as they were descending a small hill near the river, a party of Indians rushed out of a thick cane-brake, and made them prisoners. They offered no resistance, for they knew it would be useless, the odds being so great against them, but quietly handing their guns and accouterments to their captors, they signified their willingness to obey whatever commands might be given to them. In fact, for the purpose of deceiving the Indians and throwing them off their guard, they pretended to be well pleased with their new associates, and went along with them as cheerfully as if they were all out on a hunting expedition together.

So completely were the Indians deceived that they kept very little guard over their prisoners, but suffered them to do pretty much as they pleased, and treated them with marked hospitality. At night they all lay down and went to sleep, seeming to feel no apprehension that the white men might try to escape.

Thus the time passed until the seventh night, when Boone, having matured his plans, decided to make an attempt to escape. Great caution was necessary, lest the savages should awake and discover them. Any attempt to run away, where kindness and hospitality have been shown to a captive, is a mortal offense to an Indian, and can only be atoned for by the death of the offender.

Late at night, when the Indians were in their deepest slumbers, Boone gently awakened Stewart, and by signs and whispers made known his purpose. Securing their guns, knives, etc., the two hunters quietly stole away, and successfully made their escape.

They took their course as near as possible in the direction of their old hunting camp, and traveled all the balance of that night and the next day. But when they reached it they found it deserted and plundered. No trace of their friends could be found. Boone and Stewart supposed they had become disheartened and returned to North Carolina, but in this they were mistaken; and from that day to this no clue to the fate of the balance of the party has ever been discovered. The most probable conclusion is, that they were killed by the Indians, and their remains devoured by wild animals.

Boone and his companion continued their hunting, but with more caution, for their ammunition had begun to fail, and their late experience led them to be more vigilant in guarding against surprise by the Indians.

One day, early in January, 1770, while hunting in the woods, they discovered two men at some distance from them, and being in doubt as to whether they were white men or Indians, Boone and his companion grasped their rifles and sprang behind trees. The strangers discovered them at the same time, and began to advance and make signs that they were friends. But this did not satisfy Boone, who very well knew that the Indians often resorted to such tricks to deceive their enemies and throw them off their guard. So he gave the challenge, "Halloe, strangers! who are you?" The answer came back, "White men, and friends."

Imagine Boone's surprise and delight upon discovering in one of the strangers his brother, Squire Boone, who, in company with another adventurer, had come from North Carolina in search of his long absent brother, bringing news from his family, and fresh supplies of powder and lead. They had traced the white hunters by their camp fires and other signs, and only an hour before the meeting, had stumbled upon their camping place of the previous night.

This happy meeting infused new life and spirit into the entire party, and they continued their hunting with renewed energy and zeal.

But only a few days elapsed before a sad misfortune befel them. Daniel Boone and Stewart while hunting in company, at some distance from their camp, were again attacked by a party of Indians. Stewart was shot and scalped, but Boone made his escape. Still another misfortue befel them shortly after this. The man who had come with Squire Boone from North Carolina. went into the woods one morning, and did not return. The two brothers supposed he was lost, but after several days of diligent search, they gave him up, supposing he had taken that method to desert them and make his way back to the settlements. But he was never seen alive again. Long afterward, a decayed skeleton and some fragments of clothing were discovered near a swamp, and these were supposed to be his remains. The manner of his death was never known, and by some unaccountable oversight his name was never made public.

The brothers were now entirely alone, but they were not despondent or indolent. They continued their hunting during the day, and sang and talked by their fires at night. They built a rough cabin to protect themselves from the weather, and, though surrounded by dangers on all sides, they were contented and happy.

As spring approached, their ammunition began to fail, and it was decided that Squire Boone should return to North Carolina for fresh supplies.

On the 1st of May the brothers shook hands and separated. Squire took up the line of march for the settlements on the Yadkin river, more than five hundred miles distant, leaving Daniel alone in the wilderness.

For several days after the departure of his brother, he was oppressed by a feeling of loneliness, and his philosophy and fortitude were put to a severe test. In order to relieve himself from this feeling, and to gain a more extended knowledge of the country, he made long tours of observation to the south-west, and explored the country along the waters of Salt and Green rivers.

The time for his brother's return having arrived, he retraced his steps to their old camp, and upon his arrival there discovered, by unmistakable signs, that it had been visited by Indians. His absence, therefore, had doubtless saved him from capture, and perhaps death.

On the 27th of July his brother returned, and a joyful meeting ensued. He rode one horse, and led another heavily ladened with the necessaries required. His brother's family he reported to be in good health and comfortable circumstances, which afforded great consolation and relief to the long absent husband.

Convinced that the portion of country they were now in was infested by bands of Indians, and that the horses would most likely excite their cupidity and lead to their capture, they decided to change their location. Acting upon this decision, they left their old camping ground, and proceeded to the country lying between Cumberland and Green rivers, which they thoroughly explored. They found the surface broken and uneven, abounding in what are called *sink holes*, or round depressions in the earth, which are not unusual in cavernous limestone regions; the timber was scattering and stunted; the soil seemed thin and poor, and they soon became dissatisfied with that portion of the country.

In March, 1771, they returned by a north-eastern direction, to the Kentucky river, where the soil appeared more fertile, and the country more heavily timbered; and here they resolved to fix the site of their projected settlement.

Having now completed their observations, they packed up as much peltry as their horses could carry, and departed for their homes on the Yadkin river, determined, as soon as possible, to return with their families and settle permanently in Kentucky.

It was a joyful meeting that took place between Daniel Boone and his family, for he had been absent two years, during which time he had seen no other human being except his travelling companions and the Indians who had taken him prisoner, and had tasted neither bread nor salt. And of the party of six who left the Yadkin two years before, he alone lived to return. Any one less enamored of frontier life, would have been disheartened at these trials, and satisfied to spend the remainder of his days in the enjoyment of a quiet domestic home. But he seemed to regard himself, during his entire life, as an instrument in the hands of Providence for opening and settling up the western wilderness, and acted as much from a sense of duty as a love of adventure.

Notwithstanding Boone's anxiety to remove his family to the hunting grounds of Kentucky, more than two years elapsed before he had completed his arrangements for so doing. He had no trouble in persuading his wife and family to accompany him, for they were willing and anxious to follow wherever he would lead. They had seen enough of frontier life to know its dangers,

and realize the discomforts and inconveniences they would have to
endure; but these did not deter them, for the pioneer women of
those days were as daring and self-sacrificing in their sphere as
their husbands, sons and brothers. Moreover, they had bright
dreams of vast plantations and future wealth for their children
and descendants in the midst of the rich forests of Kentucky,
where land could then be had for the occupation; and these
visions no doubt had their influence in nerving them to meet the
perils of a pioneer life.

On the 25th of September, 1773, Daniel and Squire Boone,
with their families, bade farewell to their friends on the Yadkin,
and set out on their march for the distant land of Kentucky. A
drove of pack-horses carried their provisions, clothing, bedding,
ammunition, etc., and a number of milk cows, driven by the
young men, supplied nourishment for the children.

At Powell's Valley, through which their route lay, they received
an accession to their party of five families and forty well armed
men. This valuable reinforcement gave them new courage, and
they proceeded on their way with lighter hearts and increased
confidence. But they soon met with a misfortune that changed
the whole aspect of affairs, and caused the expedition to be abandoned for the time being.

Their route led them over Powell's, Wallen's, and Cumberland
mountains, it having been marked out by the brothers on their
return from their previous expedition. In the latter range, near
the junction of Virginia, Kentucky, and Tennessee, there is a
singular opening, now called " Cumberland Gap," and it was
through this the party intended to pass. As they were approaching it, seven of the young men, who had charge of the cattle,
and who had fallen some five or six miles in the rear of the main
body, were suddenly and furiously attacked by a party of Indians. Six were killed on the spot. The seventh, though unarmed, made his escape, and the cattle were dispersed in the
woods. Among the slain was James Boone, the eldest son of
Daniel, who, in the opening promise of manhood, thus fell a victim
to savage ferocity.

The rest of the party heard the firing, and hastily returned to
the scene of the massacre, but too late to save their friends. The
Indians were driven off, and the dead buried, in the midst of the
lamentations and tears of their friends and relatives.

The emigrants were so disheartened and terrified by this calamity, that a retreat was resolved upon; and they returned to the settlements on Clinch river, in the south-western part of Virginia, forty miles from the scene of the massacre.

Here Boone remained until June, 1774, when a messenger from Governor Dunmore arrived in the settlement, with a request from him that Daniel ·Boone would go immmediately into the wilderness of Kentucky and conduct from thence a party of surveyors, who were believed to be in great danger from the Indians. Boone was now in his fortieth year, with finely developed physical powers, and a mind well trained for the work that lay before him. He set out immediately, in company with another pioneer named Michael Stoner, and in sixty-two days they had performed the journey, accomplished their object, and returned home, having traveled in that time, eight hundred miles, on foot.

Among the party of surveyors which Boone and his companion had thus rescued, were Thomas Bullet, Hancock Taylor, James Harrod, and James, Robert, and George McAfee, several of whom afterward settled in Kentucky, and established families that are still in existence in that State.

During Boone's absence in Kentucky, several tribes of Indians, whose country lay to the north-west of the Ohio river, commenced open hostilities against the white settlers, and upon his return he was appointed to the command of three contiguous garrisons on the frontier, with the commission of captain. Several skirmishes ensued at different times, and the campaign finally ended with the battle of Point Pleasant, at the junction of the Great Kenhawa and Ohio rivers, in which the Indians were routed and dispersed, although their numbers greatly exceeded those of their opponents. The white troops consisted of eleven hundred men, in three regiments, commanded by General Andrew Lewis. The Indians were commanded by the celebrated chief Cornstalk, who led them with great courage and sagacity.

At the close of hostilities, Boone returned to his family, and spent the following winter in hunting.

Early in 1775, he was employed by a company of land speculators, called the *Transylvania Company*, who had purchased large bodies of land in Kentucky, from the Indians, to explore the country and open a road from the settlements on the Holston to the Kentucky river. He was supplied with a company of well armed men, and proceeded at once to the task assigned him, which he found to be a very difficult one. Hills, mountains, and rivers had to be crossed, thick cane-brakes and dense forests penetrated, and all in the face of a vigilant, wily, and treacherous Indian foe.   On the 22d of March, 1775, when they had arrived within fifteen miles of the future site of Boonesborough, they were fired upon by the Indians, and two of the party were killed and two wounded.   Three days afterward they were again fired upon, and two more men were killed and three wounded.

The following letter from Boone to Col. Richard Henderson, president of the land company by which he was employed, explains these two affairs in his own language:

"APRIL 1ST, 1775.

" DEAR COLONEL,
     " After my compliments to you, I shall acquaint you with our misfortune.   On March the 25th, a party of Indians fired on my company about half an hour before day, and killed Mr. Twitty and his negro, and wounded Mr. Walker very deeply, but I hope he will recover.

     " On March the 28th, as we were hunting for provisions, we found Samuel Tate's son, who gave us an account that the Indians fired on their camp on the 27th day.   My brother and I went down and found two men killed and scalped, Thomas McDowell and Jeremiah McPeters.   I have sent a man down to all the lower companies in order to gather them all to the mouth of Otter Creek. My advice to you, Sir, is, to come or send as soon as possible. Your company is desired greatly, for the people are very uneasy, but are willing to stay and venture their lives with you; and now is the time to flusterate their (the Indians') intentions, and keep the country, whilst we are in it.   If we give way to them now, it will ever be the case.   This day we start from the battle ground, for the mouth of Otter Creek, where we shall immediately erect a fort, which will be done before you can come or send; then we can send ten men to meet you, if you send for them.
                    " I am, Sir, your most obedient
                                        " DANIEL BOONE.

     " N. B.   We stood on the ground and guarded our baggage till day, and lost nothing.   We have about fifteen miles to Cantuck, at Otter Creek. "

Boone having selected a site on the banks of the Kentucky river, they began, on the 1st day of April, to erect a stockade fort, which was called *Boonesborough*.   This was the first permanent settlement of whites within the limits of Kentucky.

During the building of the fort they were constantly harrassed by the Indians, who seemed stung to madness at the idea that white people should presume to erect houses on their hunting grounds. But they could not prevent the work from progressing, and by the middle of June the fort was so far completed as to afford protection against their assaults.

This fort was built in the form of a parallelogram, about two hundred feet long, and one hundred and seventy-five broad. At the four corners there were projecting block-houses, built of hewn logs, fitted close together, and well supplied with port holes for rifles. The spaces immediately adjoining these block-houses were filled with stockades for a short distance, and the remaining spaces on the four sides, except the gateways, were filled with rough log cabins, built close together, and likewise supplied with port holes for rifles. The two gates were placed on opposite sides, and were constructed of puncheons or split slabs, strongly barred together, and hung with heavy wooden hinges. The plan of this fort was followed in the construction of all the others that were subsequently erected, both in Kentucky and Missouri.

The fort having been completed, Boone left his men to guard it and prepare ground for a crop of corn and vegetables, while he returned to Clinch river for his family.

Nothing of importance occurred during this trip, or the return to Boonesborough, which they reached in safety. Mrs. Boone and her daughters were the first white women that ever stood on the banks of the Kentucky river, which are now in the midst of the blue-grass region, so famous for its beautiful and accomplished women.

Shortly after the arrival of Boone and his family, three other families joined them, viz : McGary, Hogan, and Denton. These were soon joined by others, and the little settlement began to assume a flourishing aspect.

In the summer of 1775 other stations and settlements were established in the new territory; and the strength and confidence of the whites increased daily. Harrod's and Bryan's Stations, and Logan's Fort were built about this time. Bryan's Station was besieged by the Indians several times, and a number of fights occurred at and near it; so that it became one of the principal points among the white settlements. The city of Lexington was also established during the summer of 1775. A party of hunters while encamped on the site of the future town, were joined by an emigrant, who brought news of the opening events of the revolution, and the battle of Lexington. Excited by their patriotic

2

feelings, the hunters immediately decided to name their encampment Lexington, in honor of the first battle for freedom.

The spring of 1776 opened auspiciously for the new settlers. The Indians, though by no means friendly, made no direct attacks upon them, and being comparatively unmolested, they proceeded to clear away the brush and "deaden" the timber around their stations and forts, preparatory to planting the summer's crops. In the mean time their food consisted of the game they killed in the woods, and such supplies as they had brought with them from the older settlements.

Thus the time passed quietly away until the 14th day of July, 1776, when the whole country was thrown into a state of excitement and anxiety by the capture of Jemima Boone and Betsy and Frances Callaway, daughters of Col. Richard Callaway, who had moved to Kentucky early that spring. The girls were about fourteen years of age, were devoted friends, and spent most of their time together. On the evening of their capture they were amusing themselves by rowing along the river in a canoe, which they handled with great dexterity. Anticipating no danger, and, being governed by the desire that possesses all human beings, to know what lies beyond them, they crossed over to the opposite shore. Here the attention of the girls was caught by a cluster of wild flowers, and desiring to possess them, they turned the prow of the canoe toward the shore. The trees and shrubs were thick, and extended down to the water's edge, affording a safe shelter for a band of Indians who lay concealed there. Just as one of the girls was in the act of grasping the flowers, an Indian slid stealthily down the bank into the water, and seizing the rope that hung at the bow of the canoe, turned its course up stream, in a direction to be hidden from the view of the fort by a projecting point. At the same time four other Indians appeared with drawn tomahawks and knives, and intimated to the girls by signs and motions that if they caused any alarm they would be killed on the spot. But, terrified at their sudden and unexpected capture, the girls shrieked for help. Their cries were heard at the fort, but too late for their rescue. The canoe was the only means the garrison had of crossing the river, and that was now on the opposite side and in possession of the enemy. None dared to swim the stream, fearing that a large body of Indians were concealed in the woods on the opposite bank.

Boone and Callaway were both absent, and night set in before their return, and arrangements could be made for pursuit. The following account of the pursuit and recapture of the girls is given by Col. Floyd, who was one of the pursuing party:

"Next morning by daylight we were on the track, but found they had totally prevented our following them, by walking some distance apart through the thickest canes they could find. We observed their course, and on which side we had left their sign, and traveled upwards of thirty miles. We then imagined that they would be less cautious in traveling, and made a turn in order to cross their trace, and had gone but a few miles before we found their tracks in a buffalo path; pursued and overtook them on going about ten miles, just as they were kindling a fire to cook. Our study had been more to get the prisoners, without giving the Indians time to murder them after they discovered us, than to kill them.

"We discovered each other nearly at the same time. Four of us fired, and all rushed on them, which prevented them from carrying away any thing except one shot gun without ammunition. Mr. Boone and myself had a pretty fair shot, just as they began to move off. I am well convinced I shot one through, and the one he shot dropped his gun; mine had none. The place was very thick with canes, and being so much elated on recovering the three little broken-hearted girls, prevented our making further search. We sent them off without their moccasins, and not one of them with so much as a knife or a tomahawk."

As stated elsewhere, Jemima Boone afterward married Flanders Callaway, a son of Col. Richard Callaway, and brother to her young friends with whom she was captured.

After this incident the settlers were more cautious, being convinced that the country was infested by bands of hostile Indians, who were watching each station for the purpose of picking up any stragglers that might come in their way. Guards were therefore placed around the corn fields where the men worked, and these were relieved from time to time by the laborers in the fields, who, in their turn, stood guard.

During the remainder of the summer of 1776 they were greatly harrassed by the Indians, who hardly suffered a day or night to pass without making some kind of demonstration against one or more of the stations; and when fall came, they had produced so great a panic among the whites that many of them left in consternation, and returned to their old homes. It required all the address and persuasion of the oldest and bravest of the pioneers to prevent the settlements from being entirely deserted.

The following year, 1777, was a dark one for those who remained, and many of the bravest became discouraged. The stations were frequently assailed by large bodies of Indians; individuals were shot and scalped by a concealed foe, and most of the cattle and horses were destroyed or driven away.

The forts and stations at that time were very weakly manned, and they could easily have been captured by a concentrated movement of the savages. The entire effective force did not exceed one hundred men, and these were divided between some three or four stations.

During these trying times Boone was not idle. As dangers thickened and appearances grew more alarming, he became more silent and thoughtful than usual; and as the pioneers, with their loaded rifles in their hands, sat around their fires in the evening and related tales of hair-breadth escapes from the Indians, Boone would sit silently by, apparently unheeding their conversation, and busily engaged in mending rents in his hunting shirt and leggins, moulding bullets, or cleaning his rifle. But he was their undisputed leader in everything, and no enterprise of importance was undertaken without first consulting him. Often, with one or two trusted companions, but more frequently alone, he would steal away into the woods as night approached, to reconnoitre the surrounding forests, and see if he could find any signs of the presence of an enemy. During the day, when not otherwise employed, he would range the country in the double capacity of hunter and scout, and supply the garrison with fresh game, while he kept himself fully informed as to the movements of the savage foe. On these excursions, which often extended a long distance from the fort, he would frequently meet new settlers, and conduct them in safety to the stations. Entirely unselfish, he was always more ready to assist others, and to aid in all public enterprises, than to attend to his own interests, and it was this characteristic that left him a poor man when he died.

During the winter of 1777-78 the people began to suffer greatly for salt, the cost of bringing so heavy an article across the mountains on horseback, being so great that but few of them could afford to use it. Therefore, after considering the matter, it was decided that thirty men, headed by Captain Boone, should take such kettles as could be spared, and proceed to the Lower Blue Licks, on Licking river, and there manufacture salt. They commenced operations on new year's day, 1778.

Boone filled the three positions of commander, hunter, and scout, and kept the men supplied with meat while he guarded against surprise by the Indians. They proceeded with their work without being molested, until the 7th of February, when Boone, who was hunting at some distance from the Lick, was surprised by a party of more than one hundred Indians, accompanied by two Canadians. He attempted to make his escape, but was soon overtaken by some of their swiftest runners, and captured.

This party was on a winter's campaign (an unusual thing with the Indians, and therefore unlooked for by the whites), to attack Boonesborough. This information Boone obtained soon after his capture, and knowing that the weak and unsuspecting garrison could not withstand an assault from so large a force, he was filled with apprehension for their safety, and began to devise some means to prevent the attack. He well understood the Indian character, and knew how to manage them.

Pretending to be pleased with their company, he soon gained their confidence, and then made favorable terms with them for his men at the Lick, assured that their capture would prevent an attack upon the fort, and thus save the women and children. On approaching the Lick, he advanced in front of his captors, and made signs to the salt-makers to offer no resistance. They, having perfect confidence in their leader, and knowing he had obtained favorable terms for them, did as directed, and quietly surrendered. The result proved Boone's sagacity. The expedition against Boonesborough was immediately abandoned, and the Indians, with their prisoners, set out at once for their own country. The generous usage promised before the capitulation was fully complied with, and the prisoners were treated with all the hospitality that could be expected from savages. They arrived at Old Chillicothe, the principal Indian town on the Little Miami, on the 18th of February, where most of them were subsequently ransomed by the British authorities, and returned to their friends.

Boone was afterward court-martialed for his conduct in this and subsequent affairs, but upon investigation he was not only honorably acquitted, but promoted for his sagacity and foresight

On the 10th of March, 1780, Boone and ten of his companions were conducted by forty Indians to Detroit, where they arrived on the 30th, and were treated with great humanity by Governor Hamilton, the British commander at that post. The fame of the distinguished pioneer had preceded him, and this no doubt had much to do with the generous treatment of himself and men. The latter were ransomed and paroled, but the Indians refused a ransom of one hundred pounds sterling which the Governor offered for Boone. They professed a deep affection for him, and declared their intention to take him back to their own country and adopt him as one of their warriors. His reputation as a hunter and fighter naturally led them to believe that he would be a valuable acquisition to any of their tribes.

This decision on their part greatly annoyed him, for he was exceedingly anxious to return to his family in Kentucky, and he now realized that it would be a long time before he would have an opportunity of doing so.

But he was too shrewd to manifest any disappointment or vexation in the presence of the Indians, for anything of the kind, or the slightest attempt to escape, would have added tenfold to their vigilance over him. So he pretended to be well pleased with their determination, and expressed a desire to accompany them as soon as they were ready.

They returned to Chillicothe in April, where he was adopted by Blackfish, a distinguished Shawnee chief, after the Indian fashion, to supply the place of a deceased son and warrior.

After his adoption he was regarded with great affection by his Indian father and mother, and was treated on all occasions with marked attention as a distinguished hunter and mighty brave. He took care to encourage their affection for him, and treated all his fellow-warriors in the most familiar and friendly manner. He joined them in their rifle and musket shooting games, and gained great applause by his skill as a marksman; but was careful not to excel them too frequently, as nothing will so soon excite the envy and hatred of an Indian as to be beaten at anything in which he takes pride.

After he had been with them some time he was permitted to go alone into the woods in quest of game, but his powder was always measured to him and his balls counted, and when he returned he was required to account in game for all the ammunition he could not produce. But by using small charges of powder, and cutting balls in halves, with which he could kill squirrels and other small game, he managed to save a few charges of powder and ball for use in case he should find an opportunity to escape.

One evening early in June, he was alarmed, upon returning

from his day's hunt, to see a large body of four hundred and fifty warriors collected in the town, painted and armed for the war-path. His alarm was greatly increased a few minutes later, by learning that their destination was Boonesborough.

He at once decided to lose no more time, but make his escape immediately, and proceed as rapidly as possible to the settlements in Kentucky, and alarm the people in time to save them from a general massacre.

That night he secreted about his person some jerked venison, to sustain him during his long journey; and early the next morning he left the Indian village, with his gun on his shoulder, as if he were going into the woods for his usual day's hunt. But after wandering about for some time, as if in quest of game, in order to allay the suspicions of any spies that might follow him, and having placed several miles between himself and the town, he suddenly changed his course in the direction of Boonesborough, and set off with all his might for his beloved home. The distance exceeded one hundred and sixty miles, which he traveled in less than five days, eating but one regular meal, which was a turkey that he shot after crossing the Ohio river.

Until he left that stream behind him, his anxiety was very great, for he knew that he would be followed, and being but an indifferent swimmer he anticipated trouble in crossing the river. But he was rejoiced upon reaching its banks to find an old canoe that had floated into the brush and lodged. There was a hole in one end of it, but this he contrived to stop, and the frail vessel bore him safely to the Kentucky shore.

His appearance at Boonesborough was almost like one risen from the dead, and he was received by the garrison with joyful shouts of welcome. His capture and journey to Detroit were known by reports of prisoners who had escaped, but his friends did not expect ever to see him again. His wife, despairing of his return, had conveyed herself and some of the children, on pack-horses, to her father's home in North Carolina, and he keenly felt the disappointment at not meeting her. The tongue of calumny, too, ever ready to stir up strife, endeavored to bring about a permanent separation of these two devoted people, but without success, though it cost them both much trouble and anguish. This is a period of Boone's life that he never mentioned to his most intimate friends, and justice indicates that the historian should also cover it with the mantle of silence.

The garrison of the fort had become careless in their duties; had dispersed over the neighborhood in the pursuit of their various occupations, and had suffered the works to get out of repair. But the intelligence brought by Boone of the threatened invasion, aroused them to a sense of their danger, and great activity at once prevailed in making the necessary repairs and strengthening the fortifications. Information soon reached them, however, that on account of Boone's escape, the expedition had been abandoned for the present.

This gave them a short breathing spell, and Capt. Boone decided to improve it to the best advantage. Early in August, with a company of nineteen men, he made an excursion into the Indian country, for the purpose of frightening them, and to send out the impression that the whites were no longer so weak that they needed to stand entirely upon the defensive.

When within a short distance of an Indian village on Paint Creek, a branch of the Scioto, they met a party of thirty warriors on their march for Kentucky. A battle ensued, in which one Indian was killed and two wounded; when the rest gave way and fled. Three horses and all their baggage were captured, while the Kentuckians maintained no loss whatever.

Learning that a large body of Indians, under the celebrated chief Blackfish, who was Boone's adopted father while in captivity, supported by a few Canadians, commanded by Captain Duquesne, were on the march for Boonesborough, the heroic little band immediately started on their return to Kentucky. The army of Indians and Canadians lay between them and their destination, but they adroitly spied out their position, passed them in safety, and reached Boonesborough in time to give the alarm.

On the 7th of September this formidable army appeared before the fort, and demanded its surrender "in the name of his Britannic Majesty," with assurances of liberal treatment if the demand were complied with. It was a critical moment, for the garrison consisted of only from sixty to seventy men, with a large number of women and children. If they offered resistance, and were defeated, which seemed to be a foregone conclusion, in view of the overpowering numbers of the enemy, all alike would fall victims to the tomahawk and scalping knife; but if they accepted the terms offered, and surrendered, there was a possibility that they would be saved.

In the mean time a dispatch had been sent to Col. Campbell,

on the Holston, for reinforcements, and if they could by any means delay the attack until these were within reach, they would be safe. At this critical juncture, Boone had recourse to stratagem, in order to gain time. He requested that the garrison be allowed two days to consider the proposition to surrender, and his request being granted, the time was employed in collecting the cattle and horses within the walls of the fort, and filling every vessel with water from the spring, which was outside the palisades. (By a singular oversight, the springs, both at Boonesborough and Bryan's Station, were not enclosed within the walls of the fortifications, and on several occasions, during the different sieges that occurred, they were greatly pressed for water.) These duties were performed by the women and girls, in order that the enemy might have no opportunity to learn the real weakness of the garrison.

The arrangements having been completed, Captain Boone, toward the close of the second day, ascended one of the bastions and announced to Duquesne that the garrison had decided not to surrender, and added: "We laugh at your formidable preparations, but thank you for giving notice and time to prepare for denfence."

He expected an immediate assault, and the men were prepared for it, but on the contrary, Duquesne came forward with another proposition for a surrender. He declared that his orders were to take the garrison captives, and treat them as prisoners of war, instead of murdering them; and that they were prepared with horses to convey the women and those who could not travel on foot, to the British possessions. He further proposed that the garrison depute nine men to come within their lines and agree upon the terms of a treaty.

Boone and his companions very well understood that these fair promises had a sinister motive at the bottom, and meant treachery; but they wanted to gain time, and were willing to consent to almost any conditions that would cause delay. So they signified their acceptance of the last proposition, and appointed the place of meeting on the open plat of ground in front of the fort.

Ever ready to sacrifice himself for the good of others, Boone decided to lead the party on this hazardous adventure, and called for eight additional volunteers. Every man in the fort stepped forward in answer to this call, and eight of the shrewdest and stoutest were selected. The names of four of these have been preserved. They were, Flanders Callaway, Stephen Hancock, William Hancock, and Squire Boone.

Before leaving the fort, twenty men with loaded rifles were stationed so as to command a full view of the proceedings, with orders to fire on the Indians in case treachery should be manifested.

The terms offered by Duquesne were exceedingly liberal; so liberal, in fact, that Boone and his companions knew they did not come from honest hearts; but in order to gain time, they humored the whims of the enemy and held a long conference with them. At its close, the Indians proposed that, in order to make the terms more binding, and to revive an ancient custom on this great occasion, two Indians should shake hands with one white man, and thus manifest their friendliness. Even to this proposition, which they knew would end in an attempt at their capture, Boone and his party acceded. They were entirely unarmed, as it would have been regarded as a breach of confidence to have appeared upon the treaty ground with arms in their hands; but each man felt able to cope with two of his savage foes. When the latter approached, each grasped a hand and arm of the white men, and a scuffle immediately ensued, for the Indiams attempted to drag them off as prisoners. But at this critical moment, the guard in the fort fired upon the Indians and threw them into confusion, and Boone and his companions knocked down or tripped their antagonists, and fled into the fort. Squire Boone was the only one of the party who was hurt, and he received only a slight wound.

The main body of Indians, who were prepared for the turn affairs had taken, now rushed forward and made a furious assault upon the fort. But they met with a warm reception, and were soon glad to withdraw to the cover of the woods again.

After the first assault they remained at a respectful distance, for they had a wholesome dread of the rifles of the Kentuckians, which would shoot further and with much greater accuracy than their old smooth-bore muskets. Most of their balls were spent before they reached the fort, and fell harmlessly back from the tough oaken palisades.

Finding they could not carry the fort by assault, they attempted to set it on fire, by throwing combustibles upon the roofs; and for a time this new mode of attack seemed about to prove successful. But a daring young man climbed to the roof in the midst of a shower of balls, and remained there with buckets of water until the fire was extinguished.

Failing in this attempt, the Indians, under directions from the Canadians, resorted to another experiment, and tried to enter the fort by means of a mine. The fort stood about sixty yards from the river, and they began an excavation under the bank, which concealed them from view. But their project was detected by the muddy water seen at a little distance below, and it was defeated by the Kentuckians, who began a countermine within the fort, and threw the dirt over the palisades. While the men were engaged in digging this mine, Captain Boone constructed a wooden cannon, which was loaded with powder, balls, old nails, pieces of iron, etc. It was his intention to place this instrument at the head of the mine, and as the Indians entered, fire it into their midst. But on the 20th of the month they raised the siege and departed for their own country, having lost thirty-seven warriors killed, and many more wounded. The Kentuckians had two men killed, and four wounded. After the departure of the Indians, one hundred and twenty-five pounds of musket balls were picked up around the fort, besides those that penetrated and were made fast in the logs.

During the siege the women and girls moulded bullets, loaded the rifles, and carried ammunition to their husbands, fathers, and brothers; besides preparing refreshments, nursing the wounded, and assisting in various other ways. Jemima Boone, while carrying ammunition to her father, received a contusion in her hip from a spent musket ball, which caused a painful, though by no means dangerous wound.

While the parley was in progress between Boone and the Indians, previous to the first attack, a worthless negro deserted and went over to the enemy, carrying with him a large, long-range rifle. He crossed the river, and stationed himself in a tree, so that by raising his head above a fork, he could fire directly down into the fort. He had killed one man and wounded another, when Boone discovered his head peering above the fork for another shot. "You black scoundrel!" said the old pioneer, as he raised his rifle to his shoulder, "I'll fix *your* flint for you," and quickly running his eye along the bright barrel of his rifle, he fired. The negro fell, and at the close of the battle was found at the roots of the tree with a bullet hole in the center of his forehead. The distance was one hundred and seventy-five yards.

Shortly after the siege of Boonesborough, Captain Boone was tried by a court-martial, under several charges, the principal of which were the surrender of his men at Blue Licks while they were making salt, and friendliness toward the Indians while a prisoner among them.

Mr. Peck says the charges were preferred by Col. Richard Callaway, aided by Col. Benjamin Logan. But so far as Callaway was concerned, this is a mistake, as we learn from old pioneers still living, who were well acquainted with both Boone and Callaway, and who often heard them relate the history of those stirring times. The strongest friendship and utmost confidence always existed between Boone and Callaway, and their families after them; and neither Callaway, or any of Boone's friends, ever thought there was the least shadow of an excuse for the trumped up charges that were made against him. The trial resulted in the complete vindication of Boone, and his promotion to the rank of Major.

In the autumn of 1778, Major Boone went to North Carolina for his wife and family, who were greatly rejoiced to see him alive and well once more. But he did not remove them to Kentucky until two years later.

In 1779, the government of Virginia established a Court of Commissioners, to hear and determine all disputes relative to land claims in Kentucky, and to grant certificates of settlement and pre-emption to those who were entitled to them. This brought out a large number of families and single persons who were interested in these claims, and for a time the Commissioners were overrun with applications. Most of the titles obtained at this time were afterward declared invalid. through want of compliance with law and the indefinite location of many of the claims, and heavy losses and great distress were occasioned thereby. Major Boone sold all his property, and invested nearly everything he possessed in land warrants. He was also entrusted with large sums of money by friends and acquaintances who deputed him to make their entries for them, and while on his way from Kentucky to Richmond with this money, amounting to about $20,000, he was robbed of every cent, and left worse than penniless. Most of those who lost money by this misfortune readily gave up all claims against Boone, and freely exonerated him from any blame in the affair; but a few charged him with their losses, alleging that he was robbed through his own carelessness, and these held him to account for the money they had placed in his hands. Several years after his removal to Missouri, the venerable old pioneer returned to Kentucky and paid every cent of these claims.

The following extract from a letter written by Col. Thomas Hart, of Lexington, in 1780, to Captain Nathaniel Hart, is a fine tribute to the character of Boone under the trying ordeal through which he was at that time passing:

"I observe what you say respecting our losses by Daniel Boone. I had heard of the misfortune soon after it happened, but not of my being a partaker before now. I feel for the poor people, who, perhaps, are to lose even their pre-emptions; but I must say I feel more for Boone, whose character, I am told, suffers by it. Much degenerated must the people of this age be, when amongst them are to be found men to censure and blast the reputation of a person so just and upright, and in whose breast is the seat of virtue, too pure to admit of a thought so base and dishonorable. I have known Boone in times of old, when poverty and distress held him fast by the hand; and in these wretched circumstances I have ever found him of a noble and generous soul, despising every thing mean; and therefore I will freely grant him a discharge for whatever sums of mine he might have been possessed of at that time."

As previously stated, Major Boone returned to Kentucky with his family in 1780. In October of that year, he and his brother, Squire Boone, went to the Blue Licks on a hunting expedition, and as they were returning home they were fired upon by a party of Indians in ambush. Squire Boone was killed and scalped, and the Major was pursued several miles by the aid of an Indian dog; but he shot the dog and escaped. This calamity made a deep impression upon the old pioneer, and for a long time it preyed heavily upon his mind. His attachment to his brother was naturally very strong, and it had been increased and strengthened by fellowship in wanderings, sufferings and dangers for many years.

About this time Kentucky was divided into three counties, by the Legislature of Virginia, and a civil and military government organized. Each county formed a regiment, and John Todd, an estimable and popular man, was elected Colonel for one of the counties (Lincoln), with Boone as Lieutenant-Colonel. Colonel Clark was commissioned Brigadier-General and placed in command of the three regiments. With this military organization, and their augmented numbers, the settlers began to feel secure, and did not anticipate any more serious trouble with the Indians.

But in this they were disappointed, for late in the autumn the savages again began to commit depredations upon the outposts and exposed settlements, and did considerable damage, besides creating a great deal of alarm.   Boonesborough, however, was not molested, being now in the interior and surrounded by other forts and stations.

On the morning of the 14th of August, 1782, Bryan's Station, situated about five miles northeast of Lexington, was attacked by a large force of Indians under the notorious Simon Girty.   The garrison numbered only about fifty men, and the station was not in the best condition to withstand a siege.   Early in the morning of the 14th they were aroused by the hooting and yelling of savages, and hastily gathering into the block-houses, they saw a small party of Indians near the woods on one side of the station, yelling and dancing and gesticulating, and now and then firing a shot toward the fort.   This party was so small, and appeared so contemptible, that some of the younger men wanted to rush out and whip them immediately; but fortunately there were older heads in the fort, and experienced Indian fighters, who knew that this was merely a ruse to entice them out of their fortifications, when they would be attacked by the main body, which they felt assured was concealed at no great distance.   Runners were immediately dispatched to Lexington and other points for assistance, who, secretly making their way out of the station and passing through the corn fields, reached their destinations in safety.   Busy preparations were then commenced to get everything ready for a siege, when the startling discovery was made that they were out of water.   The spring was outside of the palisades, and water had to be conveyed from it in buckets.   The question now arose as to how they should get the water.   It would not do for the men to go after it, for that would bring on the attack at once; so it was proposed that the women and girls should be the water carriers this time.   The proposition was directly made known to them, but they did not receive it with favor.   Some murmured, and said that the men evidently thought very little of their wives and daughters, if they were willing to send them where they were afraid to go themselves, and that if they were too badly scared to go to the spring, they had better hand their rifles over to the women and let them defend the fort.   "We are not afraid," said the spokesman, "to go to the spring; but we know that if the men leave the fort we shall immediately be attacked by the entire force of the enemy, while you can go without exciting any suspicion or being in any danger, as the Indians know it is customary for you to bring the water.'' Finally, an old lady arose, got a couple of buckets, and started to the spring, saying that she was no better than a man, anyhow, and was not much afraid of the red-skins either. Her example was silently followed by the rest, and they soon returned with their buckets filled with water. But some of the younger ones manifested a good deal of haste on their return, and as they entered the gate of the fort their eyes were very wide open, while much of the water in their buckets was spattered over their dresses and on the ground. The danger they had faced was indeed very great; for in the brush around the spring there lay concealed more than four hundred painted warriors, who could almost have grasped them by their dresses if they had been so disposed.

As soon as these preparations were completed, thirteen daring young men were selected and sent out to attack and pursue the small party of Indians that were in view, while the balance of the men, with loaded rifles in their hands, were placed on the opposite side of the fort. The stratagem was successful. The small party of Indians retreated to the woods, pursued by the thirteen young men. Girty heard the firing, and supposing the main body to have left the fort, gave the signal yell, and instantly the woods and undergrowth around the spring seemed alive with yelling savages. Firing a heavy volley at the fort, they rushed furiously, with Girty at their head, against the nearest gate. But the Kentuckians were prepared for them, and their unerring rifles scattered death and destruction among their ranks. So deadly was the fire that they were seized with consternation, and fled precipitately into the woods. Here they were rallied by Girty and their chiefs, and with renewed yells came on to the second assault. But the leaden hail of the Kentucky rifles rained upon them again, and again they fled in consternation. After this an irregular fight was kept up for several hours, in which but little damage was done to either side.

About two o'clock in the afternoon a reinforcement of fifty men, on horseback and on foot, arrived from Lexington for the relief of the garrison. The Indians were aware of their approach, and lay in ambush for them. The horsemen rushed through without the loss of a man; but the footmen were not so fortunate. They first entered a cornfield, through which they should have passed to the fort, concealed as they were from the enemy; but, eager to get a shot at the redskins, they emerged into the road again, fell into the ambuscade, and lost six men.

The Indians, alarmed at this reinforcement, and expecting the arrival of other parties soon, were in favor of an immediate retreat to their own country. But Girty, furious at being foiled in his attempt to subdue the station by force, and smarting from a slight wound received in the morning, resorted to stratagem with the hope of gaining his purpose. He crawled to a stump, near one of the bastions, and demanded a parley. Commending their manly defence and bravery, he urged that further resistance was useless, alluded to the large number and fierceness of his followers, and asserted that he had a large reinforcement near at hand. with several pieces of artillery. He warned them that if they continued to resist, and were finally captured by force, they would all be massacred; but assured them, "upon his honor," that if they would surrender then, they should be treated as prisoners of war. The commander of the station would not deign to pay the least attention to him, but he was answered in a taunting and pungent manner by a young man named Reynolds, who told him that he had a worthless dog, to which he had given the name of Simon Girty, in consequence of his striking resemblance to the man who bore that name; that if he had artillery and reinforcements he might bring them on, but if he or any of the naked rascals with him found their way into the fort, they would disdain to use their guns against them, but would drive them out with whips. of which they had collected a large number for that purpose. When he ceased speaking, some of the young men began to call out, "Shoot the scoundrel!" "Kill the renegade!" etc., and Girty, seeing that his position was no longer safe, crawled back, crestfallen, to the camp of his followers, and next morning they had disappeared.

Information of the attack on Bryan's Station had spread with great rapidity all over the country, and reinforcements came pouring in from every direction. Colonel Boone and his son Israel and brother Samuel, headed a strong party from Boonesborough; Colonel Stephen Trigg brought up the forces from Harroosburg, and Colonel John Todd came with the militia from Lexington. Among the latter were Majors Harlan, McGary, McBride, and Levi Todd. Colonel Benjamin Logan, who resided at a greater distance, raised a large force, but did not arrive in time to participate in the pursuit and the disastrous battle which followed.

A council of the officers was held to decide upon what course should be followed. A large majority were eager for a fight, and favored immediate pursuit; but Colonel Boone, knowing the strength of the enemy, and realizing how hard it would be, in the midst of a battle with the Indians, to successfully control a body of raw militia, hastily collected together, without organization or drill, deemed it advisable to await the arrival of Colonel Logan and his force.

But his wise counsels were not heeded. Colonel Todd was heard to say that Boone was a coward, and if they wanted the glory of a victory they should press forward immediately.

The opinions of the majority prevailed, and the men were marched out to follow the trail. Boone and the more experienced ones soon became convinced that the Indians wanted to be followed, for instead of trying to hide their trail, as usual, they had taken pains to make it as plain as possible. The trees were marked with their tomahawks, the ground was much trodden, and their camp-fires were few, showing a design to mask their numbers.

But no Indians were seen until the Kentuckians reached the bluffs of the Licking, opposite the Lower Blue Licks, when a few were discovered leisurely marching over a ridge on the opposite side of the river.

Colonel Todd now ordered a halt, for further consultation before crossing the river, and, notwithstanding his intemperate language of the morning, especially solicited the views of Colonel Boone. He was still of the opinion that they had better await the arrival of Colonel Logan, for the Indians were very strong, and he had no doubt were well posted in ambush on the opposite side of the river. But in the event of a determination to proceed, he advised that the troops be divided into two parties, one of which should proceed above the bend of the river and cross in the rear of the enemy, while the other, crossing at the ford, where they then were, should proceed along the trail and attack them in front.

The position selected by the Indians was a strong one. The river, by making an abrupt curve to the north, or opposite side from the army, encircled a ridge for a mile or more in extent. Near the top of this ridge, on opposite sides, two ravines headed and ran down to the water's edge. They were filled with

3

brushwood and trees, forming an admirable hiding place for the five hundred warriors who lay concealed there. The army, in following the trail, would be enclosed, as if in a net, by these two ravines, and exposed to a raking fire on all sides, while the enemy was completely sheltered from their fire and hidden from view.

While Boone and Todd were still consulting as to what course should be pursued, Major McGary, who was a warm friend of Boone, and who had become incensed at the intemperate language used by Colonel Todd, in the morning, in reference to him, raised the war whoop, spurred his horse into the river, and called out, "All who are not cowards, follow me, and I will show you where the Indians are." On the impulse of the moment, nearly the entire army followed him, yelling and whooping, to the opposite shore ; and the rest, with Boone and Todd, soon followed. The latter rode up to Major McGary and demanded, in an excited manner, what he meant by his rash conduct, when McGary replied, "You wanted to fight, and, by g—d, I thought I would give you a chance."

Colonel Boone now advised that some scouts be sent forward to examine the ground, and, if the enemy were present, ascertain his position. Those who had been eager for the fray in the morning, were now, in the presence of the enemy, willing to heed the advice of the old pioneer, who still remained as cool and collected as if nothing unusual were transpiring.

Two bold and experienced scouts were selected and sent forward, but, though they proceeded half a mile beyond the ravines, no Indians were discovered.

Orders were now given to march, and the army advanced, Colonel Todd commanding the center, Trigg the right, and Boone the left.

They proceeded to within forty yards of the ravines, when suddenly the entire body of Indians poured a destructive fire into their ranks, from both sides of the ridge. The dead and wounded fell thick at the first discharge, but the brave Kentuckians stood their ground like heroes, notwithstanding they were greatly outnumbered and fought at such a disadvantage. Colonel Trigg fell at the first fire, and with him a large number of the Harrodsburg troops. Major Harland's advance guard maintained their ground until three men only remained, their commander having fallen covered with wounds. Colonel Todd was mortally wounded near the commencement of the battle, and when last seen he was reeling on his horse, with the blood streaming from his wounds. Major McGary fought like a tiger, but escaped unhurt. Colonel Boone was as cool as if he were merely on a hunting expedition, and gallantly led his men into the thickest of the fight.

The army having been thrown into confusion, the Indians rushed upon the men with hideous yells and drawn tomahawks, and the retreat commenced at once. The fugitives rushed down the slope of the ridge to the river, and plunging in, waded or swam across, followed closely by the Indians. Many of them would have been killed in the river except for the presence of mind of a man named Netherland, who on former occasions had been called a coward, but in this instance acted like a hero. Being mounted on a spirited horse, he had outrun the main body of his retreating comrades, and had safely reached the opposite bank of the river. Looking back, he saw the Indians rushing into the river to kill those who were struggling with the current, and wheeling his horse, he called out to some ten or a dozen men who were near him, "Halt! fire on the Indians, and protect the men in the river." His loud, stern command had the desired effect, and a volley from a dozen rifles checked the savages and gave the men an opportunity to cross in safety.

Many of the Indians swam the river above and below the ford, and continued the pursuit for more than twenty miles, killing some, and taking a few prisoners. The defeated army never halted until it reached Bryan's Station, thirty-six miles distant.

Colonel Boone was one of the very last to leave the battle field, and when he saw that the rout was hopeless, he directed all his energies to the preservation of as many lives as possible. Just as he was leaving the field, he came upon his son, mortally wounded. For a moment he was overcome by the feelings of a tender and loving father, and, with tears streaming from his eyes, raised the dying form of his boy in his arms, and made his way toward a place of safety near the river, below the curve and the ravine, where he knew he could easily cross the current.

He had proceeded but a few steps when a powerful Indian, with raised tomahawk, sprang before him; but in a moment the contents of Boone's gun entered his body, and he fell lifeless to the ground. Before he reached the bank of the river, his son expired in his arms, when, straining him to his bosom as he took a last look at the beloved face, he laid the still and lifeless form gently on the ground, and made his escape.

This event made so deep an impression on the mind of the old pioneer, that, to the day of his death, he could not mention it without shedding tears. His brother, Samuel was severely wounded, but escaped.

Of the one hundred and eighty-two persons who went into battle, about one-third were killed, twelve wounded, and seven carried off prisoners. These were put to death by torture after they reached the Indian towns.

This disastrous battle covered Kentucky with mourning, for nearly every family in the little settlements had a relative or friend killed.

The following report of the battle, made by Colonel Boone to Gov. Harrison, of Virginia, will be read with interest, as being one of the few official documents that remain from his pen:

> " BOONE'S STATION, FAYETTE COUNTY, }
> "August, 30th, 1782.   }

" SIR,

" Present circumstances of affairs cause me to write to your Excellency as follows. On the 16th instant, a large number of Indians, with some white men, attacked one of our frontier stations, known by the name of Bryan's Station. The siege continued from about sunrise till about ten o'clock the next day, when they marched off. Notice being given to the neighboring stations, we immediately raised one hundred and eighty-one horsemen, commanded by Colonel John Todd, including some of the Lincoln county militia, and pursued about forty miles.

" On the 19th instant, we discovered the enemy lying in wait for us. On this discovery, we formed our columns into one single line, and marched up in their front within about forty yards before there was a gun fired. Colonel Trigg commanded on the right, myself on the left, and Major McGary in the centre, and Major Harland the advanced party in front. From the manner in which we had formed, it fell to my lot to bring on the attack. This was done with a very heavy fire on both sides, and extended back of the line to Colonel Trigg, where the enemy was so strong they rushed up and broke the right wing at the first fire. Thus the enemy got in our rear, with the loss of seventy-seven of our men, and twelve wounded. Afterwards we were reinforced by Colonel Logan, which made our force four hundred and sixty men. We marched again to the battle ground; but, finding the enemy had gone, we proceeded to bury the dead.

" We found forty-three on the ground, and many lay about. which we could not stay to find, hungry and weary as we were. and somewhat dubious that the enemy might not have gone off quite. By the sign, we thought that the Indians had exceeded four hundred; while the whole of this militia of the county does not amount to more than one hundred and thirty. From these facts your Excellency may form an idea of our situation.

" I know that your own circumstances are critical; but are we to be wholly forgotten? I hope not. I trust about five hundred men may be sent to our assistance immediately. If these shall be stationed as our county lieutenants shall deem necessary, it may be the means of saving our part of the country; but if they are placed under the direction of General Clark, they will be of little or no service to our settlement. The Falls lie one hundred miles west of us, and the Indians northeast; while our men are frequently called to protect them. I have encouraged the people in this county all that I could; but I can no longer justify them or myself to risk our lives here under such extraordinary hazards. The inhabitants of this county are very much alarmed at the thoughts of the Indians bringing another campaign into our country this fall. If this should be the case, it will break up these settlements. I hope, therefore, your Excellency will take this matter into your consideration, and send us some relief as quick as possible.

"These are my sentiments, without consulting any person. Colonel Logan will, I expect, immediately send you an express, by whom I humbly request your Excellency's answer. In the meanwhile, I remain, &c.

"DANIEL BOONE."

The day after the little army of one hundred and eighty-two had left Bryan's Station, Colonel Logan arrived there at the head four hundred and fifty men. Fearful of some disaster, he immediately ordered a forced march, and set out on the old trail. They had proceeded only a few miles when they met the first party of fugitives, who, as usual in such cases, could give only an excited and unsatisfactory account of the affair. Colonel Logan now decided to return to the station and await the arrival of more of the survivors, in order that he might obtain additional information, and know better how to proceed. By night they were all in, and the true story became known.

Late that night, Colonel Logan, accompanied by Colonel Boone and a few of the survivors, started for the battle-ground, which they reached at noon the next day. The Indians were gone, but the sight was horrible. Dead and mutilated bodies were strewn through the timber, submerged in the river, and spread over the rocky ridge. Immense flocks of vultures were hovering in the air, perched in the trees, or feeding on the bodies of the slain. The savages had mangled and scalped many, the wolves had torn others, and the oppressive heat of August had so disfigured their faces that in many cases their friends could recognize them only by their clothing. They were buried as decently as circumstances would admit, and Logan and his men returned to Bryan's Station.

As soon as the intelligence of the defeat at Blue Licks reached General Clark at Louisville, he began to make arrangements for a formidable expedition into the Indian country, and, with his usual energy and determination, was soon on the march at the head of a large force. Colonel Boone went along as a volunteer scout, preferring that position to any command that could be given him.

The march was conducted so rapidly and with so much secrecy, that the army came within half a mile of Girty and his party, on their return from Kentucky, before they were aware of its presence, or that such a force was even in existence. Two Indians, loitering in the rear, discovered the Kentuckians, and hastily fleeing to their companions gave the alarming intelligence that a mighty army was close upon them.

They instantly evacuated their camp and fled, dispatching runners to all the surrounding towns to give the alarm. The towns were abandoned, and when General Clark and his men entered them they found nothing but deserted lodges. Upon entering Old Chillicothe they found fires still burning and provisions in process of cooking.

Of this expedition Colonel Boone said:

"The savages fled in the utmost disorder, evacuating their towns, and reluctantly left their territory to our mercy. We immediately took possession of the town of Old Chillicothe without opposition, it being deserted by its inhabitants In this expedition we took seven prisoners and five scalps, with the loss of only four men, two of whom were accidentally killed by our own army."

The troops destroyed four other towns, cut the standing corn in the fields, and desolated the whole country. The destruction of their towns and property paralyzed the Indians more than a defeat or battle would have done, and the expedition, by teaching them the superiorty of the white people, both in numbers and means of carrying on war, put an end to their raids and depredations, and the people of Kentucky, except in some of the frontier settlements, which were visited occasionally by small parties of Indians, were allowed to enjoy the blessed fruits of peace.

Colonel Boone, with his receipts for military services, and the proceeds of his own industry, was enabled to pay for several tracts of land, on one of which he built a comfortable log cabin, and cleared a farm, where he expected to spend the remainder of his days. For several years he cultivated his crops, and, during the hunting season, amused himself at his favorite occupation.

His last encounter with the Indians in Kentucky was of an amusing rather than a dangerous character, and was in substance as follows, as related by himself:

Boone never used tobacco, but he had raised about one hundred and fifty hills of the weed, on his farm, for the use of his neighbors. When it was ripe and ready to be housed, he built a pen of fence rails, about twelve feet high, and covered it with cane and grass; and in this enclosure the tobacco was hung in three tiers, one above the other, to dry and "cure." In a short time it was so dry and crisp that it would crumble into powder upon being rubbed or roughly handled.

One day while removing the sticks of tobacco from the lower tier to the upper ones, and while standing with his feet on the poles of the lower tier, he was startled to hear the gruff Indian salutation of "How!" immediately under him. Looking down, he saw four Indians, with guns in their hands, who had entered by the low door, and were now looking up at him. Seeing that he observed them, they addressed him as follows: "Now, Boone, we got you. You no get away any more. We carry you off to Chillicothe this time. You no cheat us any more. Damn!" Boone recognized them as some of his old friends who had captured him at the Blue Licks in 1778, and addressing them pleasantly, he said, "Ah! old friends! Glad to see you. Just wait one moment, and I'll come down." He parleyed with them for some time, asking about old acquaintances, and pretending to be pleased with the opportunity of going with them; until, having diverted their attention from him, he gathered a bundle of dry tobacco and threw it down upon their upturned faces, at the same time jumping upon them with as much of the tobacco as he could gather in his arms. Their mouths, eyes, and noses were filled with the pungent dust, which blinded them and set them to sneezing violently; and in the midst of their discomfiture Boone rushed out and made his way to his cabin, where he had the means of defence. But notwithstanding his narrow escape, he could not withstand the temptation to look back and see the result of his achievement. The Indians were groping about with outstretched hands, feeling their way out of the pen, calling him by name, and cursing him for a rogue, and themselves for fools.

In 1792 Kentucky was admitted into the Union as a State. As courts of justice were established in every community, litigation increased, and was carried to a distressing extent. Many of the old pioneers, who had cleared farms in the midst of the wilderness, and were prepared to spend the remainder of their days surrounded by peace and plenty, had their homes wrested from them, through lack of legal titles, by greedy and avaricious speculators, and were cast adrift in their old age, to again fight the battle of existence. Colonel Boone was among the sufferers. Every foot of his land was taken from him, and he was left penniless. His recorded descriptions of location and boundary were defective, and shrewd speculators had the adroitness to secure legal titles by more accurate and better defined entries.

Disgusted with legal quibbles and technicalities, and disheartened at his misfortunes, Boone decided to once more seek a home in the wilderness. About the year 1790 he removed to the Kenhawa Valley, in Virginia, and settled near Point Pleasant, where he remained until 1795, when he removed to Missouri, or Upper Louisiana, as it was then called. His son, Daniel M. Boone, had already settled in that country, and gave such glowing accounts of the climate, soil, game, etc., that the old pioneer's imagination was captivated. About the same time he received an invitation from the Spanish Lieutenant-Governor, Zenon Trudeau, to remove there, offering as an inducement a large grant of land. He at once decided to accept the invitation. Accordingly, gathering up such articles as were convenient to carry, and with his trusty rifle, "Old Checlicker," on his shoulder, his chattels, and a portion of his family on pack-horses, he started on his journey to the new land of promise. All his family subsequently followed him, except his two daughters, Lavinia and Rebecca, who, as previously stated, lived and died in Kentucky. His son Jesse remained in the Kenhawa Valley, where he had married, until 1819, when he too came to Missouri.

For several years after Colonel Boone's removal, Upper Louisiana remained under Spanish rule, and the promise of the Lieutenant-Governor was faithfully fulfilled. On the 24th of January, 1798, he received a concession of 1,000 arpents of land, situated in Femme Osage District. He afterward made an agreement with the Spanish authorities to bring one hundred families from Kentucky and Virginia to Upper Louisiana, for which he was to receive 10,000 arpents of land. The agreement was fulfilled on both sides; but in order to confirm his title to this grant, it was necessary to obtain the signature of the direct representative of the crown, who resided in New Orleans. Colonel Boone neglected this requirement, and his title was declared invalid when the country came into the possession of the United States.

His title to the first grant of 1,000 arpents was also declared invalid, but was subsequently confirmed by special act of Congress. Both the Spanish and American governments required actual settlement of lands granted in the ordinary way, to confirm the title; but in 1800 Boone received the appointment of Commandant of Femme Osage District, and was informed by Don Charles D. Delassus, who had succeeded Don Zenon Trudeau as Lieutenant-Governor, that as his duties as Commandant would require a considerable portion of his time, the Spanish government would dispense with his actual settlement of the land in order to confirm his title. Relying upon this promise, he neglected to have the proper entries made upon the records, and when the United States government purchased Upper Louisiana there was nothing to show that Boone had fulfilled the requirements, and his claim was declared invalid.

He subsequently petitioned Congress to have his title confirmed, and the petition was granted. The following is a copy of his petition, with the report of the committee to whom it was referred, as given in the *American State Papers*, vol. 2, page 10:

To the Senate and Representatives of the United States in Congress assembled. The petition of Daniel Boone, at present an inhabitant of the territory of Louisiana, respectfully showeth:

That, your petitioner has spent a long life in exploring the wilds of north America; and has, by his own personal exertions, been greatly instrumental in opening the road to civilization in the immense territories now attached to the United States, and, in some instances, matured into independent States.

An ardent thirst for discovery, united with a desire to benefit a rising family, has impelled him to encounter the numerous hardships, privations, difficulties, and dangers to which he has unavoidably been exposed. How far his desire for discovery has been extended, and what consequences have resulted from his labors, are, at this time, unnecessary to be stated.

But, while your petitioner has thus opened the way to thousands, to countries possessed of every natural advantage, and although he may have gratified his thirst for discovery, he has to lament that he has not derived those personal advantages which his exertions would seem to have merited. He has secured but a scanty portion of that immeasurable territory over which his discoveries have extended, and his family have reason to regret that their interest had not been more the great object of his discoveries.

Your petitioner has nothing to demand from the justice of his country, but he respectfully suggests, that it might be deemed an act of grateful benevolence, if his country, amidst their bounties, would so far gratify his last wish, as to grant him some reasonable portion of land within the territory of Louisiana.

He is the more induced to this request, as the favorite pittance of soil to which he considered he had acquired a title under the Spanish government, has been wrested from him by a construction of the existing laws not in his contemplation, and beyond his foresight. Your petitioner is not disposed to murmur or complain; but conscious of the value and extent of his services, he solicits some evidence of their liberality.

He approaches the august assemblage of his fellow-citizens with a confidence inspired by that spirit which has led him so often to the deep recesses of the wilds of America; and he flatters himself that he, with his family, will be induced to acknowledge that the United States knows how to appreciate and encourage the efforts of her citizens, in enterprises of magnitude, from which proportionate public good may be derived.

DANIEL BOONE.

The following is the report of the committee to which the petition was referred, as presented to the Senate, January 12, 1810:

That, at a period antecedent to the revolutionary war, Daniel Boone, the petitioner, possessing an ardent desire for the exploration of the (then) Western wilderness of the United States, after traversing a length of mountainous and uninhabited country, discovered, and, with a few bold and enterprising fellows, established, with a perilous hardihood, the first settlement of civilized population in the (now) State of Kentucky. That, in maintaining the possession of that country until the peace of 1783, he experienced all the vicissitudes of a war with enemies the most daring, insidious, and cruel, and which were aided by Canadians from the British provinces of Upper Canada; and that during that contest he lost several children by the hands of the savages.

That it appears to the committee, that although the petitioner was not *officially employed* by the government of the United States, yet that he was *actually engaged* against their enemies, through the whole of the war of the revolution.

That in the exploring, settling, and defending of that country, he eminently contributed to the early march of the American

Western population, and which has redounded to the benefit of the United States. That your petitioner is old, infirm, and, though dependent on agriculture, by adverse and unpropitious circumstances, possesses not one acre of that immeasurable territory which he so well defended, after having been the pioneer of its settlement. The petitioner disclaiming all idea of a *demand* upon the justice of his country, yet requests, as a grateful benevolence, that Congress would grant him some reasonable portion of land in the territory of Louisiana. The committee, upon the whole circumstance of the merit and situation of the petitioner, beg leave to report the bill without amendment.

Notwithstanding this favorable report, and the justice of the petition, the Board of Land Commissioners reported adversely to the grant, and it was not until three years after (December 24, 1813,) that Boone was confirmed in his title to the 1,000 arpents of land conceded to him by the Spanish government.

The territory of Louisiana was at that time overrun with greedy land speculators, who would resort to perjury, forgery, and even murder, to obtain their object; and it was very essential that the Land Commissioners should be careful in granting titles. Hence the difficulty Boone encountered in securing meager justice.

In every community there were drunken, worthless fellows who acted as standing witnesses for these speculators, and would sign any paper, or swear to any statement that was required of them. One of these characters, Simon Toiton, by name, gave the following evidence in a case tried at Kaskaskia, in August, 1807:

"I, Simon Toiton, being in my sober senses, having taken no drink, and after mature reflection, having been apprised that I had given a great number of depositions relating to land titles, as well those derived from donations as from improvements; that, by means of those depositions, great quantities of lands have been confirmed to different persons in whose favor I have given these depositions; I do consequently declare, as I have already declared to several persons, that I am ignorant of the number I may have given, since I was drunk when I gave them, a failing to which I am unfortunately addicted; and that, when I am in that state, any one, by complying with my demands, may do what they please with me If this work had been proposed to me when in my senses— [Here something has been omitted.] I declare that I recollect that, on the last day of November, 1806, I was sent for; before setting out, I drank a quart of liquor; and that there might be no want of it, I took it again on my arrival: before beginning the certificates, I took another quart, and this continued until midnight nearly. I recollect at that time to have given twenty-two or twenty-three depositions; that is to say, I copied them from models, to which I made them conform; observing to those persons that what I did could be of no validity. They told me not to mind that, that it would be of service to those for whom I gave them; and that I aught not to fear anything, or make myself uneasy. I declare solemnly that all these last depositions are false, as well as those I had given previously to that time, no matter in whose favor I may have given them; because, to my knowledge, I have never given any except when I was in liquor, and not in my sober senses. I furthermore declare that I am not acquainted with any improvements in this country."

Is it any wonder, in view of the above, that it was hard for the gallant old pioneer to secure a title to a small portion of the lands which he justly owned, or that he lost the greater portion of those which had been granted him by the liberality of the Spanish government? More than one-half of the applications for titles to lands, made at that period, were rejected; and against the names of most of the disappointed applicants the significant words, "Forgery," "Perjury," etc., are written in the records of the land office at Washington. Among the names are some that stood high in public affairs, and have come down to posterity as disinterested patriots and honest pioneers.

Colonel Boone and his family were the first Americans that settled within the present limits of the State of Missouri. The French had established trading posts at several points, and had formed a village of four or five hundred inhabitants at St. Louis, but there were no regular settlements beyond these.

Louisiana was discovered, settled and held in possession by the French until 1762, when, by a secret treaty, it was transferred to Spain. The few inhabitants at the different trading posts knew nothing of this treaty for several years afterward, and when it became known it was a source of great sorrow to them. But the new rule was so mild that they soon ceased to regard it as a misfortune.

It was the policy of the Spanish authorities to encourage emigration from the United States. Fears were entertained of an invasion of the country by the British and Indians from Canada, and the American people, being regarded as the natural adversaries of the British, it was supposed they would readily fight to repel an invasion. In 1781 St. Louis was attacked by a small army of British and Indians, as a retaliation for the part the king of

Spain had taken in favor of the independence of the United States. Fifteen hundred Indians, and a small party of British soldiers, constituted the invading force, which came down the Mississippi. In the battle that ensued, more than sixty of the inhabitants were killed, and about thirty taken prisoners. At this crisis, Gen. George R. Clark, who was at Kaskaskia with several hundred men, besides the Illinois militia, appeared on the opposite side of the river. The British immediately raised the siege and retreated, and the Indians, declaring that they had no hostile intentions against the Spanish government, but had been deceived by the British, dispersed to their villages.

This event caused the Spanish authorities to increase their efforts for the encouragement of American immigration, and the most liberal offers were made and disseminated throughout the Western settlements. The result was that the American population increased rapidly, and when the country was transferred to the United States in 1804 more than three-fifths of the population were Americans.

During the Spanish administration, no religious sect was tolerated except the Roman Catholic. Each emigrant was required to be a Catholic, but this requirement was evaded by a pious fiction in the examination of the Americans; and Protestant families of all denominations settled in the province, obtained land grants, and were undisturbed in their religious beliefs. Protestant ministers came over from Illinois and preached in the cabins of the settlers, unmolested by the Spanish officers; although, for the sake of keeping up a show of authority, they were occasionally threatened with imprisonment in the *calabozo* at St. Louis.

The late Reverend John Clark, a devoutly pious, but rather eccentric preacher, whose residence was in Illinois, made monthly excursions to the Spanish territory, and preached in the houses of the religious emigrants. He was a man of great simplicity of character, and much respected and beloved by all who knew him, amongst whom was M. Trudeau, the gentlemanly Commandant at St. Louis. M. Trudeau would delay till he knew Mr. Clark's tour for that occasion was nearly finished, and then send a threatening message, that if Monsieur Clark did not leave the Spanish country in three days, he would put him in prison. This was repeated so often, as to furnish a pleasant joke with the preacher and his friends.

During these times, Mr. Abraham Musick, who was a Baptist,

and well acquainted with the Commandant, and who likewise knew his religious principles, presented a petition for leave to hold meetings at his house, and for permission for Mr. Clark to preach there. The Commandant, inclined to favor the American settlers secretly, yet compelled to reject all such petitions official-ly, replied promptly that such a petition could not be granted. It was in violation of the laws of the country. "I mean," said the accomodating officer, "you must not put a bell on your house, and call it a *church*, nor suffer any person to christen your children but the parish priest. But if any of your friends choose to meet at your house, sing, pray, and talk about religion, you will not be molested, provided you continue, as I suppose you are, *un bon Catholique*." He well knew, that, as Baptists, they could dispense with the rite of infant baptism, and that plain, frontier people, as they were, could find the way to their meetings without the sound of the "church-going bell."

As early as the year 1800, the population of Femme Osage District had increased so much that some sort of a local govern-ment was required, and on the 11th of June of that year Colonel Boone was appointed Commandant of the District. The powers of his office were both civil and military, and were almost abso-lute, if he had possessed either the means or the desire to make them so. His decision of all questions was final, except those in regard to land titles, which could only be decided by the crown or its direct representative.

But few crimes or misdemeanors were committed, and then summary justice was dealt out to the offender. Whipping on the bare back was generally the punishment, and so just and equita-ble were Boone's sentences that the most abandoned characters never thought of raising objections to them or harboring resent-ment afterward.

In 1801 the territory of Upper Louisiana was ceded back to France by Spain, and in 1803 the country was purchased from France by the United States. During that interval the French did not again assume the government of the province, but the Spanish laws remained in force. The formal transfer of the coun-try to the United States was made in March, 1804, and one year later the territory of Louisiana was regularly organized by act of Congress. As a temporary arrangement, the Spanish laws re-mained in force for a short time, and Colonel Boone continued to exercise the authority of his office. In fact, during the remainder of his life he had more to do with the government of his settlement than the laws, or the officers elected and appointed under them. The people had such unbounded confidence in his wisdom and justice that they preferred to submit their disputed questions to his arbitration, rather than to the uncertain issues of law.

During the first few years of their residence in Upper Louisiana, Colonel Boone and his wife lived with their son, Daniel M., who had built a house in Darst's Bottom, adjoining the tract of 1,000 arpents of land granted to his father by the Spanish government. This entire tract, with the exception of 181 acres, was sold by Daniel M. Boone, who had charge of his father's business, to pay the old Colonel's debts in Kentucky, of which he had left quite a number upon his removal to the Spanish dominions, and although his creditors never would have made any demands upon him, yet he could not rest easy until they were paid. All his earnings, which he derived from peltries obtained in his hunting excursions, were carefully saved, and at length having made a successful hunt and obtained a valuable supply of peltry, he turned it all into cash, and visited Kentucky for the purpose of paying his debts. He had kept no book accounts, and knew not how much he owed, nor to whom he was indebted, but, in the honest simplicity of his nature, he went to all with whom he had had dealings, and paid whatever was demanded. When he returned to his family he had half a dollar left. "But," said he to his family and a circle of friends who had called to see him, "now I am ready and willing to die. I have paid all my debts, and nobody can say, when I am gone, 'Boone was a dishonest man.'"

There is only one deed on the records in St. Charles signed by Daniel Boone, and that is for 181 acres of land (being a portion of the 1,000 arpents) sold to Wm. Coshow, August 6, 1815, for $315. The witnesses were D. M. Boone and John B. Callaway.

Colonel Boone and his son laid off a town on the Missouri river, and called it Missouriton, in honor of the then territory of Missouri. They built a horse mill there, which was a great thing for those early days, and for a while the town flourished and promised well. At one time an effort was made to locate the capital of the territory there, but it failed, and the town soon declined. The place where it stood has since been washed away by the river, and no trace of it now remains. There is still a post-office in the neighborhood, called Missouriton, but the town no longer exists.

The settlers did not experience much trouble with the Indians until after the commencement of the war of 1812, and the settlements rapidly extended over a portion of the present counties of St. Charles, Lincoln, Warren, Montgomery, and Callaway; and in 1808, a settlement was formed in (now) Howard county, near the salt springs, called Boone's Lick.

Salt was very scarce among the first settlers, and it was so expensive that but little was used. It had to be transported on horseback from Kentucky, or shipped in keel-boats and barges from New Orleans up the Mississippi river to St. Louis, from whence it was distributed through the settlements by traders, who charged enormous profits.

Sometime early in the commencement of the present century, Colonel Boone, while on a hunting expedition, discovered the salt springs in Howard county; and during the summer of 1807 his sons, Daniel M. and Nathan, with Messrs. Baldridge and Manly, transported kettles there and made salt, which they floated down the river that fall in canoes made of hollow sycamore logs, daubed at the ends with clay.

The making of salt at these springs subsequently became a regular and paying business, and, assisted by the tide of immigration that began to flow there, led to the opening of the Booneslick road, which for years afterward was the great thoroughfare of Western emigration.

The remaining incidents of Colonel Boone's life, of interest to the public, are so closely connected with the events of the Indian war of 1812-15, that we cannot give them without going into a history of those times, and as that would interfere with the arrangement of this work, we must now bring this sketch to a close.

On the 18th of March, 1813, Colonel Boone experienced the saddest affliction of his life, in the death of his aged and beloved wife. She had been the companion of his toils, dangers, sorrows and pleasures for more than half a century, participating in the same generous and heroic nature as himself. He loved her devotedly, and their long and intimate association had so closely knitted their hearts together that he seemed hardly able to exist without her, and her death was to him an irreparable loss.

She was buried on the summit of a beautiful knoll, in the southern part of (now) Warren county, about one mile southeast of the little town of Marthasville. A small stream, called Teuque creek, flows by the foot of this knoll, and pursues its tortuous course to where it empties into the Missouri river, a few miles to the southeast. Her grave overlooked the Missouri bottoms, which are here about two miles in width, and now, since the timber has been cleared away, a fine view of the river can be obtained from that spot.

Soon after the death of his wife, the old pioneer marked a place by her side for his own grave, and had a coffin made of black walnut for himself. He kept this coffin under his bed for

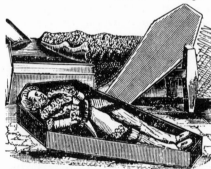

several years, and would often draw it out and lie down in it, "just to see how it would fit." But finally a stranger died in the community, and the old man, governed by the same liberal motives that had been his guide through life, gave his coffin to the stranger. He afterward had another made of cherry, which was also

DANIEL BOONE TRIES HIS COFFIN.

placed under his bed, and remained there until it received his body for burial.

The closing years of his life were devoted to the society of his neighbors, and his children and grandchildren, of whom he was very fond. After the death of his wife, wishing to be near her grave, he removed from his son Nathan's, on Femme Osage creek, where they had lived for several years previously, and made his home with his eldest daughter, Mrs. Flanders Callaway, who lived with her husband and family on Teuque creek, near the place where Mrs. Boone was buried. Flanders Callaway removed from Kentucky to Missouri shortly before the purchase of the territory by the United States, and received a grant of land from the Spanish government.

Frequent visits were made by the old pioneer to the homes of his other children, and his coming was always made the occasion of an ovation to "grandfather Boone," as he was affectionately called. Wherever he was, his time was always employed at some useful occupation. He made powder-horns for his grandchildren and neighbors, carving and ornamenting many of them with

4

much taste. He repaired rifles, and performed various descriptions of handicraft with neatness and finish.

Twice a year he would make an excursion to some remote hunting ground, accompanied by a negro boy, who attended to the camp, skinned and cleaned the game, and took care of his aged master. While on one of these expeditions, the Osage Indians attempted to rob him, but they met with such prompt and determined resistance from Boone and his negro boy, that they fled in haste, and molested them no more.

One winter he went on a hunting and trapping excursion up the Grand river, a stream that rises in the southern part of Iowa and empties into the Missouri river between Carroll and Ray counties. He was alone this time. He paddled his canoe up the Missouri and then up the Grand river, until he found a retired place for his camp in a cave among the bluffs. He then proceeded to make the necessary preparations for trapping beaver, after which he laid in his winter's supply of venison, turkey, and bear's meat.

Each morning he visited his traps to secure his prey, returning to his camp in such a manner as to avoid discovery by any prowling bands of Indians that might be in the vicinity. But one morning he had the mortification to discover a large encampment of Indians near his traps, engaged in hunting. He retreated to his camp and remained there all day, and fortunately that night a deep snow fell and securely covered his traps. He continued in his camp for twenty days, until the Indians departed; and during that time he had no fire except in the middle of the night, when he cooked his food. He was afraid to kindle a fire at any other time, lest the smoke or light should discover his hiding place to the savages. When the snow melted away, the Indians departed, and left him to himself.

On another occasion he took pack-horses and went to the country on the Osage river, accompanied by his negro boy. Soon after he had prepared his camp he was taken sick, and lay for a long time in a dangerous condition. The weather was stormy and disagreeable, which had a depressing effect both upon the old Colonel and his servant boy. Finally the weather cleared up, and there came a pleasant and delightful day. Boone felt that it would do him good to walk out, and, with the assistance of his staff and the boy, he made his way to the summit of a small eminence. Here he marked out the ground in the shape and size of a grave, and told the boy that in case he should die he wanted to be buried there, at the same time giving full instructions as to the manner of his burial. He directed the boy, in case of his death, to wash and lay his body straight, wrapped in one of the cleanest blankets. He was then to construct a kind of shovel, and with that instrument and the hatchet, to dig a grave, exactly as he had marked out. Then he was to drag the body to the spot and push it in the grave, after which he was to cover it, placing posts at the head and foot. Poles were to be placed around and over the surface, to prevent the grave from being opened by wild beasts; the trees were to be marked, so the place could be found by his friends, and then the boy was to get the horses, pack up the skins, guns, camp utensils, etc., and return home, where he was to deliver certain messages to the family. All these instructions were given with entire calmness, as if he were directing his ordinary business affairs.

In December, 1818, Boone was visited by the historian, Rev. John M. Peck, who was deeply and favorably impressed by the venerable appearance of the aged pioneer. Mr. Peck had written his biography, and expected to obtain some additional notes from him, but was so overcome by veneration and wonder, that he asked only a few questions. If he had carried out his first intention he would no doubt have given us a perfectly correct account of the life of this remarkable man, but as it was, a number of mistakes crept into his work, and many events of interest that occurred during the last few years of Boone's life were lost forever.

In the latter part of the summer of 1820, Boone had a severe attack of fever, at his home at Flanders Callaway's. But he recovered sufficiently to make a visit to the house of his son, Major Nathan Boone, on Femme Osage creek. The children had heard of his sickness, and were delighted to see grandfather again, and everything was done that could be to make him comfortable. For a few days he was happy in their society, and by his genial disposition and pleasant manners diffused joy and gladness throughout the entire household.

One day a nice dish of sweet potatoes—a vegetable of which he was very fond—was prepared for him. He ate heartily, and soon after had an attack from which he never recovered. He gradually sank, and, after three days' illness, expired, on the 26th of September, 1820, in the 86th year of his age.

He died calmly and peacefully, having no fear of death or the future state of existence. He had never made any profession of religion, or united with any church, but his entire life was a beautiful example of the Golden Rule—" do unto others as you would that they should do unto you." In a letter to one of his sisters, written a short time before his death, he said that he had always tried to live as an honest and conscientious man should, and was perfectly willing to surrender his soul to the discretion of a just God. His mind was not such as could lean upon simple faith or mere belief, but it required a well considered reason for everything, and he died the death of a philosopher rather than that of a Christian. His death was like the sleep of an infant—quiet, peaceful and serene.

HARRIS & CO. ENG. ST. LOUIS,

THE HOUSE IN WHICH DANIEL BOONE DIED.
(The first stone dwelling-house erected in Missouri.)

We present on this page a picture of the house in which Daniel Boone died. At the time of his death he occupied the front room on the first floor, to the right of the hall as you enter.

It has been stated in many of his "lives" that he died at a deer "lick," with his gun in his hands, watching for deer. In others, that he died, as he had lived, in a log cabin. But on the contrary, the house was, and is—for it is still standing, just as represented in the picture—a neat, substantial, and comfortable stone building.

The remains of the departed pioneer were sorrowfully placed in the coffin he had prepared, and conveyed, the next day, to the home of Mr. Flanders Callaway. The news of his decease had spread rapidly, and a vast concourse of people collected on the day of the funeral to pay their last respects to the distinguished and beloved dead.

The funeral sermon was preached by Rev. James Craig, a son-in-law of Major Nathan Boone; and the house being too small to accommodate the immense concourse of people, the coffin was carried to the large barn near the house, into which the people crowded to listen to the funeral services. At their close the coffin was borne to the cemetery and sadly deposited in the grave that had been prepared for it, close by the side of Mrs. Boone.

At the time of Boone's death the Constitutional Convention of Missouri was in session at St. Louis, and upon receipt of the intelligence a resolution was offered by Hon. Benjamin Emmons, of St. Charles, that the members wear the usual badge of mourning for thirty days, in respect to the memory of the deceased, and adjourn for one day. The resolution was unanimously adopted.

The Boone family were noted for longevity. George Boone, a brother of Daniel, died in Shelby county, Ky., in November, 1820, at the age of eighty-three; Samuel, another brother, died at the age of eighty-eight; Jonathan at eighty-six; Mrs. Wilcox, a sister, at ninety-one; Mrs. Grant, another sister, at eighty-four, and Mrs. Smith, a third sister, at eighty-four. There is no record of the deaths of the rest of Boone's brothers and sisters, except those given heretofore, but they all lived to be old men and women.

When Colonel Boone made choice of a place of burial for himself and family, and was so particular to enjoin his friends, if he died from home, to remove his remains to the hill near Teuque, he did not anticipate an event which occurred a quarter of a century after his death, and which resulted in the remains of himself and wife finding their last resting place on the banks of the Kentucky river, in the land he loved so well.

The citizens of Frankfort had prepared a tasteful rural cemetery, and, at a public meeting, decided that the most appropriate consecration of the ground would be the removal of the remains of Daniel Boone and his wife. The consent of the surviving relatives was obtained, and in the summer of 1845, a deputation of citizens, consisting of Hon. John J. Crittenden, Mr. William Boone and Mr. Swaggat, came to Missouri on the steamer *Daniel*

Boone, for the purpose of exhuming the relics and conveying them back to Kentucky.

The graves were situated on land belonging to Mr. Harvey Griswold, who at first objected to the removal, as he intended to build a monument over them, and beautify the place. Mr. Griswold was supported in his objections by a number of influential citizens, who claimed that Missouri had as much right to the remains of Daniel Boone as Kentucky, especially as the old pioneer had selected the location of his grave, and had given such particular instructions in regard to his being buried there.

The gentlemen from Kentucky finally carried their point, however, and on the 17th of July, 1845, the remains of Daniel Boone and his wife were removed from their graves. The work was done by King Bryan, Henry Angbert and Jeff. Callaway, colored. Mrs. Boone's coffin was found to be perfectly sound, and the workmen had but little difficulty in removing it; but Colonel Boone's coffin was entirely decayed, and the remains had to be picked out of the dirt by which they were surrounded. One or two of the smaller bones were found afterward, and kept by Mr. Griswold as relics.

The remains were placed in new coffins prepared for their reception, and conveyed to Kentucky, where they were re-interred, with appropriate ceremonies, in the cemetery at Frankfort, on the 20th of August, 1845. A vast concourse of people from all parts of the State had collected to witness the ceremonies. An oration was delivered by Hon. John J. Crittenden, and Mr. Joseph B. Wells, of Missouri, made an appropriate address.

The graves on the hill near Teuque creek were never refilled, but remain to-day as they were left by the workmen, except that the rains have partly filled them with dirt, and they are overgrown with weeds and briars. Rough head stones had been carved by Mr. Jonathan Bryan, and placed at the heads of the graves. These were thrown back on the ground, and are still lying there. Recently, pieces of the these stones have been chipped off and sent to Kentucky as mementoes.

PART II.

EARLY DAYS IN MISSOURI.

ONE hundred years ago the territory west of the Mississippi river was as unknown to the civilized races of mankind as the wilds of Central Africa are to-day. Eighty-one years ago there was not an American settlement west of Kentucky, and the Indians of Illinois, part of Ohio, and all that vast territory lying to the north, west and south-west, were undisturbed in their hunting grounds. There were doubtless tribes in the remote West who had never heard of white men, or of the coming of a superior race that was to drive them, finally, into the Pacific Ocean. Now this immense continent is dotted with large cities, thriving villages, and neat farm houses; in every valley is heard the puffing of the iron horse; and there is hardly a foot of ground that has not been trod, time and again, by the feet of white men. School houses and workshops have pushed the smoky wigwams aside, and leviathan steamboats plow and churn the waters over which the stealthy canoe once glided. There are places which we call old, and view with reverence as the abode of our ancestors, that have not yet seen a century! We talk of antiquities, and proudly point out to strangers our "old landmarks," and yet there are men and women still living who remember when Daniel Boone came to—Upper Louisiana, or New Spain. St. Louis was then an insignificant French village—now it is the third city of the United States and the metropolis of the Mississippi Valley! The Mississippi Valley! A continent within itself, that numbers its population by millions! St. Charles was an Indian trading post, and the country twenty miles west of it had been visited by only a few bold hunters. When Daniel Boone came, he went away out into the wilderness, among the Indians and wild animals—twenty miles west of St. Charles! and there he settled. When the grandfather of the writer arrived in St. Louis, seventy-six years ago, the Spanish commandant would not give him a permit to settle near the present town of Cap-au-Gris, in Lincoln county, because it was too far out on the frontier, and exposed to attacks from the Indians!

No one can view the astonishing growth of this great country without amazement. It has sprung up as if by the conjuration of some mighty magician, and one who lives in this good year of 1876 can hardly realize what Missouri and the West were eighty-one years ago.

In 1764 a company of French merchants settled where the great city of St. Louis now stands. They had received from the Director-General of Louisiana an exclusive license to trade with the Indian nations on the Missouri, and they called their settlement, or encampment, St. Louis, in honor of their sovereign, the king of France. In the autumn of the previous year (1763) a French settlement had been established at Ste. Genevieve; and as early as 1720 Fort Chartres, in Illinois, had been built by the French. In 1762 the territory west of the Mississippi was ceded to Spain, but the little band of merchants at St. Louis did not hear of the treaty until three years after. Communication between the old and the new world was not so rapid then as now.

In 1705 a party of French traders and explorers ascended the Missouri to the Kansas river, on the now extreme western boundary of the State of Missouri. They found the Indians friendly, and glad of the opportunity to trade with them. The French have always been very fortunate in their intercourse with the red men.

For many years after its discovery, America was supposed to abound in gold and silver, and most of the early expeditions were undertaken for the purpose of seeking those precious metals. In 1719 the Sieur de Lochon was sent out from France, by the Company of the West, to seek for precious metals within the present limits of Missouri. He commenced digging on the Meramec, and drew up a large quantity of ore, from which he obtained, according to his account, two drachms of silver; but his statement was generally disbelieved. He subsequently obtained a small amount of lead, and then returned to France. Other expeditions were sent out at different times, but their success was not gratifying. In 1719 Sieur Renault, one of the directors of a private company, left France with two hundred artificers and miners, provided with tools, and whatever else was necessary for carrying the object of the company into effect. In his passage he touched at the island of St. Domingo, and purchased five hundred slaves to work in the mines. Entering the Mississippi, he pursued his voyage up that river to New Orleans, which he reached some time in 1720, and soon afterward proceeded on his way to Kaskaskia, in Illinois. Establishing himself near that place, he sent out mining and exploring expeditions into different parts of Illinois and Louisiana. These parties were headed either by himself or M. La Motte, an agent, who was well versed in the knowledge of minerals, and whom he had brought with him from France. In one of these expeditions, La Motte discovered the lead mines in St. Francois, which still bear his name; and Renault discovered the extensive mines north of Potosi, which are still called after the discoverer. Numerous other mines were discovered and extensively worked, and the remains of their antique works, overgrown with brush and trees, are still to be found. The lead was conveyed from the interior on pack-horses, and sent to New Orleans, from whence it was shipped to France.

The war between France and Spain, which commenced in 1719, extended to the territory of Louisiana, and agents of the rival governments were constantly at work among the Indians, each endeavoring to stir up their animosity against the other. Some time between 1720 and 1724, the French sent an expedition up the Missouri river, which landed on an island a considerable distance above the mouth of the Osage. Here a fort was built, which they called Fort Orleans. On the arrival of this force, the different tribes of Indians in the vicinity were engaged in a bloody war, which greatly diminished the trade and rendered intercourse with them extremely hazardous. The French, therefore, desired to bring about a general peace, and commenced negotiations for that purpose. Their efforts were crowned with the desired success in 1724. Soon after this event, however, Fort Orleans was attacked and totally destroyed, and all the garrison massacred. It was never known by whom this bloody work was done.

The French now began to experience trouble with the Indians, and for sixteen years a desultory warfare was kept up. Renault, however, remained in the colony, and continued to work the lead mines until 1742, when he returned to France.

Four years after the treaty of 1762, Spain made an attempt to take possession of her newly acquired territory, but there was so much opposition on the part of the inhabitants, that the Spanish Governor and his troops were compelled to abandon their design and return to Havana. The government continued to be administered in the name of the French King until 1769, when it was peaceably transferred to the Spanish government, the people having become reconciled to the change, from a conviction that it was inevitable. Louisiana was re-ceded to France in 1800, and three years afterward it was ceded by France to the United States. Its substantial growth may be dated from that period. The beneficent laws and institutions of our republic, united with an unsurpassed climate, a soil exhaustless in its fertility, and a people distinguished for their intelligence and enterprise, could not fail to produce a great and prosperous country. Its progress, however, has been more rapid than the wildest enthusiast could have imagined, and, though less than a century old, our institutions rank with those of the oldest and most progressive nations of the world. Having accomplished so much in two-thirds of the first century of our existence, what may we not hope and expect of the century which is to follow?

FIRST AMERICAN SETTLEMENTS.

THE first American settlements within the present limits of the State of Missouri, were made in 1795, on Femme Osage creek, in what is now St. Charles county. From that time they rapidly extended in all directions, except during a period of three years, while the Indian war lasted, when everything remained at a stand-still. The first American settlements in the present counties of Warren, Montgomery, and Callaway were made from 1800 to 1815.

When Daniel Boone came to Missouri (which was then called Upper Louisiana or New Spain), in 1795, there was a French village and Indian trading post at St. Charles, at that time the most remote settlement of white people on the continent of North America. The place was then called *Les Petite Cotes* (little hills), which was afterward changed to *Village des Cotes* (the village of the hills), which names were applied to it on account of its beautiful, elevated location. When the Americans began to settle there and in the vicinity, they found the name hard to pronounce and understand, and it was changed to St. Charles, but by whom or when is not positively known.

The foundation of this town is shrouded in some degree of mystery, as well as romance. Widely different dates are given as to its first settlement, by equally reliable authorities, and the exact date will probably never be known. Several authorities give 1780 as the year of its settlement; others 1762; others again place it at 1766 and 1769. One of the two latter dates is doubtless correct, and we incline to the belief that 1766 is the one. This belief is strengthened by a dim tradition among old citizens of that vicinity, that 1766 was the year in which the village was founded. In this connection we give the following highly colored and very improbable romance, from "Hopewell's Legends of the Missouri and Mississippi," stating in advance, however, that we put no reliance in it, from the fact that it is written in the dime novel style, and is full of improbabilities and absurdities from first to last. But it will doubtless interest some of the readers of this unpretentious book, and we therefore present it as we found it. Here follthe romance:

In the year 1765, a daring Frenchman, called Blanchette Chasseur, animated by that love of adventure which characterizes all who have lived a roving and restless life, ascended the Missouri, with a few followers, for the purpose of forming a settlement in the then remote wilderness.

He was one of those who encountered perils and endured privations, not from necessity, but from choice; for he had been born to affluence, and had every indulgence consistent with wealth and station, but from a boy had spurned, with Spartan prejudice, every effeminate trait, and had accomplished himself in every hardy and manly exercise. When he had attained his majority, he sailed for America, then the El Dorado of all the visionary, roving and restless spirits of the age. He loved the Indian and the wilderness, and after a sojourn in the wilds for some months, the attractions of La Belle France were forgotten, and Blanchette Chasseur became the leader of the hardy pioneers of civilization at that early period. So assimilated had he become to the scenes in which he lived and mingled, that he forgot his *caste*, and con-

descended to mingle his noble blood with that of the aborigines
of the country, by taking as partners of his itinerant wigwams
young squaws of the tribes which were in the vicinity of his wanderings.

At the period which we have mentioned, Blanchette Chasseur
had but three followers—two Canadian hunters, and a half-breed
Indian. It was near sunset one afternoon in October, when they
rowed up the swift-running current of the muddy Missouri. The
vast forests skirting the river had that rich golden hue found only
in America, and the tops of the trees, flooded with the dazzling
glory of the sunbeams, looked gorgeous beyond description.
There were several small hills at a little distance, and from one
of these they saw the smoke ascending from a camp-fire.

Blanchette Chasseur, feeling confident that he was in the vicinity of a party of Indians, with that fearlessness and curiosity which
made up, so largely, a portion of his character, determined to see
and learn, if possible, their business in the neighborhood and to
what tribe they belonged. He landed his little boat where some
bushes grew thick upon the banks, and, armed with his rifle, proceeded alone toward the encampment. When he was within a
hundred yards of the camp-fire, seeing that he was discovered by
the Indians, he stopped in his course, and taking a soiled piece
of cloth from his pocket, tied it to the end of his gun, and waved
it in token of friendly intentions.

At this signal of friendship from Blanchette Chasseur, an old
Indian, of low stature but herculean build, came towards him.
He was followed by a band of warriors, who as well as he, were
begrimed with paint; but the old Indian, from his rich display
of beads and the plumage of birds, together with the deference
paid to him by the band, was evidently the chief. The whole
party had been on the war-path, for several fresh scalps dangled
from the belts of some of the warriors; and the cincture of the
old chief, through its whole circumference, was frizzled with the
hair of the enemies subdued in many conflicts, but was totally unlike the fabled girdle of the Paphian goddess, which gave to its
possessor transcendent loveliness—for the old chief was as hideous in his features as the veiled prophet of Korassan.

Blanchette Chasseur, with his ever-glowing courage, felt some
slight chilling sensations glide through his frame, as he looked
upon such a number of war-like Indians, besmeared with paint,
with their reeking trophies of savage prowess. Nevertheless, he
addressed them in an Indian tongue with which he was familiar, telling them he was a white man ascending the Missouri, and that
he loved the Indian. The old chief gazed upon him with a full,
attentive smile, and mollifying somewhat his rugged features, told
him he was welcome, and to call his followers, whom Blanchette
had left with the canoe.

The half-breed Indian, from the departure of Blanchette, had commenced to show symptoms of alarm, and when he saw the painted warriors, with their bows and arrows, their tomahawks and scalp-locks, some of which were still gory, his philosophy forsook him, and, darting from the canoe, and with almost the fleetness of a deer, endeavored to place as much distance as possible between himself and the supposed enemies. The old chief told his warriors to give chase, and capture without injuring him. With a yell that rang loud and echoing through the solitude, the fleet-footed warriors started after the fugitive, and, in a short time, the poor half-breed, more dead than alive, was brought to the encampment. His swarthy face looked pale with excessive fright; he kept one hand upon the crown of his head, as if he expected every moment that an attack would be made upon his scalp, and made such horrible grimaces, that the old chief shook with excess of laughter. Blanchette Chasseur, pitying his follower—who, though a coward, was faithful—calmed his fright by telling him that his scalp was as safe upon his head as the crown upon the imperial monarch of France.

All excitement being allayed, the old chief and warriors, and Blanchette Chasseur and followers, then sat, side by side, at a large fire, and smoked the pipe of peace—an essential proceeding among the Indians, as significant of friendship. Blanchette Chasseur then told one of his men to go to the boat, and bring, from beneath a seat, a jug well filled with the fluid which causes the tongue to rattle, the heart to expand, and the reason to sleep.

At the sight of the jug, the old chief rose quickly to his feet, seized it in his large hands, extracted the cork in a twinkling—and placed his nose to the aperture. He then gave vent to the most extravagant rapture. He cut a caper in the air that would have been creditable to an equestrian clown, embraced Blanchette Chasseur with the ardor of a newly accepted lover; and, spreading wide his short legs, so as to have a secure base, placed the large jug to his lips, and took a long suck of its contents. He then took a little pewter mug, that Blanchette Chasseur had in his hands, and dealt a sparing allowance to the warriors, and, after serving all with the diligence, if not the grace of a Ganymede, he threw aside the cup, and, again fortifying himself like a Colossus of Rhodes, he drank long and deeply; then drawing a long breath, he said, turning to Blanchette, " *C'est bon; j'en ai assez,*" (it is good; I have enough.)

Both Blanchette Chasseur and the old chief had a good supply of dried provisions, and all were soon in the humor to do justice to a supper. During the repast, the desirable jug was several times called upon to contribute freely, and such was the potency of its power over the usually cold stoicism of the savages, that, in a short time, they commenced to laugh and boast of their re-

cent exploits, and became on the most familiar terms with their
new friends.

The old chief, seeing everything on the most friendly footing,
with his stomach overflowing with whisky and dried beef, became
very garrulous and familiar.   Blanchette manifesting some surprise at his readiness in speaking the French language, he told
him, if he were not too sleepy, he would relate to him some of
the stirring incidents of an eventful life.

Blanchette signifying a wish to hear the narrative, the old warrior thus began:

THE NARRATIVE OF BERNARD GUILLET, THE CHIEF OF THE DAKOTAHS.

" My good friend, the first thing I have to tell you is, that I
am a Frenchman, and not an Indian. I was born near Marseilles,
in the southern part of France, of poor, but respectable parents,
who died within three months of each other, when I had attained
eleven years of age.   My mother died last, and a few hours before her death, with a feeble effort, she took a rosary which she
kept constantly suspended from her neck, and hung it upon mine,
murmuring some indistinct words.   I have thought of them often
since, and I know that they were blessings.   After losing my
parents my troubles commenced.   It is not worth my while to
dwell upon trivial incidents; let it suffice to say that four months
after I lost my parents, I was, by the authorities, apprenticed to a
tanner.   I was worked hard and almost starved; and, from the
wrongs that I had continually heaped upon me, I date the change
in my disposition, which was naturally gentle, into fierce and
vindictive elements.   I was kicked about much more than a sorry
cur we had in the establishment, named Carlo.   However, I looked
upon Carlo as my only friend, and he loved me in return.   We
were bedfellows.   Things continued in this way until I became
seventeen years of age, at which time my mind became sufficiently developed to comprehend, to its fullest extent, the unjust treatment I received from my master, who still continued to beat me as
usual for every trivial fault or fancied omission.   My blood often
boiled during the chastisements, and I felt ready to exterminate the
wretch upon the spot.   One evening, in a paroxysm of rage, I
killed him.   Working hours were over, and as usual I was looking
over some books that I had gradually collected together, so as to
improve my mind.   My rosary was in my hand, and the current
of my thoughts had floated from my book to the by-gone days,
with which was associated the image of my mother.   My master
came in, and seeing me with the beads, snatched them from my
hands and gave me a buff upon the cheek, saying, I was a good-
for-nothing, lazy fellow.   I entreated him to return the rosary,
telling him it was the last gift of a deceased mother.

" 'Your mother, you vagabond?' replied he; 'who was she
but a strumpet?'

"Blood swam before my eyes—my heart was on fire, and the voices of all the devils whispered vengeance! I sprang at his throat with a yell of rage, and clenched it like a vice! When I released the hold he was dead, and I, Bernard Guillet, was a murderer!

"I fled that night to Marseilles, where a vessel was just leaving for the new world. I offered myself as a common sailor, and as the captain was short of hands, I was taken without any inquiries. We were soon out of the harbor, and I was comparatively safe from pursuit.

"After a voyage of three months, we reached the shores of America, and fearing that I might be pursued for the murder of my master, I went far into the interior of Canada, and engaged with a man who traded for furs with the Indians. Somehow or other, I became attached to the vagabond life I led. I soon learned to speak the tongues of several of the Indian tribes; engaged in business on my own account; hunted with the hunters; and, took to wife one of the daughters of a chief of the Senecas. After thus linking myself by a new tie to the Indians, I threw off the few civilized habits which still clung to me, and adopted all the wild independence of my new relations. I still visited, however, yearly, the trading posts of the whites, chiefly for the purpose of gaining powder and lead, and a good proportion of whisky. We were engaged in several wars with the neighboring tribes, and I became a distinguished warrior. In all probability, I had passed my life with the Senecas, had not my wife died in childbed. I sincerely mourned her loss; not that I can say that I really loved her; but I had lived with her for seven years, and she was obedient to my slightest wish. She had borne me four children, all of whom died.

"After the death of my wife, I became desirous of change, and determined to go far into the West, and lead the life of a trapper and hunter. One evening, unknown to anyone, about nightfall, I took my tomahawk, rifle, a good supply of ammunition, and departed upon my long journey. I easily subsisted upon the proceeds of the chase, for then game was everywhere. I traveled through many regions, and followed the course of many rivers, yet always keeping towards the setting sun; sometimes, tarrying in a place two or three weeks, so as to try effectually what it would yield in the way of furs and peltries.

"On the banks of the Muskingum river, I was nearly losing my life. It was a warm day; and, being somewhat fatigued and drowsy, about midday, I lay beneath a large maple, which offered a fine shade, that I might take a comfortable nap. I know not how long I lay there; but I felt a dead, heavy weight upon my breast that nearly mashed me. I thought I had the nightmare, and tried to struggle with the witch that was riding me, when the effort awoke me, and I found a large red skin bestriding my body, and another commencing to bind me with thongs. I was then under thirty, and as strong as a buffalo.

" With a sudden effort, I threw the red devil who was making a pack-horse of me, and gaining my feet, struck the other a blow with my fist that made him whirl as a top. I then had time to draw my knife, as the Indian I had thrown from my breast gained his feet. He was soon finished ; but the other had seized Nancy (a name I had given my rifle, in honor of my mother), and had it pointed, with sure aim, at my heart. Sacre Dieu! how funny I felt when I was thinking of the ball that was coming through me ; but Nancy snapped—I don't know whether from accident or not ; but I have always thought that the name of my mother had something to do with it. You may smile ; but it does me good to think that her spirit can now and then come near me. I killed the Indian with a blow of my tomahawk, and took the scalps of them both. They were of the Miamis.

" I still kept westward," said the old chief, taking another pull from the bottle ; " and, after some fifteen months, came to the banks of the Mississippi. Then I got so far from civilizatian that I determined to give up all idea of trading with whites, for a time, and to find some locality to pack furs for a few years ; by which time I calculated that plenty of trading posts would be established in those parts. I coursed along the Mississippi for a few days, and, seeing a large river flowing into it, I crossed over in a canoe I found hidden on the bank of a river, and ascended it by coursing along its banks, until I reached the neighborhood in which we now are. That was, as near as I can guess, about twenty or twenty-five years ago. Here I found plenty of deer and beaver, and determined to stop. So I built a little hut and commenced trapping beaver and muskrats. I was very successful during the first year, when, all of a sudden, I found that my luck had stopped. I soon suspicioned the cause—my traps had been robbed. I determined to find out the thief. One night I lay near one of my most successful traps, and about daylight, or a little before, I saw the outlines of an Indian going to the spot where my trap was. He had a beaver in his hand, which he had taken from one of my other traps. I leveled Nancy, and he fell dead. After scalping him, I let him lie.

" A few days afterward, walking by the spot, I discovered that his body had been removed. I was much alarmed, for I knew the Indians had been there, and had taken away the dead body of their comrade. I fortified my little cabin as well as possible, and went out but seldom. About two months afterward, I was surprised one morning, before sunrise, by the sound of a war-whoop in front of my cabin, accompanied by efforts to break open the door. I thought that my hour had come, but I determined to die game. I seized Nancy, put my rosary into my bosom in case I fell, that I might call on the Virgin for grace from the Son, and jumped to a loop-hole I had prepared before. There were ten savages, and they used no precaution, thinking that the mere sight of their numbers would make me surrender. One fell dead at the call of Nancy, then another, and, in the space of an hour, a third. They then became cautious, and, surrounding my cabin at all points, succeeded in firing it. *Tonnerre de Di·u*, how it burned! I stood it some time, and, when I was almost roasted, I jumped from the blazing roof. I had no chance. Directly I touched the ground I was overpowered and bound.

"I felt as if my doom was sealed, for I was a captive in the hands of the Dakotas, who had come a long distance to take my scalp for killing one of their tribe—him who had robbed my traps. I was destined to a terrible death, and I knew it by their conversation on the journey. My skin peeled from my limbs, leaving a mass of raw flesh, so severely was I burned, but I was compelled to journey in my sufferings. After many days' travel we came to the chief village, and warriors, old men, women, and children, came to meet us. They all commenced abusing me, spitting upon me, and beating me. It was horrible to feel that I was all alone among the savages, sick and weak from the burns I had received. My only consolation was thinking of my mother.

"A council of the old men and chiefs of the nation was held, and, as I had expected, I was doomed to the fire-death. For two days there were great preparations for barbecuing me; and, when all was complete, I was delivered to the executioners. I was stripped perfectly naked, and my feet unbound. I had first to run a gauntlet. A row of boys and women were on each side of the way I had to run, and, when I started for the goal, flaming firebrands were thrust in my skin; spears and arrows pierced my flesh, and blows from clubs came in showers upon my defenceless body. I gained the goal, and fainted as I gained it.

"When I recovered consciousness, I found myself tied to a tree, and the Indian boys preparing to shoot at me for a target. The arrows stuck in my body in all directions, but did not touch any vital part, the object being not to kill but torture me. I tried by sudden efforts to twist my body so as to disappoint their aim, that I might be killed, but I was too tightly bound and had to suffer. After amusing themselves until I was a mass of bleeding wounds, it was determined to end the scene by placing me at the stake. I was bound to a post around which were piles of resinous wood. The torch was ready to be applied, and my last thoughts were on meeting my mother, when an Indian woman rushed to the stake, and claimed me as her husband, in place of one she had lost. No one disputed her claim, and I was led to her lodge, and my rifle, and all other property that the Indians

5

had brought from my hut, were restored to me. She bestowed every attention on me, and I slowly recovered. I was formally adopted by the nation and became a great favorite, doing them great service in their wars against the Pawnees and Chippewas. The chief of the tribe gave me his only daughter for a wife, and he dying I was made chief of the nation, and am so still.''

Blanchette Chasseur thanked the chief for his interesting history, and after drinking each other's health from the jug, which effectually exhausted its contents, they lay down, and were soon following the example of their snoring followers.

Next morning, Bernard Guillet, the chief of the Dakotas, invited Blanchette Chasseur to visit him in his remote home, saying that he would never get as far east again, as he was advancing in years, and was tired of taking scalps.

''Bernard,'' said Blanchette Chasseur to the old chief, before his departure, ''when you lived here did you give any name to your home?''

''I called the place 'Les Petites Cotes,' '' replied Bernard, ''from the sides of the hills that you see.''

''By that name shall it be called,'' said Blanchette Chasseur, ''for it is the echo of nature — beautiful from its simplicity.''

The two friends then separated. The chief of the Dakotas with his warriors wended their way back to their tribe, and Blanchette Chasseur again descended the Missouri, determined in a short time to return to Les Petites Cotes, and there form a settlement. He did so. In 1769 (four years after) he formed a settlement, and called the town that he laid out, '' Les Petites Cotes.'' It soon grew to a thriving village, and many years afterward was changed to St. Charles.

Femme Osage creek derived its name from the drowning of an Osage squaw. Many years prior to the date of the first American settlements, some Indians of that tribe were hunting in that part of the country, and one of their squaws, having been on an errand somewhere, was returning to her people. The stream was swollen from recent rains, and in attempting to cross it on her pony, the current swept them away from the ford, and she was drowned. The Indians, therefore, called the stream *Femme Osage*, or Osage woman's creek.

Most of the pioneers of Missouri were from the States of Kentucky and Virginia, with a few from North and South Carolina, Maryland, Pennsylvania, and Tennessee.

They were a hardy, honest, friendly class of people, addicted to hospitality and neighborly intercourse. Most of them came to the West because they wanted to be free — free from the restraints and shams of society, and the domineering influence of money and aristocracy. A few came to evade the penalty of the laws which they had violated at home, but there were not many of this class, and their standing and character being soon found out, they were shunned by the better class of people.

With the exception of the Boone families, their relations and friends, most of the pioneers were strangers to each other; but every newly arrived stranger met a hearty welcome, and was treated as an old friend, merely because he had come, probably, from the same State in the East or South. It was enough to know that he had come from the *home* State, and at once he was treated like an old acquaintance and friend. Or, if he happened to be a stray sheep, from some of the outside States, he was still treated as a friend — because they all wanted to be friendly.

Rev. Timothy Flint, an educated Presbyterian minister of New England, who lived in St. Charles for several years during the first part of the present century, thus wrote of the people and some of their habits:

"In approaching the country, I heard a thousand stories of "gougings," and robberies, and shooting down with the rifle. I have traveled in these regions thousands of miles under all circumstances of exposure and danger. I have traveled alone, or in company only with such as needed protection, instead of being able to impart it; and this, too, in many instances, where I was not known as a minister, or where such knowledge would have had no influence in protecting me. I never have carried the slightest weapon of defence. I scarcely remember to have experienced anything that resembled insult, or to have felt myself in danger from the people. I have often seen men that had lost an eye. Instances of murder, numerous and horrible in their circumstances, have occurred in my vicinity. But they were such lawless rencounters as terminate in murder everywhere, and in which the drunkenness, brutality and violence were mutual. They were catastrophes, in which quiet and sober men would not be involved. * * * The first Sabbath that I preached in St. Charles [about 1816], before morning worship, directly opposite where worship was to take place, there was a horse-race. The horses received the signal to start just as I rode to the door. * * * But I cannot forbear to relate that six years after, when I left the place, it was after a communion, where services had been performed in a decent brick church, in which forty communicants had received communion."

The same gentleman, speaking more directly of the people whom he found here at that early period, said:

"The backwoodsman of the West, as I have seen him, is

generally an amiable and virtuous man. His general motive for coming here is to be a freeholder, to have plenty of rich land, and to be able to settle his children about him. I fully believe that nine in ten of the emigrants have come here with no other motive. You find, in truth, that he has vices and barbarisms, peculiar to his situation. His manners are rough. He wears, it may be, a long beard. He has a great quantity of bear or deer skins wrought into his household establishment, his furniture and dress. He carries a knife, or a dirk, in his bosom, and when in the woods has a rifle on his back, and a pack of dogs at his heels; but remember that his rifle and his dogs are among his chief means of support and profit. Remember that all his first days here were spent in dread of savages. Remember that he still encounters them, still meets bears and panthers. Enter his door, and tell him you are benighted, and wish the shelter of his cabin for the night. The welcome is, indeed, seemingly ungracious: 'I reckon you can stay,' or, 'I suppose we must let you stay.' But this apparent ungraciousness is the harbinger of every kindness that he can bestow, and every comfort that his cabin can afford. Good coffee, corn bread and butter, venison, pork, wild and tame fowls, are set before you. His wife, timid, silent, reserved, but constantly attentive to your comfort, does not sit at the table with you, but like the wives of the patriarchs, stands and attends on you. You are shown the best bed which the house can afford. When this kind of hospitality has been afforded you as long as you choose to stay, and when you depart, and speak about your bill, you are most commonly told with some slight mark of resentment, that they do not keep tavern. Even the flaxen-headed urchins will run away from your money.''

To such a degree was this spirit of hospitality carried that one who kept a tavern and charged for his accommodations, was looked down upon by his neighbors as not the right sort of a man to associate with.

In those days there were no railroads or steamboats, nor even stage coaches, to convey passengers from place to place, and the early settlers had to depend upon their own resources. Some built flat-boats and keel-boats, into which they loaded their goods and families, and floated down the Ohio and its tributaries to the Mississippi, and then toiled up that stream to the Missouri, and up the latter to their destination, dragging their clumsy boats by tow-lines, or forcing them along with oars and poles. Others packed their goods, and wives, and children on horses, and came through the wilderness, supplying themselves with meat from the wild game which they killed with their rifles as they came along. And still others, too poor either to own horses or build boats, shouldered what few articles of worldly goods they possessed, and came on foot.

They all located in the woods, near the water courses, and built their houses adjoining some nice, cool, bubbling spring. The idea of settling on the rich prairies never occurred to them. They imagined that the prairies never could be cultivated, because there was no water on them, and no timber to fence them. They did not know, then, that water could be had by digging ponds and cisterns, or that fences could be made by hedging and ditching, or by hauling rails from the adjoining timber. Now the prairies are more valuable than the timbered lands, because they are easier to cultivate, and it requires comparatively little labor to put them in a condition to be cultivated.

Their houses were built of rough logs, with puncheon floors, clapboard roofs, and great, broad, flaring chimneys, composed of sticks and mud. Sometimes they had no floors in their houses, except the ground, beaten smooth and hard, and swept clean every day. Iron nails were not to be had, and the boards of their roofs were fastened with wooden pins, or weighted with poles and stones. One of these old-fashioned houses—two stories high, however, and built of hewn logs—still stood, within one hundred yards of where Daniel Boone and his wife were buried, no longer than five years ago.

A house-raising was a great event, and the people would go ten, fifteen, and even twenty and thirty miles, to assist on these occasions. The women and girls went, too, and cooked rousing dinners of venison, turkey, bear's meat, corn bread, etc. These were relished with fresh honey, taken from trees in the woods, and washed down with clear water from the spring; or, occasionally, with pure, unadulterated whisky. The luxuries of tea and coffee were almost unknown, except among a few of the old ladies, who had become accustomed to them in former times and could not very well do without them. Some of these old ladies would walk to St. Charles or St. Louis, a journey of four or five days, to buy a little tea and coffee, so great was their desire for these luxuries. Others contented themselves with sassafras tea, sweetened with honey, or coffee made of parched rye or corn, which had the name and color, and imagination supplied the rest. The woods were full of bee trees, and honey was abundant. They kept it stored away in cellar-pits and spring-houses by the barrel, where it would grain and become so thick that it could be cut out in slices with a knife—sweeter and more delicious than the nicest candy that was ever made. An old pioneer, still living, often laughs and tells how his mother went to the spring-house once, and found a favorite cat smothered to death in a barrel of honey. The cat and a portion of the honey around it were dipped out, and they tried to eat the rest, but it always remained on the table untasted, and it was finally thrown away.

Milk and butter were in the greatest abundance, and the latter was sent to market at St. Charles—after that place became large enough to afford a market—by the barrel. Only a few were able to own churns, and those who did not possess that useful domestic article, used large bottles or gourds instead. The milk was placed in the bottle or gourd and shaken until the butter "came." A few, more progressive than the others, resorted to the expedient of saddling a mule or a rough trotting horse, and trotting around until the milk was churned. These same progressive persons were known, on different occasions, when in a great hurry, to walk three or four miles after a horse to ride half that distance.

The "range" was so good that cattle and horses, and other stock, did not require feeding more than three months out of twelve, and then a few ears of corn was all they wanted. They kept fat all the year round. The wild rye, grass and peavine grew so high that it would reach a man's shoulders when riding through it on horseback, and so thick that large logs and trees, that had been blown down, would be completely hid from view. This statement seems a little unreasonable, but it is vouched for by a number of persons who know it to be true.

During the summer, when the cattle and horses were not fed, they would become wild, unless salted regularly and accustomed to the voices and presence of their owners. The salting was generally done by the boys, who sometimes got themselves into great danger by their recklessness. One of these boys went into the woods, one day, to salt his father's cattle, and, thinking to have a little fun, began to bleat like a calf in distress. Instantly the whole herd of several hundred came dashing towards him with their horns lowered, and bellowing furiously. The boy sprang from his horse and climbed a small tree, just in time to escape being trampled to death by the infuriated animals, who kept him in the tree for several hours, bellowing around him and plowing the dirt with their horns and hooffs. He never tried that prank again.

The same boy and his brothers used to amuse themselves by frightening the sheep. In driving them from the sheepfold into the pasture they had to pass through a pair of bars, and it was the custom for one of the boys to lie down behind the bars, and when the sheep came near, spring up and hiss, which would frighten them and make them scatter in every direction, much to the amusement of the boys. But one morning the sheep were a little too quick, and the foremost ones had passed through the the bars and over the boy before he could spring up. Of course the whole flock followed, and the louder the boy screamed the faster the sheep came, until they were all through. His back was sore for a week, where they had jumped upon him with their feet, and he was satisfied after that to let the sheep alone.

Another anecdote about these boys will not be out of place, as it goes to show that human nature, as represented in boys, was about the same then as it is now, notwithstanding a great many good people of the present age seem to think children are worse than they ever were at any other period of the world's existence.

Nearly all of the first settlers owned negro slaves, and the black and white children generally played and worked together on equal terms. One day the boy to whom we have referred was plowing in a field with two of his brothers and a colored boy about their own age. The day being very warm, they stopped under a tree to rest and cool—and play. During their conversation the subject of hanging was broached, and the colored boy expressed a desire to know, by practical experience, how it felt. The others were not slow in announcing their readiness to gratify his wish; and, procuring a plow-line, one end of it was thrown over a limb and the other tied in a noose around the boy's neck. The agreement was that when he had hung long enough to gratify his curiosity, he was to whistle and they were to let him down. The preliminaries being all completed, they hoisted him up, and would have hanged him until he was dead, if the old gentleman, who was in the barn near by, had not seen them and ordered them to let him down. When he came down he was senseless and limber as a rag, and it was some time before he recovered consciousness. His neck was very sore for several days, and he was never afterward heard to express a desire to know how hanging felt.

A great deal of pure whisky and brandy were used in those days, and every farmer, who was able to afford it, built a small still house. They were not troubled with revenue officers and

collectors, or government stamps, and other contrivances for raising taxes, so familiar at the present time; but every one made his
own liquor, freely and openly, from the pure juice of the grain
or fruit, and then drank it himself, and gave it to his family and
neighbors to drink, without any compunctions of conscience. Men,
women and children drank whisky and brandy, because it was
pure, and they considered it healthy and pleasant to the taste.
There were perhaps more drunkards then, in proportion to population, than now, but there were fewer premature deaths, derange-
ments, and cases of *delirum tremens*, growing out of the use of al-
coholic stimulants. When one neighbor visited another, the whisky and sugar, or honey, were set before him, and all drank freely.
It was considered an insult and sufficient cause for discontinuing
friendly relations, if you visited a neighbor and were not asked to
drink. Cups and glasses could not be had, and hence they used
gourds, wild cymlings, and horns for drinking purposes. "Will
you take a horn?" was the usual mode of asking a person to
take a drink, and the expression has never gone out of use. Jugs
and barrels were scarce, and large gourds, holding several gallons,
were grown, in which whisky and other liquids were stored away.

Earthenware cups, saucers, plates, etc., were not used, as they
could not be purchased in the country; and knives and forks were
unknown until a comparatively modern date. Their plates were
made of pewter, kept scoured bright and clean, and in place of
knives and forks they used their hunting knives and pocket
knives, aided by their fingers, and occasionally wooden spoons.
Wooden trays and bowls took the place of iron and tin vessels of
modern times. Pots were sometimes made of raw hide, or green
bark, and they would last a considerable length of time, the boiling water or other liquid on the inside preventing them from burning.
For chairs they had rough stools, or frames with raw hide stretched
over them; sometimes the trunks of small trees were sawed off
the proper length, and, cushioned with bear skins or buffalo robes,
made very comfortable seats. One man is reported to have used
large pumpkins for stools, into which the rats gnawed after the
seeds, and made things lively for the man and his children. This,
however, we do not vouch for.

Nearly all the first settlers brought seeds of different kinds of
fruit with them, from which they soon obtained bearing orchards;
though the fruit, being all seedling, was generally of an inferior
quality. This, however, was not always the case, for some very

fine varieties of apples, peaches, and pears originated in those old orchards.

Very little attention was given to agriculture, the men and boys devoting most of their time to hunting and trapping, which was the most profitable employment they could engage in. The women and girls did the cooking and washing, weaving, sewing and knitting, and had a much harder time than their male relatives. Their dresses were made of cotton and lindsey, manufactured entirely by their own hands; and frequently a great deal of taste was displayed in the coloring (which was done with roots and bark) and the combination of colors in weaving. A striped lindsey dress was considerd a beautiful article of apparel. Four to five yards of cloth was generally sufficient for a dress, as they were made short and small in the skirt. The men and boys raised the cotton, and sheared the sheep, but the cotton and wool were picked, washed, carded, spun, woven, and made into garments by the women and girls. Sometimes all hands, old and young, large and small, would sit up late at night and pick cotton, the little ones being kept awake by promises of supper when they had completed their tasks. This supper consisted of nothing more than a piece of buttered corn bread and a gourd of milk, for those old-fashioned people were impressed with the idea that heavy suppers

EARLY DAYS IN MISSOURI.

were not good for children. But they were hearty and hungry,
and their bread and milk was as rich a feast to them as a king's
supper. There was no lack of children then. Every family had
ten or a dozen of them, and some had as many as twenty, all
healthy, hearty, active little fellows. The country was new, land
was cheap, and it cost nothing to support them, as they usually
made their own way ; so each little new-comer received a hearty
welcome, and was sent on his way rejoicing. In warm weather
they were not burdened with a superabundance of clothes ; a coarse
cotton shirt, hanging loose from the neck, generally constituted
their wardrobe. In winter time they were dressed in warm jeans
and lindsey, with woolen socks and buckskin moccasins on their
feet. The boys sometimes wore buckskin pants and hunting shirts
in cold weather, but, as a general thing, that suit was not donned
until they were old enough to kill the deer and tan the hide from
which their suit was made.

There was no public school system in Missouri at the time of
which we write, and the people were not so generally educated as
they are now. It was often the case that men of influence in their
communities could not write their names, and the old legal records
show a large proportion of signatures made with a mark. There
was perhaps as large a proportion of well educated people then as
now, but the mass of the people were not so well versed in the
rudiments of our language. Most of parents made an effort to
teach their boys how to read, write and cypher ; but very little attention was given to the education of girls. It was thought that a
girl's education was complete when she knew how to cook, wash,
spin, weave, attend to her domestic duties, and read the simpler
chapters of the Bible. Books were scarce and very high priced,
and those who were inclined to educate themselves had but few opportunities for doing so. Now and then some pretentious pedagogue, with the title of professor, and pretending to be able to
impart a knowledge of most of the languages and all the sciences,
would straggle into a community and teach a three or four
months' subscription school, in some disused cabin, hastily furnished as a school house, with split log benches and puncheon
writing desks. To this " academy" the youth of the community
would be sent, to study a little, and play a great deal more, while
the teacher slept away the effects of too free an intercourse with
his whisky bottle—for they nearly all drank freely. The celerity
with which they claimed to be able to impart a classical education

was truly astonishing. A few months were sufficient to master all the intricacies of the English language; and Greek, Latin, and Hebrew could be forced into the dullest intellect at a dozen lessons. Some of these teachers were also ministers, and they took great delight in quoting Hebrew, Latin and Greek, in support of their religious dogmas, to gaping congregations, who imagined them to be walking encyclopedias of learning. But while they quoted the ancient languages, with which they were about as familiar as a Choctaw Indian is with Sanscrit, they did not hesitate to "murder the king's English" in the grossest and most barbarous manner.

With this class of teachers, and so great a lack of educational facilities, it is not to be wondered at that many of the children grew up in comparative ignorance; but happily they all, by some means or other, acquired a high appreciation of the advantages of a good education, and, as soon as they were able, built school houses, employed competent teachers, and sent their children to school.

Money was exceedingly scarce, and furs and peltry constituted the principal currency of the country. Lead and gun powder also passed current, and whisky would have done likewise if it had possessed any intrinsic value. A few silver dollars found their way into the country at different times, and as that was the smallest coin in circulation, they were cut into pieces of four and eight to the dollar, and passed for quarters and bits, the latter representing 12½ cents. Hence the Western expressions, "six bits," "four bits," etc., which are rarely or never heard anywhere else. Frequently a dollar would be cut into *five* pieces and passed for quarters, or into *ten* pieces and passed for twelve and a half cents. The latter were called *sharp shiners*, and both they and the dishonest quarters were so nearly like the honest ones that they generally passed without suspicion. As the population increased and currency became a necessity, counterfeit money began to make its appearance; and the people, being easily imposed upon, received it readily, until at one time there was more spurious coin in circulation than genuine. Companies of counterfeiters were organized, and large quantities of the stuff were manufactured and sent to other localities to be passed. The excitement finally ran very high, and several suspected parties were lynched, or threatened with the penalties of the law. These vigorous measures soon put an end to the business, and the people also became shrewd enough not to be imposed upon any longer.

They were all great lovers of fun in those early days, and having no occasion or desire to lay up money, they devoted much of their time to amusement. Their house-raisings, log-rollings,.corn-shuckings, rail-splittings, and musters were generally turned into frolics, and they had more fun than work. A few would get drunk and fight—then make friends, take another drink, and fight again. Others would jump and run foot races, while perhaps the greater portion would organize a shooting match, and try their skill as marksmen. The "manly art" of boxing and fighting was practiced to a considerable extent, doubtless at first with the intention of rendering themselves able to overcome their Indian adversaries in hand-to-hand combats, but it eventually degenerated into a pernicious custom, and every public gathering had to be enlivened with a fight or two. Each neighborhood had its "bully," who was monarch of all he surveyed, and who held himself in constant readiness to accommodate any man who was spoiling for a fight. Like the fabled Irishman, who begged "some jintleman to tread upon the tail of his coat," they were never happy except when engaged in a "scrimmage." When two of these champions happened to meet at any public gathering, they generally devoted the day to the improving exercise of mashing noses, bruising faces, and gouging eyes; and it was an unusual thing for one of them to live to middle age without the loss of an eye, the disappearance of sundry teeth, or the total wreck of a nose. Each community had a nick-name, by which the people of that locality were called. Thus, in Montgomery county, those who lived on Elk Horn creek were called "heel strings," those on Camp Branch, "shake rags," and those on South Bear creek "anaruges." So when one of the champions wanted to try his prowess with any of the other champions, he would liquor himself up to the fighting point, and then announce that he could whip any *shake rag*, *heel string*, or *anaruge* (as the case might be) on the ground, and immediately his challenge would be accepted and the fighting would commence. But as school houses began to make their appearance, and intelligence increased, these worthies sought more congenial haunts, until they finally disappeared.

In addition to its fighting champion, each community had its champion jumper, whose nimble limbs were supposed to sustain the honor of their respective neighborhoods in this particular. As to marksmanship, they were all so nearly perfect in the use of the rifle that but few could lay any claim to superior excellence in that line, and they held their shooting matches more for practice and amusement than from any desire or expectation of gaining reputations as leading shots.

For years after the close of the Indian war, they kept up their military organizations and drills. Each township had a company, and each county a regiment, and four times a year they mustered and drilled. On these occasions it was customary for the officers to treat the men, and a wash-tub full of whisky was generally prepared for them, and placed on a stump, around which they would gather after the drill was over, and help themselves, some with gourds, horns and other drinking vessels, while others would insert straws in the tub and suck to their hearts' content. If the officers refused to treat, the men would not drill; but usually the treat was ready when wanted, for the officers were generally candidates for civil positions, or expected to be, and did not care to risk the loss of their popularity with the men who did the voting.

The poor women had a pretty hard time, for in addition to taking care of the children, and doing all the ordinary domestic work and house-cleaning, with none of the modern improvements to aid them, they had to manufacture cloth from the raw material and make all the clothes worn by themselves and their families. Some idea of the trials they had to pass through can be obtained from the following extract from a letter, written by one of the pioneer women of Callaway county to her sister in Kentucky, who had made inquiries as to how she liked her new home:

" The *men* and *dogs* have a fine time, but the poor women have to suffer. They have to pack water from one-half to one mile, and do all the cooking and washing. So my advice to you is, stay where you are. But if you see any one coming to this part of the country, please send me a *plank cradle* for poor little Patrick. His poor little back is full of hard lumps, and skinned all over, lying in nothing but a cradle George made out of one-half of a hollow log, with a piece [of wood] on one end for a pillow. The poor child has a hard time, for he hain't got but two shirts in the world, and both of them is made of nettle bark, that almost scratches him to death. Great dents and whelps [welts] are all over the poor little creature's back. I don't want to have any more children if the poor little things are to be treated in this way. I told George so last night, and what you reckon he said? He said it was the very thing—it would make them tough, and they could stand Bare and Deer hunting. George has got him a Buckskin hunting-shirt and pants, and he is gone hunting day and night.

"We have got some good, kind Neighbors, and we visit each other when we can.   I forgot to tell you of a wedding I and George attended last week.   They were married by an old Hard Shell Baptist preacher by the name of Jabe Ham.   He had on a long buckskin overcoat that looked so funny!   The man was in his shirt sleeves, with white cotton pants that just came down below his knees, and white cotton socks, and buckskin slippers on his feet.   The girl was dressed in a short-waisted, low-necked, short-sleeved white cotton dress, that was monstrous short for a tall girl like she was, for I don't reckon there was more than five yards of cloth in her dress.   She also had on buckskin slippers, and her hair was tied up with a buckskin string, which is all the go out here.   And when Mr. Ham was spelling and reading the ceremony from the book, the girl commenced sneezing, and the buckskin string slipped off and her hair flew all over her face, and everybody laughed."

The people of that age had but few conveniences, and were compelled to resort to many expedients and shifts that now seem ridiculous to us; but they did the best they could under the circumstances, and tried to be contented and happy.   They had no convenient markets or easy modes of transportation, and what little they had to sell generally brought a very low price.   For many years there were no stores of any kind in the country, and only two or three small trading establishments at St. Charles, where a few necessary articles of domestic use could be purchased.   Occasionally wagons would come up from St. Louis, loaded with such goods as the settlers needed, which would be exchanged for game, fresh honey, butter, etc.   The arrival of one of these wagons always created a sensation, and everybody turned out to buy and sell.   If a man had nothing to exchange for the goods in the wagon, he took his rifle and went into the woods and obtained the necessary articles.   Game was so abundant that it did not require a great length of time to supply one's self with that kind of currency.   What little money was in circulation was hoarded up and taken to the land office in Palmyra to purchase lands from the government.   But few debts were contracted, and none were sued upon.   The few necessaries that the people were compelled to purchase were paid for in barter.   New Orleans was the principal market, and the produce of the country was shipped on flat or keel boats — sometimes in canoes and pirogues.   It generally required six months to make the trip.

Corn was worth from five to ten cents per bushel, wheat thirty cents, bacon a cent and a half a pound; the best horses sold for twenty to thirty dollars, and good cows from five to seven dollars. The scarcity of money and lack of means of transportation, made everything low that farmers had to sell, and the same causes enhanced the price of every article they were compelled to buy. The little money they had was principally "*hard money*," and the people fully realized its inconvenience as a circulating medium, and its want of power to build up the commercial interests of a country. Very few who lived in Missouri at that time, and witnessed the evil effects of silver currency, could be induced to vote for the "hard money" absurdity of the present day. Metal currency will do for heathens and uncivilized nations, where trade is limited and the government so unstable that its "promises to pay" are worthless, but no enlightened commercial country can prosper, or even exist, without a paper currency. Business men cannot afford to keep a cart and a yoke of oxen to draw their money around, as the Spartans of old did, and the early Missourians learned this fact to their cost. Those who possessed considerable sums of money, and came to this country to invest in lands, were compelled either to pack their money in sacks on the backs of their horses, and thereby excite the cupidity of robbers, by whom the intervening country was infested, or exchange their silver for U. S. Bank notes, and pay a premium of several per cent. These notes even brought a premium over gold, simply because of their convenience, and the faith of the people in their stability.

The lack of money — or rather the want of a convenient currency—finally led to the establishment of "wild-cat" banks in different parts of the country. Very few of these establishments were conducted on banking principles, but they issued notes that looked like money, and the people received them gladly. Trade revived, values increased, and the country seemed to be entering upon the high road to prosperity. But after a while some of these notes began to be presented for redemption, and then the unpleasant discovery was made that the "bankers" had nothing to redeem them with. The spurious bills failed in the hands of the holders, and in a short time the country was left without a currency. Even the wealthy could hardly find means to purchase the actual necessaries of life, and the people were plunged into a depth of distress never before realized. Lands and other property at first sank in value to less than at any former period, and then would scarcely sell at all. Confidence and credit were destroyed through the influence of what were called relief laws. Missouri and Illinois suffered more than any of the other States, and for the relief of the people a banking system, called a loan office, was established. The money was redeemable in equal annual installments of ten per cent. in ten years. This money was declared by some of the courts to be illegal, and not a tender, as it had been made by the Legislature that had created it; and it immediately began to depreciate, until it fell to twenty-five per cent of its nominal value. This remedy, therefore, only aggravated the disease. The people could not obtain money to pay their taxes, or to purchase clothes for their families, and their produce, stock, etc., became almost worthless. "Hard times" were upon them in earnest, and none were exempt. Years elapsed before this dreadful condition of affairs began to grow perceptibly better. Then Senator Benton had a law passed through Congress, authorizing the recoinage of British gold, with additional alloy, and this increased the currency of the country to a perceptible degree. Shortly after the passage of this law the German immigration commenced, which gave a new impetus to trade in the Western country. Then followed the discovery of gold in California, and that did more than anything else to dispel the financial gloom. A State bank was also established, on a sound basis, and its bills circulated at par with gold and silver, sometimes bringing a premium over both. The free circulation of good money caused a revival of business, and prosperity once more smiled upon the country. In April, 1836, the first railroad convention met in St. Louis, and a committee of three, viz.: Messrs. Rollins, Bates, and Gamble, was appointed to memorialize Congress for grants of land in aid of the several proposed roads. Railroads have since been built upon all the routes suggested at that time, and nearly upon the lines designated, as will be seen from the following proceedings of the convention:

"1st. It is now expedient to adopt measures for the construction of a railroad from St. Louis to Fayette, with the view of ultimately extending the road in that general direction, as far as public convenience and the exigencies of trade may require.

" Also, a railroad from St. Louis, in a Southwestern direction, to the valley of Bellevue, in Washington county, so as to traverse the rich mineral region in that part of the state, with a view to its indefinite extension in that direction, when and as far as public interest may require. And also a branch from some convenient point on the last-mentioned road, to the Meramec iron-works in Crawford county, with a view to its ultimate extension through Cooper county to a point on the Missouri river in Jackson county.

"2d. That the proposed railroad from St. Louis to Fayette ought to cross the Missouri river at the town of St. Charles, and through or within one mile of the several towns of Warrenton, Danville, Fulton, and Columbia, the said towns being points most acceptable to the people of the counties through which the road is proposed to pass."

The first railroad in Missouri was commenced in 1836, at Marion City, in the eastern part of Marion county. It was the intention for this road to extend to the Missouri river, in Howard county, but it was never completed; and, from all the information we can obtain on the subject, it was only partially surveyed.

RELIGIOUS MATTERS.

But little attention was given to religious matters in the new settlements until after the first ten or twelve years of the present century.

The Spanish government, it is true, required all who received grants of land from the crown, to be good Catholics, but as this requirement was never enforced, the people gave it little or no attention. Protestant ministers occasionally visited the settlements and held services in the log cabins of the pioneers, but no churches or classes were regularly organized until after the territory was purchased by the United States in 1803.

The first of the pioneer preachers were Old Baptists, or what are popularly known as Ironsides, or Hardshell Baptists, and there were some very original characters among them, as we shall endeavor to show in future pages. Very few of the pioneers made any pretensions to religion, but when one of those Old Ironside preachers came into the neighborhood and preached in some good brother's cabin, they all attended, with their guns on their shoulders, and their dogs at their heels. The guns were stacked in one corner of the cabin, while the dogs remained outside and fought, or went on hunting expeditions on their own account. At the close of the services, the brother in whose house they were held would pass the whisky around, and all would take a drink, the preacher included, so that, in this respect, it was hard to tell saint from sinner.   Then they would call the dogs and take a hunt, or get up a shooting match and try their skill with their rifles.

As the settlements became thicker, and the population increased, churches of different denominations were organized, and a religious fervor began to prevail.   Camp-meetings became popular, and were largely attended by all classes of people.   By this time, also, the rough frontier dress had, in a measure, been discarded, and in place of buckskin hunting shirt and leggins, there appeared home-made jeans pants and coats, with now and then a "round-about," while the feet were clad in home-made leather shoes instead of buckskin moccasins.   The good old sisters would take their babies in their arms and their shoes and stockings in their hands, and walk barefooted to the camp-ground, to save their shoes.   They would sometimes walk twenty or thirty miles to a camp-meeting, and upon arriving near the camp-ground, would stop at some spring or water course, and wash their feet and put on their shoes and stockings.   They were generally accompanied on these occasions by their husbands, who also carried

GOING TO CHURCH IN MISSOURI IN 1820

their shoes in their hands, and their rifles on their shoulders, while the older children, clad in the most primitive style, and the dogs, brought up the rear.

It was about the year 1814, as near as we can ascertain—for there was no record kept of the matter—that the singular religious phenomenon called the "jerks" began to make its appearance at the camp-meetings. It was first developed at a camp-meeting in Tennessee, and threw all the surrounding country into a state of the wildest excitement. From Tennessee it spread to other parts of the country, and soon became prevalent all over the West. It was a nervous affection, and persons under its influence lost all control over their movements, though they rarely became insensible. They would jerk violently from side to side, and backward and forward, sometimes shouting "Glory to God," and at others cursing and swearing in the most awful manner. Sometimes their heads and necks and bodies would be jerked and twisted and distorted until it would seem that every joint and bone in them must be dislocated or broken; but no physical harm ever resulted from these attacks. Some attributed the phenomenon to the agency of the devil, others imagined that the preachers understood some sort of black art which they practiced upon those who came near them or shook hands with them; but the greater portion of the people, led by the ministers themselves, considered it to be the manifestation of the Spirit of God, and gave Him praise accordingly. A few incidents, illustrative of this subject, will give a better understanding of its characteristics.

In a certain community there lived a young man and his sister, in an elegant mansion, left them by their parents. They were aristocratic and proud, and associated only with their own class of people. They rarely attended religious services, except when they could visit some fashionable church; and the Methodists, Baptists, and other primitive religious people, were regarded by them with a certain degree of contempt. On one occasion, prompted by curiosity, they visited a Methodist camp-meeting near their residence; and during the day the young lady began to feel the influence of the religious atmosphere by which she was surrounded. The young man, alarmed lest she should join the despised Methodists, threatened if she went to the altar he would carry her away by force. Finally, being deeply impressed, she did go to the altar, and requested the prayers of the members of the church. Her brother, who was at the time in a distant part of the congregation, was soon informed of his sister's action, and immediately started forward to carry out his threat.   Under the arbor, where services were held, rough board seats had been erected for the accommodation of the people, and the young man had to cross these in going to the altar.   He had proceeded about half way when he was suddenly attacked by the jerks, and could not advance another step.   Unwilling to submit to the power that restrained him, he made desperate efforts to go forward, but every time he advanced a step he would be jerked violently back over the seats, and thrown from side to side, as helpless as an infant, but raving and swearing like a madman.   He tore his hair with his hands, and frothed at the mouth, and his limbs were jerked about and distorted in a most horrible manner.   When he stood still, or retreated, the influence deserted him, and he became quiet and assumed his normal condition; but the moment he attempted to advance he would be seized with renewed power and hurled back with increased violence.   He wore a suit of fine black broadcloth, and a large spur on the heel of each boot, and the prongs of the spurs, catching in his clothes, tore them into shreds, until, when he finally submitted to the invisible power and left the ground, he was almost naked.   His sister remained at the altar, and experienced what is known among Methodists as a change of heart; and the young man was also converted at a subsequent period.   This was one of the most singular incidents that occurred during the prevalence of the jerks, but its truth is fully vouched for by several persons who witnessed it.

A young girl, a daughter of Mr. Jonathan Bryan, who lived on Femme Osage creek, having visited several camp-meetings and witnessed a number of cases of the jerks, learned to imitate them, and was rather fond of exhibiting her proficiency in that line. But one day, while sitting on the stiles in front of her father's house, she was attacked by the genuine jerks, and thrown to the ground.   Her head and body were thrown backward and forward with great force, and her long hair, coming loose from its fastenings, cracked like a whip.   She was jerked and thrown around for a considerable length of time, and then left in an almost exhausted condition.   After that she never imitated the jerks again —one genuine experience satisfied her.

Rev. Jesse Walker, a Methodist minister, and Rev. David Clark, an Ironside Baptist preacher, once conducted a camp-meeting together, on Peruque creek, in St. Charles county.   During the meeting the jerks made their appearance, and a number of persons were brought under their influence. One day a man named Leonard Harrow was looking on and laughing at some of the penitents who were jerking, when he was suddenly attacked himself, and, throwing his arms around a sapling near him, he began to butt his head violently against it, and would have knocked his brains out if he had not been restrained by several persons who stood near him.

Sometimes, after the jerks deserted them, they would fall into a trance or stupor, and remain unconscious, and often apparently dead, for hours and even days at a time. A few incidents are mentioned where persons were actually laid out and prepared for burial, their friends supposing them to be dead; but eventually they would recover their consciousness as suddenly as they had lost it, and astonish the watchers by rising up in their grave clothes. A colored woman, who belonged to Mr. Burrell Adams, of Montgomery county, was subject to attacks of this kind, and would remain unconscious and motionless for a day or two at a time.

Occasionally the jerks would assume a ludicrous aspect, and cause their victims to perform such ridiculous actions that the most sedate could hardly restrain their laughter. On one occasion, at a camp-meeting near Flint Hill, in St. Charles county a man who had been standing for sometime as if in a profound study, suddenly commenced jumping up and down, snapping his thumbs and fingers, and shouting at the top of his voice, "Slick as a peeled onion! Slick as a peeled onion!" His emotion lasted only a few minutes, and upon being questioned by his friends as to its cause, he replied that he had just received the Holy Ghost, and it came so easily that he could compare it with nothing more appropriate than the slickness of a peeled onion.

Mrs. Williamson, who lived near Loutre, in Montgomery county, often had the jerks; and so did her daughter, Miss Katy. At a camp-meeting held by the Cumberland Presbyterians, a short distance southeast of Danville, many years ago, Miss Katy was attacked by the jerks, and some men who were standing near began to laugh at her. Directly she started toward them, in a jumping, unearthly fashion, when the men became frightened and ran away. About the same time several large dogs attacked the girl and tore her dress into shreds, leaving her almost naked, when some of the preachers came down from the pulpit and drove the dogs away.

Subsequently, at a camp-meeting in Warren county, Miss Katy had an attack of the jerks, and getting down on her hands and feet, she began to crawl about like a measuring worm, when some of her friends carried her away and secured her in a tent.

Rev. James E. Welch, whose history is given elsewhere, relates the following incidents that occurred under his own observation: When a mere boy, he attended a camp-meeting held by a body of religious enthusiasts who had seceded from the Presbyterian church, and who called themselves New Lights. This meeting was held near the line between Kentucky and Tennessee, in the region of country where the New Lights, as well as the jerks, originated. One day during the meeting, the boy's attention was directed to four women, who, though in the midst of the congregation, were carefully binding up and securing their long hair. Having completed their arrangements, they all took the jerks, and commenced dancing backward and forward, over a space of about ten feet, giving a slight but very peculiar jerk of the body and head at each turn. During the performance the hair of one of the women came down, when she very deliberately stopped and re-arranged it, and then proceeded with her dancing as though nothing had occurred to interrupt her. When the horn blew for dinner, they all quieted down, and went to the table and ate as heartily as any one.

Young Welch afterward became a minister in the Missionary Baptist Church, and in 1814 came to Cape Girardeau, Mo., on some private business. He remained several months, and during his stay was invited to go to a place about twenty-five miles west of Cape Girardeau, on the waters of the St. Francois river, and hold religious services. He did so, and organized a Baptist church at that place. One day, just after he had announced his text and commenced his discourse, a young woman immediately in front of him, took the jerks. This was his first experience with that phenomenon since he had commenced preaching, and it startled him. The girl's body, as she sat on the bench, was jerked violently backward and forward, until her head almost touched the benches in front of and behind her, and the minister expected every moment to see her back break; but she was not injured in the least. In the midst of her contortions her hair came loose, and the rapid motions of her head caused it to hiss

and whiz so loud that it could be heard at a distance of thirty or
forty yards; and at every jerk she gave a peculiar shriek cr yelp
that almost made the blood curdle. It cannot be exactly represented in print, but sounded very much like "yeouk." Mr.
Welch was so overcome by his emotions at witnessing the strange
exhibition, that he could not proceed with his sermon, but stopped
and gazed in wonder at the girl. As soon as he ceased preaching,
she sank back exhausted upon the ground, and remained apparently unconscious. He thereupon resumed his discourse, when
she again began to jerk, and this was repeated three times before
he closed his sermon.

Mr. Welch was accompanied on his return to Kentucky by a
young man, whom he found to be a very pleasant traveling companion, and whose society was none the less appreciated on account of the loneliness of the road. The settlements at that time
were very scattering, and they often traveled fifty to seventy-five
miles without seeing a house. One evening they stopped at a
cabin, in the midst of a dense wilderness, fifty miles from any
other human habitation, and inquired if they could obtain lodging
for the night. The man, who was a genuine specimen of the
backwoods hunter, answered them that they were welcome, if they
could put up with his fare; and being thankful to obtain any kind
of a shelter, they gladly availed themselves of his hospitality,
and alighting from their horses, they entered the cabin, which
contained but one room, furnished in the usual frontier style.
The family consisted of the man, his wife, and a grown daughter,
and, notwithstanding their lonely surroundings, they seemed contented with their lot and happy in each other's society. After a
substantial supper of venison, corn bread, and milk and butter,
they seated themselves at the door of the cabin, where they could
enjoy the cool breeze, and spent several hours in pleasant conversation. The cabin contained two beds, one on either side of the
room, and when it was time to retire, one of these was given to
Mr. Welch and his companion, while the man and his wife occupied the other, the girl sleeping on a pallet between them. The
light had scarcely been extinguished when the girl began to pound
the floor in a very demonstrative manner, with her elbows and
feet, and upon inquiry as to what was the matter with her, the man
replied that she had the jerks. "Caught 'em," said he, "from one
of the preachers, at a Methodist camp-meeting." "For God's
sake," exclaimed Mr. Welch, "light the candle and let us see

what is the matter with her." The man complied, and as soon as
the light was struck the girl sprang to her feet, and, ducking her
head like a sheep, she ran to the door and butted it with great
violence, taking care, however, not to strike her head against any
portion of it that was solid enough to knock her brains out. She
kept this up for some time, running wildly back and forth across
the room, until Mr. Welch, becoming alarmed for her safety,
asked the man to catch and hold her. "I cant't do it," he replied; "I have tried it often, but there is no power on earth that
can hold her. You may try, if you want to." Availing himself
of the privilege thus granted, Mr. Welch awaited his opportunity, and suddenly tripping her feet from under her, he laid her
gently on the pallet. But immediately she began to whirl over
and over, and rolling herself in the pallet, seemed as if she would
tear it into shreds. Seeing that nothing could be done with her
in her wild condition, Mr. Welch requested the man to blow out
the light, and they all retired to bed again. In a few minutes the
girl became quiet and fell asleep, and they heard nothing more
from her during the remainder of the night. But the incident
made so deep an impression on the minds of the travelers that
they never forgot it.

The jerks usually made a deep and lasting impression upon the
minds of those who beheld them, and a revival of religion generally followed their appearance in a community; though the intelligent reader will fail to see any connection between such absurd
freaks of nature and religion. We can vouch for the truth of the
incidents here recorded, but shall not presume to give a reason
for them. The reader can do that for himself. It has been more
than twenty years since a case of genuine jerks was witnessed, and
it is to be presumed that no one regrets their disappearance.
Shouting and clapping of hands, and other exciting demonstra-
tions of some sort of emotion—whether religious or otherwise we
cannot say—are still occasionally witnessed at rural camp-meetings, and among the colored people, but they do not, in any manner, resemble the jerks, which made such a sensation during the
first part of the present century. The diffusion of knowledge, and
the consequent banishment of superstition, have taught people to
worship their Creator in a more reasonable and becoming manner,
and it is not probable that another case of the jerks will ever be
witnessed.

AFFAIRS OF GOVERNMENT, ETC.

THE pioneers of Missouri, as previously stated, were not a lawless or vicious class of people, but, nevertheless, some sort of a government was required to restrain the reckless characters that lived in the country. When the territory came into possession of the United States, one of the most intelligent and influential men in each community was appointed Justice of the Peace, before whom all transgressors were tried and all legal disputes adjusted. Very few of these men knew anything about law, and some of their decisions and legal documents would be regarded as curiosities in these modern times. But if they knew but little law, they understood the meaning of justice, and their decisions did not often miss the mark.

As there were no jails to confine offenders in, breaches of the peace, thefts, and other light misdemeanors were punished by fines, or if flagrant in character, by whipping. The fines were generally paid with furs and peltry, which were sold for the benefit of the government; but where whipping was the penalty, it was administered in a summary manner, and the offender was permitted to go about his business as though nothing unusual had occurred. On one occasion a man who had stolen a hog was taken before Daniel Boone for examination. His trial and the infliction of the punishment occupied half an hour, and while returning home he was met by an acquaintance, who inquired how he had come out. "Eh gad! whipped *and cleared*," was his laconic reply. In those days when men fell out and fought, they never thought of taking their cases into court, but the one who got whipped yielded with as good a grace as he could command, to the superior strength or dexterity of his antagonist, and, after taking a drink and shaking hands in token of friendship, let the matter drop until he got an opportunity to pay off his score with interest.

But few murders were committed, and generally the murderer made his escape, and was never heard of again; for if he remained in the community he was almost certain to be killed by the friends of the man he had murdered, even if he escaped immediate lynching.

We give below a literal copy of the first indictment found in St. Charles county, by the first American grand jury that sat under the United States government, in the territory of Louisiana. It was signed by twelve men, all of whom, except the foreman, had to make their marks, being unable to write. It will be seen from the wording of the instrument that considerable effort was made to give it a legal and solemn sound, in order, no doubt, that it might make a deep impression on the minds of all concerned. It reads as follows:

"That one James Davis, late of the District of St. Charles, in the Territory of Louisiana, Laborer, not having the fear of God before his eyes, but being moved and seduced by the instigation of the Devil, on the 13th day of December, in the year of our Lord one thousand eight hundred and four (1804), at a place called Femme Osage, in the said District of St. Charles, with force and arms, in and upon William Hays, in the peace of God and the United States, there and then being Feloniously, wilfully, and with his malice aforethought, did make an assault, and that the said James Davis, with a certain rifle gun, four feet long, and of the value of five dollars, then and there loaded and charged with gun powder and one leaden bullet, with said rifle gun the said James Davis, then and there in his hands had and held, fired and killed William Hays."

Davis gave bond in the sum of $3,000 for his appearance at court, and Daniel Boone went his security. He stood his trial and was cleared.

As the country settled up and the population increased, the number of civil suits grew larger, and people began to feel the need of educated attorneys. At first a few pettifoggers, possessing a little learning and vast pretensions, were imported from other localities, and they came expecting to have everything their own way, and to astonish the natives by their profundity. But they soon found themselves eclipsed by the practical, common-sense backwoodsmen, and very naturally settled down to their proper places. There were others, however, who possessed fine talents and a liberal amount of learning, and these were respected by the people, and sooned gained a large influence. Among the first prominent attorneys was Edward Hempsted, an unlettered man, but one who possessed strong sense and a fine talent for special pleading He had a sharp, fierce, and barking manner of speaking, which had a great effect upon jurors, and generally awed them into acquiescence with his own views. His style became very popular, and was widely imitated by young attorneys. At the head of the profession stood Col. Thomas H. Benton, whose fame afterward extended over the whole country, and who represented Missouri for thirty years in the U. S. Senate. One who knew him in the early days of his practice here, thus described him: "He is acute, labored, florid, rather sophomorical, but a man of strong sense. There flashes 'strange fire' from his eye, and all that he does 'smells of the lamp.'"

Edward Bates also became prominent at an early day, and he was probably the most learned of any of the lawyers of that time. He was a classical scholar, and exhibited the fruits of his attainments in his arrangement and choice of language. His manners were gentlemanly and pleasing, and his language concise and to the point; but these were often thrown away upon the jury in a region where noise and flourish were sometimes mistaken for sense and reason.

Unlimited puffing was resorted to then as now, and with like success. The man who could make the finest show and induce the greatest number of people to talk about him, *in the right way*, generally won fame and distinction, and became the leader of his portion of the country. But these things gradually passed away as the country became more enlightened, and men were esteemed for their real worth and integrity rather than for shallow display and great pretensions, unsupported by genuine merit.

THE INDIAN WAR.

Owing to the exposed position of Missouri, and the thinness of the population, it suffered severely from the effects of Indian hostility a short time previous to and during the war of 1812. The celebrated Tecumseh, doubtless the most accomplished and courageous Indian chief that ever lived, endeavored to engage all the Indian nations in a common cause against the Americans; but although he gave the signal by commencing warlike operations on the Wabash, the Missouri Indians continued for sometime to give proofs of peaceful intentions. But large presents were continually made by the British agents, and every argument used to induce them to take up the tomahawk. They, however, remained quiet, with the exception of a few murders and thefts committed by hunting parties in remote settlements, until the summer of 1811, when they committed some outrages in the settlements in St. Charles district, and on Salt river. Gen. Clark, who had command of the department, made every exertion to detect the murderers, but as the American force was not yet organized, it proved unavailing. During the winter of 1811–12 murders became more frequent, and the people began to experience the dreadful effects of an Indian war. From Fort Madison to St. Charles men, women and children were butchered by the savages and their habitations consigned to the flames. Orders were sent to Colonel Kibby, who commanded the militia of St. Charles, to call out a portion of his men, and the Governor himself immediately left for that district. Upon his arrival there he organized a company of rangers, consisting of the most hardy woodsmen, who, by rapid movements, scoured the country in all directions. With these, and the aid of a small detachment of troops from Bellefontaine, under command of Lieutenant Mason, he was enabled to afford some degree of protection to the distressed inhabitants.

Early in May, 1812, a grand convocation of chiefs met in St. Louis, for the purpose of accompanying Gen. Clark to Washington City, a plan which was thought would have a good effect. The Little Osages, Sacs, Reynards, Shawnees, and Delawares were represented by their chiefs, and after their departure for the national capitol there was a visible decrease in the number of outrages for a considerable time. But Tecumseh and his brother, the Prophet, were becoming more and more popular among the Indians; and so long as this was the case, no favorable termination of the contest could be expected. On the 26th of June, 1812, a council was held between the following Indian nations, under the direction of Tecumseh and the Prophet, viz: the Winnebagoes, Pottawatamies, Kickapoos, Shawnees, Miamies, Wild Oats, Sioux, Ottos, Scas, Foxes, and Iowas. A large majority of these tribes were in favor of war, and upon the return of their chiefs to their various nations, active hostilities were commenced all along the frontier. Murders and other outrages soon became frequent in the vicinity of St. Charles, Portage des Sioux, and Fort Madison.

In the spring of 1814 a garrison was established at Prairie du Chien, for the purpose of restraining the movements of the Indians, and preventing as far as possible their raids upon the settlements. But most of the men who composed this garrison had been enlisted for only sixty days, and when their time expired they returned home, leaving only about one hundred men to guard the fort. As this post was too important to be abandoned, it was determined to send a reinforcement at once, and Lieutenant Campbell was dispatched, with forty-two regulars and sixty-five rangers, in three keel-boats, accompanied by a fourth belonging to the sutler and contractor, to the relief of the garrison. The rangers were commanded by Lieutenants Rector and Riggs, the latter of whom was subsequently with Captain Callaway at the time of his defeat and death at Loutre creek, in Montgomery county. They reached Rock river, within 180 or 200 miles of their destination, without an accident, or any incident worthy of mention; but as soon as they entered the rapids they were visited by large numbers of Sacs and Foxes, who pretended to be peaceably inclined. The officers were deceived by their friendly overtures, and were thus led unsuspectingly into the catastrophe which followed. The boat belonging to the sutler and contractor had arrived near the head of the rapids, and proceeded on its course, having on board the ammunition, with a sergeant's guard; the rangers in their boats followed, and were about two miles in advance of Lieutenant Campbell and his regulars, whose boat had grounded within a few yards of a high bank, covered with a thick growth of grass and willows. The wind being very high, rendered the boat unmanageable, and the commander deemed it advisable to remain until it abated. Sentinels were sent on shore and stationed at proper intervals, while several of the men began to prepare breakfast. In a few minutes the report of guns announced an attack, and at the first fire all the sentinels were killed. The rest of the men on shore started for the boat, where their guns were, but before they could reach it fifteen out of thirty were killed or wounded. In a few minutes from five to seven hundred warriors were assembled among the willows on the bank, within a few yards of the bow and stern of the boat, and with loud yells and whoops they commenced a tremendous fire. The men on the boat, undaunted by the loss of their companions, the overpowering numbers of the foe, or the suddenness of the attack, cheered lustily, and returned the fire from their rifles and a small swivel which they had on board. At this critical juncture, Lieutenants Rector and Riggs saw the smoke, and, judging that an attack had been made, turned their course and pulled down stream as rapidly as possible,

to the relief of their comrades.   Riggs' boat ran aground about a
hundred yards below Campbell's, and Rector, to avoid a similar
misfortune, and to preserve himself from a raking fire, anchored
above. A brisk fire from both boats was immediately opened upon
the Indians, but as the latter were under cover, but little execution was done.   The unequal contest lasted for more than an
hour, when Campbell's boat was discovered to be on fire, and in
order to save the men, Rector cut his cable and falling alongside
of the burning boat took the men on board.   Finding that it was
impossible to withstand the   overwhelming   numbers   which
were opposed to them, a retreat was ordered, and the boats
fell away from the shore to a safe distance.   The Americans lost
twelve killed and between twenty and thirty wounded.   The expedition was abandoned, and about the same time the garrison at
Prairie du Chien surrendered to the British.

In the meantime the American settlers north of the Missouri
river, perceiving the approaching storm, had taken measures for
their own defence.   Several companies of rangers had been organized, who remained on the borders of the settlements and constantly scoured the country in all directions.   As soon as Indian
" signs" were discovered, the alarm would be given to the people, who would prepare themselves against surprise or attack.
Stout wooden forts were erected at various points, in which the
people would take shelter as soon as an alarm was given, and remain there until the danger was over.   These forts were located
in the following order:

Daniel M. Boone's Fort, in Darst's Bottom, which was the largest and strongest of the entire list.   Howell's Fort, on Howell's
Prairie.   Pond Fort, on Dardenne Prairie, a short distance southeast of the present town of Wentzville.   White's Fort, on Dog
Prairie.   Kountz' Fort, on the Booneslick road, eight miles west
of St. Charles.   Zumwalt's Fort, near the present town of O'Fallon.   Castlio's Fort, near Howell's Prairie.   These were all within
the present limits of St. Charles county, and a glance at the map
will show their positions.   Kennedy's Fort was located near the
present town of Wright City, in Warren county.   Callaway's Fort
was near the Missouri river, at the French village of Charrette, a
short distance from the present town of Marthasville.   The site of
this fort and village has long since been washed away by the river.
Woods' Fort was where Troy, in Lincoln county, now stands, and
was so far out on the frontier that it was abandoned before the

war closed. Clark's Fort was four miles southeast of Troy, and Howard's Fort near the present site of Cap-au-Gris. Fort Clemison stood on Loutre Island, in the present limits of Warren county. It was also abandoned, being too remote from the main settlements. In addition to these, there was a fortification at the French village of Cotesansdessein in what is now Callaway county ; and the settlements at Boone's Lick, in the present limits of Howard county, were also protected in like manner. These were separated from the other settlements, and depended upon their own resources for protection, being too remote to admit of communication.

These forts were all built after the same general plan, viz: In the form of a parallelogram, with block-houses at the four corners, and the intervening spaces filled with log cabins and palisades. They would not have withstood the fire of artillery, but afforded ample protection against rifles and muskets. None of them, however, were ever attacked by the Indians, for their number and convenient locations, with the constant watchfulness of the rangers, afforded the savages no opportunity of doing any very serious damage.

The most serious calamity that befel the settlers during the Indian war, was the defeat of Captain James Callaway and a portion of his company, and the death of their leader, at Loutre creek, near the line of Montgomery and Callaway counties. Captain Callaway was a son of Flanders Callaway, and grandson of Daniel Boone, and being distinguished for his intelligence, fortitude and courage, was elected to the command of a company of rangers at the commencement of the difficulties, and up to the time of his death was one of the most efficient, active, and daring scouts that the country afforded.

Inasmuch as Captain Callaway occupied a prominent position in the affairs of the country at that period, and many of his relatives are still living, we insert the following sketch of his life, public services, and death, as given by his sister, Mrs. Susannah Howell, corroborated by Mr. William Keithley and Rev. Thomas Bowen, all of whom are still living (1875). (Keithley and Bowen were members of Callaway's company, though not present at the time of his death.)

James Callaway, eldest son of Flanders Callaway and Jemima Boone, was born in Lafayette county, Kentucky, September 13, 1783. He received a liberal education for that period, and in

1798 came with his parents to Upper Louisiana, where he remained a short time, and then returned to Kentucky to complete his education.

Having finished his course, he came west again, and on the 9th of May, 1805, he married Nancy Howell.   After his marriage he built a cabin and settled near the northwest corner of Howell's Prairie, in St. Charles county, on a small stream which he named Kraut Run.   Three children resulted from this marriage—Thomas H.. Wm. B., and Theresa.

Captain Callaway is described as a tall man, with black hair and eyes, high forehead, prominent cheek bones, and erect as an Indian, but very bow-legged.   He was more than usually kind and affectionate toward his family, by whom he was devotedly loved; and his intelligence and strict integrity as a man gave him the confidence, respect and friendship of all his neighbors.

He served as deputy sheriff of St. Charles county for several years, under Capt. Murray, and in 1813 he raised his first company of rangers for service against the Indians.   This company was composed of the following named men, as shown by the muster roll, which is still preserved:

Captain, James Callaway; First Lieutenant, Prospect K. Robbins; Second Lieutenant, John B. Stone; First Sergeant, Larkin S. Callaway; Second Sergeant, John Baldridge; Third Sergeant, Wm. Smith; Cornett, Jonathan Riggs; Trumpeter, Thomas Howell.   Privates—Frank McDermid, John Stewart, John Atkinson, Robert Fruit, Francis Howell, Joseph Hinds, Richard Berry, Thomas Smith, Adam Zumwalt, Enoch Taylor, Aleck Baldridge, Lewis Crow, Benjamin Howell, Anthony C. Palmer, Daniel Hays, Boone Hays, Adam Zumwalt, Jr., John Howell, and James Kerr.

This company was enlisted for a term of only a few months, and Captain Callaway organized several others before his death. The roll of his last company was in his possession when he was killed, and it was lost, but from the memory of old citizens we are enabled to give a pretty correct list of the names of the men, as follows:

Captain, James Callaway; First Lieutenant, David Bailey, Second Lieutenant, Jonathan Riggs.   Privates—James McMullin, Hiram Scott, Frank McDermid, Wm. Keithley, Thomas Bowman, Robert Baldridge, James Kennedy, Thomas Chambers, Jacob Groom, Parker Hutchings, — Wolf, Thomas Gilmore,

John Baldridge, Joshua Deason, James Murdock, Wm. Kent, and John K. Berry. We have been particular in giving the names of these men, because their descendants, and a few of the men themselves, are still living in the country they helped to defend.

Early in the morning of the 7th of March, 1815, Captain Callaway, with Lieutenant Riggs and fourteen of the men, viz: McMullin, Scott, McDermid, Robert and John Baldridge, Hutchings, Kennedy, Chambers, Wolf, Gilmore, Deason, Murdock, Kent and Berry—left Fort Clemson, on Loutre Island, in pursuit of a party of Sac and Fox Indians who had stolen some horses from settlers in the vicinity. They swam Loutre slough on their horses, and followed the Indian trail, which led them up the west bank of the main stream. (Loutre slough runs from west to east, parallel with the Missouri river, from which it flows, and into which it empties again, at a distance of seven or eight miles below. Loutre creek flows from northwest to southeast, and empties into the slough at nearly right angles.) The trail being very plain, they had no difficulty in pursuing it, and they made rapid progress. Reaching Prairie Fork, a branch of Loutre, they swam it on their horses, a distance of seventy-five yards above where it empties into Loutre creek. It was now about noon, and feeling sure that they were not far in the rear of the Indians, they advanced with caution, in order to avoid surprise. About two o'clock in the afternoon, and about twelve miles from where they had crossed Prairie Fork, they came upon the stolen horses, secreted in a bend of Loutre creek, and guarded by only a few squaws. These fled upon the approach of the rangers, and the latter secured the horses without further trouble. They were not molested in any manner, and not a sign of an Indian warrior could be seen anywhere, although the appearance of the trail had proven conclusively that the party numbered from eighty to one hundred. These circumstances aroused the suspicions of Lieutenant Riggs, and obtaining the consent of his Captain, he reconnoitered the locality thoroughly before they started on their return. No signs of Indians could be discovered; still his suspicions were not allayed, but on the contrary, they were increased, and he suggested to Callaway that it would be dangerous to return by the route they had followed in the morning, as the savages were evidently preparing an ambuscade for them. Captain Callaway was an experienced Indian fighter, and as wary as he was brave, but on this occasion he did not allow himself to be governed by his better judgment. He declared that he did not believe there were half-a-dozen Indians in the vicinity, and that he intended to return to the fort by the same route they had come.

Seeing that further expostulation was useless, Riggs said nothing more at the time; and the rangers were soon in the saddle and on the march for the fort.

Upon reaching a suitable place, about a mile from the mouth of Prairie Fork, they stopped to let their horses rest, and to refresh themselves with a lunch. Riggs availed himself of the opportunity, and again represented to the Captain the danger they were incurring. He anticipated an attack at the crossing of the creek, and entreated Callaway, for the sake of the lives of the men, to at least avoid that point. He showed that the Indians would have all the advantages on their side; they outnumbered the rangers three to one, were not encumbered with horses, and would, no doubt, fire upon them from their concealment behind trees and logs, where the fire could not be successfully returned.

But Callaway, instead of heeding the good advice of his Lieutenant, flew into a passion, and cursed him for a coward. He declared, also, that he would return the way he had come if he had to go alone.

Riggs said nothing more, but reluctantly followed his Captain into what he felt sure was almost certain death.

Hutchings, McDermid, and McMullin were in advance, leading the stolen horses, while Callaway, Riggs, and the rest of the company were fifty or a hundred yards in the rear.

The three men in advance, upon reaching Prairie Fork, plunged their horses into the stream, which was swollen from recent rains, and were swimming across, when they were fired upon by the entire body of Indians, concealed on both sides of the creek. They were not harmed by the first volley, but succeeded in reaching the opposite shore, where they were killed.

At the first sound of firing, Callaway spurred his horse forward into the creek, and had nearly reached the opposite shore, when he was fired upon. His horse was instantly killed, while he received a slight wound in the left arm, and escaped immediate death only by the ball lodging against his watch, which was torn to pieces. He sprang from his dead horse to the bank, and throwing his gun into the creek, muzzle down, he ran down the stream a short distance, then plunged into the water and commenced swimming, when he was shot in the back of the head, the ball passing through and lodging in the forehead. His body sank immediately, and was not scalped or mutilated by the Indians.

In the meantime Lieutenant Riggs and the rest of the men were hotly engaged, and forced to retreat, fighting as they went. Several were wounded, but none killed. They could not tell what execution was done among the Indians. Scott and Wolf became separated from the main body, and the former was killed. Wolf escaped to the fort, and was the first to bring the news of the disaster, which he greatly exaggerated, supposing himself to be the only one who had escaped death.

Riggs and the men under him fell back about a mile, and turning to the right, crossed Prairie Fork about the same distance above its mouth, and making a wide circuit, escaped, without further molestation, to the fort.

The following day a company of men returned to the scene of the fight for the purpose of burying the dead. The bodies of Hutchings, McDermid, and McMullin, had been cut to pieces, and hung on surrounding bushes. The remains were gathered up and buried in one grave, near the spot where they were killed. It is said that Hutchings and McDermid, shortly before their deaths, had a bitter quarrel, and had agreed to fight it out with rifles as soon as their term of service expired. But their quarrel was brought to a sudden and tragic termination without any intervention of their own, and now their bodies slumber together in the same grave. Thus death ends all animosities.

Captain Callaway's body was not found until several days after his death, when, the water having receded, it was discovered by Benjamin Howell, hanging in a bush several hundred yards below the scene of the fight. His gun had been recovered several days before. It was found standing upright, with the muzzle sticking fast in the mud at the bottom of the creek. Lewis Jones swam in and brought the gun to the shore, and it fired as readily as if it had never been in the water. It had an improved water-proof flint-lock, which water could not penetrate.

Flanders Callaway, learning of the death of his son, had come from St. Charles county with a company of men, to assist in searching for the body, and he was present when it was found. The body was wrapped in blankets, and buried on the side of an abrupt hill overlooking Loutre creek. Several months afterward the grave was walled in with rough stones, and a flat slab was laid across the head, on which was engraved:

CAPT. JAS. CALLAWAY,
March 7, 1815.

The slab had been prepared in St. Charles county, by Tarleton Goe, a cousin of the dead ranger.

The diagram of the battle-field, which we give on this page, was drawn on the spot, and presents a correct view of the situation.

DIAGRAM OF BATTLE GROUND.

A. The ford, where Callaway was first shot. B. Where he jumped into Prairie Fork after he was shot. C. Where his body was found. D. & E. Where the Indians were concealed. F. Where Riggs and his men left the main trail, and crossed Prairie Fork at G. H. Grave of Hutchings, McDermid and McMullin. I. Callaway's grave.

Lieutenant Riggs served with distinction during the remainder of the war, and afterward became a prominent citizen of Lincoln county. He was the first County Judge of that county, and was subsequently elected Sheriff. During the Black Hawk war he was commissioned Brigadier-General of Volunteers, and afterward served as Brigadier-General of militia. He was a daring, but cautious and prudent officer, and if the unfortunate Callaway had listened to his advice, his life and the lives of his men would have been spared.

It is not known for certain whether any of the Indians were killed in this battle or not, but one of their chiefs, named Keokuk, a man of some distinction, was wounded, and died shortly after. He was buried in the prairie, one and one-half miles northeast of the present town of Wellsville, in Montgomery county. In 1826 his remains were taken up by Dr. Bryan and several other gentlemen, and upon his breast was found a large silver medal, containing his name, rank, etc.   He was evidently a giant in stature, for the jaw bone, which, with several other bones of the body, are still preserved by Mrs. Dr. Peery, of Montgomery county, will fit over the face of the largest sized man.

MURDER OF THE RAMSEY FAMILY.

The next most important event of the Indian war, was the murder of the Ramsey family, which occurred on the 20th of May, 1815.

Robert Ramsey lived about two miles northwest of the present town of Marthasville, in Warren county.   His family consisted of himself, his wife, five children, and a little half-breed Indian boy whom they had adopted.   Mr. Ramsey was a one-legged man, having received a hurt in a fall from a horse, which necessitated the amputation of one of his limbs, and he wore a wooden peg-leg.   Their location was considered dangerous, and they had been repeatedly warned by the rangers to move to a less exposed locality ; but, like most of the people of those days, they regarded the Indians with contempt, and had a very poor opinion of their bravery and fighting qualities.   Ramsey, with his one leg, felt competent to whip a score of the red skins, and therefore he paid no attention to the repeated warnings of the men who knew better than he the dangers to which he and his family were exposed.

The day before the attack on this family, the Indians watched the house of Mr. Aleck McKinney, who lived four or five miles west of Ramsey's.   McKinney's family consisted of only himself and wife, and their location, being so far out on the frontier, was considered so extremely dangerous that a man was generally detailed by the rangers to stay with them as a guard.   On the day referred to, McKinney was plowing a piece of young corn that lay between the house and a field of wheat, that was just beginning to turn ripe.   He had two fierce dogs which exhibited signs of great distress during the morning, running into the wheat and barking fiercely, and then as suddenly running out again, with their bristles turned as if they had been close upon some unfamiliar and frightful object.

McKinney, becoming uneasy, stopped plowing, and called to a ranger named Housley, who was staying with them at the time, and who was then engaged in shooting squirrels in a piece of timber on the opposite side of the house. Housley soon joined him, and the two examined the wheat as closely as they could without venturing into it. The dogs continued to exhibit signs of alarm and uneasiness, and the men unhitched the horse and went to the house, in order to be better prepared for an attack should one be made. But no Indians showed themselves. Upon examining the wheat sometime afterward, however, the places where six of them had lain were discovered, and early next morning news was received of the murder of the Ramsey family by a party of six Indians, supposed to be the same.

The attack was made about sunrise in the morning. Mrs. Ramsey was in the lot milking the cows, her husband and four of the children were in the yard near her, and the other two children—one of whom was the little half-breed Indian—had gone to the spring, which was some distance from the house, for water. The first intimation of the presence of the Indians was given by the cows. They snuffed the air, shook their horns, bellowed, and attempted to jump over the lot fence—for the cattle knew and dreaded the common enemy. At that instant, with whoops and yells, the Indians dashed out of the woods and rushed forward with uplifted tomahawks, intending to brain and tomahawk the whites without resorting to the use of their guns. Mrs. Ramsey started to run to the house, but was fired upon and mortally wounded; and just as she reached the bars that separated the lot from the yard, an Indian, who had run close up to her, aimed his tomahawk at her head. She threw herself forward, fell through the open bars, escaped the blow that was intended for her, and succeeded in reaching the house. Mr. Ramsey, who had not yet put on his wooden leg, and could therefore make but slow progress, started toward the house upon the first alarm, but was shot and severely wounded just as he reached the door. As he fell he reached his hand above the door and got a long tin trumpet which was kept there, and commenced blowing it. This was understood by the Indians as a signal of alarm to the rangers, and they turned and fled as suddenly as if they had been fired upon by a body of troops. Every family kept a trumpet in those dangerous times, to be used when in danger or distress, and its sound never failed to bring the rangers, if they were in hearing. The Indians knew this, and never delayed after the trumpet was sounded.

In the meantime, three of the children had been tomahawked in the yard, and one of them, a little girl thirteen years of age, was scalped. She lived four days in great agony, when death kindly came to her relief. The fourth child, a little thing just able to walk, squatted, like a frightened rabbit, in some weeds in the corner of the fence, and escaped unhurt. The two children who had gone to the spring heard the firing, and knowing what it meant, fled to the house of a neighbor, several miles distant, and were saved. The half-breed Indian boy, whose name was Paul, lived to be past middle age, and is still remembered by citizens of St. Charles, where he resided many years.

A lad named Abner Bryan, a son of Jonathan Bryan, was boarding at the house of Jesse Caton (who lived near the present site of Marthasville), attending school, and had been sent to Ramsey's that morning on some errand. He left only a short time before the attack, and no doubt narrowly escaped death. Jesse Caton, Jr., a son of the gentleman just mentioned, was hunting some of his father's horses in the woods, and while crossing a ravine near Ramsey's house, discovered the tracks of the Indians, and immediately afterward the yelling and firing commenced at the house. He ran home as quickly as possible, and gave the alarm, and several members of the family started at once to warn their neighbors. By eight o'clock the news had spread all over the settlements, and a large party of armed men were in pursuit of the Indians, while others remained to take care of the wounded. Colonel Boone, who was in Callaway's Fort, at Charrette, was sent for to dress their wounds, his long experience in such matters having rendered him very efficient. The news of the massacre had preceded the messenger, and when he arrived at the fort Boone was pacing up and down in front of an open space in the stockades, which had not been completed, with his gun on his shoulder, and whistling in his usual undisturbed manner.

Mrs. Ramsey gave premature birth to a child, and died shortly afterward, but her husband recovered from his wound and lived several years. Two of the children who had been tomahawked died during the day, but the other lived until the fourth day.

An eye witness, who arrived upon the scene about ten o'clock, describes it as most heart-rending. The children were lying upon the floor, two of them in the agonies of death, and every time they struggled for breath the blood and brains oozed out at the wounds made by the murderous tomahawks. Mrs. Ramsey was in an adjoining room, but her groans of agony could be plainly heard. Her husband was lying upon a bed in the front room, and Boone was engaged in extracting the bullet, which had passed through the groin and lodged near the surface on the back of the hip. The old pioneer was quiet and unexcited, as usual, but his lips were compressed and a fire gleamed from his eyes that indicated danger to any savage that might have come within his reach at that time. Strong men, looking upon those murdered children, wept and silently vowed vengeance against the inhuman foe.

Thirty experienced scouts were on the trail of the Indians, and their escape seemed almost impossible. After going a short distance they separated into three parties, two in each party, and then soon divided again, and each pursued his course alone. This rendered it difficult to follow the various trails, and necessitated a division of the pursuers also. At night the Indians came together again at a designated point, where they received reinforcements, and on the following day a fight occurred between them and a party of rangers from near Howard's Fort. Capt. Craig and a few men were in the fort, and Capt. Musick and a small party were camped two miles distant, on Cuivre river. During the day the men at the latter place heard what they supposed to be wild turkeys "calling," on the other side of the river, and Lieutenant McNeice, a Mr. Weber, a Mr. Burnes, and one or two others, got into a bark canoe that lay at the camp and crossed over, to see if they could find the turkeys. They proceeded along the stream some distance before crossing, and had not reached the other shore when they were fired upon by the Indians, who were concealed in the woods, and had been imitating the "call" of wild turkeys in order to decoy them. McNeice and several of the men were instantly killed. Weber, who was unhurt, sprang out of the canoe and swam back to a raft in the river, where he was followed by a large Indian, who pretended that he wanted to be friendly. But looking back he saw another Indian swimming toward the raft with a knife in his mouth, and knowing that he meant mischief, he sprang into the water and dived toward him, drawing his knife from his belt while he was under water. He came up by the side of the Indian, and stabbed him to the heart, killing him instantly; and then swam some distance to an island, where he climbed a tree, and began to call to the men in the fort. They recognized his voice, and several men, among whom was "Indian Dixon," the noted scout, started to his rescue. They got into a bark canoe and turned it toward the island, but had proceeded only a short distance when the frail craft capsized. Some of the men swam to the shore, and the rest were picked up by Capt. McMann, who came up just at that moment with a keel boat loaded with supplies for Fort Howard. The following day George Burnes and three Frenchmen went in a canoe down to Old Monroe, about a mile and a half below the fort, to get a grindstone. On their return they stopped in the woods to get some pawpaw bark, to use in stretching deer skins; and while they were peeling it from the bushes, they were attacked by a party of Indians. Two of the Frenchmen were killed instantly, and the third was struck in the back of the head with a tomahawk. He ran about one hundred yards with the weapon sticking fast in his skull, and then fell dead. Burnes escaped, and reached the fort unhurt. Simultaneously with their attack upon him and the Frenchmen, the Indians made a demonstration against the fort, by showing themselves and firing their guns in that direction. One spent ball fell in the yard of the fort, and was picked up by Mrs. Frances Riffle. As soon as they had discharged their guns the savages withdrew, and, after some consultation among the rangers, it was decided to follow them. The men of both Craig's and Musick's commands joined in the pursuit, which was irregular and without order, each man going on "his own hook," as they termed it. The Indians took refuge in a sink-hole about half a mile southwest of the fort, and fortified themselves behind some rocks that lay at the bottom. Here they were surrounded by the rangers, and a fight was kept up until dark, during which Capt. Craig and his lieutenant, Stevens, and one man in Captain Musick's company, were killed. One Indian was also killed. The rangers at first attempted to advance from tree to tree down the sides of the sink-hole, but Craig and Stevens having been killed, without producing any effect upon the Indians, they abandoned that plan, and constructed a moveable breastwork upon the wheels of a cart, intending to push it before them as they advanced upon the savages. But it proved ineffectual, being so clumsy that they

could not guide it around the trees on the steep sides of the sink-
hole. It was while they were experimenting with this contrivance
that Capt. Musick's man was killed. He spoke to a comrade
near him, saying he intended to shoot an Indian in the mouth,
and stepping to one side of the breastwork he deliberately took
aim and fired. At the same moment a flash came from the
bottom of the sink-hole, and the man fell dead.

During the day reports had come in, stating that a large body of
Indians, numbering 800 or 1,000, had crossed the Mississippi river from Illinois, and were advancing upon the settlements. These
reports proved to be false, but they bore evidence of truth, and
the rangers, deeming it unsafe to remain outside the walls of
the fort over night, withdrew at the close of the day and left the
Indians unmolested. Early the next morning they returned to
the scene of the previous day's fight, and, as they expected,
found that the Indians had disappeared. But on the margin of
the sink-hole lay the dead ranger, with an Indian, stark and stiff
in death, sitting astride of his body. It was a singular and re-
volting spectacle, and was not soon forgotten by those who witnessed it. This was the only Indian that was killed during the
fight, but from the amount of blood with which the rocks where
they lay were sprinkled, the rangers judged that several of them
had been wounded. They felt that they were in a very close
place, and were heard frequently during the fight to call on the
Great Spirit for assistance, promising him that if he would help
them out of that scrape they would never get into another like it.

An incident occurred at the fort on the day of the fight that is
too good to be omitted. When the rangers had decided to follow
the Indians, after their first assault, one man refused to go, and
endeavored to screen his cowardice behind the plea that it was
not safe to leave the women and children unprotected. The
women declared that they were able to defend themselves, and
tried to drive the man out of the fort. But he stubbornly refused
to go, and flying into a passion, he struck his fist with great
violence on the top of a pork barrel that stood near him, and
swore a terrible oath that he could whip any woman *or pork barrel* in the fort. His fighting qualities, however, did not extend to
Indians, and he took care to remain in safe quarters.

The report that a large body of Indians had crossed the river
very naturally created great excitement and alarm, and the people of the border settlements, acting upon the advice of the

rangers, abandoned their homes and fled to the strong forts in the interior, where they were joined by the rest of the inhabitants, until the entire population was gathered into one or two of the larger forts, principally Daniel M. Boone's Fort in Darst's Bottom. But in a day or two scouts came in and allayed the fears of the people by announcing that the alarming reports which had been circulated were entirely without foundation in truth, and that there were no hostile Indians near the settlements. So the people returned to their homes and resumed their usual occupations.

This unnecessary fright was the cause of a serious loss to Col. Boone. He had been engaged for some time in the preparation of his autobiography, undertaken at the earnest and repeated solicitations of his friends, and the work was more than half completed. When the fort at Charrette was abandoned, his manuscripts, Bible, and a number of other articles, were placed in a pirogue to be conveyed down the river to Boone's Fort. Flanders Callaway and another man had charge of the craft, and while passing down a very swift place in the river, it struck a snag and capsized, emptying its contents into the river. Callaway and his companion barely escaped with their lives. Boone was a poor scribe, and as writing was very laborious to him, he never undertook the task again, and thus many valuable facts connected with his eventful life were lost.

FIGHT AT COTESANSDESSEIN.

The village of Cotesansdessein, in Callaway county, was settled by some French explorers previous to 1800, and was once a thriving place. One of the hardest fights of the Indian war took place there, as well as one of the most remarkable exhibitions of courage and fortitude that has been recorded in the history of any country. It was an isolated place, situated equidistant between the settlements in St. Charles district and those in the Boone's Lick country, too far from either to expect succor in case of an attack.

At the time of which we write, the little blockhouse at this place was occupied by only five persons — a Frenchman named Baptiste Louis Roi, two other men, and two women; but they successfully withstood a protracted siege and repelled repeated assaults from a numerous and very determined band of Indians. The attack, as usual with the savages, commenced suddenly and without previous warning; but the little garrison, with the ex-

ception of one man, flew to arms, and soon had the satisfaction
of seeing their red enemies retire in confusion to the cover of
the woods, carrying several dead bodies with them.   One of the
men, observing how greatly the Indians outnumbered them, became panic-stricken at the commencement of the attack, and
devoted himself to fervent prayer and humble penitence throughout the siege, leaving his companions and the women to fight the
savages.   The women, the wife and sister-in-law of Roi, lent
efficient and indispensable aid to the two soldiers.   At the commencement of the attack, they were but poorly supplied with
bullets, but while the men were firing, the women busied themselves moulding balls and cutting patches, so as to keep up the
defense in a steady and uninterrupted manner.   Fourteen of the
Indians had been killed, and many more wounded; when at last,
becoming desperate under their severe punishment, they made a
combined assault upon the blockhouse, but were driven back in
disorder, with the loss of several more of their warriors.
The assault was repeated two or three times, but always with a
similar result.   Finding they could not carry the fort by storm or
siege, they resorted to the use of fire.   Fastening combustible
materials to their arrows, they were ignited and then shot into
the roof of the blockhouse; but as often as this was done the
women extinguished the fire by a judicious use of the little water
they had within the building.   The blockhouse stood near the
river bank, but the garrison was too weak to risk a single life by
going after the precious liquid, and they watched with appalling
interest the rapid decrease of their scanty stock.   Each new
blaze was heralded with demoniac yells from the assailants;
and at last the water was exhausted — the last drop in the last
bucket had been used!   The next instant the roof over their heads
was in a blaze, and despair stamped itself upon the features of
the devoted little band.   But at this critical moment one of the
women produced a gallon of milk, and the flames were again
extinguished.   Soon another shower of blazing arrows fell
upon the roof, and it was soon on fire again.   Roi and his brave
comrade looked silently at each other, and then glanced sorrowfully toward their wives.   They felt that their time had come,
and well they knew the fate worse than death that awaited the
loved ones should they fall into the hands of the infuriated savages.   For a moment Mrs. Roi disappeared in an adjoining room,
and when she came out again, her face was lighted up with a

smile of triumph. In her hands she held a vessel, familiar in all bed-chambers, that contained a fluid more valuable now than gold. Again the fire was extinguished, and then the little garrison sent forth a shout of exultation and defiance. Three times more the roof was set on fire, but each time the mysterious vessel supplied the needed liquid, and the flames were extinguished. At last, the Indians finding themselves baffled at every turn, screamed a bitter howl of rage and resentment, and withdrew. But before leaving the settlement, they collected a dozen small kettles, and having broken them in pieces, they piled them around a large unbroken one, as a sign to other savages who might follow in their trail, that one white man had slain many of their braves.

At the commencement of the war, a man named O'Neil was living on King's Lake, in Lincoln county. His family consisted of himself, his wife, two sons, two daughters, and an orphan child two years old, that his wife had adopted. Their position was very much exposed, being upon the very outskirts of the settlements, and they very naturally felt some apprehension in regard to an attack. One day O'Neil went to the house of a neighbor, some distance from where he lived, to consult with him in regard to a definite plan of defence, and upon his return home the mangled remains of his murdered wife and children met his horrified vision. During his absence the Indians had crossed the river on the ice and murdered his entire family. The little orphan child had endeavored to escape by secreting itself in the chimney, but the heat drove it out, and the inhuman monsters seized it and threw it into a large kettle of boiling water that stood upon the fire, and there its remains were found by its adopted father upon his return to his desolated home. The poor man was nearly crazy with grief, but had to submit to the fate which he could not avert.

One of the Indians belonging to this party afterward met a death that he richly deserved, and which he brought upon himself by his vain boasting. After the close of the war, when a treaty of peace with the Indians was being made at Rock Island, there was present with the American troops a ranger named McNair, who understood the Indian tongue. Some of the savages were relating their exploits, and one in particular was telling, with great delight, how he had killed and scalped one of the O'Neil boys, and how his victim grinned when in the agonies of death. McNair, enraged at what he heard, closely watched this Indian, determined, as soon as an opportunity presented itself, to kill him, notwithstanding it would be a gross violation of the treaty then in progress, and punishable with death. "I'll make *you* grin, you red devil!" he thought, as he saw the Indian stalking about in the midst of his companions. Awaiting his opportunity, when the attention of the American officers was engaged, he sent a bullet crashing through the brain of the boasting savage, and then mounting his horse he escaped before any attempt could be made to arrest him. The incident caused great excitement at the camp, and came near bringing the treaty to an abrupt and hostile termination; but quiet was finally restored, and the negotiations proceeded to their termination. But the Indians took care not to boast any more in the presence of the rangers.

The same Indians who murdered the O'Neil family also killed several other persons in the vicinity, and then escaped to their own country.

A ranger named David Reeland was wounded in a fight that occurred between the Indians and a party of rangers who were ascending the Mississippi river on a keel-boat. After he had partially recovered, he went early one morning to the house of a man named Keeley, and while sitting on his horse conversing with the latter, he was shot by an Indian who had crept close to them in the woods, and instantly killed. Keeley ran into his house, and, securing his gun, shot the Indian dead as he was in the act of scalping the fallen ranger. During the previous night a party of Indians had attacked the house of Mr. Christopher Hostetter, and while trying to get into the house one of them fell into a well in the yard. His comrades helped him out by means of an Indian ladder, which they left in the well, and then, overcome by superstitious fear, they abandoned the attack and departed.

OTHER INCIDENTS OF THE INDIAN WAR.

We are indebted for the following adventures and incidents of the Indian War to the editors of the *Lincoln County Herald*, who are publishing sketches of the early history of that county in their excellent paper, and who kindly gave us the use of their files.

Wood's Fort, where Troy now stands, and the settlement

around it, were in a state of almost constant siege. Bands of Indians were prowling about the country, watching opportunities to pick up stragglers who might'fall in their way. Much of the time the fort was closely invested, and it was a favorite maneuver of the savages, on dark nights, to gallop their horses up nearly to the walls of the fort, whooping and yelling like a pack of demons, fire a few shots, and then disappear as suddenly as they came. This kind of warfare entailed great hardships, privations and danger upon the inhabitants, and gave them but few opportunities of retaliating upon their enemies. Farming operations had to be abandoned; but a small patch in the present limits of Troy was cultivated by the rangers, when they were at home in sufficient numbers to afford a guard, and by this means starvation was kept from their doors. But provisions were very scarce, and children often cried from hunger when there was nothing to satisfy them. The people dressed almost entirely in buckskin.

The Indians who caused the troubles were principally Sacs and Foxes, led by Black Hawk, who afterward became famous as a warrior and statesman. This savage chief possessed a most remarkable intellect, united with boundless ambition and great courage and perseverance, and had he possessed the advantages of civilization and education, he would have been an ornament to the age in which he lived.

Early in the commencement of the war (about 1813), four young rangers, named Hamilton McNair, Peter Pugh, Big Joe McCoy and Little Joe McCoy, went from Wood's Fort to Sulphur Lick, to hunt deer. (It was Hamilton McNair's brother who killed the Indian at Rock Island after the close of the war.) This lick is formed by a spring, strongly impregnated with sulphur, iron, salt, and other minerals, and is situated about a quarter of a mile east of North Cuivre, and a mile and a half north of Rigg's ford. The place had been settled some time before the war; a cabin had been built and a small patch of ground cleared around the spring; but it was abandoned soon after the commencement of hostilities. While encamped at the spring, the rangers were attacked by a party of Indians under Black Hawk. Big Joe McCoy, who had gone a short distance into the woods, discovered the Indians before the attack was made, and immediately secreted himself. At the commencement of the attack, McNair fled, but was pursued into the old field about one hundred yards from the spring, where he was overtaken and tomahawked.

Pugh and Little Joe McCoy stood their ground and fought desperately. The former screened himself behind his horse, and fired only when he was sure of his aim. Four Indians bit the dust before his unerring rifle; but the unequal struggle was soon over. The savages rushed in and killed both of the rangers, and in revenge for the bloody work done by Pugh, they hacked his body in pieces. Big Joe McCoy's hiding place was soon discovered, and the Indians began to close in upon him. Among all the rangers there was none more fleet of foot or active than he, and bounding out from his concealment he started in a swift run on a direct line for the fort, with the Indians howling after him. One warrior, more active than his comrades, soon took the lead, and held him a tight race for a mile or more. A large oak tree had fallen, and its branches lay directly in the path. Without swerving in the least, McCoy made a desperate leap and went flying clear over the tree top. The Indian stopped and gazed in amazement at the retreating form of his white foe, and then exclaimed in broken English, "Whoop! heap big jump! Me no follow!" and immediately abandoned the pursuit. McCoy's legs had re-commenced their office before he touched the ground, and he never stopped until he met a party of rangers from the fort, who had become alarmed at the prolonged absence of the four men, and had started out to seek them. After listening to McCoy's story, they hastened on to the scene of the fight, but the Indians had disappeared, doubtless having observed their approach. The remains of the three men who had been killed were collected and buried on the bank of a small ravine near where they fell. Many years after their bones became exposed, by the washing away of the earth, and they were taken up and reinterred.

On another occasion a party of rangers from Wood's and Clark's forts crossed the Mississippi below the mouth of Cuivre, and attacked the Indians in their own country. Being greatly outnumbered they were compelled to retreat, but without the loss of any lives. One man, named Isaac White, had both thumbs shot off while in the act of discharging his gun.

In 1803 William McHugh came to Lincoln county, and settled near where the present road from New Hope to Cap-au-Gris crosses Sandy Creek, on the farm now occupied by B. J. Locke. One day during the following summer he sent his three sons, James, William and Jesse, mere lads, to hunt the horses, which, as usual in those times, were allowed to graze at will in the woods. They found the horses about a mile from home, and having secured them, started on their return. They were soon joined by a famous Indian scout named Dixon, whom the boys, of course, regarded with great admiration. They offered him a seat on one of their horses, and invited him to go to their father's house and remain all night. He gladly accepted the invitation, and mounted in front of the youngest boy, a lad ten or twelve years of age; the other two boys riding each a horse. They reached the ford of Sandy creek, and stopped to let their horses drink. They had barely halted when they were fired upon by a body of Indians concealed in the brush near them, and the two elder boys and the horses they rode were instantly killed. Dixon's horse, wild with fright, sprang up the steep bank of the creek, when the girth of the saddle broke and his two riders fell to the ground. But springing to their feet, they started on a race for their lives while the Indians, yelling frightfully, followed close after them. The scout outran the boy, and the little fellow, almost in the clutches of the savages, cried out in tones of agonized fright, "Oh! Mr. Dixon, don't leave me!" The next instant a murderous tomahawk sank into his brain, and his cry of terror was smothered by the death gurgle. This was a trying moment to Dixon. It seemed like base ingratitude to leave the little fellow to his fate, yet the Indians were so numerous that any attempt on the part of the scout to resist them, unarmed as he was, would have been simply a surrender of his own life into their hands, without any benefit to the boy. The savages pursued him nearly a mile, and up to the very fence that surrounded McHugh's yard, and then turned and fled. The three murdered boys were buried in one grave, on a point near where they fell, their only coffin being rude puncheons laid over them, upon which the earth was thrown. A leaning white oak marks their grave, as if weeping over their cruel and untimely fate. The Indians who committed this deed were commanded by Black Hawk himself, and the fact that peace existed at the time between the two races, made it one of the most dastardly acts that was ever committed. They afterward excused themselves by saying that some white men on the Mississippi river had killed three Indian dogs, and they had come into the settlements for revenge, and were satisfied with the killing of the three boys. But in truth they were a treacherous, bloodthirsty people, and were governed solely by their hatred of the white race, and their instinctive love of cruelty and murder.

One morning, after the commencement of active hostilities in the year of 1812, a party of men and boys left the fort and went to a place known as the Lindsay Lick, to gather greens. Among the party were Benjamin Allen, Francis Riffle, Durgee, William McHugh, and John Lindsay. After obtaining the greens, they started on their return, and had reached McLane's creek, when they were fired upon by a party of Indians. Durgee was instantly killed, but the rest of the party escaped uninjured. Two boys, sons of the man who was killed, sprang into the creek and swam across, and concealed themselves in a hollow log. They were barely settled in their place of concealment when an Indian jumped upon the log, and stood for some time peering into the surrounding woods. The boys could see him plainly through a small aperture, and they held their breath to avoid attracting his attention. Directly he gave a loud whoop, which made their hearts jump into their throats, and then disappeared in the woods. As soon as all was quiet on the outside, the fugitives crawled out and ran as fast as their legs could carry them in the direction of the fort. On the way they saw a party of Indians, but eluded them and escaped in safety to the fort. One of these boys, named Charles Durgee, lived to be an old man. He settled near Canton, Mo., built a large mill, and became wealthy. He died a few years since, much respected for his many good qualities as a citizen and a man.

Mr. Samuel Howell settled in Lincoln county in June, 1827, having emigrated from Franklin county, Ga. Soon after he came to the county, he and a small party went down to the Mississippi for a week's hunt. During the afternoon of the first day, a fine buck was killed not far from the camp. The next morning, after the others had been gone some time, Mr. Howell took his rifle and walked down the river about half a mile. Approaching the bank, and happening to look toward the opposite side, he saw an Indian shove his canoe into the water and step into it. At that distance he appeared to be a very large and powerful man, and Mr. Howell watched his movements with a considerable degree of interest, for the Indians in the upper country, under the celebrated chief Black Hawk, had begun to be troublesome, and it was not known at what time they might make a raid upon the white settlements. For several minutes the warrior remained motionless, as if listening, and then seating himself, he began to ply his paddle, and the canoe sped swiftly up the stream, hugging close to the shore as if to screen itself under the overhanging bushes. Reaching a point opposite the hunters' camp, it turned and made directly across the stream. Mr. Howell, suspecting mischief, returned as quickly as he could to the camp, which he reached a few minutes in advance of the Indian. The latter was unarmed, but advanced directly toward the camp, without showing by a sign or an expression of his countenance whether he meant friendship or enmity. Stepping up to Mr. Howell, he grasped his hand and grunted out the usual Indian salutation of "How do?" which was probably all the English he knew. The next instant he snatched the rifle out of Mr. Howell's hand, with the same show of rough cordiality, and with a complacent smile proceeded to carefully examine every portion of the weapon from the muzzle to the breech. Mr. Howell was not sure but that the smile meant mischief, and blamed himself severely for allowing the gun to be taken from him; but the movement was so unexpected and sudden that he had not the power to resist it. He deemed it prudent, however, not to betray any signs of uneasiness, but to await further developments. Having finished the examination with many evidences of satisfaction, the Indian made signs, by taking aim, imitating the noise of the discharge of the piece, going through the motions of a wounded deer, and then pointing to the skin and the spot where the deer had been killed, to show that he had been a witness on that occasion. He then handed the rifle back, and with many smiles and nods of pleasure and approbation, proceeded to examine the other equipments of the camp. No harm came of this adventure, but Mr. Howell never ceased to regret his carelessness in allowing the Indian to snatch his gun.

Shortly afterward, Mr. Howell went with another hunting party to near the mouth of Cuivre river, and while riding out one day, they came upon an Indian tent, in the door of which sat a venerable-looking old warrior. On the inside was an old squaw, engaged in cooking, while a young and very pretty one sat a little distance from her, on a mat of deer skins. The hunters thought she was the most handsome woman they had ever seen, and cast many admiring glances toward her, which greatly annoyed her. The fire of anger gleamed from her beautiful eyes, but this manifestation of her displeasure producing no effect, she covered her face with a deer skin, and remained covered while the interview lasted. The old squaw gave each of the visitors a piece of jerked venison, and poured a little salt into the palm of each one's hand. The venison had been dried in the sun, was very hard, and did not have the appearance of being extra clean; but politeness demanded that they should eat it. The longer they chewed it, the larger it seemed to get, and they were compelled either to gulp it down or spit it out, and most of them finally chose the latter alternative. The old warrior related, in broken English, and by signs, how the Indians often caught great numbers of deer by driving them into the overflowed bottoms and drowning them; and the hunters were inclined to believe, from the taste and smell of the venison they were trying to eat, that the red men were not always in a hurry about dressing their meat after it had been secured.

The Sioux Indians were allowed to hunt in Lincoln county for several years after the Black Hawk war, but they had learned discretion from past experience, and gave the white people but little trouble.

THE NEW MADRID EARTHQUAKES.

A SKETCH of early days in Missouri would not be complete without some notice of the terrible earthquakes which occurred in the southeastern part of the State in 1811 and 1812. They were the most terrible in character of any shocks that have visited the North American continent, since its discovery and occupation by white people. Numerous slight convulsions had occurred in that region before, and the people were so accustomed to them that they did not dread them. When they were awakened at the dead hour of night by the clatter of furniture in their chambers, and the uncertain heaving of the ground under them, they sank to rest again, with the drowsy remark, "It is only an earthquake!" But when the terrible shocks of 1811-12 came, they left an impression on the minds of those who felt them, and witnessed the destruction which they wrought, that never could be effaced. Whole tracts of land were plunged into the bed of the river. The grave-yard at New Madrid was precipitated into the bend of the stream. Large lakes of twenty miles in extent, were made in an hour, while other lakes were drained of their contents by the convulsions which altered the entire face of the country. The whole region, to the mouth of the Ohio in one direction, and to the St. Francois in the other, including a front of three hundred miles, was convulsed to such a degree as to create lakes and islands almost without number. In many places the surface of the ground was covered with water to the depth of four feet. Trees were split in the midst and lashed one with another, until they inclined in every direction and in every angle to the earth and horizon. The undulations resembled waves, increasing in elevation as they advanced, and when they had attained a certain fearful height, the earth would burst, and vast volumes of water, sand, and coal would be discharged as high as the tops of trees. Many persons were attacked by severe sea-sickness. Whole districts were covered with white sand, so as to be uninhabitable. Birds lost all power and disposition to fly, and nestled in the bosoms of men for protection. A bursting of the earth just below New Madrid, arrested the course of the river and caused a reflux of its waters, by which many boats were swept out among the trees and left upon dry land when the waters receded.

The shocks were distinguishable into two classes — those which had a horizontal motion, and those which moved perpendicularly. The latter were attended by explosions and terrible noises, but were not so destructive as the former. The general impulse, when the shocks commenced, was to run; but when they reached the severest point, locomotion became impossible, and people were thrown upon their faces at every step. A gentleman, escaping from his house, left an infant behind, and in attempting to climb the steps to rescue it, he was thrown to the ground a dozen times. The chasms in the earth extended from the southwest to the northeast, and the people observing this, felled the tallest trees at right angles across them, and stationed themselves upon their trunks. By this means many were saved, for the chasms frequently occurred beneath the trees on which they were seated. Horses, cattle, and other stock, together with the harvests, were nearly all destroyed.

After the earthquakes had moderated in violence, the country presented a most melancholy appearance. Deep chasms were plowed through the earth, trees were thrown down and twisted in every imaginable angle and degree, houses were ruined, and the whole face of the country was covered with the carcasses of dead animals. For some time after the shocks had ceased, the people did not dare to build houses, but they passed that winter and the succeeding one in booths and lodges of so light a texture as not to expose the inhabitants to danger in case of their being thrown down. They obtained an abundance of provisions, however, from the boats which had been wrecked in the vicinity. Flour, beef, pork, bacon, butter, cheese, apples, and other articles of food were so plentiful that there was no longer any sale for them. The face of the country had been so altered by the earthquakes that the boundaries of estates were lost, and much difficulty was experienced in locating lines. For the relief of the suffering people, Congress passed an act, allowing them to locate the same amount of land they had possessed previous to the convulsions, in any part of the territory where lands were not covered by prior claims. But most of these claims passed into the hands of speculators, and were of but little benefit to those for whom they were intended.

During an interval of the shocks there came a brilliant and cloudless evening, in which the western sky, undimmed by a single cloud, was in a continual glare of vivid flashes of lightning, from below the horizon. It was afterward remarked that these singular phenomena occurred at the same time with the fatal earthquake at Carraccas, in South America, and the people supposed that the flashes and subterranean thunder were parts of that terrible event.

SOME OF OUR ANTIQUITIES.

There are abundant evidences to prove that this Western country, and in fact nearly the entire continent of America, was, at some remote period of the world's history, thickly populated with a comparatively enlightened race of people. The burial mounds along the rivers and water courses, and on benches overlooking fertile valleys that were formerly the beds of lakes or rivers, are filled with human bones and strange relics of an extinct race. Some of these mounds present evidences of great labor in their construction, and the same general features which characterize them show that they were erected by one nation of people, for one general purpose. Specimens of earthenware, silver and cop per ornaments, ancient weapons, skeletons and bodies in a partial state of preservation have been taken from them in large numbers. Those ancient people were an entirely different race from the Indians, and lived at such a remote period that not the slightest tradition in reference to them has ever been found among even the most intelligent aboriginal tribes. They were small in stature, and were evidently inclined to the pursuits of peace rather than of war. They had large cities, and a comparatively dense population, by whom the arts and sciences were cultivated, and the earth made to bring forth its fruits for their subsistence. A large cemetery was discovered at an early day on the Meramec river, in St. Louis county, from which many partially preserved skeletons were exhumed. They had been buried in stone coffins, and in some instances the bones were nearly entire. The length of the bodies was determined by that of the coffins, and they averaged from three feet and a half to four feet. In Tennessee two bodies were found in a limestone cavern, and neither of them exceeded four feet in height. The teeth were separated by considerable intervals, and were small, long, white, and sharp. The hair seemed to have been sandy, or inclined to yellow. Great pains had been taken to preserve the bodies, and much labor had been expended in making the funeral robes in which they were folded. Two splendid blankets, woven with the most beautiful feathers of the wild turkey, arranged in regular stripes and compartments, encircled them. The cloth on which these feathers were woven, was a kind of linen of neat texture, something like that which is made from the fibres of the nettle. One of these persons, a female, had evidently died from the effects of a blow on the skull, as the marks of the coagulated blood could still be traced, where the blow fell, when the body was exhumed. The skulls and face bones of all the mound builders are of a peculiar shape, somewhat resembling the head of a squirrel or fox, and very small; the face and chin protruding, the forehead narrow and retreating. There are evidences to show that this pigmy race of people lived cotemporaneously with the mastodon, that immense antediluvian animal which has been extinct for unnumbered centuries.

The pottery which has been taken from the mounds is unbaked, the glazing is incomplete, and it presents evidences of having been moulded by hand. A drinking cup, taken from a mound in St. Charles county, is thus described by the gentleman who owned it: "It was smooth, well moulded, and of the color of common grey stoneware. It had been rounded with great care, and yet, from slight indentations on the surface, it was manifest that it had been wrought in the palm of the hand. It would contain about two quarts, and had been used to hold animal oil; for it had soaked through and varnished the external surface. Its neck was that of a squaw, known by the clubbing of the hair, after the Indian fashion. There seemed to have been an attempt at wit in the outlet. It was the horrible and distorted mouth of a savage, and in drinking you would be obliged to place your lips in contact with those of madam, the squaw.''

What became of the mound builders is a question that will probably never be settled. That they were exterminated by a stronger and more warlike race, there is but little doubt; but, then, who were their destroyers, and what, in turn, became of them? They were certainly not our modern Indians or their progenitors, for in that case some tradition of so great a conquest would have remained among them. When we contemplate this subject the mind runs far back into the misty realms of imagination, and is not satisfied. It is an insoluble mystery, which only eternity can unravel. One who studied the subject long and earnestly, and assisted his studies by personal observation, says: '' Here must have been a race of men on these charming plains, that had every call from the scenes that surrounded them, to contented existence and tranquil meditation. Unfortunate, as men view the thing they must have been. Innocent and peaceful they probably were; for had they been reared amidst wars and quarrels, like the present Indians, they would doubtless have maintained their ground, and their posterity would have remained to this day. Beside them moulder the huge bones of their cotemporary beasts, which must have been thrice the size of the elephant. * * * The unknown race to which these bones belonged, had, I doubt not, as many projects of ambition, and hoped as sanguinely to have their names survive, as the great of the present day.''

PART III.

HISTORIES OF FAMILIES.

ST. CHARLES COUNTY.

THE County, or District of St. Charles, as it was originally called, had no definite limits. It extended from the Missouri river on the south, to the British possessions on the north; and from the Mississippi river on the east to the Pacific Ocean on the west. It retained these dimensions until 1816, when Howard county was cut off from the western part of St. Charles, and organized into a separate municipality. Cedar creek, which now forms the eastern boundary of Boone county, was established as the line between St. Charles and Howard. In December, 1818, Montgomery and Lincoln counties were organized, and St. Charles was reduced to its present dimensions.

In 1818 the people of the Territory of Missouri petitioned Congress for authority to form a State government, and a bill was accordingly introduced during the session of 1818-19; but it contained a clause prohibiting slavery, and, though it passed the House, it was rejected by the Senate. At the ensuing session the bill was again brought up, and a lengthy and exciting debate took place, lasting several weeks. A compromise was finally effected, by which it was agreed that slavery should be tolerated in Missouri, but in no other part of Louisiana, as ceded by France to the United States, north of 36 degrees 30 minutes north latitude. Under this bill a Convention was called for the purpose of framing a State Constitution. The Convention met in St. Louis in June, 1820, and formed a constitution which was laid before Congress early in the session of 1820-21. It was accepted, and the State formally admitted into the Union.

During the following summer an election was held for members of the Legislature and other State officers, and in the winter of 1821-22 the first Legislature of the State of Missouri met in St. Charles. Its sessions were held in a room in the second story of a house on Main street, still standing, the lower room of which is now occupied by Mr. Fred Heye as a tin shop.

The Constitution had made liberal provisions for remunerating the Governor and Supreme and Circuit Judges, but one of the first acts of the Legislature was to reduce the salaries of these officers to a very low figure, in conformity with the stringency of the times. The Governor was allowed $1,500, the Supreme Judges $1,100, and the Circuit Judges $1,000. It was expected by many persons that this reduction of salaries would prevent men of ability from seeking those positions, but at the next election there was as great a scramble for office as there had been at the preceding one, under the large salaries fixed by the Constitution. Those salaries seem small and mean to us now, and would hardly be sufficient to support the family of an ordinary mechanic; but they were sufficient for those primitive times, when a family could live in considerable style on five or six hundred dollars a year. They had "hard money" and "hard times" then; and if the hard money advocates of our own day succeed in driving the country into the adoption of their suicidal policy, we may have to go back again to the condition of our ancestors. "Hard money," low prices, and "hard times" are inseparable.

Most of the members of the first Legislature, as well as the Governor and other high dignitaries, rode to St. Charles on horseback, and their horses were kept during the session by Mr. Archibald Watson, a farmer, who lived a few miles below St. Charles, on "the point." The members boarded at private houses, and at the few hotels that were in the town at the time, at the rate of $2.50 per week. The remuneration proved to be insufficient, and those who kept boarding houses generally lost money. Uriah J. Devore, who boarded a number of the members, lost everything he had. Pork was worth 1½ cents per pound; venison hams 25 cents each; eggs 5 cents per dozen; honey 5 cents a gallon, and coffee $1 per pound. Sugar was not in the market, and those who drank coffee sweetened it with honey. Some of the members were rough characters, and they all dressed in primitive style, either in homespun and home-made clothes, or in buckskin leggins and hunting shirts. Some wore rough shoes of their own manufacture, while others encased their feet in buckskin moccasins. Some had slouched hats, but the greater portion wore caps made of the skins of wild cats or raccoons. Governor McNair was the only man who had a fine cloth coat, and that was cut in the old "pigeon-tail" style. He also wore a beaver hat, and endeavored to carry himself with the dignity becoming a man in his position.

While St. Charles was the temporary seat of government, a newspaper was published there called *The Missourian*, by Robert McCloud, a practical printer, and step-son of Joseph Charless, Sr., one of the founders of the *Missouri Republican*. This was succeeded by the *Clarion*, which was established by Nathaniel Patten, of Howard county, and published by him until his death, which occurred in 1837. After his death the paper was continued by his widow, under the editorial management of Hon. Wm. M. Campbell. (Mrs. Patten subsequently married Wilson B. Overall.) The paper then passed successively to Messrs. Julian & Carr, as the *Clarion*, in 1839; to Berlin & Knapp, as the *Free Press*, in 1840; to Overall, Julian & Carr, as the *Advertiser*, in 1842; to Douglass & Millington, as the *Western Star*, in 1846; to Orear & Kibler, as the *Chronotype*, in 1849; to Orear & McDearmon, in 1852; to N. C. Orear, in 1853; to King & Emmons, as the *Reveille*, in 1854; to Hinman & Branham, in 1856; to Hinman in 1858; to Edwards & Stewart, in 1865; to Emmons & Orrick, as the *Cosmos and Sentinel*, in 1867; and to W. W. Davenport, as the *Cosmos*, in 1868. This paper, therefore, running back through several suspensions, and numerous changes of name and proprietors, is, perhaps, the oldest paper in the State, except the *Missouri Republican*.

The first church in St. Charles was organized by the Catholics, at a date so early that there is no record of it. The first church record that has come down to the present day, was made in 1792 by Rev. Peter J. Didier. It recorded the birth of Peter Beland, who was born in St. Charles on the 7th of June, 1792. Since that time the Catholics have preserved a regular church organization in St. Charles, and have, doubtless, possessed a larger membership than any other church in the place. The next church established there was the Presbyterian, which was founded August 30,

1818, by Rev. Salmon Giddings, assisted by Rev. John Matthews. The following persons were enrolled as members at that time: John Braskin, Theophilus McPheeters, Thomas Lindsay and wife, James Lindsay and wife, Ebenezer Ayers and wife, and Elizabeth Emmons, mother of Hon. Benj. Emmons, Sr. Thomas Lindsay and Archibald Watson were chosen elders, and Rev. Chas. S. Rob inson was elected pastor. The third church organization in St Charles was effected by the Methodists, probably not many years after the advent of the Colliers, who came in 1815; but they had no house to worship in until 1830, when they were supplied with one by the liberality of Mrs. Collier. These were the first regular church organizations in the place, but ministers of nearly all other denominations held services there and in the surrounding country on various occasions. The other church organizations of St. Charles are of a comparatively modern date. Rev. James Crittenden, of Kentucky, was a very popular Baptist preacher in those early times, and many children born then were named for him.

Among the old institutions of St. Charles, Lindenwood Female College is one of the most prominent. It was founded by Major George C. Sibley, in 1828, who erected a house upon his own grounds, and dedicated it to the cause of education. Since then a school has been sustained there almost without intermission, and about twenty-four years ago the institution was incorporated by the Legislature. The original building was improved and enlarged from time to time, but eventually became entirely inadequate for the purpose for which it was intended, and a large, handsome, and well arranged building was erected in its stead. The modern building occupies a commanding position, and a splendid view of the surrounding country can be obtained from its observatory. A boarding house and chapel are situated on the grounds adjacent to the college, and the institution is at present in a prosperous condition. Major and Mrs. Sibley donated one hundred and twenty acres of valuable land to Lindenwood College, most of which has been sold for the benefit of the institution; but one lot of twenty acres, upon which the buildings are situated, is forever inalienable. It has been tastefully improved, and presents a beautiful appearance.

St. Charles College, another of the old institutions of this place, is noticed in connection with the history of its founders.

On the hill near the clerks' offices in St. Charles, overlooking the town and river, there once stood an old, quaint looking, round stone building, which was known as the "Round Tower." No one ever visited St. Charles without observing it, and wondering what it was intended for. It was about thirty feet in diameter, and three stories high, and its commanding position and singular appearance never failed to bring it into notice. There were port-holes for rifles at regular intervals around the walls, and persons of a romantic turn of mind were disposed to believe that it was an old Spanish or French fort, erected by the first explorers of the country, for protection against the Indians; but the most authentic account of the building says that it was erected by one Francis Duquette, for a wind-mill, not many years after the founding of St. Charles. There is a tradition, however, to the effect that it was an old dismantled fort when Duquette came to St. Charles, and that he merely repaired it and used it for a mill. We cannot say which is correct, but are inclined to believe that the tradition had some foundation in truth. The building was never used for military purposes after Duquette came into possession of it, though at one time an Indian was confined in it for some misdemeanor; but he made his escape by climbing out over the top of the wall. The fort erected for protection during the Indian war, was situated under the hill, near where the court house stands. Waiving the doubtful origin of the round tower, it was beyond dispute the oldest building in St. Charles, and ought to have been preserved as a relic of early days. But it was torn down some ten or twelve years ago to make room for a brickyard, and the older citizens of the place are the only ones who remember where it stood.

The following French families were living in St. Charles in 1818, and out of the entire list only one of the original stock is left. We refer to Mr. Louis Gerneau, who gave us the names, as follows: Louis Gerneau, Antoine Janis, Gabriel Lattraille, Bazile Bruziere, Michael Belland, John Baptiste Deau, Joseph Pereau, Louis Cardinal, John Martineau, Joseph, Louis, and Charles Tayon, Gregoire Kiercereau, Mr. Souliere, John Aubuchon, Jacques and Peter Dubois, Joseph Reynal, John B. Proulx, Mackey Wherry, Francis and Baptiste Dorlaque, Joseph Baptiste, Aleck Cote, John and Baptiste Lucier, Peter Beauchemin, Joel and Toussaint Rocque, and Peter Pallardie.

The following is a list of the first Justices of the Peace appointed in St. Charles county after Missouri was admitted into

the Union as a State in 1820. Township of Portage des Sioux—
James Perras, Francis Lessieur, Daniel Griffith, Joseph Sumner,
Ebenezer Ayres. Femme Osage Township—William Hays, Isaac
Fulkerson, John B. Callaway. Upper Cuivre Township —Roger
Taylor, Felix Scott, Thomas Gilmore. Lower Cuivre Township
—James Audrain, Francis Allen, James Thomas. St. Charles
Township — Daniel Colgan, Sr., James Green, John Slayter,
Philip A. Sublette, Charles Phillips, Ruluff Peck, Joseph W.
Garraty, Benjamin Walker. Dardenne Township — Biel Farns-
worth, John B. Stone, John Naylor, Thomas. D. Stephenson.

FAMILIES OF ST. CHARLES COUNTY.

ALLEN.—William Allen, of Henry county, Virginia, was married twice. The name of his second wife was Ann Smith, by
whom he had Susan, Robert, Joseph, Pines and Frances. Susan
married William Wells, who was Probate Judge of Henry county,
Virginia. Robert was a talented man, and a fine orator, and represented his native county in the State Legislature for many
years. He married Celia Mullens, and their son, WilliamL ., was
State Senator in Mississippi for a number of years. Joseph S.,
the second son of Robert Allen, was a distinguished Methodist
minister. He settled in St. Charles county in 1828. He was
married twice, and by his first wife he had one son, named William. The name of his second wife was Rachel May, and they
had William M., Robert L., Elizabeth M., John P., Joseph J.,
Susan A., and Rachel. William M. married Mary M. Shelton, and
they had six children. Mr. Allen represented his county in the
House of Representatives four years, and four years in the State
Senate. He was a prominent and influential citizen, and now resides in Wentzville, Missouri. Robert L. was married first to Anna
Pendleton, by whom he had five children. After her death he
married Louisa B. Harnett, and they had three children. Mr.
Allen was County Judge of Warren county for some time, and
represented that county in the Legislature two years. Elizabeth
M. was married first to Henry Simpson, and after his death she
married J. D. May. She had three children. John P., who was
a physician, married his cousin, Martha L. Allen, and they had
one child. Joseph I. came to Missouri in 1850, and died soon
after. Susan A. died unmarried —Pines, son of William Allen,
was married first to Charlotte Bailey, of Tennessee, and settled
in St. Charles county in 1829. Their children were—Robert B.,
Mary J., Joseph J., John B., Charles C., and Martha L. Mrs.
Allen was married the second time to Nancy Hughes, of Virginia,
and they had Lucy A., Susan M., Pines H., William M., Smith B.,
and Columbus S. Robert B. married Louisa Chambers, and they
had ten children. He was a prominent Methodist, and an influ-

ential citizen. Mary J. married Marshall Bird, who settled in Missouri in 1833. They had seven children. Joseph J., married Sarah McClenny, and they had three children. John B. was married first to Elizabeth Lacy, by whom he had four children. He was married the second time to Lucy Harnett, and they had five children. Mr. Allen is an attorney, and lives near Flint Hill. He was a soldier in the Black Hawk war. Charles C. married Fanny Pendleton, and they had but two children. Martha L. was married first to John Taylor, and they had one child. She was married the second time to Thomas H. Lacy. They had no children.

ABINGTON.—John Abington, of Scotland, came to America and settled in Montgomery county, Maryland, sometime before the revolution. His wife was Mary Watson. She died, leaving him a widower, after which he moved to Henry county, Va. The names of his children were, Bowles, Lucy, John, Elizabeth, and Henry. Bowles, at the age of 18 years, joined the American army and served during the revolutionary war. He married Sarah Taylor, daughter of William Taylor and Sarah Scruggs, of Virginia, and they had seven children—William N., John T., Susannah, Taylor, Bowles, Henry, and Lucy. William N. was a Methodist preacher, and died in North Carolina. John T. married Rebecca Taylor, and settled in Tennessee. Susannah married Thomas Travis, and settled in St. Charles county, Mo., in 1830. Taylor married Amanda Penn. Bowles married Mary Baldridge, and died ten days after. Hon. Henry Abington, the only one of the family now living, married Maria Smith, and settled in the western part of St. Charles county, where he now resides. He is an influential, public-spirited citizen; has served three terms in the Legislature of his State, and has held the position of Justice of the Peace for many years.

AYERS.—Ebenezer Ayers came from one of the Eastern States, and settled on what is known as "the point," in St. Charles county, at a very early date. He built the first horse-mill in that region of country. He was also a large fruit-grower; and made a great deal of butter and cheese. He lived in a large red house, in which the first Protestant sermon in "the point" was preached. In 1804 he and James Flaugherty and John Woods were appointed Justices of the Peace for St. Charles district, being the first under the American government. Mr. Ayers had four children, one son and three daughters. Two of the latter died before they were grown. The son, Ebenezer Davenport Ayers, married Louisiana Overall, and settled where Davenport, Iowa, now stands, the town being named for him. His surviving sister, Hester Ayers, married Anthony C. Palmer, who was a ranger in the company commanded by Captain James Callaway. Mr. Palmer was afterward elected sheriff of the county, and served one term. He had a good education, was an excellent scribe, and taught school a number of years.

AUDRAIN.—Peter Audrain was a native of France, but came to America at an early date, and settled in Pennsylvania, where he married Margaret Moore. He subsequently moved to Detroit, Michigan, where he became an influential citizen, and was Marshal of the Territory at the time of his death. He had seven children, three of whom, James H., Peter G., and Margaret, settled in Missouri. James H. was born in Pennsylvania, December 29, 1782, and was married to Mary E. Wells, of Louisville, Ky., December, 23, 1806. He settled at Fort Wayne, Ind., and engaged in merchandising. During the war of 1812 he was commissioned Captain of volunteers, and saw some hard service. He was afterward appointed Colonel of militia. In 1816 he moved his family to Missouri, in a flat-boat, and after remaining a short time at St. Louis, he settled on Peruque creek, in St. Charles county, where he soon after built a mill and a distillery. The mill was run by a tread-wheel, on which he worked young bulls, and he often had as many as twenty of these animals at one time. This led a loquacious citizen of the community to give it the name of "Bull's Hell Mill," by which it became generally known. In 1830 Col. Audrain was elected a member of the Legislature, and died November 10, 1831, at the house of Gov. Clark, in St. Louis. His remains were conveyed to his home in a hearse, which was the first hearse ever seen in St. Charles county. When Audrain county was organized in 1836, it was named in honor of Colonel Audrain. Mrs. Audrain died about three years after the death of her husband. Their children were, Samuel W., Peter G., James H., Margaret, Benjamin O., Ann A., Francis B., Thomas B., and Mary F. The latter was born on the flat-boat, in 1816, while they were ascending the Mississippi river. Col. Audrain and his wife were baptised in Peruque creek, below his mill. The Colonel was a very stout man, and won a wager of $10 in St. Charles, one day, by carrying eight bushels of wheat, at one time, up three flights of stairs.

BIGELOW.—Moses Bigelow, the son of Zachariah Bigelow, of Pittsburg, Pa., came to St. Charles county, Mo., in 1821. He married Parthana, eldest daughter of Jonathan Bryan, who was a widow at the time, having previously married her cousin, Joseph Bryan. Mr. Bigelow had $1,000 in cash when came to Missouri, and by keeping that sum constantly at interest it made him a comfortable fortune before his death, which occurred in 1857. Several years before his death his wife, while on a visit to a married daughter, was thrown from her horse while returning from church, and one of her limbs was so badly fractured that it had to be amputated. She, however, outlived her husband, and died in 1873, of cancer. They had six children—James, Rufus, Rutia,

Abner, Agnes, and Phœbe. James was married three times; first to Mary E. Hopkins, second, to her sister, Amanda Hopkins, and third, to Angeline Callaway. Rufus married Henrietta Eversman. Rutia married Charles E. Ferney. Abner married Hulda Logan. Agnes died single. Phœbe married Fortunatus Castlio.

BIGGS. — Randall Biggs settled in St. Charles county in 1799. He married Susan Perkett. They were both of German descent. Their children were—William, Malinda, Lucretia, Elvira, Mary, and Silas P.

BOWLES.—John Bowles and his wife emigrated from England and settled in St. Mary's county, Maryland. They had seven children—William, John Baptist, Joseph, Jane, Susan, Henrietta, and Mary. In 1789 John Baptist, Joseph, James, and Mary, moved to Kentucky and settled in Scott county. Joseph married Alice Raley, and lived and died in Washington county, Ky. Jane married Ignatius Greenwell, and their son Robert married Maria Twyman, and settled in St. Charles county, Mo. Mary married William Roberts, and their daughter Elizabeth married John Burkman, who settled in Montgomery county, Mo. John Baptist married Henrietta Wheatley, and they had eight children—Walter, James, Leo, Clara, Elizabeth, Catharine, Matilda, and Celicia. Walter married Rosa McAtee, and settled in St. Charles county, Mo., in 1828. He was a soldier in the war of 1812, and is still living (1875), in his 87th year. James married Susan Luckett, and settled in St. Charles county in 1835. They had six children. Leo married Teresa McAtee, and settled in St. Charles County in 1831. They had seven children. Clara married Dennis Onan, and they lived in Kentucky. Catharine married Stephen T. McAtee, who settled in St. Charles county in 1834. They had eight children. Mr. McAtee and his youngest son, George, died the same day, and were buried in the same grave. Matilda married Walter Barnes, and they lived in Kentucky. Celicia married James W. Drury, who settled in St. Charles county in 1835. They had thirteen children.

BOYD.— ——Boyd came from the northern part of Ireland, and settled in Virginia at a very early date. In 1772 he was killed by the Indians, and left a widow and three children—William, Margaret, and John. William was appointed Indian agent for the State of Mississippi, where he lived and died. Margaret married —— Garvin, and they settled in Pennsylvania, where they raised a large family of children. Three of their sons, Alexander, John, and Benjamin, settled in St. Charles county in 1822. Alexander married Anna Mattison, and their children were— Margaret, Anna, Permelia, Jane, Alexander, and Fannie. John Boyd was quite young when his father was killed, and he was

9

raised by a Mr. Gordon of Virginia. During the revolutionary war he served as a ranger and scout in the American army. He was married in 1800 to Elizabeth Davis, of Virginia, and they had nine children—Gordon D., Cary A., William A., Margaret E., James H., Mary S., John N., Amasa P., and Maria. Gordon D. was a physician, and moved to Mississippi. He died of cholera, in New Orleans, in 1832, while on his way to Texas. Cary A. married Elizabeth Bailey, and settled in Pike county, Mo. William A. settled in St. Charles county in 1837. He married Elizabeth Poague, of Kentucky, and she died, leaving eight children. Her father was a Justice of the Peace in St. Charles county for ten years. Margaret E. married Major James G. Bailey, a soldier of the war of 1812, and they settled in St. Charles county in 1830. She died, leaving four children. James H. lived in Jackson, Miss., where he engaged in the mercantile business, and was elected Mayor of the town. Mary S. married Edmond P. Mathews, of Kentucky, and they settled in St. Charles county, Mo., in 1836. She had five children, and is still living in Pike county, Mo. John N. settled in St. Charles county in 1839. He married Mahaley Hughes, and they both died, leaving two children. Amasa P. died in Mississippi. Maria died while a child.

BATES.—Thomas F. Bates was an early settler of Goochland county, Va. He was a Quaker, but when the war of the revolution commenced he buried his religion in patriotism and became a soldier. He married Caroline M. Woodson, and they had twelve children—Charles, Matilda, Tarleton, Fleming, Nancy, Richard, James W., Sarah, Margaret, Susan, Frederick, and Edward. Charles lived and died in Virginia, where he became eminent in the profession of law. Matilda married Captain Gett, and died, leaving a daughter (Caroline M.) who was adopted by her uncle, Edward Bates, and died in St. Louis. Tarleton was killed in a duel at Pittsburg, Pa. Fleming lived in Northumberland county, Va., of which he was county clerk. He left several children at his death. Nancy married Thomas H. Walton, who was killed by lightning. He left one son, Robert A., who came to Missouri and married a daughter of Hon. Frederick Bates. Richard studied law, but died young. He was an intimate friend of Gen. Winfield Scott, and had the promise of becoming a distinguished man. James W. lived and died in Arkansas. He was a delegate to Congress from that Territory before its admission as a State. Sarah never married, but came with her mother to Missouri in 1818. Mrs. Bates died in 1845, aged ninety years. Margaret was married twice—first to John Speers, and second to Dr. Orton Wharton, both of Virginia. She was left a widow the second time, and came to St. Charles county, Mo., in 1838. Susan died while a young lady, in Virginia. Frederick Bates was well educated and became a distinguished man. President

Jefferson appointed him Secretary of the Territory of Michigan, and about the commencement of the Aaron Burr conspiracy, he was transferred to Upper Louisiana, as Secretary of that Territory. He afterward became Governor of the Territory of Missouri, and was the second Governor of the State after its admission. He married Nancy Ball, a daughter of Colonel John S. Ball, who was a soldier of the war of 1812. Mr. Bates died in 1825, leaving four children—Emily C., Lucas Lee, Woodville, and Frederick, Jr. During the latter part of his life he resided in Lincoln county. His daughter, Emily C., married Robert Walton, and is now living in St. Charles, a widow. Lucas Lee married a daughter of Samuel Conway, and lives in St. Louis county. Woodville died in his youth. Frederick, Jr., married Lavinia Merideth, and died, leaving one child. His widow married Samuel Conway, who also died, and she then married a Mr. Kerney. Hon. Frederick Bates was Governor of the Territory of Upper Louisiana from May, 1807, to October, 1807; from September, 1809, to September, 1810; from November 29, 1812, to December 7, 1812; and he was Governor of the Territory of Missouri from December 12, 1812, to July, 1813. He was elected second Governor of the State of Missouri in 1824, and died in 1825, before the expiration of his term. Edward Bates, brother of Frederick Bates, served as a private soldier in the war of 1812, having enlisted before he was of age; but he was promoted to sergeant before the expiration of his term. He settled in St. Charles county in 1814, and on the 29th of May, 1823, he was married to Julia D. Coalter, daughter of Hon. David Coalter. They had seventeen children. Mr. Bates was a man of a superior order of talents, and held many positions of trust and influence during his life. He studied law under Hon. Rufus Easton, and became eminent in his profession. He was distinguished for a faithful and conscientious discharge of every duty entrusted to him, whether great or small, and he possessed the confidence of all classes of his fellow-citizens in the very highest degree. He represented St. Louis as a delegate in the first Constitutional Convention of Missouri; served in the Legislature and State Senate for a number of years, and was a member of Congress in 1826. At the commencement of President Lincoln's administration he was honored with a seat in the cabinet as Attorney-General. He died in 1870, in his 76th year. His widow is still living, in her 78th year.

BAUGH.—The Baughs were doubtless of German descent; but there is no authentic record of the origin of the family, beyond the fact that three brothers of that name settled near Jamestown, Va., at an early date. Abram, a son of one of these brothers, married Judith Colman, of Powhatan county, and by her he had— Joseph, Thomas M., Edsa, William, Alexander, Abram, Jesse,

Mary, Judith, and Rhoda.   Joseph married Nancy Gentry, and
settled in Madison county, Ky., in 1781; and in 1816 he removed
to St. Charles county, Mo.   He served five years in the revolutionary war.   His children were—William, Benjamin, Judith, Alsey, Nancy, Mary, Patsey, and Lucinda.   William married Susan
Carter, of Kentucky, and settled in St. Charles county, Mo., but removed from there to Montgomery county in 1832.   His first wife
died, and he was married the second time to Mrs. Nancy V. Haslip, whose maiden name was Chambers.

BRYAN.—William Bryan, a native of Wales, came to America
with Lord Baltimore, about the year 1650, and settled in Maryland.   His wife was of Irish descent, and they had three children
—William, Morgan, and Daniel.   Of the succeeding two or
three generations of this family nothing is definitely known, but
early in the eighteenth century, William Bryan, a descendant of
the original stock, settled in Roan county, North Carolina.   He
married Sally Bringer, who was of German descent, and they
had eleven children—William, Morgan, John, Sally, Daniel,
Henry, Rebecca (who became the wife of Daniel Boone), Susan,
George, James, and Joseph.   During the revolutionary war six
of the sons served in the American army, and one (probably
Joseph) cast his lot with the Tories.   He was promoted to the
position of Colonel, and served with Tarleton during his campaign
in the Carolinas.   On one occasion his regiment of Tories, being
in the advance, was atttacked by the patriots and forced to retreat.   As they were falling back in great confusion, they met
Tarleton, who had heard the firing, and, accompanied by only a
few of his staff officers, was riding leisurely toward the scene of
conflict, blowing his bugle as he came.   The patriots, hearing the
sound of the bugle, and supposing that the entire British army
was advancing upon them, gave up the pursuit and retired.
When Bryan met Tarleton, he demanded, in an angry tone, why
he had come alone, instead of marching his army to his assistance.   Tarleton replied that he wanted to "see how the d—d
Tories would fight."   This so enraged the Tory leader that he
came near resigning his commission and retiring from the service,
and would probably have done so if he could have returned home
in safety.   Two of the brothers who were in the American army
(James and Morgan) were at the bloody battle of King's Mountain, and from the best information that we can obtain, their
Tory brother fought against them in the same battle.   The war
feeling ran so high that they would have shot him if he had come
within range of their rifles.   Three of the brothers (James,
William, and Daniel) followed Daniel Boone to Kentucky, and
built Bryan's Station, near Lexington.   Shortly after their
arrival, William and two other men left the fort and went some
distance into the woods, for the purpose of obtaining a supply of

game for the garrison. During their absence they were attacked by the Indians; Bryan's companions were both killed and scalped, and he was shot through the knee with a rifle ball. But notwithstanding his severe and painful wound, he rode to the fort, a distance of thirty miles, through the thick woods and brush, and gave the alarm in time to save the place from falling into the hands of the Indians. They soon began to suffer greatly for provisions, being so closely watched by the Indians, that hunting parties did not dare to venture out, and they were reduced to the necessity of boiling and eating buffalo hides in order to avert starvation.—James Bryan was a widower, with six children, at the time of the removal to Kentucky, and it was his branch of the family that afterward came to Missouri, the descendants of the other two brothers remaining in Kentucky. The names of his children were—David, Susan, Jonathan, Polly, Henry, and Rebecca. David married Mary Poor, and came to Missouri in 1800. He settled near the present town of Marthasville, in Warren county. His children were — James, Morgan, Elizabeth, Mary, Willis, John, Susan, Drizella, Samuel, and William K. Mr. Bryan reserved half an acre of ground near his house for a grave yard, and it was there that Daniel Boone and his wife were buried. He also had a large orchard, which he grew from apple seed that he carried from Kentucky in his vest pocket.—Susan Bryan married Israel Grant, of Kentucky. They had three children, James, William, and Israel B.—Jonathan married Mary Coshow, a widow with one son, William. (Her maiden name was Mary Hughes.) In 1800 he moved his family to Missouri in a keel-boat, and landed at the mouth of Femme Osage creek, on Christmas day of that year. He settled first in Lincoln county, near the present town of Cap-au-Gris, but there they were greatly exposed to attacks from the Indians, and the location proving to be a sickly one, he moved and settled on Femme Osage creek, near Nathan Boone's place, where he lived during the remainder of his life. In 1801 he built the first water-mill west of the Mississippi river. The stones were carried from Kentucky on horseback, a spring branch supplied the water power, and an old musket barrel formed the sluice or water race. The children of Jonathan Bryan were — Parthena, Phœbe, Nancy, Elijah, Abner, Mary, Alsey, James, Delila, and Lavinia.—Henry Bryan married Elizabeth Sparks, and settled in St. Charles county in 1808. They had eight children — Susan, Joseph, Rebecca, Elizabeth, Cynthia, Johannah, John W., and Polly. Rebecca (daughter of James Bryan) married Hugh Logan, of Kentucky, and they had five children— William, Alexander, Hugh, Henry, and Mary. Mr. Logan died, and she was married the second time to James Smith, of Kentucky. They had two children, when he also died; and in 1810

Jonathan and Henry Bryan moved their sister and.her family to Missouri. She settled on South Bear creek, in Montgomery county, and died twenty years later. Her two children by Smith were named Susan and James. Susan married a man named King, and James married Susan Ellis.

BALDRIDGE.—Robert Baldrige was a native of Ireland, but emigrated to America and settled in Kentucky, where he married Hannah Fruit. He subsequently moved to Missouri, and was one of the first settlers of St. Charles county. He obtained the Spanish grant of land on which Pond Fort was built. His children were—Daniel, James, Malachi, John, Robert, jr., Alexander, Elizabeth, Mary, Grace, and Nancy. Malachi and two companions, Price and Lewis, were killed by the Indians while hunting on Loutre Prairie. Shortly after, Daniel, in order have revenge for his brother's death, tracked a party of Indians to their camp at night, and shot their chief as he sat by the camp-fire. He then concealed himself in the tall grass, and watched the Indians searching for him; but they failed to find him. James and John were successful business men, and always had money to loan. A man named Hutchings once borrowed $300 in silver quarters from John, and carried the money home in a calico bag. Finding that he would not need it, he returned the money at the end of three months, and offered to pay interest. But Baldridge said he could not think of accepting interest from a man who had kept his money safe for him that length of time; "because," said he, "if I had kept it, some rascal would have stolen it." When James died he had several boxes filled with gold and silver money. Robert, jr., planted a cherry tree, and when it grew large enough, he had it manufactured into lumber, from which he had his coffin made, and when he died he was buried in it. Robert and John were rangers in Callaway's company during the Indian war. After the close of the war John moved to the Gasconade country, and built a large saw mill in the pineries; but it did not prove to be a paying investment, and subsequently passed into the hands of other parties. Elizabeth Baldridge married John Scott, and their son, Hiram, was killed at Callaway's defeat. He was a man of great daring, and Callaway placed much confidence in him. Daniel married Kate Huffman. James married Margaret Zumwalt. Robert, jr., married Peggy Ryebolt. Grace married John Howell, and Nancy married Frederick Price.

BURDINE.—General Amos Burdine, as he was called, was a native of Kentucky, where he married Jennie Davidson, and came to Missouri in 1811. He settled in Dog Prairie, St. Charles county, and built his cabin on the James Mackey claim. Soon after he came to Missouri, the earthquakes at New Madrid occurred, and the shaking of the earth caused the boards that composed the roof of his cabin to rattle so that he imagined there were Indians up there trying to get in. So, arousing his sons (for it was at night), they secured their guns and began to fire through the roof, which they so completely riddled with bullets that it would not turn the rain any more. He was a believer in witches, as were many of the early settlers, and used to brand his cattle in the forehead with a hot shoe hammer, to keep the witches from killing them. He had a flock of geese, and several of the birds died of some disease peculiar to the goose family. The General imagined that the witches had been at work; so he built a large log fire and commenced burning the dead birds one by one. When the third bird was thrown on the fire it gave signs of life, and the General always declared, that all the others came to life and flew around the fire and drove the witches away. On another occasion he imagined that he had been shot in the hip with a hair ball, and called on a physician to have it extracted. But of course no such ball could be found. Burdine was a great hunter, and killed more deer than any other half-dozen men in the vicinity. He used the skins of the animals that he killed for beds and bed clothing, which was a common thing among the people of that day. He had a habit of naming the trees in the woods where he killed deer, and his sons knew the woods so well, and the names of the different trees, that when he sent them to bring the game in, they never had any trouble in finding it. His little pony, Ned, was so well trained that he knew

when to run, walk, or stand still by the simple motion of the bridle, and, being as fond of hunting as his master, he never failed to obey commands. The General could mimic the cry of any animal or bird, and often imitated wolves or panthers for the purpose of scaring deer out of the brush, so he could shoot them. A party of hunters heard him one day screaming like a panther, and imagining they were in close proximity to one of those ferocious animals, they put spurs to their horses and rode away for their lives. He gave names to nearly all of the

BURDINE'S ATTEMPT TO WEIGH HIS WIFE. streams in his vicinity, and

Chain-of-Rocks, on Cuivre, owes its appropriate title to him. Burdine was a man of medium size, but his wife was very large and heavy. One day he undertook to weigh her with a pair of old-fashioned steelyards. They were fastened to the rafters of the porch in front of his house, with a grape vine, and he tied another grape vine to the hook on the under side of the steelyard for his wife to sit in. Mounting on a barrel, so as to be high enough to handle the beam, he signified to his wife that he was ready, and she took her seat. But immediately the beam ascended to the roof, carrying the General with it; and he hung suspended in the air until some members of the family came to his assistance and helped him down.

Hon. Wm. M. Campbell, of St. Charles, began to write a history of the General's life, but died before the book was completed. It would no doubt have afforded a rich mine of humor and adventures. Some amusing anecdotes of this original character will be found under the head of "Anecdotes and Adventures" in this book. The General's wife died of cholera in 1832. Some years afterward suit was commenced against him for the land on which he lived, the title being vested in another party. He lost the suit and his home, and becoming dissatisfied with the new order of things in Missouri, he moved his large family to Arkansas, where they were not crowded with neighbors.

BOYD.—John Boyd, of Ireland, came to America before the revolution. He had two sons, John and William. The latter was a gunsmith, and in the war of 1812 he was commissioned Captain of volunteers. In his company were six of his apprentices, all of whom were killed in the same battle. Capt. Boyd married Ruth Carr, of Pennsylvania, and settled in Spencer county, Kentucky, in 1792. In 1829 he came to Missouri, and, selecting a location in St. Charles county, for his future residence, he returned to Kentucky, but died before he had completed his arrangements for moving. His widow and children came to St. Charles county in 1830. The names of the children were—Elizabeth, John, Elijah, Hiram, Jane, James, Emeline, William, Ruth, Alexander T., and Thomas C. John married a Miss Clemens. Elijah married Fannie Thomas. Jane was married in Kentucky, to Joseph Brown. Emeline married James Cochran. Aleck T. married Medora McRoberts. Thomas C. married Ruth Allen. Ruth married Wade Munday. William went to California, and died there. James never married, and died in St. Charles county. Hiram married Rebecca Datson, of Lincoln county. Elizabeth married Alex. W. Thomas, and settled in Kentucky.

BALL.—James Ball and his wife, Nancy Smith, were natives of Fauquier county, Va. The names of their children were—Margaret, Judith, Sheltile, Taliaferro, Lucy, Elizabeth, James, John, and Casay. John, Sheltile, James, and Nancy all settled in Missouri. John married Elizabeth Ellis, of Virginia, and settled in St. Charles county in 1834. He is dead, but his wife survives. Nancy married William Ellis, and settled in St. Charles county in 1835. James married Peggy Smith, and settled in St. Louis county in 1835. Sheltile married Polly Elliott, of Virginia, and settled in St. Louis county, Mo., in 1834. He died some time afterward, and his widow and children moved to St. Charles county. The names of the children were—John, Bernadotte, Benjamin, Sheltile, Jr., and Bushrod. The rest of the Boyd children, with the exception of James, who died of yellow fever in New Orleans, lived and died in Virginia.

BRAUN.—Cipler Braun and his wife, Magdalene Keeler, were of Baden, Germany. They emigrated to America and settled in St. Charles county in 1832. Their children were — Martin, Antoine, Clarissa, Agnes and Godfrey. All of these, with the exception of Martin, married and settled in St. Charles county. Martin, while sick of fever, wandered into the woods, where he died, and his body was eaten by the hogs. His shirt, with his name upon it, was found sometime afterward, and except for that his friends would never have known what became of him.

BROWNING.—Daniel F. J. Browning was a native of Kentucky, where he married a wealthy widow, from whom he afterward separated. He was always an unlucky man, and attributed his ill fortune to the fact that he once volunteered to hang a negro. The sheriff of the county where he lived, being averse to executing the criminal, offered $10 to any one who would drive the cart from under him. Browning accepted the offer, and drove the cart from under the negro; but after that his life became a burden to him. He lost his property, separated from his wife, and then came to Missouri, where he supported himself for several years by teaching school. He taught in White's Fort, and at several other places. During the Slicker war he kept a ferry at Chain-of-Rocks, and was ordered by the Slickers not to put any anti-Slicker men across the river at that place. But he paid no attention to the order, and a party of Slickers went to his house one night to lynch him; but he heard them coming, and mounting his horse, swam the river and escaped. Sometime afterward a friend met him in Lincoln county, and inquired where he was going. Browning pulled out a little pistol, about two inches long, and replied that he was "going to kill every d—d Slicker he met." But the places where he buried his dead have not been discovered.

BABER. — Hiram Baber married a daughter of Jesse Boone. He was sheriff of St. Charles county one term, and was a reckless, fun-loving sort of a man. He built a brick residence in St. Charles, and carved over the door, in large letters, "Root Hog, or Die." He moved from St. Charles to Jefferson City, and became one of the leading men of the State.   He made a great deal of money, and spent it as freely as he made it.   He would often, in braggadocio, light his pipe with bank bills, to show how easily he could make money and how little he cared for it.

COSHOW. — William Coshow, a native of Wales, married Mary Hughes, an Irish girl, and, emigrating to America, settled in North Carolina.   He went with Daniel Boone on one of his expeditions to Kentucky, and was killed by the Indians at the head of Kentucky river.   He had but one child, a son, named William.   His widow married Jonathan Bryan, several years after the death of her first husband, and they came to St. Charles county in 1800.   Her son was raised by his step-father who loved him as one of his own children.   He served in the war against the Indians, and afterward married Elizabeth Zumwalt, of St. Charles county.   They had three children, Andrew J., Phœbe A., and John B., all of whom are still living.

CAMPBELL.—Dr. Samuel Campbell and his wife, Sally Alexander, were natives of Rockbridge county, Va.   They had ten children, of whom William M., the subject of this sketch, was the fifth.   He was born in January, 1805, and after having received a fair education at home, was placed under the instruction of Rev. Wm. Graham, at what was then called the " Log College," but which was subsequently named Washington University, and is now known as Washington and Lee University, at Lexington, Va.   Here he qualified himself for the practice of law, and at the age of twenty-four came to Missouri with his brother-in-law, Dr. Robert McCluer, who settled in St. Charles county.   Young Campbell remained two years with his brother-in-law, hunting and amusing himself, and then went to St. Charles and commenced the practice of law.   He remained in St. Charles until 1843, when he removed to St. Louis, where he died, January 2, 1850.   Mr. Campbell wielded a large influence in his adopted State, and served as a member of the Legislature during the greater portion of his residence here.   He was editor of the St. Charles *Clarion* for some time, and also of the St. Louis *New Era*, by which means his influence and reputation were greatly extended.

COTTLE. — Warren Cottle, of Vermont, was a soldier in the war of 1812.   He had six children — Warren, Ira, Oliver, Stephen, Marshall, and Letitia.   Warren was a physician, and came with his father to Missouri in 1799.   He married his cousin, Salome Cottle, and they had eight children — Oliver, Alonzo, Fidelo, Alvora, Lorenzo, Paulina, Ora, and O'Fallon.   Ira also married his cousin, Suby Cottle, and they had six children — Levi, Harriet, Warner, Ira, Joseph, and Mary J.   Oliver married Charity Lowe, and they raised thirteen children — Royal, Leroy, Oliver, Mary,

Orville, Priscilla, Lethe, Juliet, John, Ira, Julius, Ellen, and Cordelia. Stephen married, but died without issue Marshall died single. Letitia married and died childless. Lorenzo Cottle, son of Dr. Warren Cottle, founded the town of Cottleville, in St. Charles county, in 1840.

COALTER. — The ancestors of the Coalter family of St. Charles were members of the Presbyterian colony that settled in Augusta county, Va., at an early date. From among them we have obtained the following names—David, John, Polly, Jane, and Ann. John was married four times. His third wife was a Miss Tucker, sister of Judge Beverly Tucker, and half-sister of John Randolph, of Roanoke. They had two children — St. George and Elizabeth. The latter married John Randolph Bryant, of Flovanna county, Va. David married Ann Carmicle, of South Carolina, and the names of their children were — John D., Beverly T., Maria, Catharine, Fanny, Caroline, and Julia. Polly married Judge Beverly Tucker, who became eminent as a jurist. They had no children. Jane married John Naylor, of Pennsylvania. They settled in Kentucky, but removed to Missouri in 1818. They had seven children — James, John, William, Thomas, Caroline, Sophronia, and Ann. The boys all died about the time they were grown. Ann married a Mr. Ward, of Kentucky. — (Children of David Coalter.) John D. married Mary Meanes, of South Carolina, and settled in St. Charles county, where he lived until two years prior to his death, when he removed to St. Louis. He had but one child. Mr. Coalter was a talented and influential attorney, and also a leading member of the Legislature of his State. Beverly T. was a physician. He married Elizabeth McQueen, of Pike county, where he resided. They had three children, one son, and two daughters. Dr. Tucker was a gentleman of fine business qualifications. Maria married Hon. Wm. C. Preston, of South Carolina, and died, leaving one daughter, who died when she was about grown. Catharine married Judge William Harper, of South Carolina, who removed to Missouri and became Judge of the Court of Chancery. They had several children, but only one survives. Fannie married Dr. David H. Meanes, of South Carolina. The Doctor removed to Missouri and remained a short time, and then returned to South Carolina, where his wife died. They had several children. Caroline married Hamilton R. Gamble, of St. Louis. They had two sons and one daughter. Julia married Hon. Edward Bates, and is now a widow, living in St. Louis. (Children of Jane Naylor, nee Coalter.) Caroline Naylor married Dr. William B. Natt. They removed to Livingston, S. C., where Dr. N. died, leaving a widow and five children. Sophronia married James W. Booth, of Pike county, Mo., who subsequently removed to St. Louis, and became a commission merchant. Their children were —

John N., Thomas, Edward B., and George.   Ann married a Mr.
McPheeters, who died, leaving two sons, James and Theophile,
who removed to Mississippi, where they married and raised large
families.

CASTLIO.—John Castlio, of Tennessee, married a widow named
Lowe, whose maiden name was Harrison.   They settled in St.
Charles county in 1806.   The names of their children were —Ruth,
Lottie, Mahala, Sinai, John H., Nancy, and Hiram.   Lottie married William Keithley.   Ruth married Frank McDermid, who
was killed at Callaway's defeat.   They had two children, Rhoda
and Viletta.   Mahala married Benjamin Howell, and they had
eleven children.   Sinai married Absalom Keithley.   John H.
married the widow of Capt. James Callaway, whose maiden name
was Nancy Howell.   Nancy married Felix Scott.   Hiram died
when he was about grown.   The names of John H. Castlio's
children were—John C., Fortunatus, Jasper N., Othaniel C., Hiram
B., and Zerelda E.

CAMPBELL.—James Campbell, of Scotland, settled in Essex
county, Virginia, and married a Miss Montague.   They had
only one child, James, Jr., when Mr. Campbell died,
and his widow married a Mr. Stubbs, of Richmond.   James, Jr.,
married Lucinda S. Gautkins, of Virginia, and they had ten children—Mary M., Thacker, Charles G., Nancy H., Catharine L.,
James E., Elijah F., John, Caroline, and Lucy H.   Mrs. Campbell died, and her husband was married a second time to Catharine Heihm, of Lynchburg.   He was a soldier in the war of 1812,
and died in 1872, in his eighty-fifth year.   His widow still lives
(1875), in her eightieth year, but is sorely afflicted, being both
blind and deaf.

CANNON.—Joseph Cannon married Nancy Sitton, of North Carolina, and settled first in Tennessee, where he remained until 1811,
when he removed to St. Charles county, Missouri.   During the Indian war he and his family lived in Kennedy's Fort.   Mr. Cannon
was a great hunter and Indian fighter, and had a great many adventures.   He once tracked a bear to a hollow log, and began to kindle a fire to smoke it out; but as he was stooping down to blow
the flames, the bear sprang out of the log and threw him on his back,
and then ran away.   He was so badly scared that he never saw
the bear any more.   The names of Mr. Cannon's children were
Phillip, Sarah, Rachel, Keziah, and Nancy.   Phillip married Elizabeth McCoy, and they had ten children—George, Julia A., Rachel, William R., Nancy, Ellen, John, David M., Sarah, and
Mathaneer.   Sarah married Jerry Beck, of Lincoln county, and
is now a widow.   Rachel married Raphael Florathey, and lives
in Iowa.   Nancy married John Creech, of Lincoln county.
Keziah died single.

CARTER.—Thomas Carter, of Virginia, married Judith Mc-

Crawdy, and their children were—Jesse, Thomas, Edward, Lawson, Christopher, and Dale. Thomas married Nancy Hutchings, of Virginia, and settled in St. Charles county in 1836. Christopher married Mary Soizes, whose father served seven years in the revolutionary war. They settled in St. Charles county in 1830. The names of their children were Frances, Rebecca, James, Jane, Christopher, Judith, Thomas M., Mary, George, and Rolla. Thomas M. is the present sheriff of Lincoln county (1875).

Collins.—The father of William Collins was an Englishman. At an early age William was bound out to learn the carpenter's trade, but becoming dissatisfied, he ran away and got married, which suited him better. He married Jane Blakey, of Warren county, Virginia, and they had six children—George, John, Reuben, Fanny, Elizabeth, and William. John married Fanny Curtley, and settled in Franklin county, Missouri. George married Jane Eddings, of Warren county, Virginia, and settled in St. Charles county, Missouri, in 1825. They had seventeen children—Sarah, Elizabeth, Frances, Smith, Eliza, Nancy, Clarissa, James, Elijah, Thomas, William, Tandy, George, Sandy, Jane, Mary, and Joseph. Sandy, Joseph, and Mary died before they were grown. Elizabeth, Eliza, and Clarissa married and remained in Virginia. Sarah and Nancy married and settled in Warren county, Missouri. Smith married Emily Wyatt, and moved to Oregon. Thomas, William, and Frances settled in Henry county Missouri. Elijah settled in Arkansas, and George in Warren county, Missouri.

Collins.—Nicholas Collins, of England, married Margaret Long, of Va., and they had two children, John and Lucy. John married Elizabeth Yager, of Virginia, and settled in St. Charles county, Missouri, in 1831. His children were—Sarah, Lucinda, Mary, Ann, Elizabeth, William K., and John J., all of whom, except Sarah and John, settled in St. Charles county.

Carr.—Elijah Carr was of Irish descent. He settled first in Hagarstown, Maryland, and in 1798 removed to Shelby county, Kentucky, from whence, in 1829, he removed to St. Charles county, Missouri, where he died in 1832. He kept a distillery, and was a keen, shrewd, horse trader. His children were—Ruth, James, and John. Ruth married William Boyd, of Missouri. James was a zealous member of the Old Baptist Church, but joined the Misssionary Baptists when the division took place. He married Susan Jones, daughter of Silas Jones, of Shelby county, Kentucky, and they had nine children—Sally, Elizabeth, Hellen, Mary R., John, William, Susan L., James, and Eliza J. Mrs. Carr died in 1834, and he died in 1836. John Carr married Mary Dorsey, of Kentucky, and they had nine daughters. They lived at Louisville, Kentucky, where Mr. Carr died in 1865.

Collier.—The father of John and George Collier lived in the

State of New Jersey, not far from the city of Philadelphia. He died when they were quite young, and their mother being an energetic, industrious woman, determined to do the best she could for herself and family. She purchased two milk cows with the little money that her husband had left her, and opened a small dairy. It was not long until she owned and milked one hundred cows, and in a few years had accumulated a handsome fortune. Desiring to come West, she sold her dairy and other property, and, in 1815, came to St. Charles with her two sons and $40,000 in cash. The two boys, being no less energetic than their mother, supplied themselves with a small stock of goods, and for several years followed the tiresome and dangerous calling of country peddlers, carrying their goods on their backs. They made money, and in a few years opened a store in St. Charles. Here they rapidly augmented their means, and, desiring to extend their business, they established a branch store at Troy, in Lincoln county, and shortly after another in St. Louis. Mrs. Collier bought a residence in St. Charles, and kept several negro women busy making coarse shirts and various other kinds of garments, which her sons sold in their stores. She was a devoted Methodist, and as earnest and zealous in her religion as in everything else. She always entertained the Methodist ministers when they came to St. Charles, and kept a room in her house exclusively for their benefit, no one else being allowed to use it. In 1830 she had erected upon her own grounds the first Methodist house of worship in St. Charles, which was occupied by her congregation for religious services, free of rent. She also authorized the occupancy of the house as a common school room, reserving, by way of rent, the privilege of sending four pupils of her own selection, at the then customary tuition price of $1 per month, each. The school progressed so satisfactorily that Mrs. Collier determined to appropriate $5,000 to the building of a school house for Protestant children in the village; and after giving the subject mature deliberation, she broached it to her son George. He not only heartily commended her plan, but desired to build the house himself—a larger and better one than $5,000 would procure— and that his mother's donation should constitute an endowment fund for the institution. This was agreed upon, and in 1834 the building, which has since been known as St. Charles College, was erected, at a cost, including the grounds, of $10,000. Beriah Cleland, well known to the older citizens of St. Charles, was the builder. The College was opened in 1835, under the presidency of Rev. John F. Fielding; and for many years the President's salary was paid out of Mr. Collier's private purse. The College prospered beyond expectation under the liberal patronage of its generous benefactor, who gave in all fully $50,000 to the institution. George Collier did more for the cause of education in his adopted State than any other man, and has received but little credit for it. The alumni of the College spread through Mississippi, Louisiana, and the western part of this State, and opening schools and other institutions of learning diffused the benefits of science and knowledge throughout an immense extent of country. Many of the leading men and educators of this State studied the sciences under the roof of this parent institution. Mrs. Collier died in 1835, but made provision in her will for the carrying out of her part of the philanthropic enterprise. By some mistake the sum donated by her was lost, but it was promptly replaced by her son, and at his death, in 1852, he left an endowment of $10,000 for the College, on condition that the County Court of St. Charles county donate a similar amount for the same purpose. The Court complied with the requirements of the will, and the College was promptly endowed with $20,000. George Collier married Frize Morrison, daughter of James Morrison, of St. Charles. She was a Catholic, and according to the rules of her Church, could not be married by a Protestant minister; but Mr. Collier refusing to be married by a priest, the ceremony was performed by Judge Benjamin Emmons. Mrs. Morrison wanted her daughter to be re-married by a priest of her Church, but Mr. Collier objected, saying that he was married well enough to suit him, and then added, good-humoredly, that if she wanted her daughter back again, she could take her. But the old lady concluded to let the matter drop, and said nothing more about the second ceremony.

COLGIN.—Daniel Colgin was a tailor by trade, and settled in St. Charles county (where the poor house now stands) in 1806. He made a deep cellar under his log cabin, and placed a trap door in the floor, just inside of the door, and every night when he went to bed this trap door was unfastened, so that if the Indians attacked the house and broke the door open they would fall into the cellar. He also kept an ax and a sledge hammer near his bed, to use in tapping Indians on the head; but his house was never attacked, and his ingenious contrivances were never brought into use. In 1812 he removed to St. Charles, and opened a tailor's shop in that town. Here he dressed deer skins and manufactured them into pants and hunting shirts, from which he derived a comfortable income. In 1814 he was elected Justice of the Peace, and made a rather eccentric officer. (Some of his official acts are noticed under the head of "Anecdotes and Adventures.") His dwelling house and shop were one and the same, and there was but one window in the house, which contained only two panes of glass. The old gentleman kept a pet bear chained in his yard, and the boys of the town used to torment the poor beast until it would become furious. One day while they were teasing the bear, it broke the chain, and ran the boys all off the place. After that they let the bear alone.   Colgin's wife was a native of Kentucky, and his daughters were said to be the prettiest girls in St. Charles.

CRAIG.—Rev. James Craig married a daughter of Col. Nathan Boone.   He was a Hard-Shell Baptist preacher, and preached and taught school in St. Charles for several years.   He baptized, by immersion, in the Missouri river, the first person that ever received Protestant baptism in St. Charles.   The candidate was a colored woman named Susan Morrison.   Daniel Colgin assisted Mr. Craig to perform the ceremony, by wading out into the river and measuring the depth of the water with his cane, singing as he went—

"We are going down the river Jordan,
As our Saviour went before."

Revs. John M. Peck and Timothy Flint were present, and joined in the singing.

CHRISTY.—William Christy, Sr., and William Christy, Jr., were cousins, and natives of Pittsburgh, Pa.   In 1800 the elder settled in St. Louis, where he opened a hotel and made a fortune.   The younger was quartermaster for the troops at Bellefontaine during the war of 1812, and after the return of peace, he settled in St. Charles, and went into the mercantile business, which he followed for two years.   He then went into politics, and was at different times clerk of the County and Circuit Courts.   He was also Receiver and County Treasurer, and Clerk of the Supreme Court. He married Constance St. Cyr, of St. Charles, and they had nine children—William M., Ellen, Leville, Martha T., Israel R., Mary A., Eliza, Louisa, and Clarissa.   Mrs. Christy was well educated, and did a great deal of writing for her husband.   They also kept boarders while the Legislature sat in St. Charles, and had so much patronage that they were compelled to hire beds from their country friends for the accommodation of their guests.   They paid 25 cents a week for the beds.   Mr. Christy had an apple tree in his yard that bore 40 bushels of apples one summer, and his son, William M., who was a little fellow at the time, sold them on the street, and to the members of the Legislature, at 25 cents per dozen, thus reaping a handsome income from the one apple tree.   William M. Christy is still living in St. Charles.   He served as sheriff and deputy sheriff of the county for sixteen years, and organized the first express company in St. Charles. He acted as express agent for ten years.

CHARLESWORTH. — Walter Charlesworth, of England, being captivated by the glowing tales of life in the New World, ran away from his parents at the age of eighteen years, and came to America.   He remained a while at Wheeling. Va., and then went to St. Charlesville in Ohio, where he engaged in shipping pork to New Orleans and the West India Islands.   He married Mary A.

Young, and in 1827 he came to St. Charles, Mo. They had two children, Walter J. and Eliza. The latter died, but the former is still living in St. Charles. Mrs. Charlesworth died sometime after the removal to St. Charles, and her husband subsequently married Mary St. Louis, of Canada, who died, leaving no children. Charles Charlesworth, a brother of Walter, came from England with his wife, in 1840, and settled in St. Charles. Here his wife went blind, and subsequently died, when he started on his return to England, and died at New Orleans. They had six children—George, Martha, Ann, Charles, Mary, and Hannah.

CONOIER.—Peter Conoier was a Frenchman, and settled on Marais Croche Lake at an early date. He was very fond of hunting wild hogs, which he lassoed, being so expert in that art that he could throw the lariat over any foot of the hog that he chose, while it was running at full speed. He was married three times, and had several children. One of his sons, named Joseph, while going to school, was chastised by the teacher, for some misdemeanor, and the old gentleman was greatly incensed thereat. He determined to whip the teacher in turn and went to the school house next morning for that purpose. Arriving at the school house, he drew his knife out and began to whet it on his foot, whereupon the teacher drew *his* knife, and invited him to "come on," if that were his game. But concluding that discretion was the better part of valor, he put up his knife, bade the teacher a polite good morning, and went home.

DARST.—David Darst was born in Shenandoah Co., Va., December 17, 1757, and died in St. Charles Co., Mo., December 2, 1826. He married Rosetta Holman, who was born in Maryland, January 13, 1763, and died in Callaway Co., Mo., November 13, 1848. She was buried in a shroud of homespun wool, which she made with her own hands when she was about middle-aged. Mr. Darst removed from Virginia to Woodford Co., Ky., in 1784, and in 1798 he left Kentucky with his wife and seven children, and settled in (now) St. Charles Co., Mo., on what has since been known as Darst's Bottom. Some of the leading men of Kentucky gave him a very complimentary letter to the Spanish authorities in St. Louis, which enabled him to obtain several grants of land for himself and children. The names of his children were—Mary, Elizabeth, Absalom, Isaac, Sarah, Jacob, Samuel, Nancy, and David H. Mary married Thomas Smith, of Callaway county, and died; he then married her sister Elizabeth. Isaac married Phœbe, daughter of Jonathan Bryan. Sarah and Samuel died before they were grown. Jacob lived in Texas, and was killed by the side of Col. Crockett at the battle of the Alamo. Nancy married Col. Patrick Ewing, of Callaway Co. David H. married Mary Thompson, and lived and died in Darst's Bottom. They had thirteen children—Violet, Rosetta H., Mar-

10

garet R., Elizabeth I., Nancy E., Harriet, Mary T., David A.
Lorena, Henry, Martha, William, and Julia. Mr. Darst was a very
systematic man, and for many years kept a book in which he recorded every birth and death, and all important incidents that
occurred in the community. This book would have been very
interesting, but it was destroyed by fire several years ago.

DAY.—Robert Day, of England, emigrated to America and
settled in Maryland, where he had two sons born, Frank and
Robert. The latter died while a boy. Frank moved to Wythe
Co., Va., where he married Mary Forbish. They had twelve
children—Nancy, Polly, Aves, Peggy, Elizabeth, Rebecca, Jane,
Frank, jr., Nathaniel, George, Nilen, and James. Nancy was
killed by a horse. Polly married in Kentucky, and settled in St.
Louis in 1815. Aves died single. Peggy married Solomon
Whittles, of St. Charles Co., Mo. Jane married John Proctor,
and settled in Warren Co., Mo. Frank, Nathaniel, and George
all died bachelors, in Missouri. Nilen married Susan Wilson.
James married Emily Rochester, of Virginia, and settled in St.
Charles Co., Mo., from whence he removed to Lincoln county,
where he still resides. When quite a boy he and a young friend
of his spent a night at Amos Burdine's, and slept on a bed that
had a buckskin tick. During the night they felt something very
hard and uncomfortable in the bed under them, and determined
to find out what it was. They had no knives to cut the tick with,
so they gnawed a hole in it with their teeth, and drew out a
buck's head with the horns attached, after which they did not
wonder that they had slept uncomfortably. During the operation
of drawing the horns out of the bed, the boys broke out several
of their front teeth. Mr. Robert Day settled in Dog Prairie, St.
Charles Co., in 1819, and spent the rest of his life there.

DAVIDSON.—Andrew Davidson, of Kentucky, came to Missouri
in 1811, but returned in 1813, and married Sarah Johnson. In
1830 he came back to Missouri and settled in St. Charles county.
His children were—Susan, Greenberry, William, Angeline, Eliza
J., Salome, and John. The old gentleman was a great friend of
the Indians, and in order to manifest his good feelings, he kept a
lot of tobacco with which he would fill their pouches when they
stopped at his house. One of his sons, a mischievous lad,
poured a pound of gunpowder into the tobacco, and several of the
Indians got their faces and noses burnt in attempting to smoke it.
This, of course, was taken as a mortal offence, and it was with
the greatest difficulty that Mr. Davidson kept the Indians from
killing himself and family.

DRUMMOND.—James Drummond, of England, settled in Fauquier Co., Va., prior to the American revolution, and served in
the patriot army during the war. He had two sons, James, jr.,
and Milton, who came to Missouri. James married Martha

Lucas, of Virginia, and settled in St. Charles Co., Mo., in 1834. He was a soldier in the war of 1812. He had seven children— Elias, Harrison, Mary, James, Catharine, William, and Elizabeth. Mary married Wm. E. Jackson, and settled in St. Charles county in 1835. Catharine married George M. Ryan, of Virginia, and is now living in St. Charles county. William and Elizabeth died in Virginia. Elias lives in St. Louis. Harrison married Elizabeth Wilkinson, and settled in St. Charles county in 1834. James settled in Mississippi.

DYER.—John Dyer, of Greenbriar county, Virginia, married a Miss Roley, and they had six children—George, James, John, Polly, Pauline, and Marktina. George married Margaret Hayden, of Kentucky, and settled in Pike county, Missouri, in 1838; in 1840 he removed to St. Charles county. His children were— Rosana, Elvira, Mary J., William C., Eliza, Martin V., Lucy, and Elizabeth. Rosana married Pleasant Colbert, of Lincoln county. Elvira married Dr. Sidney R. Ensaw, an Englishman, who settled in St. Charles county, in 1836. Eliza married James McNanone, of St. Louis county, who died, and she afterward married John J. Sthallsmith, of St. Charles county. Elizabeth married Frederick Grabenhorst, of St. Charles county. Martin V. is a Catholic priest, and lives in New York.

DENNEY.—Charles Denney, of Germany, settled within the limits of the State of Missouri while the country belonged to Spain. He married Rachel Clark, and they had eight children— Christine, Magdalene, Mary, Adeline, Ann, Charles, John, and Raphael. Mr. Denney was an herb doctor, and treated the simpler classes of diseases. He was also something of a dentist, and pulled teeth for people when they came to him for that purpose. He lived on Dardenne creek, where he built a water mill, which supplied the people of the vicinity with meal and flour for many years. He finally grew tired of milling, and erected a distillery, but this did not pay so well, and he went back to his former occupation. In the meantime his wife had lost her sight, but could still recognize her old acquaintances by their voices. She could give the history of every person in the county, and it was quite interesting to hear her converse about early times in Missouri. Denney finally sold his mill, and removed to the Fever River lead mines, where he was unfortunate, and lost all his property. He then returned to Dardenne, and with the assistance of his old neighbors re-purchased his mill.

DAVIS.—Lewis Davis, of Albemarle county, Virginia, had seven children—Edward, Matthew, Rachel, William, Rhoda, Martha, and Virginia. Edward married Miss Walton, of Virginia, and settled in St. Charles county, Missouri, in 1829. The names of his children were—Mary A., Joel A., and Lucy M. Mary A. married Ira Shannon, of New York. Joel A. married Frances A.

Guthrie, of Virginia.   Lucy M. married Peter Randolph, of Virginia.   Edward Davis was a blacksmith, and had a shop on McCoy's creek.   Like most of the early settlers, he was fond of a good article of whisky, and when his supply ran out he would take a sack of corn on his horse, go the distillery, and have it made into whisky, without the fear of revenue officers before his eyes, for they had no such encumbrances then.

EDWARDS.—Ambrose Edwards and his wife, whose maiden name was Olive Martin, were married in Albemarle county, Virginia, in 1775.   They had ten children—Brice, James, John, Childs, Henry, Joseph, Booker, Carr, Susannah, and Martha. Brice was a Major in the war of 1812.   He married Martha Barksdale, of Virginia, and settled in Warren county, Missouri, in 1836.   James never married, and died in Virginia.   John married Patsey Johnson, of Virginia, and settled in St. Charles county, Missouri, in 1837.   Childs married Nancy Hughlett, of Virginia, and settled in Howard county, Missouri, in 1834.   Henry married Sarah M. Waller, a daughter of Carr Waller and Elizabeth Martin, of Virginia, and settled in St. Charles county, Missouri, in 1835. Their son, W. W. Edwards, was United States District Attorney, and is now Circuit Judge for the St. Charles circuit.   His brother, A. H. Edwards, served two terms as Representative of St. Charles county in the Legislature, and is now State Senator from that district.   Both are talented and able men, and their prospects for future advancement are good.   Their father died in 1844, but their mother is still living (1875).   Joseph Edwards lived and died a bachelor, in St. Charles county.   Booker also died a bachelor, in Virginia.   Carr married Lavenba Lanier, of Virginia, and settled in St. Charles county, Missouri, in 1835.   Susannah married Carr Waller, of Virginia.   Martha married Milton Ferney, who settled in St. Charles county, Missouri, in 1837.

EMERSON.—John Emerson, of England, emigrated to America, and settled in St. Charles county, Maryland.   His youngest son, Edward D., married Elizabeth Downs, of Maryland, and settled in Pike county, Missouri, in 1818.   He was married three times, and raised a large family of children.   His son, Daniel, married Catharine Smiley, and they had thirteen children.   His first wife died, and he was married the second time to Ellen Boice, of St. Louis, who bore seven children.   Mr. Emerson was Captain of militia in Pike county for four years.   He removed to St. Charles county in 1840.   When he was a young man, courting his first wife, he went to see her one day, and got very wet in a heavy shower of rain that fell while he was on the road.   When he got to the house he found no one at home, so he built a fire and lay down before it, and went to sleep.   He slept sometime, and was awakened by his buckskin pants drawing tight around his legs and body as they dried.   They were so tight that he could not straighten himself, and while he was in that condition his sweetheart came. She laughed at him a little, and then procured him dry clothing in which to dress.

EMMONS.—Benjamin Emmons and his wife came from one of the Eastern States and settled on Dardenne Prairie, near the present town of Cottleville, in St. Charles county. Several years afterward he removed to the town of St. Charles and opened a hotel. He was also elected Justice of the Peace, and, being a man of education and intelligence, was chosen by the people of his county to represent them in the first State Constitutional Convention, which met at St. Louis in 1820. He afterward served in both houses of the Legislature for several terms, to the entire satisfaction of his constituents. In 1832 St. Charles was visited by that dreadful pestilence, the Asiatic cholera, and many persons were swept into untimely graves. Mr. Emmons fearlessly offered his assistance to the afflicted, and nursed the sick night and day; thereby saving many lives. He was assisted in this good office by a Mr. Loveland, proprietor of the ferry at St. Charles. Mr. Emmons had two children —Daphney, and Benjamin, Jr. Daphney married a Mr. McCloud, who was the first editor of the St. Charles *Gazette*. He died, and she afterward married Alonzo Robinson, a school teacher, who moved to California and died. Benjamin, Jr., was County and Circuit Clerk of St. Charles county for many years, and is now practicing law in St. Louis.

EASTON.—Col. Rufus Easton, a well known lawyer of St. Louis, removed to St. Charles at an early date, and entered upon the practice of his profession there, in which he was very successful, and accumulated a considerable fortune. He raised a large family of children, whose names were — Alton, Joseph, Langdon, Henry, Mary, Louisa, Joanna, Rosella, Adda, Sarah, and Medora. Mary Easton, the eldest daughter, married Major George C. Sibley, who served in the war of 1812. He was appointed by the Governor of Missouri, a number of years afterward, to survey the route to Pike's Peak and New Mexico. During his residence in St. Charles he improved the beautiful place now owned by Capt. John Shaw, and donated the land upon which Lindenwood College is built. His wife, before her marriage, traveled over a large portion of the United States, on horseback, in company with her father. She made several trips to New York, Philadelphia, and Baltimore in that way. After the death of her husband she visited Europe several times, and made preparations to go as a missionary to China, but death prevented her from carrying out her intentions. She and her husband did a great deal for the cause of education and religion in St. Charles, and will long be remembered by the citizens of that place.

FULKERSON.—James Fulkerson, of Germany, came to America and settled first in North Carolina, and afterward removed to

Virginia. He had twelve children—Peter, James, John, Thomas, Abraham, Jacob, Isaac, William, Polly, Catharine, Hannah, and Mary. Isaac married Rebecca Neil, of Lee county, Va., in 1799, and came to Missouri and settled in Darst's Bottom in 1814. He served in the State Senate one term. He had ten children—William N., James P., Virginia, Bathsheba V., Frederick, Catharine H., Isaac D., Margaret A., Peter H., and Jacob. William N. married Ellen Christy, and they had nine children. James P. married Louisa Stanbark. Virginia married Caleb Berry. Bathsheba married Judge John A. Burt. Frederick married Ann Miller. Catharine H. married Shapley Ross. Isaac married Mary Wheeler. Margaret A. married Gordon H. Waller, who was Judge of St. Charles County Court one term. Peter H. married Martha V. Montague, and they had fifteen children. Jacob died in infancy.

FERRELL.—Benjamin Ferrell, of Mecklenburg county, Va., had two children—Hutchings and Martha. Hutchings was a merchant, and married Mary Pennington, of Virginia. They had four children—Frederick, Benjamin P., Martha, and Hutchings, Jr. Frederick settled in St. Charles county in 1833, and never married. Benjamin P. came with his mother to St. Charles county in 1832. He married Sally Hutchings, and they had two children—Ann and Alexander. Martha died single, in 1828. Hutchings, Jr., married Ann Hutchings, and settled in St. Charles county in 1832. They had four children—Martha S., Robert W., William P., and Benjamin H. Mrs. Ferrell died, and he was married the second time to the widow of John McClenny, who had one child—Redman M. By his last wife Mr. Ferrell has had six children—Mahala, Henry, Drucilla, Susan, Julia, and Jennie.

FRAZIER.—David Frazier, of Virginia, settled in St. Charles county in 1804. He had two sons, Jerry and James. Jerry was killed in Virginia. James married Jane Anderson, of Pennsylvania, who was of Irish birth, and settled in St. Charles county in 1804. They had twelve children—David, James, John, William, Thomas, Martin, Sally, Elizabeth, Polly, Catharine, Jane, and Abigail. David married Elizabeth Fry, and lived in Virginia. James married Polly Crow. John was married first to Mary Shuck, and after her death he married Sally T. Hall. The latter was a grand-daughter of Alexander Stewart, who was captured by the British during the Revolutionary war, and taken to England, where he was kept in prison one year. When he returned he found all his property advertised for sale, his friends supposing him dead.

FLINT.—Rev. Timothy Flint, a Presbyterian minister of Connecticut, settled in St. Charles in 1816. He was an educated man and devoted much of his time to literature. Several interesting works were written by him; but in many instances he allowed his vivid imagination to lead him aside from the facts of history, and his writings are not to be relied upon in regard to accuracy. A number of his imaginary sketches of Daniel Boone have been accepted as true, and copied into leading histories of our country. One of these, representing a desperate hand-to-hand contest between Boone and two savages, in which the former slays both of his antagonists, has been represented in marble, and adorns the Capitol at Washington City. But the incident originated wholly in Mr. Flint's imagination. He was a poet, also, and wrote some passable verses. He organized a church in St. Charles, and performed a great deal of laborious missionary service in different parts of Missouri and Illinois, supporting himself and family by teaching school, assisted by his wife, who was also an excellent teacher. He opened a farm on Marais Croche Lake, where he raised cotton, and made wine from wild grapes. He resided in St. Charles county for a number of years, and then went to the South for missionary service, where he died soon after.

GREEN.—James Green emigrated from North Carolina in 1797, and settled first in St. Louis county, where he remained two years. In 1799 he removed to St. Charles county and settled on what has since been known as Green's Bottom, where he obtained a Spanish grant for 800 arpents of land. Mr. Green, who was a plain, honest farmer, had a passion for running for office, and was a candidate at nearly every election. He was always defeated, but did not seem to mind that, being satisfied, apparently, with the pleasure it afforded him to be a candidate. The largest number of votes he ever received at an election was 70, and the smallest 11. He married in North Carolina, and raised five children—Robert, John, James, Squire, and Elizabeth.

The next settler in Green's Bottom was James Flaugherty, who came there in October, 1799. He received a Spanish grant for 600 arpents of land. The next settlers in Green's Bottom, that we have any record of, were Peter, Joseph and James Jerney, who came there with their families at a very early date. All received grants of land, and the liberality of the Spanish authorities soon filled the Bottom with enterprising settlers.

GATY.—George Gaty, of Italy, came to America and settled first in Pennsylvania, where he married Christiana Smith. In 1797 he came to Missouri, and settled in what is now called St. Charles county. He had five children—John, Mary, Theresa, Christiana, and George N. John married Jerusha Burkleo, and they had thirteen children. Mary married Samuel Burkleo, and they had five children. Theresa was married first to Isaac Robinson, and after his death she married Allen Turnbaugh. She had ten children in all. Christiana married William Burns. George N. married Edna Burkleo, and they had eleven children.

GRIFFITH.—Samuel Griffith, of New York, settled on the point below St. Charles in 1795. He was therefore one of the very first American settlers in the present limits of the State of Missouri. Daniel M. Boone had been here previous to his arrival, and the rest of the Boone family must have come about the same time that Mr. Griffith did. They all came the same year, at any rate. Mr. Griffith was married in North Carolina, and had four children —Daniel A., Asa, Mary, and Sarah. Daniel A. married Matilda McKnight, and they had five children. Asa married Elizabeth Johnson; they had five children. Mary married Wilson Overall, and Sarah married Foster McKnight.

GUTHRIE.—Robert Guthrie was a native of Scotland, but emigrated to America and settled first in Virginia, from whence he removed to Williamson Co., Tennessee. He had five children— William, David, Samuel T., Robert, and Finley. Samuel T. and Robert settled in St. Charles Co., Mo., in 1819, and the former assessed the county in 1820. In 1821 he removed to Callaway county. Robert married Matilda H. Maury, a sister of the celebrated Lieutenant M. F. Maury, of the U. S. Navy. They had nine children—Diana, Eliza L., Harriet, Richard M., John M., Matthew F., Robert M., Cornelia J., and Mary. These are all dead except Eliza, Matthew F., Robert M., and Mary.

GILL.—John Gill, of Scotland, married Margaret Pitner, of Cumberland Co., Va., and they had four children—Mary, Elizabeth, Sally, and John. Mary married Archibald Bilboa, of Kentucky, and after their deaths their children moved to Indiana. Elizabeth married James Martin, and they removed to Missouri and settled in St. Charles county; they had five children. John married Mary Watts, and settled in St. Charles Co., Mo., in 1821. He was a carpenter, and worked two years in St. Louis before he went to St. Charles. They had ten children—Margaret A., Peter W., Sarah A., Elizabeth M., William I., John P., Bently T., Adam F., Lucy G., and Mary B. Mrs. Gill had a sister (Mrs. McFall,) who was scalped by the Indians, but recovered.

GIVENS.—James Givens, of Augusta, Co., Va., had the following named children—Robert, Samuel, James, Jr., John, Benjamin, and Martha. They all settled in Lincoln Co., Ky., in 1780. Benjamin married Hannah Riggs, of Kentucky, and settled in Howard Co., Mo., in 1821. John married Martha Robinson, of Kentucky. They had seven children—James, Margaret, Samuel, Robert, Jane, Alexander R., and Martha. Of these children, Martha and Margaret died single in Kentucky; Robert, Jane, and Alexander married and settled in Johnson county, Missouri; Samuel married Sarah S. Organ, of Indiana, and came to Missouri in 1823, and in 1825 he removed to St. Charles county. He was a soldier in the Black Hawk war. They had eight children, five of whom are living. Mr. Givens brought his wedding coat (a blue "pigeon-tail") with him when he came to Missouri, and his wedding boots, which had never been wet. He also brought the gammon stick which he used for hanging hogs at butchering time. These articles are still preserved in the family.

GRANTHAM.—Joseph Grantham, of England, came to America, and settled in Jefferson county, Va. The names of his children were—John, Lewis, Mary, and Jemima. John married Mary Strider, of Virginia, and they had one child, a son, which they named Taliaferro. He married Mary D. Ashley, daughter of Major Samuel Ashley, of the war of 1812, who was the son of Captain John Ashley, a soldier of the Revolution. Mr. Grantham settled in St. Charles county in 1835, and in 1836 he laid out the town of Flint Hill, which he named for Flint Hill, of Rappahannock county, Va. He built a house in the new town the same year, and kept it as a hotel. When the war with Mexico began Mr. Gratham enlisted and was commissioned Captain of volunteers. He had six children—Samuel A., Charles W., Jamison M., Martha C., Mary C., and Maria.

GARVIN.—Alexander Garvin, of Pennsylvania, married Amy Mallerson, and settled in St. Charles Co., Mo., in 1819. His cabin was built of poles, and was only 16x18 feet in size, covered with linden bark weighted down with poles. The chimney was composed of sticks and mud. The house was built in one day, and they moved into it the next. Mr. Garvin and his wife had seven children—Amy, Margaret, Permelia, Alexander, Jane R., Julia A., and Fannie D. Amy, Julia and Permelia all died single. Margaret was married first to Thomas Lindsay, and after his death she married Joles Dolby, and is now a widow again. Alexander married Elizabeth Boyd. Jane R. married Robert Bowles. Fannie D. married Robert Roberts.

HEALD.—A Mr. Heald, of England, settled in Massachusetts at a very early date. He was married twice, and by his first wife he had two sons, Nathan and Jones. Nathan was born in April, 1775. He received a military education, and entered the army as Lieutenant, but was soon afterward promoted to the rank of Captain, and at the commencement of the war of 1812 he was placed in command of Fort Dearborne, where Chicago now stands. Here they were attacked by a large body of Indians, who captured the fort, murdered the garrison, and carried Capt. Heald and his young wife away as prisoners into their own country. (See "Anecdotes and Adventures.") During his captivity he was promoted to the rank of Major, but did not receive his commission until after he had been exchanged. In 1817 Maj. Heald came to Missouri with his family, and settled in St. Charles county, not far from the present town of O'Fallon, where he spent the remainder of his life. He died in 1832, leaving a widow and three children—Mary, Darius, and Margaret. Mary married David McCausland. Darius is now living on the old place. He was married twice; first to Virginia Campbell, and second to Mattie Hunter. He has seven children. Margaret died unmarried, in 1837.—Jones Heald, brother of Major Nathan Heald, never married. He lived in St. Louis until after the death of his brother, when he went to St. Charles county, and lived part of the time at the home of his sister-in-law, and part at Judge Bates'. He died in St. Louis not many years ago.

HUFFMAN.—George Huffman was a native of Pennsylvania, but removed to Buckingham county, Va., where he married and lived until 1789, when he brought his family to Missouri. He had five children—Peter, Christina, George, Catharine, and Elizabeth. Peter was a soldier in the war of 1812. He married Susan Senate, of Kentucky, and they had thirteen children. (The names of eleven of the children were—Elizabeth, Margaret, John, Sarah, George, Abraham, Maria, Lucinda, Lucretia, Elijah, and Cassander.) Christina married Daniel Baldridge. George married Catharine Wolff, and they had five children—Peter, Elizabeth, William, Abraham, and James. Catharine married Henry Haverstakes. Elizabeth married John Weldon.

HUTCHINGS.—Charles and Peter Hutchings lived in Virginia. Peter married Elizabeth Brim, and they had eight children—John, Peter W., Elizabeth W., David, Washington, Charles, Ann, and Sally. David, Washington, Charles, Ann, and Sally all came to St. Charles county in 1831. Susan married William Peebles, and settled in Williamson county, Tenn. The other two children remained in Virginia. David was married twice, first to Sally Butler, and second to Polly Lett. Washington also married twice, first to Nancy Wooten, and second to the widow Brumwell, whose maiden name was Elizabeth Harris. Ann married Hutchings Ferrell. Sally was married twice, first to Benjamin Ferrell, and second to Robert McIntosh.

HOWELL.—John Howell was born in Pennsylvania, but moved to North Carolina, where he had three sons—John, Thomas, and Francis. John moved to Tennessee, where he died, leaving a widow and four children. Thomas lived in South Carolina until after the revolutionary war. He married a Miss Bearfield. Francis married Susan Stone, daughter of Benjamin Stone, of South Carolina, and emigrated to what is now the State of Missouri in 1797. He first settled thirty miles west of St. Louis, in (now) St. Louis county, where he lived three years, and then removed to (now) St. Charles county, and settled on what has since been known as Howell's Prairie. Soon after his settlement there he built a mill, which was called a "band mill," because it was run by a long band. This was doubtless the first mill erected north of the Missouri river, except perhaps a small one at St.

Charles. Some time afterward Mr. Howell built another mill on his farm, which was run by a large cog-wheel and was called a cog-mill. His place was a noted resort during early times. Musters and drills were frequently held there, and Indian agents in conducting Indians to and from St. Louis, often stopped there for supplies. Mr. Howell died in 1834, in his 73d year, and his wife died eight years afterward. They had ten children—John, Thomas, Sarah, Newton, Francis, Jr., Benjamin, Susan L., Lewis, James F., and Nancy. John was married three times, and died in his 87th year, leaving nine children. He was a ranger in Capt. James Callaway's company. Thomas married Susannah Callaway, sister of Capt. Callaway, in whose company he also served as a ranger. They had fourteen children. Mr. Howell died in his 85th year, but his widow survives, in her 87th year. (See "Anecdotes and Adventures.") Newton married the widow Rachel Long. They had ten children, and he died in his 74th year. Francis, Jr., married the widow Polly Ramsey, who was the daughter of James and Martha Meek. He died in his 82d year, and his widow is still living, in her 87th year. They had no children. Mr. Howell served as a ranger two years, part of the time in Capt. Callaway's company, and was Colonel of militia for five years. Benjamin married Mahala Castlio, and they had twelve children. He died in his 63d year. He was Captain of a company of rangers for two years. Susan married Larkin S. Callaway, son of Flanders Callaway, and died at the age of 33 years. She had seven children. James F. married Isabella Morris, and died in his 33d year. Nancy was married twice, first to Capt. James Callaway, and after his death she married John H. Castlio. Lewis received a classical education, and followed the profession of a teacher for many years. Some of the best educated men and women of the State received instruction from him. His life has been an eventful one, dating back to the very earliest period of the existence of our commonwealth, and as it cannot fail to be of interest to the reader, we here present the following autobiographical sketch, which he kindly prepared for this work, at the solicitation of the compilers:

"When I was eight or nine years old I went to school to an Irishman, about a year and a half, who taught school near where I lived. In about a year and a half after this, I went to school a few months to a gentleman by the name of Prospect K. Robbins, from Massachusetts, and when I was nearly twelve years old I went to the same gentleman again for a few months, and made considerable progress during this term in arithmetic. The war of 1812 then came on, and I was nearly stopped from pursuing my studies. I studied as I had an opportunity. After the war I was placed by my father in a school in the city of St. Louis, taught by a Mr. Tompkins, who afteward became one of the

Supreme Judges of this State. I did not continue in this school long, but was brought to St. Charles and placed in the care of Mr. U. J. Devore, with whom I remained several months. English grammar was my principal study while at St. Louis and St. Charles. I was now about sixteen, and when about seventeen, as my old teacher, U. J. Devore, had been elected Sheriff, he selected me for his deputy. I was accordingly sworn in and entered the service, young as I was. There were but two counties at this time north of the Missouri river— St. Charles and Howard—the former of which embraced now the counties of St. Charles, Warren, Montgomery, Lincoln, and Pike. There were no settlements any further West at this time, until you came to the Booneslick country, embraced in Howard. I had to ride over the five counties before named, collecting taxes, serving writs, etc. I continued in this business a few months, when I relinquished the office of Deputy and entered the store of J. & G. Collier, in St. Charles, as one of their clerks. I remained with them a few months, and as my father and Mr. John Collier, the elder of the brothers, could not agree on the terms of remaining with them, I went back to my father's farm, where I labored a short time, when my father, having some business in Kentucky, took me with him to that State. On our return to Missouri we overtook a small family on the road, moving to our State, by the name of Reynolds, originally from the city of Dulin, in Ireland. He and my father got into conversation, and he appeared so well pleased with the description my father gave him of this section that he determined, before we separated, to come to the neighborhood where we were living. With this gentleman, whom I believe was a profound linguist, I commenced the study of the Latin language. I can say without egotism, that I am very certain I was the first person that commenced the study of Latin between the two great rivers, Missouri and Mississippi. I found it very difficult to get the necessary books, and had to send to Philadelphia for the authors which my teacher recommended. With him I read Ovid, Cæsar, Virgil, Horace and a few others. Shortly after this (as Mr. Reynolds had left the State) I went and spent a few months with my old teacher, Gen'l. P. K. Robbins, where and with whom I studied a few mathematical branches, and this closed my literary studies at school. I finally gave out studying medicine, which I had long contemplated, and came home to my father's. I was now about twenty-one years of age, and several of the neighbors and some of my relations being very anxious that I should teach school for them, I at last, yet somewhat reluctantly, consented, and accordingly taught school a few months, and was not very well pleased with the avocation.

"About this time there was considerable talk about the

province of Texas, and about the inducements that were held out for persons to emigrate to that country. In consequence of this stir about Stephen F. Austin's colony, a company of us agreed to pay it a visit and examine the country and ascertain the prospects of getting land; but all finally gave out going except my brother Frank and myself. We, therefore, alone, left Missouri January 22, 1822, for the Spanish province of Texas, which, however, we never reached. Having gone fifty or sixty miles south of Red river, my brother, who was seven or eight years older than myself, and of more experience, thought it was imprudent to proceed further, on account of the difficulties in the way. We therefore retraced our steps and arrived at home between the first and middle of March. I labored on my father's farm until fall, and in October, when a few months over twenty-two, I left home for the State of Louisiana. I took a steamboat at St. Louis and landed at Iberville early in November. This place was about ninety miles above New Orleans, where I remained until spring, having been employed by a physician (a prominent man of the parish) to teach his and a neighbor's children, and to regulate his books, etc., he having an extensive practice. I was treated rather badly by him, and in the spring I went down to the city of New Orleans and took passage on a steamboat, and returned to Missouri, and commenced farming, my father having given me a piece of land which I commenced improving. A year or two previous to this I went a session to a military school, taught by an old revolutionary officer. I took, at this time, a considerable interest in military tactics, and a year or two after this I was appointed and commissioned Adjutant of the St. Charles Militia, my brother Frank being Colonel of the regiment. This office I held for several years, when I resigned, it being the only military office I ever held; and the only civil office I ever had was that of Deputy Sheriff, as already stated. After this time, I turned my attention to teaching and farming, and in June, 1833, I married Serena Lamme, the daughter of William T. and Frances Lamme, and great-granddaughter of Col. Daniel Boone, the pioneer of Kentucky. I was then in my thirty-fourth year. We have had six children, three of whom have already gone to the grave, the youngest of those living being now about twenty-two years old. I still continued teaching, and kept a boarding school, and had my farm also carried on, until the close of the civil war, when I stopped farming, as the servants I owned had been liberated. I therefore rented out my farm, moved to the little village of Mechanicsville, where I built and commenced a boarding school, being assisted by an eminent young lady, a graduate of one of the female seminaries of Missouri. This school was carried on for five sessions, the last two or three mostly by the young lady before named, as my health had somewhat failed.

"I have relinquished all public business whatever. I cultivate my little garden with my own hands; am now in my seventy-sixth year; enjoy tolerably good health for one of my age; can ride 35 or 40 miles in a day, and I believe I could walk 20. I am a member of the Presbyterian Church, to which I have belonged upwards of fifty years. I attribute my health and advanced age to my temperate habits, having never yielded to dissipation of any kind.

HATCHER.—John Hatcher was a soldier in the revolutionary war, and afterward served twenty-one years in the Legislature of Virginia. He married Nancy Gentry, of Cumberland Co., Va., and they had sixteen children, of whom the following lived to be grown—Nancy, Susan, Polly, Joseph, Samuel, John, Elizabeth, Martha, Henry, and Frederick. John and Henry came to St. Charles county in 1837. John had previously married a Miss Flippin, and after remaining in St. Charles county a short time, he returned to Virginia. Henry married Susan A. Speares, daughter of John Speares and Margaret Bates. They had twelve children—Ann M., Caroline, Charlotte V., Frederick, Martha, Mary E., Sally M., Permelia, Worthy, John H., Henrietta, and Samuel. Ann M. married Strother Johnson. Caroline married Hon. Barton Bates, son of Hon. Edward Bates. Charlotte V. married Daniel H. Brown. Frederick never married. Martha died in childhood. Mary E. married George W. Jackson. Sally M. married Peyton A. Brown. Permelia married William E. Chaneyworth. Worthy died when she was a young lady. John H. married Caroline Harris. Henrietta and Samuel are unmarried.

HILL.—James Hill, of Ireland, came to America and settled in Georgia. His children were—William H., Alexander, Middleton, Thomas, James B., Oliver, and Jane. Alexander was in the war of 1812. He married Miss Nancy Henry, of Tennessee, where he first settled. In 1817 he removed to Missouri and set-in Lincoln county. The names of his children were—Malcolm, James B., Jane, and Thomas A. The latter married Isabella Brown, of North Carolina, and settled in St. Charles Co., Mo. He had four children—William H., Andrew F., John A., and Middleton. Malcolm, son of Alexander Hill, settled in Texas, and his brother, James B., settled in Wisconsin. Thomas, son James Hill, Sr., married Elizabeth Henry, of Tennessee, and settled in Lincoln Co., Mo., in 1817. His children were, James A., Mary, Nancy J., and Thomas L. Nancy J. married John Wright, who settled in St. Charles county, and after her death he married her sister Mary. James Hill, Sr., was a great hunter, and spent most of his time in the woods. He died at the age of seventy-two years.

HAYDEN.—Russell Hayden, of Marion Co., Ky., married Mary

Roper, and they had nine children—Ellen, Nancy, James K., Margaret, Leo, Joseph T., Eliza, Mary J., and William B. James K. married Penina Williams, and settled in Pike Co., Mo. Margaret married George Dyer, who settled in St. Charles Co., Mo., in 1838. Mary J. married Richard Hill, who settled in Missouri in 1838. William B. settled in St. Charles county in 1838. He married Mary Freymuth.

HENDRICKS.—John Hendricks was a blacksmith, and had a shop, first at Audrain's mill on Peruque creek, but afterward removed to Mr. David K. Pittman's. He married a daughter of Phillip Sublett, and sister of William Sublett, the noted mountaineer. Hendricks was an eccentric genius, and fond of playing pranks on other people. While he was living at Audrain's mill he played a trick on his neighbor, Mr. Robert Guthrie, that came near being the cause of his death. A stream of water ran through Mr. Guthrie's farm, across which he had felled a log that he used as a foot-bridge. One night Hendricks sawed the log nearly in two, from the under side, and next morning when Mr. Guthrie went to cross the creek upon it, it suddenly sank with him into the water, and he had a narrow escape from drowning, as the water was very deep at that place. At another time Hendricks found some buzzard's eggs, and sold them to Mrs. Felix Scott for a new kind of duck's eggs. She was very proud of her purchase, and took a great deal of pains to hatch the eggs under a favorite old hen. But when the "ducks" came, and she saw what they were, she passed into a state of mind that might have been called vexation. Hendricks once had a large wen cut out of his hip, and during the operation he coolly smoked his pipe, as if nothing unusual were transpiring.

HIGGINBOTHAM.—Moses Higginbotham, of Tazewell county, Va., had eleven children. His third son, whose name was Moses, married Jane Smith, of Virginia, and settled in St. Charles Co., Mo., in 1838. They had the following children—Hiram K., Elizabeth, Sidney, Ellen, George W., and Minerva. Hiram K. married Millie Evans, and raised a large family of children before his death. Elizabeth married William A. Hawkins, of Warren county, Mo. Sidney and Ellen both lived in Virginia, where they married. George W. married Sarah A. Byer, and is still living in St. Charles county. Minerva never married, and is now living in St. Charles county.

IMAN.—Daniel Iman and his wife, whose maiden name was Barbara Alkire, settled in St. Charles county in 1818. They had nine children—Washington, Adam, Isaac, Daniel, Henry, Solomon, Katy, Mary, and Mahala. Washington married Louisa Griggs. Adam was married first to Nancy Hancock, and after her death he married Virginia Thornhill. Daniel was married first to Elizabeth Hancock, second to Martha A. McCutcheon, and third to Ann Brittle. Mary married John Urf, and Mahala married Benjamin F. Hancock.

JOHNSON.—George W. Johnson was a native of England, but emigrated to America, and settled in Northumberland Co., Va., where he married Mildred Dye, daughter of William Dye, by whom he had—Eliza J., Henry V., Robert A., George C., William B., and Amanda N. Henry, Robert, and William all died single. Eliza, George, and Amanda married and settled in Missouri.

JOHNSON.—John Johnson, of England, settled in Albemarle Co., Va., at a very early date. He had two sons, Bailey and James. Bailey married a Miss Moreland, and they had nine children— Beall, Susan W., Bailey, Jr., John, Pinckard, Smith, George, Charles, and Presley. Bailey and Charles were the only ones who left Virginia. George was a soldier in the revolutionary war. He married Elizabeth Blackmore, of Virginia, and they had nine children—Elizabeth, Hannah, Catharine, Nancy, Charles, Edward, George, Bailey and Jemima. Nancy, Edward, Catharine, and Jemima died in childhood, in Virginia. Charles was married twice, first to Rachel Woodward, and second to Harriet Ficklin, both of Virginia. By his first wife he had three children, and by the second four. In 1836 he bought Nathan Boone's farm and settled in St. Charles Co., Mo., but in 1846 he removed to Illinois. Elizabeth married Rodman Kenner, who settled in St. Charles county in 1834. Hannah married Joseph B. Stallard, who settled in St. Charles county in 1835. George S. married Mrs. Eliza A. Hunter, whose maiden name was Gautkins. She was a daughter of Edward Gautkins and Mary Oty, of Bedford Co., Va. Bailey was married twice, first to Catharine Forshea, and after her death to Nancy Campbell.

JOHNSON.—John Johnson, of Tennessee, settled on "the point" below the town of St. Charles, in 1805. His father was killed by the Indians when he was a small boy, and he grew up with a natural antipathy to the race. He became a noted Indian fighter, and never let an opportunity pass to slay a red-man. On one occasion, while the people were collected in the forts, during the war of 1812, he saw an Indian hiding behind a log not far from the fort, disguised as a buffalo, with the hide, to which the horns were attached, thrown over his body. The disguise was so transparent that Johnson had no difficulty in penetrating it, and he at once decided to give the Indian a dose of lead for the benefit of his health. So he cautiously left the fort, and making a wide circuit, came in behind the savage, who was intently watching for an opportunity to pick off some one of the inmates who might come within range of his gun. But a ball from Johnson's rifle put an end to his adventures here, and sent him speeding on his way to the happy hunting grounds of the spirit land. For more than five years after his removal to Missouri Johnson dressed in the Indian garb, and never slept in a house, preferring to repose in the open air with nothing but the heavens for a shelter. He was thirty-seven years of age when he came to Missouri, and when the Indian war commenced he joined the company of rangers commanded by Capt. Massey, and was stationed for some time at Cap-au-Gris on the Mississippi river. Before he left Tennessee he was married to Nancy Hughlin, of Nashville, and they had six children—Daniel, Elizabeth, Levi, Dorcas, Evans, and Susan. Daniel married Susan Smelzer. Elizabeth married Asa Griffith. Levi married Esther Bert. Dorcas married Thomas Fallice. Evans was married four times; first, to Susan Miller; second to Susan Sullivan; third, to Angeline Lefavre, and fourth, to Sarah M. McCoy. Susan married William Roberts.

JOHNS.—John Jay Johns was born in Buckingham county, Va., in 1819. His father was Glover Johns, a tobacco planter, and a magistrate, an office of great honor in the Old Dominion in those days. He removed to Middle Tennessee in 1831, and from thence to Mississippi in 1834. In 1836, John Jay, then in his seventeenth year, went to the Miami University at Oxford, Ohio, where he graduated in 1840. He was married the same year to Catharine A. Woodruff, of Oxford, Ohio, and returning to Mississippi, engaged in the planting business. In the spring of 1844 he removed to St. Charles county, Mo. That was the memorable year of the great overflow of the Missouri and Mississippi rivers, by which untold suffering and sickness were entailed upon the population. In 1845, attracted by the rich lands in the Point Prairie, below St. Charles, Mr. Johns settled there. St. Charles, at that time, was a small, unprepossessing village, and many of its merchants and citizens were struggling against financial ruin, which threatened them on account of the stringency of the times. In 1846 Mrs. Johns died, leaving two daughters. There were a few scattering farms on the Point Prairie when Mr. Johns settled there, but its prospects soon began to improve, and a number of enterprising persons located there. Among them were Willis Fawcett, B. H. Alderson, Abner Cunningham, John Chapman, Charles Sheppard, and James Judge. On the 2d of November, 1847, Mr. Johns was married to Jane A. Durfee, daughter of Rev. Thomas Durfee and his wife, Ann Glendy, who was the niece and ward of Thomas Lindsay. The ceremony took place at the old Thomas Lindsay farm, near St. Charles. In 1849, Mr. Johns, B. A. Alderson, Willis Fawcett, and John Stonebreaker bought the first McCormack reaper that was ever brought to the State. This gave a new impetus to the production of wheat in this great wheat growing county In 1851, Mr. Johns removed his family to the city of St. Charles, where they have since resided. He had a large family of thirteen

11

children, of whom ten are still living, four daughters and six sons. Believing a cultivated and well trained mind to be more valuable than wealth, he gave all his children a good education, and those who are grown occupy honorable and useful positions in society. Mr. Johns has been an Elder in the Presbyterian Church since he was twenty-one years of age.

KEITHLEY.—Jacob, John, Joseph, Daniel and Samuel Keithley, came from North Carolina and settled in Bourbon Co., Ky. John married and raised a large family of children, some of whom settled in Texas and California. Joseph married in Kentucky, and had but one son, John, who settled in Boone Co., Mo. Daniel married Mary Mooler, and the names of their children were— Joseph, John, Isaac, Daniel, Jr., William R., and Katy. Samuel lived and died in Tennessee. Jacob married Barbara Rowland, and moved to Warren Co., Ky., where he died. His children were—Absalom, Jacob, John, Samuel, Obadiah, Rowland, William, Levi, Daniel, Absalom, Tabitha, Isaac, Polly, Elizabeth, Katy, Patsey, Sally, and one not named, making eighteen in all. Daniel Keithley, son of Daniel, Sr., married a Miss Hostetter, and they had a daughter named Kate, who was the largest woman in the world, weighing 675 pounds. She died when twenty-two years of age. (CHILDREN OF JACOB KEITHLEY, SR.) Abraham married Tennie Rowland, and settled in Missouri in 1806. He had four children, and was killed by his horse, on Cuivre river, in 1813. His widow afterward married John Shelley. John married Polly Claypole, and lived and died in Kentucky. Joseph married Elizabeth Burket, of St. Charles Co., Mo. Samuel settled in the city of St. Charles in 1808. He was married twice, first to Polly Burket, and second to Mrs. Nancy Pulliam. He had twenty-two children by his two wives, and shortly before his death he gave a dinner to his children and grandchildren, of whom there were eighty-two present. He died in 1871. Rowland was married twice. He settled in St. Charles county in 1816, where he remained two years and then moved to Pike county. William came to St. Charles county in 1812. He joined the rangers under Nathan Boone, and served with them one year, when he joined Capt. Callaway's company. He was married first to Charlotte Castlio, who died in 1857, and he then married the widow Duncan, who was a daughter of James Loyd. Mr. Keithley is still living, in his eighty-fourth year. He had eight children, four of whom are living, viz.: Mrs. Paulina Sharp and Mrs. Elizabeth Wray, of St. Louis, Mrs. Ruth Savage, of Wentzville, and Mrs. Adeline Ward. The names of those who are dead were —John, Samuel W., Lucy, and Francis M. Samuel came to St. Charles county in 1818, and died in 1862. He was married twice, first to a Miss Owens, and second to Emma Wellnoth. He had six children. Absalom settled in St. Charles county in 1818.

He married Cenia Castlio, and they had eleven children. Obadiah settled in St. Charles county in 1825, and moved to Texas in 1869. He was married twice. Polly married Isaac Hostetter, of Kentucky, who settled in St. Charles county in 1806. Elizabeth married Joseph Rowland, who came to Missouri and remained one year, and then returned to Kentucky, where he died. Katy married Peter Graves, and lived in Tennessee. Patsy married Alfred Dithmyer, and settled in Illinois.

KILE.—George A. Kile was a native of Germany, where he married and had two children. He then came to America with his wife and children and settled in Maryland, where they had six children more. George, the youngest son, married Nancy Marshall, of Maryland, and moved to Kentucky, where he died, leaving a widow and eight children. The names of the children were —Ephraim D., Hezekiah, Alexander M., Humphrey F., Lucretia P., Susan, Stephen W., and Alfred S. In 1837 Susan, Stephen W., and Alfred S. came to Missouri with their mother, and settled in St. Charles county. Mrs. Kile died in August, 1872. Of the children we have the following record: Hezekiah was married twice. Stephen D. died a bachelor. Alexander was married twice, lost both of his wives, and then went to Colorado. Humphrey never married, and is still living. He once had a hen that laid a *square* egg, and from the egg was hatched a pullet that lived to be sixteen years old; when she was eight years old she turned perfectly white, and remained so the rest of her life. During the sixteen years of her life she laid 4,000 eggs and hatched 3,000 chickens.

KIBLER.—Jacob Kibler, Sr., a native of Virginia, settled in St. Charles in 1820. He married Victoire Cornoyer, who was born in St. Charles, and belonged to one of the old French families. Their children were—George, William, Jacob, Jr., Catharine, and Louis. George died at the age of twelve years. Jacob, Jr.. married Mary L. Drury, who died in 1873. Mr. Kibler has been identified with the press of St. Charles during the greater portion of his life. He was one of the founders of the *Chronotype;* also of the *Democrat,* one of the oldest German papers in the State, now owned and published by the Bode Brothers. Arnold Krekel, now Judge of the U. S. District Court, was editor of the *Democrat* during Mr. Kibler's connection with the paper. Catharine Kibler died young. Louis resides in Virginia. In the early days of St. Charles, Jacob Kibler, Sr., was a hatter and dealer in furs. He died in September, 1875, at the advanced age of eighty-five, his wife having preceded him to the grave by several years.

KENNER.—In 1834 Rodman Kenner, of Virginia, came to Missouri and settled near Missouriton, on Darst's Bottom, where he lived one year, and then moved out to the Booneslick road and opened a hotel where the town of Pauldingville now stands. Mr. Kenner was a first-class landlord, and his house became a noted resort during the palmy days of staging on the Booneslick road. Col. Thomas H. Benton and many other well known and leading men of earlier times, often stopped there; and in fact, no one ever thought of passing Kenner's without taking a meal or sleeping one night in his excellent beds. Travelers always had a good time there, and would travel hard two or three days in order to reach the house in time to stay all night. Mr. Kenner made a fortune, and died in June, 1876, in the 86th year of his age. (See "Anecdotes and Adventures.")

LUCKETT.—Thomas Luckett was a native of Maryland, but removed to Virginia, and settled there. He married Elizabeth Douglass, and they had ten children—John, Richard, Thomas, William, Nathan, Joanna, Nancy, Polly, Elizabeth and Ignatius. William married Nancy Combs, daughter of Ennis Combs and Margaret Rousseau, and settled in St. Charles county, Mo., in 1835. He served in the war of 1812. He had six children—Elizabeth D., Thomas H., Jane N., Gibson B., John C., and Benjamin D.

LOGAN.—Hugh Logan, of Ireland, was one of the pioneers of Kentucky. He married Sarah Woods, of Virginia, and they had ten children—Nancy, David, Ellen, Cyrus, Jane, Green, William C., Harriet, Sally, and Dorcas. William C. settled in St. Charles county, in 1829, and died in 1844. He married Sarah B. Bell, of Virginia, and they had eleven children—Francis A., James F., Hugh B., Sarah W., Mary D., Samuel F., Maria E., Harriet J.. Helen P., Charles J., and William C., Jr. Green Logan married Fannie McRoberts, of Lincoln county, Ky., and settled in St. Charles county, Mo., in 1829. His children were—Sarah J., Anley M., George, Mary F., and Fannie G.

LEWIS.—Joseph Lewis, a Frenchman, settled in St. Charles county during the Spanish administration. He married Nancy Biggs, daughter of John Biggs, of Virginia, who also settled in Missouri during the Spanish administration. They had one son, James, who was born in 1806. He married Elizabeth Gross, of Kentucky, and they had fifteen children. After the death of Joseph Lewis, his widow married Edward Smith, and they had four children—Randall, Frances, Mildred, and Lucinda.

LINDSAY.—The original Lindsay family of the United States sprang from seven brothers, who came from England before the revolution. Their names were William, Samuel, James, John, Robert, Joseph, and Alexander. William married Ellen Thompson, of Ireland, and settled in Pennsylvania. Their children were—James, Jane, Elizabeth, Samuel, William, Henry, and Joseph. Henry Lindsay and his brother-in-law, Col. Robert Patterson, who married Elizabeth Lindsay, were the joint owners of the land on which the city of Cincinnati now stands. They built the first cabin there, and dug a well one hundred and twenty-two feet deep, when they struck a large walnut stump, and being unable to remove it, and having become dissatisfied with the location, they abandoned it. They were both in the battle of Tippecanoe. Henry Lindsay married Elizabeth Culbertson, and they had one son, William C., when Mrs. Lindsay died, and he afterward married Margaret Kincaid, daughter of William Kincaid, of Dublin, Ireland, who had settled in Greenbriar county, Va. By his second wife he had—Ellen K., James, Nancy B., Preston, John K., Henry C., and Margaret J. William C. Lindsay settled in St. Charles county in 1827, and died in 1861. He was married twice, first to Mary Hamilton, and after her death, he married the widow Lewis, whose maiden name was Maria Bell. Ellen K. died single in Kentucky. James died in Lincoln county, unmarried. Nancy married Alexander McConnell, of Indiana. Preston studied medicine, and married Jane Mahan, of Kentucky. John K. married Hannah Bailey, of Lincoln county, where he now resides. Henry C. was also a physician. He settled in St. Charles county in 1835, and died three years after. Margaret J. married Dr. John Scott, of Howard county, Mo. William Lindsay, Jr., was married in Pennsylvania to Sarah Thompson, and settled in Pike county, Mo., in 1829.

LINDSAY.—Thomas Lindsay and his family lived in Scotland. The names of his children were—Thomas, Jr., James, John, Martha, Mary, Ann, and Jane. James was married in Scotland to Charlotte Kettray, and came to America and settled in St. Charles county, in 1817. His children were—William, Ann, Thomas, James, Jr., John, Agnes, and Isabella. Ann married John H. Stewart, and settled in Carroll county. Agnes married Addison McKnight, of Tennessee, who settled in St. Charles county in 1817. His mother settled in Missouri in 1800. She was a very brave and resolute woman, and killed several Indians during her life. On one occasion she had a horse stolen, which she followed forty miles, alone, found it and brought it back home. Mr. McKnight was the owner of McKnight's Island, on the Mississippi river. Isabella Lindsay married Nathaniel Reid, of Virginia, who settled in St. Charles county in 1839. Mr. Reid was a carpenter and contractor, and built the Insane and Blind asylums, and Westminster College, at Fulton. William Lindsay died a bachelor in St. Charles county. Thomas married Margaret Garvin, and was drowned in 1841, leaving a widow and five children. James was married first to Jane Black, of Virginia, and after her death he married the widow of Dr. Benjamin F. Hawkins, whose maiden name was Sarah Fleet. Mr. Lindsay is an intelligent gentleman, and we are indebted to him for many interesting items of family history. John Lindsay married Mary Stewart, of

Monroe county, Mo. Thomas Lindsay, Jr., settled in America in 1800, and in St. Charles county in 1816. He married Margaret Breckett, of South Carolina. John, son of Thomas Lindsay, Sr., settled in South Carolina, where he died. Ann, his sister, married Peter Glendy, of South Carolina, and settled in St. Charles county in 1817. The names of their children were—James, Ellen, Thomas, Ann, and Andrew.

LÉWIS.—Joseph Lewis, of England, settled in Rock Castle county, Ky., and married Sarah Whitley, the sister of William Whitley, the noted Indian fighter. They had eight children— Ruth, Sarah, Isabella, Mary A., Samuel, Joseph, William, and Benjamin. Samuel, who was a brick mason, married Mary Day, and settled in St. Charles in 1816. His children were— Joseph F., Victor, Andrew, Samuel, Jr., Avis, William, Mary A., Margaret J., and Adeline. Joseph, William, and Benjamin, sons of Joseph Lewis, Sr., settled in Palmyra, Mo. The children of Samuel Lewis, with the exception of Andrew and Samuel, Jr., settled in St. Charles county.

LACKLAND.—James C. Lackland, a native of Montgomery Co., Md., came to Missouri in the fall of 1833, and brought his family, consisting of his wife and nine boys. He settled first near Florissant, in St. Louis county, but in 1835 he removed to St. Charles, where he engaged in the saw-mill business until within a few years previous to his death, which occurred in July, 1862, at the age of 71 years. Mr. Lackland was a model man and citizen, and made friends of all who became acquainted with him. The names of his boys were—Richard, James, Jeremiah, Augustus T., Benjamin F., Eli R., Norman J., Henry C., and Charles M. Jeremiah died the first year after the arrival of the family in Missouri, sometime between his 16th and 21st year. Benjamin F. was killed in St. Charles, at the age of twenty-one, by P. W. Culver, who was intoxicated at the time. Culver was tried and sentenced to the penitentiary, but was pardoned without serving his term. Norman J. and Charles M. live at Mexico, Mo., the former engaged in the mercantile business, and the latter in the cattle trade. Eli is chief clerk of the Scotia Iron Mines, near Leasburg, Crawford Co., Mo. Henry C. is a prominent attorney at St. Charles. He was Professor of Mathematics in St. Charles College from 1856 to 1859, and also taught classes in Greek and Latin. He held the position of School Commissioner from 1859 until the office was abolished. In 1875 he was elected a member of the State Constitutional Convention for the district composed of the counties of St. Charles, Warren, and Lincoln, receiving almost the unanimous vote of the district. Only eight votes were cast against him in his own county. He was one of the leaders of that able body of men, and made an enviable record for himself as a legislator and parliamentarian.

LUSBY.—Thomas Lusby, of Ireland, settled first in Illinois, and in 1800 moved and settled in Portage. des Sioux, St. Charles county. He married Fanny Scott, and they had one child, Elliott, who was the first white child born in Portage des Sioux. Elliott married Avis Lewis, of Kentucky, and the names of their children were—Julia A., William W., Sarah, Margaret, Thomas, Louisa, Mary, Ellen, Samuel, Fanny, and Joseph, and in addition to these there were three who died in infancy. When Mr. Lusby was married he borrowed a dollar to pay the parson; and, having no horse, he raised his first crop of corn with an ox.

LEWIS.—Capt. John Lewis and his wife, whose maiden name was Peggy Frog, were natives of Ireland. They came to America and settled in Virginia, and their son, Charles A., married Judith Turner, by whom he had—Mary, Timothy P., Margaret, Catharine E., Isabella S., and Louisa. In 1817 he removed to St. Charles county and settled on "the point." Mary, the eldest daughter, married Samuel Watson, and rode on his horse behind him to their home, carrying all of her wardrobe in her lap. Timothy P. died single. The rest of the children, except Louisa, returned to Virginia with their mother, after the death of their father. Louisa married William Ferguson, for whom Ferguson Station in St. Louis county was named. The land was first owned by Charles A. Lewis, who sold it for six dollars per acre, and moved to St. Charles county. Mr. Ferguson gave ten acres of the land to the railroad company, to secure the station. Mrs. Lewis once saved her house from burning by having a churn of buttermilk convenient. She kept some of her clothes in a large chest, and one evening while looking through them with a torch in her hand, the clothes caught fire, and they and the chest were entirely consumed, and the house would have been burned except for the churn of buttermilk, which Mrs. Lewis used in extinguishing the flames.

MURDOCK.—James Murdock was born and raised in Dublin, Ireland, but came to America prior to the revolution, and took an active part on the American side in that war. In one of the battles in which he was engaged he received a severe wound in his heel, and died from its effects two years afterward. He had seven children—Nancy, Grizey, Mary, James, Alexander, John, and George. Nancy married James Clay, who settled in St. Charles county. Alexander settled in St. Charles county in 1806, and married Mary Zumwalt. John married Lucy Grider, and settled in St. Charles county. George married Catharine Kennedy. James married Lydia Bell, and settled in Missouri in 1808.

MOORE.—John Moore, who is still living in St. Charles county, near St. Peters, in his 89th year, is of German parentage. His father came from South Carolina to Philadelphia, and learned the

hatter's trade. There he became acquainted with and married
Elizabeth Bobb, and they had three children—Thomas, Maria,
and John. The two former died in infancy, and John learned
the cooper's trade. He remembers well when Gen. Washington
died, and saw him frequently before his death, as he often passed
his father's shop. When John was twenty-one years of age he
went to Kentucky, and lived in Lexington two and a half years.
He then returned to Philadelphia, where he remained five years,
and then removed to West Virginia. In 1822 he settled in St.
Charles county, where he has since resided. He was married
three times—first to Frances Dawlins; second, to Margaret Mc-
Coy, and third to the widow Eller, who abandoned him soon
after their marriage.

McKay.—Patrick McKay came to St. Charles from Florissant,
St. Louis county, about the year 1825, and died in 1834, his
wife having died two years previously. Their children were—
Susanna, Margaret, and Gregory. Susanna became a member of
the order of the Sacred Heart, and remained such for thirty-seven
years. She died in 1861. Margaret married Sir Walter Rice,
who held the various official positions of County Surveyor,
Recorder, Justice of the Peace, and Postmaster. He was also a
trustee of the Church of St. Charles up to the time of his death,
which occurred in 1859. Gregory died at the age of 21. His
widow is still living, in her 70th year; is healthy and active, and
bids fair to live to see many more years. She is well educated,
and retains her memory in a remarkable degree.

McElhiney.—Dr. William G. McElhiney and family, (at that
time four in number) came from Beriar, Hartford county, Md., in
1837. He bought a farm and settled on the Booneslick road, about
five miles above St. Charles, where he lived twenty years, and
then removed to the city of St. Charles. The Doctor was born
in Baltimore, November 15th, 1798, and retains a remarkable
degree of mental and physical vigor for a man of his age. He
graduated in medicine at the University of Maryland, in Baltimore, and was soon afterward appointed Brigade Surgeon by the
Governor of the State; he also held the same position in Missouri
after his removal. He was for many years a prominent leader of
politics in his adopted State, but of late has retired, in a measure,
from the political arena. He was elected by the Democrats
to represent St. Charles county in the Legislature, his opponent on the Whig ticket being Wilson Overall. He was
one of the messengers that notified Franklin Pierce of his
election as President of the United States, and was a
delegate to the Baltimore Convention that nominated Breckin-
ridge and Lane as candidates for President and Vice-President.
He has served as Curator of the State University at Columbia,
and was appointed by the Governor as one of the commissioners

to locate the State Insane Asylum. The names of his children were—Martha M., Virginia, Cassandra, William H., James P., Missouri, Georgia, Florida, Louisiana, Henrietta, William J., Mary Julia, Robert H., and Emma. Martha, Cassandra and Emma died young, and Virginia died at the age of twelve years. William H. was drowned. James P. is a graduate of the Old School University of Pennsylvania, at Philadelphia, and resides near Cottleville, where he is engaged in the practice of medicine. He married Edna Gaty. Missouri married Thomas Gallaher, who died in 1867, at Minneapolis, Minn., where his widow now resides. Georgia married W. W. Orrick. Florida married William H. Gallaher, who died at Minneapolis two years ago, and she now resides in St. Charles. Louisiana married Robert F. Luckett; they reside in St. Charles. Henrietta married Lee Gaty, and lives in St. Charles. Mary Julia married Edward S. Lewis, son of Hon. Edward A. Lewis, the distinguished jurist, and died in Augusta, Kansas. Robert H. graduated in medicine at the Missouri Medical College, St. Louis, and is now practicing at New Melle, St. Charles county.

McDEARMON.—James R. McDearmon and family came to St. Charles county in 1834. Mr. McDearmon was an educated man, having graduated at St. Mary's College, Virginia. After his settlement in St. Charles he became an active participant in the politics of his adopted State, and proved himself to be an able advocate of the principles of the Democratic party. The Whigs at that time were in the ascendency, but his popularity, ability and honesty were recognized by his political opponents, who repeatedly entrusted him with important public affairs. He was Judge of the County Court, and in 1844 became a candidate for the Legislature, but was defeated by the superior numbers of the Whig party. The following year he was appointed by Gov. John C. Edwards to the position of Auditor of State, which at that time was designated as Auditor of Public Accounts. He held this office until his death, which occurred in 1848. He had eight children —Aurelia, John K., Thomas H., James R., Francis L., William N., Theodoric F., and Albert G. John K. has for many years been prominent in the politics of his State and county, and, like his father, is a staunch advocate of Democratic principles. He was a student of the State University at Columbia, but was prevented from graduating by the death of his father. He read law at Jefferson City under General Monroe M. Parsons, who was killed in Mexico by Mexican soldiers, since the late war between the North and South. He finished his readings in the office of Robert H. Parks, at St. Charles; was admitted to the bar, and practiced his profession for about two years. He was Public Administrator in 1852–53, and is at present County Clerk, a position to which he has been elected several times. His wife

was Lucy A. Orrick.   Thomas H. McDearmon was elected
County Clerk in 1853, but died before he entered upon the discharge of the duties of his office.   James R. died in his 19th year,
and was at the time editor of tne St. Charles *Chronotype.*   Francis L. died in his 18th year.   William N. married Laura Sigerson,
and lives in Kansas City.   He is connected with the St. Louis,
Kansas City and Northern R. W., and is one of the Police Commissioners.   Theodoric is a prominent attorney of St. Charles,
and his name has been mentioned as a candidate for Congress on
the Democratic ticket.   Albert G. married Mary Ferguson.
Aurelia is a distinguished teacher, having been engaged in that
profession for more than eighteen years.   The widow of James
R. McDearmon is still living, in her 75th year.

MURPHY.—John Murphy, of Ireland, settled in Virginia.   He
married Elizabeth Maling, of England, and they had three children—Alexander, Nancy, and Travis.   Alexander moved to Kentucky, and from there to Ohio, and died a bachelor.   Nancy
married John Gaff, of Fauquier Co., Va.   Travis settled in St.
Charles county in 1834, where he is still living, in his 95th year.
He married Sally Campbell, of Virginia, in 1799, and they had six
children—Alfred, Eliza, John A., Rosanna, Julia, and William A.
Alfred lives in Georgia.   Eliza married Richard B. Keeble, who
settled in St. Charles county in 1833.   John A. died at Independence, Mo.   Rosanna married Henry Lawler, of Virginia, who
settled in St. Charles county in 1834.   Julia was married first to
Humphrey Best, and second to John Overall, and now lives in St.
Louis.   William A. died single.   Travis Murphy was a soldier in
the war of 1812, and has never been afraid to stand up and
fight for his rights.

McATEE.—James McAtee and his wife, whose maiden name
was Ellen Montgomery, were natives of Montgomery Co., Maryland; their parents came from Ireland.   They had several
children, among whom were three sons, Elias, James, and
Ignatius.   Elias married Henrietta Magruder, who was of Scotch
descent, and settled in Union Co., Ky.   The names of their children were—John R., Stephen T., Mary, Elizabeth, Rose, Teresa,
and Maria.   John R. became blind, and died in Kentucky, unmarried.   Stephen T. married Catharine Bowles.   Mary married
Vernon Brown, who settled in Madison Co., Mo., in 1823.   Elizabeth married Benedict Wathen, of Illinois.   Rose married
Walter Bowles.   Teresa married Leo Bowles, and Maria died in
childhood.   Stephen T. McAtee removed from Kentucky to Missouri and settled in St. Charles county in 1834.   Mr. McAtee
was prompt and reliable in all the transactions of life, and was
universally respected by all who knew him.   He held the office
of Justice of the Peace for seventeen years, and died in 1863, at
the age of sixty-four years.   His widow is still living at the old

homestead, in her 78th year. Their children were—Walter P., Mary H., John P., James E., (the two latter were twins) Stephen H., Thomas J., Phillip C., and George A.

MOORE.—Zachariah Moore, of Maryland, was of English parentage. He married Elsie Born, and in 1810, with his wife and eight children, settled in St. Charles Co., Mo., on the Missouri river. The names of their children were—Elsie, Caroline, Creene, Maria, Thomas, Harriet, James D., and Elizabeth. Elsie married James Gillett, and moved to Texas, where they both died, leaving seven children. Caroline married James Beatty, who lives in St. Louis. Creene married John Boone, and they both died, leaving several children. Maria married Horace Moore, her cousin. They died without children. Thomas settled first in Texas, and afterward moved to California. Harriet was married first to Mr. Dezane, and they had one child. After his death, she married Cyrus Carter, and died, leaving two children by him. James D., better known as "Duke" Moore, married Catharine Ward, daughter of William Ward and Catharine Frazier. The father of the latter owned the land upon which the first battle of the revolution was fought. He joined the American army and served during the war. Elizabeth Moore married Horace Beatty, and settled in Morgan Co., Mo.

McCLUER.—John McCluer was a soldier in the war of the revolution. He married his cousin, Nancy McCluer, the ceremony being performed at the Natural Bridge, in Virginia. They were of Scotch-Irish descent. The names of their children were—Arthur, John, Nathan, Robert, Catharine, Jeannette, Nancy, and Elizabeth. Nathan married Jane McClenny. Catharine married Samuel McCarkill. Jeannette married her cousin, John McCluer. Elizabeth married a Mr. Tedford. Nancy married James Alexander, who settled in St. Charles county in 1829. They had four children—John, William A., Agnes, and Elizabeth, all of whom, with the exception of William A., who is a prominent lawyer of St. Charles, removed to Virginia, and settled there. Mr. Alexander and his wife died in St. Charles county; the latter in 1833, and the former in 1835. Robert McCluer was a physician. He also served as a soldier in the war of 1812. He was married in 1816 to Sophia Campbell, a daughter of Dr. Samuel L. Campbell and sister of Hon. William M. Campbell. In the fall of 1829, he settled in St. Charles county, with his family, consisting of his wife and five children—Jeannette C., Samuel C., John A., Susan T., and Sally. Two other children, Nancy and Robert, were born after they settled in Missouri. Dr. McCluer died in 1834, at the age of 42 years, and his wife died in 1866, in her 72d year. John, Susan, and Sally McCluer died young. Jeannette married John B. Muschany, and had seven children. He died in 1861. Samuel C. married Lucretia

C. Fawcett, and they had ten children. Nancy married Rev. Thomas Watson. They had nine children. Robert married Ellen S. Brown, and they had eight children.

MEEK.—William Meek and his wife, of Greenbriar Co., Va., settled in Woodford Co., Ky., in 1804, and in 1806 they removed to Missouri, in company with David Kincaid and family. They left Kentucky on a flat-boat of their own construction, on which they had their families, their horses, sheep, cows, hogs, and household goods. The boat sank before they reached the mouth of the Ohio river, and they then transferred their families and household goods to keel-boats, and drove the stock through by land. While Mr. Meek lived in Virginia, his mother, wife and two children (James and Rebecca) were captured by the Indians, but were rescued three days afterward by a party of white men who had gone in pursuit. The Indians placed Mr. Meek's mother on a wild young colt, thinking it would run away and kill her, but the colt, seeming to appreciate the value of his burden, acted like an old, gentle horse, and she was not hurt. Mr. Meek and his wife had fourteen children, five of whom died young. Those who lived were—John, Rebecca, James, Samuel, Sally, Polly, Benjamin, Joseph, and Isaac. John was drowned in Kentucky. Rebecca, James, Samuel, Sally, Benjamin, Joseph, and Isaac all returned to Kentucky, where they lived and died. Polly was married in 1807 to John Ramsey, son of Capt. William Ramsey. They walked fifteen miles to the house of a Justice of the Peace to be married, who performed the ceremony free of charge. Polly Bryan, wife of David Bryan, who was an old lady and wore a cap, acted as bridesmaid, while Henry Bryan, her brother-in-law, officiated as groomsman. Mr. Ramsey was an invalid, and died in 1815. He was compelled to make frequent visits to Kentucky to consult his physician, as there were no physicians in Missouri at that time, and his wife always accompanied him. These trips were made on horseback, and they often had to swim the rivers that lay in their course. On one occasion they were accompanied by David McKinney, Aleck McPheeters, and a Mr. Crawford, and on reaching White river they camped for the night. Next morning they all prepared to swim the river on their horses, and McPheeters went first, carrying their bag of provisions, and his saddle-bags containing his clothing, etc. The current was very strong, and it carried away his saddle-bags and the bag of provisions, and they had to go without anything to eat for two days, as there were no settlements where they could obtain supplies. After the death of Mr. Ramsey, his widow married Col. Francis Howell, in December, 1816, who died a few years ago, and left her a widow again. She is living at Mechanicsville, St. Charles county, in her 88th year.

McGOWEN.—Henry McGowen, of Ireland, was a soldier of the

revolutionary war. He married Atha Ratcliff, of Maryland, and they had six children—Daniel, Mary A., Margaret, Julia A., Henry, and Martha. Daniel served as a soldier in the war of 1812. He married Frances Corley, and settled in St. Charles county in 1833. They had ten children—Henry C., Sarah E., Arthur M., Daniel T., George I., Francis M., Polly A., Luther A., James A., and Martha J.

MALLERSON.—Thomas Mallerson, of Connecticut, married Amy Newton, and moved to Alleghany county, Pa. Their children were—Elijah, Elizabeth, Lucinda, and another daughter, who married a man named Thankful Hays. Elijah married Miranda Robbins, of Pennsylvania, and settled in St. Charles county in 1818. Their children were—Amy, Lucinda, Elias, Moses N., Abigail, Frances W., Thomas, and Walter P. Amy married Michael Shue, of St. Louis. Lucinda married John C. Mittleberger, of St. Charles county. Elias, Abigail, Thomas, and Walter P. all died unmarried. Frances W. married Nicholas Ficklin. Moses N. married Margaret V. McCluer, daughter of James A. McCluer, of Pike county.

MACKEY.—James Mackey, of Scotland, came to America in 1776, when he was seventeen years of age. He settled in St. Louis, and was the first English speaking white man who ever came west of the Mississippi river. Mr. Mackey was well educated, and understood surveying, which secured him employment for a number of years under the Spanish and French governments. He was out four years on an exploring and surveying expedition, accompanied by a Frenchman and three Indians, who acted as chain-bearers and flagmen, and during their absence they came near starving to death. In 1803. Mr. Mackey was appointed Commandant of the territory of Upper Louisiana, with his headquarters at St. Louis. At forty years of age he was married to Isabella L. Long, who was in her seventeenth year. Her parents came from Virginia to St. Louis in 1800. Mr. Mackey died in 1821, but his widow lived until 1860. The names of their children were—John Z., Eliza L., Catharine M., Julia J., William R., George A., James B., Amelia A., and Isabella L. John Z. married the widow Kerker, whose maiden name was Maria Robinson. Eliza L. married Reuben Coleman, of Kentucky. Catharine M. married Louis Guion, of St. Louis. Mr. Guion's mother brought a small trunk with her when she came to America, that is now two hundred years old, and is in the possession of Mrs. Thomas Chapman, of Montgomery county, Mo. Julia J. Mackey married David Bowles. George A. married Fannie Miller, of Jefferson county, Mo. William K. died in childhood. James B. married Sarah Hall, of Franklin county, Mo. Amelia A. married William A. Coleman, of Kentucky. Isabella L. married Simeon L. Barker, of Kentucky, and their son, S. M. Barker, is now the

County Clerk of Montgomery county. Mr. Mackey built the first brick house in St. Louis. On the 13th of October, 1797, the Spanish authorities granted him 13,835 arpents of land, lying on both sides of Cuivre river, now in St. Charles and Lincoln counties; also 545 arpents in another tract, on the same river; 5,280 arpents on the Mississippi river, and 10,340 arpents in St. Charles district. These grants were made for services rendered the Commercial Company of the Missouri river, on a voyage of discovery up that stream, made by order of Baron de Carondelet. It was intended that the party should be absent six years, but they returned in four, having exhausted their supplies. In addition to these grants, Mr. Mackey received 30,000 arpents of land for his services as Commandant in 1803. This last grant embraced a considerable portion of land within the present limits of St. Louis, and he donated a graveyard to the city, which is now covered with valuable buildings. Mr. Mackey was a fine musician, and brought with him from Scotland a violin and flute, both of which are in the possession of his grandchildren. The violin has been in use so long that a hole is worn through it by the friction of the chin.

McCoy.—Daniel McCoy, for whom McCoy's creek is named, came to Missouri, or Upper Louisiana, in 1797, in company with his brothers, John and Joseph, and his father-in-law, Henry Zumwalt. In 1804 Mr. McCoy was commissioned Lieutenant of a company of militia in St. Charles district, and served until the close of the Indian war in 1815, when he was discharged. His discharge papers were signed by Capt. Bailey, who was First Lieutenant in Capt. Callaway's company before the death of the latter. Mr. McCoy married Rachel Zumwalt, by whom he had eight children—John, Frances, Sarah, Nancy, Elizabeth, Mahala, Margaret, and Joseph. John died single. Frances married her cousin, William McCoy, a son of James McCoy, who settled in St. Charles county in 1814. They had ten children—Nathan, Rachel, Susan, Lucinda, John, Elizabeth, Mary, William, James M. and Frances. Sarah McCoy married Fred. Keishler, who settled in Lincoln county. Nancy married John Cain, who settled in St. Charles county. Elizabeth married Phillip Cannon, of St. Charles county. Mahala married James Cain, of St. Charles county. Margaret married James Tenney, of St. Charles county. Joseph died a bachelor, in St. Charles county, in 1849. (Children of James McCoy, Sr.) James, Jr., came to Missouri with his father in 1814. He married Rachel Doty, and settled in Lincoln county. Four of his brothers, John, Martin, Benjamin, and David, also settled in that county. John McCoy, Sr., brother of Daniel, had four sons—David, John, Joseph, and Timothy. David and John settled in Texas. Timothy, usually called Tim, was an original character, and we give some anecdotes of him elsewhere. He married Sarah Van Burkleo, daughter of William Van Burkleo.

MORRISON.—William, James, and Jesse Morrison, were natives of the State of New Jersey. William settled at Kaskaskia, Illinois, and made a fortune merchandising. James and Jesse settled in the town of St. Charles, in 1800. In 1804 James went to New Orleans and purchased a hogshead of sugar, and as he returned he peddled it out to the settlers, but had enough left, upon his arrival in St. Charles, to supply the wants of the people of that county for three years. Several years afterward he and his brother bought the salt works at Boone's Lick, and operated them for sometime. James finally bought his brother's interest in the works, and the latter went to the lead mines at Galena, Illinois. The two brothers married sisters, French ladies, named Saucier, of Portage des Sioux. James Morrison had six children —Adeline, Caroline, Frize, William, James, and another son whose name we could not obtain, and who was killed by an accidental discharge of his gun, the ramrod passing through his head. Adeline married Judge Francis Yosti of St. Charles. Caroline married William G. Pettis. Frize married George Collier. When James Morrison courted his sweetheart she could speak only a few words of broken English, and he could not speak a word of French. So their courtship had to be carried on principally by those glances of the eye which speak love from one soul to another, and it would doubtless have been a very slow process if the lady had not, with true French tact, brought matters to an immediate crisis. When she met him at his second visit, she blushingly inquired: "What for you come here *so much?* Do you want to marry me? If you do, you must marry me to-morrow, or there is another man who will marry me in two days." That settled the matter, and they were married forthwith.

MILLINGTON.—Dr. Jerry Millington, and his brothers, Seth and Ira, were natives of the State of New York. They settled in St. Charles county at a very early date, and the Doctor was the first physician that located in that county. Seth Millington settled on a farm in 1818, and planted a large orchard. He also planted mulberry trees, and procured silk worms and made silk. Ira was a wheel-wright, and built the first shop of that kind in St. Charles.

McNAIR.—David McNair was a brother of Governor McNair. He lived in St. Charles at an early date, and built the first ice house ever erected there. He married a Miss Florathay, and they had two children, a son and daughter.

McPHEETERS.—Theophilus and Dr. James McPheeters settled in St. Charles county in 1816. The former bought forty acres of land near the city, and went to farming. He had two horses, which he brought with him, and every time they could get out of the lot, they would swim the river and go back to their old home.

Mr. McPheeters was an educated man, and would farm during the summer and teach school in the winter.   He built a house with a very steep roof, and the cone was so sharp that all the birds that lit upon it had their toes cut off.   (We don't believe this yarn, but anybody else that wants to, can.)   Dr. McPheeters went South to practice his profession.

MILLER.—Judge Robert Miller and his brother, Fleming, of Virginia, settled in St. Charles county, near Cottleville, in 1824. They married two sisters, named Simons.   The Judge was a staunch Democrat, and a shrewd politician, and represented his county in the Legislature several times.   He was also a good farmer, and always got the premium on wheat.   He had nine children, three sons and six daughters.

McDONALD.—Archibald McDonald, of Scotland, had four children, two sons and two daughters.   One of the sons, named Donald, married Sarah Crittenden, of Hampton Co., Va., and their son, Dennis, married Frances Orrick, daughter of Nicholas Orrick and Mary Pendleton, of Virginia, by whom he had fifteen children, viz: Donald, Elenora, Edward C., Lucy V., Mary F., John W., Louisa, Orrick, Agnes, Glenroy, Scotland, Dennis, Maud, and two who died in childhood.—John, a son of Donald McDonald, married Elenora Tidball, and settled in St. Charles county in 1836.   Their children were—Anna E., James B., Lucelia, Frances, Gertrude, Edgar, Scott, and Elenora.

NICHOLS.—Rev. Joseph Nichols, of England, came to America and settled in Pennsylvania in 1830; and in 1334 he removed to St. Charles county, Mo.   He afterwards removed to Warren county, where he resided until his death, which occurred in 1872, in his eighty-fourth year.   He belonged to the Missionary Baptist Church, and organized a church at Mount Hope, in St. Charles county, and one at Warrenton.   He married Martha R. Cook, of England, and their children were—Ebenezer, Reuben, Emma, Rhoda, and Edwin.   Rhoda married Frank A. Freymuth, of St. Charles county, who is a native of Prussia.   His father came to America with his family in 1834, and settled in St. Charles county. The names of Mr. Freymuth's children were—Elizabeth, Clara, Gertrude, Frank A., Mary B., Frederick A., Joseph A., Theresa A., Frances, Phillip, and Albert.

OVERALL.—Wilson L. Overall, Sr., of Davidson county, Tenn., was killed by the Indians.   The names of his children were— Isaac, William, Nathaniel, Wilson L., Jr., and Elizabeth. Nathaniel settled in St. Charles county in 1797.   He married Susan Squires, and they had four children—Louisiana, Isaac, Jackson, and Eliza.   Wilson L., Jr., also settled in St. Charles county and became County Judge.   He married Mary Griffith, and the names of their children were—Ezra, Daniel, William, Samuel, Wilson, Asa, Richard H., Lucretia, and Mary.   His first wife died, and he was married the second time to the widow Gould, by whom he had one son, Oscar. His second wife died, also, and he was married the third time to the widow Patton, by whom he had three children—Hannah M., John H., and Eliza. Elizabeth, daughter of Wilson L. Overall, Sr., married William R. Miller, who was killed by the Indians while on a hunting and trapping expedition, and his head was cut off and placed on a pole by the roadside.

ORRICK.—The parents of Capt. John Orrick were natives of Virginia, but of English ancestry. The Captain was born at Bath, or Warm Springs, Berkeley Co., Va., January 5, 1805. His father was a planter, and he followed the same occupation until he was thirteen years of age, when he was apprenticed to learn merchandising, at Reading, Pa., where he remained nine years. He then went to Lancaster, Pa., where he resided three years. In the meantime he had saved a portion of his earnings, and during the excitement in the Pittsfield coal regions he purchased, with the assistance of his former employer, some property, from the sale of which he realized a profit of $1,000 in the short space of six weeks. He then removed to Boonesboro, Md., and, in partnership with his brother, went into the mercantile business. But their success did not meet their expectations, and in 1833 they sold out, emigrated to Missouri, and located in St. Charles, where they resumed their mercantile business, and met with great success. But unfortunately they made heavy advances to parties engaged in the fur trade in the mountains, and in 1836, owing to the low stage of water, which obstructed navigation, and the hostility of the Indians on the upper rivers, they met with heavy losses, and were compelled to suspend. Previous to this misfortune Capt. Orrick had been elected Justice of the Peace, and in 1840 he was elected Sheriff of the county, on the Whig ticket. At the expiration of his term he was re-elected, and served four years in all. In 1844 the Whigs elected him to represent the county in the Lower House of the State Legislature. At the close of his term he engaged in farming, which occupation he followed for about two years, and then went into the boating business. In 1851 he took the United States census for St. Charles county, and when the North Missouri railroad was built he became one of the directors, in which capacity he served about four years. Capt. Orrick was married in 1833, to Urila Stanebru, of Washington Co., Md. One of his sons, Hon. John C. Orrick, represented St. Charles county in the State Legislature two terms, and was chosen Speaker of the House the last term. He is a graduate of St. Charles College, having received his diploma from Dr. Anderson. He is at present a prominent attorney of St. Louis, and a leader of the Republican party of the State.

12

PEREAU.—Joseph Pereau was born in Montreal, Canada, March 15, 1775, and settled in St. Charles, Mo., sometime during the latter part of the Spanish rule. On the 13th of January, 1807, he was married to Marie Louise Savoy, who was an only child, by whom he had—Charles, Joseph P., Isidore, Catharine M., Mary L., Sulpice P., Alexander, Ursula M., and Eleanor M. Mr. Pereau died of cholera in 1833. He possessed many good qualities of head and heart, and is remembered with pleasure by the older citizens of St. Charles. After his death his widow married Mr. Lattraille, whom she also survived. Her death occurred in 1847. Charles Pereau married Louise Dodier, and died a month after. His widow subsequently married Mr. Lorain, and she died about four years ago. Joseph P. married Martha Martineau, who died five years afterward. In 1833 Mr. Pereau, in company with his brothers, opened a brickyard in St. Charles, after which he spent twenty-five years in the employ of the American Fur Company, under the various firms of Chouteau, Sarpie, and the Baker Brothers, at Forts Union and Benton, in the capacity of Indian trader and trapper. He is now living in Richardson Co., Nebraska. Isidore Pereau died in his 17th year. Catharine M. died in infancy. Mary L. married her cousin, William S. Pereau, who came to St. Charles from Montreal, Canada, in 1831. They were married by Rev. Charles Van Quickenborn, S. J., under whose supervison the Church of St. Charles was built. Mrs. Pereau and others were the last who received their first communion in the old log church, which stood on Main street, part of the square being now occupied as a lumber yard by Holrah & Machens, and which is well remembered by the older Catholics of St. Charles. A portion of the square was used as a cemetery in early days. Of that party of young communicants only three are living, viz: Miss Louise Chauvin, (at present residing in St. Louis), Mrs. Iott, and Mrs. Pereau. The pastor at that time was Rev. P. J. Verhægan, S. J., who died in 1868. He was closely identified with the early history of the Church, and his memory will ever be cherished by his parishoners. Mrs. P. was also one of the first who was confirmed in the then new stone church, which was torn down several years ago to make room for the new, large, and handsome brick structure erected within the last eight years by Rev. John Roes, S. J. Bishop Rosati administered confirmation to the applicants. Sulpice Pereau died at the age of twenty. Alexander married the widow of Holland Rice, whose maiden name was Eliza Earl. In 1864 he went to California, from Lexington, Mo., and is supposed to be dead, as he mysteriously disappeared from his family and has never since been heard from. His family reside in Oakland, Cal. Ursula M. married Samuel J. Tyner, and died in Hopkinsville, Ky., in 1862. Two of her children, Eleanor B. and Andrew, are living in St. Charles county, the former having married Christy P. McAtee; another, Mary J., living near Grenada, Miss., married Samuel Harper; Thomas J. is practicing medicine in Memphis, and Samuel is living in Christian Co., Kentucky, also her other children. Eleanor M. was married twice. Her first husband was William L. Earl, who died in Lexington, Mo., in 1852. They had two children, one of whom died. The other, James A., married the eldest daughter of August Gamache, and resides in South St. Louis, Station B. She was married the second time to Joseph Pourcillie, of South St. Louis, Station B, where she now resides. Wm. S. and Mary L. Pereau had six children—Thomas C., Priscilla L., Joseph H., William A., Mary U., and Chas. B. Thomas C. and Charles B. died in infancy. Priscilla L. married Benjamin Parham, and died in 1856. Joseph H. married his cousin, Martha P. Pereau. During his youth he traveled extensively over California and Mexico, operating in the mines. He subsequently returned to St. Charles, and in October, 1871, in company with his brother, William A. Pereau and William S. Bryan, established the St. Charles *News*. The following year he disposed of his interest in that paper and removed to Nebraska, where he has since resided, engaged in agricultural pursuits. William A. Pereau is well known in St. Charles, from his connection with the various newspaper establishments of that place. He was a soldier of the "Lost Cause," and participated in a number of the hottest contests of that war. In February, 1873, after having disposed of his interest in the St. Charles *News*, he went to Texas and traded in "long horns," and, in a financial point of view, got badly "hoisted." Mary U. married Joseph McDonald, of St. Charles county, and is now residing near Dawson's Mill, Richardson Co., Nebraska.

PEARCE.—Gideon Pearce, of England, settled in the State of Maryland, on the Chesapeake Bay, about the year 1675. He had a grandson named Thomas Pearce, who was married three times. The name of last wife was Ann Evert, by whom he had five children—Gideon, James, Thomas, Jr., Elizabeth, and Bartrus. Gideon, James, and Bartrus died in Maryland, unmarried. Thomas, Jr., married Catharine Comegys, of Maryland, and settled in St. Charles county, Mo., in 1820. They had ten children—Anna, Maria, Elinga, Miranda, Caroline, William, Catharine, Thomas, Matilda, and Benjamin. Anna married Cautious Money, and returned to Maryland. Maria was married twice, first to Richard Talbott, and second to Henry Rengo. Elinga married, lived and died in Maryland. Miranda and Catharine died young. William married Eve Baldridge. Thomas married Mrs. Elizabeth Wetmore. Matilda married Jonathan Zumwalt. Benjamin married Martha Camp.

PITMAN.—The grandfather of the Pitman families of St. Charles and Montgomery counties came to America with the Penn colony in 1681; but he afterward settled in Campbell county, Va. His grandchildren were—William, Thomas, John, and two daughters, Mrs. Hall and Mrs. Gill, whose first names we could not obtain. William was one of the early pioneers of Kentucky, on the Daniel Boone order. He lived and died in that State. Thomas married a Miss Berry, of Warren county, Ky., and they had five sons and several daughters. One of the daughters, named Rachel, married Christopher Hutchings, who settled in St. Charles county in 1811. They had—Albert G., Beverly T., Christopher, Melvina, and Nancy. Richard B., a son of Thomas Pitman, married Lucinda Hutchings, and settled in St. Charles county in 1811. They died and left two sons, James M. and Andrew J. The former moved to Quincy, Ills. John Pitman, a brother of Thomas, settled in St. Charles county in 1810. He married Dorothy Robinson, of Virginia, by whom he had three sons and one daughter —Chriscopher I., Irvine S., Peyton R., and Mary I. His first wife dying, he was married the second time to the widow Burns-Price, of Virginia, whose maiden name was Magdelene Irvine. She bore him one son, David K., and died in 1830. Mr. Pitman died in 1839, in his eighty-sixth year. Christopher, the eldest son of John Pitman, died in infancy. Irvine S., was married first to Nancy Talbott, daughter of Col. Hale Talbott, whose wife's maiden name was Jane Irvine. After her death he married Rachel Sweet. Mr. Pitman was a tanner by trade, and built a tanyard on Massey's creek, in (now) Warren county. In 1821 Gov. McNair commissioned him Colonel of the 15th regiment of Missouri State militia. He was also the first Sheriff of Montgomery county, and served as County Judge of that county for several terms. Mr. Pitman was a good violinist, and very fond of dancing. Mary I. Pitman married Thomas D. Stephenson, of Kentucky. David K., now living in St. Charles county, was married first to Caroline L. Hickman, of Clark county, Ky., who was a daughter of Richard Hickman and Lydia Callaway. His second wife was Eliza H. Baker. Mr. Pitman has for many years been a leading member of the Southern Methodist Church, and has filled many prominent and responsible positions to the entire satisfaction of his brethren. He has had much to do with the educational institutions of that Church, and his son, Prof. R. H. Pitman, Principal of the Methodist Female College at Fayette, Mo., is well known all over the State as an experienced and successful educator.

PRICE.—Mike Price, a German, settled in St. Charles county at a very early date. He married Nancy Weldon, and they had— William B., John, Absalom, Miletus, George, and Allen. William B. married and had but one child, a daughter, who married an Irishman named Tim Sweeney. Rev. Thomas Watson performed the ceremony, and as soon as he was done, Tim pulled out his pocket-book and paid the fee, before he had seated his bride. He had provided a jug of good whisky, which he left on the outside, and the marriage fee having been satisfactorily arranged, Tim invited the parson out to take a drink, which he, of course, declined. Tim went home that night without his bride, and came back after her the next day. In about twenty years they had twelve children, and Tim surprised the district school master one morning by presenting himself at the door of the school house with nine of them to be placed under his charge. He said he would have brought three more, but their mother had n't finished their clothes. They were promptly on hand next morning, and increased the number of pupils to respectable proportions.

PALLARDIE.—Pierre Pallardie is probably the oldest native-born citizen of St. Charles county. He was born in that county in 1800, and has lived continuously in the city and county ever since. His father came to St. Charles at an early date, and died on Peruque creek, twenty-five years ago. Mr. Pallardie has lived at his present residence on Fifth, between Lawrence and Lewis streets, for thirty-nine years. In his boyhood days that locality abounded in deer, wild turkeys, and other game, and a man could kill all he wanted, and more too, without exhausting the supply. After he began housekeeping he frequently had as many as two hundred smoked venison hams ahead of his immediate wants, and often fed them to the hogs in order to get them out of the way. The howl of the wolf broke the stillness of the woods at night, and sheep-raising was a precarious business. They also had black-tailed elk and a few bear. Their plows in those days were made entirely of wood, and the only vehicle which approximated a wagon was the French *charrette*, a two-wheeled concern, with no tires on the wheels. Tar was unknown, and they greased the axles with *fiante de vache*, and at a later date soft soap. Mr. Pallardie is still able to do a day's work in the harvest field, and he possesses great activity for a man of his advanced age. His health has always been good, probably because he relied more upon nature to keep his system in tone than upon nostrums and medicines. He remembers the following physicians who practiced in St. Charles city and county during his younger days—Reynal, Millington, Wilson, Stoddard, Graham, Twyman, Lay, and Watson. The latter came to St. Charles in 1833. Mr. Pallardie has been married three times; first to Elizabeth Cornoyer; second to Eulalie Sarie, and third to Sarah Jane Cole. He has had twenty-one children in all, only ten of whom are living. His first wife had two children, both of whom are dead. A son of one of these children resides in Montgomery county. By his second wife he had twelve children, four of whom are living—Francis L., August, Elizabeth, and John. Francis L.

has been in the Indian country for many years, and has made frequent visits to Washington with delegations of Indian chiefs, as interpreter. When last heard from he was traveling toward the Black Hills. August is a broom maker, and lives with his father. Elizabeth married Louis McDonald, and lives in Livingston county. John resides at Colorado Springs. By his last wife Mr. Pallardie had seven children, five of whom are living, the other two having died in infancy. The names of the survivors are—Sophie, Alberteen, Michael, Mary E., and George. Sophie married Edward Deversia, and lives near Florissant, in St. Louis county.

RIGGS.—General Jonathan Riggs, whose name has frequently been mentioned in this work, and particularly as Lieutenant under Capt. Callaway at the time of his death, was the son of Rev. Bethel Riggs, a Baptist preacher, of Campbell Co., Ky. In 1812 he removed to Missouri, and settled within the present limits of Lincoln county; and in 1813 he organized the Sulphur Springs Baptist Church. His son Jonathan married Jane Shaw, of Campbell Co., Ky., and they had ten children—Samuel, Franklin, Tucker, Clinton, Nancy, Epsy, Lucinda, Matilda, Eliza, and Sally. Samuel was killed in Texas, by a runaway team. Franklin died in Wisconsin. Tucker lives in California. Clinton lived in Louisiana, Mo. Nancy married James Shaw. Epsy married Eli H. Perkins. Lucinda married a lawyer, named Raymond. Matilda married John Massey. Eliza married John Mitchell. Sally married Daniel Draper. General Riggs settled in Lincoln county, three miles north of Troy, on the Auburn road, where he died, in 1835. His widow died in 1873, and was buried at Louisiana, Mo. The remains of several of the children, who had died and were buried in Lincoln county, were removed in 1874, and re-interred by the side of their mother's grave.

RICE.—An Englishman named Rice settled on the point in St. Charles county at a very early date, and started a large dairy. His wife made cheese and sold it to the soldiers at Bellefontaine Barracks, in St. Louis county. On one occasion, as she was returning home after having sold her load, she met a Mr. Loveland, a widower, who wanted to buy some cheese. She told him she had just sold out, but her daughter had some, and if he would go· home with her he could buy it. So he went along and bought the cheese, and then courted the girl and married her. The old gentleman often said, afterward, that that was the most successful trip his wife ever made — she had sold all of her own and her daughter's cheese, and found a husband for the daughter besides.—Holland Rice, a brother of this girl, was a farmer and cheese maker also, and had a happy turn of utilizing his resources. Being in need of a smoke house, he sawed off a large hollow sycamore tree, about fourteen feet from the ground, and covering it with clapboards, had as neat a smoke house as he could desire. He then built a shed room at the side of the tree, which he used as a cheese house.

RAMSEY.—Capt. William Ramsey, a revolutionary soldier, came to Missouri in 1800, and settled on a small stream in St. Charles county, which has since been known as Ramsey's Creek. He removed from there and settled within the present limits of Warren county, not far from the village of Marthasville. Capt. Ramsey was at the battle of Yorktown, and witnessed the surrender of the British army under Lord Cornwallis, and during the Indian war in Missouri he commanded a company of rangers. He died in Boone Co., Mo., May 22, 1845, aged 104 years. He was married twice, and by his first wife he had—Robert, John, William, Jr., India, Elizabeth, and Peggy. Robert married a Miss Smith, and lived near Marthasville. (A history of the murder of his family at that place has already been given.) India married Thomas Gillmore, who was a ranger under Capt. Callaway, and present at his defeat. Elizabeth married Dabney Burnett. Peggy and William married Bryans. John married Polly Meek, and after his death his widow married Francis Howell.

ROBBINS.—Prospect K. Robbins was a native of Massachusetts, but came to Missouri and settled in St. Charles county in 1810. He served as first Lieutenant in Callaway's first company of rangers. He was a finely educated man, a good surveyor, and taught school for a number of years in St. Charles county. He was the first, and for many years, the only teacher of surveying in that county. He subsequently removed to Ste. Genevieve county, where he died.

RICHEY.—John Richey, of Pennsylvania, married Cynthia Mallerson, and settled in St. Charles county in 1818. He built a small log cabin and covered it with linden bark, and sixteen persons lived in that one little cabin. One summer they were all sick of fever, and not one well enough to wait on the others. The names of Mr. Richey's children were—Rosana, Emma, John, Thomas, and Cynthia.

ROBBINS.—Thaddeus Robbins, of Pennsylvania, settled in St. Charles county in 1818. He was a mill-wright by trade. The names of his children were — Thaddeus, Welcome, Miranda, Sophia, Moses B., Frederick, Abigail, Thomas J., and Samuel. Thaddeus died single, while on his way to Pennsylvania. Welcome married Maria Mittleberger. Moses D. married Polly Best. Frederick and Samuel died single. Abigail married David McKnight. Thomas J. married Elizabeth Ewing. Miranda married Elijah Mallerson, of Pennsylvania, who settled in St. Charles county in 1818.

RUTGERS.—In 1801 Aaron Rutgers received a grant of 7,000

arpents of land, on condition that he would build a saw and grist mill, and open a store on Dardenne creek, not far from where Cottleville now stands. He built several mills before he got one to stand, and was at a very heavy expense.

REDMON.—George W. Redmon, with his wife and four children, emigrated from Clark county, Ky., in 1828, and settled in St. Charles. He was one of the citizens who, in conjunction with Nathan Boone, took the first steps toward incorporating the town of St. Charles, and laying off the commons, which were leased for a period of nine hundred and ninety-nine years. Mr. Redmon died in 1833, but his widow is still living near St. Charles, at the age of 85 years. Their children were—John W., Thomas J., Permelia A., and Lucinda. John W. is an active business man, and has acquired a comfortable fortune. He married Anna Miller, of Columbia, Mo. Thomas J. was a volunteer in the Black Hawk war; also in the Seminole war in Florida. He died in 1842. Permelia married Charles Wheeler, a lawyer, of Lincoln county, where she now resides. Lucinda married Major N. C. Orear, and died in 1852. Major Orear was for many years connected with the press of St. Charles, and was for a long time intimately connected with the manufacturing and commercial interests of the city and county. He removed to St. Louis a few years since, and is now engaged in the real estate business in that city.

STALLARD.—Walter Stallard and his wife, Hannah Pitts, were both of Virginia. Their son, Randolph, married Mary Bullett, of Culpepper Co., Va., and they had seven children—Susan, Maria, Lucy, Thomas, Joseph B., Randolph, and Harrison. Joseph B. was a soldier in the war of 1812. He married Hannah Johnson, and settled in St. Charles county in 1836. They had seven children—Maria L., Mary E., Amanda M., Mortimer, Adelia, Benjamin H. and George R., who died young. Mary E. married B. H. Boone; Maria L., J. C. Luckett; Amanda M., A. S. Clinton; Adelia, Col. Thomas Moore; and Mortimer, Amy Craig.

SHELTON.—Capt. James Shelton was an officer in the war of 1812, and died in 1814. He married Frances Allen, daughter of William Allen, and they had—Nancy M., Pines H., Mary M., and James N. Mrs. Shelton and her children came to Missouri in 1830. Nancy M. married William Frans, and had four children. Pines H. was married three times, first to Rebecca Carter, second to Mary Wyatt, and third to Mary Scales. He had ten children in all. Mr. Shelton represented St. Charles county in the Legislature several terms, and was in the State Senate four years. He subsequently removed to Texas, and served several terms in the Legislature of that State. He now lives in Henry Co., Mo., and is an influential and highly esteemed citizen.

Mary M. married William M. Allen, her cousin.   James N. married Jane Carter, and removed to Texas, where he died, leaving a widow and several children.

SMITH.—A Mr. Smith and his wife, of Germany, settled in Baltimore, Md., at an early date, where they made a fortune, and died. Their son, John A. Smith, was a soldier of the revolution, and became noted for his daring and bravery.   After the close of the war he married, moved to Kentucky, and settled on Licking river, where he remained two years, and in 1799 he came to Missouri, and settled in St Charles county.   He had two sons and one daughter—John A., Daniel, and Elizabeth.   John A. married Elizabeth Shelly, and they had—John A., Jr., Rebecca, Job, Asa, and Daniel.   Mr. Smith died of cholera.   Daniel married Elizabeth Hostler, and they had—Levi, Jesse, Isaac, John, Mahala, Eliza, and Daniel, Jr.   He was married the second time to Polly Drummond, and they had one child, Duke Y.

SMITH.—William Smith and his wife, Joice Humphrey, settled in Montgomery Co., Ky., in 1790.   They had—George, Daniel, William, Jr., Henry, and Enoch.   Mr. Smith's first wife died, and he was married the second time to Mary E. Holley, of Virginia, by whom he had — John, Robert T., Elkanah, Sarah, Elizabeth, Mary, and Lydia.   John married Elizabeth Lyle, and settled in St. Charles county in 1819.   Elkanah was married first to Fanny Botts, of Kentucky, and after her death he married Sarah Green, of Missouri.   He settled in Callaway county, Mo., and built a wool factory in Fulton, in 1826.   Elizabeth married Micajah McClenny, an early settler and prominent citizen of St. Charles county.   Sarah married Richard Crump, who settled in Callaway county in 1820.   Nancy married Ira Nash, of Boone county.   Henry came to Missouri and settled in Warren county in 1831.   He married Nancy Davis, and they had—George, Mary, Salley, Nancy, Elizabeth, Owen, Maria, John D., Rebecca, and William.   George was a distinguished lawyer, and died in Kentucky.   Mary married Anthony Wyatt, of Warren county.   Nancy married James McCluer.   Elizabeth married James J. Smith.—The ceremony was performed by Rev. Dr. Smith, and they had seventeen attendants, all named Smith.—Owen married Eliza Post, of Callaway county.   Maria married Hon. Henry Abington.   John D. married Susan Gizer.   Rebecca was married twice; first to Grenade Harrison, and second to Thomas Travis. She is a widow again, and lives in Warren county.   William married Elizabeth Wright.

SULLIVAN. — William Sullivan, of Maryland, married Susan Simons, of Virginia, and their children were—Jerry, Charlotte, Elizabeth, Virenda, Nancy, Davis, and St. Clair.   Jerry served in the war of 1812, and married Frances Collins, of Albemarle Co., Va.   They settled in St. Charles Co., Mo., in 1825.   Mr.

Sullivan was a school teacher, and a member of the Old or Iron-side Baptist Church. His children were—Harriet J., Susan F., Nancy E., Clarissa A., and Mary C. Harriet married Pleasant Kennedy, of Warren county. Susan F. married Jesse E. Darnell, of St. Charles county. Nancy E. died single. Clarissa A. married Fielding C. Darnell. Mary C. married James Love, of Warren county. Davis married Mary Summers, of Virginia, and settled in St. Charles county in 1835. The names of their children were—Frances, George, St. Clair, and William.

STEWART.—William Stewart settled in Green's Bottom, St. Charles county, in 1798. He married Sally Howell, by whom he had—Susan, John, Nancy, Francis H., Elias C., and Melcina, all of whom married and became substantial citizens. E. C. Stewart was Sheriff of St. Charles county several times, and was a man of considerable influence in the public affairs of his county. William Stewart had a brother named Jackey, who belonged to the rangers during the Indian war; and on the day that Captain Callaway was killed he and Jacob Groom were hunting and scouting in the woods not far distant, when they were attacked by the Indians, who fired upon them and wounded Stewart in the heel. Both of their horses were also wounded, Stewart's mortally, and after running a short distance it fell from exhaustion and loss of blood. The Indians were close upon them, and it was impossible for Stewart to escape on foot, wounded as he was. But Groom, with great generosity, gave him his horse, and they both succeeded in escaping to Fort Clemson. A man named Dougherty was killed by the Indians the same day, in the vicinity of Groom's farm. Jackey Stewart married Lucy Crump, and they had—William, Edward, Joseph, Coleman, Mary, Sarah, and George.

SCOTT.—Felix Scott, of Monongahela county, Va., settled in St. Charles county in 1820. He was educated for a lawyer, and represented St. Charles county in the Legislature several times, and also in the State Senate, and was Justice of the Peace in Dog Prairie for many years. He was a great fighter, but never got whipped. His son-in-law once challenged him to fight a duel, and Scott accepted the challenge. They were to fight with double-barrelled shot-guns, and Scott was not to fire until after his son-in-law had discharged his piece. When the fight came off, Scott waited patiently until his son-in-law had fired, and then, instead of shooting him, he laid his gun down, and gave him a good pounding with his fists. In 1846 Mr. Scott removed to California, and from there to Oregon. He was an ambitious stock raiser, and exhibited some of his fine cattle at the Oregon State Fair, but did not secure a premium. Determined not to be beaten in future, he went to Bourbon county, Ky., and purchased a herd of blooded cattle, which he drove across the plains to Oregon. But when he was within a day's travel of home, he was killed by a man who accompanied him, and his murderer ran away with the cattle, and was never heard of again. Mr. Scott was married twice. The names of his children were—Taswell, George, Presley, Herma S., Nancy, Ellen, Harriet, Julia, Felix, Jr., Maria, and Marion.

SPENCER.—George Spencer married Sally McConnell, of St. Charles county, April 14th, 1307. Their marriage certificate was the first that was issued in St. Charles district under the American government. The ceremony was performed by Ebenezer Ayres, a Justice of the Peace. They settled on the Salt River road, about three miles above St. Charles, and raised sixteen children. Robert Spencer, brother of George, was the first Judge of the Court of Common Pleas for the District of St. Charles, receiving his appointment in December, 1804. He lived on the point below St. Charles, and in 1822 built the first brick house in that locality. During the overflow of 1824, the water came up into the second story, and not long after, the house was set on fire by lightning, and destroyed. Mrs. Spencer was a very energetic woman. She milked thirty cows, and made large quantities of butter and cheese for market. Wild cats and catamounts were abundant in that region, and her cows would sometimes come home with holes eaten in their shoulders by these animals. The names of Mr. Spencer's children were—Robert, Jr., Harriet, William, Joseph, Rebecca, John, Sally, and Maria. The girls were all well educated, and taught school. Maria was the only one that married.

SUBLETT. —William Sublett and David Swope, both of Kentucky, settled in St. Charles in 1818, and put up the first billiard table in that place. Sublett served as a Constable in St. Charles, and afterward went with Gen. William H. Ashley on his Rocky Mountain expedition. He had nothing but his rifle and a buckskin suit that was given him by the citizens of St. Charles. He was absent five years, and walked all the way back, traveling at night and lying by during the day, for fear of Indians. Gen. Ashley, who had formed a strong friendship for him, fitted him out with a stock of goods, and sent him back to the mountains, where he made a fortune trading with the Indians. He then returned to St. Louis and opened a large store, in company with Robert A. Campbell. Sublett thought a great deal of the Indians, and had a wigwam built in the rear of his store, where he maintained a family of them during his life-time. He had no children, and at his death he willed his property to his wife, with the condition that it should belong to her so long as she did not change her name. His intention was that she should not marry again, but she afterward married her husband's brother, Solomon, and retained the property while she evaded the intention of the will.

SHAW.—Samuel S. Shaw, of England, settled in Philadelphia, where he married Charlotte Wood, by whom he had Samuel S.,

Jr., and John.   The latter entered the service of the United States Navy, where he died.   Samuel S., Jr., married a widow named Wilson, of Boston, whose maiden name was Ann B. Thompson, a daughter of Aaron Thompson and Margaret Davidson.   Mr. Shaw settled in St. Charles in 1819, and went into the mercantile business in partnership with a man named Mechatt. He died in 1823, and his widow continued the business for sometime in partnership with Mechatt.   She afterward married Dr. Ludlow Powell, by whom she had one daughter, Ann, who married Major Ross, of St. Charles.   The names of Mr. Shaw's children were—Charlotte W., John S., and Julia K.   The latter died young.   John S. married Mary J. Elbert, of Lexington, Ky.

TAGGART.—James Taggart, of North Carolina, was the father of the following named children—Sally, Anna, Elizabeth, Jane, Richard, Andrew, William, and James.   Sally, Richard, Andrew, William and James came to St. Charles county at an early date.   The first died single.   Richard married Margaret Johnson. Andrew married Rachel Evans, and they had sixteen children. William married Margaret Thompson, daughter of James Thompson, and they had—Reason A., Sarah, Ann, Margaret, and Franklin.   Reason A. married Nancy Baldridge.   Sarah was married first to Elijah Goodrich, and after his death to Wm. M. Mason.   Ann married Creed Archer, of Warren county.   Margaret married Andrew Taggart.

TALLEY.—Dr. John A. Talley, although not one of the pioneers of Missouri, is so well known, and has been engaged for so many years in the practice of medicine and surgery in St. Charles county, that a sketch of his life will not be out of place in this connection.   He was born in Cumberland Co., Va., June 5, 1813.   At an early age he became well versed in the English classics and the principal Greek and Latin authors, having been thoroughly instructed in them by a private tutor at home ; and at the age of seventeen he was sent to Randolph Macon College, where, after a rigid examination, he was at once placed in the advanced classes.   He remained at this institution two years, when he entered the University of Virginia, and graduated in medicine and surgery in 1840.   Soon after receiving his diploma, he was appointed assistant surgeon at the alms house in Richmond, Va., where he learned the practical application of the theories which he had studied in college.   He subsequently practiced a year and a half with his brother, Dr. Z. Talley, and in the fall of 1840 he started, on horseback, for Missouri, followed by his favorite pointer dog.   He located in St. Charles county, and boarded at the house of Col. C. F. Woodson, who resided a few miles south of the present site of Wentzville.   He soon gained a large and remunerative practice, and during the sickly season of 1844 he was kept so constantly in the saddle that he could not procure the requisite amount of rest, and came near sacrificing his own life in his efforts to save others. In 1845 he married Paulina C. Preston, a daughter of Col. W. R. Preston, of Botetourt Co., Va. The Preston family is one of the most distinguished and extensive in the United States, and from it have sprung statesmen, soldiers and scholars of the highest renown. Two sons resulted from this marriage, William P. and Edwin. The former graduated in medicine at the University of Virginia, and is now practicing his profession at Wentzville. Dr. Talley is advanced in years, but retains his mental and physical vigor unimpaired, and faithfully attends to his extensive and laborious practice.

TAYLOR.—Richard Taylor, of Virginia, was a commodore in the U. S. Navy. His son, Roger, married Hannah Fishback, of Virginia, and settled in St. Charles county in 1818. His wife was noted for being an extremely neat housekeeper, and as carpets were not fashionable then, she kept her floors waxed. When gentlemen came there on business or to visit her husband, she had them take their boots off, and gave them slippers to wear while in the house. The names of Mr. Taylor's children were—Lucinda, James T., Sally S., Samuel, Matilda, Mary, Letitia, Caroline, Colby, Eleanor, William, and Jacob. Lucinda married William Ross, who settled in St. Francois county. Sally S. was married three times—first to Lawrence Ross, second to Frank Taylor, and third to Dr. B. English. Matilda married Colburn Woolfolk. Mary married James Clark. Letitia married Dr. Daniel McFarland. Caroline married Robert Nusom. Eleanor married George Parton. Samuel was drowned in McCoy's creek.

TAYON.—Charles Tayon, a Frenchman, was commandant at St. Charles for sometime, under the Spanish government. He had a little farm just above town, which he cultivated with a yoke of oxen, which were driven by an old negro named Larabe. The yoke was tied to the horns of the oxen with rawhide strings, instead of being fastened around their necks with bows, and they drew their load by their horns. Mr. Tayon had one son and two daughters. The Spanish government never paid him for his services as commandant, and he finally went to Spain to see if he could have the matter arranged ; but he neglected to procure the proper credentials, and was arrested as an impostor and imprisoned for three years. When he was finally released and returned to America, his property had all been squandered, and he was left a poor man.

THOMPSON.—John Thompson, of Pennsylvania, was one of the early settlers of St. Charles county. He built the first two-story barn that was erected on "the point," and used the second story for treading out wheat. The floor was made of plank, which he sawed with a whip-saw, and it was laid so that the grain when it was trodden out would fall down on the lower floor and leave the chaff and straw above. He had several children, all of whom, with his widow, returned to Pennsylvania after his death.

VAN BURKLEO.—William Van Burkleo settled near the junction of the Mississippi and Missouri rivers, in St. Charles county, in 1798. He was married three times, first to Nellie Fallice, second to Mary Black, and third to Clarissa J. Gilderland, who was younger than some of his grandchildren. Mr. Van Burkleo followed the occupations of farming and horse-racing. The names of his children were—Edna, Samuel, Sarah, Eleanor, Mary, William, James, John, George, Joshua, Stephen, Elizabeth, Henry, Rebecca, Harrison, and Lee, sixteen in all. Mr. Van Burkleo was a ranger in Captain Musick's company, and was killed by the Indians about the close of the war. (See "Anecdotes and Adventures.")

WALKER.—Joel Walker, of Rockingham Co., N. C., was married twice. His second wife was Sally Bass, of Ireland, by whom he had two children, Warren and Benjamin F., both of whom came to St. Charles Co., Mo., with their mother, in 1830, after their father's death. Warren had married Mary B. Meyers, of North Carolina, and they had—Robert A., Mary D., Sally A., Benjamin F., Warren W., Elizabeth A., Harriet U., and Charles J. Benjamin F., the brother of Warren, married Julia A. McRoberts, and they had George, Joseph, Milton, Henry, John, Sally, Martha A., and Louisa. The mother of Warren and Benjamin F. was married the second time to John Griffin, and they had two children, Joseph and John.

WATTS.—Samuel R. and George W. Watts settled in St. Charles county in 1830 and 1834. Samuel R. was married twice, first to Sally Pemberton, and second to Lucy Sanders. George W. was also married twice; first to Martha Matthews, of Virginia, and second to Paulina Ferrell. He died in Ralls county.

WATSON.—Thomas Watson and his wife, Elizabeth Donnell, of Ireland, had three sons—Thomas, Robert, and William. Mrs. Watson having died, her husband came to America with his three sons, and settled in North Carolina. Robert and William died young. Thomas married Sarah T. Harris, daughter of John Harris, a revolutionary soldier, and settled in St. Louis in 1837. There he became associate editor of the *Missouri Argus*, and subsequently purchased the paper. In 1842 President Van Buren appointed him Postmaster at St. Louis, a position that he filled for four years. He was subsequently appointed Land Agent for the State of Missouri by President Polk. Mrs. Watson died in 1865, in her 73d year, and he died in 1870, in his 83d year. They had nine children, five of whom survived their parents, viz: Henry, Emily, Julia, Sarah, and Thomas. Henry was married twice; first to Miss Hay, of Tennessee, and second to Maria Bergen. He resides in St. Louis. Julia lives in Mississippi, unmarried. Sarah married John Jordan, of Pensacola, Florida. Thomas has been a Presbyterian minister for thirty-two years, and is one of the leading divines of that denomination in this State. He is pastor of Dardenne Church, in St. Charles county, which was organized in 1819, and was the first Presbyterian church established west of St. Louis. Mr. Watson married Nancy McCluer.

WATSON.—Archibald Watson and wife were natives of the northern part of Ireland. About the year 1789 they emigrated to America, and settled in Pennsylvania, near Easton, on the Susquehanna river, where Mr. Watson engaged in merchandising, and where a town called Watsonville subsequently grew up. In 1802 the family removed to Erie county, and settled on a farm, where they remained until 1819, when they came to Missouri. The voyage was made on a keel-boat, which they launched on French creek, and floated down that stream to the Alleghany river, from thence to the Ohio, down that river to the Mississippi, and then cordelled their boat up the latter stream to the town of Louisiana, Mo., which at that time consisted of only half-a-dozen log cabins. During that summer there were three hundred Indians encamped on a creek at the lower end of the town. The following year Mr. Watson removed in his boat to St. Charles, and purchased a farm about four miles below town, where he resided until his death, which occurred in 1826. His wife died in 1824. Their children were—Mary, James, Archibald, Jr., William, Johnson, Samuel S., John, and Martha. It was Archibald Watson, Sr., who kept the horses of the members of the Legislature while that body sat in St. Charles. After the death of his father, Samuel S. purchased the interest of his brothers and sisters in the home place, where he remained and became a successful and prosperous farmer. In September, 1826, he married Mary A. Lewis, daughter of Charles and Judith Lewis, who at the time was only fifteen years of age, and after the ceremony was over she rode home on horseback behind her husband, carrying her wardrobe in her lap. They remained on the farm until 1859, and prospered far beyond their expectations. Having acquired a comfortable fortune, they removed to their present beautiful residence near Lindenwood College, in the city of St. Charles, where they have since resided, enjoying the society of their numerous friends, and the comforts of an elegant and refined home. Mr. Watson has always been liberal in the support of religious and educational enterprises. He is one of the incorporators of Lindenwood College, and was for a number of years a member of the board of incorporators of Westminister College, at Fulton, to both of which institutions he has contributed

largely.   In 1865 he was appointed by Governor Gamble, one of
the Judges of the County Court, and at the end of the term he
was solicited to become a candidate for the same office, but
declined, having no desire to mingle in the turbulent affairs of
politics.   Mr. Watson was born in Erie Co., Pa., February 18,
1804, united with the Presbyterian Church at Erie, Pa., in 1819,
and was chosen an Elder in the First Presbyterian Church at St.
Charles in December, 1832, a position which he has held without
intermission since that time.

WELLS.—Carty Wells, of Stafford Co., Va., settled in Kentucky
about 1797.   He had two sons and five daughters, and four of the
daughters married four brothers.   The names of only four of the
children can be ascertained now, viz.: Hayden, John, Sally, and
Margaret.   Hayden died in Kentucky, and left a large family.
John was married in Prince William Co., Va., to Anna Brady and
settled in Shelby Co., Ky., in 1810, and in St. Charles Co., Mo.,
in 1827.   He settled at a place called Williamsburg, where he
was appointed postmaster, and died in 1837.   His children were
—Carty, Jr., Joseph B., James, John C., Thomas F., Jeptha D.,
Helen B., Euphemia, and Jane S.   Carty, Jr., studied law and
became prominent in that profession.   He was circuit and county
clerk of Warren county, became a member of the State Senate,
and was Circuit Judge for a number of years.   He removed to
Lincoln county in 1839, and died in 1860.   His wife was Mahala
Oglesby, of Kentucky, by whom he had nine children, viz.: Mary
F., Euphemia, Anna, Catharine, Richard H., James, Alfred C.,
Joseph D., and Thomas L.   Mary F. married Judge Samuel F.
Murray, of Pike county.   Euphemia married William W. McCoy.
Anna married William A. Bevan.   Catharine married Thomas
Hammond.   Richard was married twice, and removed to Texas.
James was a physician, and lived in Osage Co., Mo.   Alfred C.
married a Miss Sharp, and lives in St. Louis.   Joseph D. married
a Miss Guthrie.   Thomas L. never married.—Joseph, brother of
Judge Carty Wells, was also a prominent attorney, and was a
member of the Constitutional Convention of 1855.   He removed
to California, and entered into the practice of law in San Fran-
cisco, in partnership with Judge Crockett.   He subsequently
returned to Missouri, and died at Troy, Lincoln county, in 1858.
He never married.   James Wells married Catharine Johnson,
daughter of Charles Johnson, who bought Colonel Nathan Boone's
place on Femme Osage creek.   John C. Wells was a physician.
He married Catharine Carter, and lived in Troy.   Thomas F.
married Martha Shelton.   Joseph D. studied law, and died about
the time he began to practice.   Helen B. married Richard H.
Woolfolk,, of Kentucky.   Euphemia married John Snethen, of
Montgomery county.   Jane S. married Solomon Jenkins, who
was an architect, and planned the lunatic and deaf and dumb

asylums and Westminster College, located at Fulton, Missouri.

WOOTON.—Mr. Wooton, of Kentucky, married Miss Marion of that State, and settled in St. Charles county in 1816. They had four children—Marion, Elijah, John, and Elizabeth. Elizabeth married Calvin Gunn, and their daughter, Mary, married ex-Gov. B. Gratz Brown.

WHITE.—Jacob White, of Kentucky, married a Miss Stone, and settled in the town of St. Charles in 1816. He was a great bee raiser, and had an idea that no one could be successful in that business unless he stole a swarm to commence with. One of his neighbors wanted to purchase a swarm from him one day, but White told him that they would do him no good unless he stole them. The man took him at his word, and stole the bees that night, but they stung him nearly to death as he was carrying them home. Mr. White had four children, all daughters, whose names were—Harriet, Angeline, Elizabeth, and Mary. They all remained single except Elizabeth, who married Mr. Whitney, of Boston, who settled in St. Charles and opened a shoe store at an early date. Their children were—William F., Martha E., and Frank W. William F. married a daughter of Hon. A. H. Buckner, member of Congress from the thirteenth district. Martha E. married Hon. A. H. Edwards, at present a member of the Missouri State Senate.

YOSTI.—The father of Judge Francis Yosti, of St. Charles, whose name was Emelieu Yosti, was a native of Italy. He came to St. Louis with some Spanish troops sometime during the latter part of the eighteenth century, and engaged in the mercantile business. He possessed only a limited capital, but by persever-ance and tact he accumulated a fortune. He married Theotes Duran, a daughter of one of the old French families of St. Louis, by whom he had six children. The first court in the Territory of Missouri, under the American government, was held in his house ; and at one of its sessions a murderer named John Long was con-victed and sentenced to death. Mr. Yosti died in 1812, and his wife in 1824. Francis Yosti, the eldest child, was born in St. Louis on the 7th of August, 1798. He settled in St. Charles in 1829, and married Emily Adeline Morrison. He subsequently engaged in the mercantile business with a Mr. Morrison, at Frank-lin, in Howard county, where they remained one year. They then loaded their goods into wagons, and started across the plains to Santa Fe, New Mexico. They made the trip in ninety days, and immediately opened their goods and went into busi-ness. The following year Mr. Yosti returned to Missouri, but went back to Santa Fe the next spring. During that summer they disposed of their stock of goods, and Mr. Yosti, in company with nine others, started back to Missouri. They took the south-

ern route down the Arkansas river, in order to avoid the cold of
a northern latitude, and when near the confluence of the Mex-
quite and Canadian rivers, they were attacked by about 150 Indians.   Two of the party and all their horses were killed, but the
bodies of the latter were piled in a circle and afforded a safe
breast-work, behind which the survivors gallantly withstood the
assaults of the overwhelmning numbers of the enemy. They killed
and wounded a large number of their assailants, and when night
came on they succeeded in making their escape, but were compelled to abandon all their property, and travel with empty guns,
as they had expended all their ammunition in their defence.
They traveled seventeen days on foot, through swamps, and over
hills and rocks, with nothing to eat but roots, bark, and sumac
buds.   Finally, when nearly exhausted and almost famished,
they heard firing on the opposite side of the Arkansas river,
which they had followed into the Indian Territory.   They
rightly conjectured that they were in the midst of friendly Indians, and hastily constructing a raft, they crossed the river
and made their presence known.   The Indians received them
in the most friendly manner, and kindly cared for them several days, until their strength was sufficiently restored to resume
their journey, when they furnished them with ponies and accompanied them to Fort Gibson, where they embarked on a boat for
St. Louis.   Mr. Yosti located in St. Charles in 1834, and again
engaged in mercantile pursuits.   He was also interested in the
milling business with George Collier.   In 1857 he began to deal
in grain, in company with Capt. John Orrick, and continued in
that business for sixteen years.   He then retired to private life,
and now enjoys the fruits of his labors in his elegant home, surrounded by his cultivated and intelligent family.   The names of
his children were—Virginia, James M., Emily Jane, William,
Euphrasia, and Mary.   Emily Jane and William were twins.
Virginia died in childhood, and James M. died at the age of
twenty-five years.   Emily Jane married John K. Lintz, and Mary
married John A. Keller.   Mr. Yosti was Judge of the County
Court during six years of his life.

YOUNG.—William Young, of England, came to America and
settled in Halifax county, Va.   He served as a soldier in the
American army during the revolutionary war.   He married Elizabeth Stegale, and they had—Archibald, Marland, Milton, Peyton, Wiley, Samuel, Frances, and Judith.   Archibald, Marland,
and Milton fought in the revolutionary war.   The former married and settled in Kentucky, and the two latter in Smith Co.,
Tenn.   Samuel died in Virginia, and Wiley settled in East Tennessee.   Frances and Judith married and lived in Virginia.   Peyton married Elizabeth Oglesby, and they had—Celia, George,
Nancy, Oglesby, William, Peyton, Elizabeth, and Araminta.

Oglesby settled in St. Charles county in 1829.   He married Jane
Love, daughter of Robert Love and Esther Bevan.

ZUMWALT.—Jacob Zumwalt, of Germany, emigrated to America, and settled first in Pennsylvania, where the town of Little
York now stands.   He purchased the land upon which the town
was subsequently built, and erected a cabin upon it.   Being afflicted with a cancer, he removed to Virginia, where he could obtain medical aid, and settled on the Potomac, not far from
Georgetown.   But he grew worse instead of better, and soon
died.   In the meantime the deed to his land in Pennsylvania had
been destroyed, and his children lost what would have been a
princely fortune to them.   This valuable paper was lost in a
rather singular manner.   One of the girls, while hunting about
the house for a piece of pasteboard to stiffen her new sun-bonnet,
found the deed, and, being unable to read, she supposed it
was some useless piece of old paper, and used it in her bonnet.
The deed had never been recorded, and therefore could not be
restored, and the heirs to the property never succeeded in establishing their title.   Mr. Zumwalt was married twice.   By his first
wife he had—Henry, George, Dolly and Lizzie ; and by his second
he had—Christopher, Jacob, John, Adam, Andrew, and Catharine.   Christopher and Jacob settled in St. Charles county, on
Peruque creek, in 1796, and in 1798 Jacob built the first hewed
log house that was ever erected on the north side of the Missouri
river.   It is still standing, on land owned by Mr. D. Heald, about
one and a half miles northwest of O'Fallon Station, on the St.
Louis, Kansas City and Northern Railway.   The house was used
as a fort during the Indian war, and often as many as ten families
found shelter within its walls at the same time.   The first Methodist sacrament in Missouri was administered in this house, by
Rev. Jesse Walker, in 1807.   The wine was made by Mrs. Zumwalt and Mrs. Col. David Bailey, from the juice of polk berries,
sweetened with maple sugar ; and for bread they used the crusts
of corn bread.   Adam Zumwalt came to Missouri in 1797.   He
placed his family and $800 worth of goods, with his stock, con-
sisting of 30 head of cattle, 11 sheep, and 12 horses, on board a
flat-boat, and came down the Ohio and up the Mississippi river to
St. Charles county with his clumsy craft.   He settled near the
present town of Flint Hill, where he erected two still houses and
made whisky to sell to the Indians, who were camped near his
place.   The great chief Black Hawk made his home at Mr. Zumwalt's for sometime, and was a regular and frequent visitor until after the commencement of hostilities between the whites and the Indians.   He often·danced with Mr. Zumwalt's daughters, and was
so fond of his whisky that he frequently became very drunk ; but
he never caused any disturbance or acted in an ungentlemanly
manner.   In very cold weather the whisky would freeze and be-

come solid ice, in which state it was sold to the Indians by the cake, and they often bought as much as a $100 worth in a single day.   Mr. Zumwalt was a friend of the preachers, and whenever they came into the neighborhood they held services in his house. Rev. Jesse Walker and a German minister named Hostetter preached there as early as 1800.   During the Indian war Mr. Zumwalt's family took shelter in Pond Fort, while he and his son Jonathan remained at home to protect the property and prevent the Indians from destroying it.   Jonathan had learned to use his gun when only five years of age, and was as quick and accurate a marksman as could be found in the country.   When he was six years old he killed a large buck, which plunged about so in its death agonies that he became frightened and ran home, and lost his gun in the woods.   On one occasion the Indians crossed the Mississippi river on the ice, and murdered an entire family of twelve persons, who lived near Mr. Zumwalt's place. He assisted in burying them.   The bodies were wrapped in quilts and buried under the house, in a place that had been used as a cellar.   The Indians burned the house soon after, and the bodies were devoured by the flames.   On another occasion an Indian chief died at Mr. Zumwalt's house, and was buried with a loaf of bread in one hand and a butcher-knife in the other, and his dog was killed and buried at his feet.   These preparations were made in order that when he reached the happy hunting grounds he would have something to eat, and a dog to find game for him.   The names of Mr. Zumwalt's children were—John, Elizabeth, Andrew, Rachel, Mary, Catharine, Jonathan, and Solomon. —John Zumwalt, a brother of Adam, settled on Darst's Bottom, in St. Charles county, in 1806.   The names of his children were—George, John, Barbara, Mary, Elizabeth, Adam, Andrew, Jacob, Henry, and William.—Andrew Zumwalt was a devoted Methodist, but his three daughters joined the Baptist Church, and their mother said she was glad of it.   But the old gentleman was very angry, and said he hoped, now that his family was divided among the churches, that some of them would find the right one and get to heaven, and be contented when they got there, and not want to go somewhere else.—There were five Jacobs in the different Zumwalt families, and they were distinguished as Big Jake, Little Jake, Calico Jake, St. Charles Jake, and Lying Jake.

OTHER FAMILIES OF ST. CHARLES COUNTY.

The following additional histories of families in St. Charles county were obtained after the preceding pages of this work had gone to press.

ALEXANDER.—The Alexanders were among the early Colonial settlers. They located in Virginia prior to the revolution, and John Alexander, the first of whom we have any definite record, was an officer of the American army during the struggle for independence. His son, James H., who who was a Virginia farmer, came to Missouri in the fall of 1829, and settled on a farm in the lower part of Dardenne Prairie, where he resided until his death, which occurred in 1836. His wife died in 1833. They left four children, two sons and two daughters, the latter being the younger. One of the sons, William Archibald, better known by the familiar name of Arch, was twelve years of age when his father died, having been born in Rockbridge Co., Va., June 15, 1824. He was taken back to Virginia by a family of relatives, and educated for the legal profession. He devoted three years to study in the literary department of Washington College, now Washington and Lee University, when he returned to St. Louis and entered the law office of Spaulding & Tiffney, as a student. The following year he was admitted to the bar, and began the practice of his profession in the office of Hon. Wm. M. Campbell, where he remained until the death of the latter. He then returned to Virginia and spent a year in traveling through the South, when he came back to Missouri and located in St. Charles. There he met with marked success, and was soon elected Public Administrator. He was subsequently elected to the office of Commissioner of Public Schools, and in 1870 was chosen Mayor of the city of St. Charles, an office which he filled with great credit to himself and to the satisfaction of his constituents. In 1872 he was elected Prosecuting Attorney of the county, and was re-elected in 1874. He possesses a pleasant address, a fine flow of language, a handsome personal appearance, and is universally popular. He was married December 10, 1861, to Agnes Behrens, daughter of Dr. Henry and Bertha Behrens, of St. Charles.

ANDERSON.—Robert A. Anderson, of Kentucky, settled in St. Charles Co., Mo., in 1838. His wife was Rachel Givens, of Kentucky, by whom he had—Harriet J., Margaret A., America, Alexander G., and Sarah L. Sarah and Margaret married Preston B. Scott, at present of St. Louis. America married Alcana Delana

Fortunatus Fleming Trout, of Warren county, who was noted for his unusually numerous names and eccentric disposition. Major A. G. Anderson was married in Vernon county, to Mary Roberts, and they now live in St. Louis. He was a Major in the famous First Missouri Brigade, on the Confederate side, during the late war, and is well known all over the State. He is a man of fine address and more than ordinary ability.

ATKINSON.—John Atkinson moved from Louisville, Kentucky, and settled in St. Charles about the year 1843. Prior to that time he was extensively engaged with his brother in the milling business at Louisville, Ky., and Richmond, Va. He bought the large stone mill on the river bank in St. Charles, from George Collier, and operated it successfully for many years. The flour manufactured by him attained a high reputation, in the South and in New York and Liverpool; and it might be said with propriety that he was one of the first millers in the West who helped establish the reputation of St. Louis and St. Charles flour, and gave it that high standing it has since enjoyed, both at home and abroad. Cotemporary with him, were Edward Walsh, A. W. Fagin and Dennis Marks, prominent millers of St. Louis, who, with him, may be said to have been the founders of the present immense milling business St. Louis and St. Charles; an interest that has grown to such gigantic proportions and which has contributed so largely to the wealth and commercial prosperity of the two localities. About 1850 Mr. Atkinson purchased a large mill in Pekin, Ills., intending to carry on both establishments, and had just completed thorough and extensive repairs on the property, when it was destroyed by fire, inflicting on him a severe loss from which he never fully recovered. He returned to St. Charles, and operated the mill there till about the breaking out of the war, after which he did not again engage in active business. During his business life in St. Charles his operations were on a large scale, and gave employment to a great number of men in his mill and in connection with it. He was one of the most prominent and highly esteemed citizens of the place, and his memory is held in kind remembrance by the older people here, who knew him, and esteemed him in the highest degree for his sterling qualities as an upright, honorable business man, and for his genial and social traits. He married his first wife, Virginia Davidson, of Petersburg, Va., in Louisville, Ky. She bore him eight children, of whom only three are living—Robert and John, well known and prominent merchants of St. Charles, and Virginia, wife of E. E. Chase, Esq., an extensive hardware merchant of Edina, Missouri. His second wife, formerly Miss Lockwood, of Binghampton, N. Y., survives him. Mr. Atkinson was a gentleman of the old school, with the strictest sense of honor, a man of warm and generous impulses, charitable and kind hearted. He was a public spirited citizen, contributing liberally to all deserving enterprises, and taking a warm interest in all undertakings tending to advance the interests of his section of the country. He was one of the original projectors and a strong friend of the North Missouri Railroad, and lent his aid and influence toward securing its success.

BARADA.—Louis Barada was born in St. Louis, and settled with his parents in St. Charles about the year 1800, where he resided during the rest of his life. He died in March, 1852, and his wife died in February, 1873. Mr. Barada followed various occupations, but devoted most of his time to the butchering business and milling. He assisted in the building of the famous old stone flouring mill, in which he at one time owned an interest. He also helped to build the old stone Catholic church, and was one of its trustees for many years, serving in that capacity until his death. He married Ellen Gagnon, by whom he had eleven children—Louis, Jr., Danaciene, Louise, Ann N., Mary, Pierre, Benoist, Ellen, John B., Lucille and Eulalie. Louis, Jr., Danaciene, Benoist and Eulalie died in childhood, and Pierre died at the age of ten years. Louise married David Knott, who died in St. Louis in 1848. His widow still resides in that city. Ann N. married Antoine LeFaivre, who died in 1853 ; she is still living. Mary married Charles Cornoyer, who died in St. Louis in 1871, and his widow still resides there. Ellen was married twice ; first to John LeFaivre, who died two years afterward, and she subsequently married Joseph Widen, who died from injuries received from the explosion of the steamer *George C. Wolf*. His widow lives in St. Louis. John B. was clerk on the steamer *Robert*, and died in St. Louis of Yellow fever, contracted in New Orleans. Lucille married Lucien F. LaCroix, and died in St. Louis in 1863. Mr. LaCroix married again, and is living in Helena, Montana, publishing the *Daily Independent*.

BOYSE.—Matthew R. Boyse was born in Wexford Co., Ireland, in 1788. In 1814 he married Ann Cullin, and in 1825 they emigrated to the United States. They settled first in Wheeling, Va., but came to St. Louis, Mc., in 1827. In 1837 they removed to St. Charles, but returned to St. Louis in 1843, where they resided the rest of their lives. Mr. Boyse died December 25, 1864, and his widow died in 1874, aged 79 years. They had fifteen children, of whom the following lived to be grown—Mary, Ellen, John, Clement, Martin, Ann, Matthew, Jane and William. Mary married Samuel Maxwell, of St. Louis, and died in 1872. Ellen married Daniel Emerson, of Dog Prairie, St. Charles county. John married Mrs. McKinney, whose maiden name was Celeste Cornoyer, and died in 1868. Clement married Martha A. Drury. Martin married Johanna Casey, of Washington county. Ann married Michael McGuire, of St. Louis. Matthew married Ellen Murphy,

of St. Louis, and died in 1857.   Jane married John O'Brien, of
Lincoln county.   William married Susan E. Drury.

CUNNINGHAM.—Col. Thomas W. Cunningham came to St.
Charles, from Virginia, in 1830.   His life has always been
governed by motives of purity and honesty, and there is no
man in the county or State who enjoys the esteem and respect of
his fellow-citizens in a higher degree than Colonel Cunningham.
Public duties entrusted to him have been as faithfully and carefully attended to as if they were his own private affairs ; and it can.
be truly said of him that he has never shirked a responsibility or
evaded a duty.   He is now in his 77th year, has laid aside the
cares of business, and enjoys himself in the society of his family
and the companionship of his books.   He has been a close student
for many years, and his library is one of the rarest in the county.
The first civil office to which the Colonel was elected was that of
Public Surveyor of St. Charles county, a position which he filled
for a number of years in the most satisfactory manner.   He was
subsequently chosen Mayor of the city of St. Charles, and made
one of the best executive officers the city ever had.   During the
Black Hawk war he served as Colonel of a regiment, and retained
his sword until the late war between the North and South, when
he was forced to reluctantly surrender it to the military authorities.   Colonel Cunningham married Elizabeth A. Christman, of
Lincoln county, and they had six children—Josepha, Theresa,
Henry A., John C., Thomas S., and Bettie Barr.   Josepha married
J. H. Aikin of Virginia, and at present resides in Warren county,
Missouri.   Theresa and Bettie Barr died in infancy.   Henry A. is a
prominent attorney of St. Louis.   He graduated at St. Charles.
College and studied law in his father's office.   His success at the
bar has been brilliant, and though a young man, he has acquired a
considerable fortune.   He has managed a number of cases with
great ability in the United States Supreme Court, is at present a
prominent candidate for Judge of the Court of Appeals of Missouri, and will probably be elected, as he is supported by Democrats and Republicans without regard to party affiliations.   He
has traveled extensively in the United States and Europe, is pol-
ished and gentlemanly in his manners, and universally popular.
John C. Cunningham died at the age of twenty-seven.   Thomas
S. studied law in his father's office, was admitted to the bar, and
is meeting with good success for a young attorney.   He was elected to the office of Public Administrator. two years ago.

CUNNINIGHAM.—Edward C. Cunningham was born in Frederick
county, Maryland, February 22, 1809.   He married Margaret
Buxton, of Montgomery county, Maryland, on the 27th of January, 1831, and emigrated to Missouri in 1836.   He remained one
year in St. Charles county, and then removed to Warren, but remained there only a short time, when he came back to St. Charles,

where he has since resided. In the spring of 1838 Mr. Cunningham was appointed Collector of revenues for the city of St. Charles, and the following August was elected Constable of the township. In 1844 he was elected Sheriff of the county, as an independent candidate, and was re-elected in 1846. Since the expiration of his second term of office he has been employed in various branches of business, such as farming, stock raising, dealing in stock, and butchering; and at present he is cultivating his farm near St. Charles, attending to the butcher's business, and operating a coal mine. He purchased the Wardlow farm in 1847, and is still proprietor of the place. The stepping plank to the horse-block at his front gate, was placed there by Mr. Wardlow forty-four years ago, and it is still sound and used for the same purpose. In 1845 Mr. Cunningham introduced a new variety of wheat, from Frederick county, Maryland, called the Zimmerman, which has since become the standard wheat of St. Charles county, and has given a reputation to the wheat and flour of that county which extends over a large portion of the civilized world. In 1840 he imported from Albany, New York, the first Berkshire hogs that had ever been introduced into St. Charles county, and since that time the county has become celebrated for its fine pork. By his first wife Mr. Cunningham had four children—Mary, Nancy E., Charles W., and Margaret S. Mary and Margaret S. died in infancy, Nancy E. died in her thirteenth year, and Charles W. died in his eighteenth year. Mrs. Cunningham died August 28, 1836, and her husband afterward married Elizabeth Slagle, of Frederick county, Maryland, by whom he had—Sarah N., Frederick S., Edward L., Ann E., John M., and Elizabeth S. Ann E.. Elizabeth S., and Sarah N. died in infancy. Frederick S. married Ann Taylor. He was at one time postmaster of St. Charles, but, being in bad health, he resigned the office and went to California, where he died, April 23, 1865. His widow afterward married Charles A. Cunningham, and now resides in Carrollton, Missouri. Edward L. married Mary Stewart, and lives in Texas. John M. is in business with his father. Mrs. Cunningham died May 1, 1854, and on the 21st of December, 1854, he married Teresa Johnson, of Cumberland, Maryland, who died August 16, 1855.

CRUSE.—Francis and Elizabeth Cruse were natives of Prussia. They emigrated to America and settled in St. Charles county in 1834, and were married soon after. They had five children. Mrs. Cruse died in 1844, but Mr. Cruse survived until 1853. Their eldest son, Joseph, was born October 20, 1837, and is now a prominent citizen of his native county. He learned the carpenter's trade at the age of sixteen, with F. Smith & Co., of St. Louis; but preferring agricultural pursuits he purchased a farm in Cuivre township, where he has since resided. He has been three times elected to the office of Justice of the Peace in his township, and was appointed Notary Public by Gov. Fletcher in 1871. In 1870 he was elected one of the Judges of the County Court, and at the expiration of his first term was re-elected to the same position. He has made a faithful and efficient officer, and enjoys the confidence and esteem of his fellow-citizens. He is a leading member of the Catholic Church, and possesses a friendly, sociable disposition. He was married in 1860 to Josephine Beckman.

DURFEE.—Rev. Thomas Durfee came to St. Charles from Fall River, Mass., in 1827. He was a graduate of Brown University, Rhode Island, and of the Theological Seminary at Andover, Mass. In 1828 he was married to Miss Ann Glenday, who was a neice of Thomas Lindsay, and then living with him. Mr. Durfee lived several years after his marriage in Callaway county, as pastor of the Presbyterian Church at Auxvasse. He afterward returned to St. Charles, and was agent of the American Bible Society, and in 1833—the great cholera year—he died at the house of Thomas Lindsay. Mr. Durfee was a man of great worth and a fine preacher. He left two daughters, Jane S., who afterwards was married to John Jay Johns, and Margaret, Lindsay, who is now the wife of E. P. Borden, of Philadelphia. Mrs. Durfee, after the death of her husband, continued to live with her uncle, Thomas Lindsay, till his death in 1843. At her uncle's death she was, by his will, possessed of his old homestead, where she continued to reside till 1850, when she went to live with her son-in-law, John Jay Johns, with whom she still resides. She is a great enthusiast on the subject of education, and is using her means freely in educating her grand children. Her eldest daughter, Mrs. Johns, was educated at Monticello, Ills., and Mrs. Borden at Bradford Seminary, in Massachusetts.

HILBERT.—Jacob F. Hilbert and wife came from Carlile, Cumberland Co., Penn., to St. Charles county in July, 1836. For about seven years after his arrival in that county, Mr. Hilbert was engaged in the distilling business with his brother John; but it did not prove remunerative, and he removed to the city of St. Charles, where he remained until his death, which occurred May 7, 1848. In 1843 he acted as Deputy Sheriff of the county, and Councilman for the city of St. Charles. He was afterward elected Assessor of the county, and was performing the duties of that office at the time of his death. He married Cresentia Yeally, of Pennsylvania, before his removal to Missouri, and they had five children, three of whom are living, viz: Julius, Jerome, and Jacob. Mr. H. was upright and prompt in all his transactions with his fellow-men, and his death was an irreparable loss to the community. His estimable widow lives in the house that he purchased thirty-three years ago. John Hilbert, a brother of Jacob, settled in St. Charles county in 1836. He came from Elizabethtown,

Pa. During his residence in St. Charles he held the various offices of Constable, Councilman, and Mayor, and always discharged his duties in a conscientious manner and to the best of his ability. He possessed considerable force of character, and was firm in his adherence to principle and the measures which he deemed just and right. He married Eliza Close, and they raised five children. He died in 1871, and his widow resides in St. Louis. Aloyseus Z. Hilbert, another brother, came from Rochester, N. Y., to Franklin Co., Mo., in 1826, where he married Sarah Johnson, and with his wife removed to St. Charles. He had the reputation of being one of the best millers in the West, and did the first stone dressing that was ever done on the buhrs of the old Collier mill. He was a member of the firm of Woods & Hilbert, flour manufacturers, of New Orleans, twenty-seven years ago; and during Mayor Pratt's administration he was flour Inspector of St. Louis. His first wife died, and he afterward married Mrs. Martha Spencer, who now resides in Iowa. Mr. Hilbert was killed in St. Louis, in 1873, by a fall down a flight of stairs at the hotel where he was stopping. He received a wound in the head from which he died in an hour. He had gained an extended reputation as a miller, and among his effects were found strong letters of recommendation from Messrs. Chouteau, Jules and Felix Valle, and J. & E. Walsh, the latter stating that the popularity of their brand of flour in the South and South America was due in no small degree to the skill and intelligent services of Mr. Hilbert.

McROBERTS.—John McRoberts and wife settled in Lincoln Co., Ky., about 1785. They had a son named George, who married Sally Embree, by whom he had—Milton, Fannie, Harvey, Nancy S., Preston, John, Harrison, Julia A., and Mary B. In 1824 they removed to Missouri and settled in Boone county, where Mr. McRoberts and his son Harvey died the same year. The widow and the rest of the children then returned to Kentucky, but in 1828 they came back to Missouri and settled in St. Charles county. In the meantime Milton had married Harriet Logan, and settled in St. Charles county in 1826. Nancy married Frank Hun, who settled in St. Charles county in 1830. Preston married Fannie Wade, of Lincoln county. John returned to Kentucky, married Nancy Massey, and remained in that State. Harrison was married twice; first to Harriet J. Anderson, and second to Rachel E. Phillips. Julia A. married Benjamin Walker.

PHILLIPS.—Jenkin Phillips, of Virginia, married Rachel Grubb, by whom he had—Rhoda, William, Benjamin, Rachel, and Jenkin, Jr. Mrs. Phillips died in Virginia, and her husband, with his son Jenkin, Jr., and daughter Rhoda, settled in St. Charles Co., Mo., in 1838, where he died in 1857. Jenkin, Jr., was married twice; first to Margaret Kinnear, who died in 1844; and second to Martha Smith. Rhoda died single in 1844.

HISTORIES OF FAMILIES.

WARREN COUNTY.

WARREN County was organized January 5, 1833, out of the surplus territory of Montgomery county. The first settlement within its limits was made by some French emigrants, who built a village at the mouth of Charrette creek, at a date so early that we have no record of it, and who gave it the name of that stream. A fort was erected at that place during the Indian war, but both fort and village have long since disappeared, and the place where they stood was washed away by the river many years ago.

The first American settlement within the limits of Warren county was made by David Bryan, in 1800. He built his cabin near the bank of Teuque creek, on a hill overlooking the Missouri river bottom, about a mile and a half southeast of Marthasville. Not many years afterward he built a double hewed log house, the first of the kind that was erected in that part of the country, and which at the time was considered a very fine structure. Men came thirty miles to help raise it. The boards of the roof were fastened to the rafters with wooden pins, because nails could not be procured. This house remained standing, and was occupied as a dwelling, until about six years ago, when it was torn down to make room for a handsome brick edifice.

The next American settler in Warren county was Flanders Callaway, who came about the same time Bryan did, and built his cabin in the bottom, about half-way between the bluff and river, and about half a mile from each.

Sometime previous to 1802, William and Robert Ramsey settled to the northwest of the two families just mentioned, the former about half a mile east of the present site of Marthasville, on land now owned by Frederick Griswold, Jr., and the latter about two miles northwest of Marthasville, where several members of his family were afterward massacred by the Indians.

Thomas Kennedy settled in the northern part of the county, about a mile southeast of the present town of Wright City, sometime between 1807 and 1812. He built a fort on his place during the Indian war, and it became one of the most noted places of that period.

Other settlements were made from time to time, but the population increased so slowly that when the county was organized it did not contain more the 4,000 inhabitants.

A place called New Boston, on Charrette creek, was the first county seat; but in 1835 the town of Warrenton was laid out, and established as the permanent seat of justice. In 1838 a brick court house was erected there, at a cost of $2,600. It was at that time one of the largest and most handsome buildings in all North Missouri, and the people complained about having to pay taxes to build so fine a house. This building was used for its original purposes until 1869, when it was torn down, and a more elegant structure, costing $35,000, erected on its site. The first County Court was organized on the 20th of May, 1833, at the house of Mordecai Morgan, not far from the future town of Warrenton. The members of this court were, Tilman Cullum, President; Morgan Bryan, and Thomas N. Graves. Absalom Hays was Sheriff, Carty Wells Clerk, and Walter Dillon deputy Clerk. James Pitzer was County Surveyor. The first license was granted to Frederick Griswold, to keep tavern at Pinckney, for which he paid $15. Walter Dillon also obtained a license at the same court to keep tavern at Hickory Grove.

The first grand jury of Warren county was composed of— Thomas Talbott, foreman; Grief Stewart, Samuel Doherty, Benoni McClure, Andrew G. Long, Isaac Kent, Jr., William Camron, James Miller, Edward Pleasant, Turner Roundtree, Jonathan D. Gordon, Benjamin Hutchinson, W. A. Burton, Thomas Chambers, George Clay, James B. Graves, John B. Shaw, and Jared Irvine.

Pinckney was the first town founded within the limits of Warren county, after the French village of Charette. It was laid off in 1819, and named for Miss Attossa Pinckney Sharp, daughter of Benjamin Sharp. It was situated on the Missouri river, in the southern part of the county, and was the first county seat of Montgomery county. The original site of the town has fallen

into the river, and a country post office in the vicinity, called
Pinckney, is all that is left to mark the location of a once flourishing town.   (For a history cf Pinckney, see Montgomery
county.)

FAMILIES OF WARREN COUNTY.

ARCHER.—Charles C. Archer, of England, emigrated to America and settled in Virginia previous to the revolutionary war.   He
married Elizabeth Prior, daughter of David P. Prior and Mary
Cunningham, of Buckingham county, Va.   They had—William,
Mary A., Thomas D., Charles C., Elizabeth P., Creed T., Fields,
and John.   William C. married Kittura Kahale, and settled in
Montgomery county, Mo., in 1832.   Elizabeth C. married Presley
T, Oaks, and settled in Warren county in 1832.   Creed T. married Anna Taggart, and settled in Warren county in 1832.   Fields
married Frances L. Wood, and settled in Warren county in 1832.
John was married first to Winney Giles, and after her death he
married Matilda Shelton.   He also settled in Warren county in
1832.

BURGESS.—Thomas Burgess, son of Reuben Burgess, of North
Carolina, moved to Tennessee with his family in 1814.   In 1830 he
was drowned in the Cumberland river, and left a widow and eleven
children, viz: Elizabeth, George W., Charles, Anderson, Margaret, Joel, Thomas, William, Polly, Hiram, and Nelly.   Two of
these, Anderson and Thomas, settled in Missouri.   The latter was
in Nathan Boone's company of rangers during the Indian war,
and also served in the Black Hawk war.   He subsequently removed to Arkansas.   Anderson married Elizabeth Whiteason,
daughter of William Whiteason and Ann Wiser, and settled in
Warren county in 1831.   Their children were—Malissa, Wayman
L., Celina, Polly A., Elizabeth, Sarah, Dudley H., Valentine,
and Adolphus.

BROWN.—William Brown, of Tennessee, was married twice.   By
his first wife he had—Delila and William ; and by his second wife,
whose maiden name was Katy Nave, he had—Gabriel, Levy, and
Joseph.   Mr. Brown settled in Lincoln county, Mo., in 1817.
His son William married Sally Hopkins, and settled in Warren
county in 1820.   Levi married Polly Odin, and Joseph married
Polly Hopkins, and both settled in Warren county in 1820.

BIRD.—John Bird and his wife, Sarah Harvey, lived and died
in Franklin county, Va.   They had a son named Bartlett, who
married Jane Jameson, by whom he had—Mary, Edward, Abner,
Marshall, and Sally.   Mary was married first to Henry Morris,
who died in Virginia.   She then married Richard Stegall, who
settled in Warren county, Mo., afterward removed to Jackson

county, and now resides in Texas. Edward died single, in Virginia. Abner died in Nashville, Tennessee. Marshall married Mary J. Allen, and settled in Warren county in 1834. His children are—Samuel, Sallie, Martha J., John B., Charles E., Charlotte V., and Fannie. Sallie, daughter of Bartlett Bird, married Edward Moorman, who settled in St. Charles county, Mo., in 1831.

CARNEFAX.—William Carnefax, of England, settled in Campbell county, Va., and married Esther Maxey, by whom he had— Edward, John D., Charles, William, Benjamin, Nancy, Lucy, Rebecca, Mary, and Rhoda. John settled in Warren county in 1832, and married Jane W. Leavell.

CULLUM.—Tilman Cullum, of Kentucky, came to Missouri at an early date, and settled on Loss creek, in what is now Warren county. His wife was a Miss McDurmid, of Kentucky, and they raised a large family of children. Mr. Cullum was a good business man, a large trader and money loaner, and accumulated a fortune during his life-time. He was one of the first County Judges of Warren county, but resigned the position to administer upon the estate of Daniel Shobe.

CRAVENS.—Armon Cravens was born in Montgomery county, Maryland, but removed to Kentucky in 1776. He married Abigail Hathaway, of Maryland, and they had eighteen children, only nine of whom lived to be grown. Their son John was a soldier in the war of 1812, and married Elizabeth Burton, of Kentucky, by whom he had—James S., Paulina, Permelia, Hudson, William, Louisa, John, and Louisiana. Hudson married Virginia Walden, of Virginia, and settled in Missouri in 1836. In 1852 he left Missouri and went to Texas, but was so disatisfied with the country that he did not unload his wagon. He came back to Missouri and was satisfied. While in Texas he experienced several "northers," and came near freezing to death. He asserted that his dog was frozen fast in the mud, and that he had to pile all his bed clothes on his horses to keep them from freezing. William Cravens settled in Montgomery county in 1843, and married Louisa Walden. James S. and John settled in the same county at a later date.

CAIN.—Jesse Cain settled on Charrette creek, in now Warren county, about 1812. He joined Nathan Boone's company of rangers, and served with them during the Indian war. He was an eccentric character, and generally managed to afford his associates a great deal of amusement. His children were—Polly, Sally, Paulina, Vina, Jack, James, Jesse, Jr., Harvey, and Eli.

COIL.—Jacob Coil settled on Loutre Island in 1817. He was born in Pendleton county, Virginia, in 1780, and died in 1845. He was married twice, and had nine children. His eldest son by his first wife, named Jacob, Jr., was married first to Sarah Gibson and second to Mrs. Taylor, who was a daughter of Stephen Quick.

CARTER.—Ithiel Carter, a native of Scotland, married an English girl named Louisa Deming, emigrated to America, and settled at Hartford, Connecticut. During the revolution Mr. Carter enlisted in the American army, and fought for the rights of his adopted country. He had only two children, Cyrus and Orion. Cyrus came to St. Charles in 1822, as a clock peddler, and sold to Benjamin Emmons, Sr., the first patent clock ever sold west of the Mississippi river, the price being $40. Mr. Carter was married first in 1838, to the widow Derang, whose maiden name was Harriet Moore. His second wife was the widow of Samuel W. Williams, whose maiden name was Martha Johnson, daughter of John Johnson and Mary M. Wooldbridge of Chesterfield county, Virginia.

CHAMBERS.—John Chambers, of Ireland, settled in North Carolina, and married Mary Thompson, of Kentucky, by whom he had —John, Jr., William, Sarah, James, Thomas, Alexander, Nancy, and Jane. In 1798 Mr. Chambers came to Missouri and settled in St. Louis county, and in 1800 his wife died. After that he lived with his son Thomas, in St. Charles. Thomas married Eleanor Kennedy, and the names of their children were—Prospect, Riley, Sarah, Julia, Harriet, Davis H., Ellen, Rhoda, and Thomas, Jr. Thomas and Alexander Chambers were rangers together in Captain Musick's company, and were at the battle of the sinkhole in (now) Lincoln county. Alexander married the widow of Frank McDermid, who was killed at Callaway's defeat. Her maiden name was Ruth Costlio. James, son of John Chambers, Sr., was a tanner and lived in (now) Warren county.

CLYCE.—William Clyce, of Virginia, was an early settler near Pinckney, in Warren county. He married Nancy Hart, and they had—Milford, Elizabeth, and Preston. His first wife died, and he was married the second time to Polly Wyatt, by whom he had —Nancy, Frank, William, Gabriella, and Thomas. Milford married in Kentucky, to Priscilla Williams. Elizabeth married and settled in Linn county, Missouri. Preston and Frank died single, in Kentucky. Nancy married a Mr. Swasey, of Canada, who settled at Pinckney, in Warren county, and opened a store. William married Christina Cheeseman, a German lady. Gabriella married Cunningham Parsons. Thomas married Rebecca Anderson, and lives in High Hill, Missouri.

CALLAWAY.—John B. Callaway was the eldest son of Flanders Callaway and Jemima Boone.* He was a fine scribe and an excel-

---

*It is stated elsewhere that Capt. James Callaway was the eldest son, but it is a mistake, as we have learned since that portion of the book was printed.

lent business man, and was Justice of the Peace and Judge of the County Court for many years. A large proportion of the old legal papers of St. Charles county have the name of John B. Callaway attached to them as Justice of the Peace. He had a mill and a distillery on Femme Osage creek, and the water for the distillery was carried some distance in troughs, made by hollowing out poles, which were kept free of mud by crawfish, placed in the troughs for that purpose. Mr. Callaway died in 1825. His wife was Elizabeth Caton, and their children were— Emaline, Verlenia, James, and Octavia. Emaline married Hayden Boone, a son of Squire Boone, who was a nephew of Daniel Boone. Verlenia married John Bryan, a son of Henry Bryan. James married Mary McKinney, daughter of Alexander McKinney. They live in Mexico, Mo., where Mr. Callaway, who is a capitalist, is engaged in the banking business. Octavia married Schuyler Rice, who was from New England.

CATON.—Jesse Caton, of Kentucky, settled near the present site of Marthasville, in Warren county, in 1811. He married a Miss Sparks, who was a sister of Henry Bryan's wife, and their children were—Noah, Jonas, Jesse, Jr., Elizabeth, Nancy, Jemima, Mahala, Rebecca, Fannie, and Hester. Noah married a Miss McDermid. Jesse, Jr., married Missouri Lamme. Elizabeth married John B. Callaway, son of Flanders Callaway. Nancy married Adam Zumwalt. Jemima and Mahala married John Carter. Rebecca married a Mr. McCutchen. Fannie married Daniel Gillis. Hester married a man in Southwest Missouri, but we could not obtain his name.

DAVIS.—Louis Davis, of England, came to America and settled in Virginia, prior to the revolution. He had one son, Louis, Jr., who married Agnes Walton, and they had nine children— Lourena, Mary, Saluda, Sally, Jincia, Edna, Louis, Thompson, and John K., all of whom married and lived and died in Virginia. Isaac T., the second son of John K. Davis, married Martha Langford, and settled in Warren county in 1835. They had five children.

ELLIS.—Charles Ellis, of Virginia, married his cousin, Nancy Ellis, and they had—Thomas, Polly, Stephen, Elizabeth, Nancy, Charles, Joseph, Martha, James M., and Susan. Mr. Ellis removed from Richmond, Va., to Shelby Co., Ky., in 1815. Stephen married Mary Young, of Kentucky, and settled in Warren Co., Mo., in 1826. In 1847 he removed to St. Charles county, where he died. His children were—James, Charles, Nancy, Sarah C., Martha F., Mary H., and William T. Joseph Ellis was married twice; first, to Nancy Netherton, by whom he had—Henry C., Mildred C., Charles M., Ann E., Lucy B., Paulina, Joseph, Stephen E., John G., William S., and Martha L. After the death of his first wife Mr. Ellis married the widow of

14

Benjamin Pitts, whose maiden name was Susan R. Simms. Martha Ellis married Thomas Moffitt, of Virginia, who settled in St. Charles Co., Mo., in 1830. Elizabeth married Edward R. Kelso, who settled in St. Charles Co., Mo., in 1831. The most of their children moved to Texas.

FINES.—Vincent Fines, of Germany, settled first in Pennsylvania, from whence he removed to Tennessee, where he was killed by the Indians. His children were—Thomas, William, Abraham, Isaac, Phœbe, and Sally. After the death of her husband, Mrs. Fines married Rueben Bedford, by whom she had three children. Thomas married Mary Nave, of Tennessee, by whom he had—Levi, Abraham, Sally, Delila and Amy. Mr. Fines was killed by an accidental discharge of his gun, and in 1817 his widow and children came to Missouri. Abraham married Cynthia Harper, in 1819. The nearest Justice of the Peace was James Duncan, of Lincoln county, who lived sixteen miles distant, and was too old to go so far to marry people. But he agreed to meet them half way. Accordingly on the day of the wedding they set out on foot, and walked to the designated place, where the 'Squire met them and performed the ceremony, and they walked back home the same day. Mrs. Fines still has the dress that she wore on that memorable occasion. Mr. Fines was a very active man, and no one could beat him on a foot race. He was one of the first grand jurymen of Montgomery county. He says that while out hunting one day, he came upon a den of rattlesnakes, whose heads were so thick where they stretched themselves out of their den that they looked like corn stubbles in a field. He fired into them with his gun and then ran away without looking back to see what execution he had done. Levi Fines married Nancy Oden. Sally married Jacob Oden. Delila married Nicholas Shrumb. Amy married Joseph Shrumb. Phillip, a brother of Vincent Fines, settled in St. Louis county in 1800. He was a small man, and had a small wife and daughter. Their aggregate weight was two hundred and fifty pounds.

FOURT.—Dr. Andrew Fourt was born in Maryland in 1780. When he was fourteen years of age his parents removed to Kentucky, where, in 1807, he married Sarah Wyatt. In 1810 he came to Missouri with his wife and two children, on pack horses, and settled near Charrette village in (now) Warren county. When the Indian war began he joined Capt. Callaway's company of rangers, and served twelve months. When Montgomery county was organized, Dr. Fourt was appointed one of the commissioners to locate the county seat, and Pinckney, near the Missouri river, was chosen as the place. The Doctor subsequently located there, and opened the first hotel in the place, which he kept three years, and then removed to the head of Pinckney Bottom, where he lived until his death, which occurred on the 27th day of November, 1852. He had eight children—Emsley, John T., Peter W., Pullyan M., Elizabeth, Martha S., Sarah J., and Louisa. Six of the children married and raised families.

GRISWOLD.—Harvey and Frederick Griswold, of Connecticut, were cousins. They emigrated to the West, and settled in (now) Warren county, Mo., at a very early date. Frederick married Rebecca Shobe, and opened the first store in Pinckney. They had no children. Harvey came to Missouri when he was only about sixteen years of age, and walked from St. Louis to Pinckney, carrying his wardrobe and all the property he possessed tied up in a cotton handkerchief. His cousin Frederick at first hired him to clerk in his store, but afterward bought a store at Marthasville, and sent him there to take charge of it. He subsequently purchased the store on his own account, and followed the mercantile business for many years, acquiring a comfortable fortune before his death. He married Mahala Shobe, a sister of Frederick Griswold's wife, and they had sixteen children, only six of whom lived to be grown, viz: Rebecca, William, Sylvanus, Prudence, Angeline, and Frederick. Mr. Griswold owned the land on which the graves of Daniel Boone and his wife were situated, and he bitterly opposed the removal of the remains, but in vain. It was his intention to erect a monument over the graves, and otherwise beautify the last resting place of the old pioneer and his wife.

GILKEY.—John Gilkey, of Ireland, married Jemima Pattenger, of Virginia, by whom he had—Allen, John, David, Elizabeth, Samuel, Barbara, William, and Thomas. David married Sally A. Murdock, by whom he had—Erasmus D., John G., William L., Sarah E., James P., and Ellen W. Mr. Gilkey settled in Warren county in 1824, and his wife died in 1830 He afterward married Polly Wyatt, when he was seventy-five years old. William L. Gilkey married Elizabeth Liles. Sarah E. married James Bowen. Jemima P. married William C. Gilkey, her cousin. Ellen W. married Samuel Kennedy.

GRAVES.—Thomas Graves, of Culpepper county, Va., was a soldier and Quartermaster in the revolutionary war. He married the widow Simms, by whom he had—Thomas N., Elizabeth, Nancy, Lucy, and Waller. Thomas married Mary Mason, of Virginia, and in 1806 he removed, with his father and sisters Elizabeth and Nancy, to Barbour county, Ky., from whence, in 1820, they came to Warren county, Mo. The names of Thomas' children were—James B., William M., Candice A., Henry B., and Lucy M. Mr. Graves was Judge of the County Court of both Montgomery and Warren counties. James B., his eldest son, moved to Oregon. William M. disappeared in a mysterious manner while in New Orleans, Louisiana. Candice married Usurdus Brainbridge, of St. Charles county. Henry B. married Lucinda Howell, and lives in California. Lucy M. married Woodson A. Burton, who settled in Warren county in 1830. Warren, the brother of Thomas Graves, settled in Warren county in 1826. His children, whose names were John, Henry, Mary, and Ann, remained in Virginia.

GIBSON.—Archibald Gibson, of Ireland, emigrated to America and settled in Virginia. He had a son named Joseph, who served in the war of 1812. Joseph married Susan Hudson, and settled in Lincoln county, Mo., in 1818. His children were— Mary, Elizabeth, Archibald, Nancy, John, William, Patsy, Susan, Lucinda, and Malinda. Mr. Gibson was married the second time to the widow Caffer, whose maiden name was Matilda Wright. By her he had Rufus, Mary, Waller, Matilda, Martha, Richard, Emma, and Thomas J. Mr. Gibson died in Lincoln county in his 87th year. Archibald, Elizabeth, and John married and settled in Warren county. John married Sarah A. Wright. He was at a camp-meeting, once, where a woman near him took the jerks, and fell into his arms. Never having seen anything of the kind before, he was astonished and bewildered, and called out at the top of his voice, "Here, Mr. Preacher, your attention, please. Here's a woman with a fit!" But the "fit" soon left her, and he was relieved. Lucinda Gibson married Felix Kountz, and settled in St. Charles county. Martha married Mr. Patton, of Warren county. Malinda married Mr. Spencer, and settled in St. Charles county.

GIBSON.—Guion Gibson came from Duck River, Tennessee, and settled in (now) Warren county in 1810. His children were— Sarah, Rachel, Ellen, Samuel, Joseph, John, Polly, Guion, Jr., and James. Sarah married Thomas Kennedy. Rachel married Lawrence Sitter. Ellen married Phillip Sitter. Samuel married Tabitha Kennedy. Joseph married Elizabeth Armstrong. John married Polly Sitter. Polly Gibson married John Shrumb. Guion, Jr., married Saloma Sitter. James married Diana Sitter. James, John, and Guion, Jr., were rangers in Callaway's company.

GRAY.—When Robert Gray was a small boy he lost his father, while they were moving from North Carolina to Tennessee. He had four sisters—Polly, Dorcas, Elizabeth, and Jane. After the death of his father, his mother proceeded on her way to Tennessee, with her children; and they remained in that State until 1809, when they came to (now) Warren county, Mo. During the Indian war they lived the greater portion of the time in Castlio's Fort, in St. Charles county. Polly Gray married Rueben Thornhill, Dorcas Barney Thornhill, and Jane Bryant Thornhill, all of whom were early settlers of Warren county. Elizabeth married Job Stark, who was also an early settler of Warren county. Robert married Elizabeth Liles, by whom he had—James, Milton, Henry, Elizabeth, and Jane, only a part of whom lived to be grown.

HUGHES.—James Hughes, of Ireland, settled in Pennsylvania. His son James married and settled in Sullivan county, Tennessee. By his first wife he had but one child, a son named Alexander; and by his second wife a daughter, named Gertrude, who married James M. Owings. Mr. Hughes built a keel-boat, in which he conveyed his family and property to Missouri, coming down the Holsten, Tennessee and Ohio rivers, and up the Mississippi and Missouri.

HOWARD.—Cornelius Howard, of Kentucky, was married first to a Miss Griggs, by whom he had—Rachel, Cynthia, Elizabeth, Martin, John, and two others whose names we could not obtain. He was married the second time to the widow Hunt, but had no children by her. She had eight children of her own at the time he married her. One of the Misses Howard was a very beautiful girl, and one day she handed some water to a stranger who called at the gate and begged for a drink. The stranger fell desperately in love with this beautiful Rebecca, and married her two days afterward. In 1816 Mr. Howard settled on Brush Creek, in Warren county, and lived there two years. He cleared a field and raised two crops of corn, but now the field is covered with large oak trees, and the Brush Creek Presbyterian Church stands about the center of it. In 1818 he moved and settled on South Bear creek, wher he died many years afterward.

HAYS.—Jeremiah Hays, of Ireland, married Jane Moore, of Scotland, and came to America and settled in Bourbon county, Kentucky, where they had—Mary, Delila, Nancy, Joanna, Absalom, Jane, Thomas, Joseph, and Mahala. Mr. Hays, with his wife and two daughters, Jane and Mahala, started to Montgomery county, Mo., but when they reached St. Louis he died. His widow and children settled near Marthasville. Jane married Oliver McCleur, of Pennsylvania, who was a blacksmith, and settled in Warren county. Mahala maried John Ward, of Kentucky, who was a hatter, and also settled in Warren county. Absalom and Joseph Hays came to Missouri with Dr. John Young, in 1816. Joseph married Kate Mahoney, and settled in Montgomery county. Absalom was the second Sheriff of Montgomery county, and after the organization of Warren, he was elected the first Sheriff of that county, which office he held alternately until 1845. He married Anna Skinner, of Montgomery county, by whom he had—Jeremiah, Susan, John A., Jane, and Mary C. The year after Mr. Hays' marriage he had to attend court at Lewiston, and took his wife and little child with him to her father's, who lived on Camp Branch, to remain while he was at court. But the session lasted longer than he expected, and his wife, impatient to be at home, persuaded her father to go with her. The journey was too long for one day, and they stopped over night at the house of Mr. John Wyatt. During the evening Mrs. Wyatt put on her spectacles, and after scrutinizing Mrs. Hays and her child very closely for some time, she turned to Mr. Skinner and said she was "monstrous" glad that was not his wife and child, for "of all things she did despise upon this earth was an old man with a young wife and child; for," she added, "it is the most bominubler thing in the world." Mr. Hays was lame from his birth, and sometime before his death he was thrown from a horse and received an injury from which he never entirely recovered. After the death of her husband, Mrs. Hays continued to live on the farm near Marthasville, until the late war, when she was broken up, and has since lived with her children. She now resides in Jonesburg, Montgomery county, with her daughter Jane, and still enjoys good health for a person so advanced in years.

HANCOCK.—William Hancock was a pioneer of both Kentucky and Missouri. In the former State he helped to fight the Indians and guard the forts, and experienced the dangers and privations of those times. He came to Missouri among the first Americans who sought homes here, and was the first settler on the Missouri river bottom, in Warren county, which has since borne his name. He was married in St. Charles county to a Miss Mc-Clain, by whom he had three children, two daughters and a son named William, Jr. The latter died at home, unmarried. One of the daughters, named Mary, married Capt. Hamilton, and they now live on the old homestead. Capt. Hamilton served with distinction in the war with Mexico. The other daughter married Dr. George Y. Bast, of New Florence, Mo. Mr. Hancock was a jovial man, and fond of practical jokes. He and Anthony Wyatt and Jacob Darst once took a flat-boat loaded with pork and peltries to Natchez, Miss., and while there they concocted a plan to show Darst—who was a devil-may-care sort of a man—as a wild man of the forest. Accordingly they rigged him out in an appropriate costume, and exhibited him with great succes, the room being crowded with visitors during the entire exhibition. Darst enjoyed the joke equally as well as his two companions, and they all reaped a substantial reward for their pains. Hancock and John Wyatt ran for the Legislature once, and the vote was a tie. They tried it over, and tied again, when Hancock withdrew and let Wyatt have the office.

HOPKINS.—William Hopkins, of South Carolina, removed to Kentucky, where he married Jane Stone, and in 1810 he came to

Missouri, and lived for some time in Captain James Callaway's house. In the spring of 1819 he settled in (now) Warren county. His children were—Cynthia, Isaac, Walker, Polly, Sally, Thomas, Jane, Matilda, Lucy, Anna, Benjamin, John, and Susan. Isaac married Elizabeth Brown. Walker married Nancy Gibson, by whom he had twenty children. He was married a second time to Jane Beck, a daughter of one of the first settlers of Warren county. Thomas married Lydia Beck. Jane married Joseph Hatfield. Matilda married James Stark. Lucy married John Zumwalt. John married Sally Cops. Susan married John Corker. Anna and Benjamin died of measles

HART.—Capt. Hart was a native of the State of New Jersey, where, during the French and Indian war, previous to the American revolution, he raised a company of men and was commissioned Captain. He was with General Wolf's army at the battle of Quebec, in Canada, in 1759, where that gallant young general fell. Capt. Hart's company behaved with great gallantry on that occasion, and the men, who were dressed in blue uniforms, were afterward known as the "Jersey Blues." Honest John Hart, as he was called, was a son of Capt. Hart, and one of the signers of the Declaration of Independence. Nathaniel, the fourth son of Honest John Hart, settled in Mason county, Ky., in 1795. His son, also named Nathaniel, was born May 5, 1794, and came to Missouri in 1819. He settled first in St. Charles county, where he remained one year, and then, in 1820, removed to Warren county, and settled near Pinckney; where, on March 6th, 1823, he was married to Unity L. Marshall, daughter of John Marshall, of Montgomery county, Ky., who was one of the first settlers of Warren county. Mr. Hart is now living in Boone county, in his 83d year. He had several children, but they all died in infancy, except two sons, Joseph E. and Alfred H., who also live in Boone county. He has in his possession a cane that belonged to his grandfather, Honest John Hart.

HUGHES.—John Hughes, of England, came to America and settled in Virginia, where he married and raised three children— John, Jr., Nancy, and Mary A. John married in Virginia, and had seven children. One of his sons, named Andrew, married Elizabeth Thompson, by whom he had—Sarah, Thomas S. T., Reason, Elizabeth, Louisa, Harriet, Waddy, Susan, Joseph, and George. Thomas S. T. came to the City of St. Louis in 1830, where he was married, first to Rebecca Downs, and second to Rebecca Wells. Andrew Hughes settled in St. Charles county in 1839, and his daughter, Reason, married Samuel Abington. Elizabeth married John Williams, of Warren county. Louisa married Thomas Royston, who died in North Carolina. Harriet married Sidney Woods, of St. Charles county. Susan married St. James Matthews, of St. Charles county, and after his death she married Archibald Caruthers. Waddy died single. Joseph married Sarah Carycoe, and settled in Warren county. George settled in Colorado.

HOWARD.—David Howard, of Mount Sterling, Ky., married first to Margaret Fourt, and settled on Charrette creek, in Warren county, 1819. His children were—James, Peter, Thomas, Polly, John, and Jackson. After the death of his first wife, Mr. Howard married the widow McCutchen, whose maiden name was Rebecca Caton. By her he had Elizabeth, George, and Naoma. Mr. Howard was a great hunter and sugar maker, and made the best maple sugar in the country. He was also a zealous Methodist, and his name is prominetly identified with the early history of that church in his county. His son, John Howard, is at present Sheriff and Collector of Warren county.

IRVINE.—Jared Irvine was one of the early settlers of Warren county. He married Mary Peebles, and they had—Eliza J., Louisa, and John. Mr. Irvine served as a soldier in the war of 1812, when he was only sixteen years of age. He was captured in one of the battles and taken to Canada, and after his exchange he walked from Canada to his home in Kentucky. He was a member of the first grand jury of Warren county, and was a leading and influential citizen.

JAMES.—Benjamin James married Nancy Fourt, of Kentucky, and settled in (now) Warren county in 1811. He joined the rangers during the Indian war, and saw some active service. His children were—William, John, Walter, and Peter. John fell from a mill dam on Charrette creek, and was drowned. Peter lived in St. Louis county, and never married. Walter married Sally Wyatt, and they had—Frank, Mary A., William J., John, Elizabeth, Walter R., Joseph, and Lycurgus.

JONES.—Henry Jones, of Wales, emigrated to America, and settled in Henry county, Va., where he married and had the following children—Fielding, Joseph, Lewis, Peter, Willis, Delila, and Elizabeth. Lewis married Fannie Lamb, of North Carolina, and settled in Missouri in 1837. His children were—Henry, Zero, Joseph, George, Elizabeth, Willis Malinda, Lewis, Delila, and Fielding, all of whom married and settled in Missouri. Willis is a Baptist preacher, and married Margaret C. Burson, of Virginia, whose father was also a Baptist preacher.

JONES.—Giles Jones was an Englishman, but came to America and served as a soldier in the revolutionary war. His son John came to Missouri in 1817, and studied medicine under Dr. Young. Dr. Jones married Minerva Callaway, daughter of Flanders Callaway, and granddaughter of Daniel Boone, and settled near Marthasville. They had the following children—James, Caroline, Emily, Daniel, John S., Ellen, Paul, Samuel, George, and Anna.

The Doctor became celebrated as a physician, and had an extensive practice. He was also very fond of hunting, and had a horse named Nick, that he generally rode on his hunting expeditions. Sometimes, just as he would be in the act of firing at a deer or some other game, Nick would move and cause him to miss his aim. The horse did this one day just as he was drawing a bead on a fine buck, and the buck escaped unhurt, which so enraged the Doctor that he determined to give him a whipping. So he alighted and cut a keen switch, and placed the bridle under his feet to keep old Nick from running away while he whipped him; but the horse jerked his head up at the first cut of the switch, threw the Doctor on the back of his head, and nearly killed him. After that, when he tried to whip old Nick, he held the bridle in his hand. Dr. Jones took a prominent part in ferreting out the counterfeiters and horse thieves with which the country was infested from about 1835 to 1844, when the "Slicker" organization put a stop to their rascally practices. By so doing he incurred the enmity of the gang, and the 22d of January, 1842, he was shot and killed in his own yard, by an assassin who was concealed in the woods near the house. The whole country was thrown into a state of excitement by this murder, and the repeated outrages which led to it, and companies of regulators and patrols were organized in every community. But notwithstanding the most delight and thorough search was made for the murderer, no trace of him could ever be found. Several suspected parties were arrested and tried, but they generally had but little difficulty in proving their innocence.

KABLER.—Rev. Nicholas C. Kabler, of Campbell Co., Va., was a son of Rev. Nicholas Kabler, of the same county. He married Sarah Goldon, of Virginia, and settled in Warren Co., Mo., in 1830. He was a Methodist minister, and traveled with Rev. Andrew Monroe for a number of years. His children were—Ellen, Simeon, William A., Lucy, Anna, Parks, and Charles. Ellen married William McMurtry, of Callaway county. Simeon and Lucy died in Virginia. William A. married Lucy J. Pendleton, of Warren county, whose father and mother, James Pendleton and Nancy Sharp, settled in that county in 1833. Her brothers and sisters were—Robert, Frances, Patrick, Elizabeth, James L., and Caroline. Anna Kabler married Marcellus C. Poindexter, of St. Louis. Charles lives in California, unmarried.

KENNEDY.—John Kennedy and his wife, whose maiden name was Margaret Rowan, of Ireland, came to America and settled in Virginia many years before the revolution. They had eight children—John, James, William, Thomas, George, Abraham, Margaret, and Jane. John was killed by the Indians while assisting to cut a road from Knoxville to Nashville, Tennessee. James settled in South Carolina, where he died. William was captured by the British, while serving in the continental army, and died on board one of their prison ships.   George and Margaret were killed by the Indians, where Nashville, Tenn., now stands.   Their mother died shortly after, and was the first white woman who died a natural death in the State of Tennessee. Abraham emigrated to Missouri in 1808, and joined Nathan Boone's company of rangers in 1812.   He removed to Texas in 1834, where he died.   His wife's maiden name was Rhoda Cartleman, of South Carolina.   Thomas was in the 5th regiment of Virginia volunteers during the revolutionary war, and was at the massacre of Beaver Creek, South Carolina.   After that he served as a scout in Capt. Murphy Barnett's company, until the close of the war.   He then went to Tennessee, but remained only a short time, when he returned to South Carolina, and married his second wife, whose name was Sarah Gibson.   In 1807 he came to St. Charles Co., Mo., where he remained until the commencement of the Indian war, when he removed to near the present town of Wright City, and built a fort there.   His children were—James, Gayem, Abraham, Pleasant, Royal, Ellen, Tabitha, Rhoda, Sarah, Ann, Dinah S., Narcissa, and Amanda.   James was a ranger in Capt. Callaway's company, and was present when he was killed. He married Sally Lyle.   Gayem married Elizabeth Sitten.   Abraham married Sally Rice. Pleasant married Harriet Sullivan.   Royal was married twice; first to Caroline McKezell, and second to Margaret E. Huntchinson.   He has long been a prominent citizen of Warren county, having served as County Judge for several terms, and in 1860 he was elected a member of the Legislature. —Ellen Kennedy married Thomas Chambers.   Tabitha married Samuel Gibson.   Rhoda married Allen Jamison   Sarah was married first to Thomas Livingston, and second to William Perkins.   Ann married Benjamin F. Ruggles.   Dinah S. married Isaac Kent.   Amanda married Levi Tilson.

KITE.—Martin Kite, of Virginia, was of German descent.   He married a Miss Cheeley, of Virginia, by whom he had George and Kitty, and several other children whose names we could not obtain.   George and Kitty both live in Warren county.   Mr. Kite settled in that county in 1835, and built a mill on Charrette creek.   The lumber from which most of the flat-boats of that period were built, was sawed at Kite's mill.

KETCHERSIDES.—A man named Ketchersides, a cooper by trade, came from Tennessee at a very early date, and settled on Massey's Creek in (now) Warren county.   He remained only one year, when he sold out and returned to Tennessee.   In about another year he made his appearance in Missouri again, but remained only a short time, when he went back to his old State. He continued in this way until his death, remaining in one State only so long as it was necessary to get money enough to take him back to the other.

KENT.—Isaac Kent, of Kentucky, lost his parents when he was quite young, and was "bound out" to be raised. When he was of age he married Lucy Hopkins, and they had—John, William, Jane, Andrew, Robert, Elizabeth, Polly, Thomas, Isaac, Dozier, Louisa, and Lucinda. Mr. Kent came to Missouri and settled in Warren county in 1819. His son John married Catharine Zumwalt. William married Mary A. Zumwalt, and was killed by Waller Graves, who was insane, at the house of Newton Howell, on the 2d of October, 1830. Andrew Kent enlisted as a soldier in the Mexican war, and was burned to death in one of the forts captured by the Americans. Robert, Elizabeth, Isaac, Polly, and Thomas all moved to Oregon. John Kent was a ranger in Callaway's company.

LEEPER.—Thomas Leeper was born in Jefferson Co., Va., and came to Missouri in 1821, with John Reynolds, when he was only eight years of age. He married his first wife, whose name was Elizabeth Edwards, in 1838, and they had three children. After her death he married Ruth A. Griggs.

LONG.—Lawrence Long, of Culpepper Co., Va., settled in St. Louis Co., Mo., in 1797, and built a saw and grist mill. His children were—Gabriel, John, William, James, Nicholas, Nancy, Sally, and Elizabeth. John married Rachel Zumwalt, by whom he had—Lawrence and Andrew J. He died soon after, and in 1823 his widow and her two sons removed to Warren county, where she married Newton Howell. Lawrence married Malinda Hutchings, of St. Charles county. Andrew J. married Mary W. Preston of St. Charles county.

LANGFORD.—Parrish Langford married Sally Lawrence, of North Carolina, and they settled first in Virginia, from whence they removed to Smith Co., Tenn. They had five children—William, Arthur, Jesse, Henry, and Moses. William, who was a soldier in the war of 1812, married Sally King, of South Carolina, and settled in Warren county in 1818. Their children were—Elizabeth, Polly, Nancy, Sally A., Delila, Lawrence, Arthur, Joshua, Jesse, Richard W., John, William, and Henry. Nancy and Delila married and settled in Pike Co., Mo. Lawrence, Henry, Jesse, William, and Arthur married and settled in Warren county. Joshua settled in Lawrence Co., Mo. Lawrence married Polly McCann, a daughter of Neal McCann, who was an early settler of Warren county.

LAMME.—William T. and James Lamme were sons of Robert Lamme, of Bourbon Co., Ky. William T. settled in (now) Warren Co., Mo., in 1803. He was 1st Lieutenant in Nathan Boone's company of rangers, and was afterward Major of a regiment. He married Frances Callaway, daughter of Flanders Callaway, and granddaughter of Daniel Boone, by whom he had ten children—Serena, Zarina, Hulda, Cornelia, Missouri, Josephine, Jackson, Leonidas, Achiles, and Napoleon B. Mr. Lamme had a good education, was a fine business man, and left his family in good circumstances at his death. Zarina Lamme married Willis Bryan, a son of David Bryan, who was the first settler within the present limits of Warren county. Hulda married John Bryan, called "Long Jack," on account of his extraordinary height, who was also a son of David Bryan. Missouri married Jesse Caton. Josephine married Campbell Marshall. All of the above are dead except Hulda, who lives with her son, John C., who is Recorder of Franklin county, and a pominent and influential citizen. Achiles Lamme lives in Montana, where he carries on an extensive mercantile business. Napoleon B. lives in California. Serena married Lewis Howell.

LILES.—Hugh Liles and his wife and children, whose names were—Robert, Polly, William, James, Elizabeth, Sally, and Ann —settled in (now) Warren county in the year 1809. Robert, the eldest son, married Polly Walker, and settled in Audrain county, Mo. Polly married Joshua James, and settled in Warren county. Sally married James Kennedy. Ann married a German. Hugh Liles was a great hunter, and belonged to the rangers.

MARTIN.—James Martin, of Campbell county, Va., married Caroline Burton, by whom he had—William, Elizabeth, Oliver W., Frances A., Edward M., Caroline W., Cynthia P., Sarah, and Thomas J. Mr. Martin settled in Warren county in 1830. William and Elizabeth remained in Virginia. Caroline W. married Garret Pratt, and lives in Warren county. Cynthia P. married William H. H. Simpson, of St. Charles county. Sarah married Charles A. Womack, of Lincoln county.

McKINNEY.—John McKinney, of Staunton, Virginia, served in the American army during the latter part of the revolution, and had his thigh broken by a musket ball, which lamed him for life. He settled at Lexington, Kentucky, where he taught school, and was elected Sheriff of the county. He married a Mexican woman, by whom he raised a large family. In 1805 he came to Missouri on a trading and prospecting tour, and in 1809 he moved his family here. When the Indian war began, he took his family back to Kentucky, to get them out of danger. His son Alexander remained, married Nancy Bryan, who was only sixteen years of age, and settled near Charrette creek, in (now) Warren county. He was a surveyor and a fine business man, and accumulated a fortune before his death. He also served in the State Legislature during several sessions. His sister Elizabeth married John King, who settled near Marthasville. John McKinney traveled back and forth between Kentucky and Missouri as long as he lived, trading in land and land warrants.

MORGAN.—Mordecai Morgan, of Shelby county, Kentucky, married Catharine Turner, and settled in (now) Warren county, Missouri, in 1814. He was a noted pioneer of that county, and the first County Court was held in his house. His children were Malinda, Hiram, Rachel, Maranda, Matilda, Missouri, Martha, and Minerva. Malinda married James Bryan, a son of David Bryan. Hiram was a ranger in Nathan Boone's company. He died of cholera, at Rock Island, in 1832. Rachel married Samuel Dougherty, of Warren county. Maranda married Louisa Harper, of Lincoln county. Matilda married Levi Hinds, of Tennessee, who settled in Warren county. Missouri died single. Martha married William Harper, who is at present a banker in Mexico, Missouri. Minerva married Edward Pleasants, of Virginia, who settled in Warren county, Missouri, in 1830.

NORTHCUT.—John Northcut, of Kentucky, married Jane Trimble, and settled on Charrette creek in 1820. He was an ardent Methodist, and used to exhort and preach in a style peculiar to himself. He had three daughters, and was very much opposed to their getting married. He was not willing for them to learn to write, lest they should send letters to their sweethearts; but they all contrived to get married in spite of his precautions. The names of his children were—Elizabeth, George, John, Polly, Joseph E., Stemmons, and Jane. Elizabeth married Mr. Keithey, of St. Charles county. George married Kitty Welch, and raised a large family before his death. John married Kitty Kite, of Warren county. Polly married Nathan Keithley, and lives in Lynn county, Missouri. Joseph E. married Miss Welch, daughter of John Welch, of Warren county. Stemmons married a daughter of Henry Welch, of the same county. Jane married James Welch.

OWINGS.—George Owings, of Maryland, married a Miss Wells, by whom he had twelve children. He was married the second time, and had twelve children more. Two of his sons, John and Thomas, by his first wife, came to Missouri in 1816, and settled in Warren county. Thomas married Mary O'Brien, and moved to Illinois. John was in the war of 1812. He married Hattie McGarvey, by whom he had fifteen children—James M., Richard, George W., David R., Joseph E., John B., Thomas, William H., Wesley, Rachel, Nancy, Julia, Maria, Eliza J., and Emily. All the children lived to be grown, and all married except Wesley and Rachel. Mr. Owings was a devout Methodist, and built a church near his house, which he called Ebenezer. He came to Missouri in a cart, drawn by two horses, one before the other. He kept this cart for many years, and used it on his farm.

PRATT.—Thomas Pratt, of Culpepper county, Virginia, married a Miss Smith, by whom he had Thomas B., Elizabeth, and Ann. His first wife died, and he was married the second time to Martha Terrell, by whom he had—Jonathan, Milton W., Lucinda, Mary, and Martha. Mr. Pratt settled in Warren county in 1831, with all of his children except Thomas B., and most of them now reside in that county.

PRINGLE.—Norman Pringle, of Connecticut, settled in Warren county in 1819. He was a very intelligent man, and was frequently solicited to run for office, but always refused, because he had so great a dislike for politics. He married Sally Kellogg, by whom he had nine children—Jane, Judith, Helen, Harriet, Huldah R., Virgil, Mark, Norman O., and Charles W. All of the children except Mark (who died a bachelor) married, and most of them live in Warren county.

PRESTON.—John Preston was left an orphan when very young, but at eight years of age he was adopted by an old gentleman and his wife, who were very kind to him. They took him to Rock Castle Co., Ky., and educated him, as though he had been their own son. When he was of age he married Jane Day, and came to St. Charles Co., Mo., in 1820. They had eleven children, only five of whom lived to be grown. Their names were—Frank L., Mary W., Caroline V., Liberty M., and Fanny H. Mr. Preston and his wife were the first members of the Old Baptist Church at Warrenton.

PRICE.—Lemuel Price, of North Carolina, settled on the Boone's Lick road, near Camp Branch, in (now) Warren county, in 1815. He came to Missouri the year previous, but as the Indians were very troublesome at that time, he remained in one of the forts until the following year, when he erected his cabin at the place mentioned above. It was the first habitation erected on Camp Branch. Isaac VanBibber, Patrick Ewing, Boone Hays, and Lewis Jones assisted in raising the cabin. Mr. Price had eight children—James, Lamb W., Parthena, Margaret, Miles, Job, Caroline, and Alfonso. James married and moved to Texas. Parthena married John Thurman. Margaret married Joseph Thurman. Miles married the widow of John Skinner. Job married a Miss Bryan. Caroline married a man named Williams. Alfonso married Sarah Gammon, and they had—Lamb, Benjamin Elizabeth, Lucinda, John, Timothy, Virginia, Alfonso, and Anna.

SHERMAN.—David Sherman, who was a millwright by trade, settled in Warren county in 1819. His wife's maiden name was Margaret Root, and their children were—David, William, Lucinda, Ira, Frank, Mary A., Charles, Electa M., and George W. All these, except David, married and settled in Missouri.

SIMPSON.—James Simpson was the owner of Simpson's Ferry on the Kentucky river. He had a son named Erasmus, who married Mary Bartlett, of Virginia, and they had—Fortes B., Elizabeth, Thomas, James W., Martha, William H. H., John L., Mary, Julia, and Jeptha D. Fortes B. settled in Warren county in 1828. Elizabeth married William B. King, and they settled in St. Charles county in 1830. Martha married Sidney S. Wood, who settled in St. Charles county in 1835. Julia married Joseph I. Carter, and settled in St. Charles county in 1836.

TICE.—John Tice, a German, and an uncle of the celebrated Prof. Tice, of St. Louis, settled in Warren county about 1809, and was the first settler on Pinckney Bottom. When the overflow of 1824 came he refused to leave his house, but moved his family upstairs and waited patiently for the water to subside. But in order to be prepared for escape in case of an emergency, he tied two meat troughs together to be used as a canoe. Some of his neighbors who had fled to the hills, became alarmed at the absence of Tice and his family, and went to their house on a raft, to see what had become of them. They found them safe, but unwilling to abandon their home; so they left them. Fortunately the water did not sweep the house away or reach the second story, and they remained in safety until the river receded into its banks. When Mr. Tice first settled on Pinckney Bottom, the country was infested by hostile Indians, and they had to be always on the lookout for them. One day Tice went into the woods near the river, for some purpose, and came close upon a white man who was making an ax helve, without perceiving him. The man, thinking he would have a little fun, rapped upon the ax helve with the blade of his knife, making it sound like the snapping of a gun, which frightened Tice so badly that he sprang into the river and swam to the other side. The names of Mr. Tice's children were—John, Joseph, Mary, and Sally. The latter was a splendid ball player, and played with the boys at school, who always chose her first, because she could beat any of them.

WYATT.—Frank Wyatt was a native of North Carolina, but settled and lived in Montgomery Co., Ky. He came to Missouri five times to look at the country, but could never make up his mind to move here. He had four sons—John, Anthony, Douglass, and Joseph. John was a Captain in the war of 1812. He settled in Missouri in 1817, and married Attossa Sharp, by whom he had seven children—John, Jr., Sarah, Harriet, Catharine, Margaret, Lucy, and Mary. Anthony came to Missouri in 1816. He married Mary Smith, daughter of Henry Smith and Nancy Davis (who were natives of Wales), and by her he had—Henry S., James W., Joseph, Martha A., Nancy J., and Frank. Douglass Wyatt settled in Missouri in 1817. He married Elizabeth See, of Montgomery county, and they had—Hayden, Amanda,

Emily, Frank, Douglass, Jr., Joseph and Mary. Joseph Wyatt, son of Frank, Sr., died a bachelor, in Franklin Co., Mo. (Children of Anthony Wyatt.) Henry S. married Sarah Hopping. James W. married Martha A. Pearle. Joseph married Susan Griswold. Martha A. married Thomas J. Marshall, of Mexico, Mo., who was County Clerk of Warren county for eighteen years. Nancy J. married John Jones, of Mexico, Mo. Frank was married twice; first to Eliza A. Jones, and after her death, to Maria Farsdale. Mr. Wyatt built a ferry boat for Thomas Howell, who paid him in gold, and then offered to run a foot race for the money he had paid him. But Mr. Wyatt did not consider it safe to take the risk, notwithstanding he was a young man and Mr. H. was sixty-seven years old.

WALLER.—Thomas Waller, of Spottsylvania Co., Va., was born in July, 1732, and his wife, Sarah Dabney, was born in October, 1740. They had nine children—Mary, Anna, Agnes, Dolly, Carr, Dabney, Comfort, Elizabeth, and John. Carr married Elizabeth Martin, by whom he had—Sarah M., William I., Joseph G., and Martha M. Sarah M. married Henry Edwards. William I. married Maria Norval. Joseph G. married Virginia McDonnell, and settled in Warren Co., Mo., in 1830. They had nine children—Susan, Martha, Agnes, Jane, Collin, John, Louisa, Joseph, and Eliza.—Martha M. Waller married Henry Pritchett, who settled in Missouri in 1835. Their children were—Carr W., Lizzie, Sarah, William I., Julia D., Joseph H., John F., Martha P., Edwin, and Mary E. Joseph H. is a distinguished Methodist minister, and Carr W., principal of Pritchett Institute at Glasgow, Mo., is one of the most highly educated men in the State. The Waller and Pritchett families are well educated and intelligent, and exercise a large influence for good in their respective communities.

WRIGHT.—Richard Wright, of Culpepper county, Va., was a soldier of the war of 1812. He married Ann Smith, of Virginia, and settled in Warren county, Mo., in 1822. In 1858 he removed to Lincoln county, where he died. His children were—Elizabeth, Henry C., Susannah, Ann M., George W., and Francis M. Elizabeth married Marion Ross, who settled in Lincoln county. Henry C. is a physician. He settled in Warren county, and when the North Missouri Railroad was built he laid off a town on his farm, and called it Wright City. The place now numbers some five or six hundred inhabitants, and is a thriving town. Dr. Wright represented his county in the Lower House of the Legislature two terms, and one term in the State Senate. He at present resides in St. Louis, and enjoys a comfortable fortune. Susannah Wright married Presley Ross, of Lincoln county. Ann M. married James Taylor, who died in California. George W. married Judith Carter, of St. Charles Co. Frank M. married Nancy Gizer, of Lincoln Co.

WILLIAMS.—Edward Williams, of North Carolina, went to Kentucky with Daniel Boone, and lived for some time at Boonesborough, where he married Jemima Anderson, daughter of Major Jack Anderson. Their children were—Daniel, Joshua, Pernell, Casper, Susan, and Caleb. The latter married Elizabeth Woodland, of Kentucky, and settled in Warren county in 1818. They had nine children—William, Dulcinea, Laurel, Abihue, Heath, Jane, Zuima, Elizabeth, and Caleb C. Dulcinea married Everett Creech, who settled in Warren county in 1819. Jane married William Guerdo, son of Jared D. Guerdo, who settled in St. Charles county in 1806. Elizabeth married William Anderson, who settled in Warren county in 1832. Caleb Williams was Justice of the Peace in Warren county for many years.

WYATT.—Frank Wyatt, of North Carolina, had the following children—John, William, Frank, Jr., Ricks, Polly, Elizabeth, and Sally. John, William, and Ricks settled in Lincoln county, Kentucky, at a very early date, and the former served as a soldier in the revolutionary war. He married Polly Pearle, of Virginia, and settled in Warren county, Mo., in 1817. They had—Martha, Frank, Susan, Elizabeth, Sarah, Rebecca, William S., Mary A., Anna E., and Nancy. Frank was a soldier of the war of 1812, and died of consumption in Kentucky. Nancy, Martha, and Anna E. all died unmarried. Susan married James Pennington, of Kentucky, who settled in Warren county in 1817. Their children were—Frank M., John T., Liberty S., Mary C., Ephraim, Rebecca, Isabella J., Martha F., and Lavinia W. Elizabeth Wyatt married William James, who settled in Warren county in 1809. Their children were—John W., Martha A., Benjamin S., William F., and Lucian A. Mr. James was Judge of the County Court for some time, and Sheriff two terms. Sarah Wyatt married Walter T. James, who settled in Warren county in 1709. They had—Frank W., Mary A., William S., John B., Elizabeth, Joel P., Rex, and Lycurgus. Rebecca Wyatt was married first to Joel Pearle, who settled in Warren county in 1828. They had two children—John H., and Mary A., when Mr. Pearle died, and his widow subsequently married Joseph Rattsburn, of Ohio. William S. Wyatt married Patience Pearle; but they had no children. Mary A. married and settled in Missouri.

WHEELER.—Chester Wheeler, of Vermont, settled in (now) Warren county, Mo., in 1810 or 1812. He married Joanna, daughter of Henry Bryan, and they had a large family of children. Their son, Samuel H., who is at present Treasurer of Montgomery county, and a leading and influential citizen, was raised by his uncle, John Davis. He married Margaret Fulkerson, daughter of the late Col. Robert Fulkerson, of Danville.

YOUNG.—Leonard Young, of Virginia, married Mary Higgins, and settled in Fayette Co., Ky. They had thirteen children—

15

Nancy, Elizabeth, William, James, Richard, Frances, Jane, John, Aaron H., Henry, Mary, Catharine, and Benjamin. James married Nancy Booker, by whom he had—Elizabeth, William, Richard, Mary, Martha, Nancy K., Booker, James S., Sarah J., Frances A., Caroline, John H., and Elenora E. William and Mary came to Missouri. The latter married Stephen Ellis, of Kentucky, who settled in St. Charles Co., Mo., in 1826. William was born in Shelby Co., Ky., in March, 1803. He settled in the town of St. Charles in 1827; but the following year he removed to Troy, in Lincoln county, where he practiced law for many years. He was also County Judge. He was married first to Martha A. Boyd, daughter of Hon. William G. Boyd, of Shelby Co., Ky., by whom he had but one child, who died in infancy. Mrs. Young also died, and he was married the second time to Sarah C. Russell, of Kentucky, by whom he had—James R., Richard, Samuel, William H., Anna B., and Susan F. E.—John, Aaron H., and Benjamin Young also came to Missouri. John was a physician, having graduated at the Philadelphia Medical College. He came to Warren county in 1816, and laid off the town of Marthasville, which he named for his first wife, Martha Fuqua. He was married twice; first, to Martha Fuqua, of Virginia, in 1805, who died without children. In 1811 he married Sarah Scott, of Virginia, who also died without children. The Doctor moved to St. Louis in 1827, and died while on a visit to some of his wife's relations in Alabama, in 1832.—Aaron Young was married in 1804, to Theodosia Winn, of Fayette Co., Ky., and came to Missouri and settled near Marthasville in 1819. His children were—James, Martha, Elizabeth, Leonard, and Mary. Mr. Young served as County Judge for several terms, and finally moved to St. Louis county, where he died.—Benjamin Young was born in Fayette Co., Ky., in 1791. He married Mary Maaro, and came to Warren county in 1819. He settled at Marthasville, and opened a store, being the first merchant of the place. In 1820 he removed to Callaway county and settled in Ham's Prairie, at a place called Elizabeth, which was the first county seat of Callaway county. In February, 1821, he was appointed the first County Judge, by Gov. McNair, which office he filled for a number of years with credit to himself and the county. Mr. Young was a man of superior talents, and represented Callaway county in both Houses of the State Legislature for a number of years. He was also a member of the Constitutional Convention of 1845. Unfortunately he had an impediment in his speech, and always had to go through a certain formula before he could speak, which was as follows: "Be-kase, be-kase, be-kase, sir, by g—d," at the same time advancing with a short hop at the utterance of each word. He was married twice, and by his first wife had—Hannah, Mary, Margaret, Elizabeth, and William M. By his second wife he had Anna and Martha.

YATER.—Conrad Yate , of Germany, came to America and settled first in Virginia, where he married. In 1818 he came to Missouri and settled in Warren county. During his residence here he built four mills (one run by water, two by horses, and one by oxen), and one distillery. His children were—Joseph, Peter S., Polly, Elizabeth, Nancy, Henry, Sarah, Catharine, Charles, and George W. Joseph married Polly Phœnix, and settled in Pike Co., Mo. Polly married John Johnson, of Pike county. Elizabeth married Joseph King, of Montgomery county. Nancy married Colonel Reuben Pew, of Montgomery county. Henry married Susan Shields, of Pike county. Sarah married Israel Sitters, of Callaway county. Catharine married Nicholas Bradley, of Callaway county. Charles married Judith Jamison, of Callaway county. George W. married Elizabeth Coil, and settled in Warren county. Peter S. married Miss Slonce, of Kentucky, and settled in Warren county in 1818. He built a stone chimney 8x9 feet in size, and afterward built a cabin to the chimney. He obtained assistance from St. Charles county to raise his cabin, and as he furnished plenty of good whisky, it took them a week to finish it. When the house was completed he gave a dance, and during the night the floor gave way and let them all down into the cellar. Thomas Howell played the fiddle, and Rev. Thomas Bowen, who was a young man then, danced as vigorously as any of the other guests.

HISTORIES OF FAMILIES.

MONTGOMERY COUNTY.

THE county of Montgomery was organized December 14, 1818, out of surplus territory of St. Charles county. It was named for Montgomery county, Ky., because so many citizens of that county had settled here. The statement that it was named in honor of General Montgomery, who fell at the battle of Quebec, soon after the commencement of the American revolution, is erroneous.

The seat of justice was first located at Pinckney, on the Missouri river, and within the present limits of Warren county. This town was named for Miss Attossa Pinckney Sharp, daughter of Maj. Benjamin Sharp, the first Clerk of the County and Circuit Courts of Montgomery county. It was once a flourishing place, but the removal of the county seat to Lewiston proved its death blow, and the town disappeared many years ago. The spot where it originally stood has fallen into the river, and a postoffice in the vicinity, with perhaps one store, are the only reminders of its existence. The land upon which the town was built was originally granted to Mr. John Meek, by the Spanish government, but he failed to comply with the terms, and it reverted to the United States government upon its purchase of the territory. It was sold at the land sales in 1818, and bought by Mr. Alexander McKinney, who sold fifty acres of the tract to the County Commissioners, for the use of the county, for which he received $500. The Commissioners were, David Bryan, Andrew Fourt, and Moses Summers. The first public building erected in the place was the jail, which was built in 1820, at a cost of $2,500. During the summer of the same year, Nathaniel Hart and George Edmonson built a frame house there, which was the first frame house erected in Montgomery county. It was 25x30 feet in size, and was rented to the county for a court house, at $100 per year. The rent was paid with county scrip worth 25c to the dollar. The same sum-

COL. WILLIAM TALBOTT
MONTGOMERY CO.

MAJ. BENJAMIN SHARP
1ST CO. & CIRCUIT CLERK
OF MONTGOMERY CO.

MRS. BENJ. SHARP

BISHOP E. M. MARVIN.
OF THE M. E. CHURCH, SOUTH.

HENRY SHOCK
AUDRAIN CO.

HON. JOHN JAMESON
CALLAWAY CO.

MAJ. JOHN HARRISON
CALLAWAY CO.

CHAS. JUEHNE LITH ST. LOUIS

mer Frederick Griswold built a log store house, and opened the first store in Pinckney. The next house erected in the place was a mill, partly built by Hugh McDermid, who sold it to two Germans named Lineweaver and Duvil, who completed it.

The first Judges of the County Court were, Isaac Clark, Moses Summers, and John Wyatt. At the first meeting of the Court Mr. Clark resigned, and Maj. Benjamin Sharp was appointed to fill the vacancy. He also resigned soon afterward, and Hugh McDermid was appointed in his place, after which there was no other change in the Court until the removal of the county seat to Lewiston. Previous to his appointment as Judge of the County Court, McDermid was a member of the Territorial Legislature, and when the line was established between Montgomery and St. Charles counties he acted as one of the Commissioners for the former county.

Irvine S. Pitman was the first Sheriff of Montgomery county. John C. Long was appointed first County and Circuit Clerk, by Governor McNair, after the admission of the Territory into the Union, but he sold the offices to Jacob L. Sharp before assuming his duties; so that Mr. Sharp became the first incumbent of those two offices under the State government, which he held by election for many years afterward. Robert W. Wells was the first Prosecuting Attorney, and Alexander McKinney was the first County Surveyor.

Andrew Fourt built the first hotel in Pinckney, and on court days he generally had a lively time. Men would come to town and get drunk, and then quarrel and fight in and around the hotel, which they regarded as a public place, where they could do as they pleased. Among the most noisy characters of that class was a man known as Big Ben Ellis, of South Bear creek, and one day he became so demonstrative that Fourt offered him a dollar to leave the house. He took the money, stepped out at the door, came right back again, and told Fourt that if he would give him another dollar he would go home. He finally compromised on fifty cents, and took his departure.

The first criminal case tried in Pinckney was against a man named Jim Goen, who had stolen a pair of shoes from his sweetheart. He was sentenced by the court to receive twenty-nine lashes at the whipping post, which, at that time, was a familiar instrument of justice, as there was one at every court house in the State. As soon as the sentence was pronounced, the pris-

oner started to run, and the Sheriff (Mr. Irvine Pitman) gave
chase. It was a pretty close race until they came to a fence,
which Goen attempted to jump, but failed and fell on his back.
Pitman secured him, took him back to the whipping post, and inflicted the punishment, which was the first and last sentence of
the kind ever executed at Pinckney.

In 1826 or 1827, the seat of justice of Montgomery county was
removed to a place called Lewiston, situated a short distance
south of the present site of New Florence. Every vestige of the
town has long since disappeared. It was named in honor of Col.
Merriwether Lewis, generally known from his connection with
Lewis and Clark's famous expedition to the Pacific Ocean, and who
was also the second Governor of the Territory of Upper Louisiana. The land upon which the town was situated was entered in
1818, by Amos Kibbe, who donated to the county a sufficient
quantity of land for the public buildings. Several courts were
held in Mr. Kibbe's house, but in 1824 a log court house and jail
were erected. The jail was built by Charles Allen. It was eighteen feet square, and composed of two walls, one a few inches
outside of the other, with hewn timbers set on end in the space
between. The court house was the same size as the jail, built of
logs, and floored with puncheons. The roof was composed of
clapboards, weighted down with poles. During the intervals between courts this house afforded a shelter for Mr. Kibbe's sheep,
which were driven out the day before the commencement of
each session, and the house swept clean. The materials for the
jail and the court house were furnished by various individuals,
who were paid with county warrants, with which some of them
liquidated their taxes for the next ten years.

Mr. Kibbe laid off and sold lots, and a small town soon came
into existence. George Bast and William Knox opened the first
store in Lewiston, and hauled their goods from St. Louis in a
wagon drawn by oxen. They sold principally for skins and furs,
which they bartered in St. Louis for new goods. Not long after
they began business they met with a serious misfortune, which
ruined them financially for the time being, and compelled them to
suspend. They had been to St. Louis with a load of furs, and
started home with a stock of new goods in their wagon. When
they drove on board the ferry-boat at St. Charles it sank, and
their team, wagon and goods were all lost. This misfortune left
them without means to carry on their business, and they suspended.

In 1834 Danville was laid off by Judge Olly Williams, on land belonging to him, and the same year the seat of justice was established there. This place is situated about five miles west of where Lewiston stood, and was, for many years, the most flourishing town in that part of the country, but when the North Missouri railroad was built, it was left several miles to the south, and since then it has not prospered. It suffered severely from guerrilla raids during the late war between the North and South, during one of which the court house was burned and all the public records were consumed, and several prominent citizens killed. A proposition will be submitted to the voters of Montgomery county this fall, for the removal of the seat of justice to Montgomery City, and the friends of the measure confidently expect to carry it. A similar attempt was made several years ago, but failed.

In this connection the following letter from Mr. Alfred Kibbe, a son of the founder of Lewiston, to the compilers of this work, will be interesting. Mr. Kibbe at present resides at Dallas, Texas, where his letter was dated, and as he has a great many friends in Montgomery county, we have endeavored to preserve, as nearly as possible, his characteristics of expression in copying his letter, thinking they would be glad to recognize something that would call up memories of the olden time.

MR. KIBBE'S LETTER.

"You wanted to know something about my father. Amos Kibbe. Well. he was born in the State of Connecticut, and emigrated West when he was seventeen or eighteen years of age, in company with his brother Timothy, who was a Colonel in the United States army. My father parted with his brother somewhere in the State of Ohio, and went to Little Sandy Salt Works in Greenup county, Kentucky. After remaining there several years he became a partner of Jesse Boone, son of old Daniel Boone, and they carried on the salt making business for a number of years. They finally sold out, in 1816, to a Louisville man named David Dellward, and my father came to St. Louis, Missouri, and kept hotel on the corner of Pine and Main streets for several years. In 1818 or 1819, (I can't remember which,) Missouri was admitted into the Union as a State,* and the first session of the Legislature was held in St. Louis.† The Legislature was then removed

---

* This, of course, is a mistake, as the State was not admitted into the Union until 1820.

† This is also incorrect. A session of the Legislature was held in St. Louis, commencing on the third Monday of September, 1820, which was three months before the commencement of the session of Congress at which the Territory was admitted into the Union. This session was held under authority of the State Constitution, which

to St. Charles, and my father moved there with it, and built a hotel, which he kept for several years. After the removal of the Legislature to Jefferson City [in 1826], my father sold his hotel to a man from Kentucky, named Whitley, and moved to Callaway county, six miles north of Fulton. We were the first settlers in that part of the county. Our nearest neighbor was a man named VanBibber, who lived fifteen miles east of us on Loutre creek. We lived at that place one year, and during that time my mother died of consumption, and we buried her sometime in August, 1822. My father then sold out to a man by the name of McKinney, from Kentucky, and moved back to St. Charles. He had not received all the pay for his hotel, and went back to collect the balance that was due him; and after doing so he moved to Montgomery county, and settled in a little prairie eleven miles from Camp Branch, where the Booneslick and Cotesansdessein roads forked. While we were living there the county seat was moved to that place, and my father donated half his land to the county. A town was laid out by the county, and called Lewiston, for the man that crossed the Rocky Mountains with General Clark. In a few years the county seat was moved again, to a place called Danville, about eight miles up the Booneslick road. This place was settled by a man named Olly Williams, who was from one of the Eastern States, and was a very industrious man. He was a mechanic, and built a mill with an inclined wheel, with which he ground our wheat and corn. He afterward attached a wool carding machine and cotton gin and wheel to the same mill. The people raised only enough cotton for their own use. A man named.Whitesides, who lived twelve miles from Williams' mill, was the first to raise cotton in Montgomery county. Olly Williams was the most useful man in the country, owing to his great skill as a mechanic. He ground our corn and wheat, carded our wool, ginned our cotton and spun it into thread. He built a fine brick house, which was used as a hotel after the county seat was moved to Danville. His property increased rapidly in value, and he finally sold out for a good price and moved to St. Louis county, and bought property close to the city, which made him rich. He had a large family.

"My father was married twice. The maiden name of his first wife, who was my mother, was Sidney Bragg, a daughter of Thomas Bragg, who lived on the Ohio river at a place called Lewisburg, in Lewis county, Kentucky. About one year after the death of my mother, my father married a widow lady by the name of Finch. She had two children, and he had six living and

had been adopted by the Convention, but not yet accepted by Congress. An act passed this Legislature on the 28th of November, 1820, fixing the seat of government at St. Charles, where the next Legislature met in the winter of 1821-22, so that the first Legislature of the *State* of Missouri met in St. Charles. The seat of government remained there until October, 1826, when it was removed to Jefferson City.

one dead. My eldest brother, Preston, died of typhoid fever, a disease which had just made its appearance and was considered incurable. Its victims died suddenly, and nearly every one that was attacked died. It was a long time before the doctors learned how to cure the disease.

"My father had six children by his second wife. Some of my half-brothers went to St. Louis to live, and after they had been there a while they sent for the old folks, who were growing old and helpless. My father died a short time after he went to St. Louis, at the age of seventy-five or seventy-six years. He was a postmaster at the place where he lived in Kentucky, in 1793, and some time after he settled in Montgomery county, he was appointed postmaster again, and held the office for a number of years. He was also county magistrate for some time. My stepmother lived for a number of years after the death of 'my father, and finally went to live with a son-in-law, on the Illinois river, where she died.

"I will now give you some of the names of the old settlers of Missouri. There was a large family by the name of Talbott that settled first on Loutre Island. The next was Colonel Pitman, who married a Talbott. In the eastern part of the State [St. Charles county] there was a large family by the name of Callaway, which was related to Daniel Boone's family by marriage. Then there were the Bryans, McKinneys, Hayses, Sharps, Wyatts, and Griswolds. Fred. W. Griswold was a merchant in the town of Pinckney, which was the first county seat of Montgomery county. That part of the country was quite thickly settled, but no one lived on Loutre Prairie near where my father settled except Jonathan Smith, whose house was about a mile below my father's, on the Booneslick road. North of Lewiston lived John Dutton, Glover Dozier, Bass Farrow, John Custer, Hensley, and some few others. In the upper part of the county lived a noted man by the name of Isaac VanBibber, whose house was at a place called Loutre Lick, where the Booneslick road crosses Loutre creek. He was raised an orphan boy by old Daniel Boone, and was a very kind, generous hearted old man. He could tell a great many things about the early settlement of Missouri, and the trouble they used to have with the Indians. It was quite interesting to hear him talk about old Grandfather Boone, who always came to see him once a year, and would spend several weeks or months at his house. It was at Isaac VanBibber's that I first met Daniel Boone and got acquainted with him. I would rather sit and hear him talk than to hear any other man I ever saw in my life, and I have seen several of the greatest men of this nation, among whom were Henry Clay, Andrew Jackson, General Harrison, Thomas H. Benton, General Taylor, Andrew Johnson, and last, but not least by any means, General Clark. Isaac Van-

Bibber's nearest neighbor was Lewis Jones, who was a brother-in-law of Mrs. VanBibber. He crossed the Rocky Mountains with Lewis and Clark. Samuel Boone, a cousin of Daniel Boone, and Isaac Clark, a very considerable man, lived in the same region of country. Clark's eldest daughter married a man named Knox, and their eldest son, named Henry, married a Miss Talbott, of Loutre Island. Families by the name of Logan, Davis, and Ellis lived on Bear creek, and Enoch and Aleck Fruite lived on Nine Mile Prairie. They were the first settlers there. Jesse Boone, a son of Daniel Boone, settled in that part of the country in 1820, and John Clark, a brother of Isaac Clark, settled on Nine Mile Prairie in 1825. Israel and William Grant lived in the southwestern corner of that prairie, where they settled in 1819. Israel was afterward killed by two of his negroes, who waylaid him on the road about three miles from home as he was returning from Fulton, where he had gone to collect some money. They killed him with clubs and knives. The next settlers there were two brothers, named McMurtry, who bought out the Fruites. Boone and Samuel Hays, relatives of Daniel Boone, also lived in that part of the country.

"The first saw mill in Montgomery county was built by Colonel Pitman, on Loss creek. It was run by water.

"A man named Lomax, who was one of the early settlers of Callaway county, was taken very sick and sent for a physician at Fulton, who gave him calomel and salivated him very badly; and in order to stop salivation he poured cold water on him, which caused him to lose all his teeth.

"When my father lived in Callaway county, we had to go forty miles to mill, and take our own team to grind with. We went three times a year.

"In the year 1817, while we were living in St. Louis, I saw the first steamboat that ever landed at that place. It was simply a large barge, with an engine and smoke stack. The first newspaper I ever saw was the *Missouri Republican*. It was published then by a man named Charless, who was the father of Joseph Charless.

"While we were living in St. Charles my father made the first cradle for cutting grain that was ever seen in that county, and the old French settlers viewed it with as much curiosity as their friends in St. Louis did the first steamboat. When harvest came my father sent several negro men with cradles to assist a farmer named John East in cutting his wheat. When harvest was over East wanted to pay several dollars per day for each of the hands, the customary price being one dollar, 'because,' said he, 'each of them did as much work as two or three men with sickles.'

"My grandmother's name was Lucy Bragg. She was born on the Shenandoah river, in Virginia, and lived to be 113 years old.

She was a widow for more than fifty years.   Her mother was born in Paris, France, and lived to be 120 years old.   My grandmother gave my mother a negro woman who had eight children at the time; she afterward had eleven more, making nineteen in all.   The woman lived to be 110 years old, and died in St. Louis.

"Yours, etc.,

"ALFRED KIBBE."

The first person hanged in Montgomery county, by judicial process, was a negro named Moses, who had killed his master, John Tanner, who lived on Cuivre river, in the northern part of the county.   This murder was committed in 1828.   The negro had run away and hid in the woods, where he remained several weeks.   In the meantime he was furnished with a gun by a man who had a grudge against his master, and with this weapon he crawled up to the house and shot Tanner through an opening in the wooden chimney, which had not been completed.   The house was an ordinary log cabin, such as the people universally occupied in those days, and it had a partly finished puncheon floor.   When Tanner was shot he was sitting on this floor with his feet in his wife's lap, and his face toward the chimney.   The entire discharge entered his breast.   He sprang to his feet and called to his wife to hand him his gun, but before she could do so he fell on his face outside of the door, and expired immediately.   The negro was arrested and tried at Lewiston, and hanged in the spring of 1829.   Henry Clark was Sheriff at the time, and rode in a cart with the negro, seated on his coffin, to the scaffold.   The last act of the condemned man before his execution, was to sing the hymn commencing,

"Show pity, Lord; O Lord forgive,"

which he did in such an affecting manner that nearly all who were present shed tears.   No other scene like it was ever witnessed in Montgomery county.   The body was given to Dr. Jones, of Marthasville, who dissected it for the benefit of his students.

It may not be generally known that the ancestor of the notorious Younger boys was an early settler of Montgomery county.   His name was Charles Younger.   He came from Mount Sterling, Ky., and settled near Pinckney, then in Montgomery, but now in Warren county, about 1819, where he lived until 1822, when he removed to Callaway county, and settled on Auxvasse creek.   He was a horse racer and gambler in Kentucky, and followed the same pursuits in Missouri.   One day in Kentucky, he placed his little son on a fine horse to run a race.   The horse threw the child and killed him, but Younger dragged his body out of the way and placed another son on the horse, who won the race.   In 1823 he sold his place on the Auxvasse to David Henderson, and removed to Clay county, where he died soon after.   His son, Coleman Younger, who was the father of the boys who have become so well known as outlaws in this State, was a delegate from Clay county to the Convention that nominated General Taylor for President in 1848.

Bear Creek, in Montgomery county, was so named by Daniel Boone, because he found a great many bears in that locality. North Bear creek was named by Presley Anderson, who settled in Montgomery county in 1817.   The name originated in an adventure which he had with some bears, one day, while hunting on that stream and which nearly cost him his life.   While stalking through the woods looking for game, he saw two cub bears run up a tree, a short distance from him, and desiring to capture them alive, he set his gun down and climbed after them.   Pretty soon he heard a fearful snorting and tearing of the brush under him, and looking down he saw the old mother bear just beginning to climb the tree after him, with her bristles on end and her white teeth glistening between her extended jaws.   He knew she meant business, and began to wish himself somewhere else.   To go down by the angry brute was impossible, and it was equally impossible to ascend higher, as the slender branches would not sustain his weight.   If he remained where he was he must sustain a hand-to-hand contest with the old bear, which he knew would result entirely in her favor.   He had only one way to escape, and that was to play the squirrel and jump to another tree.   It was a desperate chance, but he felt the hot breath of the old bear close to him, and determined to take it.   Gathering himself up for a desperate spring, he made it, and safely landed among the branches of a neighboring tree.   Then hastily sliding to the ground, he secured his gun, and killed all the bears.   This incident led him to name the adjacent stream Bear creek, but as main Bear creek had already been named, he designated the former as North Bear creek, by which name it has been known ever since.

On a small stream in the southern part of Montgomery county there is a huge, singular looking rock, known as Pinnacle Rock. It stands alone in the midst of a small valley, and rises perpendicularly on all sides except one, to the height of seventy-five feet. It covers an area of about one acre, and the top is flat and covered with trees, grass, etc. A shelving path on one side affords a safe ascent, and the people of the vicinity often collect there on picnic occasions and Fourth of July celebrations. During the last few summers the Pinnacle has been used as a preaching place, and the praises of God are often heard ascending from its romantic summit.

The dates of the organizations of the various churches in Montgomery county are difficult to obtain. Some of them are given in connection with the histories of families. On the 16th of April, 1824, a Baptist church called Freedom was organized at the house of John Snethen, on Dry Fork of Loutre, by Revs. William Coats and Felix Brown. The following members were enrolled at the time: John Snethen and wife, Nancy Skelton, Sarah Elston, William Hall, Mary Allen, and Jonathan Elston. Mr. Snethen was chosen Deacon, and Jonathan Elston Clerk. A small log church was erected the following July, and their meetings were held in it for a number of years. In this church, on January 4, 1825, Alexander Snethen and Jabez Ham were ordained ministers, by Revs. William Coats and Absalom Brainbridge. During the first four years of the existence of this church the collections for all purposes amounted to $1.75. On one occasion two of the members were sent as delegates to a Baptist Association south of the Missouri river, and they concluded to swim the river on their horses, and save the money which had been given them to pay their ferriage. After swimming the river they invested the money in whiskey, and both got "tight," for which offence they were tried and suspended.

About 1838 another church building was erected on South Bear creek, also called Freedom, but owing to its location near some stagnant water, it subsequently received tne facetious appellation of "Frog Pond." The association was afterward removed to Jonesburg, and retained the name of Freedom.

FAMILIES OF MONTGOMERY COUNTY.

ALLEN.—Charles Allen and his wife, Elizabeth Powell, settled in Kentucky in 1800, and came to Montgomery Co., Mo., in 1823. Their children were—Joseph H., David P., Charles P., Polly E., Elizabeth B., Anna A., Martha C., Tabitha W., Lucy J., and Catharine C. Mr. Allen was a carpenter by trade, and built the jail at Lewiston. His son, Joseph H., who was a physician, died at Troy, in Lincoln county. David P. was married first to Ann Boone, by whom he had two children. After her death he married Nancy Courtney, of St. Charles, and they had eight children. He died in 1874. Charles P. married Eliza J. Courtney, by whom he had thirteen children. Tabitha and Catharine died before they were grown. Polly and Elizabeth married brothers named Simpson. Anna married William Cowherd, and their children were—Charles A., James D., William R., Catharine C., Martha E., and Elizabeth P. Charles and William died before they were grown. James married Ella Logan, of Montgomery county. Martha married Joseph Crane, of Callaway county. Elizabeth married Charles Blades, of Montgomery county.

ADAMS.—James Adams, of Virginia, settled in St. Louis Co., Mo., in 1818. He married Sally Brown, and their children were—Burrell, James, Polly, Sally, Elizabeth, Lucy, Rebecca, Martha, and Nancy. Burrell was a soldier in the war of 1812. He came to Missouri in 1816, with Judge Beverly Tucker, and was married in 1818 to Harriet Allen, a daughter of John Allen, who died in 1830. Mr. Adams died in Danville, Mo., during the summer of 1876, in his 82d year. He had eight children—William B., B. T., J. B., James B., Susan F., John A., C. C., and Sarah E. William B. is a physician, lives in Danville, and has a practice that extends for many miles over that portion of the country. He is a very intelligent man, and exercises a large influence in the affairs of the county, which he has represented in the State Legislature. He possesses a large fund of ready wit and humor, and is an entertaining conversationalist.

ANDERSON.—Presley Anderson and his wife, Elizabeth Steele, settled in Montgomery Co., Ky., in 1779. Their children were John A. S., James, William, Presley, Jr., Lucy, and Eliza. John A. S., better known as Captain Jack, was a remarkable man in his day, and is well remembered by the old citizens of Montgomery and Callaway counties. We give his history elsewhere. Presley, Jr., married Euphemia Jones, of Tennessee, and settled first in Warren Co., Mo., in 1814, from whence he removed to Montgomery county in 1817, and settled near Brush creek. He brought his family to Missouri on pack-horses, and they occupied Robert Ramsey's house, near Marthasville, soon after the murder of the family of the latter. The blood was still upon the floor when they went into the house, and Mrs. Anderson scoured it up before they put their furniture in. During the Indian war Mr. Anderson served as a ranger in Capt. Hargrove's company, in Illinois. He was a devout Methodist, and the preachers of that denomination held services in his house for many years. The names of his children were—Presley, Jr., Joseph, James,

William, John, Margaret, Lucy, Elizabeth, and Eliza. James Anderson married Eliza Journey, of St. Charles county, and settled on Brush creek, in Montgomery county. He afterward removed to St. Louis county, where he died. Eliza Anderson married John Dabney, who settled near Middletown in 1830.

ANDREWS.—William Andrews, of Virginia, had a son Robert, who married Nancy Edmonds, and settled in Missouri in 1833. Their children were—William, Samuel, Sally, Mary J., and Catharine.

ANDERSON.—John Anderson, of England, had a son John, who married Letitia Stewart. They also had a son John, who married Jane Clark, and they had—Gustavus A., William E., Theresa J., Robert S., Eliza C., and John W. Gustavus A. graduated in medicine, and settled in Missouri in 1836. He was married first to Jemima E. Fisher, and after her death to Mary A. Talbott, daughter of Major Kit Talbott, of Loutre Island.

BUSH.—William Bush, of Fayette, Co., Ky., had—Benjamin, Ambrose, Levi, and Matilda. Benjamin married and settled in Illinois, on the bank of the Mississippi river, and was murdered under the following circumstances: Parties on the opposite side of the river owed him a considerable amount of money, and he went over on the ferryboat, one day, to collect it. As he was returning that evening he was robbed while on the boat, and then thrown into the river.—Levi and Matilda Bush both married and lived and died in Kentucky. Ambrose married Nancy Douglass, and settled first in Illinois, near his brother Benjamin, where he remained one year, and then (in 1818) he removed to Missouri and settled at Charrette, in Warren county. In 1818 he settled on Dry Fork of Loutre, in Montgomery county. Mr. Bush was a shrewd business man, and made a fortune by trading in horses and other stock. He had a low, soft voice and gentlemanly manners, and was a general favorite with his neighbors. He died in 1873, at the advanced age of 88 years. His wife died many years previous. Their children were—Greenberry, Maria, Edward D., William, and Ella. Greenbury married Sarah Cundiff, and they had— William D., Eliza A., Nancy J., Amanda G., Caroline, Mary, Clay, Edward W., Virginia, and Susan. Mr. Bush served as Sheriff and Assessor of Montgomery county for several years. He was also elected to the Legislature one term. Maria Bush was married first to Aaron Groom, and after his death she married William M. Wright. Edward D. married Virginia Mosley, and died in 1863. His children were—Lavinia, John, Greenberry B., William T., Judith A., Lydia, Benjamin F., Emma, and Fannie.

BAKER.—David Baker, son of Robert Baker, of England, married Mary Anderson, in November, 1756, and settled in Norfolk, Va. They had—Elizabeth, Mary, Benjamin, David, Robert,

Sarah, Dempsey, Thomas, and James. David was born in November, 1763. He married Judith Johnson, and they had—Sylvester, Thomas J., and John. Sylvester, who was born in 1791, married the widow of John Johnson, whose maiden name was Elsey Ward, and settled in Montgomery Co., Mo., in 1820. His children were—Judith, David W., Sylvester, Jr., William M., and John F. Capt. John Baker was born in 1795. He married Lizzie Johnson, and settled in Montgomery county in 1820. They had—Sylvester C., Elsey A., Robert W., John J., Mary K., Judith M., Margaret E., and Dicey B. V. Capt. Baker built a water mill on Loutre creek, and a rather singular circumstance happened to it one day. The mill was running at full speed, with a heavy head of water on, when the wheel suddenly blocked and the machinery stopped with a jar and crash that shook the mill to its foundation. Upon examining the wheel a large catfish was found in it. The fish was taken out, a handspike run through its gills, and two tall negroes hoisted it on their shoulders and carried it to the house; and it was so long that its tail dragged on the ground. This is a considerable fish story, but it is true.

BAKER.—Rev. Robert Baker came from Tennessee to Missouri at a very early date, and was one of the first Methodist preachers in Montgomery county. He organized the first church of that denomination in this county, at the house of Rev. Drury Clanton, who was also a Methodist preacher. His house was situated on a branch called "Pinch," about five miles southwest of Danville, and the church was organized in 1819. Baker was an old revolutionary soldier and drew a pension from the government, all of which he gave to his church and the Sunday-school cause. He had two sons, Jacob and Esau, who were as much unlike each other in personal appearance as it was possible for them to be; Jacob being six feet two inches in height, while Esau measured only four feet five inches. The former settled in Callaway county, near Readesville. He had an old yellow dog that he thought a great deal of, and in order to keep him from running away, he drove a honey locust stake in the yard and tied him fast to it. The stake took root and grew to be a large tree, and its branches cast a grateful shade over the yard and dwelling.

BAST.—George Bast settled in Montgomery county in 1819. His father was a native of Germany, but came to America and settled in Baltimore. George was married first to Sarah Clark, of Lexington, Ky., by whom he had—Alonzo, John, George Y., and William H. Mrs. Bast died in 1816, and her husband subsequently married Emily Courtney, by whom he had two children. She also died in 1823, and Mr. Bast was married the third time to Elizabeth Ford, by whom he had three children—Sarah, Anna, and Edward. Mr. Bast was killed by the falling of a tree, in

February, 1829, and his widow married Sirenus Cox. Alonzo, the eldest son, married a Mexican lady, and lived and died in Camargo, Mexico. At his death he left a widow and several children. John married Harriet Kibbe, by whom he had—Mary, Julia, Harriet, Charles, and George. George Y., son of George Bast, Sr., is a physician, and lives at New Florence. He is a prominent and influential citizen of the county, where he is widely known and respected. He was married first to Leonora Hancock, and they had one son,—William. After the death of his first wife he married Sophia Jacobs, and by her had two sons— George and Charles. William H. Bast is a merchant at Montgomery City. He also has a store in Kansas City, Mo., and is a wealthy and influential citizen. He lives at his beautiful country residence, a short distance south of Montgomery City, and enjoys himself in the society of his family and neighbors. He was married first to Epsey McGhee, by whom he had—William, Mary, and Alonzo. After the death of his first wife, he married Louisa Gordon, and they have one child—a daughter.

BEST.—Stephen Best, of Ireland, emigrated to America many years before the revolution, and settled in Pennsylvania. His children were—Isaac, Humphrey, Stephen, Jr., and Ebenezer. He also had several daughters, but their names are lost. Ebenezer never married, but he educated sixty children that claimed him for their father. He was one of the celebrated horse racers of Madison Co., Ky., and also indulged in chicken fighting. He once fought ten times with his chickens in one day, and gained seven of the fights, winning $1,000 each.—Isaac Best and his wife came to Missouri in 1808, from Garrard Co., Ky. They rode two old horses, on which they also carried their bedding, furniture, cooking utensils, etc. They settled on the bottom in Montgomery county, which has since borne their name. Mr. Best, like his brother, was fond of amusement, and delighted in horse racing. When the Indian war broke out he built a fort on his farm, but had to give it up before peace was declared. The Indians became so troublesome that he was afraid to leave his family in the fort any longer, and conveyed them for greater security to Fort Clemson, on Loutre Island. The following day his fort was captured by the Indians, but they found nothing to reward them for their trouble. The names of Mr. Best's children were—John, Stephen, Isaac, Jr., Humphrey, Ebenezer, Polly, Phœbe, Sally, and Peggy. John was married twice ; first to his cousin Polly, a daughter of Humphrey Best, and second to Sarah Quick, daughter of Alexander Quick. By his first wife he had— Polly, Catharine, and Margaret; and by his second—Stephen, John, Jr., Rice, Nancy, Rhoda, and Elizabeth. Isaac Best, Jr., died when he was nineteen years of age. Stephen, Humphrey, Ebenezer, Polly, Sally, and Margaret all accompanied their father

16

to Texas, to which State he removed a number of years ago.

BEARD.—Edwin Beard and his wife, Mary Bell, of Ireland, came to America and settled in Augusta Co., Va. They had— William, John, David, Charles, and Samuel. The latter was a soldier in the revolutionary war, and was present at the surrender of Lord Cornwallis at Yorktown. He married Sarah Craig, of Staunton, Va., and settled first in Pennsylvania, from whence he removed to Kentucky in 1792, and to Missouri in 1827. His children were—John, William, David, Samuel, Absalom, James, Mary B., Sarah L., and Elizabeth. William was a soldier in the war of 1812, under Gen. Harrison. He married Elizabeth Finley, of Lincoln Co., Ky., and settled in Missouri in 1830. David married Mary DeJarnette, and settled in Missouri in 1827. Samuel married Rebecca Fisher, and settled in Ohio. Absalom died unmarried, in New Orleans. James was married first to Mary J. Logan, and second to Martha A. Briggs, and settled in Missouri. Mary married Gabriel Reeds, of Kentucky, and settled in Lincoln Co., Mo., in 1830. Sarah was married first to William C. Finley, and after his death she removed to Lincoln Co., Mo., where she married McKenly Hays. She died, and Hays married her sister Elizabeth.

BUSBY.—Matthew Busby, of Ireland, was a weaver by trade. He came to America and settled first in Delaware, from whence he removed to Bath Co., Ky., at an early date. He had seven sons, one of whom, James, married Nancy Lewis, of Delaware, by whom he had eleven children—Isaac, Rolley, John, James, Hiram, Lewis, Granville, Elizabeth, Lucretia, Amanda, and Malinda. Lewis and James settled in Missouri. The former married Eliza McClannahan, of Kentucky, and settled in Missouri in 1835.

BARNES.—James Barnes, of Virginia, settled in Kentucky at an early date. He had three sons—James, Jr., Noble, and John. The two latter settled in Illinois, where they lived and died. James, Jr., settled in Missouri. He married Sarah Callaway, daughter of Flanders Callaway, and they had twenty-two children, sixteen of whom lived to be grown, viz.: James, John, Larkin, William, Callaway F., Flanders C., Lilborn, Volney, Andrew, Rhoda, Jemima, Minerva, Margaret, Hulda, Cynthia, and Elizabeth. Flanders C. married Obedience Grigg, and lives in Montgomery county. He has in his possession a knee-buckle and silk stocking that belonged to his grandfather, Daniel Boone. In his youth Mr. Barnes was a great swimmer, and from being in the water so much he contracted inflammatory rheumatism, from which he suffers greatly in his old age.

BUNCH.—David W. Bunch, of Kentucky, settled in Montgomery Co., Mo., in 1826. He married Elizabeth Wright, by whom he had fourteen children—Thompson H., John J., William F.,

Lucretia, Patsey A., Sterling L., Lewis W., Nancy D., Amanda J., Hamilton V., Eliza M., David W., Cordelia, and Elizabeth.

BERGER.—Jacob Berger, of Germany, came to America and settled first in Pennsylvania, but subsequently removed and settled in Pittsylvania Co., Va. His sons were—William, Jacob, George, and John; and he had several daughters whose names we could not obtain. William was killed in the war of 1812, having volunteered to serve in place of his brother George, who had been drafted, and who, being a married man, could not leave his family. George married Mary Boatright, of Virginia, by whom he had—Thomas A., Jacob, Louisa J., Lucy A., William J., Appalana F., Polly, David, Elizabeth, and Marialmnel. Jacob and Polly died young, in Virginia. The rest of the children came with their parents to Missouri in 1838, and settled in Montgomery county. Thomas married Ellen Stone, of Virginia. Louisa married Pleasant Davis, of Missouri. Lucy married Buckner Jefferson, of Missouri. Appalana married Erasmus McGinnis, of Missouri. Elizabeth married William Anderson.

BOWLES.—Gideon Bowles and wife, of Dublin, Ireland, were members of the St. James Colony that settled in Goochland Co., Va. Anderson Bowles, their son, married Jane Thomas, and settled in Cumberland Co., Va. Their children were—Caleb, Sarah, James, Gideon, Ann, Anderson, Jr., Virginia, Elizabeth, Augusta, and David. Ann and Gideon died in Virginia. The rest of the children came with their parents to Madison Co., Ky., in 1806, and in 1811 they all settled in St. Louis Co., Mo., where Mr. Bowles died the following year. His widow lived until 1834. Caleb, the eldest son, was Judge of the County Court of St. Louis county several terms. He was married twice, and finally settled in Saline county, where he died. Sarah married Stephen Maddox, of Virginia, who settled in St. Louis county. They had fifteen children. James was a ranger in Captain Musick's company, and was killed by the Indians at Cap-au-Gris in 1814, in his 20th year. Anderson settled in Mississippi, where he died. Virginia married Richard Ripley, of St. Louis county, and died soon after. Elizabeth married Richard Sapington, and lives in Illinois, a widow. Augusta married Jacilla Wells, who removed to Texas and died there. David, the youngest son living, was married first to Julia Mackay, a daughter of Capt. James Mackay, of St. Louis, by whom he had—James A., Jane, Jesse, Nathan Z., Mary E., George R., John B., Julia V., Gustave, Jefferson R., and David J. Mr. Bowles settled in Montgomery county at an early date, and still resides there. He is a tanner by trade, but has pursued the avocation of a farmer the greater portion of his life, and has prospered in more than an ordinary degree. After the death of his first wife he was married, in his old age, to the widow Giles, of Lincoln county, and in that connection his neighbors tell a story on him to the following effect: When he got his new wife home, he was so overjoyed that he danced about the room and waved his hat over his head in an excess of delight, when he happened to strike the lamp that was standing on the mantel, and threw it on the floor, where it was dashed to pieces. In a moment the house was on fire, and it was only by the most prompt and energetic efforts that they were enabled to save it from destruction. Mr. Bowles was a great hunter during the earlier years of his residence in Montgomery county, and during one winter he killed 120 deer, three elk, and 400 raccoons, besides gathering 350 gallons of honey from the various bee trees that he found. The same year he killed the famous buck which the hunters had named General Burdine, and which had thirty-three prongs on his horns. But one day his favorite dog got hung by a grape vine in the woods, and he has not hunted much since. During the late war he was bold and fearless in the expression of his political sentiments, which were favorable to the South, and on that account he suffered severely from the depredations of the militia.

BROWN.—William Brown settled on Clear creek, near its mouth, in 1819. He built his house under a high bluff that ran parallel with the creek, and cut his fire wood on the top of this bluff, and rolled it down to the door of his house. When the wood gave out he moved his cabin to another place, and when it gave out there he moved it again, preferring to move his house rather than haul his wood.

COX.—Sirenus Cox, of New York, settled in Montgomery county in 1820. He married a daughter of Col. Isaac Van-Bibber, and raised a large family. His wife died, and he afterward married the widow of George Bast, and moved to St. Joseph, Mo., where they now reside.

CLEMENTS.—Benjamin A. Clements was a soldier of the revolution. He married his cousin, Susan Clements, and they had nine children—six sons and three daughters. Two of the sons, Robert and David, settled in Missouri. Robert was born in Fluvanna Co., Va., January 19, 1783, and is still living in Montgomery Co., Mo., in his 94th year, being the oldest man in the county. He was a soldier in the war of 1812, and settled in Montgomery county in 1842. He married Elizabeth Thomas in 1809, and they had eleven children, six sons and five daughters.

CRAIG.—Victor Craig, of England, came to America in 1760, and settled in Maryland. He had four sons, William, James, Robert, and Samuel. William and James lived in Albemarle Co., Va. Samuel was drowned in the Susquehanna river. Robert was a soldier of the revolutionary war. He was married first to Susan Carter, of Virginia, who was afterward killed by the Indians.

She lived nine days after having been scalped. Mr. Craig was married the second time to Sarah Ellington, of New Jersey, by whom he had—John, David, Victor, Jonathan, Jacob, Cynthia, Nancy, and Sally. Mr. Craig settled in Montgomery county in 1829, and died the following year. His eldest son, John, married Nancy Cobb, and settled in Montgomery county in 1826. He was a blacksmith by trade, and the first one at Danville. In 1831 he built the Dryden horse-mill, on the Booneslick road, below Danville. The mill was run by a cog wheel, and it required three or four hours to grind a bushel of grain. The hermit, Baughman, whose history is given elsewhere, carried the stones of this mill to his cave, many years after the mill ceased running, and arranged them so he could do his own grinding, by hand. He still uses the same stones.—Col. David Craig, brother of John, settled in Montgomery county in 1817, and is still living, in his 87th year. He lived two years, when he first came to Missouri, with Major Isaac VanBibber, at Loutre Lick. The Colonel remembers many amusing and interesting incidents of early days in Montgomery county, and takes great pleasure in relating them to his friends. When he came to Missouri he brought two black cloth suits with him, and one Sunday morning, while staying at Major VanBibber's, he dressed up in them and went down to breakfast. The clothes made quite a sensation, and VanBibber and all his family crowded around to look at them, having never seen anything of the kind before. One of the girls came close up to Craig, and touched his coat with one of her fingers, and then sprang back with the exclamation, " Oh, ain't he nice! " But her father, who did not relish so much style, replied, " Nice, h—l! he looks like a black-snake that has just shed its old skin." Soon after his arrival in Missouri the Colonel paid Mrs. Robert Graham a dollar in silver, and made 300 rails for her husband, for one pair of wool socks. Aleck Graham, who was a little boy then, remembers the splitting of the rails, for Col. Craig agreed to give him a picayune (6 1-4 cents) for keeping the flies off of him while he slept on the logs at noon; but for his life he cannot remember whether he ever paid the picayune or not. The Colonel served in the war of 1812, and was in Gen. McCarthy's division at the battle of Brownsville. He also served with Nathan Boone in the Black Hawk war, and was elected Colonel of militia in 1834. He was married in 1819, to Sarah Webster, and they had eleven children—Narcissa, Cynthia A., Mary A., Susan T., David, George R., Green, Martha, William A., Francis, and James W.—Victor Craig settled in St. Francois county. Jonathan and Cynthia lived in Kentucky. Jacob died in Ohio. Nancy married Greenberry Griffith, of Pettis Co., Mo.

CARTER.—Peter Carter, of Kentucky, had twelve children. Larkin G., one of his sons, married Judith Jones, and settled in

Montgomery county, Missouri, in 1819. He was a soldier in the war of 1812, under General Harrison, and acted as Colonel of militia in Montgomery county for several years. He died in 1847, having raised thirteen children.

CRANE.—George W. Crane was born in 1792, in King and Queen county, Virginia, was married in 1818 to Nancy Gresham, of Franklin county, Kentucky, and settled in Montgomery County, Missouri, in 1824. He was Assessor of Montgomery County four years, and Sheriff eight years. He was a member of the Baptist Church, and the first clerk of New Providence Church on Loutre. His children were—C. C., Thomas J., Joseph G., George W., C. D., Mildred A., Martha E., and Mary.

CLARK.—Henry Clark, of Scotland, emigrated to America, and settled in Kentucky, where he married Sarah Jones. They had—Benjamin, Isaac, John, Henry, Susan, Mary A., and Sally. Benjamin died in Kentucky, and his widow moved to Boone county, Missouri. Isaac Clark was a man of superior talents, and represented his county in the Legislature for several terms; he was also Assessor four years. He brought with him from Kentucky a set of China ware, the first that was ever in Montgomery county, and used it on a puncheon table. He was married first to a Miss Campbell, of Virginia, and settled in Montgomery County in 1819. They had three children—Harold, Cynthia, and Jane. Harold died single. Cynthia married Enoch Fruite, who settled in Callaway county in 1819. Jane married John French, of Callaway county. Mr. Clark was married the second time to Mary French, and they had—Henry, William, Isaac, Benjamin F., Sally, Susan, Polly A., Elizabeth M., and Mary H. Henry was married first to Susan A. Talbott, and they had two children. After her death he married Catharine Jacobs, and they had one son, Henry. William Clark married Elizabeth Snethen, and they had eleven children. Isaac died at 18 years of age. Benjamin F. married Prudence N. Snethen, and they had six children. Mr. Clark is an influential citizen, and an ex-Judge of the County Court. Sally Clark married William Knox. Susan A. married David Talbott. Polly died in childhood, and Elizabeth died at the age of twenty-two. John Clark, a brother of Isaac, was Clerk of the County Court of Christian Co., Ky., for many years. He was married first to Lucy Elliot, and settled in Callaway Co., Mo., in 1820. His children by his first wife were—Edward, Narcissa, Nancy, Susan, Sally, Jane, Lucy A., James, and John. He was married the second time to the widow Samuels, by whom he had one child, Melvina. He was married the third time to the widow of Alexander Read, whose maiden name was Elizabeth Chick, by whom he had—Logan, Isaac, Shelby, Elizabeth J., Samuel, Fanny, and Benton. Mr. Clark was a good business man, a kind husband and father, an excellent neighbor, and was held in high esteem by all who knew him.

CARSON.—Lindsay Carson came from Kentucky to Missouri in 1810, with Col. Hale Talbott, who had partly raised and educated him. He settled on Loutre Island, but the following year he sold out to Colonel Talbott, and moved to the Boone's Lick country, where he was killed in 1819, by the falling of a limb from a burning tree that he was cutting down. Mr. Carson was married twice. By his first wife he had—William, Anderson, Moses B., and a daughter who remained in Kentucky. By his second wife he had—Robert, Hamilton, Christopher, and four daughters. Christopher Carson, called "Kit," became famous as an Indian fighter, scout, and army officer. He was named for Colonel Hale Talbott's eldest son.

CLARE.—There were six brothers and two sisters named Clare, who came from Germany with their parents and settled on James river in Virginia. The names of the brothers were—Thomas, Allen, George, Jacob, Daniel, and Frank. George and Jacob married and remained in Virginia. Thomas, Allen, Frank and Daniel settled in Pulaski Co., Ky., and Thomas married and died there. Allen married Leah Foley, and settled in Lincoln Co., Mo., in 1834. Frank and Daniel built a tan yard at Summerset, in Pulaski county, and carried it on until the war of 1812 began, when they both enlisted in the army, and were together at the battle of the Thames, where Frank was killed. After the war Daniel married Jane Hansford, of Virginia, and settled in Lincoln Co., Mo., in 1830. He had six children at the time, whose names were—Frank, Jacob, Thomas, John, William, and Margaret. The rest of the children were born in Missouri, and their names were—Susan, Walden, Fountain S., and Horatio. Frank, son of Daniel, married Polly Gray, and lived Lincoln county. Jacob and Thomas died when they were young men. John married Sarah McClane, and settled first in Lincoln county, but afterward removed to Montgomery county. William married Sarah Maupin, and died, leaving a widow and six children. Margaret was married first to Hiram Palmer, and after his death to Armistead Uptegrove, of Montgomery county. Susan married John Jameson, of Lincoln county. Walden married Nancy Gilleland, and settled in Montgomery county. Fountain studied medicine, and practiced his profession for some time. He then went to merchandising; was subsequently elected Collector of Montgomery county, and then Circuit Clerk, which position he now holds. He married Hannah Hogue. Horatio married Ellen Sitton, and settled in Lincoln county.

COPE.—James Cope, of East Tennessee, settled in Montgomery county in 1837. He married a Miss Hutton, of Tennessee, whose father was a soldier of the war of 1812. On one occasion the portion of the army with which he was acting met

with some reverses, by which it was cut off from its base of
supplies, and the soldiers were reduced to the verge of starvation.   As a last resort, Mr. Hutton cut off a portion of his horses'
tail, and ate it, and thus saved his life.   The horse seemed to
experience very little inconvenience from the loss of his caudal
appendage, and Hutton rode him during the rest of the war.
The children of James Cope were—Malinda, Hannah, Isabella,
Samuel W., and Susan, all of whom settled in Montgomery
county in 1837.   Malinda was married in Tennessee, in 1835, to
John Kizer, a blacksmith, who came to Missouri and settled in
Troy, Lincoln county, the same year.   He remained there two
years, working at his trade, as a journeyman, for $30 per month.
He also worked nearly every night, for which he received extra
wages, and at the end of the two years had saved a small sum of
money.   He then came to Montgomery, and with his own money
and $50 that he borrowed from the County Treasurer, he bought
a tract of land, on which he opened a farm, and resided there
until his death, which occurred in 1869.   He hunted a great deal
during the first part of his residence in Montgomery county, and
on one occasion killed forty-five deer in a single day.   At another time he killed three deer at one shot.   He had nine children,
eight daughters and one son, and his widow and children, six of
whom are married, still reside in Montgomery county.   Hannah
Cope married her cousin, James Cope.   Isabella also married her
cousin, John Cope.   Samuel W., who became a Methodist minister, and is now a Presiding Elder in his Church, was married
twice; first to Louisa Stewart, and after her death to Jane Scott.
He lives, at present, in Chillicothe, Mo.   Susan Cope married
David Glover, of New Florence, Montgomery county.

CRUTCHER.—Samuel Crutcher and his wife, Elizabeth Lee, were
natives of Patrick Co., Va.   Their children were—Elizabeth,
Cornelia, Frank, Charles, and Samuel.   The latter married Nancy
James, of Virginia, and settled in Lincoln Co., Mo., in 1810,
from whence he removed to Montgomery county in 1830.   Their
children were—William, John, Sophia, Lucella, and Samuel, Jr.
John was married first to Clemency White, and after her death to
Mary J. Williams.   Sophia married Sandy Jones, who settled in
Montgomery county in 1831.   Samuel, Jr., was married three
times; first to Eliza Holladay; second to a widow named Holloway, and third to the widow Randolph, whose maiden name was
Jane Winter.   Lucella married John Darby, who settled in Randolph Co., Mo.—Samuel and John Crutcher settled near Middletown, and the first goods sold in the northern part of Montgomery
county were sold in one end of Samuel's house, in 1836, by Matthew Willburger and Samuel King.   The latter sold out to Samuel
Crutcher, and Willburger & Crutcher moved their stock of goods
to the present site of Middletown, into a little log cabin, which was

burnt soon after, and they were both ruined. Willburger surveyed and laid out Middletown in 1836, and John Dugan built the first house there. Stewart Slavens owned a part of the land on which the town was built.

CAMP.—Hardin Camp, of South Carolina, was of English parentage. He served his country in two of its principal wars—the revolution and the war of 1812. He married Sarah Hawkins, and settled in Warren Co., Ky. Their children were—Josiah, Thomas, Hawkins, Joseph, Sarah, and Elizabeth. Thomas married Sarah Middleton, of Kentucky, and settled in Missouri in 1842. He died soon after, leaving a widow and nine children. Joseph married Nancy Shackelford, of Madison Co., Ky., and settled in Warren Co., Mo., in 1836. His children were—Hiram H., Josiah, Mahala, Angeline, Sarah, Elizabeth, Martha, Judith A., and Mary. Mr. Camp had intended to settle in Howard, Co., Mo., but when he reached Jones' farm, where Jonesburg now stands, his wagon mired down, and he concluded to stop there. So he bought land in the vicinity, and settled upon it. He was Judge of the County Court of Warren Co., Ky., before he left that State.

COBB.—Samuel Cobb, of Kentucky, married Magdalene Peverley, and settled in Montgomery Co., Mo., in 1823. They had six children—Philip, Samuel, Jr., Adam, Easter, Nancy, and Sally. All are dead except Samuel, Jr., who is still living in the 86th year of his age. He was married first to Sally Sayler, of Kentucky, by whom he had ten children. He was married the second time to Lenora Taylor, and they had three children. Mr. Cobb belongs to the old-fashioned style of men, and does not believe in many of our modern inventions and innovations. His brother Adam was a soldier in the war of 1812. He married Delilah Bodkin, and settled in Montgomery county in 1823. They had ten children. Adam was the great Fourth of July orator of his day, and had a glowing speech about George Washington, of whom he was an ardent admirer, that he delivered with great oratorical effect whenever called upon. We have obtained a copy of this speech, and present it elsewhere.

CUNDIFF.—William Cundiff, of Virginia, settled in Montgomery county at a very early date. His children were—Joseph, John, William, Jane, Uraney, Elizabeth A., and Polly. Joseph married Sally McFarland, of Kentucky. John Married Polly Snethen. William died a bachelor. Jane married William Groom, a son of Jacob Groom. Polly married Joseph McFarland. Elizabeth A. married Nelson Hunter.

CHAPMAN.—Stephen Chapman, of England, came to America when he was only fifteen years of age. When the revolution began he joined the American army under Washington, and fought throughout the whole war. After the close of the war, he married Eliza Floyd, of Virginia, by whom he had—Frank,

George, William, James, John, Andrew, Isaiah, Benjamin, Rachel, and Peggy. Frank was a soldier in the war of 1812. He married Nancy Chester, of Virginia, whose father, Dr. Stephen Chester, was a surgeon in the American army during the revolution. Their children were—Sally, Polly A., John W., James B., and Wesley. James B. married Susan Fipps, of Virginia, and settled in Montgomery Co., Mo., in 1838. Mr. Chapman was a cabinet maker by trade, and before he left his home, in Virginia, he made the coffins for the parents of General Joseph E. Johnston, who became so celebrated during the late war between the North and South. After he came to Missouri Mr. Chapman took up the carpenter's trade, and became one of the most rapid workmen in his part of the country. He possessed great powers of endurance, and on one occasion, while building a house for George Britt, he worked sixty hours without stopping, for which he received $25 in gold. When he first came to Montgomery county there were no roads through the prairies, and the grass was nearly as high as his horse's back. When he traveled anywhere he would tie a small log to his horse's tail, and drag it through the grass, so it would make a trail he could follow back home. He raised his first apple orchard by cutting off small pieces of the branches of apples trees, and sticking them in Irish potatoes, which he planted, and the branches grew to be bearing trees.

CLANTON.—Drury and Henry Clanton, of Tennessee, settled on a branch called "Pinch,"* about five miles south of Danville, in 1818. Drury Clanton was a Methodist preacher, and it was at his house that the first Methodist church in Montgomery county was organized, by Rev. Robert Baker and himself, about the year 1819. A Sunday-school was also organized at the same time and place, and the first camp-meeting in Montgomery county was held there, on what was called the Loutre camp ground. Drury Clanton married a Miss James, of Tennessee, and their children were—John, James, Thomas, William, Eliza, Nancy, Angeline, Rebecca, and Patsey.—Henry Clanton was married twice, and his children were—Wesley, Alonzo, Sally, Martha, and Mary. Martha and a negro woman were burned to death on the prairie in Montgomery county.

COLE.—Mark Cole, of Tennessee, came to Missouri in 1817, and settled in Montgomery county. He married Dorcas Hall, a daughter of William Hall, who settled on Dry Fork of Loutre in 1817. Mr. Cole was a hatter by trade, and the first that settled in Montgomery county. He made "Boss" Logan's famous hat, which he wore twenty years. It was composed of twenty ounces of muskrat fur, mixed with thirteen ounces of raccoon fur, and

---

* Captain John Baker gave the name to this branch, because the people who lived upon it were always "in a pinch" for something to live on.

would hold an even half-bushel. The crown was eighteen inches high, and the brim six inches wide. Mr. Cole died in 1854, but his widow is still living. Their children were—Stephen H., William C., John W., Henry W., David D., James A., Robert T., Marcus L., Jerusha A., Mary M., Elizabeth S., Sarah A., and Nancy J., all of whom are still living except James A. and Nancy J.

CUNDIFF.—Richard Cundiff, the grandfather of the Cundiff family of Montgomery county, was killed at the battle of Point Pleasant, 1774. His sons, Louis and William, settled in Missouri, the former in 1818, and the latter in 1819. Louis married Elizabeth Towers, by whom he had—Polly, Elizabeth, Richmond, James, Louis, Sally, and Levisa. William married Sally Maddox, by whom he had—Joseph, James, John, William, Polly, Jane, Sally, Maria, and Elizabeth A.

DIGGS.—Simon Diggs, of Lancaster County, Virginia, had a son named William, who married a Miss Goe, of Middlesex county, Virginia, by whom he had one son, named Christopher. His first wife died, and he was married the second time to Mary Seeton, by whom he had—William, Isaac, Simon, John H., Dudley, Rowland, Barbee, Cole, Nancy, Polly, and Elizabeth. John H. married Sarah Hathaway, who lived to the age of 103 years. Their children were—Lawson, Christopher Y., John H., Jr., Cynthia, Malinda, Nancy, Elizabeth, and William C. Lawson and John H., Jr., were ship carpenters. The former married Sarah Diggs, of Virginia, and settled in Missouri in 1834. John H., Jr., followed the sea for a number of years, but finally abandoned that dangerous calling and emigrated to the West. He came to St. Louis in 1834, and worked on the first steamboat built in that city. In 1339 he settled in Montgomery county, where he still lives. He married Jane Jeter, a daughter of Pleasant Jeter, of Richmond, Virginia, and sister of the eminent Rev. Dr. Jeter, of that city. —Cole Diggs was born February 25, 1791. He served as a soldier in the war of 1812, and in 1817 he settled in Kentucky, and married Jane Pace, a daughter of Rev. John Pace, of Virginia. In 1832 he removed to Missouri and settled in Montgomery county, where he still resides (1875), in the 85th year of his age. He kept hotel at Danville, for some time after he came to Missouri, and served as Justice of the Peace for many years.

DRURY.—Lawson Drury was a native of Worcester Co., Mass., but removed to New Hampshire, where he married Elizabeth Johnson. Their children were—Lawson, Jr., Charles, and Ruth. His first wife died, and he was married the second time. His children by his second wife were—George, John, James, and Sarah. Mr. Drury removed from New Hampshire to Ohio, where he became Judge of the County Court for the county in which he lived. After the death of his second wife he came to Missouri and lived with his son Charles, at Danville, where he died in July, 1835, in

his 65th year.   Charles Drury came to Missouri at a very early
date, and was the second merchant in Montgomery county, Daniel Robinson being the first.   Drury's first store was at Loutre
Lick, but in 1834 he removed to Danville.   He was an honest,
enterprising man, and was highly esteemed by all who knew him.
He married Sally A. Wiseman, of Boone county, who was a
daughter of James Wiseman and Mary Tuttle.   Their children
were—Lawson, James H., Susan B., Charles J., Jarrett, Joseph,
Andrew M., Richard B., Mary E., and Elizabeth.   Mr. Drury
died in Danville in 1848, in his 47th year.   Five of his children,
James H., Jarrett, Joseph, Andrew M., and Elizabeth, died
unmarried.   Lawson was married twice; first to Margaret Frazier, and second to Catharine Wilson.   He lives in Kansas City,
Mo.   Susan B. (who was the first child born in Danville) married
Dr. William B. Adams.   Charles J. and Richard B. live in Atch-
ison, Kansas.   Mary E. married Capt. Stuart Carkener, of Danville.—Joseph Wiseman, a brother of Mrs. Charles Drury, married Elizabeth Robinson, of Callaway county, and became one of
the early settlers of Danville.

DAVIS.—John Davis, of Jonesburg, familiarly known as "Uncle
John," is the oldest son of the late Thomas Davis, of Shenandoah Co., Va.   John was born October 30, 1791, in Shenandoah
county, and is now nearly 85 years of age.   When he was about
sixteen his parents removed to Bourbon Co., Ky., and when the
war of 1812 began, he enlisted in the army and served under
Generals Winchester and Payne.   He was stationed at Forts
Wayne and Laramie, in Ohio, for some time.   In 1820 he came
to Missouri, and stopped a short time in St. Louis, which then
had only one principal street, and most of the houses were made
of square posts set upright, with the spaces between filled with
straw and mud, the chimneys being built of the same material.
The court house was surrounded by a post-and-rail fence, and
young Davis was sitting on this fence when the announcement was
made that the Territory of Missouri had become a State.   From
St. Louis Mr. Davis went to Pike county, and settled in Clarksville, where he lived forty-six years.   In those days rattlesnakes
were much more abundant than they are now, and the old pioneers would occasionally go on "snaking" frolics.   They always
came back vomiting from the effects of the poisonous smell of the
snakes.   On one occasion Mr. Davis and his neighbors went to a
knob near Clarksville, and killed seven hundred rattlesnakes in
one day.   This is a pretty large snake story, but it is nevertheless true.   Mr. Davis had failed in business in Kentucky before
his removal to Missouri, but he worked hard for ten years after he
came here to get money to pay those debts; and he often says
that that was the happiest period of his life.   Bankrupt and
exemption laws had not been invented then, and when men

entered into obligations they generally endeavored to fulfill them. For many years after he settled at Clarksville, the population was so thin that it required all the men within a circuit of ten or fifteen miles to raise a log cabin. At that time the government sold its public lands at $2 per acre, payable in four equal installments, with interest on the deferred payments. But in 1825 a new system was adopted, and the public lands were sold at $1.25 per acre, for cash. Mr. Davis has a son living at Navoo, Illi., who is 62 years of age ; and his brother-in-law, Rev. Thomas Johnson, was Indian missionary where Kansas City now stands, many years ago. His children still reside in that vicinty.

DAVIS.—Jonathan Davis, of Pennsylvania, married Elizabeth Bowen, and they had six children—James, John, Elijah, Septimus, Jonathan, and Elizabeth. John and James came to Missouri in 1800. John was a great hunter and trapper, and spent most of his time in the woods, often being absent for months at a time. He married Susan Bryan, a daughter of David Bryan, and his children were—James B., Jonathan, Joseph C., John H., Unicia, and Elizabeth. James, the brother of John Davis, married Jemima Hays, a granddaughter of Daniel Boone, her mother being Susanna Boone. After his marriage he returned to Kentucky and remained until 1819, when he came back to Missouri and settled in Montgomery county. His children were— John, Elizabeth, Jesse, Susan, Narcissa, Marcha, Daniel B., Unicia, and Volney.—Jonathan Davis, brother of James and John, came to Missouri in 1820, and married Mahala Hays, a sister of his brother James' wife. They had thirteen children, only four of whom are living (1875.)

DAVIDSON.—Alexander Davidson, of South Carolina, married Sarah Ellis, and settled in Kentucky, from whence, in 1821, he removed to Missouri and settled in Montgomery county. They had three children—John, Abraham and Rachel. Abraham was married first to Mary Branson, by whom he had twelve children —Alexander, Alfred, Abraham, Stout B., Franklin, Hezekiah, Elizabeth, Sarah, Rachel, Mary, Louisa, and Martha. His first wife died and he was married the second time to the widow Hubbard, by whom he had William and John A. Mr. Davidson was not out of the county during the last forty-five years of his life.

DRYDEN.—David Dryden, of Pennsylvania, married Barbara Berry, and settled in Washington county, Va., where he and his wife both died. Their children were—Jonathan, David, Nathaniel, William, Thomas, Rebecca, Elizabeth, and Mary. Jonathan married Fanny Duff, and lived and died in Kentucky. David was married twice, the name of his second wife being Jane Laughlan. He settled in Blunt county, Tenn. Nathaniel was also married twice; first to Ellen Laughlan, a daughter of Alexander and Ann Laughlan, but she died without children. Mr.

Dryden was married the second time to Margaret Craig, a daughter of Robert Craig, who was a son of a revolutionary soldier, and they had—Frederick H., John D. S., Ellen E., Mary R., Jane R., Louisa W., Thomas A., Margaret, David C., Caroline, and William P. Mr. Dryden represented Washington county, Va., in the Legislature of that State before he came to Missouri, and after he settled in Montgomery county in 1829, he represented that county in the Missouri Legislature several terms. He also held other important positions in the county, and was an influential and highly esteemed citizen. He died in 1858, in his 75th year; his widow still survives, in her 83d year. Thos. Dryden built a horse mill near Danville, soon after his arrival in Montgomery county, which, being something unusual for those times, attracted a great deal of attention. It was situated on a high point of ground, where the wind had a fair sweep against it, and several persons came near freezing to death while grinding grain there during cold weather. The capacity of the mill for grinding was from three to five bushels per day. Mr. Dryden was a leading member of the Methodist Church, and strict in his observance of its rules; but one day he needed some whisky for some purpose, and went to Danville and procured a jugful of that fiery liquid. On his way back home he met Rev. Andrew Monroe, his pastor, who was bitterly opposed to the use of intoxicating liquors in any manner, and was very strict in his enforcement of the rules of the church against it. Mr. Dryden saw him coming, and wondered what he should do—he a Steward in the church, with a jug of whisky in his hands! But a happy thought struck him. He remembered that Monroe had once entertained the Governor in his house at Danville, and had sent to the saloon to get a bottle of whisky for his benefit, as he had none in the house, and the Governor had called for a stimulant. When they met, Monroe's first question was, "Well, Brother Dryden, what is that you have got in your jug?" Dryden promptly answered, "It's some whisky that I have just purchased for the Governor, who is at my house." Monroe saw the point, and let Brother Dryden off without a reprimand. Thomas Dryden, brother of Nathaniel, married Elizabeth Craig, and settled in Montgomery county. He died in 1874, in his 74th year.

DAVAULT.—Henry Davault was born in France, but married Catharine Maria Grover, of Germany. They emigrated to America about the year 1764, landed near Philadelphia, and settled near Hanover, York Co., Pa., where they lived and died. Mr. Davault served in the revolutionary war, under General Washington. He died at the age of 85, but his wife lived to the remarkably old age of 97 years, 4 months and ten days. They had the following children — Philip, Margaret, E.izabeth and Gabriel (twins), Catharine, Mary, Henry, Valentine, Frederick,

Julia, and Jacob. Philip was one year old when his parents arrived in America. He married Catharine Long. Margaret married Samuel Long. Elizabeth married John Kitzmiller. Gabriel married Mary Kitzmiller. Catharine married Nicholas Keefauver. Mary married Martin Kitzmiller. Henry married Kitty Gross. Valentine married Louisa Range. Julia married Jacob Warts. Jacob married Rachel Kitzmiller. Philip Davault had the following children — Mary, Kate, Margaret, Lydia, Louisa, Daniel, and Eliza. One of these children married John Harshey, and died in Maryland. Another married William Roberts, and lived in Baltimore. Another married William Landers and lived in Illinois. Another married John Kitzmiller, and lived in Tennessee. Another married Mary Kitzmiller, and lived in Tennessee. Another married James Larrimore, and lived in Ohio. The children of Frederick Davault were—Henry, Peter, David, Mary, Elizabeth, John, Louisa, Kitty, and Samuel. Most of these children settled and lived in Tennessee. Henry settled in Montgomery county in 1831, and married Virginia Maughs, by whom he had—Mary, Elijah, and John. Peter married Mary Hays, of Tennessee, and settled in Montgomery county in 1831. He conditionally donated the land to the county on which Danville now stands. His children were—Henry, Laban, Catharine, Frederick, Alfred, John, Emma, Louisa, and Mary V. The latter died in childhood. Mr. Davault died in 1872. His sister, Kitty, married a Mr. Crawford, of Tennessee, and removed to Kansas but afterward died in Missouri. Mary Davault married James Duncan, who settled in South Carolina. Elizabeth married Joseph Duncan, and remained in Tennessee. Louisa was married twice, to two brothers, named Rankin, and remained in Tennessee.

DUTTON.—Natley Dutton and wife, of England, settled in Maryland some time after Lord Baltimore began to colonize that State. Their son, Natley, Jr., was born and raised in Maryland. He had a son, named John H., who was born in 1790. Mr. Dutton died when his son was eleven years of age, and two years afterward his mother had him bound out to learn the ship carpenter's trade. He worked at that business fourteen years. In the meantime his mother had married a Mr. Elton, whose father was a Quaker and came to America with William Penn. They had a son named Thomas T. Elton, and in 1818, he and his half-brother, John H. Dutton, in company with Philip Glover, started to Missouri. They traveled in a wagon to Wheeling, Virginia, where they bought a flat-boat, and loading their wagon and team into it, they floated down to Maysville, Kentucky, where they traded their flat-boat for a keel-boat, transferred their property to it, and proceeded to Louisville. There they sold their boat and came by land to Missouri. They located first in St. Charles county, where

they rented land and lived two years.   They then entered land
on North Bear creek, in Montgomery county, and settled there.
Mr. Elton married Eleanor Glover, and raised a large family of
children.   He subsequently removed to Grant county, Wisconsin,
where he now resides.   Mr. Dutton married Mary Bruin, of St.
Charles county, whose father settled there in 1808.   They had
—John H., Jr., Eveline, Timothy B., Eleanor, James M., and
Elizabeth.   The two latter lived to be grown, but died unmarried.   John H., Jr., lives in Warren county.   Eveline married J.
B. Shelton, of Montgomery county.   Timothy B. lives in Montgomery City.   Eleanor married Edmond F. Adams.   John H.
Dutton, Sr., and his wife were members of the Baptist Church,
of which he was a deacon for twenty years.   He was Justice of
the Peace for a long time, and Judge of the County Court for
eighteen consecutive years, twelve years of which time he was the
presiding Justice.   He was a man of fine business qualifications,
and was highly esteemed for his many excellent characteristics.
He died the death of a Christian, June 9, 1853?   His widow survived him thirteen years.

ENGLAND.—Joseph England married Mary Reed, of Virginia,
and settled in Montgomery Co., Mo., in 1833.   Their children
were—David, William, Joseph, Jr., James, John, Riley, Elizabeth, and Nancy.   James married Elizabeth Russel, who died in
1874.   John died in California, unmarried.   The rest of the children married and settled in different States.

ESTELL.—Benjamin Estell, of Kentucky, married Anna Claugh-
naugh, and settled in Boone Co., Mo.   They had ten children,
and one of their sons, named James, married Matilda VanBibber,
daughter of Major Isaac VanBibber, and settled in Montgomery
county.   Their children were—Horatio, Elizabeth A., William
K., Isaac V., Pantha, Colelia C., Robert G., Jonathan, Arrata,
James W., Benjamin, and Sarah N.—Philemon Estell, a brother
of James, settled in Montgomery county, and was married three
times.

ELLIS.—Benjamin Ellis settled on South Bear creek in 1815.
He was a wheelwright and chair maker, and also had a hand-mill.
He had ten children.—James Ellis settled on Bear creek in 1819.
He married Elizabeth Bowen, and they had six children—Edmund,
Benjamin, Leeper, William, Fanny, and Martha.   Benjamin mar-
ried Catharine McGarvin, and now lives in Callaway county.

FULKERSON.—(This name in the native tongue, was Volkerson,
but after the removal of the family to America they began to
spell it as it is pronounced.)   James Fulkerson, of Germany,
came to America at an early date and settled in North Carolina.   There he became acquainted with and married Mary Van-
Hook, and subsequently removed to Washington Co., Va.   The

names of their children were—Peter, James, John, Thomas, Abraham, Jacob, Isaac, William, Polly. Catharine, Hannah, and Mary. Peter married Margaret Craig, and they had—Polly, Robert C., James, Benjamin F., Jacob, Peter, Jr., John W., Margaret, Rachel, David C., and Frederick. Of these children Robert C., Benjamin F., and Frederick settled in Missouri. The former (Robert C.) was born in Lee Co., Va., August 27, 1794. He served as a soldier in the war of 1812, was afterward elected Colonel of militia, and took part in the Black Hawk war in 1834. He first came to Missouri in 1816, with Major Benjamin Sharp, but remained only a short time, when he returned to Virginia, where he resided until 1828. During that period he served his county for seven years in the capacity of Sheriff, an office which at that time was beset with many dangers and hardships, requiring a man of nerve and determination to discharge its duties. So faithful was he in the performance of his labors, that he received the special commendation of the Judge who presided, by an order entered upon the records of the county. He was married in 1827 to Lavinia Dickerson, and the following year he came with his family to Missouri. He settled first in Randolph county, where he remained only a short time, and then removed to Grand Prairie in Callaway county. In 1836 he removed to Montgomery county, and lived for a short time on the old Isaac VanBibber farm. In 1840 he purchased and removed to a farm near Danville, where he resided until his death, with the exception of a portion of the years 1851-52, when he crossed the plains to Oregon. He served as Treasurer of Montgomery county for ten years, and the people never had a more faithful and vigilant officer. His first wife died in 1852, and the following year he married the widow Davidson, who survives him. He had seven children, whose names were—Peter, John, Robert, Margaret, Rebecca, Amanda, and Anna. Only three of the children are living, two sons, one in Oregon and one in Missouri, and a daughter, Mrs. Samuel A. Wheeler, who lives on the old homestead near Danville. Colonel Fulkerson died at the latter place on the 17th of March, 1876, and was buried in the family graveyard, close by the side of a number of the intimate associates of his earlier life. The funeral ceremonies were conducted by the Masonic fraternity, of which he had long been an honored member. He had also been a member of the Methodist Episcopal Church, South, for a number of years, and died in the full faith of the Christian religion.

FREELAND.—Nelson Freeland, of Virginia, married Myra Woodruff, settled in Montgomery county in 1828, and died the same year. Their children were—Sultana, John W., William M., Mace D., Ann, Amanda, and Hiram.—William F., a brother of Nelson Freeland, married Susan Woodruff, and settled in Mont-

17

gomery county in 1828. They had—Robert, Charles, Amanda, and Eveline.

FARROW.—The parents of George Farrow came from Scotland, and settled in Fauquier Co., Va., where George was born. He was a soldier of the war of 1812. He married a Miss Massey, and they had — George, Jr., Nimrod, John, and Benjamin—also two daughters. Benjamin married Lucy Smith, of Virginia, and they had—John P., George, Mortimer, Joseph, Margaret, Sarah, Liney M., Mary L., and Amanda M. John P., Sarah, and Margaret came to Missouri. Sarah married William Browning, and settled in St. Charles county, but afterward removed to Lincoln county. Margaret married James B. Barton, and settled in St. Charles county. John P. was married in Virginia, to Susan M. Smith, and settled in St. Charles county in 1836. He subsequently removed to Troy, where he was employed in a store, and in 1844 he settled in Montgomery county, where he was elected Judge of the County Court, and held the office for twenty years. He afterward removed to Crawford Co., Mo.

FIPPS.—William Fipps, Jr., son of William Fipps and Rebecca Kendrick, of Washington Co., Va., married the widow of John King, whose maiden name was Barbara A. Stroup. They removed to Montgomery Co., Mo., in 1836, where Mr. Fipps died in 1857, at the advanced age of 111 years. He had voted for every President from Washington down to Lincoln. He had twelve children—John, Mary A., Sarah, Elizabeth, Rachel, William, Jr., George, Joseph, David, Robert, Susannah, and Margaret—all of whom lived to be grown except Robert, who died when he was fifteen years of age. John, David, Sarah, Susannah, Joseph, and Mary, all live in Montgomery county. Mrs. Fipps died last spring, at the residence of her son, Joseph, three miles west of Montgomery City, aged 106 years. She lived to see the fourth generation of her descendants, and at her death she left surviving her six children and one hundred forty grandchildren of the second, third and fourth generations. Her youngest child was born when she was in her 54th year. She had been a member of the Methodist Episcopal Church for 53 years, and was a consistent Christian woman, dying in the full faith of that religious belief.

FITZHUGH.—Richard Fitzhugh was born in North Carolina, but while he was a boy his parents removed to Davidson Co., Tenn., where he was raised. He married Mary Watson, who was also born in North Carolina and raised in Tennessee. They came to Montgomery Co., Mo., in 1818, and settled on the east side of Loutre creek. Mr. Fitzhugh was a hard-working man, and he and his son Hopkins sawed a great deal of lumber with a whip-saw, and sold it in Danville. He once met with a misfortune by which he had several of his ribs broken, and after that he would eat nothing but milk and mush, which he imagined kept the broken ribs in their places. His children were—Hopkins, Mary A., Matilda, Louisa J., John S., Thomas B., and Catharine.

FORD.—Calvin Ford came from Ireland, and settled in Charlotte county, Virginia, where his son Hezekiah was born. The latter married Ann Garrett, by whom he had thirteen children, eleven of whom he raised. Their names were—Calvin, James, Claiborne, Laban, Marley, Thomas, William, Elizabeth, Morning, Susan, and Martha. William, James, Elizabeth and Martha came to Montgomery county with their mother, who was a widow, in 1835. William was married first to Martha A. Eperson, of Virginia, and after her death he married Margaret H. Nettle. James was married first to Mary Robinson, and after her death he married the widow Natton. Elizabeth married John Buster, of Virginia, who settled in Montgomery county in 1835. Martha married Simeon Hovey, of Virginia, and after his death she was married the second time to Andrew Britt, of Virginia.

FARTHING.—William Farthing, of Albemarle county, Virginia, married Polly Vaughn, and settled in Kentucky. They had—Sarah, Elizabeth, William, John, Thomas, and Shelton B. Sarah married James Hunt, who settled in Montgomery county in 1836. Elizabeth married William P. Hill, of Kentucky, who also settled in Montgomery county in 1836. William married Nancy Wood, and settled in Iowa. John married Lucena J. Moran, and settled in Missouri City, Missouri. Shelton B. married Lucy A. Glenn. and settled in Montgomery county in 1836.

FISHER.—Solomon Fisher, of Virginia, married Mary A. Petty, by whom he had—Adam, George, William, John, Solomon, Jr., Eunice, Maxmillian, Parthena, Selemer, and Emmarilla. All of the family came on a keel-boat to Louisiana, Missouri. Adam married Dulcinea Powers, of Virginia, and settled in Pike county, in 1824. They had Mary A., Sally, William P., and Joseph. William P. married and lives in Montgomery county. George Fisher died in California, and Solomon died in the United States army. Mr. Adam Fisher laid off the town of Frankford, in Pike county.

GRAY.—George Gray, of Scotland, emigrated to America previous to the revolution, and when that war began he joined the American army and served during the entire struggle. He had several brothers in the British army during the same war. Before leaving Scotland, he married Mary Stuart, and they settled first in Philadelphia, but afterward removed to North Carolina, and from there to Bryan's Station in Kentucky. Here their son Joseph married Mary Finl y, and settled in Warren county, Kentucky. In 1818 he removed to Missouri, and settled on Brush creek in Montgomery county, where he died in 1830. His children were—Hannah, William, Isaac, George, Sarah, Rachel, James, and Mary.

Hannah married Asa Williams, who was an early settler of Montgomery county. William, Isaac and George married sisters, named Price, of Kentucky. William had three children, who settled in Missouri after the death of their parents. Isaac and George also settled in Montgomery county, but the latter removed to Clark county in 1837, where he still resides. Sarah married Stephen Finley, who settled in Wisconsin in 1846. Rachel married John P. Glover, who settled in Oregon. James married Margaret Williams, of Ohio. Mary married Presley Anderson, who died in 1848, and who was Sheriff of Montgomery county at the time. He left a widow and five children, who still live in Montgomery county.

GENTRY.—David Gentry, of Virginia, married Jane Kendrick, and settled in Madison county, Ky. They had—Bright B., Pleasant, David, Dickey, Martin, Bailey, and five daughters. Bright B. married Martha Jones, and they had—James, Margaret, David, Jonathan J., Eliza, Susan, Albert, and Fanny. David settled in Montgomery county in 1833, and married Polly A. Groom. Jonathan also settled in Montgomery county in 1833, and married Elizabeth McFarland.

GROOM.—William Groom, of England, emigrated to America, and settled in Kentucky, where he married Sally Parker. They had—Abraham, Isaac, Moses, Jacob, Aaron, Susan, Elizabeth, and Sally. All except Susan came to Missouri. Abraham and Isaac settled in Clay county. Jacob and Aaron settled in Montgomery county in 1810. Jacob was a ranger under Captain Callaway, and, in company with Jackey Stewart, was scouting in the woods the day Callaway was killed. A man named Dougherty was killed the same day, at Salt Peter Cave, not far from Groom's farm. After they had killed him the Indians cut his body into pieces, and hung them on a pole. As Groom and Stewart approached the cave, they discovered the horrible spectacle, and about the same instant were fired upon by the Indians. Both horses were wounded, Stewart's mortally, and he also received a a gunshot wound in his heel. After running a short distance, his horse fell, and soon expired; and he being unable to walk, on account of his wound, Groom generously helped him on to his own horse, and they both succeeded in making their escape to Fort Clemson. Groom was an uneducated man, but generous hearted and possessed of strong common sense. He was a leading politician of his day, a Democrat of the Andrew Jackson stripe, and was elected to the Legislature several times. He was a member of the first State Legislature, which met in St. Charles in 1821-2. He dressed in a buckskin suit, wore a band of hickory bark around his hat, and always had independence enough to express his honest convictions on every subject that came up for discussion. We give several characteristic anecdotes of him elsewhere. He married Sally Quick, and they had—Aaron, Maria, William, Lucinda, Sally A., and two other daughters, one of whom married a Mr. Hubbard and the other a Mr. McGarvin, all of whom lived in Montgomery county.

GILL.—Samuel Gill, whose father lived in Maryland, settled in Virginia, where he was married twice, one of his wives being a Miss Kidwell. His sons, James and Presley, came to Missouri in 1831. The former settled in Callaway county, and married Matilda Darnes, by whom he had eight children. Presley settled in Montgomery county, and lives at New Florence. He learned the trade of a gunsmith, and is also a doctor.

GRAVES.—Peyton Graves, of Pittsylvania county, Virginia, married Charlotte Pinkard, and they had nine children   Jane, the eldest, married Thomas Jefferson, a nephew of President Jefferson. William, John, and Washington, sons of Peyton Graves, came to Missouri and settled in Montgomery county. William married Lucy Berger. John married Mildred George. Washington married Melcina Berger. The rest of Peyton Graves' children, with the exception of one, lived and died in Virginia.

GRAHAM.—John Graham, of Kentucky, married a Miss Dugan, and they had—Robert, John, Alexander, Catharine, and Isabella. Alexander died in Kentucky, and John died in Mississippi. Catharine married Tocal Galbreth. Isabella married Alexander Collier. Robert, who was a physician, married Isabella Galbreth, a daughter of Tocal Galbreth by his first wife, and settled in Montgomery county in 1816. He bought a Spanish grant of land, situated on Loutre creek, from Daniel M. Boone, and built an elm bark tent upon it, in which he lived four years. The Doctor was a very small man, but of determined will and a nerve that could not be shaken. He was a staunch Democrat, a voluminous reader, and a great admirer of Benjamin Franklin. He was the only physician in that part of the country at that time, and had as large a practice as he cared to attend to. He was fond of hunting, and devoted much of his time to that occupation. One day a large wolf got caught in one of his steel traps, broke the chain, and dragged the trap away with him. The Doctor, Joseph Scholl, and Major VanBibber tracked the wolf and came upon it where it had gone into the creek and was struggling in the water. Graham waded into the creek for the purpose of killing the wolf with his knife, when it caught one of his hands and bit it nearly off; but he succeeded in killing it. On another occasion the Doctor and a party of hunters ran a large bear into his cave, and tried to smoke him out, but could not succeed, and finally shot him. After the bear was dead the Doctor was the only one of the party who had nerve enough to crawl into the cave and drag the carcass out. Wolves were plentiful then, and one day while out hunting he

killed thirteen of them.—The children of Dr. Graham were—
John F., Alexander W., James W., Benjamin R., Robert D.,
Franklin D., Doctor F., Patrick H., Maria, Catharine, and
Clara A.

GLENN.—James Glenn and his wife, Sarah Grigg, with their
two children, James and Nellie, came from Ireland to America,
and settled in Virginia. After their settlement there the following children were born—Polly, William, Thomas, and Whitehill.
Mr. Glenn and his three sons, William, Thomas, and Whitehill,
moved to Ohio; the rest of the children married and settled in
Kentucky. James, William, and Thomas were in the war of
1812, and the former was killed at the battle of New Orleans.
The other two were with the armies that operated in Canada and
the northern part of the United States. After the war Thomas
married Lucinda T. Kendall, of Kentucky, and came to Missouri
in 1815. He came in a wagon, which contained, in addition to
his family and furniture, a set of wheel-wright's tools, a gun and
a dog. Mr. Glenn settled first on Cuivre river, but made
about twenty settlements in all before he could find a location to
suit him. These were all within the present limits of Montgomery
county. He was a great hunter, and during the first year
of his residence in Missouri killed fifty-six deer, one elk, and
one bear. The names of his children were—Julia A , Emily H.,
Sarah E., James M., and William I.

GODFREY.—George Godfrey lived at Ritford, England. His
son Peter married Dorothea Learey, of England, by whom he
had—Thomas, John, Edward, George, Charles, and Mary.
Thomas came to America and settled in Canada. John went to
California, and died on his return to England. Edward lives in
Mercer county, Pa. George married Mary Ostick, of England,
and settled in Pittsburg, Pa., in 1830, in St. Louis in 1836, and
in Montgomery county, where Jonesburg now stands, in 1838.
His children are—Mary A., George, Edward, William O., John
W., Henry M., and James A. Mary A. married Rev. George
Smith, a Methodist minister, who came to Montgomery county in
1836. Mr. Godfrey has been a devoted Methodist for many
years, and a leading member of his church. His brother Charles
settled in Louisville, Kentucky, and his son, Charles, Jr., lives in
Fulton, Mo.

GAMMON.—Benjamin Gammon, of Madison county, Va., mar-
ried Sarah Maddox, and settled in (now) Montgomery county,
Mo., in 1812. They had—John, Henry, Anderson, Stephen,
Jonathan, Benjamin, Jr., Harris, Elizabeth, Julia, and Sarah.
John, Anderson, and Benjamin all died unmarried. Jonathan
married Martha Dickerson, and lives on Hancock's Prairie, in
Montgomery county. Sarah married Alfonzo Price. The other
children married and settled in different States. Mr. Gammon,

Sr., built a hand-mill on his farm, which was the first in that part of the country, and it supplied his own family and his neighbors with meal for some time. The meal for his own family was generally ground just before it was required for use, and he allowed two ears of corn for each individual; but one day Jacob Groom took dinner with them, and they had to grind *three* ears for him, as he was very fond of corn bread. The grinding was done by the children, and it was said that Mr. Gammon "broke all his children at the mill."

GREENWELL.—John Greenwell, of Kentucky, had a son Joseph, who married a Miss Taylor, and they had—Ellen, Richard, Joseph, Jr., John, and William. Richard was married first to Eveline Raymond, of Kentucky, and second to Mrs. Counts, whose maiden name was Rachel Davidson. The rest of the children married and remained in Kentucky.

HUGHES.—Major Thomas Hughes, of Bourbon county, Kentucky, married Lucy Tandy, and their children were—William, Gabriel, Thomas, Henry C., Elliott M., James and Susan T. The Major's first wife died, and he subsequently married her sister, who was a widow at the time. Major Hughes held the position of Justice of the Peace, in Paris, for forty years, and all his decisions were sustained by the higher courts. He also represented Bourbon county in the Kentucky Legislature. His eldest son, William, married his cousin, Margaret Hughes, and settled in Boone county, Missouri. Elliott M. received a classical education, and came to Missouri when a young man, and taught school in and near Danville for several years. He then returned to Kentucky, where he married Jane S. McConnell, and soon after came back to Montgomery county, where he remained until his death, which occurred on the 14th of January, 1862. He exercised a large influence in his community, and was a general favorite with all who knew him. He was fond of practical jokes. was full of wit and humor, and became a prominent member of the Evanix Society of Danville. The names of his children living in 1876, are—Blanche A., Duncan C., Susan C., Elliott M., Jr., R. H., Arnold, and Tandy. Elliott M., Jr., is Prosecuting Attorney of Montgomery county, and is a rising young lawyer, with a promising future before him.

HUNTER.—This name in German is Yager, but when translated it means Hunter. Andrew Hunter, and his wife, of Germany, came to America and settled in Greenbriar county, Virginia, where they had—John, Tobias, Philip, William, Peter, Elizabeth, and Sarah. Peter, who changed the family name from Yager to Hunter, married Margaret Wood, and settled in North Carolina in 1816, and in 1819 he and his family and his two sisters, Sarah and Elizabeth, came to Missouri and settled in Montgomery county. The change of the name was the cause of the family losing a large estate in Germany, as the heirs could not be traced after the change was made. Peter's children were—James, Robert, Andrew, Ephraim, William, John N., Tileson, Nancy, and Elmira. All married and lived in Montgomery county.

HALL.—William Hall and Elizabeth Hicks, who was his second wife, came from East Tennessee and settled in Montgomery county in 1817. Their children were—Sarah, Elizabeth, Dorcas, Nancy, Laney, David, and Henry. Sarah married John Morrow, and they had thirteen children. Elizabeth married Elijah Waddell. Dorcas married Mark Cole, who was the first hatter in Montgomery county. Nancy Hall married John R. Crawford, who built his cabin in Montgomery county, in 1818. Among others who were present and assisted him to raise the cabin, were Daniel Boone and his sons Nathan and Jesse. Lewis Jones killed the game and cooked the dinner, and found a bee tree not far distant, from which they obtained fresh honey for their dinner. Crawford was noted for his ability to tell humorous yarns, and entertain a crowd. Laney Hall married Ephraim Hunter. David married Fanny Morrow. Henry married his cousin, Polly Hall.

HOWARD.—Charles Howard, of Halifax county, Virginia, married Nancy Lewis, and settled in Warren county, Kentucky. One of their sons, named Joseph, married Malinda Lennox, and settled in Montgomery county, Missouri, in 1818. Their children were—Sylvesta, Cynthia E., Elijah, Rachel, Estelle, Cordelia, and Malinda. Mr. Howard's first wife died, and he was married again to Phœbe Saylor, by whom he had John and George. She also died, and he married a lady named McCormack, by whom he had—Greenup, Nancy, and Matilda. He was married the fourth time to Sydney Hall, by whom he had Joseph W. and a daughter. He was married the fifth time to Nancy Bladenburg, but they had no children.

HARPER.—Capt. John Harper was a native of Philadelphia, and followed the sea for many years after he was grown. In 1750 he settled in Alexandria, Va., where he died in his 87th year. He was married twice, and had twenty-nine children, eighteen sons and eleven daughters. Charles, the youngest son by his first wife, married Lucy Smither, who was of Scotch descent, and by her he had two children. He was married the second time to a Miss January, by whom he had nine children. The second son of his last wife, whose name was Charles B., was born in Culpepper Co., Va., in May, 1802. He was married in 1823 to Anna C. Price, of Pittsylvania Co., Va., and settled in Montgomery Co., Mo., in 1830. He was engaged in merchandising at Danville for five years, and one year on his farm. He brought the first demijohns to Montgomery county, and sold a great many as curiosities, most of the inhabitants having never seen anything of the kind.   Soon after his arrival in Montgomery he went over to Callaway county, one day, to get a load of corn, and wore his usual every-day clothes, made of home-spun cloth.   On his way back the road led him by a house where Jabe Ham was preaching, and he stopped to hear the sermon.   During the services the minister called on the congregation to kneel in prayer, and all knelt except Mr. Harper, who leaned his head upon his hand, and remained in that position.   Ham noticed him, and prayed that the Lord would bless "that Virginia man, who had on store clothes, and was afraid or too proud to get down on his knees." Mr. Harper represented his county four years in the State Senate, and has always been a good citizen.   He had eight children.

HAM.—Stephen Ham lived and died in Madison Co., Ky.   He was the father of John, Jabez, and Stephen Ham, Jr.   John was born in Kentucky in 1786, and came to Missouri in 1809, and settled in St. Charles county.   He joined Nathan Boone's company of rangers, and served during the Indian war.   In 1816 he and Jonathan Crow built a bark tent on Auxvasse creek, now in Callaway county, and lived in it for some time, while they were engaged in hunting.   They were, therefore, probably the first American settlers within the limits of Callaway county.   Ham cut his name on a lone tree in the prairie, which has since borne his name.   He was a Methodist preacher.   He was married twice, first to a Miss Bennett, by whom he had two children.   She died when the children were quite small, and their father took them to their relatives in Kentucky, performing the journey on horseback, with one of the children before him and one behind.   When he came to water courses that were deep enough to swim his horse, he would tie one of the children on the bank, swim across with the other, tie it, and go back for the one he had left.   He afterward married a Miss Thomas, and they had six daughters. Mr. Ham was a daring hunter, and there were but few who possessed nerve enough to follow him in all his adventures.   He once smoked a bear out of its cave and then knocked it in the head with an ax.   In 1823 he built a house on the Auxvasse, about five miles above its mouth; and the following year the big overflow came and washed away his smoke house, filled with bear and deer meat.   He followed it in a soap trough, which he used as a canoe, and overtook the floating house where it had lodged against a large elm tree.   He took his meat and hung it in the tree, and when the water subsided he had to cut the tree down in order to get his meat.   Mr. Ham subsequently removed to Illinois, where he died in 1869.—Jabez Ham, brother of John, was born in Madison Co., Ky., in 1797, and came to Missouri in 1817. He had no education, was of a roving disposition, and did nothing for several years but hunt and fish.   His mind was naturally bright, and if he had been educated he would have made a re-

markable man. Rev. Aley Snethen and Lewis Jones taught him the
alphabet and learned him to read, and in 1824 he began to preach,
having united with the Old or Hard Shell Baptist Church. In
1826 he organized a church of that denomination on Loutre
Creek, and called it New Providence. For some time after he
began to preach he always carried his gun with him when he
went to church, both on week days and Sundays, and often killed
deer on his way to and from his preaching places. He also manufactured powder, which he had a ready sale for at high prices;
and by this means and from the proceeds of his rifle he made a
living and did well. He was a large, stout man, and often added
emphasis to his opinions by the use of his fists. On a certain
occasion he forgot the text that he had intended to preach from,
and when he arose in the pulpit he announced the fact by saying
to the congregation that he had a text when he left home, but had
lost it, and he had looked for it, and Hannah (his wife) had
looked for it, but they could not find it; but to the best of
his belief it was "somewhere in the hind end of Job, or there-
abouts, and it went about this way—'Do any of you all know
the good old woman they call Mary, or Sal of Tarkus, who
said you must not put new wine in old bottles, for the bottles will bust and the good stuff will all be spilled.'" Mr.
Ham often compared his sermons to an old shot-gun loaded
with beans, which, when it went off, was almost sure to hit somebody, or somewhere. He died in Callaway county in 1842, and
was buried at New Providence Church, in Montgomery county.
His wife was Hannah Todd, of Kentucky, and they had fourteen
children.—Rev. Stephen Ham, brother of John and Jabez, married
Jane Johnson, of Kentucky, and came to Missouri in 1828. He
settled in Montgomery county, where he still lives, in his 72d
year. He also is a Baptist preacher. He had eight children, and
John and Hardin Ham, the well known and popular merchants of
Montgomery City, are his sons.

HUDNALL.—William Hudnall, of England, married Fannie Mc-
George, of Ireland, and their children were—John, Thomas,
William, and Richard. The latter was a soldier of the revolu-
tionary war. He married a Miss Cresey, and they had a son,
Jack, who settled in Missouri in 1835. William was married
twice. By his first wife he had—Polly, Catharine, Lucy, and
Elizabeth. He was married the second time to a widow, whose
maiden name was Nancy Williams, and by her he had—Jabez,
Samuel, Patsey, Nancy, Parthena, Susannah, and William R.
Catharine and Lucy married and settled in Howard Co., Mo.
Samuel (now living in Callaway county) married Julia A. Hewett,
and settled in Montgomery county in 1837. He got a good
ducking in Loutre creek, one day, in the following manner. He
was sitting on his horse, about the middle of the creek, talking to

Ned Hudnall and William Elliott, who were engaged in a playful scuffle on the bai k. Ned finally threw Elliot into the water, which amused Hudnall so that he became convulsed with laughter, and rolled off of his horse into the creek. He happened to roll into deep water, and had to swim to the bank, while his horse swam out on the other side. Mr. Hudnall says he will never forget the first deer he killed. The weather was very cold, and the deer froze fast to him while he was carrying it home on his shoulder. When he got to the house he had to build a fire and thaw it before he could get away from it.—Susannah Hudnall married William Elliot, who settled in Missouri in 1835.

HARDING.—Alexander Harding, of Halifax Co., Va., married Mary Hightower, and they had—Archibald, Anna, Benjamin, Elizabeth, Mary, and Sally. Mr. Harding died in 1816, and his widow married Josiah Rodgers, and moved to Alabama. Archibald married in Virginia, and settled in Missouri in 1833. Anna married James Anderson, and settled in Montgomery county in 1833. Benjamin served in the war of 1812. He married Mary Nunnelly, of Virginia, and settled in Montgomery county in 1831. They had but one child, who died when nineteen years of age.

HENSLEY.—Samuel and Benjamin Hensley were sons of an English family that settled on the Potomac river in Virginia, at an early date. Samuel married a Miss Landers, and they had Samuel, Jr., and William. His first wife died, and he was married again to Susan Taplett, by whom he had several children. William, son of Samuel, Jr., by his first wife, married Elizabeth Appleberry, of Virginia, and they had—James, Benjamin, William, Jr., Thomas, Fleming, Judith, and Elizabeth. James, William, Jr., Thomas, and Fleming came to Montgomery county in 1826, and all except Thomas afterward married and settled in Jefferson Co., Mo. Thomas Hensley was born in Albemarle Co., Va., in 1796, and when eighteen years of age he enlisted as a soldier in the war of 1812. He afterward married Harriet Rust, who was a daughter of Samuel Rust and Mary Lee Bailey, who was the daughter of James Bailey and Nancy Smith. Mr. Hensley with his wife and four children, embarked in a keel boat of his own make, on the Pocotalico river, and floated down to the Big Kenhawa, and thence to the Ohio, on their way to Missouri. They reached Louisville in safety, but just below that place their boat sank, and it was with the greatest difficulty that they succeeded in reaching the shore in safety. Here they built a cabin and remained one year, in order to recruit and build another boat. At the end of that time, their boat being complete, they re-embarked and proceded on their journey. When they reached the Mississippi they found the current so strong that they could not stem it, so Mr. Hensley gave his boat away, embarked his goods and furniture on a French barge, and conveyed his family by land to Jefferson Co., Mo., where they remained one year, and then settled in St. Louis county, seven miles from the city of St. Louis. Here he entered 80 acres of land, which he still owns, and which has become very valuable. Mr. Hensley and his wife had nine children, and they now reside in Montgomery City, Mo. He has been a Baptist minister for many years, having made a solemn promise while on a bed of sickness, which he expected would be his last, that if allowed to recover he would go to preaching and devote the remainder of his life to the service of the Lord. He recovered, and has faithfully kept his promise. His courtship and marriage were somewhat romantic, and happened in this wise, as related by Mrs. Hensley herself: The first time she ever saw him he stopped at her father's house to inquire the way to a place he was trying to find, and during the conversation she stepped to the door, dressed in a home-made striped lindsey dress, with a frying pan in her hand, from which she was sopping the gravy with a piece of bread. The next day Mr. Hensley returned, *lost again*, and made some additional inquiries. A week from that time he came back again, but not to see her father. This time he wanted to know if she was engaged to anybody else, and if not, how she liked his looks. His inquiries were satisfactorily answered and it was only a few weeks until the minister's benediction was given to help them on their way through life.

HASLIP.—Robert Haslip was a native of Maryland, but settled and lived in Virginia. He had two sons, Samuel and John. The latter was a soldier in the war of 1812. He married Lucy Johnson, by whom he had—Robert, James N., Samuel, John, William, Malinda, Jane, Elizabeth, and Polly. James N. settled in Montgomery Co., Mo., in 1838. His wife was Esther Clements, by whom he had ten children. Robert, brother of James, settled in Lincoln county in 1837, and in 1860 he was killed by a wagon running over his body.

HENLEY.—Hezekiah Henley, of Virginia, had a son named Thomas O., who was married first to Martha Bugg, by whom he had—William, Samuel, Thompson, John, Nancy, Martha, and Polly. After the death of his first wife he married Mary Herndon, by whom he had—Allen, Wilson, Thomas, Archibald, Schuyler, Sarah, Lucinda, Amanda, and Catharine. Samuel was married twice, and settled in St. Charles county. Allen settled in Montgomery county in 1838. He married Lucy Thomas, and they had ten children.

HUGHES.—Thomas Hughes, of Abingdon, Va., settled in Tennessee, where his son, William, married Sallie Green, and settled at Middletown, Montgomery county, at an early date. They had thirteen children.

HARRIS.—James Harris, of Wales, married his cousin, a Miss Harris, and settled first in the eastern part of Virginia, but afterward removed and settled in Albemarle county. Their children were—Wise, Thomas, Joel, James, and Nathan. Thomas married Susan Darby, of Virginia, by whom he had—Anna, Elizabeth, Garrett, William, Robert, Mary, Sarah, and Thomas, Jr. Anna and Elizabeth came to Montgomery county, and the latter married' Bernard B. Maupin. Garrett married Jane Ramsey, and settled in Montgomery county in 1837. Their children were—William R., Mary B., Anna J., Garrett T., Margaret M., Sarah E., and Susan D. William R. is an influential citizen of Montgomery county. He is at present Probate Judge, has served eight years as County Judge, and several terms as Representative in the Legislature. He is a substantial, upright citizen, and enjoys the confidence and respect of all who know him. He married Margaret N. Bethel, of Virginia.—Joel, son of James Harris, Sr., married Anna Waller, by whom he had—Clifton, Ira, and Joel, Jr. Clifton married Mary Lewis, by whom he had Decatur, who married his cousin, Isabella Harris, and settled in Montgomery county.—Waller C., Charles W., Mann H., Merriwether L., Susan, Catharine B., Matilda and Caroline, children of Ira Harris, settled in Montgomery county.—William, son of Thomas Harris, Sr., married Patsey Maupin, and settled in Montgomery county; also his brother Thomas, who married Elizabeth Turk.

HENTON.—Jesse Henton of Logan Co., Ky., was in the war of 1812. He married Sarah Hughes, of Kentucky, and settled in Pike Co., Mo., in 1827, His children were—John, James L., William, David, Wesley S., Rolla W., Mary J., Benjamin, Sarah A., Elizabeth E., and Harriet D. Rolla W. married Elizabeth L. Jamison, of Pike county, and settled in Montgomery. Samuel, son of John Henton, settled in Pike county in 1826. He married Mary Estens, and subsequently settled in Montgomery county.

HICKERSON.—John Hickerson, of Fauquier Co., Va., married Elizabeth Baker, and their son, Thomas, came to Missouri in 1816, as teamster for John Ferguson, who settled in Darst's Bottom. In 1818 Hickerson moved to Montgomery county and settled on the west bank of Loutre creek, near Loutre Lick. He soon after married Susan VanBibber, daughter of Major Isaac VanBibber, by whom he had thirteen children—Melissa, Thomas A., James, Isaac V., Robert L., Alfonzo, and Susan J. The other six children died in infancy.—Ezekiel Heckerson, a brother of Thomas, married Elizabeth Hayden, of Kentucky, and settled in Pike Co., Mo., in 1823, and in 1827 he removed to Illinois. His children were—Elihue W., William B., Nancy A., James, Samuel, Silas L., Joseph L, and Mary A. Silas L. married

Jane Allen, of Callaway county, and now lives in Mexico, Mo.

HOPKINS.—The parents of Price, William, John and Patsey Hopkins, were natives of Queen Anne county, Va., but settled and lived in Bedford county. Their children married and lived near the old home place, in the same county. Price was married twice ; first to a daughter of Rev. James Price, a pioneer preacher of Virginia, and second to a Miss Slater. By his first wife he had William M., John, Ann, and Sally; we have no record of the names of his children by his second wife. William M. was born July 14, 1802, and was married to Nancy Hudnall, of Bedford county, in 1832. In 1837 they bade farewell to their native place, and started toward the setting sun to find a new home. They settled on Loutre creek, in Montgomery county, near Bryant's store, in the fall of the same year, and Mr. Hopkins set diligently to work in the cultivation and improvement of his farm. He was an industrious, honest, upright man, and enjoyed the esteem and respect of his fellow-citizens in the highest degree, who manifested their confidence in him by repeatedly electing him to the important position of Justice of the Peace. He was an excellent farmer, and rarely ever complained of short crops or hard times, as his barns and cribs were always full of grain, and his stock never had to live on short allowances. He remained on his farm on Loutre until 1855, when he removed to a farm near Montgomery City, where he resided until his death, which occurred on the 11th day of August, 1875. He became a member of the Baptist Church some twenty years before his death, and ever afterward lived a consistent Christian life, doing all he could for the cause of morality and religion in his community. He took an active interest in everything that promised to advance the good of the people with whom he had cast his lot, and when he was called away his neighbors felt that they had lost a friend and counsellor whose place could not easily be filled. His widow and six children survive him. He had nine children in all, but three preceded him to the grave. By his frugality and industry he was enabled to leave his family in good circumstances, and they can now attribute the prosperity which they enjoy to his kind and fatherly interest in their future welfare.

HANCE.—Adam Hance was born in Coblin, a French province of Alsace, and, as usual with the people of that country, spoke both German and English. He came to America and settled near Germantown, Pa., in 1722, where he married a German lady, and raised a large family. His younger son, also named Adam, married a Miss Stoebuck, of Pennsylvania, in 1768, and settled in Montgomery county, Va. When the revolutionary war began, fired by the prevailing patriotic feelings of the day, he joined the American army under Washington, and served during the entire war. He was in the battles of Brandywine, Yorktown, and several others, and experienced a great deal of very hard service. He had six children, viz.—Henry, Peter, Martha A., Priscilla, William, and John. Henry was Sheriff of his native county for a number of years, and afterward became a successful merchant in Newburn, N. C. Peter was married first to Elizabeth Harper, of Virginia, by whom he had—Mary, Anna, Margaret, Sabrina, William, and James. After the death of his first wife, he married Mrs. Juliet Hewett, whose first husband was drowned in Kentucky about 1815. By her he had—Robert, Elizabeth, Harvey, and Juliet. Mr. Hance settled in Montgomery county, Mo., in 1829, on what is now the Devault place. (Children of Peter Hance.) Mary never married, and died in Virginia at the age of sixty years. Sabrina married Isaac C. Bratton, of Virginia, who settled in Greenville, Tennessee, in 1831, and while living there had a suit of clothes made by Andrew Johnson, who afterward became President of the United States. Mr. Bratton settled in Montgomery county, Missouri, in 1833. Several of his children live in Kansas, and his son, Peter, who is a great fox hunter and conversationalist, lives near Montgomery City. Anna Hance married Dr. Samuel H. Gordon, of Gordonville, Va., who also settled in Greenville, Tenn., in 1831, and had a suit of clothes made by Andrew Johnson. In 1836 he removed to Missouri, and settled in Montgomery county, where he practiced medicine and taught school for a number of years. In 1846 he removed to St. Louis. His children were—Philip Doddridge, James H., Nathaniel D., Mary E., Louisa H., and Isabella V. Margaret Hance married William H. Alexander, of Tennessee, who settled in Montgomery county in 1833. His children were—Robert, Elizabeth (Mrs. J. P. Busby), Thomas, Marston, and James G. William Hance settled in Illinois about 1825, and raised a large family. James Hance settled at the Virginia lead mines, Franklin county, in 1838, where he married Evelina Hurst, and died soon after. They had one son, James R., who was born after the death of his father, and is now an enterprising merchant of Montgomery City. Robert Hance married and settled in Rushville, Ill., and is supposed to have been killed in the Confederate army. Elizabeth Hance married Rev. Jacob Siegler, a Methodist minister, and a merchant at Shelbyville, Mo., by whom she had three children. Harvey Hance married Mary Caplinger, and settled in Hannibal, Mo., where he died. Previous to his death he was intimate with Samuel L. Clemens, better know as Mark Twain. Juliet Hance married John Marmaduke, at that time a merchant in Shelbyville, Mo., but at present a resident of Mexico, Mo. (Children of John Hance.) John, the son of Adam, and brother of Peter Hance, married Kittie Hewett, and settled in Montgomery county, Mo., in 1832. Their children were—Henry W., Charles, Edward, Virginia C., Jane,

Martha, and Melcina. Henry W. lives in St. Louis. Charles was in the Confederate army during the late war, and lost an arm. He is at present County Clerk of Randolph county. Edward is a painter by trade. Virginia C. married Joseph C. Brand, and is now a widow, living in St. Louis. Jane married a Mr. Freeman, and died at Glenwood, Mo. Martha married Benjamin Douglas, a farmer of St. Louis county. Melcina married Charles Lewis of St. Louis county, and is now a widow.

HUDSON.—John Hudson and his wife, who was a Miss Allen, lived in North Carolina. They had six sons—Isaac, Drury, Thomas, William, John, and Jesse. Drury and Isaac were in the revolutionary war. The latter settled in Georgia, where he married Polly Shipper. He afterward removed to South Carolina, and from thence, to Kentucky, and in 1818 he came to Missouri. The names of his children were—Elizabeth, Nancy, Sally, John, Thomas, William, and Charles. Elizabeth married Lemuel Cox. Nancy married Garrett Ingram. Sally married James Owings. John was married three times; first to Lucinda Morris, of Kentucky; second to Nancy Holloway, and third to a widow lady named Carolina W. King. Thomas married Polly Hammond, and settled in Pike county. Charles and William married sisters, and settled in Lincoln county. William's first wife died, and he afterward married Sarah Hamlet.

INGRAM.—Jonathan Ingram married Barbara Mennefee, of Virginia, and settled in Logan Co., Ky. Their children were—Rhoda, Jonas, Samuel, Garrett, James, Anna, Polly, and Barsheba. Garrett married Nancy Hudson, and settled in Pike Co., Mo., in 1818. Their children were—Polly, John, Barbara, Elizabeth, Jonathan, Samuel, Nancy, and Sally.—Rhoda Ingram settled in Indiana, and James and Polly in Illinois.

JACOBS.—John Jacobs, of Germany, came to America and settled in Virginia, where he married Sarah Crawford. Their children were—David, John, Peter, William, Elizabeth C., and Susan H. William married Margaret A., daughter of Daniel McDaniel and Mary Anderson, who were natives of Edinburg, Scotland. By her he had—Charles A., George R., Mary, Anna, Sallie, Sophia, and Catharine H. Mr. Jacobs died in Virginia in 1828, and in 1831 his widow removed to Missouri and settled in Montgomery county, where she died in 1850. Charles, who was a wealthy merchant of New Orleans, died without marrying. George R., who was a physician, married Louisa Parsons, of Virginia, and settled in Montgomery Co., Mo., in 1831, but subsequently removed to Boone county. Mary and Anna died single, in Montgomery county, one in 1843 and the other in 1844. Sophia married Dr. Gorge Y. Bast, of New Florence. Catharine H. married Henry Clark, Sr.

JONES.—Ezekiel Jones, of Buckingham Co., Va., married Rhoda

Gill, and they had—James, John, Andrew, Polly, Nancy, and Sallie. John married Anna Herron, and lived in North Carolina. They had eight children. Andrew was married first to a Miss Wilson, daughter of a Congressman of that name from South Carolina. He was married four times in all, and lived in Arkansas. Polly married John Lapping, and they had five children. One of their sons married and had thirteen daughters. Nancy married Joseph Tate, of North Carolina. Sallie married Jesse Orr, of North Carolina. James married Elizabeth Wardlow, daughter of Patrick Wardlow and Esther Connor, both of Ireland, but who settled in Buckingham Co., Va., previous to the American revolution. He was married in 1811, and settled in Montgomery county, where Jonesburg now stands, in 1829. The town was named for him, and he was the first postmaster at that place. He also kept hotel and the stage office, and after the railroad was built he was ticket agent for some time. He had seven children—Calvin, Julia A., Patrick, Luther, Thomas, William, and James F.

JONES.—Richard Jones, who was born in England, married a Miss Love, and settled in Botetourt Co., Va. He was a member of the Baptist Church, but had to give a hogshead of tobacco every year for the support of the Episcopal Church. The names of his children were—William, John, and Silas. William married Elizabeth Metcalf, and settled first in Shelby Co., Ky., from whence he removed to Missouri and settled on Darst's Bottom, St. Charles county, in 1818. In 1820 he removed to Callaway county, and built a horse-mill, under the shed of which the Baptists held religious services for a number of years. The mill was kept by his son, William M., who afterward became a Baptist preacher, and is now a merchant at Montgomery City. William Jones' children were—Jane, Richard, Elizabeth L., Susan, William M., Minerva, Maria, Martha, and Narcissa. Jane married Robert Saylor. Richard married Unicia Davis. He afterward died of consumption, and the day before his death he was taken to the creek, on his bed, placed in a rocking-chair, and baptized, chair and all, by Jabez Ham.—Elizabeth L. Jones married William McCormack. William M. married Elizabeth Jones, and they had twelve children, one of whom, Judge Robert W. Jones, has been Judge of the Probate Court of Montgomery county, and is now editor of the *Standard* at Montgomery City. —Minerva married Anderson Hunter. Maria married Martellus Oliver. Martha married Benjamin Proctor. Narcissa married William Metcalf, of Kentucky.

JONES.—William R. Jones was born in the State of Georgia. His father's name was John Jones, and the maiden name of his mother was Robinson. William R. came to Missouri in 1819, a single man, and settled in Montgomery county, where he was

18

married the same year to Mary Whitesides, by whom he had—
John H., James H., Amanda, Mary M., Emeline, Nancy J., William R., Jr., Sylvesta M., Samuel A., Thomas S., and Perry S.
All the children, except three, who are dead, live in Montgomery
county. Mr. Jones was a Methodist preacher.

KNOX.—David Knox was born in Ireland, in 1700. He had a
son named Andrew, who was born in 1728. In 1732 Mr. Knox
came to America, bringing his little son with him, and settled in
Philadelphia county, Pa. Andrew married Isabella White, of
Pennsylvania, and they had—Robert, David, Martha, James,
John, William, Mary, and Andrew, Jr. Mr. Knox was a soldier
in the revolutionary war, and having taken an active part in the
events of the day, a reward was offered for him, dead or alive, by
the British authorities. On the night of the 14th of February,
1778, he was at home visiting his family, and during the night his
house was surrounded by a party of Tories, who had come to
capture him for the reward. They announced their presence by
firing a volley of balls through the door, and then broke it down*
with the breeches of their guns. But before they could effect an
entrance, Mr. Knox and his son Robert met them with drawn
sabres, and laid about them so vigorously that they were soon
glad to retreat, with several of their party bleeding from the
gashes and cuts they had received. Some American troops in the
vicinity were notified of the attack, and immediately started in
pursuit. Several of the wounded were captured, as they could be
easily traced by the blood on the snow; but the rest made their
escape. Those who were captured were tried by court-martial,
condemned as spies, and shot. David, son of Andrew Knox, was
born in Pennsylvania in 1760. He married Isabella Caldwell, of
Charlotte county, Va., and settled in Mercer county, Ky. Their
children were—William, George, Mary, Andrew, John C.,
Robert, Davis C., James, Samuel, Benjamin F., and David R.
William was born in Mercer county, February 3, 1792. He enlisted as a soldier in the war of 1812, and in 1818 he settled in
Montgomery county, Mo. On the 18th of December, 1828, he
married Sarah Clark, and the children resulting from this mar-
riage were—David F., Mary I., Isaac H., William S., and Davis
R. David F. married Catharine Davault, who died in 1875. He
has been Sheriff of Montgomery county several times, and is a
prominent and influential citizen. Mary I. married Dr. D. F.
Stevens, of New Florence. Isaac H. was married first to Sarah
Clark; second to Elizabeth Clark, and third to Caroline Snethen.
Davis R. married Alice Dyson.

KING.—Isaac King, of Germany, settled in Wythe county, Va.,
and married Barbara Stroup (late Mrs. Fipps, of Montgomery
county, Mo.), by whom he had one son, John P. The latter
settled in Montgomery county in 1835, and married Susan Steph-

enson, a granddaughter of James Heller, of revolutionary fame, and who was at the battle of Bunker Hill.

KING.—Isaac King, of South Carolina, married Lydia Sitton, and settled in Tennessee. Their children were—Joshua, Abraham, Sarah, and Joseph. Joshua, Abraham, and Sarah settled in Lincoln county, Mo., in 1817. Joseph married Elizabeth Yates, and settled in Montgomery county, in 1823. They had six children— Conrad, Isaac, John, Charles, and Sarah. Mr. King built a horse mill, which was run principally by his wife. He took a great deal of interest in politics, and was elected Justice of the Peace and Captain of militia.

KERR.—The father of William Kerr, whose name was Thomas, died when he was six years of age. They were originally of Virginia, but at the time of Mr. Kerr's death they were living in Mercer county, Ky. William was bound out by his mother, who did not feel able to raise him; and in 1827 he came to Montgomery county. Here he married and had—James H. H., George W., Elizabeth, William A., John T., Melissa C., Benjamin, Sophia, William, Douglass M., and Milton. Two of the children are dead, and all the others, except one, who resides in Lincoln county, live in Montgomery county. William Kerr was a stage driver for sixteen years, on different routes, but most of the time on the route between Fulton and St. Charles, over the Booneslick road. He was one of the best drivers that could be found, and his services were sought by all the contractors. The horses were herded on the prairies, like cattle, when they were not in use.

LEAVELL.—Edward Leavell, of Virginia, married Elizabeth Hawkins, and settled in North Carolina. They afterward removed to Garrard Co., Ky., where they both died. Their children were—Benjamin, Joseph, James, John, Edward, Nathan, Mary, Nancy, Elizabeth, Catharine, Sally, and Mildred. Benjamin, Joseph and John lived in Kentucky. Nathan died in North Carolina. James married Rebecca Stinson, who cut the throat of a mad wolf, that had bitten her father, while he held it. Their children were—Margaret, Elizabeth, Jane, Julia A., William H., James M., Benjamin F., and Edward. Margaret married John Stephens. Elizabeth married Randolph Boone. Jane married Mr. Carnifix. Julia A. married M. B. Snethen. William H. was married three times. James M. died single. Benjamin F. married Sarah Nunnelly, and they had one child, James. Edward married Rhoda Sallee. Mildred, daughter of Edward Leavell, Sr., married Nicholas H. Stephenson, of Kentucky, and is now a widow in her 86th year. Mr. Stephenson and his family started to Missouri in 1813, on horseback, but after crossing the Ohio river they purchased a wagon and traveled in that some distance, when the roads became so bad that they could use it no longer. They then sold the wagon and performed the rest of the journey on horseback, arriving in St. Charles county in 1814, having been on the road one year. Mr. Stephenson settled first in Howell's Prairie, where he built a tanyard, and in 1818 he removed to Montgomery county. He had two children, James and Mildred A.—Thomas D. Stephenson, a brother of Nicholas, settled in Howell's Prairie, St. Charles county, in 1812, where he married Mary Pitman. In 1844 he removed to Warren county, where he died. He was County Judge and Justice of the Peace for some time, and was an influential citizen.

LEACH.—John Leach, of England, settled in Prince William Co., Va. His son William was married first to Fanny George, and they had Henry and Fanny. He was married the second time to Martha Clark, by whom he had William, Reason, Louisa, Martha, and Mary E. Henry married Frances Horton, and settled in Montgomery Co., Mo., in 1830. They had two sons and eight daughters. Fanny married John Robinson, who settled in Montgomery county in 1830. William died in infancy. Mary also died young. Reason, Laura, and Martha settled in Montgomery county.

LEWIS.—Edwin Lewis, of North Carolina, pitched his tent in Montgomery county in 1830. He married Elizabeth Evans, by whom he had—Wormley, Mary, Edward, Francis, Hiram, Bentley, Susan, Ann, and Lucretia. Mr. Lewis' first wife died and he afterward married Mrs. Rebecca Wallpool, a widow, by whom he had—Thomas, James, Elizabeth, Amanda, Margaret, Caroline, and Jane.

LAWSON.—Henry Lawson, of Shelby Co., Ky., married Rebecca Lewis, by whom he had—Henry, James, Joseph, William, John, Cynthia A., Mary, Laura, Rebecca, and Nancy. Mr. Lawson settled in Montgomery Co., Mo., in 1822. He and his wife were present at the organization of Macedonia Church, on Cuivre, of which they became members.

LEWIS.—Æsop Lewis, a blacksmith, was of English parentage, and lived in the State of New York, from whence he removed to Vermont. The names of his children were—Rufus, Benjamin, Eli, Chandis, Salina, and Hannah. Rufus, who was a cooper by trade, married Elizabeth Gilbert, of Connecticut, and moved with his parents to Ohio in 1816. They went from there to Kentucky, and in 1819 they came to Missouri in keel-boats, landing at St. Genevieve. They settled in Washington county, and in 1839 Rufus Lewis, with his wife and son, Enos W., came to Montgomery county. They had three children besides Enos W., viz.: Mary A., George W., and Elizabeth. The latter was married first to Commodore C. Lewis, and after his death she married Joseph Charles. Mary A. and George W. married and settled in Missouri. Enos W. lives in Montgomery county, and is a substantial, well-to-do farmer, fond of fun and frolic, and nearly always has a joke to tell on somebody. He married the widow Cotes, whose maiden name was Nancy Smith.

LEWELLYN.—Jacob, son of Samuel Lewellyn, had a son Samuel who settled in Pike Co., Mo., at a very early date, and died in 1837. He left a son, John W., who married Jane Trabue, of Kentucky, in 1824, and had ten children, nine of whom are still living. Mr. Lewellyn lived for some time in Clarke Co., Mo., where he was Judge of the County Court for eight years. He settled in Montgomery county in 1839, having lived in St. Charles county in 1818, and in Pike county in 1820.

LOYD.—William Loyd, of Wales, emigrated to America, and at the commencement of the revolution he sided with the Americans and enlisted in their army. He settled and lived in Virginia. His son William married Mary Hill, and they had—Kirtley, Richard, William, Willis, Robert, James, Anna, Mary, Sarah, and Margaret. Kirtley lived in Virginia until 1860, when he removed to Missouri. Richard married Martha Ellis, and settled in Montgomery county in 1838. William married the widow Davault, whose maiden name was Virginia Maughs. Robert married the widow Brown, whose maiden name was Cynthia A. Bush. James, Sarah, and Margaret lived in Virginia. Anna married James D. Wood, who settled in Missouri in 1835. Mary married Thomas Nunnelly.

LOGAN.—Hugh Logan was born in Ireland. At the age of fourteen years he had a difficulty with his father, and ran away from home and went to sea. He followed the life of a sailor for three years, and then landed at Philadelphia, and made his way from there to Kentucky, during the first settlement of that State. He married Rebecca Bryan, a sister of Jonathan, David and Henry Bryan, who had been raised by her aunt, Mrs. Daniel Boone; her mother having died while she was young. Their children were— William, Alexander, Hugh, Jr., Henry (called "Boss") and Mary A. Mr. Logan was drowned in Fleming's creek, Ky., while attempting to swim a race horse across the stream, and his body was not found until twenty-four hours afterward. The night before his death he had a singular premonition of his approaching fate, in a dream, in which the catastrophe of the following day was clearly depicted. He related the dream to his wife, who tried to persuade him not to go near the creek that day; but he laughed at her for being scared at a dream, and met his death as above stated. William Logan, the eldest son, married Nancy H. Hobbs, daughter of Joseph Hobbs and Nancy Hughes, and came to Missouri in 1820, with his wife and one child, on horseback. They had twelve children in all. Mr. Logan died in 1852, but his widow is still living, on the old place in Teuque Prairie, in her 81st year. Her memory is bright as ever, and she takes great pleasure in relating incidents and adventures of early days in Missouri and Kentucky. She still has her wedding dress, which is made of home-spun cloth and striped with copperas.—Alexander Logan married Elizabeth Quick, and settled in Callaway county, Missouri, in 1817, but the following year he moved and settled on South Bear creek, on the line between Warren and Montgomery counties. He was a man of iron constitution, and could endure the greatest extremes of cold and heat without apparent inconvenience. His will was as strong as his constitution, and he governed his family and everything that came under his control with the strictest discipline. One day he accidentally killed a fine donkey, for which he had paid $500, while trying to teach it "horse sense" with a clapboard.—Hugh Logan married a Miss Massey, and settled in Warren county. He was very fond of hunting, and became subject to rheumatism from exposure in the woods. But he was cured one day by an adventure with a bear, which is related elsewhere.—Henry Logan came to Missouri when he was quite a boy, and at the age of fourteen he accompanied Daniel Boone and John Davis on a hunting expedition to Grand river. His father having died while he was young, he was bound out to learn the tanner's trade, and when he became able, he opened a tanyard in Montgomery county, and carried on the business for many years. He was more eccentric than any of the other boys, and many amusing anecdotes are related of him. He was a member of the Old Baptist Church, and a regular attendant upon religious services. He would often carry his hat full of grapes to church and pass them around to the ladies and children during services. In warm weather he went barefooted, with his pants rolled up nearly to his knees; and it is said that he courted his wife barefooted. He asked her father, Jacob Quick, for her hand, late one Sunday night, long after the family had retired to bed. It seems that, about twelve o'clock, he obtained the consent of his sweetheart, and immediately knocked at the door of her father's sleeping room, in order to secure his sanction. Mr. Quick, startled at the unexpected summons, sprang up and demanded what was wanted, to which Logan replied in a loud voice, "I want your daughter Sally." The old gentleman, who was vexed at the disturbance and the abruptness of the demand, replied angrily, "Take her and go to the d—l with her." Mr. Logan wore a hat for twenty years that was made by Mark Cole, out of raccoon and muskrat fur. It would hold an even half-bushel of corn, and its owner frequently used it to measure grain with. He once had a bushel of seed corn that he was saving for a neighbor, when another neighbor came along one day and wanted it, but Logan told him he could not have it unless he would prove himself to be the better man of the two. The neighbor said he was willing to try, and so they went at it on a big pile of tan bark. The result was that Logan lost his corn. Late one night, a stranger stopped at his house and begged to stay all night, when Logan gave him the following characteristic reply: "No, sir, you can't stay *all* night at my house, but if you feel like it you may spend the *balance* of the night with me." Notwithstanding his eccentricities, he was a kind-hearted man and a good neighbor, and was respected by all who knew him. Two years ago he started to California to visit one of his sons, and not long after the train had left Omaha he fell from the car and was killed.

McFARLAND.—Joseph McFarland, of Ireland, came to America before the revolution, and settled at Norfolk, Va. He joined the American army when the war broke out, and was killed in battle. He left a widow and one son, Robert, who settled in Madison Co., Ky., where he married Rhoda Quick, and they had—Sarah, Joseph, and Rachel. Mr. McFarland's first wife died, and he subsequently married Eva Farmer, of Virginia, by whom he had—Eleanor, Lucinda, Elizabeth, Permelia, Eliza, and Robert. Joseph McFarland settled in Montgomery county in 1825. He married Polly Cundiff. Lucinda married James McGarvin, of Montgomery county. Eliza married Jonathan G. Gentry.

MORROW.—Daniel Morrow, a soldier of the war of 1812, married Fanny Hall, and settled in South Carolina, but afterward removed to Tennessee. Their children were—John, Fanny, Sarah, and Elizabeth. John married Sarah Hall, and settled in Montgomery Co., Mo., in 1816. They had—William, Bethel C., John H., David P., James A., Washington J., Lucinda, Elizabeth, and Sarah M.

MASSEY.—Thomas Massey, Sr., married Nancy Hill, of Kentucky, and settled in Montgomery county in 1809, and in 1813 he settled at Loutre Lick, having obtained permission to do so from Nathan Boone, who owned the land on which the Lick is situated. His son, Thomas, Jr., was a ranger in Boone's company. There were eleven children in all, viz.: Israel, Thomas, Jr., Harris, Ann, Agnes, Sally, Nancy, Matilda, Elizabeth, and Docia.

MAUPIN.—Gabriel Maupin, eldest son of Thomas Maupin, of Albemarle Co., Va., married Anna Spencer, by whom he had—John, Thomas, Joel, Clifton, David, Arthur T., Susan, Nancy, Polly, Rosana, and Patsey. Arthur T. and Joel married and settled in Montgomery Co., Mo., in 1838.

McGINNIS.—John McGinnis and his wife came from Ireland, and settled first in Virginia, from whence they removed to Kentucky. Their son, Greenberry D., married Sallie Lewis, of Kentucky, and settled in Lincoln Co., Mo., in 1832. His children were—Elizabeth, Margaret B., William B., Jane, Nancy, Thomas S., Maria, Milton, Sarah E., and Mary E. Milton married Mar-

garet Williams, and settled in Pike county.   Elizabeth married
Enoch Sevier, and lives in Lincoln county.   William B. married
twice and settled in Illinois.   Jane and Nancy died single.   Sarah
E. married John Harris, and settled in Illinois.—Samuel, son of
John McGinnis, Sr., was married twice, and by his first wife he
had—John, Dora, Samuel, Jr., Polly, and Elizabeth.   He was
married the second time to Mrs. Mary McGinnis, by whom he
had, Erasmus T., William, and Jesse G.   Erasmus was married
first to Miss Stewart, and second to Fanny Berger.   He lives
in Montgomery county.   William also married a Miss Stewart,
and lived and died in Montgomery county.

MABREY.—Cornelius Mabrey, of Pittsylvania Co., Va., was a
mill-wright by trade.   He was married twice, but of his first wife
and her children we have no account.   His second wife was
Polly Chaney, by whom he had—Patsey, Pleasant, Letitia, Elizabeth, Polly, and Philip.   Mr. Mabrey moved to middle Tennessee and lived there several years.   He afterward settled in Logan
county, Ky., where, after a residence of several years, he was
drowned.   In 1828 his widow and her children came to Missouri,
and settled in Lincoln county, where she died two years afterward.   The eldest daughter, Patsey, married George Huss, who
also settled in Lincoln county.   Pleasant married Barsheba
England, and is now living in Pike county.   He had seven children, five of whom live in Montgomery county.   Letitia married
James Eidrum, of Kentucky.   Elizabeth married Shelton Cobert.
Polly married Elbert Enert.   The three latter all live in Lincoln
county.   Philip, who lives in Montgomery county, was married
twice; first to Polly Uptegrove, and second to Eliza J. Hughes.
He is a carpenter by trade, and has done well in his battle with
life.   In his younger days he was very intimate with Dr. McFarland, of Troy, and they went to all the quiltings and dances
together.   They were both very tall men, and the lofts of the
cabins had to be taken out before they could dance without striking their heads against the boards.   When the dance was over
they would assist in replacing the loft.   Young men and women
often came to these frolics barefooted; but they generally
went prepared with buckskin, from which they made moccasins to
dance in, before the dance began.

McCARTY.—Ezekiel and Ira McCarty were sons of James Mc-
Carty and Jane Harding, of Virginia.   They settled in Clark
county, Kentucky, in 1806, where they lived and died.   They had
twelve sisters, all of whom married and settled in Kentucky.
Ezekiel was a soldier of the war of 1812, and was in the battle
known as Dudley's Defeat.   He married Elizabeth Sidebottom, of
Kentucky.   Their children were—Shelton A., Eli, James, Sally,
George W., John W., Joseph K., and Alfred S.   Mr. McCarty
removed to Missouri and settled in Danville in 1836.   He died

in 1866, and his wife in 1873. Eli, George W., and Alfred are the only surviving children. George W. is a Justice of the Peace and a prominent citizen. Ira McCarty, brother of Ezekiel, married a Miss Moore, of Kentucky, and settled in Boone county, Mo., where he raised a family of seven children.

MAUGHS.—Nathaniel Maughs was of Loudon county, Va. His children were—David, William, John, Moses, Elijah, Stephen, Vinson, Mary, Sally, and Eli. Mr. Maughs removed from Virginia to Fleming county, Ky., and his children all came with him. David and William were Baptist preachers, and the former settled in Lincoln county, Mo. Elijah married Mary Smith, by whom he had—Mordecai M., Milton M., Sophronia F., Lucinda S., Elijah C., Daniel M., and Mary S. V. Mr. Maughs died, and his widow married his brother Stephen, who settled in Montgomery county, Mo., in 1822. They had—Jerry S. D. S., and George M. B. Mordecai Maughs, who was a physician, was married first to the widow Jane Scott; second to Dorothea Stephenson, and third to Lizzie Offutt. He had sixteen children in all. The Doctor was an educated, intelligent man, full of wit and humor, and very fond of practical jokes. He lived at Danville for many years, but finally removed to Callaway county, where he died. Sophronia Maughs married Dr. William Proctor, of St. Louis. Mary V. S. was married first to Henry Davault, and second to Willis Loyd, both old settlers of Montgomery county. Jerry died a bachelor in Montgomery county. George M. B., son of Stephen Maughs, is a physician. He married Anna Anderson, of Callaway county, and settled in St. Louis, where he has become distinguished in his profession.

MORRIS.—The parents of Joshua and Samuel Morris died in Virginia. Joshua married Narcissa Vallandigham, and settled in Missouri in 1821. Their children were—William H., Samuel J., Lewis R., Sarah J., and Rachel A. Samuel Morris, brother of Joshua, was a saddler by trade, and made such good saddles that they became popular all over the country, and he had all the work he could do. He settled in Missouri in 1821, and married Esther Bryan, daughter of Henry Bryan. Their children were—Joshua, Chester, Marion, Naoma, Cynthia, Lucinda, Julia, Virlena, and Alice. Mr. Morris lives in Saline county; his wife has been dead several years.

McGHEE.—John McGhee, a native of Ireland, married Margaret Adams, who was born in England. They settled in Shelby county, Ky., where they had—Lynch, Emily, Margaret, James, Washington, Nancy, and Rice. Lynch was a physician. He married Margaret Shackelford, and settled in Louisville, Ky., but removed to St. Louis, Mo., in 1838. Washington married Julia Sibley, of Kentucky, and died in 1828, leaving a widow and four children—Mary H., Robert L., Harriet, and Epsey. Mrs. Mc-

Ghee and her children settled in Montgomery county, Mo., in 1841, and she is still living, in her 76th year.

MOORE.—James Moore was born in Campbell county, Va., in 1761. He was married in 1795 to Priscilla Reed, by whom he had—John G., William R., Sarah, Thomas, James G., Mary, and Martha. He was a Captain in the war of 1812. In 1839 he came to Missouri and settled on Dry Fork of Loutre, in Montgomery county, where died in 1858. His wife died one month later. Mr. Moore was a member of the Methodist Church, a quiet and inoffensive man, and highly esteemed by his neighbors and friends. His son, William R., married Mary Hubbard, of Virginia, and settled in St. Joseph, Mo. Sarah married William Farris, and remained in Virginia. Thomas married Edetha Reynolds, of Virginia, and settled in Montgomery county in 1839. James G. never married. He settled in Montgomery county in 1839, and is the only one of the original family still living. Mary married William McDaniel, who settled in Montgomery county in 1839. Martha married Peter G. Hunter, of Montgomery county.

NOWLIN.—James Nowlin and his wife, Martha Collins, were natives of Scotland. They came to America prior to the revolution, and brought all their household and kitchen furniture with them. They settled first in the eastern part of Virginia, but afterward removed to Pittsylvania county. Their only son, Bryan W. Nowlin, was a Captain in the American army during the revolution. He married Lucy Waide, of Virginia, and they had fifteen children, thirteen of whom lived to be grown, and twelve of them married. The eldest son, Peyton, married Lucy Townsend, and settled first in Kentucky, from whence he removed to Saline county, Mo., previous to 1820, and raised a large family of children. Richard Nowlin, brother of Peyton, married Celie Shelton, and settled first in Kentucky, and afterward in Saline county, Missouri. Samuel Nowlin married Fannie Paul, of Virginia, by whom he had Joseph and David. His first wife died, and he was married the second time to Elizabeth Everson, by whom he had two daughters, both of whom are living in Virginia. Joseph Nowlin lived and died in Lynchburg, Va. David studied law at the University of Virginia. In 1835 he married Elizabeth Berger, of Virginia, and the following year he came to Missouri and settled in Montgomery county, where he practiced his profession, and was elected to several official positions in the county, which he filled with credit to himself and his constituents. He was also a Baptist preacher, and possessed more than ordinary powers as a pulpit orator. His son, Samuel S. Nowlin, is an attorney, and lives at Montgomery City. He has served his county as Circuit Clerk, and made one of the best officers the county ever had. He possesses a large influence, and his prospects for future political advancement are good.

NUNNELLY.—Peter Nunnelly was a "bound boy" to a horse doctor and jockey, and was with Lord Cornwallis' army at Yorktown, when it was captured. After the war he settled in America, and was married twice; first to Elizabeth Smart, by whom he had —Peter, Jr., Absalom, Benjamin, Gillum, Buckner, Littleberry, James, Ephraim, Mildred, Martha, and Judith. Ephraim married Elizabeth Williams, and his son Ephraim married Eveline Scholl, and lives in Callaway county. His children were—James, Anderson, Daniel, John, Lucy, Mary H., Elizabeth, Sarah L., and Susan A. James is a bachelor, and lives in Montgomery county. Anderson married Violet Patton, and lived and died in Montgomery county. Daniel married Catharine Lee. John and Lucy died young. Mary H. married John McMahan. Elizabeth married Granville Nunnelly, her cousin. Sarah L. married Benjamin F. Leavell. Susan A. married Granville L. Gregory.

ODEN.—John Oden, of England. settled in Loudon county, Virginia. His children were—Hezekiah, Thomas, John, Lewis, William, and Vinson. Hezekiah married Elizabeth Leach, of Virginia, and settled in Pike county, Mo., in 1828. They had— John, William, Vinson, Harriet, Maria, Polly, Sally, and Alfred. Vinson married Mary House, and lives in Montgomery county. William and Polly died in Kentucky. Sally was married first to Joseph Thomas, and second to Garland T. Hudson. She is a widow again, and lives in Audrain county. Maria and Alfred married and remained in Pike county. Harriet married John King, who moved to New Orleans, La.

PRICE.—Miles Price, of Wales, settled in Lincoln county, N. C., prior to the revolutionary war. He married a Miss Sharp, and had a son named Thomas, who was a soldier of the revolution. He married Isabella Sharp, and they had Elizabeth, Thomas, jr., Reese, Isaac, James, John, Isabella, and Ellen. Zohn married Anna Barber, of North Carolina, and they had four children previous to their removal to Missouri, viz. : Elizabeth L., Cynthia, Miles S., and Thomas J. They came to Missouri and settled in Pike county in 1819, after which they had the following children —Robert B., John H., Sallie A., Emily I., and Lucinda J. All of his children except Miles S., who is a member of the County Court of Montgomery county, settled in Lincoln county. Mr. Price, was Constable and Justice of the Peace in Pike county for thirty years. He was also a great snake killer, and every spring he and his neighbors would have a snake hunt. One spring they killed 9,000 rattlesnakes.—Isaac Price first settled in St. Charles county, and afterward in Lincoln. He married Tabitha Wilkerson, of the former county.

PEGRAM.—The parents of Daniel Pegram were Scotch. Daniel was born in Petersburg, Va., but settled and lived in Bedford county, where he raised ten children, six sons and four daughters, each of whom was more than six feet in height. Thomas, a son of Daniel Pegram, married Nancy Hopkins, whose mother's maiden name was Clark, and who had a brother, Chester Clark, who drew $100,000 in a lottery. Thomas had but three children—James L., Edward T., and William. The latter died in Virginia in his 19th year. James L. married Julia R. Oley, of Virginia, and settled in St. Charles county, Mo., in 1839, and in Montgomery county in 1845. Mrs. Pegram died in 1863. They had eight children, four sons and four daughters. Edward T. Pegram married Mildred Crane, of Montgomery county, and had two children, a son and a daughter. (See "Anecdotes and Adventures.")

PEVERLEY.—Peter Peverley and his wife, Libbie Myers, of Kentucky, had the following children—Polly, Peggy, David, Daniel, Elizabeth, Jacob, and Peter. The three daughters married and settled in Montgomery county, Mo. David died in Texas. Daniel married Miss Cassety, of Kentucky, and settled in Montgomery county in 1824. Jacob married Crecy Bunch, of Montgomery county. Peter married Jane Dungom.

PATTON.—Jacob Patton and his wife, Rebecca Barnett, of North Carolina, had four children—James, Thomas, Mary, and Rebecca. They settled on Loutre Island, in Montgomery county, in 1810. James, the eldest son, married Violet Douglass, and they had— Robert, William, Jesse, Samuel D., Amelia, Cynthia A., and Violet. Jesse married Nancy Burrell, and lives in Boone county. Amelia married Eli Johnson, and is now a widow in Callaway county. The rest of James Patton's children are dead. Thomas, brother of James Patton, was bitten by a mad wolf, at his home on Loutre Island, in January, 1816, and died of hydrophobia on the 16th of the following August, in the 43d year of his age. His wife died in December, 1867, in her 90th year. Their children were— James, William, Robert H., Thomas H., Elizabeth, Rebecca, Jane, Violet, and Mary. Rebecca, daughter of Jacob Patton, married John Gibson. She is now in her 88th year, a widow, and resides in Callaway county. Mary married Thomas Patton, and their children were—James B., William, Robert H., Thomas H., Eli M., Elizabeth, Rebecca, Jane, Violet, and Mary.

PEW.—Reuben C. Pew was left an orphan at a very early age. According to the custom of those days he was "bound out" for his living, and got a very poor one. His master treated him badly, worked him hard, and gave him no education. When he was sixteen years of age he could not read or write, and his master, desiring to get rid of him, induced him to sign the muster roll of a company that was recruiting for service in the revolutionary war, telling him it was only a common piece of writing, and could do him no harm. The consequence was that he had to go into the army, very much against his will. He was captured soon after his enlistment, and held as a prisoner for several years, during which time he experienced all the horrors of the British prisons of those times. After the war he married a Miss Smith, and settled in North Carolina, where he and his wife died, leaving seven children, viz.: Reuben P., Benjamin F., Anderson S., Frances, Jemima, Polly, and Zilphey. Reuben P. was born in 1789. In 1810 he married his cousin, Sarah Park, who died in Kentucky in 1818, leaving four children—Erasmus D., Permelia H., James S., and William H. When the war of 1812 began, Mr. Pew enlisted, and was taken prisoner at Dudley's Defeat, but afterward exchanged. After the death of his wife he came to Missouri, and made a contract to haul a lot of tan bark to St. Louis. He returned to Kentucky, got his team, came back to St. Louis, fulfilled his contract, and cleared $1,200. He then returned to Kentucky, and removed his family to Montgomery Co., Mo., where he settled in 1819. Here he married Nancy Yater, by whom he had eight more children—Anderson J., George W., Amanda C., Frank M., Sally, Frances S., Mary J., Judith E., and Nancy E. Mr. Pew built the first horse-mill in the northern part of the county, and made good flour, which was a rarity in those days. He put the flour into sacks, and sent his boys on horseback to peddle it out over the country, at the rate of one cent per pound. They frequently went as far as thirty miles from home to sell a few pounds of flour.—Benjamin F. Pew married Elizabeth Clark, of Kentucky, and settled in Audrain county. Andrew S. married Anna Betheuram, and settled in Montgomery county in 1836. They had—William D., Reuben C., Mary A., Jane H., Eliza A., and David A. Mr. Pew and his wife died at the same time, in 1844, and were buried in the same grave. Frances and Jemima married and settled in Grundy Co., Mo. Polly married Simpson Stewart, who came to Missouri in 1821, but afterward removed to Illinois. Zilphey married a Mr. Polk, who settled in Indiana.

PEERY.—George, William, and James Peery emigrated from Scotland and settled in Tazewell Co., Va. George married Martha Davidson, of Ireland, and they had three sons and nine daughters. Joseph, the youngest son, married Elizabeth Hall, of Virginia, and settled in Montgomery Co., Mo., in 1836. Their children were—Charles, Albert G., Gordon C., Thomas, Andrew, William H., Joseph A., and George. The members of the Peery family are a genial, hospitable people, and highly esteemed by their neighbors and acquaintances. Dr. Thomas Peery, who died in 1875, was especially distinguished for his many excellent qualities, and his loss is deeply felt by the community in which he lived.

PURVIS.—John Purvis and his wife, Margaret Strother, of Virginia, had—Frank, George, Strother, John, William, Thomas, Elizabeth, Frances, Harriet, and Mary. Strother married Elizabeth Sterne, and settled in Montgomery county in 1839. They had nine children.

POWELL.—William G. Powell, of Holland, settled in Albemarle county, Virginia. His son, Lewis G., had three sons, James, Buck, and Lewis, Jr. James married Nancy Shelor, of Germany, and settled in Montgomery county, Missouri, in 1820. They had—John W., James W., William L., Thomas J., and two daughters, who died in infancy. After the death of James Powell, his widow, who lived for many years afterward, proved herself to be a woman capable of managing the business affairs of life and carrying them to a successful issue. During the cold winter of 1831-2 she had what is called a "jumping sleigh" built, and went in it to Virginia, one thousand miles distant, by herself, and brought back some negro slaves in another "jumper" similar to her own. Very few women have ever accomplished such a feat as that.—Buck Powell was a very stout man, and it is said that he could lift a barrel of whisky by his teeth and drink from the bung hole. He won a bet of fifty cents one day, by biting a ten penny nail in two, and he certainly earned his money.—Thomas J., son of James Powell, is a prominent attorney and citizen of Montgomery county, and lives at New Florence. He has been Sheriff of the county several times, and wields a large influence in political matters.

PEARLE.—William Pearle, of Virginia, settled in Lincoln county, Kentucky, among the first settlers of that State. During a portion of the Indian troubles he took refuge with his family in the fort at Crab Orchard. His son, Henry, married Polly Owsley, sister of Governor Owsley, of Kentucky, by whom he had twelve children, seven of whom lived to be grown. The names of the latter were—Samuel, William S. F., Patience, Joel, Henry, Nudigit O., and Catharine. Samuel married Sally Dugan, and settled in Warren county, Missouri, in 1830. Joel married Rebecca Wyatt, and settled in Montgomery county. Henry married his cousin, Sally A. Pearle, and settled in Montgomery county in 1833. He was a school teacher and farmer, and concluded once that he could preach as well as anybody. So he gave out an appointment at the school house, and when the time arrived, a large congregation was in attendance to hear him. He gave out the hymn, sang, and led in prayer as well as any one, but when he arose to preach his subject "flew from his brain," as he graphically expressed it, and he could not preach at all. He apologized by saying, " We thought we could preach, but we can't preach," and took his seat. Another incident of an entirely different character, but equally embarrassing, happened to him soon after he came to Montgomery county. Four or five of his horses strayed away, and he spent several months in hunting them, during which time he rode four or five hundred miles, and at last found his horses within five miles of home, where they had been all the time, grazing on the prairie.—Patience Pearle married William S. Wyatt, of Warren county, and settled in Montgomery county in 1836. The rest of the Pearle children settled in Montgomery county at a later date.

POINDEXTER.—Joseph Poindexter, of Bedford county, Virginia, was a Captain in the revolutionary war. He married Elizabeth Kenerly, and they had a son, Richard, who married a Miss Ford, of Virginia, and settled in Montgomery county in 1837. They had—Elizabeth A., Parthena S., Caroline K., Hezekiah F., Eliza, Edward L., Joseph C., James W., John D., and Mary L., most of whom settled in Montgomery county.

QUICK—Jacob Quick, of Germany, married a widow named Morris, whose maiden name was Rhoda Moore, of Ireland. They first settled in Maryland, where they had—Aaron, Alexander, Jacob, Jr., Sarah, and Rachel. Mr. Quick then removed with his family to Kentucky, and in 1811 he came to Missouri and settled on Loutre Island, in Montgomery county. Previous to his removal to Kentucky his children had never tasted corn bread. In 1812 he built a block-house, for protection against the Indians, in Best's Bottom, on the place that was settled by John Hancock, for whom Hancock's Prairie was named. Mr. Quick died at this place in 1822, and his wife in 1834. During their residence there an old Indian named Phillips lived with them for several years. He finally left them, and his body was afterward found away out in the western wilderness, with his gun lying by his side.—Aaron Quick, the eldest son, died a bachelor. Alexander married Nancy Gilbert, of Kentucky, where they resided thirteen years, and then came to Missouri. Their children were—Elizabeth, William, Stephen, Sarah, Samuel, Aaron, Rhoda, Alexander, James, and Gilbert. Jacob, Jr., married Phœbe Copps, of Kentucky, and settled in Montgomery county, on Whippoorwill creek, in 1811. They had eight children—William, Jacob, Sampson, Polly, Patsey, Sally, Peggy, and Elizabeth. Sarah Quick married Jacob Groom. Rachel married Robert McFarland, of Kentucky. They had only two children, Joseph and Sally, both of whom settled in Montgomery county.

ROCKAFELLOW.—Peter Rockafellow, and old revolutionary soldier, was of German descent. He married the widow McGlathan, and settled in Montgomery county, Missouri, in 1822. (He lived a short time in St. Louis county, when he first came to Missouri.) He had but one child, Anna, who married Andrew Hunter.

RUSSELL.—Robert Russell, of Campbell Co., Va., settled in Montgomery Co., Mo., in 1830. His wife's maiden name was Bridget Bryant. Their children were—James, Harrison, John, Mary, Susan, Elizabeth, and Sarah. Mr. Russell died in 1831, and was the first person buried in the noted old Virginia grave yard, of Montgomery county, which received its name from the fact that nearly all who were buried there were Virginians.

RICE.—William B. Rice was a revolutionary soldier. Previous to his enlistment in the army he accompanied Daniel Boone on one of his expeditions to Kentucky.   He married Rebecca Arlington, by whom he had—David, William G., Benjamin, Samuel, Callier, and Sophia.   Mr. Rice settled in Montgomery county in 1825, and died in his 95th year.   His eldest son, David, married Elizabeth Henderson, by whom he had a daughter named Louisa, who married Judge William G. Shackelford, son of John Shackelford, of Virginia.   The Judge was left an orphan at four years of age, and was raised by his uncle, Samuel Lawrence, who educated him for a lawyer.   He came to Montgomery county in 1835, where he lost his wife, by whom he had six children.   He afterward married Anna Rice, daughter of William G. Rice, by whom he had six other children.   Judge Shackelford was Judge of the County Court of Montgomery county for twenty-one years. He was a successful farmer, also, but never had a cart or wagon on his place.   His corn and other produce were gathered in baskets and carried to the barn.—William G. Rice was married first to Mary Vandiver, by whom he had three children.   His second wife was Sally Vandiver, by whom he had nine children.

Mr. Rice was elected Assessor at a time when the county was in debt, and he made such a thorough and accurate assessment that he paid the debt and left some money in the treasury.   It is said that he rode an ox most of the time as he traveled over the county, and although the assertion cannot be substantiated, it is universally believed, and is doubtless true.

MR. RICE ASSESSING MONTGOMERY COUNTY ON AN OX.

But no matter what sort of an animal he rode, he made one of the best assessors Montgomery county ever had, and his horned steed no doubt greatly assisted him in climbing over the mountainous region that borders upon the head waters of Loutre.   Mr. Rice also kept tavern on the Booneslick road, where Mrs. Davault now lives, and when a traveler asked the price of dinner he would be told that he could get corn bread and "common fixins" for 25 cents, but if he wanted wheat bread and "chicken fixins" it would be 37½ cents. If the trav-eler decided to take both kinds of "fixins," he paid 62½ cents, ate his dinner, and departed, much amused at the singular terms of his eccentric host.

RODGERS.—James Rodgers. of Pennsylvania, settled in Nelson Co.; Ky., where he raised a large family of children, and gave each of them a Bible. Presley Rodgers, his son, married Eliza-beth Folay, of Kentucky. by whom he had—Matha A., Mary E., James. John. Phœbe, Felix G , Elizabeth E., Nancy, Julia A.. Pernesia, and America. Mr. Rodgers came to Missouri in 1831, and settled in Howard county, afterward in Boone, then in Saline, and finally in Montgomery. He was a blacksmith, and worked at his trade until his death, which occurred in December, 1863. He built the first blacksmith shop in Montgomery City. Eight of his eleven children are still living. and seven of them reside in Mont-gomery county.

STROBE.—Christian Strobe, of Pennsylvania, removed first to Indiana, and from thence to Audrain Co., Mo. His wife was Marry Miller, of Kentucky, and they had—William H., Eliza, James. Isabella, George, Rebecca, Mary, and Christian, Jr., most of whom have families, and live in Audrain and Montgom-ery counties.

SANDERS.—Christopher Sanders settled near Loutre Lick, in Montgomery county, at an early date. He was a great hunter, but somewhat indolent, and generally depended upon borrowing a gun to shoot his game with rather than perform the labor of carrying one. (See "Anecdotes and Adventures.") He raised four sons and two daughters—Jack, James, Joseph, William, Nancy, and Rachel. William married Ibby Slavens, a daughter of Stewart Slavens, of Middletown.

SHARP.—Thomas Sharp was a native of Ireland, but emigrated to America, and settled first in Pennsylvania, from whence he removed to Washington Co., Va. He was married twice, and by his first wife he had—John, Thomas, Jr., and Benjamin. By his second wife he had but one child, David, who became a Methodist minister, and lived and died in Virginia. Thomas, Jr., settled in Kentucky. Benjamin was a soldier in the revolutionary war, and was in Colonel Campbell's command at the battle of King's Mountain He married Hannah Fulkerson, of Virginia, and their children were—James F.. John D., Polly C., Jacob L.. Cath-arine E., Attosa P., Hannah D., Peter L , Elvira E., Malinda M., Margaret J., and Benjamin F. In 1816 Mr. Sharp removed to Missouri with all his family except John and Malinda, and settled in (now) Warren county, three miles east of Pinckney. When Montgomery county was organized in 1818, he was ap-pointed Clerk of the County and Circuit Courts. and held the position until the State was admitted into the Union. A small log

19

cabin was built in his yard and used as a court house, until the county seat was located at Pinckney, which was named for his daughter, Atossa Pinckney Sharp. Mr. Sharp died at the old homestead in 1843; his wife died two years previous. Their son James married Catharine Neil. Polly C. married Jerry H. Neil. Jacob L married Harriet Vance. After the organization of the State government he bought the offices of County and Circuit Clerk from a man named Long who had been appointed by Gov. McNair. He paid $100 for those offices, and continued to hold them by election until 1865. He was a bald-headed man, and wore his hat on all occasions, including the sitting of the Courts, a privilege which all the Judges allowed him. While the county seat was located at Lewiston he made a regular practice of taking the prisoners out of the jail and exercising them. He died in 1869. Attossa Sharp married Capt. John Wyatt, a soldier of the war of 1812. Hannah D Married Beston Callahan. Peter L. married Jane Johnson. Elvira married James Hughes. Catharine E. married Conrad Carpenter. Margaret J. married Frederick Hamilton, who was editor of the Columbia, Mo., *Patriot*. Benjamin F. is a physician, and is the only one of the twelve brothers and sisters who is still living. He married Mary H. McGhee, and resides on his farm near Montgomery City, respected and honored by all who know him. Samuel T. and Benjamin F., sons of Jacob L. Sharp, are well known and prominent citizens of Montgomery county.

SEE.—The See family is of German origin. Three brothers, Adam, George, and Michael, with seven sisters, were raised in Hardy Co., Va. Their father, George, and a negro man were all killed by lightning while stacking hay. The girls married and settled in Kentucky and Ohio. Adam was a prominent lawyer, and lived and died in Virginia. Michael married Catharine Baker, of Hardy Co., Va., by whom he had—Mary, Elizabeth, Adam C , Barbara, Anthony, Jacob, John, Solomon, and Noah. Mr. See was a soldier of the war of 1812. He settled in Montgomery Co., Mo., in 1837. His daughter Elizabeth married Hugh Hart, who settled in Montgomery county in 1839. Barbary married Thomas McCleary, who settled in Mongomery county in 1840 Jacob married Rachel Morrison, and settled in Montgomery county in 1837. He has been Justice of the Peace and Deputy Sheriff, and is now the Representative of his county in the State Legislature. He was also a prominent member and officer of the Evanix Society, in Danville. Mr. See is very fond of fine stock, and in 1871 he raised eighteen hogs that averaged from 700 to 1000 pounds each. He took them to St. Louis, had them made into bacon, and sent the hams to Memphis, Tenn. But they were shipped back, with a statement from the commission merchant that they were not buying *horse hams*. Mr. See also raised, and still has in his possession, the largest ox in the world. He has made a good deal of money by exhibiting this mammoth brute in various parts of the United States, and everywhere he goes crowds gather to see the wonder.—John See married Margaret Stewart, and settled in Montgomery county in 1839. Noah See was married first to his cousin, Margaret See, and after her death he married Mary A. Saylor, and settled in Montgomery county in 1839. He is an influential and wealthy citizen, and has been County Surveyor for a number of years.

SAYLOR.—Emanuel Saylor and his wife, Ann Hulett, were early settlers of Montgomery county. They had James, John H., and Thomas. James married Libbey Cobb, and they had eleven children. John H. married Virginia M. Perkins, of Kentucky. Thomas married Maria Rice, and after his death his widow married John Hays.

STEVENS.—Richard Stevens was a noted hunter and trapper. He married Sally Ambrose, and settled in Montgomery county in 1831. The first day after his arrival in Montgomery he killed six deer, and during his residence in the county he killed 400 deer, 40 bears, and so many wild cats, raccoons, etc., that he could not keep an account of them. He had six children—Hiram A., Emily, Willis, Lucretia, Virginia, and Joseph. Hiram A. married Sarah A. Garrett, and lives in Montgomery county. Emily married Evans B. Scale, and also lives in Montgomery county. The rest of the children settled in other States.

STEVENS.—Thomas Stevens emigrated from England and settled on the James river, 120 miles above Richmond, Va., prior to the revolution. His children were—John, William, Susan, Delila, Elizabeth, and Lucy. John married Amanda Thornhill, of Virginia, and they had—Thomas, William, Absalom, Elizabeth, Nancy, Susan, and Hope. Thomas was a soldier in the revolutionary war. He married Agnes Perkins, and settled in Missouri in 1826. His children were—John, William, Agnes, and Eliza. He was married the second time in Missouri. William, who was a Baptist preacher, was born in May, 1786. He married Frances A. Ferguson, daughter of Dougal Ferguson and Elizabeth Archer, whose father was the third owner of Bermuda Hundreds on James river. William Stevens settled in Montgomery county in 1830. His children were—Dougal F., William H., John A., Thomas, Eliza, Mary S., Frances A., and Virginia. Nancy, daughter of John Stephens, married Jacob Maxey, who settled in Montgomery county in 1835. They had—William B., Joseph, Redford, Jacob, Elizabeth, Mary, and Nancy.

SINGLETON.—Spiers Singleton was the son of George Singleton, of North Carolina. He married Lucinda Whitesides, of Christian Co., Ky., and settled in Illinois, where he died, leaving a widow and seven children. Her brother, James Whitesides, brought

her and the children to Montgomery county, and attended to their
wants until the children were grown, and at his death he left
most of his property to them. The names of the children were—
James W., Ewell D., John S., Emeline, Cynthia A., Polly, and
Mary A.

SNETHEN.--Abraham Snethen and his wife, Elizabeth Stewart,
were natives of Germany. They emigrated to America and settled in New Jersey, where they had eleven children, of whom
the names of only seven are now remembered. They were—
William, John, Reuben, Polly, Lydia, Elizabeth, and Margaret.
William married and settled in Kentucky in 1792, and in 1810 he
removed to Ohio, where he lost his wife. He then started to return to New Jersey, but died of cholera, at Hagerstown, Md.
John was born in March, 1789, and when he was eight years old
his mother died. He was then bound out to a man in Elizabethtown, N. J., to learn the trade of wheel-wright. He remained
with the man seven years, and then having had a misunderstand-
ing with his landlady, he ran away and went to Philadelphia,
where he embarked on board a ship as a sailor He followed the
sea seven years, and during the latter part of that period, while
the ship was returning from the West India Islands, with a cargo
of sugar and coffee, the yellow fever broke out among the crew.
and all of them died except Snethen, the cook, and one sailor. They
succeeded, however, in bringing the vessel safely into port, and
delivering her to the owners, whose admiration of Snethen's
bravery and skill was so great that they proposed to educate him
and give him command of a ship. He accepted their offer, but
in the meantime paid a visit to his friends in New Jersey, who
persuaded him to abandon the sea. He then went to Kentucky,
and arrived at Maysville (then called Lewiston) in December,
1799. Here he first heard of the death of General Washington.
From Maysville he went with his brother Reuben to visit their
brother William, who lived in Estell county. There he became
acquainted with and married Susan Box. He remained in that
county seven years, and bought several tracts of land, all of
which he lost on account of defective titles. In 1808 he placed
his wife, three children, and all their household goods and chattels on a two-year old filley and a little pony, and came to
Missouri. He settled four miles above Loutre Island, on the
Missouri river, where he remained one year. During that time
he was visited by a party of French hunters, who expressed surprise that he had settled in the bottom, "For," said they, "our
fathers have seen the water over the tops of the sycamore trees."
He became alarmed at their statement and removed seven miles
northward, and settled on Dry Fork of Loutre, where several
other families soon gathered about him. In 1812 he removed to
Howard county, in company with Muke Box, Elisha Todd, James,

John, and William Savage, William Warden and Robert Benton, and their families. They placed their families in Kincaid's Fort, and joined the rangers, to assist in protecting the settlement against the Indians. Mr. Snethen afterward removed his family to Hempstead's Fort, which was larger and stronger than Kincaid's. They remained there until 1814, when they removed to Cooper's Fort. On the night of the 14th of April of that year, Capt. Sarshall Cooper was killed by some unknown person, who picked out the chinking of his chimney and shot him through the opening as he was seated in his cabin. Mr. Snethen was seated by his side at the time, but was not hurt. In 1818 Mr. Snethen returned to his old place on Dry Fork of Loutre, where he remained until his death, which occurred on the first of January, 1859. He raised twelve children of his own, and twelve negro children, and there was not a death on his place for forty-five years. He saw eighty-one of his grandchildren before his death. Mr. Snethen and his wife were both members of the Old Baptist Church. Their children were Aley B., John, Jr., Polly, Elizabeth, William, Sally, Reuben G., Muke B., Nancy, Emeline, David S., and Matilda. Aley B. was a Baptist preacher and a physician. He married Caroline Johnson, and had fourteen children. John, Jr., was a merchant at Troy, Mo., for thirty-seven years, but has retired from business. He is an intelligent gentleman, and can give a vivid portrayal of the dangers and trials of pioneer life. He went to school with Kit Carson in Cooper's Fort, and received most of his education while they were living in the forts during the Indian war. He married Euphemia Wells, a sister of Carty Wells, by whom he had six children. Mr. Snethen clerked in the store of Charles Drury, at Loutre Lick, from 1824 to 1826. Polly Snethen married John Cundiff; and they had fourteen children. Elizabeth married William Clark. William married Susan Groom, and they had eleven children. Sally married Holland Whitesides. Reuben G. was married three times; first, to Rebecca Dixon; second to Catharine Hunter, and third to Lucinda J. Sallee. He had twelve children in all. Muke B. married Julia A. Leavell, and they had five children. Nancy was married first to James Russell, second to Alfred Windsor, and third to Newton J. Hunter. Emeline married Toleson Hunter. David S. married Keziah Felkniff. Matilda married Benjamin F. Clark. Reuben Snethen, brother of John, Sr., married a Miss Smith, and settled on Duck river, in Tennessee. Abraham, another brother, was married twice, and lived in Callaway county.

STEWART.—John Stewart, of Bath Co., Va., was of Irish descent. He married Hannah Hickland, of Virginia, and their children were—James, John, Edward, Jacob, Miranda, David, Margaret, Nancy, and Jennie. John married his cousin, Mary

Stewart, and they had—Octavia, Tabitha, Osborne, Margaret, Alonzo, Emily, Martha and Cortez. Mr. Stewart settled in Montgomery county in 1839. His three younger children died before they were grown. Octavia married Frank Devine. Tabitha married Rev. Martin Luther Eades, who died in old age, and she afterward married Lewis Busby. Margaret married John See.

SUBLETT.—Hill Sublett, of Green Co., Ky., married Delphi Jennett, of Virginia. In 1817 he came to Missouri on a prospecting tour, returned to Kentucky and brought his family out in 1822. He had ten children, six daughters and four sons.

SLAVENS.—William S. Slavens was born in Greenbriar Co., Va., September 15, 1787. He was married five times; first to Anna Hawkins, by whom he had three children, second to Mary Riggs, third to Elizabeth Elsbury, by whom he had seven children, fourth to the widow Thomas, whose maiden name was Rebecca Stanley, by whom he had two children; and fifth to the widow Meyers, whose maiden name was Paulina Hunt. Mr. Slavens settled in Montgomery, on Brush Creek, in 1820, and removed to near Middletown in 1829. He owned part of the land that Middletown was built upon. Mr. Slavens came to Missouri in company with his brother Thomas and a Mr. McCarta, in a little horse cart. Their stock consisted of one cow, the property of William Slavens, which they drove before them and for which he was offered forty acres of land within the present limits of St. Louis; but thought his cow was worth more than the land, and kept her. Mr. Slavens had $640 in money, which he loaned to Mr. McCarta, who invested it in Irish potatoes, and planted them on ten acres of land in Illinois. The potato crop was a failure, and the money was never repaid. The names of Mr. Slavens' children were—James H., Sarah, Isabella, Lydia A., Martha A., Aaron, William N., Henry B., Euphemia, Louisa, Elizabeth, and Mary S. The youngest son, now in his 47th year, has sixteen children and ten grandchildren.

SUMMERS.—Caleb Summers was raised in Montgomery county, Maryland, where he married Rachel Crawford. In 1796 he settled in Jefferson county, Kentucky. His children were—Polly, Benjamin, Robert, Thomas, and Malinda. Robert married his cousin, Grace Summers, and settled in Pike county, Missouri, in 1834. His children were—William B., Elizabeth, Caleb L., Noah, Benjamin F., George, Robert A., and Thomas. William B. married the widow Tucker, whose maiden name was Margaret J. Bryan, and settled in Montgomery county in 1840. Caleb L. married Sallie A. Bryan, and settled in Montgomery county in 1840. Benjamin F. married Antoinette Sharp, and settled in Montgomery county in 1842. Noah married and settled in Montgomery the same year. Benjamin, son of Caleb Summers, Sr., married

Polly Raferty, and settled in Montgomery county in 1839. The father of Caleb Summers. Sr., came to America in 1750, and the boots he wore then are in the museum at Cincinnati.

SPRY.—Enoch Spry came to Missouri from Clark county, Kentucky, with Simon Griggs and Cornelius Howard, when he was fifteen years of age. He married Mary A Logan, the only sister of William, Alexander, Hugh and Henry Logan, and settled in Montgomery county in 1817. They had eight children. Soon after steamboats began to navigate the Missouri river, Mr. Spry, happening to be in the vicinity of the river one day, heard a boat blow its whistle, at which he became very much frightened, and ran home. He told his neighbors that a panther had caught a man down on the river, and he never heard any one halloo like he did. His story created so much excitement that a company was organized and went in pursuit of the "panther," which, of course, they could not find.

SMITH.—Col. John Smith, of the revolutionary war, lived in Franklin county. Virginia, where he married Frances Burk. by whom he had—William, Calum. Stephen, John, Wyatt, Henry, Susan, Mary, and Frances William married Elizabeth Ferguson, of Virginia, by whom he had—Samuel, Thomas, Stephen. William H., Mary, Frances, Susan. Martha, Elizabeth, Sarah P., and Julia. Mary married Kemcol C. Gilbert, who settled in Callaway county. Frances married Colonel Peter Booth. of Kentucky. Susan married Colonel F. A. Hancock, who settled in Alabama. Martha married Thomas J. Holland, who settled in Montgomery county in 1832. He represented the county in the State Legislature one term, and was Justice of the Peace in Warren county for a number of years. He died in 1862. Sarah P. Smith married her cousin, Wright Smith, who settled in Warren county in 1837. Julia married John Craighead, who settled in Callaway county.

TRIPLETT.—Thomas Triplett, of Buncomb county, North Carolina, had the following children—James, William, George, John, Rebecca, Nancy, and Lydia. William married Hannah Cox, of North Carolina, and settled in Montgomery county in 1830. He was a blacksmith and wheelwright by trade; and a staunch member of the Baptist Church. It was at his house that Macedonia Church was organized by Jabez Han, in 1831. His children were—Olive, Mary, Margaret, Harriet D., Rebecca C., Narcissa J., Lydia, Thomas, Zaccheus, David, Isaac M., and William H. Mary married William E. Wells, who settled in Montgomery county in 1830.

TALBOTT.—Matthew Talbott, of England, had a son named Hale, who was born in December, 1754. He married Elizabeth Irvine, who was born in September, 1778. Their children were—Christopher, Thomas, William, David, Elizabeth, Polly, Nancy,

Sophia. and Jane.   Mr. Talbott came to the Territory of Missouri in 1809, with his eldest son, Christopher, and two negro slaves. They cleared a small farm on Loutre Island, and raised a crop of corn and vegetables.   The following year (1810) the rest of the family came out and settled at their new home.   Mr. Talbott brought to Missouri seventy-six fine mares, from which he raised horses for the Western and Southern trade.   During the Indian war he kept the greater portion of his stock on the opposite side of the river, where they could not be molested by the savages.   Christopher Talbott married Susan Parrish, by whom he had—Hale, Jr., Thomas, John, James, William, Matthew, Susannah, Martha, and Mary A.   Major Thomas Talbott, the second son, was a roving, fun-loving youth.   On one occasion his father sent him to Cotesansdessein for some apple barrels, and gave him the money to pay for them.   He was gone about a month, and came back without the barrels or the money.   In 1828 he made his first trip to Santa Fe.   He was afterward employed by the government as Indian agent, and while acting in that capacity the Indians stole a lot of mules from him that were his individual property.   The government promptly paid him $5,000 for his mules.   On one of his expeditions to Santa Fe there was a Mr. Bradus, of Kentucky, in his company, who one day accidentally shot himself in the arm   The pain of his wound soon became so great that he could not endure it. and it was decided that his arm must be amputated to save his life.   There were neither surgeon nor surgical tools in the company, but they made such preparations as they could, and successfully performed the operation. The flesh was cut with a butcher's knife, the bone separated with a hand saw, and the veins seared with the king bolt of a wagon, which had been heated for the purpose.   The man got well and lived to a ripe old age.   A number of years after this event Maj. Talbott took a number of horses and mules to South Carolina, but finding no sale for them, he loaded them on board a couple of schooners, and sailed for Cuba.   During the voyage a violent storm came up, and the rolling of the vessels excited the animals so that they began to fight one another, and several of them had their ears bitten off.   But these sold as well as the others, and the Major had a very successful trip.   That was the first importation of American horses to Cuba; but since then the business has been extensively carried on.   The Major was married twice, and became a consistent member of the Methodist Church before his death.   Colonel William Talbott, the third son, was a ranger in Nathan Boone's company, and was afterward chosen Colonel of militia.   He was married twice; first to Jane Ferguson, and after her death to a widow lady named Bascom, a sister-in-law of Bishop Bascom, by whom he had one daughter, Emma, who married a Mr. Linberger, of Boonville.   At the time of his death, which occurred June 14, 1874, the Colonel was living with his daughter in Boonville. David Talbott married Susan Clark, and they had—Isaac H., William H., Mary E., Sarah A., David R., Susan J., Adda A., and Ellen. Mr. Talbott died in November, 1852, and his wife in June of the same year. Elizabeth married Judge Matthew McGirk. Polly married James Pitzer. Nancy married Col. Irvine S. Pitman. Sophia married Fletcher Wright. Jane married Dr. James Talbott, who was in the first State Constitutional Convention, which met in St. Louis in 1820. He also represented Montgomery county in the State Legislature.

VanBibber —Peter and Isaac VanBibber, of Holland, came to America and settled in Botetourt Co., Va., previous to the revolution. Peter married Marguery Bounds, and they had—Peter, Jr., Jesse, Jacob, James, Joseph, Matthias, Nancy, Sophronia, Ellen, and Olive. James married Jane Irvine, and settled in St. Charles county in 1803. He was Coroner at the time William Hays was killed by his son-in-law, James Davis. In 1817 he removed to Callaway county, and settled on the Auxvasse. His children were—Joseph, Irvine, Frances, Lucinda, Melissa, Daniel, and Minerva. Joseph was a surveyor, and made the government surveys in range eight, west of the fifth principal meridian. Olive VanBibber married Nathan Boone. Isaac VanBibber, brother of Peter, was Captain of a company in the battle of Point Pleasant, in 1774, and was killed there. He left a widow and four children—John, Peter, Isaac, and Rebecca. John and Peter married and settled in Powell's Valley, East Tennessee. Isaac was born in Greenbriar Co., Va., October 20, 1771, and was only two and a half years old when his father was killed. He was adopted and raised by Colonel Daniel Boone, and at the early age of thirteen years acted as a scout against the Indians in Virginia. In 1800 he came to Missouri with Nathan Boone, and settled first in Darst's Bottom During the Indian war he was Major of the militia under Col. Daniel M. Boone. He was married in 1797 to Susan Hays. In 1851 he settled at Loutre Lick, now in Montgomery county. The place was first settled by Thomas Massey, in 1813. The land was a Spanish grant of 460 acres, made to Nathan Boone, who sold it to VanBibber. The latter built several cabins where he settled, and afterward erected a large frame house, which he used as a hotel, and made a great deal of money. His children were—Matilda, Marcha, Susan, Elvira, Frances, Erretta, Pantha, Isaac, Jr., Ewing, and Alonzo. Major VanBibbe died in 1836, his wife having died some time before.

Worland.—Charles B. Worland, of Maryland, married Martha A. White, and settled in Washington Co., Ky. Their children were—Benedict. Charles B., Thomas N., Maria, William T., John H , Stephen W., Edward H., James P., and Martha A. Mr. Worland, his wife, and a portion of their family settled in Montgomery county in 1839. They are excellent people; honest, industrious, intelligent, kind-hearted and friendly.

WHITESIDES.—Thomas Whitesides was a native of Virginia, but removed to and settled in North Carolina. He had a son named Francis, who married Ann Clark, of Kentucky, and settled in Montgomery Co., Mo., in 1818. Their children were—James, Holland, John C., Susan, Lucinda, Sarah J., Ann, Polly, and Nancy.

WILLIAMS —Frederick, son of Richard Williams, of Pulaski Co., Ky., married Nancy Hanford, and settled in Montgomery Co , Mo., in 1832. Their children were—Liberty. Margaret. Mary, William, Harriet, Martha, Rosa A., John, Euphema, and Clara A. Margaret married James Gray. Mary married John Crutcher. Harriet married Stephen Manning Martha married Sylvester Millsap. Rosa A. married Christopher Millsap. Euphema married John Crutcher, Jr.

WHITE.—Esquire William White settled in Montgomery county in 1836. He is a brother of Benjamin White, who lives near Danville. He married Anna Fletchrall, of Maryland, and their children were—John, Daniel, Ann, William, Benjamin, Stephen, Mary, Dorcas, and Elizabeth. Elizabeth, a sister of William White, Sr., married William Smith and settled near Jonesburg.

WINDSOR.—Sampson Windsor, of Prince William Co., Va., had four sons—William, Christopher, Burton, and Alfred. Burton married Elizabeth Tinsley, and settled in Missouri in 1833. Alfred married Sarah Clark, and settled in Montgomery county in 1833. He had a son, John R., who married Mary A. Fitzhugh, of Tennessee, and died leaving a widow and nine children, five sons and four daughters. William T., another son of Alfred Windsor, married Jane B. Bryan, a daughter of Reece Bryan and Jane Evans, by whom he had seven sons and four daughters.

WHITE.—Matthew L. White was born and raised in Virginia, but removed to East Tennessee, from there to Alabama, and in 1829 he settled in Montgomery Co., Mo., and entered the land upon which the celebrated Pinnacle Rock stands. He married Rhoda Stagdon, and they had—Nancy, William, Thomas S., James H., Isaac M., John R., Mary J., Rebecca, Samuel M., Margaret A., and Martha L.

WHITE.—Benjamin White, Sr., was a native of Wales. He married Elizabeth Smith, and their son Benjamin, Jr., married Rebecca Chesell. They all lived in Montgomery Co., Md. Benjamin, a son of Benjamin White, Jr., was born November 4, 1796. He was married in 1821 to Rebecca Darby, who died, and in 1831 he married Lucy Scott. In 1837 they came to Missouri and settled in Montgomery county. Their children were—Edward G., William H., Richard G., Benjamin, Susan, Mary A., and Sarah E., all of whom are married and living in Montgomery county.

WOODRUFF.—Charles Woodruff, of Buckingham Co., Va., married a Miss Gatewood, and their son, Wyatt P., married Mary Talphro, and settled in St. Louis Co., Mo., in 1825. In 1827 they removed to St. Charles county, and from there to Montgomery county in 1832. They had—John, Charles E., Robert H., Francis S., and David B., all of whom live in Montgomery county.

WRIGHT.—Jesse Wright and his wife, Dicey Galarby, of Amherst Co., Va., had—George G., Ellis, Shelton, William, Daniel, and Nancy. George G. married Sally Jacobs, of Nelson Co., Va., and settled in Montgomery Co., Mo., in 1837. Their children were—Margaret, Anna V., Catharine and George G., Jr. Margaret married John R. Arnor. Anna V. married Isaac H. Talbott, of Montgomery county. Catharine married Hon. Norman J. Colman, editor of *Colman's Rural World* and Lieut.-Gov. of Missouri. George G., Jr., lives in Montgomery county, is an influential citizen and a leader of the Democratic party of his locality.

WITCHER.—James Witcher, of Virginia, married Martha Watson, and they had three sons and three daughters. Ephraim, their eldest son, who was a soldier in the war of 1812, settled in Montgomery Co., Mo., and married Winifred B. Holley, by whom he had six children. He died in 1845, and his widow married Col. Reuben Pew, who also died, leaving her a widow the second time.

WADE.—Henry Wade and his wife, Lucy Turner, lived in Culpepper Co., Va. They had—Luke, Zackfill, Henry, Andrew, John, Orinda, Polly, and Sally. Henry married Mary D. Waller, in 1810, and settled in Lincoln Co., Mo., in 1835. His children were—William, Henry, John, Richard, Andrew, Martha, Judith, Lucy, Polly, and Margaret. William married Susan Sitton, of Lincoln county. Henry lives in California, unmarried. Richard died in that State. John married Levisa Wright. Andrew died in his youth. Martha was married first to Peter Shelton, and after his death to George Dyer. Judith married John Carter, and is now a widow. Lucy married James Berger, of Montgomery county. Polly was married first to John C. Whitesides; after his death to Capt. William Quick, and she is a widow again. She has in her possession her mother's wedding costume that was spun and woven with her own hands in 1810. Margaret Wade was married first to John T. Wright, and second to George Ousley.

WRIGHT.—John Wright, of England, came to America and settled in Pittsylvania county, Va. He had four children—John, William, Nancy, and another daughter. William married Isabella Thrailkill, of Virginia, and settled in Clark county, Ky. He served five years in the revolutionary war. He had twelve children, ten of whom lived to be grown, and were married. His fifth son, William, married Nancy Oliver, of Kentucky, and they had eleven children—Harvey S., James T., William M., Stephen, Isaac W., Elizabeth, Susan, Nancy, Emeline, Louisa, and Lucinda. Mr. Wright settled in Montgomery county, Mo., in 1824, on a place adjoining the present town of Danville, where he lived and kept tavern for many years. A Methodist minister named Prescott, stopped at his house one day to get his dinner, and there being no men present he went to the barn to feed his horse. While looking around for the food he saw some large flat gourds, which he supposed to be pumpkins, and fed a lot of them to his horse. After that he was called Gourd Head Prescott. In 1833 Mr. Wright sold his place to Rev. Andrew Monroe, a well known pioneer Methodist preacher, who lived there and kept tavern for some time. Isabella Wright, sister of William Wright, Sr., married John Stone, who settled in Montgomery county in 1818, but afterward removed to Arkansas.

HISTORIES OF FAMILIES.

CALLAWAY COUNTY.

The county of Callaway was named for the gallant Captain James Callaway, who was killed by the Indians at Loutre creek, on the 7th of March, 1815. The county was organized November 25, 1820, out of the territory of Montgomery county.

The first county seat was at a place called Elizabeth, situated on Ham's Prairie, about six miles south of Fulton. It remained until there 1826, when the seat of justice was permanently located at Fulton. The latter place was founded in 1824, by Mr. George Nichols, and was at first called Volney, for the celebrated French author; but the name was soon after changed to Fulton, in honor of Robert Fulton, the great applyer of steam to navigation.

The dates of the various early settlements in Callaway county, are given in connection with the histories of families, and it is not necessary to repeat them here.

FAMILIES OF CALLAWAY COUNTY.

Allen.—Captain Archibald Allen settled in Callaway county in 1822. He was born in Botetourt county, Virginia, January 7, 1795, and served his country in the war of 1812. He was married in 1815 to Anna Galbreth, of Virgina, and settled first in St. Clair county, Illinois, from whence he removed to Callaway county. Missouri, at an early date. After the death of his first wife he married Nancy Hamilton, of Missouri, in 1858, who died also. In 1875 he was married again, to a Mrs. Brown, being at the time more than 80 years of age. He died soon after. Captain Allen joined the Presbyterian Church in 1824, and was one of the first members of that organization in Callaway county. He remained a consistent and devout member until his death.

ALLEN.—David Allen and his wife, Margaret Gamble, were natives of Scotland, but came to America and settled in South Carolina prior to the revolution. Mr. Allen took part in the war, and saw some hard service in the Continental army. After the return of peace he removed to Kentucky and settled in Montgomery county. He had two sons, James and Joseph, who came to Missouri. The former married Sarah Smith, of Bath Co., Ky., and settled in Callaway Co., Mo., in 1825. Joseph married Margaret Murphy, and settled in Callaway county about the same time. The children of James Allen were—Jane, Caroline, John, Nancy, David, James, William, Milton, Mary, Harvey, Martha, and Virginia. The children of Joseph Allen were—Clarinda, Jane, Grezella, Margaret, Amanda, John, and Sally.

ARMSTRONG.—The parents of Thomas Armstrong died when he was quite young, and he was "bound out" to a man in Philadelphia, to learn the boot and shoe trade. When he was grown he married Jane Dalton, and settled in Dixon county, Tenn. His children were—William, John, James, Thomas, Charles, Abner, Lucy, Sophia, and Jane. William married Lucy Baxter, and settled in Callaway county in 1837. He had—John, Limis, Jane, Nancy, Richmond, Thomas, Felix, and William, Jr.

AUSTIN.—Hezekiah Austin, of Montgomery county, Md., married Elizabeth Odell, and settled in Christian county, Ky. They had—Barach O., Mary A., Margaret, Jane, and Elizabeth. Barach O. married Paulina J. Shirtridge, who died, and he afterward married Ellen L. Allen, and settled in Callaway county in 1836.

ALLEN.—Bethel, Sampson, and Thomas Allen, sons of Daniel Allen and Elizabeth Bethel, settled in Callaway county in 1817. Bethel married Elizabeth Read. He and Sampson were soldiers of the war of 1812.

AGEE.—Matthew and Tilman Agee settled on Coats' Prairie in Callaway county in 1817. Matthew had a large apple and peach orchard, and made brandy. In 1833 the cholera made its appearance in his family, and one of his sons, while suffering from the scourge, drank a barrel of water in twenty-four hours, and got well. Matthew Agee's wife was a daughter of Rev. William Coats. Tilman Agee married a daughter of William Thornton, when she was only thirteen years of age. The next morning after the wedding he left her to get breakfast, while he went out to work. He worked until nine o'clock, without being summoned to his meal, and then having become impatient, he went to the house to see what was the matter, and found his wife sitting on the floor playing with her dolls.

ANDERSON.—William Anderson, of Campbell Co., Va., married Sarah Easley, and they had—Jacob, John, Mary, Elizabeth,

Jerry, Lucinda, William, and James C. Jacob settled in St. Charles Co., Mo., in 1832. John settled in Gentry county in 1835. Mary, William, and Lucinda settled in Lafayette Co., Mo., and the latter married Rev. Thomas Callaway. James C. married Jane Moorman, of Virginia, and settled in Callaway county in 1831. Their children were—James W., Thomas C., Anna M., Alexander, Judith, Jerry, Sarah J., Mary F., Henry W., and George B.

ADAIR.—Joseph, son of John Adair, of Delaware, married Sarah Long, of Kentucky, and settled in Callaway Co., Mo., in 1830. They had—Lydia, John L., Samuel S., Sarah, Ann, Joseph, and Andrew. Mr. Adair was accidentally killed by a horse. Lydia married Levi James, who settled in Callaway county in 1822. Their children were—Sarah A., John, Eliza, and Joseph. John L. Adair married Elizabeth E. Pemberton, and they had—Louisa, John, Sarah, Fanny, Catharine, Noah, Jacob, and James. Sarah Adair married Hardin Wash, who settled in Callaway county in 1830. Ann married Thomas Baker, and Joseph married Sarah Adcock. The former settled in Callaway county in 1821, and the latter in 1830. Andrew was married first to Nancy Stephens, by whom he had—Lock and Elijah. After the death of his first wife he married Louisa Booker, and they had—Lulu and Louisa.

ADCOCK.—John Adcock, of England, settled in Buckingham Co., Va., and married a Miss Carter, by whom he had—John, Carter, Edward, Henry, Joseph, and Phœbe. The latter was captured by an Indian, who made her his wife. Joseph married Susan Cason, of Prince Edward Co., Va., by whom he had—Phœbe, Milly, Elizabeth, Lucy, Polly, Susan, Nancy, John, Samuel, Joel, Henry, Edward, and Cason. Joel, who was born in 1792, served eleven months in the war of 1812, principally at Richmond and Norfolk. He was married in 1820 to Elizabeth Childup, and settled in Callaway Co., Mo., in 1830. His children were—John H., Joseph Q., Aaron, Madison, Elizabeth, Sarah, Susan, and Drury W. Mr. Adcock lost his wife in 1872, and he died in the summer of 1876.

ARNOLD.—William Arnold, of Eastern Virginia, married Elizabeth Nowell, and they had—Robert, William, Pleasant, Polly, and Susan. The three latter removed to Tennessee with their parents. Robert and William were both in the war of 1812, and the latter died of measles while in the army. Robert settled in Shelby county, Ky., and was married in 1816 to Elizabeth Marion, by whom he had—William, Nancy, and Pleasant. In 1820 he removed to Missouri, and settled in St. Charles county, where he was employed two years as overseer for Nicholas Kountz. He then removed to Montgomery county, where he lost his wife in 1823. He soon after married Piercy Hamlin, daughter of John

Hamlin and Bertha Arnold, of Virginia, and settled in Callaway county in 1825. His children by his second wife were—George H., Bertha A., John W., Mary E., Robert, and Martha C. His eldest son, William, married Louisa Scholl, and died without issue. Pleasant married Caroline Scholl, and died, leaving a widow and nine children. He was an excellent man and a good citizen. Nancy married Henry Covington. George H. married Melissa Johnson, of Kentucky. Bertha A. married Benjamin F. Covington. John W. married Mary S. Lail. Mary E. was married first to James O. Johnson, of Scotland, and after his death she married James R. Covington. Robert married Elvira Allen. Martha C. married Thomas W. Higginbotham.

Adams.—John Adams, of Maryland, married Susan Wood, and had—William, Sylvester, Richard, Philip, Benjamin, Susan, and Elizabeth. Philip was married first to Fannie Powell, by whom he had—Susan, Thomas, and Mary. He was married the second time to Matilda Foster, by whom he had one son, John Booker. Mr. Adams settled in Callaway county in 1839. John Booker is still living. He was married twice; first to Miss Anna M. Allen, and second to Mrs. Sally E. Allen.

Burt.—Moses Burt was a native of Germany, but emigrated to America, and settled in New Jersey. Times were very hard then, and wages very low. A great many persons were out of employment, and glad to work for a living. Burt worked several months for a peck of corn a day, and was glad to get that. About the year 1776 he married Hannah Gru, and removed to Culpepper county, Va. In 1783 he emigrated to Kentucky, and settled in Scott county, where he lived and died. He had ten children, six sons and four daughters. The names of the former were —Benjamin, Joseph, Richard, William, John, and James. Joseph and James were soldiers in the war of 1812. The former died, and the latter was killed on Lake Erie. Benjamin and Richard lived and died in Kentucky. John settled in Indiana. William was born in Culpepper county, Va., in 1776. He married Sarah Greenup, a daughter of Samuel Greenup, and niece of Governor Greenup, of Kentucky, and they had—Julia A., Polly, Franklin, Susan, Emily, Amanda, James, and Sarah. Polly died in Kentucky, and Mr. Burt and the rest of his children, with the exception of Franklin, removed to Indiana. Franklin married Martha Craig, and settled in Callaway county, Mo., in 1835, where he has since resided. His wife died in October, 1872. The names of their children were—William D., James R., Mary E., Samuel E., Nancy J., Hiram W., Sally A., John H., and Amanda M. Mr. Burt is an industrious, honest, jovial gentleman, and a worthy and highly respected citizen. He says that when he first settled in Callaway county he raised large quantities of watermelons every year, of which he could eat more than any other man living, his daily allowance being from fifteen to twenty large ones.

BENTLEY.—The children of John Bentley, of Warren county, Ky., were—Rebecca, John, James, Thomas, George, Mary, Nancy, and Rhoda. Rebecca married Uriah Sutherland, who settled in Callaway county in 1826. Thomas married Rhoda Hickerson, and settled in that county two years later. John married Rhoda Patton, and removed to Callaway county, where she died. He then married Amanda Scott, who also died, and he was married the third time to Mrs. Harriet Yancy. George was married first to Jane Hall, and second to Polly Singer.

BERRY.—Richard, Edward, Frank, John, and Rachel Berry were children of an English family that settled in Kentucky at an early date. Richard married Polly Ewing, and settled in Darst's Bottom, St. Charles county, in 1820. Three years later he removed to Grand Prairie, in Callaway county. The names of his children were—Calep E., John, Edward G., Richard, Samuel H., Robert M., Elizabeth, Nancy, Margaret, and Mary J. Calep was at a public gathering of some kind, on a certain occasion, and seeing no convenient place to hitch his horse, he buckled the bridle to the stirrup of Colonel Warner's saddle. The Colonel's horse got loose after a while, and went home, a distance of twenty miles, taking Berry's horse with him. Both of the men had to walk the entire distance to recover their horses. Calep Berry married Virginia Fulkerson. John married Margaret Galbreth, and Edward G. married Sallie A. Galbreth. Richard was married twice; first to Elizabeth Watts, and second to Mary Hamilton. Samuel H. was Sheriff of Callaway county two years. He married Eliza Watts. Robert was married first to Permelia Martin, and second to Emily A. Scholl. Elizabeth was married first to Thomas Yocum, and second to John Watts. Nancy married John W. Johnson. Mary J. married James B. Yager.

BROWN.—Joseph Brown, of Buckingham county, Va., married his cousin, Lucy Brown, and they had—Nathaniel, Frederick, Felix, Jonathan, James, Thomas, Stephen, Polly, and Patsey. Felix married Agnes Boaz, of Buckingham county, in 1808, and settled in St. Charles county, Mo., in 1819. The following year he removed to Callaway county. His children were—Joseph, Robert J., Elizabeth, Polly, William, John, Delila T., Jane, Martha L., Harriet, James, Paulina A., and Thomas F. Mr. Brown was a soldier in the war of 1812. He was also a steam doctor, and an Ironside Baptist preacher. For many years he wore a long buckskin hunting shirt, reaching almost to his heels, which caused him to present a singular appearance. He wore this strange garb in the pulpit as well as everywhere else, and his congregations no doubt imagined that he bore a strong resemblance to the patriarchs of old. He was very positive in his opinions, and would never admit that he was in the wrong on any

20

question, if he could possibly avoid it.   He believed that he could
do anything that any other man could, and one day he endeavored
to temper a cross-cut saw that belonged to one of his neighbors.
The saw was ruined, and the owner sued him for its value.   The
case went though a number of courts, and was the source of a
great deal of amusement.

BOSWELL.—Matthew Boswell, of Albemarle county, Va., was a
cooper by trade.   He married Nancy Maire, and settled in Callaway county, Mo., in 1835.   Their children were—Barbara, Mary.
Marshall P., Elizabeth, Harriet, John H., Frances, Matthew M.,
James W., Thomas, and Martha M.   Barbara married Willis
Hall, who settled in Callaway county in 1835.   Elizabeth married
James Simpson, who became a citizen of that county in 1836.   He
subsequently died, and she was married again to John Blunkall,
who settled in Callaway county in 1834.   Harriet was married
first to Robert Ansel, and after his death to John Bentley, both
early settlers of Callaway county.   Frances married James Field.
Martha M. married Abraham Brendonburgh.

BETHEL.—Samuel Bethel, of Smith county, Tennessee, married
Rebecca Patton, and settled in Callaway county in 1820, and
was elected Justice of the Peace the same year.   He was a soldier
of the war of 1812.

BLACKBURN.—The parents of Robert Blackburn lived in Fairfax
county, Va.   Robert married Jane Fields.   It was a runaway
match, and they were married at the cross roads.   They settled
in Callaway county in 1838, and Mr. Blackburn died in 1845.
His widow still survives in her 91st year.   Their children were—
William, James, Edward, Thomas, Richard, Louis, Robert H.,
James S., Eveline, Amanda M., Mary J., and Margaret A.

BOONE.—George, a brother of Daniel Boone, married Nancy
Lingell, and their children were—Squire, John, Samuel, Edward,
George, Jr., Elizabeth, Martha, Sarah, Polly, and Maria.   Squire
married and settled in St. Charles county, Mo., where he died,
leaving five sons and several daughters.   The names of the sons
were—Samuel, Hayden, Milo, Thomas, and John.   Capt. Samuel,
son of George Boone, Sr., married Anna Simpson, of Kentucky,
by whom he had—Jeptha V., Mary A., Elizabeth C., Maxemille.
Martha L., and Samuel T.   Elizabeth C. married her first cousin,
Dr. Banton Boone, who was a son of Edward Boone, and their
son, Hon. Banton Boone, of Henry county, was chosen Speaker
of the last House of Representatives of the State of Missouri.   He
is a young man of fine abilities and has a brilliant future before
him.   Dr. Banton Boone died of cholera, at his home on Prairie
Fork creek, in Callaway county.   Capt. Samuel Boone settled in
Callaway county in 1818, and in 1820 he assisted in building the
first Baptist Church erected in that county, which was called Salem.
He was Judge of the County Court for some time, and a promi-

nent and influential citizen. Edward, son of George Boone, Sr.,
married the widow White, whose maiden name was Dorcas
Simpson. She was a sister of Capt. Samuel Boone's wife, and at
the time of her marriage with Mr. Boone she had a son, Morgan
B. White, who is still living in Callaway county. Her Boone
children were—Banton, Rodolph, William, George L., Ann, Milley,
Margaret, Maria, and Mary.

BENSON.—John and Thomas Benson settled in the State of
Maryland. John married a Miss Edmonson, and remained in
that State. Their children were—Thomas, Eden, Ruth, Elizabeth, and Margaret. Eden married Sally Bell, and removed to
Louisiana, where he made a fortune raising cotton. He then
came to Missouri, and settled in Callaway county in 1823. After
his removal to Missouri he speculated largely in lands, and at his
death he left his children, of whom he had thirteen, wealthy. Jefferson B., a son of Thomas Benson, Sr., of Maryland, settled in
Montgomery county, Mo., in 1832. He married Sarah Hays, and
they had nine children.

BROADWATER.—Charles L. Broadwater was an Englishman. He
came to America a short time before the commencement of the
revolution, and when the war began, he joined the American army
and served as a soldier during that memorable struggle. He afterward married Behethler Sabaston, and they had three children—
George, William E., and Anna M. George married Catharine
Gunnell, and they had—Ann M., Henry, Arthur, John C. H.,
Elizabeth, Thomas, and George, Jr., all of whom, except Arthur,
settled in Missouri. William E., son of Charles L. Broadwater,
married Margaret Darne, and they had three children, who, after
the death of their father, came to Missouri with their mother, and
settled in Callaway county in 1833.

BOARD.—James Board, of New Jersey, maried Nancy Skiller,
and they had a son named Philip, who married Ellen Thompson,
by whom he had—James, William, John, Eliza, and Eleanor. His
first wife died, and he afterward married a widow lady named
Mitchell, by whom he had—David, Joseph, Thomas, Cornelius,
Maria, Benjamin, and Nancy. John Board married Elizabeth
Matthews, of Kentucky, and settled in Darst's Bottom, St. Charles
county, in 1819, where he lived six years. During that time he
assisted David Darst in catching a corn thief in a steel trap, and
then helped to whip him. In 1825 he removed to Callaway county.
The trip was made on one horse, which carried the entire family
of husband, wife and child, with their household goods, etc. Mr.
Board is a stone mason by trade, and built nearly all of the
old-fashioned mammoth stone chimneys in his neighborhood. He
has been married five times, and had twelve children. He is now
in his 83d year, and stout and hearty for a man of that age. He
never wore gloves or over-shoes in his life, and his hands were

never so cold but that he could thread a cambric needle. In disposition he has always been firm, even to obstinacy, and always endeavored to have a mind of his own on every subject.

BISHOP.—James Bishop came to America with the Penn colony, and settled in Pennsylvania. He afterward married Elizabeth Penn, a sister of William Penn, by whom he had eight children. He died in his 99th year. The names of his children were—Jesse, Rachel, James, Thomas, William, Samuel, Polly, and Rebecca. Samuel married Sarah Viah, of Virginia, by whom he had—Tisa D., Mary E., David J., Granville, Beverly A., William C., Frank, Edwin L., Sarah V., Ardena F., and Samuel A. Mr. Bishop and his family settled in Callaway county, Mo., in 1835.

BASKET.—Martin, James, Jesse, and John Basket were sons of Jesse Basket, Sr., of Nicholas county, Kentucky. Martin and James settled in Callaway county, Mo., in 1821; Jesse and John married and remained in Kentucky. Martin married Jane Baker, of Kentucky, by whom he had a son and daughter. James married Mary Baker, of Kentucky, by whom he had five sons and four daughters. Mr. Basket was Circuit Clerk of Callaway county for six years, and in 1835 he was elected one of the Judges of the County Court. He was a good man, and respected by all who knew him.

BOYD.—Thomas Boyd, of Pennsylvania, married Grezelda Allen, of the same State, and settled first in Montgomery county, Ky., from whence they removed to Callaway county, Mo., in 1827. Their children were—Robert, John, Joseph, Thomas, Jane, and Eleanor. Robert married Margaret Rallston, and died in 1872, without issue. Colonel John Boyd, still living in Callaway county, was a soldier in the war of 1812. He married Mary A. Scott, of Missouri, by whom he had—William S., John R., Joseph, Benjamin F., Charles O., Edward L., Grezelda A., Lydia A., George F., Mary E., Sarah E., and Thomas A. The first seven are living. Joseph, son of Thomas Boyd, Sr., married Ann King, by whom he had—Malinda J., James E., Thomas G., Cynthia A., Robert M., John K., Grezelda M., Elizabeth S., Caroline H., Joseph W. W., and Newton C. Mr. Boyd settled in Callaway county in 1822. Thomas, son of Thomas Boyd, Sr., married Ann Davis, by whom he had—Eliza, Thomas, Grezelda, Mary J., Amanda, and Margaret. Jane Boyd married Isaac P. Howe, by whom she had—Jane, William, John, Thomas, David, Harvey, Margaret, and Mary. Ellen married Thomas Caldwell, who settled in Callaway county in 1826.

BAYNHAM.—Dr. Baynham, of London, England, settled in Virginia in 1775. His son, William, married Mary Wyatt, by whom he had—Jonah, Mary, Millie, William, Joseph, and John. The latter married Sarah Blackwell, of Halifax county, Va., and they had—Mary, William G., Harriet B., John, Joseph, Charles M., and Grief H. Mr. Baynham died in Virginia, and his wife afterward married John W. Blackwell, by whom she had twelve more children. Grief H. Baynham came to Callaway county, Mo., in 1831, with his step-father, and hired out to work on a farm, at the rate of fifty cents per day. He has since made a fortune, besides raising a large family of children. He married Martha E. Gaines, of Callaway county.

BRIGHT.—David Bright, of Pennsylvania, married Mary Gale, and settled in the western part of Virginia in 1785. Their children were—Polly, Michael, David, Jr., Jesse, and George. Polly married a Mr. Weaver, and died in Pennsylvania. Michael married Sally Price, of Virginia, by whom he had—David, Samuel, Margaret, Jesse, Elizabeth, Michael, Jr., Sarah, Mary A., Jackell, and Washington. Of these children we have the following history: David, Margaret, and Samuel remained in Virginia. Mary A. married Ephraim Howe, who settled in Callaway county at an early date. They had one child, Sally A., who is the widow of Thomas Wright, and lives in Columbia, Mo. Jesse came to Missouri, and married a widow lady named Thompson, who died of cholera, while traveling on a steamboat on the Mississippi river in 1849. Elizabeth married Robert Calhoun, of Audrain county, by whom she had—Robert O., Joshua J., Margaret, William, Virginia, and Samuel. Michael Jr., was born in Greenbriar county, Va., in 1810. He was married in 1832 to Jane McClung, and settled in Callaway county in 1837. He served as a member of the County Court for eight years. Sarah married David Patterson, of Callaway county. Washington settled in Callaway county in 1838. He married Esther Rapp, of Virginia.

BROWN.—John Brown, of Pennsylvania, married Jane Shannon, and settled in Scott county, Ky. Their children were—John, William, Mary, Jane, Nancy, and Ann. John married Elizabeth Ewing, and lived in Kentucky. William married Margaret D. Hamilton, and also lived in Kentucky. His children were—Alexander, Samuel, James, Robert, Charles, Sally, Margaret, Rachel W. J., Polly, Nancy, and Jane. Margaret married her cousin, William Brown, and they had—Charles H., John, Sarah, James, Margaret, Robert William, and George S., all of whom settled in Callaway county in 1834. Charles H., John, James, and Robert are large land owners and cattle raisers. The former married Amanda McCanny; John married Jane Robinson; Jane married Catharine F. Holman, and Robert married Mary A. Fry. George S., son of William Brown, Sr., lives in Mexico, Mo. He has been married twice; first to Margaret Smith, and second to Laura Payne. Margaret, daughter of William Brown the second, married John Bailus, and died, leaving four children.

BLATTENBERG.—Jacob Blattenberg, of Pennsylvania, married Mary Read, of Kentucky, and settled in Callaway county in 1824.

His children were—Eliza, Mary, Margaret, Emma A., Philip H., and George.

BURCH.—Leonard Burch, of Maryland, was married twice; first to a Miss Webster, by whom he had—James, Thomas, John, and Nancy; and second to a Miss Crow, by whom he had—Stiman, Stephen, Sally, Susan, and Catharine. James, the eldest son by the first wife, was married in 1806 to Mary Padgett, of Virginia, by whom he had—Lucy, Thomas, Nelson, Joseph, and Nancy. He died in 1816, and in 1841 his widow and two of her daughters settled in Callaway county, Mo., where the former died in 1853. Thomas, son of Leonard Burch, married the widow of Thomas Hall, whose maiden name was Susan S. Clarby, of Amherst county, Va. He settled in Callaway county in 1830. Joseph, son James Burch, married Elizabeth Chaney, of Boone county, Mo., and settled in Callaway county in 1831. Lucy, his sister, married James L. Whittington, of Callaway county. Nancy never married, and died in Bates county, Mo.

BRUNER.—John Bruner was of German extraction. He settled in Clark county, Ky., and was married four times. His son, Stephen, married Elizabeth Strood and settled in Boone county, Mo., in 1820. His children were—John W., James M., Mary, Jacob T., George W., Edward T., and Robert S. After Mr. Bruner's death, his widow married Stephen King, who was an early settler of Callaway county.

BOULWARE.—Richard Boulware was an Irishman by birth, but lived in Essex county, Va. He married Esther Ramsey, who was born in England, and they had six children —Catharine, Mordecai, Richard, Theodoric, Ramsey, and Martha. In the fall of 1784 Mr. Boulware and his family left Virginia and made their way on pack horses through the wilderness to Garrard county, Ky., where they settled. Theodoric was born in Essex county, Va., November 13, 1780. After he grew up he united with the Old Baptist Church, and became a minister of that sect. He was married April 17, 1808, to Sarah W. Kelley, by whom he had—Stephen G., James R., Theodoric F., Daniel R., Jane C., Cordelia A., Susan M., Jeptha, and Isaac W. In 1827 Mr. Boulware came to Missouri with his family, and settled near Fulton, in Callaway county, where he taught school and preached in various churches of his denomination for many years. He lost his wife in January, 1854, and in June, 1855, he married Mrs. Elizabeth H. Offutt, who died in December, 1857. Mr. Boulware was a man of a superior order of talents, possessed a fine flow of language, and ready wit. He was highly respected by the people of his community, and loved by the members of his church.

BRADLEY.—Thomas Bradley, of Kentucky, married Fannie Bush, by whom he had—F. B., Lucy A., Thomas, and Milton, all of whom settled in Callaway county in 1828.

BURGETT.—John Burgett lived at or near New Madrid, Mo., in 1811–12, and was one of the victims of the dreadful earthquakes at that time and place. He struggled against his misfortune for several years, but finally, in 1817, he left that part of the country and settled in Callaway county. His wife was Elizabeth Coonse, by whom he had—Josiah and Eli. The former married Polly Zumwalt, by whom he had—Jacob, Elizabeth, John T., and Sarah. His first wife died, and he was married again to Catharine Gilman, and they had—Thomas B. and Sterling P.

BROOKS.—Benjamin Brooks was a soldier of the revolutionary war. He settled first in Franklin county, Va.; removed from there to Kentucky, but soon afterward returned to Virginia. He was married twice, and had two children, Mary and William. William married Mary Sellers, daughter of Andrew Sellers, a revolutionary soldier. The student of history will remember that in early days in Virginia a number of young girls were brought from England and sold to the settlers for wives, to pay their passage across the ocean. Mr. Sellers obtained his wife in that way, paying twenty pounds sterling for her; and she made a good and loving wife. The children of William Brooks were—Andrew, John, Clifford, Ewell, Pleasant D., Irene, Drusilla, Julia, and Nancy. Pleasant D. married Frances Gilbert, and settled in Callaway county in 1834. His first wife died, and he was married the second time to a widow lady named Lovelace. Ewell, his brother, married Lourena Gilbert, and settled in Callaway county in 1837.

BARTLEY.—John Bartley was a native of Scotland; his wife was born in Turkey. They came to America a number of years before the revolution, and when the war began, their son, Joshua, who was only eighteen years of age, enlisted in the American army. He soon manifested great gallantry and fine soldierly qualities, for which he was promoted to the rank of Captain, a position which he held during the remainder of the war. Soon after peace was declared he married Elizabeth Allen, who was a niece of General Nathaniel Greene, and they had—Allen, John, James, William, George, Polly, Nancy, and Elizabeth. Mr. Bartley settled in Kentucky, and his sons, Allen, John and James, became volunteers from that State in the war of 1812. John married Winifred Bagby, of Virginia, and settled in Callaway county, Mo., in 1829, where he died in 1849. His children were—George G., John J., William W., Joshua W., Joseph D., Daniel M., Andrew J., Sarah E., and Susan A. George, the youngest son of Joshua Bartley, Sr., was educated by his brother John, and in 1820 he came to Missouri and settled in Callaway county, where he married Elizabeth Moore, and raised a large family, most of whom still live in that county. He was appointed Deputy County and Circuit Clerk at an early date, and was afterward elected Circuit Clerk, which position he held for eighteen consecutive years. He also served

as Judge of the County Court for three terms.   During his residence in Missouri he made several trips to Santa Fe, New Mexico,.
on trading expeditions.

BEAVEN.—John, Charles, and Sally Beaven were the children of
Richard Beaven, of Maryland.   Charles married Anna Saucier,
and settled in Callaway county in 1824.   His children were—
Richard, William, Robert, Zadock, Theodore, Walter, Polly,
Elizabeth, Julia A., Eliza, and Permelia.

BOYCE.—Robert C. Boyce, of Lincoln county, Ky., settled in
Callaway county in 1829.   He married Ann Murphy, by whom he
had—Marion C., Greenberry D., Harrison A., Charles L., John
R., Wharton B., Ann M., Eliza, Susan, and Sarah.

BUSH.—Frank Bush, of Clark county, Ky., married Lucy Davis,
by whom he had—William, Polly, Nancy, Elizabeth, Mary, and
Fanny.   Mr. Bush was married the second time to Rachel Martin,
by whom he had—Fielding, Jordan, Lucy, and Sally.   Fanny
married Thomas Bradley, who settled in Callaway county in 1828.
Elizabeth married Daniel Oliver, who settled in that county in
1833.   Jordan married Sally Stewart, and settled in Callaway
county in 1829.

BENNETT.—Joseph Bennett, of Maryland, married Margaret
Davis, and settled in Madison county, Ky.   In 1820 he removed
to Missouri and settled in Boone county, where he remained until
1838, when he removed to Callaway county.   His children are—
Moses, Joel, Jesse D., Milton, Elijah, Sedreia B., Elizabeth,
Nancy, Rebecca, Margaret, Emily, and Mary.   The Bennetts
are relatives of Jefferson Davis, ex-President of the late Confederate States.

BROOKS.—James Brooks married Elizabeth Holt, daughter of
Timothy Holt, and settled in Callaway county in 1819.   His children were—Robert, John, Elizabeth, Winifred, Ann, Fanny,
and James.

BRANDON.—Robert Brandon married Jane Holt, daughter of
Timothy Holt, and settled in Callaway county in 1832.   His
children are—Ann, Smith, Sarah, Frances, and Elizabeth.

BLYTHE.—John Blythe, of Kentucky, married Sallie Carter, by
whom he had—Daniel, Samuel, Matilda, John, William, Peggy,
Sally, Polly, Abbie, Patsey, and Maria.   Mr. Blythe settled in
Callaway county in 1817.   Samuel married Sally H. Russell.
William was married first to Matilda Denton, and second to Maria
Coonse.   Polly married Price Holt.   Matilda married Isaac Zum-
walt.   They live in Callaway county.

BRYANT.—William Bryant, of Kentucky, married Rachel Wilcox, by whom he had—Jerry, Hiram, Thomas, Henry, Susan,.
and Benjamin.   They settled in Callaway county in 1820.   Jerry
married Martha Plummer, by whom he had twelve children, seven

of whom lived to be grown, and married and settled in Callaway county.

BROOKS.—Thomas Brooks, of Virginia, married Elizabeth Bullard, and settled in Callaway county in 1819. His children were —Thomas, Jr., Churchill, Elcham, Theophilus, Jane, Elizabeth,. William, James, George R., Lafayette, Lorenzo, and Sarah, most of whom live in Callaway county.

BERRY.—Richard, Edward, Frank, John, and Rachel Berry were the children of an English family that settled in Kentucky. Richard married Polly Ewing, by whom he had—Frank, Caleb E., John, Edward G., Richard, Jr., Samuel H., Robert M., Elizabeth, Nancy, Margaret, and Mary J. Mr. Berry settled in Darst's Bottom, St. Charles county, in 1820, and in 1823 he removed to Grand Prairie, in Callaway county, where he died in 1843. His wife died in 1829. Frank, his eldest son, died a bachelor. Caleb E. married Virginia Fulkerson, of Darst's Bottom, and settled in Callaway county. John married Margaret Galbreth, and settled in Callaway county, where he died in 1851. Edward G. married Sally A. Galbreth. Richard was married first to Elizabeth Watts, and second to Mary Hamilton. Samuel H. married Elizabeth Wells. He was Sherff of Callaway county several times. Robert M. was married first to Permelia Martin, and second to Emily A. Scholl. Elizabeth was married first to Thomas Yocum, and second to John Watts. Nancy married John W. Johnson. Margaret married Joseph Dunham. Mary J. married James B. Yager.

BIRD.—The children of Abraham Bird, of Shenandoah Co., Va., were—George, Andrew, Marcus, and Abraham. The latter married Mary Holker, of Virginia, and they had—Nancy, John, George, Abraham, Marcus, William, Rebecca, Mary, Elizabeth, and Catharine. Marcus settled in Callaway county in 1826, and married Eliza J. Talbott, daughter of Dr. James Talbott, of Montgomery county, and she is the only one of the original Talbott family that is still living. Mr. Bird was County Surveyor of Callaway county for thirty-six years.

BARNES.—Richard Barnes, of Boone county, North Carolina, had—Elias, Equilles, Richard, Samuel, Shadrach, Amos, Abraham, and Sally. Elias, Equilles and Shadrach were in the revolutionary war, and Equilles was killed at the battle of Cow Pens. Amos, Shadrach and Sally (who married Randall Simms), settled in Madison county, Ky. Amos afterward removed to Howard Co., Mo., where he lived and died. Shadrach was married in North Carolina, to Hannah Turner, and had three children at the time of his removal to Kentucky. They went from North Carolina to Kentucky on pack-horses. Mr. Barnes subsequently removed to Missouri, and settled in Howard county. He died in Boonville, Mo., in the 92d year of his age. His children were—Elizabeth, Equilles, Philip, Sally, James, Amos, John, Abraham, Benjamin, Nellie, Thomas, and Sophia. Elizabeth married William Taylor, who settled in St. Charles county, Mo., in 1810. Equilles married Dolly Herndon, and settled in Howard county. Philip married Fanny Barnes, his cousin, and also settled in Howard county. Sally married William Ridgeway, who settled in Boone county. James married Elizabeth Burkhart, and settled in Boone county. He was one of the noted pioneer Baptist preachers of Missouri, and during the Indian war he taught school in Cooper's Fort, and the afterwards celebrated Kit Carson was one of his pupils. In 1815 he went to New Orleans with a flatboat loaded with nine different kinds of wild meat, besides honey, corn, potatoes, onions, furs, hides, deer and elk horns, etc. He died in 1875, in his 87th year. Amos Barnes married Dorcas Kincaid, and settled in Boone county. John married Sally Hubbard, and settled in the same county. Abraham married Grace Jones, and settled in Cooper county. Benjamin married Lucretia Simms, and settled on the line between Boone and Callaway counties, in 1819. He raised a large family of children, and is the only one of his father's family now living. He is a sociable old gentleman, and fond of fun and jokes. During his younger days he made seven trips to Sante Fe, New Mexico, and rode the same little pony every time. He was Captain of a wagon train, and received good pay. Nellie Barnes married Harris Jameson, who settled in Boone county. Thomas married Susan Fields, and settled in Cooper county. Sophia married Jefferson Boggs, a brother of Governor Boggs, and settled in Cooper county.

BURT.—John Burt, of Orleans Co., Vt., removed to Ohio in 1815. His three sons, John A., Henry, and George W., came to Callaway county, Mo., from 1819 to 1821. They were millwrights by trade, and built the first water mill in Montgomery county, for Col. Irvine Pitman. After a number of years the mill was moved away, and the large water wheel left standing. The action of the water of course kept it constantly turning, and the negroes and a few superstitious white people of the vicinity imagined that spirits had something to do with it, and could not be induced to go near the place. The Burts also built the first water mill in Callaway county. Henry Burt died in 1823, leaving no family. John represented Callaway county in the Legislature four years, was Judge of the County Court seven years, and died in 1855. He married Bathsheba Fulkerson, of St. Charles Co., and they had nine children. Major George W. Burt served in the war of 1812, when he was only fifteen years of age, and was captured by the British. He married Erretta VanBibber, daughter of Major Isaac VanBibber, and great-granddaughter of Daniel Boone. When he asked the consent of her father to the marriage, the old gentleman replied in a loud tone of voice that he could have her if he wanted her, but she was a "contrary stick," and if he could do anything with her he was welcome to her; but he didn't want him to send her back on his hands. Major Burt gladly accepted the "contrary stick," and obtained a good wife by so doing. They prospered beyond their expectations, and accumulated a fortune. Major Burt was a money loaner for many years, but would never accept more interest than the law allowed him. He always paid every cent he owed, and collected all that was due him. He was a good man, and respected by the entire community where he lived. He died in March, 1876, in his 78th year, leaving a widow and one son, Huron. They also had a daughter, but she died many years ago. Major Burt was in poor health for about thirty years before his death, and his complaint often carried him apparently to the verge of the grave.

CRESS.—James Cress, of Virginia, married Judith Bybee, and they had one child, William C., who settled in Callaway county in 1833. He married Martha A. Thomas, and they had four sons and three daughters. Mrs. Cress died in 1858, and her husband afterward married Frances Gannaway. Mr. Cress owns the celebrated Boone Hays place in Callaway county.

CORDER. —Benjamin Corder, of Virginia, married Rebecca Runion, and they had—John, William, James, Ephraim, Elias, Polly, Susan, Hannah, Eliza, and Rebecca. James was married twice; first to Judith Murray, and second to Leah J. Hylton. He settled first in Benton county, Mo., and removed from there to Callaway in 1838.

COVINGTON.—Melchizedec Covington was born in North Carolina, and lost both of his parents when he was quite young, consequently he received but little attention from any one, and grew up without an education. When he was grown he went to Christian Co., Ky., where, in 1799, he married Catharine Suddith, who was born in Fairfax county, Va. In 1827 they loaded their effects into a little one-horse wagon, and with their seven children, came to Callaway county, Mo. They had $15 in money when they started, and when they arrived at the end of their journey had but 50 cents left. Mr. Covington rented some land and went to work, and then as he became able he entered land and obtained a home of his own. He raised thirteen children, six sons and seven daughters, and died at the age of 86 years.

CROWSON.—William Crowson and Mary Thomas, his wife, lived in East Tennessee. Their children were—Moses, John, Jacob, Abraham, Isaac, Thomas, Jonathan, Richard, Aaron, and Jane. Thomas married Jane Vinson, whose father, Daniel Vinson, came from Tennessee to Old Franklin, Howard county, in a keel-boat of his own construction. He was on the different rivers seven months. Mr. Crowson and his wife had fifteen children, twelve of whom are living, and the youngest is thirty-six years of age. Mr. Crowson was a very benevolent man, and sold corn on credit to all who were not able to pay the cash for it. When persons came with the money, he told them to go and buy of those who would not sell on credit to poor, suffering humanity.

CHICK.—The widow of Harding Chick, of Christian county, Ky., came to Callaway county, Mo., in 1830, with eight of her children, viz. : Elizabeth, Polly, Nancy, Fanny, Frank, Lucy, Adeline, and Joseph. She had six other children—Elijah, William, Harding, Asa, Alexander, and Amanda—who remained in Kentucky. Elizabeth Chick married Alexander Reade, and they had a son, named John, who settled Readesville. John was a small man, and he married Sarah Moxley, who was a very small woman. They built a small house, bought a small cow that had a small calf, and all their dogs, pigs, and chickens were small.

COLLINS.—William Collins, of Halifax county, Va., married Martha Isbell, and settled in Sumner county, Tennessee, where they had—Elizabeth, Thomas, George, Daniel, Nancy, William, Barba, Samuel, and Martha. Mr. Collins died, and in 1808 his widow and children removed to Christian county, Ky. Barba was a soldier of the war of 1812, and was at the battle of New Orleans. He married Martha Johns, and settled in Callaway county, Mo., in 1831, where they had twelve children. Mrs. Collins died, and he was married the second time to the widow of William Reade, whose maiden name was Polly Chick. She died also, and he was married the third time to the widow McMurtry, whose maiden name was Serena Hays, daughter of Boone Hays, and great-granddaughter of Daniel Boone. Mr. Collins had nine children by his three wives, and is a widower again, in his 83d year.

CURD.—Doctors Isaac and Thomas Curd, and their sister Catharine, were born in Albermarle county, Va. Dr. Isaac married Jane Watkins, and in 1824 he removed to Ross county, Ohio. In 1831 he came to Missouri and settled in Callaway county. His children were—Catharine, Martha, John, Thomas, Isaac, Edward, and two named Martha, both of whom died while infants. Catharine married Frank Diggs, John and Isaac live in St. Joseph, Mo., and Edward is a banker in Fulton.

CASON.—William Cason married Nancy Hawkins, of Kentucky, by whom he had—Hawkins, William, Larkin, and Benjamin. Hawkins settled in Callaway county in 1827, and died a bachelor. William married Sarah J. Overton, and settled in Callaway county in 1828. Larkin married Nancy Suggett, and settled in that county in 1831. Benjamin was married first to Mary J. Hawkins, who died in 1834, and he was married the second time to Ann E. Overton, who died in March, 1872. After her death he married the widow of Dr. Thomas Hardin, of Boone county.

CRUMP.—Richard Crump, of Virginia, was born in 1772, and was married in 1796 to Sarah Smith of that State. Their children were—Lucinda, Turner, Nancy, Richard W. S., America, Thompson S., Henry S., Sally, Mary F., James S., John H., Benedict, and Lydia A. Mr. Crump settled in Callaway county in 1820. America, his third daughter, was drowned in the Kentucky river in 1819. His sons all made fortunes, and are good and highly respected citizens.

CALLERSON.—Reuben Callerson, of Augusta county, Va., married Elizabeth Mitchell, and they settled first in Kentucky, from whence they removed to Missouri. Their children were—James, John, Robert, William, Elizabeth, Isabella, Dorothea, Nancy, Polly, Jane, Martha, Margaret, and Ann. Robert, Polly, Dorothea, and Isabella came to Missouri. James married Nancy Chick, by whom he had six children. John married a Miss Lockridge, and died leaving a widow and three children. William married Nancy Moore, by whom he had eleven children. Elizabeth married Andrew Hamilton, and they both died without issue. Nancy and Martha never married. Jane married John Board, and they had three children. Ann married a Mr. Gilmore, and is now a widow.

COIL.—Jacob and Elizabeth Coil were natives of Ireland, but came to America and settled in Bourbon Co., Ky., where they had—Solomon, Noah, John, George, Elizabeth, Elijah, Polly, and Margaret. Solomon and Noah settled in Callaway county in 1825. The former died in 1842 and the latter in 1843. Noah married Elizabeth Lail, by whom he had nine children. John Coil also settled in Callaway county, and married Dinah Bradford He died in 1865. Elijah married Lucinda Lail, and died in 1863. Elizabeth, Polly, and Margaret remained in Kentucky.

CULBERTSON.—Joseph Culbertson was born in Pennsylvania, but removed to Bourbon county, Ky. He was married first to Elizabeth Martin, by whom he had—Samuel, John, Joseph, Alexander, Robert, Patsey, and Polly. He was married the second time to a Miss McClannahan, by whom he had four children. Samuel, John, Robert, and Polly settled in Indiana. Patsey married and removed to Ohio. Joseph was married in 1829, to Sallie A. Griffin, of Kentucky, and settled in Callaway county, Mo., in 1832. Their children are—Joseph M., James A. G., Amanda J., Rosa E., Mary A., Sarah A., William T., and Samuel A.

CARTER.—Adam Carter, of Virginia, married Mary A. Roberts, and they had—Joseph R., Robert H., Elizabeth, William, and Creed C. Joseph and Robert remained in Virginia. Elizabeth married Gibson Goodrich, who settled in Callaway county in

1830. Their children were—Martha P., Abraham C., Joseph, Edwin, Robert, Mary, Rebecca, and Elizabeth. William Carter died in Arkansas. Creed C. married Mary Clansburg, in 1822, and in 1830 he settled in Callaway county. They had—Thomas A., Emily J., Mary C., Nancy E., Susan E., Ann M., Phœbe E., Amanda S., and Robert C.

CROOK.—John Crook, of Pennsylvania, married Elizabeth Deen, by whom he had seventeen children. His son John married Margaret Hughart, of Kentucky, and settled in Callaway county in 1834. His children were—Martha E., Trennvilla J., Elizabeth M., Letitia E., Mary C., Sophia M., and John. Mr. Crook and his wife lived together fifty-one years, and never had a quarrel; nor did he ever quarrel with one of his neighbors. He lived in Callaway county fifty years without going beyond its limits.

COONES.—Jacob Coones, of Virginia, married Lettie Kemper, by whom he had—Nancy, Henry, Jacob, and Joseph. Nancy married Robert Evans, and died in Kentucky. Henry married Nancy Evans, and settled in Callaway county in 1836. Their children were—John W., Isaac F., Joseph N., Louisiana J., Cynthia A., Nancy M., and Mary J. Mr. Coones and his wife were members of the Christian Church. Jacob Coones married Jane Howe, and settled in Callaway county in 1830. Their children were—Joseph W., John D., Cynthia J., Amanda, and Elizabeth. Joseph Coones married Lacretia I. Dalzell, and settled in Callaway county in 1836. They had—Thomas J., William H., Joseph W., Robert, Nancy A., Isaiah, and Martha.

CRAIGHEAD.—Robert M. and Isaiah Craighead were brothers, and they had a nephew named John who was a son of their brother John, of Virginia. Robert M. married Nancy Powell, and they had—William, Solomon, Robert, Jr., Jonathan, Stephen, Elizabeth, Mary, Sarah, and Nancy. They settled in Callaway county in 1819. Isaiah married Feminine Robinson, and settled in Callaway county in 1830. His children were—John R., George, James, Isaiah W., William A. B., Jane, and Nancy P. John R. married Sarah Hall, and they had—Isaiah O., John W., Mark A., James, Patrick H., Caroline, and Lucy J. John Craighead, the nephew of Robert and Isaiah, married Julia Smith, and settled in Callaway county in 1828.

COATS.—Rev. William Coats was born in South Carolina. When grown he removed to Smith county, Tennessee, where he married Nancy Baker, by whom he had—James, William, John, Wilson, Hiram, Lemuel B., Rachel, Frankie, Tabitha, Mahala, Nancy, and Laodocea. In 1817 Mr. Coats removed with his family to Callaway county, Mo., and settled on the prairie which has since borne his name. There was no minister in that part of the country at that time, and his neighbors appointed him to preach, which duty he performed at stated intervals until his death. He organized most of the Old Baptist Churches in that region. His son James married Polly Callaway, of Tennessee, by whom he had two children—Matthias S. and Laura A. William Coats, Jr., was married first to Patsey Tracy, and second to the widow McLaughlan, whose maiden name was Celia Callaway. John married Nancy Smith. He was Sheriff of Callaway county for several years, and was a good auctioneer. Wilson married a Miss Phillips, and moved to California. Hiram married Permelia Walker, and was afterward killed by lightning. Lemuel B. married Elizabeth Maddox. Rachel married Robert Reade, and is now a widow. Frankie married a Mr. McLaughlan. Tabitha married William Callaway. Nancy married Joseph P. Callaway. Laodocea married Daniel Phillips.

CALLAWAY.—Joseph Callaway, of South Carolina, married Polly Barrett, by whom he had—John, Nancy, Joseph, Jr., Polly, Elizabeth, William, Vinson, Cenia, and Thomas. Mr. Callaway removed to Tennessee in 1804, and in 1818 he settled on Coats' Prairie, in Callaway county. His sons John and Thomas served in the war of 1812. Thomas married Elizabeth Griffith, and settled on Crow Fork, a branch of Auxvasse creek. During the night of July 4, 1831, there came a very heavy rain, which raised the creek so that it washed away his stable and smoke house. He had a horse in the stable, which by some means, climbed into the loft, got out at the window and swam ashore. The smoke house contained some meat and a barrel of whisky, which Mr. Callaway succeeded in bringing ashore with a sugar trough, which he used as a canoe. Mr. Callaway died some time ago, but his widow is still living.

CROW.—Joseph Crow, of Nelson county, Ky., married Sarah Humphreys, and settled in Callaway county in 1819. His children were—John H., Rolly H., Joseph R., Mary, Elizabeth, Nancy, and Sarah A.

CHILDS.—Benjamin Childs, of Halifax county, Va., married Elizabeth Falkner, by whom he had—John H., William F., Henry, Samuel, Keziah, Nancy, and Mary. John H. married Mary Boyster and settled in Callaway caunty in 1835. His children are—William H., John D., Benjamin F., Samuel J., Henry C., Walter S., Nathaniel R., Elizabeth, Frances, Ann, and Saladay.

CURRY.—William Curry, of Ireland, married Sarah Bigun, emigrated to America, and settled first in Virginia, from whence he removed to Mercer county, Ky. They had—William, James, Robert, Samuel, John, Ann, Polly, and Jennie. John married Polly McCamly, of Kentucky, by whom he had—William, Rosana, Sarah, and Nancy. Mr. Curry settled in Callaway county in 1828. His son William married Mary Snell. Rosana married William Nasgal. Sally married Josiah Dixon. Nancy married

Justice Murphy.   All of the above are living in Callaway county.

CHEATHAM.—James Cheatham, of Kentucky, married Miss Turley, by whom he had—David C. and Turley, both of whom settled in Callaway county in 1834.   David C. married Amanda Rice.

CRESWELL.—James Creswell, of Ireland, married a Miss Mackennon, of Pennsylvania, and settled in Kentucky, where they had—Martha, Robert, William, George, Elizabeth, John, Sally A., Jane, and James.   Mr. Creswell and four of his children settled in Callaway county in 1827.   Robert Creswell, his son, settled in St. Charles county in 1818.   He was a carpenter and did the wood work on Colonel Nathan Boone's stone house, on Femme Osage creek.   He also assisted in making Daniel Boone's second coffin.   In 1819 he and his brother William removed to and settled in Callaway county.   Robert married Nancy Nevens, and William married Eliza Nichols.   George married Elizabeth Fitzhugh.   James married Jane Allen, and Jane married Singleton Shelby.

CALDWELL.—Robert Caldwell, of Scotland, was married in South Wales, emigrated to America, and settled in Pennsylvania, where he had a son, Robert, Jr., who married Mary Stephenson, and settled in Bourbon county, Ky.   His children were—James, Robert, William, John, Alexander, Thomas and Patsey.   Thomas married Eleanor Boyd, and settled in Callaway county in 1826. He established the pottery works there, now known as Pottersville.   His children were—Robert, Thomas, Jr., James, John, Newton, and Grizella.   Robert, brother of Thomas Caldwell, Sr., married Anna Avery, and settled in Callaway county in 1844.

CLATTERBUCK.—Reuben Clatterbuck, of Virginia, settled first in Shelby county, Ky., and removed from there to Callaway county, Mo., in 1826.   His children were—John, Leroy, James, Cageby, Richard, William, Nancy, and Caroline.   John married Martha Reynolds.   Leroy married Mary Gray.   James married Permelia Howard.   Cageby married Margaret Howard.   Richard married Anna Reynolds.   William married Caroline Laford. Nancy married Reuben Gerdon, and Caroline married George W. Griffin.   All of the above settled in Callaway and adjoining counties.

COONCE.- -This name was formerly spelled Kountz, but by agreement among the different members of the family the orthography has been changed to its present form.   Jacob Coonce, of Pennsylvania, settled in St. Charles county, Mo., in 1797.   He had—John, Jacob, George, Henry, Nicholas, Polly, Elizabeth, Eliza, Nancy, Harris, and Ibby.   John married Barbara Rudy, by whom he had—Abraham, Charlotte, George W., Maria, Euphemia, Rebecca, Elizabeth, and Edna.   Henry Coonce married Mahala Buckner, and settled in Callaway county in 1835.

Sarah married Samuel Maycock, who also settled in that county. Nicholas Coonce married Rebecca McConnell, and settled on the Booneslick road in St. Charles county, where he was killed by a fall from a horse. He hunted a great deal, and was not afraid of anything. It is said that he used to crawl into hollow trees and dens, where bears were hid, and feel of them to see if they were fat enough to kill.

CARRINGTON.—Samuel Carrington, of Montgomery county, Md., married Mildred McDaniel, and settled in Montgomery county, Ky. They had—Thomas, Randolph, Timothy, John, Samuel, Elizabeth, Susan, Sally, and Priscilla. Randolph married Catharine McGarey, and they had—William, John, Samuel, Randolph, Jr., Emily, Nancy, and Permelia. They settled in Callaway county in 1826. William Carrington was Judge of the County Court one term. He married Susan Fisher. John was married first to Eliza Randolph, and second to Nancy Hyton. Samuel married Lydia A. Bowen. Emily married John Martin. Nancy married Elisha Davis. Permelia married Hiram Holt. All of the above live in Callaway county.

CLANSBURY.—Thomas Clansbury married Catharine Brown, and their daughter Mary married Creed C. Carter. They also had a son, Thomas, Jr., whose children were Susan, Mary W., William H., John A., Martha, Virginia, Elizabeth, Robert and James, all of whom settled in Callaway county.

CRAIG.—One day, a great many years ago, as a ship was sailing from an Irish Port to America, a sailor named Toliver Craig fell overboard and was drowned. The next morning a boy baby was found on the deck of the vessel, with no one to claim him or take care him. The ship was loaded with emigrants, among whom were his parents, who doubtless felt too poor to assume the care of the little fellow in the new county to which they were going; so they took that method of throwing him upon the charities of the ship's crew. After some consultation it was decided to name the little waif for the lost sailor, and he was accordingly christened Toliver Craig. He grew to be a man, married and had a son, whom he also named Toliver. The latter also grew to man's estate, married, and had a son, whom he named Toliver, Jr. The latter married Elizabeth Johnson, of Virginia, and removed to Scott county, Ky., during the early settlement of that State. The Indians were very hostile at the time, and they lived three years in a fort. They had seven children—Jack, Elijah, William, Nathaniel, Mary, Nancy, and Toliver. Jack, Elijah, William, and Nancy married and lived in Tennessee. Nathaniel married Polly Ealey, and lived in Kentucky. They had— William, Nancy, Martha, Robert, Ann, and Mary, all of whom settled in Missouri. Toliver married Patsey Wright, an English lady, by whom he had—Elizabeth, Polly, Larkin, Permelia,

Catharine, Patsey W., Sally, Nathaniel, Margaret, Fannie, Carter
T., and John T.   Larkin married Fanny Ficklin, and settled in
Callaway county at an early date.   Catharine married her cousin,
Levi Craig, who died, and she afterward married Colonel Thomas
Smith, of St. Aubert, Callaway county.   Patsey W. married
Gideon Games, of Callaway county.   Nathaniel married Easter
L. McKinney.   Margaret married Samuel Craig, her cousin.
Fanny also married her cousin, Henry Craig, and lived in Boone
county.   Carter T. married Sally S. Games, and lives in Calla-
way county.   John T. married Adelia Berger, and settled in
Callaway county.

DAVIS.—Joseph Davis, of Georgia, settled in Callaway county
in 1834.   His wife's maiden name was Mary Boxley, and their
children were—Marion, Nancy, William, Joseph, John, Susan,
Jesse, Levi, Isaiah, and Margaret, all of whom, except Isaiah,
were married by Esquire William J. Jackson, at one dollar each.

DRISKALL.—Dennis Driskall and his wife, whose maiden name
was Thacker, were natives of Ireland, but came to America and
settled in Danville county, North Carolina.   They had—Timothy,
Dennis, Jr., David, Polly, and Sarah.   Mr. Driskall died, and his
widow and children removed to Franklin county, Ky., in 1805.
Dennis, Jr. was married in North Carolina, to Barbara Craft, by
whom he had—Jesse, John, William, David, Thomas, James H.,
Dennis, Frances, Elizabeth, and Sarah.   James H. was married
in Kentucky to Martha Wallace, and settled in St. Charles county,
Mo., in 1825, and the following year he removed to Callaway
county, where he and his wife are still living.   They had eight
children, three sons and five daughters.   Mr. Driskall is called
the *working man* of Callaway county, and by industry and economy has made a fortune.   He is a carpenter by trade, and built
the first Auxvasse Presbyterian Church.   It is related of him that
he once bought a yoke of oxen and some bacon in St. Charles
county, and conveyed the bacon home, a distance of sixty miles,
by tying it around the necks of the oxen with hickory withes.   Not
long afterward, while he was lying in bed one morning, he heard
the oxen jump the lot fence, and knowing they would go back where
they were raised, he sprang up and followed them, dressed only
in his shirt and drawers, without hat or boots.   He failed to head
them, but followed them to St. Charles county, and drove them
back home, performing the journey of one hundred and twenty
miles in twenty-four hours, and with nothing on but his shirt and
drawers.

DILLARD.—The parents of John Dillard were natives of Eng-
land.   He settled in Caroline county, Va., and married Lucy
Taliaferro, whose parents were natives of Ireland.   They had—
John T., Thomas, Mary, Isabella, William, Margaret, Franklin
E., and James D.   Thomas was a surgeon in the United States

army, and lived and died in Philadelphia. John T. married Margaret Steele, of Missouri, and settled in Callaway county in 1832. Mary married John Waller, of Kentucky, who settled in Callaway county in 1831. Isabella married John French, who settled in Callaway county in 1821. William was a physician, and was married first to Martha Hockaday, of Kentucky, and settled in Callaway county in 1832. After the death of his first wife he married Elizabeth Hughes. Margaret married James Hockaday, of Kentucky, who settled in Callaway county in 1831. Franklin E. also was a physician. He was married first to Ann Bernard, who died, and he then married her sister. He settled in Callaway county in 1833. James D. married Sally A. French, and settled in Callaway county in 1833. The members of the Dillard family are distinguished for their social qualities, intelligence, hospitality, and polite manners. They possess good business qualifications and are excellent citizens.

DULEY.—James Duley married Devola Shields, of Montgomery county, Md., and settled in Scott county, Ky., in 1799. They had—Enoch, Nathaniel, Alexander, Susan, Devola, and Nancy. Nathaniel was a soldier of the war of 1812. He married his cousin, Sarah Duley, and settled in Indiana, from whence he removed to Callaway county, Mo., in 1821, and settled on the bank of the Missouri river, where he died July 11, 1832. His widow died July 10, 1843. They had—Paul H., Ferdinand C., John S., Margaret T., Samuel M., George W., Enoch C., William M., and Milton D. Paul H. was married first to the widow of Samuel B. Long, whose maiden name was Harriet Burnett, by whom he had two daughters. After her death he married the widow of Thomas Kelley, whose maiden name was Malinda Ellis. Ferdinand C. and John S. died when they were about grown. Margaret T. married Thomas Jones, and died soon after. Samuel M. was married first to Sarah Emmett, and second to Mary Wilkerson. He had three sons and three daughters by his last wife. George W. married Amanda Wilkerson, and they had one son and one daughter. Enoch C. married Minerva Wilkerson, and died, leaving a widow and two daughters. William M. married Amanda Dozier, and they had three sons and one daughter. Milton D. died in Mexico in 1847, while serving as a soldier in the war between that country and the United States. Paul H., Enoch C., William M., and Milton D. were all soldiers in the Mexican war. Thomas Duley, a brother of Nathaniel Duley's wife, settled in Callaway county in 1817, and died in 1830. He took a great deal of interest in politics, and in order to keep himself informed in regard to public affairs, etc., he subscribed for the *Missouri Republican* in 1817, and continued his subscription until his death, when his nephew, Paul H., assumed it and still takes and reads the paper.

DAY.—Thomas Day, who was born in Virginia, removed to Kentucky and married Mary Sanders, by whom he had— Louis T., William, Ackley, Sanders, Polly, Milley, Elizabeth, Truman, and Charles A. Mr. Day was married the second time to Catharine Williams, and by her had— Fanny, Rebecca, Martha, Middleton, and Dudley. Louis T. married Catharine McIntire, and settled in Callaway county in 1831. Ackley married Sally Fowler, and settled in Callaway county in 1830. Milley married Garret Davis, who settled in Callaway county in 1828. Charles A. settled in Callaway county in 1830. He was married first to Anna Speed, and second to her sister, Dinah Speed. He died in 1850, leaving two children. Mr. Day was the founder of the town of Portland, on the Missouri river.

DAWSON.—Elijah Dawson, of Nelson county, Va., married a Miss Gentry, and had—Robert, Martin, Elizabeth, and James. He was married the second time to Judith Gilliam, by whom he had—Achilles G., Mary, Samuel, and Judith. Most of his children live in Callaway county.

DYER.—Samuel Dyer was born in Bristol, England, and came to America when he was fourteen years of age, with a merchant named Breckenridge, to whom he was bound. When the revolutionary war began Breckenridge returned to England, but young Dyer enlisted in the American army and became a commissioned officer. After the war he settled in Albemarle county, Va., and married Celia Brickley, of Hanover county, by whom he had— William H., Samuel, John, Ann, Frank B., Eliza, and Robert. William H. married Margaret Bridie, of Richmond, Va., and settled in Callaway county, Mo., in 1827. Their children were— Alexander B., Eliza A., Margaret, William F., Randolph H., George M., Celia B., John N., Isaac C., and Henry. Samuel married a Miss Watkins, of Goochland county, Va., and settled in Callaway county in 1821. He was the second merchant in the town of Fulton. His children were—Thomas B., Mary J., Martha, Samuel R., Virginia, Edward B., Eliza, and Susan. John Dyer married Evilena Warren, of Missouri, and settled in Callaway county in 1822. His children were—Sarah, Helen, Emily, Samuel W., Israel G., Mary, and Ann. Ann Dyer, daughter of Samuel Dyer, Sr., married George Robinson, of Richmond, Va., who settled in St. Louis, Mo., in 1828. Frank B. and Eliza lived in Virginia. Robert married Sarah A. Morris, of Augusta county, Va., and settled in Callaway county in 1850. His children were—Catharine E., Frank M., Ann M., Robert, Thomas W., and Samuel.

DULIN.—Thaddeus Dulin, of Loudon county, Va., married Elizabeth Powell, and they had—John, Edward, James, Nancy, Sally, Fanny, Winifred, Susan, and Lydia. Most of the children came with their parents to Kentucky at an early date. Edward married Mary Gordon, and they had—Thaddeus, Sally, William, Thomas, Elizabeth, Fanny, John, Richard, Nancy, and Lydia. Thomas settled in St Charles county, Mo., in 1819, and married Mary Lyle, by whom he had two sons and four daughters. He was married the second time to a widow, whose maiden name was Maria Hill. He removed to Callaway county in 1831. Richard settled in St. Louis. He was married twice. Thaddeus settled in St. Charles county.

DUNCAN.—Roger and John Duncan were sons of Roger Duncan, Sr., of Scotland. The two brothers came to America and settled in Bourbon county, Ky. John married Elizabeth Wam, by whom he had—Thomas, John, Jr., Alexander, David, William, Ann, and Mary. He subsequently removed to Callaway county, Mo. Roger, Jr., married Sally Rodman, and remained in Bourbon county, Ky. Their children were—John, Thomas, George, Polly A., and Amanda. John married Sally J. Adair, and settled in Callaway county in 1833. His children were Eveline, George T., Angeline, Anna A., Joseph W., and Mary E. Mr. Duncan was married the second time to Nancy Loid, by whom he had—John, Hiram J., Polly J., Solomon R., Susan, Nimrod N., Benjamin R., and Nancy F.

DUNCAN.—David Duncan, of Scotland, came to America with his wife, and remained some time in Boston, after which they removed to Mercer county, Ky. They had nine children. Mrs. Duncan died, after which he married again and had eleven children more. William, the eldest son by his first wife, married Elizabeth Henderson, of Kentucky, and settled in Callaway county in 1826. His children were—Alfred R., Joshua M., William G., Nancy M., Amanda E., and Elizabeth J.

DUNCAN.—Joseph C. Duncan, of Buckingham county, Va., was of Scotch descent. He married Nancy Maddox, and settled in Christian county, Ky., in 1817. In 1829 he removed to Missouri and settled in Callaway county, where he lived the rest of his life. His wife died in 1860, and he died in 1870. They had nine children, but two of them died before they were grown. The names of the other children were—Elizabeth A., Frederick W., Ouslow G., Jerome B., Artinicia, Merrett B., and Edward. Elizabeth A. married John McMahan, and is now a widow. Frederick W. lives in Oregon. Ouslow G. married Julia A. Broadwater, and lives in Audrain county. Jerome B. married Mary George. Artinicia married Colonel Marshall S. Coats, of Coats' Prairie. Merrett B. married Mary E. Berkett. He is a prominent banker of Mexico, Mo. Edward married Martha McMahan, and lives in Monroe county. Joel and Richard were the two who died before they were grown.

DUNLAP.—Robert and David Dunlap were born in Ireland, but

came to America with their parents when they were small boys, and settled in North Carolina. Robert was born February 26, 1763, and at the age of twenty-five years he was married to Elizabeth Wile, of North Carolina, by whom he had—John, David M., Robert, Thomas, Eliza, and Elizabeth S. In 1801 he removed to Bath county, Ky., and in 1821 he and his brother David removed to Missouri and settled in Callaway county. In 1825 they settled where Fulton now stands, and Robert Dunlap gave the name to the town, which for a number of years was called *Bob Fulton* on his account. He died in 1848, his wife having died in 1834. John Dunlap married Elizabeth Gudgell, and they had two children, Robert and Jane. The former was killed in the Florida war, and the latter married Milton V. Davis, of Callaway county. David M., son of Robert Dunlap, Sr., married Polly Gudgell, of Kentucky, by whom he had—Elizabeth, Andrew, Thomas, Jane, Robert A., James, and Mary. Robert and Eliza, children of Robert Dunlap, Sr., died in childhood, and Thomas died when he was twenty-three years of age. James married Sally S. Crump, of Missouri. Elizabeth married Solomon Craighead. David, brother of Robert Dunlap, Sr., taught the first school in Fulton. He had but one leg, and supplied the place of the lost member with an old-fashioned wooden peg-leg. He married and had one daughter, and died of cholera, at Portland, in 1840. The citizens of the place had such a dread of the disease that they buried him as soon as he was dead, in the dress he had on at the time. It was ascertained soon afterward that he had $2,800 in a pocket in his undershirt, and two or three of the boldest citizens ventured to take the body up and get the money.

DARBY.—Basil Darby, son of George Darby, of England, married Rebecca Allnut, of Maryland, by whom he had—Samuel, Thomas, George, Jane, and Ann. Samuel married Jane Viers, and settled in Callaway county in 1840, where he died in 1869, in his 76th year; his widow still survives. They had two sons and eight daughters.

DAVIS.—James, Harrison, Benjamin, and Robert Davis were sons of James Davis, of Pennsylvania. Robert married Devora Hornbuckle, and settled in Callaway county in 1819. His children were—William, Emeline, James M., Thomas, Julia A., Susan, Jane H.; Amanda C., Rufus, Martha, Nancy, Elizabeth, and Sarah A. Thomas Davis married Nancy Gee, daughter of John Gee, of England, and Elizabeth Pugh, of Tennessee, who settled in Callaway county in 1822. The children of John Gee were—Nancy, Silas, Elizabeth, Emeline, Willoughby, and John J.

DAVIS.—Richard Davis, of Halifax county, Va., married Polly White, and they had—Thomas, Henry, William, John, and Daniel. William married Elizabeth Mulberry, and they had—James,

Elizabeth, Catharine, and John. James was a soldier of the war of 1812. He married his cousin, Frances Davis, and settled in Callaway county in 1826. They had—John W., George W., Richard A., James H., Cynthia E., Martha J., Delila, Polly, Elizabeth F., and Mary F.

DAVIS.—Richard Davis was a revolutionary soldier. He married Priscilla Coe, of Maryland, and they had—Matthew, Catharine, Eli, James, Elizabeth, William, John, Presley, Richard, and Alexander. Matthew married Elizabeth King, and settled in Callaway county in 1829. Jane married Baylis Reno, who set-settled in Callaway county in 1831. Elizabeth married Robert Randolph, who settled in Callaway county in 1833. William married Mary Randolph, and settled in Callaway county in 1830. John married Malinda Lutrell, and settled in Callaway county in 1837. Garret Davis, son of Eli, married Milley Day, and settled in Callaway county in 1826.

DOZIER.—Zachariah Dozier, of Pennsylvania, married Susan Evans, and they had—John, Evans, William, Thomas, and Zachariah, Jr. William married Sally Combs, of Kentucky, and settled in Callaway county in 1830.

DOUGHERTY.—Charles Dougherty, of Ireland, settled first in Baltimore, Md., and removed to Callaway county, Mo., in 1817. His children were—Hugh, John, Matthew, and Nancy. Hugh married Hannah Doyle, and they had eleven children. John married Elizabeth Hudson, and Nancy married William Wallace. They all live in Callaway county.

EVANS.—Benjamin Evans, of Charlotte county, Va., had a son named Larry B., who married Elizabeth Covington, of Halifax county, and settled in Callaway Co., Mo., in 1834. He died in 1851, leaving a widow, six daughters and an infant son in very poor circumstances. Mrs. Evans was an excellent tailor, and was the only person in that part of the county who could make fine clothing for gentlemen. She carried on the business before her husband's death, and continued it with success after his decease. She and her daughters also cultivated their farm, and did the work as well as it could have been done by men. Mrs. Evans is an excellent lady, and deserves great credit for her energy and industry.

ELLIS.—The parents of John, Abraham, Peter, and William Ellis were natives of England. The four brothers came to America and settled in Fauquier county, Va. Peter and Abraham came to Missouri in 1808, and settled first in St. Louis county. Abraham was in the war of 1812. He was married first to a Miss Lee, and second to Mary Trussell, of Tennessee. By his two wives he had—Elizabeth, Jane, Polly, Peter, Ellen, Isabella, Mary, Rosa A., John, James, Cynthia A., Malinda J., Barbara L., William, Amanda R., and one other that died in childhood.   Mr. Ellis was a member of the Methodist Church, and the first camp-meeting in Callaway county was held on his land, and for many years afterward camp-meetings were held there regularly.   Religious services were also held in private houses, and Mr. Ellis was generally selected to announce the next appointment, which he would do from the top of a stump, in a loud voice, and then would add, "Bring along your guns and dogs, and make as big a show as you can."   Peter Ellis settled in Boone county.

EVERHART.—Jacob Everhart was of German parentage.   He lived in Loudon county, Va., and his wife was Ann Waltman, a daughter of Jacob Waltman.   They had—Jacob, John, Joseph, and Sarah.   Jacob married Sarah Stuck, and they had one child, a daughter.   John was married twice, the name of his first wife being Sarah Prince.   Sarah married Henry Bruce.   Joseph was married in 1826, to Lydia Stuck, and they had—James L. and Jacob E.   Mrs. Everhart died in 1830, and her husband subsequently married Ann C. Deaver, by whom he had—Jesse D., Joseph V., Margaret A., Martha, Virginia, Catharine, John, and William B.   Mr. Everhart settled in Callaway county in 1834.   He was married the third time to the widow of William Dyson, whose maiden name was Lucinda Davis.   She was also married three times, her first husband being a Mr. Wren.

ESTENS.—James and John Estens settled in Callaway county in 1815.   They lived for two years on wild meat, without salt or bread.   They were said to be the first American settlers within the present limits of Callaway county.

EWING.—Patrick Ewing, of Ireland, settled in Maryland, where he married a Miss Patton, by whom he had—Joshua, Robert, Putnam, Samuel, Polly, Eleanor, Catharine, and William.   Mr. Ewing's first wife died, and he was married the second time to a Miss Potter, by whom he had Patrick and Elizabeth.   William settled within the present limits of Missouri while it was a Spanish province.   Joshua married Rachel George, of Pennsylvania, and settled in Lee county, Va., where they had—Robert, Patrick, Joshua, Jr., James P., Samuel, William, David C., Jesse, Margaret, Eliza S., and Polly.   Patrick, who was born in Lee county, Va., in 1792, served as soldier in the first part of the war of 1812, and in 1814 he came to Missouri and located in Darst's Bottom, St. Charles county, where he taught school for some time.   He afterward married Nancy Darst, and settled in Callaway county in 1817.   He became the second Sheriff of that county, and was Captain of a company in the Black Hawk war.   He was married the second time to Mrs. Fisher, whose maiden name was Ann Eliza Ratakin.   By his first wife he had—David D., Joshua, Jesse, Rosetta H., Rachel C., Elizabeth, Jane, Mary, and Margaret.   James Ewing, brother of Patrick, married Belinda Neil, and settled in Callaway county in 1820. Samuel married Selena Beatty, and settled in Callaway county in 1835.

ELEY.—Edward Eley, of Culpepper county, Va., had a son named Henry, who married Mary James, by whom he had—Mary, Catharine, Benjamin F., George, James, Harriet, and Sally. He was married the second time to the widow Simms, who also died, and he was married the third time to Sally Fitzhugh. Mr. Eley settled in Callaway county in 1835.

EVANS.—Major Jesse Evans, of Wythe county, Va., was married twice. His children were—John, Joseph, George, Jane, and Nancy. He came to Missouri in 1816, and settled in Cotesansdessein, Callaway county. His son John married Sally Newell, of Virginia, and settled in Callaway county in 1817. Joseph married Elizabeth Smith, of Virginia, and settled in Callaway county the same year his father did. Jane married Thomas Farmer, who settled in Callaway county in 1817. Nancy married Colonel George King, of Virginia, and settled in Callaway county in 1817. George married Hannah Pritchett, and settled in Callaway county in 1818.

FRENCH.—William and Simon French were brothers, and lived in South Carolina. William died, leaving a widow and seven children, viz.: Hugh, John, Jane, Sally, Hannah, Mary, and Susan. The widow and her children removed to Warren county, East Tennessee, in 1795. Her son Hugh married his cousin, Sally French, of Christian county, Ky., and settled in Boone county, Mo., in 1820. His children were—Simon L., William H., John N., Caroline M., Mary J., Susan A., Sarah J., and Emily E. John French settled in Callaway Co., Mo., in 1820. He was married first to Jane Clark, of Montgomery county, by whom he had—William H., Bryant, Milton, and Sally A. His second wife was Isabella Dillard, by whom he had—Hugh, Thomas and Lucy. Jane French married John Dutton. Sally married Joseph Elledge. Hannah married Samuel Cox. Mary married Isaac Clark, of Montgomery county. Susan married Samuel McRunnels. Simon French, Sr., settled in Christian county, Ky. His children were—Lewis, Pinckney, Andrew J., William N., Isaac C., Sally, Susan, and Mary A. Lewis married Louisa Simpson, of Montgomery county, Mo., and settled in Callaway county in 1821. Pinckney was married first to Devonia Clark, of Christian county, Kentucky, and settled in Callaway county, Missouri in 1836. They had—Henry, Isaac, Edward, and William. After the death of his first wife, Mr. French married Elizabeth Jones, of Christian county, Ky., and they had Albert and Virginia. Andrew J. French married Sally Towley. William N. married Comfort E. Parks. Isaac married Nancy Monroe. The three last mentioned all settled in Morgan county, Mo. Sally married her cousin, Hugh French. Susan married

Enoch French, of Morgan county, Mo. Mary A. married Bell Mure, of Christian county, Ky.

FOXWORTHY.—William Foxworthy, of Prince William county, Va., was a soldier of the revolutionary war. His children were—William, Samuel, John, Thomas, Alexander, Sally, Lilly, and Harriet. William was a soldier in war of 1812. He married Elizabeth Hesler, of Pennsylvania, and they had—Alexander, Joseph, John, Isabella, Clarissa, and Sarah. Mr. Foxworthy settled in Callaway county, Mo., in 1836, and was subsequently killed by a horse. His widow removed to California when she was 75 years of age. Alexander married Emily Bryan, of Kentucky, and they had four sons and four daughters. John married Mary Burt. Isabella married William H. Wilson. Clarissa married Galbreth Wilson. Joseph and Sarah reside in California.

FREEMAN.—John Freeman was an orphan Irish boy, and was raised in South Carolina. When he was grown he settled in Kentucky, where he married Nancy Lenox. In 1832 they came to Missouri and settled in Callaway county. Their children were—John, Thomas, Michael, David, Harvey, William, Mary, Jemima, Lucretia, Pernina, Mahala, Arnetha, Lourena, Elizabeth, and two that died in childhood. Mary married Thomas Moxley. Jemima married James Boyce. Lucretia was married first to Frank Drinkard, and second to a Mr. Blessing. Pernina married Allen Ticer. Lourena married Handy Moxley. Mahala married David Cross. Arnetha married Charles Cravens. John, Thomas, Michael, Harvey and Jemima lived and died in Callaway county.

FRUITE.—Enoch and Alexander Fruite settled in Callaway county in February, 1819. They were raised in Christian county, Ky., and lived several years in Howard county, Mo., before they settled in Callaway. Aleck Fruite lived on Nine Mile Prairie, and was the first postmaster in that part of the county. He was a hunter and trapper, and devoted most of his time to those occupations. His stock of fire wood gave out once, during a very cold spell of weather, and he and his family had a good prospect of freezing before them, until a bright idea struck him. He took down the wooden chimney of his cabin, hung a blanket across the fire place, and then built a fire of the sticks of his dismantled chimney in the middle of his cabin, the smoke ascending through the roof. By this means they kept from freezing until the weather moderated. Mr. Fruite was opposed to slavery, being what was then called an Abolitionist, and in 1832 he removed to Illinois, so he could live in a free State. Enoch Fruite also settled on Nine Mile Prairie, and devoted the principal part of his time to hunting and trapping. He was elected a Justice of the Peace, and became an influential citizen of the county. He finally sold out and removed to Monroe county. Some time afterward he had occasion to visit his old neighborhood, and while crossing the prairies in Audrain county, on his way to Callaway, he caught four young wolves, and carried them in his saddle bags to the house of William B. Douglass, whose wife kept them for him, in a chicken coop, until he returned home. The scalps of those wolves paid his taxes for two years.

FITZHUGH.—John Fitzhugh was a soldier of the revolutionary war. His youngest son, Alexander C., married Nancy Cason, and settled in Pike county, Mo., in 1823. Their children were— John, Thomas, Sarah, Lucy, Ann, Elizabeth, Hart, Mary, Permelia, and Frances, most of whom married and settled in Callaway county.

FISHER.—William Fisher, of Virginia, married Susan Peck, and they had—Thomas, James, Elizabeth, William, Joseph, Richard, Margaret, Charles W., and Mary. Thomas married Isabella Humphreys, of Virginia, and settled in St. Charles county, Mo., in 1819, and the following year he removed to Callaway county. His children were—Mary J., William H., Susan, Isabella, and Elizabeth. Joseph Fisher married Mary Craighead, and settled in Callaway county in 1826. His children were— William R., Charles P., Mary J., Elizabeth G., James M., Richard B., Joseph S., Sarah M., Catharine F. V., and Cordelia A. William Fisher, Jr., settled in St. Louis. The members of the Fisher family are nearly all zealous Methodists.

FERRIER.—Nathaniel Ferrier, of East Tennessee, settled in Callaway county in 1817. His two sons, Thomas and Samuel, and his nephew Thomas (better known as "Long Tom") came with him from Tennessee. Thomas, the son of Nathaniel Ferrier, married the widow of James H. Goodrich. Samuel married Alice Shannon, daughter of James Shannon, who was the first settler on Hancock's Prairie, in Callaway county. Mr. Shannon was a Catholic, and donated four acres of land to his church, upon which he also built a house of worship. He was a native of Ireland, where he married. After his marriage he decided to emigrate to America, but being too poor to bring his wife, he came over by himself, and after he had made money enough he sent for her. He met her in St. Louis, where they celebrated the event by drinking liberal draughts of the liquid which elevates the soul and makes the spirit glad. They drank a little too much, and began to quarrel about the time they were married, one claiming that is was during a certain year, and the other that it was altogether a different year. Being unable to agree, they decided to settle the matter by getting married again; so they repaired to a convenient priest and were soon made one again. Samuel Ferrier, in his old age, removed to Washington Territory, and soon afterward wrote a glowing letter back to his cousin, Long Tom Ferrier, who was then about eighty years old, telling him that deer, bears, and bee trees were abundant out there. Long Tom was so captivated by the description that he shouldered his gun the next day after the receipt of the letter, and, with his dogs following at his heels, started for the distant land of promise, on foot.

FERGUSON.—John Ferguson, of Virginia, whose father was a sea captain, married Frances Lucas, and settled in Callaway county in 1820. They had—Moses, Ann, John, Sarah, Nancy, Swan, Napoleon, and Mary. Moses married Jane Pew, and settled in Callaway county in 1824. Ann married Arthur Neal, who settled in that county in 1820. John married Peggy Pew, and settled in Callaway county in 1820. Sarah married Braddock Beasley, who settled in Callaway county in 1833. Nancy married Henry Neal, who settled in Callaway county in 1820. Major Swan Ferguson was born in Virginia in 1796. He married Jane Holloway, and settled in Cotesandessein, Callaway county, in 1820. He purchased a farm and lived upon it forty-six years, and raised and educated seven children, six of whom are living. On a certain occasion, as he was returning from Santa Fe, New Mexico, he was surrounded by Indians, but cut his way through them and escaped in the midst of a shower of arrows. Major Ferguson is now in his 80th year, and lives with his son-in-law, Colonel C. W. Samuels, who was formerly a member of the Legislature, and is now a merchant at Cedar City. Napoleon Ferguson married Elizabeth Allen, and settled in Callaway county in 1820. Mary married Milton Cleveland, who settled in Callaway county in 1820.

FOSTER.—Richard Foster, of Prince Edward county, Va., had a son named James, who married Eliza Taylor, by whom he had—George, William, Philip, Louisa, Ann, Eliza, Judith, Edmonia, and John J. The latter married Sarah Gilcrease, of Virginia, by whom he had—George and William. Mr. Foster settled in Callaway county in 1837.

FERGUSON.—Joshua Ferguson, of Fairfax county, Va., was a wagon master in the revolutionary war. After the close of the war he settled in Kentucky, where he married Mary Stone, by whom he had—John S., William, James, Polly, Sally, Nancy, Elizabeth, and Rachel. Mr. Ferguson came to Missouri and settled in Callaway county in 1817. His son, John S., married Mary Jones, of Kentucky, and settled in Callaway county the same year his father did. He had fifteen children, twelve of whom lived to be grown, viz.: Thomas J., Elizabeth, John R., William S., Joshua, J., Sarah, Marion, Louisa, Nancy, Emma, Jane, and Lucy. Joshua and Thomas built the first court house at Fulton, in 1826, for which they received $1,300. Such a house could not be built now for less than four or five thousand dollars. James Ferguson married Mary A. McGruder, of Kentucky, and settled in Callaway county in 1817. Rebecca married Dennis Askrens, who settled in Callaway county in 1817. Nancy married George Hirsch, who settled in Callaway county in 1823.

GALBRETH.—Torcai Galbreth, of North Carolina, married a Miss Calvin, and settled in Callaway county in 1819. They had— Neal, Catharine, Isabella, Mary, and Elizabeth. Neal died unmarried. Catharine died at the age of seventy years. She never married. Isabella married Robert Graham. Mary married her cousin, Daniel Galbreth. Elizabeth also married her cousin, James Galbreth. She was married the second time to Newton Carpenter. Torcal Galbreth was married the second time to Catharine Graham, and they had—Agnes, John, Daniel, Sally A., Margaret, and James.

GLENDY.—John and William Glendy, of Scotland, came to America at an early date, and in 1796 John was a Presbyterian minister in the city of Philadelphia. William was married twice, his second wife being Anna Robinson, of Augusta county, Va. They had— John, David, Samuel, Thomas, William, Jr., Robert, and Mary. Samuel married Mary Shields, and settled in Callaway county, Mo., in 1829. Thomas married Ellen Shields, and settled in that county the same year. Samuel is a politician, and very few persons can out-talk him.

GRANT.—Israel Grant, of Scott county, Ky., married Susan Bryan, a daughter of James Bryan, and niece of Daniel Boone's wife. They had three children—James, William, and Israel B. Mr. Grant died when his youngest son was quite small, and James the elder, educated his brothers from the proceeds of their father's farm. When Israel B. was fifteen years of age he came to Missouri with his uncle, Jonathan Bryan, and taught school one year, when he returned Kentucky, and began the study of medicine. But he soon grew tired of medicine, and bound himself to a silver smith at Lexington, Ky., to learn that trade, his term of apprenticeship to last five years. After the expiration of his apprenticeship he came to St. Louis, Mo., and worked at his trade five years in that city. He then paid a visit· to his uncle, Jonathan Bryan, who persuaded him to quit his trade and go to farming. He accompanied his nephew to Callaway county, where the latter entered a tract of land, and then returned to Kentucky, where, on the 28th of March, 1820, he was married to Letitia Warren. He brought his bride to her new home in Callaway county the same spring. Mr. Grant was elected County Judge several times, and served two terms in the State Legislature. During Christmas of 1835, he was killed by two of his negro slaves, as he was returning from Fulton, where he had gone to collect some money. One of the negroes was named Jacob. They were both hanged, and Jacob's skeleton remained in a doctor's office in Danville for many years. James Grant was married twice; first to a Miss Easton, and second to Sally Hunt. He settled in Callaway county in 1823, where he became an influential citizen, and represented the county in the Legislature one term. He was also Judge of the County Court for some time. He subsequently removed to the southwestern part of the State, and settled on the Neosho river, where he died. William Grant enlisted as a private soldier in the war of 1812, and was soon afterward promoted for gallantry to the rank of Lieutenant. He was killed at the disastrous battle known as Dudley's Defeat, under the following circumstances. After the defeat and capture of the American forces, they were driven under guard into an enclosure, where the Indians at once began to rob them of their money, watches, etc. Grant still had his sword, which had not been taken from him, and was standing with it in his hand, conversing with a friend, Captain Micajah McClenny, when an Indian came up and demanded the weapon. Grant turned to McClenny and said, "They will kill us anyhow, and I intend to sell my life as dearly as possible," and dropping the point of his sword to the level of the Indian's breast he plunged it through his body to the hilt, killing him in his tracks. The next instant Grant's body was pierced with a hundred rifle balls, and he fell dead at the feet of his friend. McClenny was not hurt, but was afterward exchanged and lived to be an old man. Grant was married before he entered the army, to Miss Mosbey, and they had a son named William, Jr., generally known as Captain Billy Grant. He was married in 1820, to Sally A. Warren, of Kentucky, and settled in Callaway county, Mo., the following year. His house was the first one in Callaway county that had glass windows and a staircase, and people came twenty and thirty miles to look at it. The names of Captain Grant's children were—Thomas W., James E., Samuel, Sally W., Mary L., Agnes, Elizabeth, Eveline H., and Martha. Captain Grant died in 1849, and his widow in 1875. Sally W. married Joseph I. Grant, a son of Samuel M. Grant, and they settled in Callaway county in 1834. Mrs. Grant died in 1875. Israel Boone Grant, who was known as Licking Grant, because he came from Licking river, Ky., was a son of Squire B. Grant and Susan Hand. He settled in Fulton, Callaway county, and was County Clerk for twenty-one years. The names of Mr. Grant's children were—James, Moses, Robert, William T., John, Agnes, Martha, and Mary.

GILBERT.—The children of Michael Gilbert, of Franklin county, Va., were—Kimwell, Preston, James, and Michael, Jr. Kimwell married Mary Smith, and settled in Callaway county in 1834. Michael, Jr., was married first to Elizabeth Ashworth, and second to Elizabeth Kemp. He also settled in Callaway county.

GOODRICH.—Benjamin and James Goodrich, sons of James Goodrich, Sr., of Tennessee, settled on Coats' Prairie, in Callaway county, in 1817. They built a horse mill and a distillery soon after they settled there. James was married in Tennessee, to Patsey Taylor, and they had—Thomas, Joseph, Mary, Sarah, Elizabeth and Ellen. His first wife died, and he was married again to Charity Phillips, who is the oldest white person living that was born in Callaway county. They had—James H., Martha, Matilda, and John B. Mr. Goodrich was one of the first grand jurymen of Callaway county, and he donated the ground upon which the Baptist church called Salem was built.

GILMAN.—William Gilman, of Virginia, married Mary Mann, and settled in Kentucky, where he had—George, William J., Elizabeth, Lucy, and Emily. George married Sallie Glazebrook, and settled in Callaway county in 1825. William J. (Dr. Gilman) married Laricia Callaway, and settled in Callaway county in 1829. Emily married John Gibner, who settled in Callaway in 1825.

GLOVER.—Robert Glover, of Virginia, married Omon Jones, and they had Jesse and Creed. Jesse was married first to Eliza Anderson, and second to Susan Williams, and settled in Callway county in 1832. He was a soldier of the war of 1812. Peter and Robert Glover settled in Callaway county in 1827. The former was Secretary of State one term. He married Patsey Mosley. Robert married Patsey Anderson.

GATHRIGHT.—William Gathright, of Virginia, had a son William who married Jane Woodson, by whom he had—Benjamin, Matthew W., William, Jr., Thomas M., John S., Malinda, Elizabeth, and Jane A. Matthew W. married Mary J. Withens, of Virginia, and settled in Callaway county in 1831. His children were—James W., William B., Matthew W., Jr., John T. Jane A., Malinda, and Mary E.

GRAY.—Alexander Gray, of Scotland, married Elizabeth Fitzhugh, and settled in Halifax county, Va. Their children were—James, John, Alexander, Robert, George, Henry, Elizabeth, Mary, and Sally. George was married in 1799, to Fannie Brooks, of Virginia, and settled in Callaway county in 1823. His children were—John B., Alexander, George W., Martha, Elizabeth, Rachel, Polly, Fannie, and Anna, all of whom were born in Virginia, but settled in Callaway county with their parents.

GILMORE.—Thomas Gilmore, of Kentucky, settled in St. Charles county, Mo., in 1808. He was a ranger in Captain Callaway's company during the Indian war, and after its close he settled at a noted place, which has since been known as Gilmore's Springs, in the western part of St. Charles county. He married India Ramsey, daughter of Captain William Ramsey, and they had—William, Thomas, Robert, Nathan, Ephraim, and John, all of whom, except Thomas, who was killed at Callaway's defeat, settled in Callaway county from 1826 to 1830.

GARRETT.—Richard Garrett was a soldier of the war of 1812.

He married Nancy Weare, of Richmond, Va., by whom he had—James,.John W., Nancy, Frances, and Agnes.   James first set-tled in Warren county, Ky., where he married a daughter of Joseph Lect, a soldier of the war of 1812, and removed to Calla-way county, Mo., in 1832.   They had—Sarah, Mary V., Mar-garet H., Nancy, Lucretia, Francis M., Lucy A., Amanda J., James T., and John P.

GARRETT.—Stephen Garrett, a Frenchman, settled in Bucking-ham county, Va.   His children were—Stephen, John, David, Eli-jah, William, Mary, and Elizabeth.   William married Mary Cole-man, of Virginia, by whom he had—Spillsberry, James, William B., Stephen, Reuben, John, Elijah, Coleman, Magdalene, Lucy, and Mary. Spillsberry married Biddie Hockett, and settled in Ralls county, where he died.   James married Nancy Brown, and set-tled in Tennessee.   William B. was born in Buckingham county, November 1, 1795.   When the war of 1812 began he was a mere boy, but, carried away by the patriotic fervor of the day, he enlisted and served during the war.   He was married on the 3d of June, 1827, to Mary Ockaman, and came to Missouri in 1829. He settled on Hancock's Prairie, in Callaway county, where, by industry and economy, united with good business qualifications, he made a fortune.   He built the first steam mill in Callaway, from which he realized a good income.   His children were—Wil-son, Jane, Leneus B., Amanda C., John A., William H., Benja-min F., George W., and James M.   Elijah Garrett married Mar-tha Glover, and settled in Callaway county in 1823.   His chil-dren were—Mary, Eliza, William E., Martha, Sedona, Chesley, and Benjamin.   James, Ann, and Magdalene all married and set-tled in Tennessee.   Coleman, Mary and Reuben married and set-tled in Illinois.   Stephen settled in south Missouri.   John lives in Virginia, and Lucy married and lived in Kentucky.

GALBRETH.—Neal Galbreth, of Scotland, settled on Tar river in North Carolina.   He had a son named Torcal, who mar-ried a Miss McLooking, and they had—Catharine, Mary, Eliza-beth, and Neal.   He was married the second time to Catharine Graham, by whom he had—Marion, Ancus, John, Daniel, Sally, Margaret, and James.   Mr. Galbreth removed from North Caro-lina to Kentucky, and in 1819 he settled on the Auxvasse in Calla-way county.   He built the first water mill in Callaway county, on that stream.   The work was done by John and George W. Burt. Mr. Galbreth had the plank sawed for his coffin several years be-fore his death, which occurred in 1825.   Sirenus Cox made his coffin.

GREGORY.—William and John Gregory, of Buckingham county, Va., settled in Callaway county in 1832.   The former had mar-ried Nancy Fuque, by whom he had—John B., Richard F., Wilson, and Martha.   Mrs. Gregory died, and her husband afterward married Nancy Robinson, by whom he had—Thomas J., William, Mary, and Sarah. Mr. Gregory is dead, but his widow still survives. The eldest son, John B., married Isabella Scholl, and is one of the wealthy men of Callaway county. Richard F. married Catharine Oliver, and lives in Montgomery county, Mo. Wilson and Martha died unmarried. Thomas J. married Bettie McCall, and lives in Callaway county. William died in California, unmarried. Sarah was married first to Samuel Gilbert, and second to Stokes McCall. Mary married John Bailey, of Williamsburg.—John, brother of William Gregory, Sr., married Elizabeth Fuque, of Virginia, and they had—Hopson, James H., John D. (a physician), Granville L., Thomas M., Eliza, Sarah, and George W. Mr. Gregory was married the second time to the widow of Jesse Scholl, whose maiden name was Elizabeth Miller, and died, leaving no children by her. She is still living. Hopson Gregory was married first to a Miss Mosley, and second to Martha A. House. James H. married Mary Scholl, and lives in Callaway county. Dr. John D. was married first to Sallie A. Groom, and second to Elizabeth Nunnelly. He lives in California. Granville L. married Susan Nunnelly, and she is now a widow in Callaway county. Thomas M. went to California, and married there. Eliza died single. Sarah married John Windsor, who removed to California. George W. married Mary White, and lives in Montgomery county. The Gregorys are industrious, energetic people and good citizens, and stand high in their communities.

GAMES.—John Games, of Scotland, came to America and settled in Maryland. His children were—Robert, Absalom, James, Basil, and Rachel. Absalom married Mary Wood, and they had—Absalom, Jr., John, Gideon, Benjamin and Elizabeth. Absalom, Jr., and John lived in Ohio, and the latter became a member of the Legislature of that State. Gideon was in the war of 1812, and was at the battle of the Thames, where the celebrated Tecumseh was killed. He saw the great chief fall after he was shot by Colonel Johnson. Mr. Games was married first to Rachel Strother, of Kentucky, by whom he had—Mary, Minerva, and Eliza. He was married the second time to Patsey W. Craig, by whom he had—Martha, Craig, Catharine, Fanny, Amanda, John, Benjamin, Gideon, Jr., Alice, and Louisa.

HARDING.—Rev. John L. Harding, of England, settled in Maryland. He had two sons, Elias and Reason. The latter married Cassandra Ford, and they had—Elias H., Charles, Loyd, John, Cassandra, Rebecca F., and Eliza. Elias H. married Harriet Hall, of Maryland, and they had—William H., Francis L., Howard D., John H., Elias H., Amanda, Henrietta, and Emeline. He was married the second time to Mary Harding, and settled in Callaway county in 1838.

HARPER.—Nicholas Harper, of Fairfax county, Virginia, had—
Thomas, Walter, Nicholas, Jr., Smith, Sally, Nancy, Rachel, and
Mary. Nicholas, Jr., married Lucy Jameson, and settled in
Callaway county in 1824. He had—Thomas J., Sarah, Louisa,
Elizabeth H., Judith A., and Catharine. Rachel Harper married
Stephen Donahue, and Sally married William Graham.

HUTTS.—Michael Hutts, of Franklin county, Va., married
Susan Owens, and they had—Owens, Nancy, William, Sally,
Leonard, Robert, Mahala, Bluford, and Sarah. Bluford was the
only one who came to Missouri. He married Rebecca W. Hippin-
stall, and settled in Callaway county in 1835. They had several
children, and Mrs. Hutts died October 2, 1867.

HUGHES.—Reece Hughes of Franklin county, Va., married
Polly Lyon, and settled in Callaway county, Mo., in 1834. They
had—John, William, Elias, Robert, Armistead, Catharine, Polly,
Lucy, Elizabeth, Sally, and two that died young.

HOBSON.—Dr. Samuel Hobson, of Kentucky, married a daughter of Judge John Clark, and came to Missouri at an early date.
He settled first in Montgomery county, on Camp Branch, where
he lost several of his negro slaves by fever. He then removed
and settled on Nine Mile Prairie, in Callaway county, where he
remained some time, and then removed to Fulton. He had two
children, Winthrop and Joseph. The latter died in his youth,
and the former is a distinguished minister of the Christian
Church. Winthrop was very wild when he was a boy, and was
called one of the worst boys in Callaway county: He was bound
to have his fun, no matter who suffered by it. Among his victims was an old colored man named Tom Nichols, whose life became a burden from the constant badgering of the young scape-
grace. When Winthrop was nearly grown, he was sent off to
school, and remained away several years, during which time he
grew to be a large, portly man. When he came back to Fulton
he met Tom on the street, who failed to recognize him. "Why,
Uncle Tom," said he, "don't you know me?" "No, sah,"
said Tom; "neber seed you afore, as I knows of." Winthrop
looked at him smilingly for a moment, and then said, "Well, Uncle Tom, who was the worst boy you ever saw?" This was sufficient. Tom immediately recognized his old tormentor, and exclaimed, "Why, Massa Winthrop, is dis you! Bless God! I
neber would 'o known you in dis world! But what made you so
fat, Massa Winthrop; has you been drinking whisky? *I bet you
has, 'fore God.*" This was a pretty rough sally for a divinity student, but Hobson took it in good part, laughed at the honest
earnestness of his old friend, and then told him of the change
that had taken place, which greatly astonished Uncle Tom.

HARRISON.—Micajah Harrison, of Kentucky, married Mary
Payne, and they had—Albert G., Micajah V., James O., Jilson

P., and Mary. Albert G. married Virginia L. Bledsoe, of Kentucky, and settled in Callaway county in 1832. He had four sons and two daughters. Mr. Harrison was a prominent lawyer, and was elected representative in Congress from his district three times, viz.: 1834, 1836, and 1838. He died in 1839. Micajah V. Harrison married Dulcinea M. Bledsoe, of Kentucky, and settled in Callaway county in 1833. He was Chief Clerk of the House of Representatives of Missouri during six sessions of the Legislature, and was Sergeant-at-Arms during several other sessions. He died in June, 1855, and a neat monument was erected by the State over his grave in the cemetery at Auxvasse Church. Jilson P. Harrison settled first in Mississippi, and removed from there to New Orleans, where he died. James O. was a lawyer, and lived in Lexington, Ky. After the death of Henry Clay he administered upon the estate of that eminent man. Mary Harrison was married first to Captain Simpson, of Kentucky, and after his death she married Dr. John Hannor, of Fulton, Mo., who subsequently removed to Kentucky.

HENDERSON.—Alexander Henderson, of Augusta county, Va., had sixteen children, and raised ten of them. The names of those who lived were—John, Samuel, Joseph, Robert, David, Alexander, Jr., William, George, James, and Daniel. The latter married Martha Steele, of Virginia, and settled on Auxvasse creek, in Callaway county, in 1823. They had four children, all of whom were born in Virginia and came to Missouri with their parents. Their names were—Alexander, James S., John S., and Jane. Alexander married Dicey Finley. Judge James S. married Emily Boone, daughter of Judge Jesse Boone. John S. was married twice; first to Mary Snell, and second to Elizabeth Pratt. Jane married Colonel Isaac Tate. Joseph Henderson, brother of Daniel, married Susan Rallef, of Virginia, and settled in Callaway county in 1835. John married Polly Burton, of Kentucky, and settled in Callaway county in 1835. William married a widow lady named Irvine, and settled in Audrain county. George and James also settled in Missouri, the former in Clay county, and the latter in St. Louis. David married Ellen Anderson, and they had—Alexander, David, Jr., Joseph, John, William, Margaret, Rachel, Elizabeth, and Elsa. Alexander, son of David Henderson, Sr., was married first to Margaret Hart, and second to Elizabeth Morrison. He had ten children by his two wives. Mr. Henderson settled in Callaway county at an early date, and taught singing school for a number of years. It is said that he and George W. Burt sang love songs so sweetly that the pupils all fell in love with them. David J., son of Alexander Henderson, Jr., married Mary R. Blackenburg, and settled in Callaway county in 1828. They had nine sons and two daughters.

HOCKADAY.—Isaac and Amelia Hockaday, of Clark county, Ky., had the following children—Irvine O., Philip B., Edmund, Isaac N., Jane, and two other daughters, one of whom married Thomas Moore, and the other John H. Field. All except Jane settled in Callaway county at an early date. Judge Irvine O. Hockaday (see portrait on frontispiece) received a good English education, and at an early age manifested good business qualifications. When quite young he was appointed to the important position of cashier of the Clark County, Ky., Bank, and discharged his duties to the entire satisfaction of his employers. He was married in 1829 to Emily Mills, daughter of Dr. John and Lucy Mills, of Winchester, Ky., and in 1821 he resigned his position as cashier of the bank and came to Missouri. He settled in Callaway county, and was appointed the first Circuit and County Clerk, also Treasurer, which offices he continued to fill for eighteen years, to the entire satisfaction of the people of the county. He was also Probate Judge of Callaway county one term, and President of the Weston Bank, in Fulton, for some time. Judge Hockaday was a man of superior talents, and associated intimately with such distinguished men as Edward Bates, Thomas H. Benton, Beverly Tucker, and Hamilton R. Gamble. He was an influential member of the Presbyterian Church for a number of years, and enjoyed the respect and confidence of his brethren and fellow-citizens in the highest degree. He died in 1864, leaving a widow, who still survives, and a large family of children. One of his daughters married James L. Stephens, a wealthy and influential citizen of Columbia, Mo. Another married J. H. Vanmeter, of Lexington, Kentucky, and died since the decease of her father. The names of his other children are—Isaac, who lives in Columbia, Mo., Mrs. R. B. Price, Irvine O., Jr., also of Columbia, Mrs. J. M. McGirk, of Lexington, Mo., Mrs. Dr. A. Wilkerson, of Fulton, Miss Lizzie, of the same place, and Hon. J. A. Hockaday, the present able Attorney-General of Missouri. Philip B., brother of Judge Irvine O. Hockaday, was an eminent attorney. He married Maria Hanson, a daughter of Judge Hanson, of Winchester, Ky., and came to Missouri in 1821. He settled first in Boone county, but afterward removed to Montgomery, where he died. The names of his children were—S. H., Amelia S., Martha J., Isaac, Philip B., Jr., Serena, and R. W. Isaac N. Hockaday also settled in Callaway county at an early date, and resided there many years; but he now lives in Pleasant Hill, Mo. He married Catharine Shortridge, of Callaway county, by whom he had three children. Mr. Hockaday is an excellent and most highly esteemed citizen. Judge George, E. O., John, and James Hockaday, cousins of the above family, settled in Missouri in 1838. Judge George Hockaday married Laura Hart, of Jefferson City, Mo., and raised a large family. He was a member of the County Court of Callaway county for six years, and also represented the county in the Legislature one term. He was a good business man and a highly esteemed citizen. John Hockaday was a merchant in Fulton for many years. He married Caroline Scott, of Loutre Island, and they had three children. He stood high in the community as a man and citizen, and was respected by all who knew him. James Hockaday was a successful farmer, and prominent citizen. He married a Miss Dillard, and they had two children.

HOUF.—Peter Houf, of Germany, came to America before the revolution. He had a son named Peter, who was born in Pennsylvania, and who served as a soldier in the war of 1812. He settled in Augusta county, Va., where he married Mary E. Summers, by whom he had—Susanna, Elizabeth, Henry, David S., Jacob, John, Polly, James, William, Martha J., Margaret, Amanda, and Louisa. Mr. Houf came to Missouri and settled in Callaway county in 1823, and died in 1851. His widow died in 1870. All the children, except John, who died in childhood, in Virginia, settled in Missouri.

HARRISON.—The Harrison family, of which there are several members in Callaway county, is one of the most distinguished in America. It sprang from some of the best blood of England, and has given to that country and America several of their most celebrated characters. John, Benjamin, and Thomas Harrison were sons of a family of English nobility, and were born in the town of Feuby, Yorkshire. John was born in 1693, and became a great inventor. Among his inventions were a chronometer and gridiron. He also invented the pendulum for clocks, for which the British crown paid him £20,000. He died in Red Lion Square, London, in 1776. Benjamin Harrison was born in 1694. He had two sons, Benjamin and Robert. The former was the father of Hon. Benjamin Harrison, one of the signers of the Declaration of Independence, and who was the father of General William Henry Harrison, President of the United States. Robert Harrison was the father of Hon. Robert Harrison, the great jurist. Thomas, the younger brother of John and Benjamin Harrison, was born in 1695. He married Hannah Morrison, of England, by whom he had six sons—John, Benjamin, Thomas, Jr., Samuel, Daniel, and James, all of whom came to America after the death of their parents, and settled in the State of Maryland. When the revolutionary war began they all enlisted in the American army, and John and Thomas were soon promoted, the former to the rank of Captain and the latter to that of Colonel. The other four brothers were killed, and each left families, but of these we have no account. Captain John Harrison married a Miss Malone, of Maryland, and settled in Botetourt county, Va. He had six sons—Thomas, Samuel, John, Benjamin, Daniel, and James. Colonel Thomas Harrison never married. He was a shrewd business man, and made a great deal of money while in the army, most of which he invested in lands in the Valley of Virginia, and at his death he left his property to his nephew, Thomas, son of Captain John Harrison.   This nephew married Margaret Billops, of Virginia, and removed with his parents to South Carolina, but returned to Virginia after their deaths, and settled in Montgomery county.   He had ten children by his first wife, of whom he raised eight, viz.: Edward, John, Thomas, Samuel, James, Elizabeth, Sarah, and Polly.   His second wife was Nancy Crawley, of Virginia, by whom he had—Nancy, Margaret, and William D.   He was married the third time to Jane Childress, of Virginia, by whom he had—Cynthia, Andrew L., Eliza J., and Benjamin R.   In the fall of 1819 he removed with his family to Missouri, and settled on the Booneslick road in Callaway county, where he died July 3, 1840, in his 75th year. His eldest son, Edward, died in Virginia.   His second son, John, was born in Boutetourt county, Va., October 7, 1791.   (See portrait; page 228.)   He volunteered in the war of 1812, and was promoted to the rank of Major.   He was married in 1816, to Mary Crockett, of Virginia, and in 1817 he came to Missouri with his family, consisting of his wife and one child, Thomas. He settled first in Saline county, but removed to Boone in 1819.   In 1827 he settled on Harrison's Branch in Callaway county, where he died February 19, 1874.   His wife died August 1, 1873.   Major Harrison had seven children—Thomas, Crockett, Benjamin F., Samuel, James M., Rebecca, and Virginia.   Thomas and Crockett were blown up on a steamboat at New Orleans in 1849, and the former was seriously injured.   Thomas, brother of Major John Harrison, married Sarah Potts, of Virginia, by whom he had—William, John T., Samuel P., Mary, Nancy, Margaret, and Lucy.   He settled on Harrison's Branch, in Callaway county, in 1819.   In 1832 he went to St. Louis on business, and on his return died of cholera, at St. Charles, on the 8th of June, in the 42d year of his age.   His widow is still living.   In early days Mr. Harrison belonged to the Regulators of Callaway county, and when the Indians, who sometimes passed through the county on their way to Washington City, would steal anything, or commit other depredations, the Regulators would catch them and whip them.   One day an old Indian set the woods on fire, and Mr. Harrison caught him and whipped him, and then took his gun lock off and kept it, so that he could not shoot any one for revenge.   Judge James Harrison came to Missouri with his brother, Major John Harrison, in 1817, and settled with him in Saline county.   In 1819 he removed to Boone county, where, in 1821, he married Rebecca Crockett.   In 1830 he settled in Audrain county, and the following year he was appointed presiding Judge of the County Court, by Gov. Boggs, but resigned the office soon after. He was Justice of the Peace for a number of years, and was elected to the Legislature three times. He died in 1875, three days before his 80th birth-day. He had twelve children—Thomas J., Samuel C., John, James, William, Margaret R., Jane, Mary A., Nancy, Sarah, Virginia, and Lucy. Samuel, brother of Major John Harrison, left Virginia for the West in 1819, and was never heard of again. He was doubtless robbed and murdered, as the route between the East and West was infested with robbers at various places, at that time. Elizabeth and Sarah Harrison married and lived in Virginia. Polly married and settled in Wisconsin. Margaret married Charles McIntire, of Audrain county. Nancy married her cousin, Abner Harrison, of Audrain county. William D. Harrison was married first to Mary E. Bourn, and after her death he married her sister, Effie. He lives in Audrain county. Cynthia married Alfred Kibbe, of Texas. Eliza J. married Jeptha Yates, of Callaway county, and died September 21, 1873. Andrew L. and Benjamin R. are bachelors, and live in Callaway county. James Harrison, son of Captain John Harrison, of the revolutionary war, married Louisa Duncan, of South Carolina, and settled in Washington county, Mo., in 1819. John and Daniel, his brothers, married and settled in Alabama, and Samuel and Benjamin married and settled in Mississippi.

HAYS.—Boone Hays was the son of William Hays, who was killed by James Davis on Femme Osage creek, in 1804. He married Lydia Scholl, his cousin, and settled in Darst's Bottom in 1801. In 1818 he removed to Callaway county, and built the first horse-mill in his part of the county. His children were— Hardin, Jesse, Alfred, Wesley, Terilda, Eleanor, Amazon, Cinderella, Samuel, Mason, and Mary B. Mr. Hays was married the second time to a Mrs. Frazier, of Memphis, Tenn., and in 1849 he went to California, where he died soon after. When Mr. Hays raised his first cabin in Callaway county, he lacked a few logs of having enough to finish it, and went into the woods to cut some more. One of the trees in falling slipped and broke his leg, and the severe pain caused him to faint. As he was reeling and about to fall, John P. Martin, who was standing near, caught him in his arms, when he too fainted, and they both fell to the ground together. A man standing near them, but who knew nothing of Hays' leg being broken, called out, " Hallo there! are you two drunk again?" Hays had his broken leg splinted and bound up, and then sat on a stump and gave directions about the completion of his cabin as if nothing had occurred. He was a man of iron nerve and robust constitution.

HATTON. —Thomas Hatton, of England, settled in Bedford county, Va., prior to the revolutionary war. He married Polly Capton, and they had—Thomas, Benjamin William, and Reuben.

Benjamin and Reuben were soldiers in the revolutionary war, and the former was killed by the Indians. Reuben married Joanna Bellew, of Virginia, and settled in South Carolina. He afterward removed to Madison county, Ky., with his wife and six children, on pack-horses. The names of his children at that time were— Frances, Polly A., William, Robert, Charles, and Nancy. After they settled in Kentucky they had—Benjamin, Elizabeth, Fleming, Stewart, Wesley, Thomas, James, Mitchell, and John. Thomas married Polly Butler, of Kentucky, and settled in Boone Co., Mo., in 1819, and the following year he removed to Callaway. Polly A. married Samuel Miller, and settled in Callaway county in 1819

HUME.—William Hume, of Bath county, Va., married Sarah Benson, and removed to Bourbon county, Ky. They had—Prub, Jefferson, Gabriel, and Joel. Gabriel married Rachel Ashbrook, of Virginia, and settled in Callaway county in 1831. He died in September, 1838, leaving a widow and eleven children, viz. : Jane, Benson, Thomas, Benjamin, Willis, Lucinda, Sarah, Ann, Margaret, James, and William D. The latter is now a large stock dealer, and a wealthy citizen of Callaway county. When he was married he had to borrow money to pay the parson; he also borrowed a pair of shoes to wear on that occasion.

HOBSON.—Thomas Hobson, of Cumberland county, Va., had a son named John, who married Permelia Robinson, and settled in Callaway county in 1839. He was married the second time to Elizabeth James, of Callaway county, and by his two wives he had eight sons and eight daughters. Mr. Hobson was a soldier of the war of 1812.

HAYS.—William Hays, of Maryland, had two children—George N. and Nellie. His wife died, and he removed to South Carolina, where he married Phœbe Jackson, by whom he had— Otho, Owen, Charlotte, John, Harmon, William, Patsey, Lavinia, and Riley. Nellie married Robert Jones, and settled in Montgomery county, Mo., in 1827. Harmon came to Missouri with Levi McMurtry and his family, when he was a boy, and rode a bull calf most of the way. He settled near Readesville, in Callaway county, in 1832, and married Minerva Scholl. Since then he has made a fortune and raised a large family of children.

HOLLAND.—Major John M. Holland, of Franklin county, Va., represented his county in the Legislature twelve years. He married a Miss Ferguson, and they had—Peter, John, Andrew, Johnson, Abraham, Ebenezer, Fanny, Mary, Julia, and Nancy.

HERRING.—George Herring, of Virginia, married Elizabeth Closby, and they had—Jonathan, George, John, and Nathan. The three last named were soldiers in the war of 1812, and they afterward married and settled in Callaway county. George married Lucy Sinco, John married Lucy Carver, and Nathan married Susan Hill.

HOLMAN.—Edward, the son of Henry Holman, of Maryland, married Abigail Williams, and their son Henry was married first to Eliza Jones, of Kentucky, by whom he had two sons and five daughters. After the death of his first wife he married Nancy Nash, of Missouri, and settled in Callaway county in 1820. Rosetta, daughter of Henry Holman, Sr., married David Darst, who settled in Darst's Bottom in 1798. Jesse, son of Henry Holman, Sr., was a noted lawyer of Indiana, and a son of his is a representative in Congress from that State.

HOWE.—Rev. Joseph Howe, of Pennsylvania, was a Presbyterian minister, but unlike ministers in general, he was wealthy. At his death he willed $20,000 to pay a church debt, and divided the remainder of his property into nine equal parts, eight of which were for his eight children, and the ninth was to be given to "the Lord." His children were—Isaac, Harvey, John D., James, Cynthia, Maria, Jane, and Eliza. Isaac married Jane Boyd, and settled in Callaway county at an early date. His children were—Wallace, Thomas, John, David, Harvey, James, Jane, Margaret, and Mary A. Harvey and John D., brothers of Isaac, also settled in Callaway county. The latter was married first to Sally Parnell, and second to Margaret Henderson. James married Ann C. Baker. Cynthia married David D. Davis. Maria married James Jameson. Jane married Jacob Coons. Eliza was married first to Joseph Henderson, and second to Mr. McAdoff.

HOPKINS.—Charles Hopkins was an Episcopal minister of England, but came to America and settled in Goochland county, Va. He was married twice, and had nineteen sons and two daughters. One of his sons, named John, married Mary Luck, of Virginia, by whom he had—George B., William L., Nancy, Adelia, Lucy, Polly, and Sarah. George B. married Ann Withens, of Virginia, and settled in Callaway county, Mo., in 1831. He served as Judge of the County Court for twenty years. In 1835 he was elected Colonel of militia, and served until 1845. His children were—James A., Anna E., Marion L., John A., and Edward W. Mrs. Hopkins died in 1852, and he afterward married Mrs. Ann Gray, who died in 1873.

HORNBUCKLE.—William Hornbuckle, of Virginia, married Jane Harding; and settled in North Carolina, from whence he removed to Kentucky, and in 1821 he settled in Callaway county, Mo. His children were—Thomas, Richard, Harding, Alfred, Rufus, Nancy, Dubby, Rebecca, Peggy, Susan, and Sally, all of whom settled in Callaway county.

HORDE.—Killes Horde, of Culpepper county, Va., had—Alexander, Daniel, Lewis, Edwin, Catharine, and Minnie. Alexander married Agnes Jones, and settled in Callaway county in 1837.

They had—Robert J., Richard L., Alexander, Julia A., Mary C., and Sarah J.   Robert J. was born deaf and dumb.   He married Martha Jones, and they had two children who are deaf and dumb also.   Richard L. married Mary T. Heard, of Virginia.   Alexander married Mary T. Jones, of Missouri.   Julia A. married John Carby, of Virginia.   Mary C. married John Waller, of Virginia.   Sarah J. married Robert Davis, of Missouri.

HYTEN.—Joseph Hyten, of Maryland, married Priscilla Caywood, and their son, Josiah, married Rebecca Caywood, and settled in Montgomery county, Ky., in 1810.   Their children were—William, Stephen H., and Otho.   Stephen H. was in the war of 1812.   He married Nancy McGary, and settled in Callaway county in 1830.   Their children were—Sampson, Landrum, Stephen, Susan, Mary, Malinda, Rebecca, Nancy, and Amanda.

HUMPHREYS.—The children of John Humphreys, of Greenbriar county, Va., were—Rachel, Samuel, James, William, Elizabeth, and Polly.   Richard married Elizabeth Nevens, and settled in Callaway county in 1818.   Samuel married Susan Smart, and settled in Callaway county in 1821.   The rest of the children settled in that county the same year.

HAMILTON.—Archibald Hamilton was a native of the northern part of Ireland, but came to America and settled in Augusta Co., Va.   He had three sons—William, John, and Andrew.   William married Patience Craig, a daughter of Rev. Jesse Craig,* and they had—Isabella, Jane, Frances, Mary, Joanna, Rebecca, John C., Hugh, and Andrew.   John C. married Sarah Craig, of Virginia, and they had—James C., Mary, John, Robert, Eliza J., Isabella, Sarah, and Frances.   Mr. Hamilton settled in Callaway Co., Mo., in 1837.—Hugh, the son of William Hamilton, Sr., married Elizabeth Clark, and settled in Saline Co., Mo.   His brother Andrew married Nancy Craig, and settled in Callaway county in 1829.   They had—James, William C., Elizabeth, Rebecca, Hugh, John S., Mary, and Margaret.   Mr. Hamilton's first wife died, and he was married the second time to Elizabeth Callison.   Joanna, daughter of William Hamilton, married Samuel Wilson, who settled in Callaway county in 1832.   Rebecca married Brydon Wilson, who settled in Callaway county in 1832.   Frances married Robert Neal, who settled in that county in 1829.   —John Hamilton, a distant relative of the above family, settled in Callaway county in 1820.   His wife was Peggy C. Baskins.

---

*Rev. Jesse Craig was the first Presbyterian minister who settled west of the Blue Ridge Mountains.   On the 28th of July, 1747, he assisted in laying the corner stone of the first Presbyterian Church erected west of those mountains, and on that occasion delivered the following address: "This is the day set apart, my friends, to lay the corner stone of the first church west of the Blue Ridge Mountains, over which I pronounce this unpremeditated benediction—'May He who is the Layer of this corner stone prosper the work and countenance this hope as long as it shall be used for His glory.   Amen.'"

He was a fast runner, and ran a race one day, with an Indian, for a horn of powder. He won the powder, and then the Indian wanted to run the race over again; but Hamilton could not see the matter in that light. The children of John Hamilton were— Anna R., William B., James G., John, Agnes G., Thomas S., George W., and Charles H. Anna R. married Albert G. Boone. Agnes G. married John H. Hamilton, of Montgomery City. The Hamiltons were a sober, industrious, hospitable class of people and highly esteemed by all their neighbors and acquaintances.

HAWKINS—John Hawkins, of Scott county, Ky., married Sarah Johnson, and they had—John, Philip, William, Margaret, Sally, Fanny, and Nancy. William married Lydia T. Francis, of Kentucky, and settled in Howard county, Mo., in 1816. They had—John, William, Mary J., Granville, and Henry. William married Catharine W. Shelby, and settled in Caliaway county in 1832. He raised a large family of children.

HOLT.—Timothy Holt, of Halifax county, Va., married Elizabeth Chambers, and they had—Abner, Hiram, Robert, John, William, Lucy E., Elizabeth, Jane, and Ann. Abner married Elizabeth Brooks, of Virginia, and settled in Callaway county in 1819. They had—Timothy, James, Robert, John, William P., Hiram, Abner, Jr., Elijah, Susan, and Elizabeth C. Hiram, son of Timothy Holt, Sr., was married twice, his first wife being Jane Stanfield, and his second her sister Nancy. He settled in Callaway county in 1826. His children were—Ann, William, Abner, Elizabeth, Jane, Emeline, Mary, Margaret, Lucy, Hiram, Jr., and Ashley.

JACKSON.—William J. Jackson was born in Chester, England, and was an only child. He came to America in 1788 and settled in Maryland, where he became a large tobacco grower. He married Mary Belt, and they had two sons and two daughters; but only one of their children, Richard B., lived to be grown. In 1811 he went to Kentucky and settled in Scott county, where he subsequently filled several offices of honor and responsibility. In 1816 he married Clarissa Greenwell, by whom he had—William J., Caroline E., Thomas J., Clarissa, Richard B., and Robert W. Mr. Jackson settled in Callaway county, Mo., in 1831, and in 1834 he was elected door-keeper of the House of Representatives at Jefferson City, which office he filled in a highly creditable manner for twenty-one years. He was also Marshal of the Supreme Court for several years. He died in 1855, in the 66th year of his age. A handsome monument was subsequently erected to his memory by the State. His son, William J., married Sarah E. Wren. He has been a Justice of the Peace for many years, and has performed the marriage ceremony for more than a hundred couples. He married an entire family of thirteen persons at $1 each. He was also a great hunter in early days, and devoted a considerable portion of his time to that exciting pursuit. One day, while out with a party of hunters, they came upon an old bear, which they found to be a tough customer. He killed or wounded all their dogs, and having shot all their ammunition away at him without bringing him down, they drove him into a neighbor's horse-lot, and killed .him with their knives. Thomas J. Jackson, brother of William J., married Orientha Sharp. Richard B. and Robert W. were killed during the late war between the North and South. Caroline E. married a Mr. Broadwater, and Clarissa married a Mr. Foster.

JONES.—William Jones was a Captain in the American army during the revolutionary war, and was killed at the battle of Guilford Court House. He had a son named David, who married Elizabeth Mosley, of Buckingham county, Va., and settled in Callaway county, Mo., in 1838. He was Postmaster at Williamsburg for some time. His children were Eliza, Robert M., Permelia, Walker, William A., and Louisa W. Eliza married James S. Mosley. William A. married Mary E. Venable, and settled in Missouri in 1831. Louisa W. married John Hobson, who settled in Callaway county in 1838.

JAMESON.—James Jameson, of Virginia, married Lucy Hackney, by whom he had—John, James, Thomas, David,· William, Zachariah, Judith, Margaret, and Nancy. Mr. Jameson removed to Kentucky in 1789. His eldest son, John, married Jalee Reeds, of Virginia, by whom he had—James, Samuel, Thomas, John, Isaac N., Sarah, Lucy, Judith, Elizabeth, and Amanda. Mr. Jameson settled in Callaway county, Mo., in 1824. His son James lived and died in Kentucky. Samuel married Malinda Harris, and settled in Callaway county, where they had—Tira H., James, Samuel, Sally A., Jalee, Minerva, Susan, and Mary. Thomas Jameson was married first to Margaret V. Martin, and second to the widow of Philip George, whose maiden name was C. A. Sallee. Col. John Jameson was born March 6, 1802. He possessed a superior order of mind, was an able speaker and reasoner, and was twice elected to Congress from his district. He wielded a large influence in that body, and ably represented his constituents. He died January 24, 1857. (See portrait on page 228). He married Susan Harris, and they had—John H., Elizabeth, Sallie T., and Malinda R. Isaac N. Jameson married Miss A. P. Smith, and died twenty-eight days after. Sarah married John Litton. Lucy married Nicholas Harper, and they had— John, Albert, Thomas J., Sarah, Louisa, Elizabeth, and Judith. Judith Jameson married Charles Yeater, and they had—John, Joseph, and Sarah. Elizabeth married Henry Wright, and they had Jameson and Jalee. All of the above settled in Callaway and Audrain counties.

JONES.—John Jones, of Mercer county, Ky., married Elizabeth

Wren, and they had—Tilman, Nancy, Polly, Robert, Margaret, Elizabeth, Hezekiah, and William. Robert was married first to Ellen Hays, and second to Tillie C. Simpson. His children were —John, Elizabeth, Mary, and George. Mr. Jones settled in Callaway county in 1831. Hezekiah, his brother, settled in that county the same year. He married Elizabeth Perkins, and they had—Elvira, Newton, Elizabeth, Milton, Virginia, Nancy, Thomas, Tilley, Lucy, and Nathaniel.

KEMP.—John Kemp, of England, married a Miss Craighead, and settled in Franklin county, Va. They had—Thomas, Robert, William, Jordan, John, and Martha. John married Fannie Dudley, and settled in Callaway county in 1832. They had—Dudley, Jordan, William, Milley, and Polly. Thomas Kemp married Esther Maxey, of Virginia, and they had—Walter, John, William, Robert, James, Mary, Martha, Susan, Nancy, Lucy, Joanna, Elizabeth, and Sarah W. Walter married Jerusha Key, and settled in Callaway county, in 1832. William married Delila Kemp, his cousin, and settled in Callaway county in 1834. Robert married Mary Holland, and settled in Callaway county in 1834. James married the widow of Robert Craighead, and settled in Callaway county in 1834. Sarah W. was married first to Peter H. Holland, who settled in Callaway county in 1836. After his death she married John Steel.

KIDWELL—Zedekiah Kidwell, of Fairfax county, Va., was born in England. His children were—Washington R., Albert, Zedekiah, Charles F., George W., Eglantine, Sarah, Virginia, and Mary. Washington R. was married at Willard's Hotel, in Washington City, in 1835, to Mary A. Wheeler, of Maryland, and settled in Callaway county, Mo., in 1839. They had—William L., John S., Z. K., Albert, Rebecca E., Mary W., Josephine, Eglantine, Sallie, and Rosa W. Mr. Kidwell died in 1864. He represented Callaway county in the Legislature one term.

KELLEY.—James Kelley, of Virginia, was of Irish descent. He married Hannah George, and they had—John R., Mahala Y., and Williamson. Mr. Kelley was Captain of a ship, and was lost in a storm at sea, which also wrecked his vessel. John R. and Mahala Y. Kelley died in childhood. Williamson married Elizabeth B. Bragg, daughter of Henry Bragg and Dinah W. Talbott, of Norfolk, Va., by whom he had three sons and one daughter. Mr. Kelley was a merchant in Virginia, and when he came to Missouri he brought his goods with him, and opened the first store in Martinsburg, Montgomery county.

KITCHEN.—Thomas Kitchen, of Smith county, Tennessee, married the widow of James Goodrich, and settled on Coats' Prairie in Callaway county, in 1817. He had no children, but adopted a little girl named Lizzie Linnville, who was five years of age at the time. When she was grown she married her adopted father,

his first wife having died.   He ·was seventy years of age at the
time.   Mr. Kitchen's first wife was a member of the Old Baptist
Church at Salem, but he never joined because he could not tell
his experience, from the fact that he had none to tell.   But he
officiated with the members, and was the business man of the
institution, which led to his being called a *dry land member*.
When Captain John Baker's mill was being built on Loutre creek,
Kitchen, who was a carpenter, assisted in the work, and one day
he slipped and fell from the top of the mill into the creek, and
struck a catfish, which he mashed into jelly, but escaped unhurt
himself.   After this event he declared that he was no longer a
a dry land member, as he had been thoroughly baptized.   He
also called himself Thomas Jonah Kitchen, because he, like Jonah
of old, had been saved by a fish.

KEY.—George Key served in the revolutionary war four years.
He afterward married Susannah Craighead, of Franklin county,
Va., and in 1831, at the age of 78 years, he came to Missouri,
and settled in Callaway county.   His children were—George T.,
Martin, Susan, Jerusha, Adonijah, Arphaxad, and Joanna.
Jerusha married Walter Kemp, and settled in Callaway county in
1831.   Joanna married Albert Agee, who settled in Callaway
county in 1830.

KING.—Stephen M. King, of Maryland, settled in Kentucky at
an early date, and married a Miss Nelson, by whom he had a son
named Stephen.   The latter was married first to a German lady,
who died; he then married Cynthia Chaney, who also died, and
he afterward married a widow' lady named Bruner, who was a
daughter of a Mr. Strood, of Clark county, Ky., who was a great
Indian fighter.   Mr. King had nine children by his three wives
and was an early settler of Callaway county.

KEMPER.—Tilman Kemper was a soldier of the revolutionary
war.   He settled first in Culpepper county, Va., where he married Dinah Hitt, by whom he had fifteen children.   He subsequently removed to Bryan's Station, in Kentucky, with three of
his children, Thomas, Anna, and Benjamin.   The latter married
Sally Adams, and they had a son named Abraham, who studied
medicine when he was grown and became a physician.   He married Sophia Wainscott, of Kentucky, and settled in Callaway
county in 1830.

KENNON.—John Kennon, of Louisa county, Va., was the son of
Joseph Kennon.   He married his cousin, Martha Kennon, and
settled in Callaway county in 1831.   He lost his wife, and was
married again to Julia Snell.

KNIGHT.—James Knight, of Maryland, married Nancy Will-
iams, and settled in Fleming county, Ky., where they had—John,
William, Elijah, Wesley, James, Selatha, Rebecca, Elizabeth, and
Sally.   William Married Eliza Hornbuckle, and settled in Calla-

way county in 1825. They had—James F., Sally, Wesley H., Rebecca A., Amanda, Elizabeth A., William S., and John H.

LEEPER.—James Leeper and his wife, whose maiden name was Margaret Henderson, were natives of Nicholas county, Ky. In 1829 they came to Missouri, and Mr. Leeper bought a New Madrid claim of 640 acres, near Concord, in Callaway county, upon which he settled. His children were—Ellen, Susan, Elizabeth, Louisa, Isabella C., Amanda, John, David, James A., and William C. Mr. Leeper was a soldier of the war of 1812.

LANGTRYE—William and Hillery Langtrye came to America from Ireland, and settled in Madison county, Va. Hillery was a bachelor, and was in the employ of the government at Washington City for a number of years. In 1861 he returned to his native country, and died there in 1869. His brother William married Kitty B. Arbuckle, of Madison county, Va., and they had—Hillery J., Anna, Archibald, Margaret, and William. Anna was married first to William Gray, of Callaway county, and second to Joseph Allen, of the same county. Archibald married Elizabeth Hamilton, and settled in Callaway county in 1837. Margaret married Madison McMullen, who settled in Callaway county in 1838. William married Sarah Hamilton, and settled in Callaway county in 1836.

LARCH.—John Larch, of Pennsylvania, had four sons and two daughters—Christopher, Joseph, Michael, John, Barbara, and Jane. Christopher and Michael settled on Clinch river, in Virginia. Joseph was killed at the battle of Tippecanoe. John married Margaret Long, of Maryland, and they had—Daniel, Joseph, John, Abraham, Isaac, Jonathan, Catharine, Rachel, Mary, and Eve. Daniel settled in Montgomery county, Md., in 1820, and married Elizabeth S. Johnson. Joseph settled in Callaway county in 1822, and married Narcissa Davis, by whom he had twelve children. Daniel and Joseph Larch are both living, the former in his 78th year, and the latter in his 76th. Daniel owned a tanyard on Loutre creek, many years ago, and bought a great many hides in Lincoln county, which he conveyed to his tanyard by tying them to his horse's tail and dragging them on the ground, a distance of twenty miles.

LAWRENCE.—David Lawrence, of Ireland, came to America, married a Miss McKinney, and settled in Shelby county, Ky. His children were—Mary A., Thomas, James M., Elizabeth, and David. Mary A. was married first to Richard Bowen, and they had—Judith A., Elizabeth, William, Richard, Mary E., and Effie Mr. Bowen died in Kentucky, and his widow subsequently married William Rodman, who settled in Callaway county. They had Margaret and Susan. Thomas Lawrence settled in Callaway county in 1824. He married Sally Riddle, and they had—Durrett, David, Thomas, James, and Russell. James M. married

Lucy D. Martin, and settled in Callaway county in 1823. They had—David R., William M., James T., Mary A., Peggy R., and Larissa W. Elizabeth Lawrence married James Metcalf, of Kentucky. David married Elizabeth Scofield, of Kentucky.

LAIL.—John Lail was born while his parents were prisoners in an Indian camp in Kentucky. When he was grown he married Susan Williams, and settled in Harrison county, Ky. They had— George, John, Charles, Elijah, Nancy, Margaret, Jane, Lucinda, Elizabeth, and Susan. George, John, Charles, Margaret and Susan all married and remained in Kentucky. Nancy married and lived in Indiana. Jane was married first to John Speirs, and after his death she married Edward Wingfield, who settled in Montgomery county, Mo., in 1834. Elizabeth was married first to Noah Coil, and second to Mr. A. Hall. She has twelve children living. Lucinda married Elijah Coil, by whom she had six children. Elijah married Harriet Allen, of Kentucky, by whom he had fourteen children. He died in 1869, leaving his children all well off.

LARRIMORE.—Abraham Larrimore, of Madison county, Ky., had one child, Eliza, by his first wife. He was married the second time to Mary Davis, of Kentucky, by whom he had—Samuel, Nancy, Henry, Elizabeth, Silas, Sally, Phœbe, John, Mary, and Susan. Nancy married Burgess Elliott, who settled in Buchanan county, Mo. Elizabeth married Fielding Lane, who settled in Jackson county. Sally married Loudon Burk, and also settled in Jackson county. Phœbe married Allen Cox, and settled in Buchanan county. Henry married Jane Thomas, and settled in Callaway county in 1835. He is one of the fine stock raisers of Missouri, and his herd of thoroughbreds is not surpassed by any in the State.

LANGLEY.—Moses Langley, of Georgia, settled in Callaway county in 1817. His children were—Moses, Isaac, Jane, Carter, John, Collett, Agnes, Uley, Sally, Polly, and Elizabeth, all of whom married and settled in Callaway county. Moses married Polly Clanton. Isaac married Nancy Chandler. James married Matilda Haynes. John married Lucy Boyd. Collett married Theresa Evans. Uley married Collett Haynes. Sallie married her cousin, William Langley.

LOVE.—Charles Love, of Maryland, married Polly Barnes, and removed to Prince William county, Va. They had—William, Philip, Thomas, Samuel, John, Margaret, Luncinda, Harriet, and Emily, all of whom, except Thomas, who died in Virginia, settled in Bourbon county, Ky. Philip married Elizabeth Sparks, of Virginia, and settled in Callaway county, Mo., in 1828. His children were—Charles, James (a physician), Margaret A., Mary F., Lucinda J., Thomas S., William H., John W., Robert T., Emily, and Stephen.

LYNES.—The parents of Joseph Lynes died when he was a small boy, and he was raised by his aunt, Mrs. Wayne. When he was grown he married Mary Miller, of Kentucky, and settled in St. Louis county, Mo., in 1805. In 1819 he removed to Boone county. His children were—William, Jefferson, Washington, Madison, Harrison, Jackson, Perry, Elizabeth, Malinda, and Paulina. Jefferson, Washington, and Jackson married and settled in Callaway county, the two latter in 1836, and the former in 1831. Jefferson married Catharine Suggett, Washington married Susan Suggett, and Jackson married Mary E. Hervey.

MARTIN.—George Martin, of Virginia, married Elizabeth Russell, and they had a son named Russell, who was a soldier of the revolutionary war. He married Peggy Vaughn, a daughter of Cornelius Vaughn, of Caroline county, Va., and settled first in Kentucky, from whence he removed to Callaway county in 1826. His children were—Nancy V., Lucy D., Fanny, John T., William, and Samuel P. Nancy V. married Matthew McGill. Lucy D. married James M. Lawrence, who settled in Callaway county in 1824. Fanny married Henry Vaughter, of Kentucky. John T. married Lucy Wayne. William married Peggy Wright, and settled in Callaway county in 1824. He was married the second time to the widow of James Davis. He founded Martinsburg, in Audrain county. Samuel P. was married first to Judith D. Wright, and settled in Callaway county in 1824. He was married the second time to the widow Sally Turner. Mr. Martin is an Old School Baptist, and a State's rights Democrat of the purest water. In early days he was a great wolf hunter. On a certain occasion he went into a wolf's den, killed the old ones, and brought out eight young ones alive. He paid his taxes for two years with the scalps of the latter. On another occasion he attacked a gang of nine large wolves that had followed a neighbor of his, an old man, several miles, trying to kill and devour him and his horse. Mr. Martin killed three out of the nine with a club, while sitting on his horse.

McMAHAN.—John McMahan, Jr., of Ireland, came to America before the revolution, and settled in Roan county, N. C. In 1780 he went to Bryan's Station, in Kentucky, where he lost his wife. He afterward married a daughter of Israel Boone, a brother of Daniel Boone, by whom he had—James, Jesse, William, John, and David. He was married the third time, but had no children by his last wife. Jesse McMahan married Polly Fox, and settled in Callaway county in 1827. His children were—John, Richard, Shem, George, and Sophia. Jesse McMahan came to Missouri in 1800, with a party of hunters, on a hunting expedition, and while on Loutre Prairie they found a man living alone in a miserable hut, and devoting his time to hunting and trapping. They took dinner with him one day, which consisted of nothing more than potatoes and buffalo milk.

McKINNEY.—Major James McKinney, of Virginia, removed to Kentucky and settled at Crab Orchard. In 1818 he came to Missouri and settled in St. Charles, where he remained two years, engaged in hauling wood to town and selling it to the citizens. In 1820 he bought Amos Kibbe's place in the southern part of Grand Prairie, Callaway county, and settled there. He was married in Kentucky to Levisa Whitney, and they had—Liberty, Esther L., Charles, Sally A., Samuel, William, and Freeman. Major McKinney was a member of the Ironside Baptist Church, and the second organization of that church in Callaway county was effected at his house. He was an intelligent man and a useful citizen, and served as County Judge from 1827 to 1832. He had twelve brothers, three of whom were killed in the revolutionary war. One of his brothers, Abraham, settled in Randolph county, Mo., at an early date, and was a great hunter. Liberty, eldest son of Major James McKinney, never married, and died in New Orleans. Esther L. married Nathaniel Craig. Charles married Mary A. Craig. Sally A. married George McCredi. Samuel married Hortense McLane. William married and settled in Kansas. Freeman joined General Walker's expedition against Central America, and was killed with his commander.

MARTIN.—John P. Martin is the son of Bailey Martin, of Virginia. He married Sally Hatcher, of Richmond, and settled in Callaway county. Mo., in the spring of 1819. They had three childred—Permelia, Polly A., and William J. Mrs. Martin died in September, 1873, in her 79th year, but her husband is still living, in his 83d year. He has been one of the most successful farmers of Callaway county, and has accumulated a fortune. In early days he raised cotton and flax, which his wife spun and wove into cloth. She made her loom with her own hands, and it was the first loom in Callaway county.

McCALL.—Robert McCall, of Ireland, came to America and settled in Franklin county, Va., from whence he removed to Bruke county, N. C. His children were—William, James, Robert, Samuel, Henry, Alexander, Nancy, and Jennie. William married Malinda Holland, by whom he had—Peter H., Lydia, Robert H., Jane, William S., Mary L., James E., John M., Thomas F., and Frances, nearly all of whom settled on and near Coats' Prairie, in Callaway county, from 1834 to 1837. Robert H. married Elizabeth M. Gilbert, and they were the parents of Dr. William S. McCall. The Doctor says that when he was learning to crawl his mother put sheep skin gloves on his hands, and padded his knees with sheep skin, so he could crawl over the rough puncheon floor without getting splinters in his hands and knees. Jane McCall married William Bell, who settled in Callaway county in 1839. William S. was married first to Martha Smith, and second to the widow Gilbert. He settled in Callaway county in 1839. Mary L. married Stephen Smith, who settled in Callaway county in 1839. James E. married Angeline Gilbert, and settled in Callaway county in 1834. Frances married Thomas Gilbert, and settled in Callaway county in 1846.

MOORE.—William Moore married Hannah Ramsey, and settled in Kentucky, where he had—William, Wharton, John, Thomas, Henry, Charles C., Samuel, Mary, Elizabeth, and Nancy. Wharton married Polly Browning, of Virginia, and settled in Callaway county in 1819. His children were—William G., James B., John B., Wharton H., Charles C., Mary C., Nancy S., Elizabeth, and Margaret J. Samuel Moore married Emily Tarleton, and settled in Callaway county in 1820. His children were—William, Alfred J., Merideth T., and John H. After the death of his first wife Mr. Moore married Catharine Tarleton, and they had one daughter, Emily. Mary Moore married James Gray, who settled in Callaway county in 1824. They had, Virginia, Mary F., Caroline, William, John, and Wharton. Elizabeth Moore married Henry Brite, who settled in Callaway county in 1813, but afterward removed to Texas, where he died. Their children were—William, Charles, Wharton, Thomas, Barton, Lucas, Hannah, Anna, and Eliza. Nancy Moore married Judge Benjamin Young, who settled in Callaway county in 1820. They had Mary, Margaret, Elizabeth, and William.

MURPHY.—Augustus H. Murphy, of Louisville, Ky., settled in Callaway county in 1829. He married Nancy Curry, by whom he had—Augustus C., Richard T., John, William, Margaret A., Sarah J., Susan J., and Charles W.

MURRAY.—Robert Murray and his family came from Scotland to America on the first ship that sailed after the revolution. They settled in Fauquier county, Va., and one of their sons, named John, married Dorcas Robinson, and settled at Bullett Station, Ky. His children were—Jesse, John, Enoch, Alfred, James, Joseph, Nancy, and Dorcas. John was killed at Dudley's Defeat in the war of 1812. Enoch was born in 1779. He married Jemima Gray, of Virginia, and settled in Callaway county, Mo., in 1817. At that time he had one son, Andrew R., and after his settlement in Callaway county the following children were born—Benjamin F., Elizabeth B., and Nancy G.

MOSELEY.—Drury Mosely, of Tennessee, married Mary Thomas, by whom he had a son named Benjamin L., who married Eliza Thomas, and settled in Callaway county in 1828. His children were—John, Robert, Joseph, Benjamin, Andrew, Jr., Frances, Sarah J., Susan E., and Eliza.

McCLELLAND.—William McClelland, of Pennsylvania, married

Martha Miller, by whom he had—Jane, Martha, Robert, William, Elisha, and James. Robert married Elizabeth Amos, and settled in Callaway county in 1827. His children were—William, Thomas, James, Elisha, Joseph, Elizabeth, and Martha. Elisha, son of William McClelland, Sr., married Sally James, and settled in Boone county, Mo., in 1827. His children were—Mary J., Martha, John, and James. James, son of William McClelland, Sr., married Polly Hunt, and settled in Boone county in 1826. His children were—Elizabeth, Julia, Oliver, Mary A., James, Noah, and Robert.

METEER.—William Meteer married Nancy Kirkpatrick, and settled in Callaway county in 1826. Their children were—Polly, Catharine, Jane and John. Mr. Meteer was married the second time to the widow Miller, by whom he had—Samuel, Sally, Ann, and Virginia.

MILLER.—Abner Miller, of North Carolina, was married three times, and settled in Kentucky. His children were—Aaron, John, Henry, Jacob, Dolly, James, Margaret, Sally and Matilda. John married Margaret Fowler, and settled in Callaway county in 1823. Henry married Elizabeth Oliver, and settled in that county 1826. His children were—William B., Isaac, Henry, John, George W., Lucinda, Elizabeth, Rachel, and Harriet.

MOSELEY.—The children of Arthur Moseley, of Virginia, were—Arthur, Daniel, Robert, William, John, Judith, Martha, and Thomas. John and Thomas settled in Kentucky in 1796. The latter married Magdalene Guerrant, by whom he had—Daniel P., Robert, Thomas, John, Polly, Magdalene, Patsey, Elizabeth, Judith, Louisiana, and Peter. John settled in Callaway county, Mo., in 1829, and married Sophia McMahan. Magdalene married Edward Sallee, who settled in Callaway county in 1829. They had thirteen children. Patsey married Peter Glover, who settled in Callaway county in 1827. They had ten children. Judith was married first to John Moseley, and after his death she married Thomas Swearinger, who settled in Montgomery county, Mo., in 1834. Louisiana married Glover Smith, who settled in Callaway county in 1827.

MANNING.—Stephen Manning settled in Callaway county in 1825. His brother Asa had settled in Montgomery county at a much earlier date. Stephen Manning came from Warren county, Ky., where he married Sally Leet, by whom he had—Asa, Robert, Rozelda, and Nancy J. Mrs. Manning was a very large woman, but her husband was very small, and his neighbors used to tease him a good deal about his diminutiveness. He would reply by saying that he and Sally would make as good a man as any of them.

MAY.—Harry May settled on May's Prairie, in Callaway

county, in 1820, where he built a horse-mill and opened a race track. This race track became a place of note in those early times, and a great many races were run upon it. On a certain occasion the Willinghams and Kilgores, of Audrain county, borrowed Sanford Jameson's fine race nag, Janus, filled her mane and tail full of sheep burs, and took her to May's race track to run against a crack pony known as Nick Biddle, which had been brought from Kentucky by Thomas, David, and Singleton Shehan. The mare presented such a poor appearance with the burs in her mane and tail, that the bets were all in favor of the pony, and nearly every one present staked some money on the favorite. Colonel Jeff. Jones, who was a boy then, was there with $7:50 in his pocket, and he bet $5 of his money on the pony. When the race came off the mare beat the pony 250 yards in a run of 600, and there were some pretty long faces in the crowd that witnessed the result. Mr. Jameson afterward sold his little mare to a gentleman from Louisiana, for a large sum of money, and the latter won $80,000 with her while he kept her. She made the fastest time on record in the United States, in a race of 600 yards. Mr. May's children were—Gabriel, Hannah (Mrs. Joseph Sitten), Frances (Mrs. Stewart), Susan (Mrs. Crump), Matilda (Mrs. Robert Arm), Richard, John, and Harry, Jr.

McFARLANE.—George McFarlane was the only son of Duncan and Maria McFarlane, of Scotland. He was born January 12, 1796, and received a classical education from his father, who taught forty-six years in a parish school in Scotland, and was a finely educated man. George subsequently studied law at Edinburg, and then wrote and studied several years more in a lawyer's office in Glasgow. In 1821 he came to the United States, and landed at Philadelphia. The vessel was forty-nine days in making the trip, which is now made in less than eight by the steamers that ply between Europe and America. Mr. McFarlane remained in Philadelphia a short time, and then went to New Orleans as supercargo of a trading vessel. In 1823 he came West, and settled in Boone county, Mo., where he taught school two years. He then (1825) settled in Callaway county, a few miles north of Fulton, where he resided until his death, which occurred in April, 1866, from injuries received by falling out of a wagon. He never practiced law in America, but would occasionally write a deed or other legal instrument for the accommodation of his neighbors. He married Catharine Bennett, of Boone county, formerly of Madison county, Ky., and they had—William W. (who is a physician), Mary M., George B., and John D. Mrs. McFarlane is still living (1876), in Callaway county.

McPHEETERS.—Alexander McPheeters, of Ireland, settled in Virginia, and married Jane Campbell, of Augusta county, by whom he had eight children. His eldest son, Alexander, was mar-

ried first to Jane Kelso, by whom he had five children. He was
married the second time to Florence Henderson, by whom he had
two sons, Robert and William. He was married the third time
to a widow lady named Arnott, of Kentucky. Robert and William McPheeters settled in Callaway county, Mo., in 1839. The
former married Jane McKee, of Kentucky, and the latter married
Mary R. Henderson, daughter of David Henderson, of Kentucky.

MADDOX.—Sherwood Maddox, of Fauquier county, Va., married Elizabeth Ferguson, and in 1795 they removed to Scott
county, Ky. Their children were—James, Jacob M., Sherwood,
David, Larkin, Frances, and Elizabath. James and Jacob M.
married and remained in Kentucky. Sherwood married America M. Jones, and settled in Callaway county, Mo., in 1830. His
children were—Uriah, Wilson, David, Jacob, Irvin, Mary E.,
Catharine, Henry L., Larkin, and Elizabeth. Larkin married
Jane Powers, of Kentucky, and settled in Callaway county in
1825. They came to Missouri in an ox cart, drawn by a yoke of
oxen and a blind horse, and after they settled in Callaway county
he and his wife used to ride the horse and one of the oxen to
church, frequently going a distance of fifteen or twenty miles,
and back home the same day. After the death of Mrs. Maddox
her husband married Emeline Belcher, of Cass county. He had
twelve children by his two wives. Mr. Maddox was an outspoken
Southern sympathizer during the late war, and fearing that the
government would confiscate a large body of land which he
owned in Johnson county, he deeded it to a friend to hold for
him until the troubles were all settled. The next day he was
killed by an accident on the cars, and the friend to whom he had
entrusted so much endeavored to keep the land, but had to relin-
quish it after four years of litigation. Mr. Maddox was killed in
the early part of 1865, about the close of the war. David and
Elizabeth, brother and sister of Larkin Maddox, remained in
Kentucky. Uriah and Wilson died unmarried in Callaway
county. Jacob married Louisa E. Morris. Irvin is a bachelor.
Mary E. married Samuel Harrison. Catharine married Thomas
Harrison. Henry S. married Nancy McIntire.

MILLER.—William Miller, of Pennsylvania, settled in Bourbon
county, Ky., in 1778. He had—Robert, Thomas, William, Mot-
ley, Jane, and two others whose names could not be obtained.
Thomas married a Miss Dodd, and settled in Callaway county in
1826. He laid off and founded the town of Millersburg. His
children were—James, Sally, and William. Horace Miller, son
of John Miller and Caroline West, of Millersburg, Ky., settled in
Callaway county in 1834. He married Nancy Vernon, of Bourbon county, Ky. The other children of John Miller were—John
T., Alvin W., Marguery, Robert W., Joseph A., Richard S., Jemima W., and Preston A., all of whom came to Missouri except

the latter. Stephen Miller, of Maryland, had ten sons and one daughter. Four of his sons came to Missouri. Their names were Philip, William, and Abraham. Philip was married twice; first to a Miss Richardson, and second to Lucy McIntire. He had twenty-one children by his two wives, and gave each of them a quarter section of land when they were grown. William Miller settled in St. Louis county in 1798, and removed to Callaway county and settled in Millersburg in 1831. He was such a large man that he could hardly pass through the door of a house. He was a ranger in Nathan Boone's company in 1814. He married Jane Martin, and they had—Elizabeth, David, Martin A., Allen D., Luretha, and Harriet. Elizabeth married Albert Caruth. David died in Callaway county. Martin A. was married first to Jane Miller, by whom he had ten children. After her death he married Mrs. Ramsey, whose maiden name was Sally D. Miller. Allen D. married Maria Reed, of Kentucky. Luretha married Zadoc Barnes. Harriet married J. E. Zerley. Abraham Miller settled in Callaway county in 1818. He married Polly Rule, of Kentucky, by whom he had—Warden, William B., Minerva, James W., Noah W., Telemachus, Leander, Lycurgus, Vernile, and Barton S., all of whom settled in Callaway county. Samuel Miller was a carpenter by trade. He settled in St. Louis county in 1817, where he married Polly A. Hatton. In 1819 he settled in Callaway county, and built the jail at Elizabeth in 1821. His children were—William P., James E., Albert H., Wesley G., Benjamin M. (a physician), John O., Elizabeth A., Angeline, Cordelia, Catharine, and Frances. Wesley G. Miller is a distinguished Methodist minister, and Professor of Theology in Central College at Fayette, Mo. Samuel Miller died in 1858, and his remains were taken up in 1875 and reinterred in the cemetery at Miller's Church. They were found to be in a perfectly sound state when the grave was opened. Mrs. Miller is still living, in her 88th year. (See portrait on frontispiece.) She resides with her youngest son, on the old homestead, and takes great pleasure in recounting the perils and adventures of pioneer life in Missouri. She was the first member of the Methodist Church in Callaway county, and the first class of that denomination was organized in her little cabin, 16x18 feet in size, in 1819. Preaching was held there regularly for thirty years, and her house was often filled, night and day, with people who had come to hear the gospel preached. They frequently came as far as twenty and thirty miles, and she would borrow beds from her neighbors for them to sleep upon. The men would bring their guns and dogs with them. The guns were stacked in one corner of the house, while the dogs remained outside and fought. On one occasion the dogs treed a catamount during services, which were immediately closed so that all could go and witness the fight. The first election in Callaway county was held under a large oak tree near Mrs. Miller's house, and she had to cook dinner for the "big men," as she called them, while the rest sat around trees and ate gingerbread that they had brought with them.

Moss —Frederick Moss, of Virginia, married Sarah Tompkins, by whom he had—John, Edward, William, Pleasant, James, Mason, and four daughters. Mason married Catharine Hogan, by whom he had—William, James, John, and Sarah. He was married the second time to Lucy Hickman, by whom he had—David H., Margaret, Benjamin F., Henry W., Clara, Thomas T., Nancy B., and Charles. Mr. Moss settled in Callaway county in 1825.

Moore.—John Moore, of Ireland, emigrated to America and settled in Halifax county, Va. He had three sons—Bird, Armistead, and Tarleton. The latter married Elizabeth Stanfield, of Virginia, by whom he had—Sarah, Banks, Armistead, Catharine, and Edwin. Banks married Elizabeth J. Wilson, of Virginia, and settled in Callaway county in 1837. He had five sons and three daughters. Bird, son of Bird Moore, Sr., married Anna G. Sitten, of Callaway county, who died, and he afterward married Sarah Blackwell.

McDonald.—Joseph McDonald, of New York, was married first to Elizabeth Ogden, and settled in Henderson county, Ky., where they lived until 1818, when they removed to Boone county, Mo. Their children were—Daniel, Susan, Hiram, Nash, and Joseph. Mr. McDonald was married the second time to Nancy Willingham, and they had—Icham, Cash, Giles, Clark, Nancy, Pinckney, and Sally. Joseph, Icham, Susan, and Nash live in Ohio, and Cash, Giles, Clark, Nancy and Sally live in Texas.

McGary.—Major Hugh H. McGary, who, it will be remembered, took a prominent part in the battle of Blue Licks, Ky., (see page 34), settled in that State and was married several times. His children were—Daniel, Robert, William R., Hugh, John, Jesse, James, Elizabeth, Nancy, Rosa, and Sally. William R. married Patsey Davis, of Virginia, by whom he had—James D., Hugh H. and America I. James D. married Nancy Murray, and settled in Callaway county in 1822. He was a member of the Legislature one term, and is now living in Texas. Hugh H. married Susan Davis, and settled in Callaway county in 1831. He was married the second time to Rosetta Ewing. America I. married Thomas W. Langley, who settled in Callaway county in 1838. She is now a widow and resides in Howard county, Missouri.

McCracken.—Ovid, Cyrus, Isaac, William, Seneca, and Elizabeth McCracken were born in Ireland, but came to America prior to the revolution. Ovid married and settled in Indiana. Cyrus settled in Kentucky, and died, leaving five children. Isaac was Captain of a company of Kentucky militia, and was killed at the disastrous battle of Blue Licks. He left a widow and two daughters. William was also Captain of a company in the same battle, and was likewise killed. When Colonel Logan's army returned to the battle field the next day, his body was found and buried in an old house, which was burned to prevent the Indians from finding the grave. His remains were afterward taken up and buried at Lexington, Ky. Seneca was married first to Rebecca Williams, and second to Rebecca Reynolds. Elizabeth married John Hamilton, who settled in Warren county, Mo. Otho, a son of Cyrus McCracken, is now living in Callaway county, in his 86th year. He was a soldier of the war of 1812. He was married in 1832, to Jane Bell, of Kentucky, who died in 1840, leaving two children. He afterward married Sarah Wilson, by whom he had three children. She died in 1875. Mr. McCracken is noted for his wit and humor, and the felicitious manner in which he can crack a joke. He can tell anecdotes all day, and never repeat the same one; but he rarely smiles even in his most humorous moments.

McCLANAHAN.—Robert McClanahan married Elizabeth McCluer, and they had—Margaret, John, and Sophronia. Margaret married and lived in Indiana. John married Mary Griffith, of Kentucky, and settled in Callaway county, Mo., in 1832. They had—Robert, Margaret, James N., Amanda S., Nancy S., John, and Samuel W. Mr. McClanahan was married the second time to Jane Martin, of Kentucky.

McCAMEY.—Robert McCamey, of Pennsylvania, married Rosanna McConnell, and settled in Kentucky. They had—Nancy, Rosa, Margaret, Elizabeth, Polly, John, and Robert. Nancy married James McAfee, who settled in Boone county, Mo., in 1826. John was married first to Margaret McAfee, of Kentucky, and after her death he married Margaret Adams, of the same State, and settled in Missouri in 1828. Robert settled in Callaway county in 1826. He married Susan McAfee, of Kentucky, by whom he had—Lucinda, William A., Amanda, James I., Joseph, and John. Lucinda married Joseph Bennett, and is now a widow, with four children. Joseph and John died unmarried. James I. is still living, unmarried. Amanda married Charles H. Brown, Sr. William H. married Angeline Scott.

MARTEIN.—Abram Martein was a native of France. He came to American and settled in Virginia. He had a son named Nicholas, who settled first in North Carolina, and in 1804 he came to Missouri and settled in Callaway county. His children were— William, Abraham, Louis, Robert, Elizabeth, and Polly. William, better known as Esquire Billy Martein, was born in 1786. He served as a soldier in the war of 1812, furnishing his own outfit and paying his own expenses during the entire war. On one occasion he assisted in capturing 100 Indians.   He was married in December, 1818, to Winifred Hardyshell, and settled in Callaway county in 1820.   He was Justice of the Peace for twenty-one years, and was a zealous member of the Regular Baptist Church.   He died in 1872, leaving a widow and twelve children.   Mrs. Martein died in 1813.   The names of their children were—Nicholas P., John L., George W., William B., Cynthia, Malinda J., Mary A., Martha C., Louisa W., Caroline M., Elizabeth C., and Virginia.

NICHOLS.—John Nichols, of Bedford Co., Va., had—Archa, John, Frall, Elisha, Jesse, Catharine, and Jane.   Archa married Julia Hatcher, of Bedford county, and they had—Daniel, Bartley C., Elizabeth, Catharine, Byer, Lucy, Julia, and Patsey.   Bartley C. married Polly Richardson, and settled in Callaway county in 1836.   His first wife died, and he was married the second time to Martha J. Love.

NEAL.—Joseph Neal and his family settled in Callaway county in 1831.   His children at that time were—William, George, Joseph J., Thomas, John, Benjamin, Carroll A., and Mary A.— Benjamin, brother of Joseph Neal, Jr., married a Miss Walker, and settled in Callaway county in 1831.

NASH.—William Nash, Jr., of England, came to America and settled in Virginia, where he married a widow lady named Bradford, whose maiden name was Mary Morgan.   Mr. Nash subsequently removed to Tennessee.   His children were—Ira, Elizabeth, and William.   Ira married and settled in St. Charles county, Mo., in 1801.   William married Rebecca Leitchworth, and settled in St. Charles county in 1813, from whence he removed to Callaway county in 1816.   His children were—Ira, Alfred, James, Jesse, Allen, Elizabeth, and Nancy.

NUSUM.—John Nusum was born in England in 1721.   He learned the blacksmith's trade, and came to America in 1757.   He died in 1761, leaving two sons, Robert and William.   The latter married Margaret Peece, of Virginia, by whom he had—John, Lewis, William, Robert, Nathan, Conrad, David, Polly, Susan, Elizabeth, and Sally.   John and Robert settled in Callaway county in 1820. The former had married Sally McLung, of Greenbriar county, Va., by whom he had—Allen, Lewis, Nathan, Samuel, Nancy, Mary J., Sally A., and Amanda.   Robert married Elizabeth Guinn, of Virginia, by whom he had—Harvey, William, David, Rebecca, Julia, Virginia, Ruth, Susan, Sally, and Polly.   Harvey was Judge of the County Court of Callaway county for two years.

NEVINS.—John Nevins, of Ireland, married Winifred Dixon, came to America, and settled in Greenbriar county, Va.   In 1819 he removed to Missouri, and settled Callaway county.   His children were—James, Joseph, John, Thomas, Elizabeth, Nancy and Virginia.

NICHOLS.—Mr. Nichols, of Pennsylvania, was of German descent. He removed from Pennsylvania to Virginia, married Elizabeth Thomas, and afterward removed to Kentucky, and settled in Clark county, near Bryan's Station, where he died at the age of 98 years. His widow died many years afterward, aged 115 years. Their children were—George, William, Robert, Frederick, James, Catharine, Frances and Elizabeth, five of whom lived and died in Missouri, and three in Kentucky. George was born in Loudon county, Va., and was married in the same county to Rebecca Davis, by whom he had—James, William, George, Jr., Garret, Felix G., Frederick, Elizabeth, Polly, Eveline, Nancy and Sally. Mr. Nichols removed with his family to Callaway county, Mo., in 1824, and entered the land upon which Fulton is situated. The town was laid off in 1825, and he donated 50 acres of his land to the county. Mr. Nichols built the first cabin in Fulton, and had to go ten miles get men to help him raise it. They came before sun-rise on the appointed day, had the cabin completed before the sun went down, and danced in it the same night. Mr. Felix G. Nichols, fifth son of George Nichols, Sr., and to whom we are indebted for this sketch, is the only member of his father's family now living in Callaway county. He says that in early days in that county bread was the most difficult of all things to get. The first mill he ever saw was a horse-mill with a large wheel over-head, around which was a raw-hide cable that propelled the stones. A hollow sycamore "gum" was used for both meal and bolting chest, the latter being turned by hand. When the blackberry season came in there was always great rejoicing. They would then throw their corn "dodgers" to the dogs, and "go for" the blackberries with the greatest relish. Buckskin shirts, pants and moccasins were all the style. At a wedding which Mr. Nichols attended in 1824, the bride was dressed entirely in cotton of her own spinning and weaving, and which she had also made into garments. The groom wore pants and shirt of white cotton, and a coat and vest of buckskin, while his low gaiter shoes were made white with tallow. He came to the bride's home six hours before the time for the wedding, amd remained until the appointed hour. They were married by a Hard Shell Baptist preacher, who was dressed in buckskin from head to foot. Mr. Nichols married Elizabeth Reno, of Missouri, by whom he had seven children. His mother, Rebecca Davis, was a daughter of John Davis, of Wales, who came to America and settled in Virginia. His brother Thomas settled in South Carolina. Their father was a silk merchant in Wales, and left an estate valued at $33,-000,000 of dollars, a portion of which the Nichols heirs are now sueing for. John Davis was married three times, and had sixteen children. He removed from Virginia to Montgomery county, Ky., where he died at the age of 107 years.

OVERFELT.—Matthias Overfelt, of Franklin county, Va., married Mary Vineyard, and they had—Charles, John, Michael, and Mary. Charles settled in Monroe county, Mo. Michael was in the war of 1812. He married Mary Ayers, of Virginia, and settled in Callaway county in 1829. His children were—Aletha, Irean, Kitburd, Bethena, Mary, Eli, John, Elijah, William, and Elizabeth.

OLIVER.—James Oliver, of Clark county, Ky., married Rachel Conkwright, and they had—John, James, and Benjamin. James married Nancy Broughton, of Kentucky, by whom he had—William, Richard, Robert, James, Taylor, Thomas, Rachel, Margaret, Ellen, and George. Margaret married Richard Swearinger. Rachel married R. F. Gregory, of Callaway county. William died unmarried. The rest of the children are living in Callaway county, unmarried.

PRICE.—Samuel Price lived and died in Virginia. He left a widow and ten children, all of whom came to Missouri and settled in Callaway county in 1836. They were about the first settlers on Grand Prairie, and were a hardy, honest, intelligent, and highly respected class of people. The names of the children were—Cyrus, Margaret, Addison, Elizabeth, Sarah, Nancy, Rebecca, Charles, John, and Mary.

PLEDGE.— William Pledge, of England, married Elizabeth Woodson, and came to America and settled in Goochland county, Va. Their children were—William, John, Arden, Frank L., Elizabeth and Nancy. John was a soldier of the war of 1812. William married Mary Gray, of Virginia, by whom he had—John A., Susan A., William N., George F., Thomas G., and Jane. Mr. Pledge removed first to Ross county, Ohio, in 1824, from whence he came to Callaway county, Mo., in 1831. Susan A. married Willis Snell, who settled in Callaway county in 1819. Jane died single. John A. married Minnie C. Warren, and settled in Callaway county in 1819. William N. married Isabella Luper, and is now living in Callaway county. He served in the Black Hawk war. Mr. Pledge was not an experienced hunter, though fond of the sport. One day he killed six buzzards, supposing them to be wild turkeys, and did not discover his mistake until he had carried them nearly home. Thomas G. Pledge married Florence Luper.

PRICE.—Major Samuel Price, a soldier of the revolutionary war, died in Greenbriar county, Va., in his 93d year. He was of Welch descent. He was married twice, and the names of his children were—Jacob, Samuel, William, James, John, Catharine, Polly, and Margaret. James settled in Callaway county, Mo., in

1828. He married Sarah McClentic, and they had—Albert, Jane, Robert, Margaret, James, Samuel, and Sarah. Mr. Price was a soldier of the war of 1812. William Price married Sarah Walker, and settled in Callaway county in 1830. He also was a soldier of the war of 1812. His children were—Margaret, Joseph, John, Elizabeth, Sarah, and William.

PHILLIPS.—John and Jonathan Phillips, sons of Jonathan Phillips, Sr., of East Tennessee, settled in Callaway county in 1817. John married Nancy Allen, and they had—Andrew, David, Mary, Jane, Moses, Bethel, Hiram R., Elizabeth, Matilda, Charity, Sarah, Sampson, Eliza, and Rosa.

PETERS.—Charles Peters, of Nelson county, Va., settled in Callaway county, on Auxvasse creek, about the year 1833. He was married twice. By his first wife he had seven children, but raised only three, viz.: Oliver, Napoleon, and Lafayette. He was married the second time to Mary A. Fulkes, by whom he had—John, Martha, Claiborne, Frank, Samuel, Mary and Maria, all of whom married and settled in Callaway county, and are all dead except three.

PRATT.—William Pratt and his wife, both natives of Ireland, came to America and settled in Smith county, Tennessee. They had—John, William, and Lavinia. Mrs. Pratt died, and her husband subsequently married Polly Aikens, of Tennessee, by whom he had—Nancy, Rebecca, Edward, Mary A., Jerusha, William, Albert G., Samuel, Araminta, and Carroll. John and William Pratt came to Missouri in 1817. The former settled in Clay county. His wife was Anna Williams, and they both died, leaving four children—Charles W., Ann, Fidella, and William. Chales W. married Sally Vaughn, and lives in Callaway county. Fidella married John Allen, of Callaway county.—William, son of William Pratt, Sr., married Jerusha Burchett, of Tennessee, and settled on Coats' Prairie, in Callaway county, in 1817. His children were—John, Thomas J., James M., Lavinia, and Elizabeth. John died of cholera, in 1833, in his 24th year. Thomas J. was married in 1839 to Lucinda Petty, by whom he had—James M., John M., and Robert. Mr. Pratt was a good citizen and a kind husband and father. He died in 1876, and his loss was much lamented by all who knew him. James Pratt died in childhood, in Tennessee. Lavina was married first to Oliver Wright, by whom she had William H. and Mary E. She was married the second time to James Hamilton, by whom she had one daughter, named Fannie. Elizabeth Pratt married Hon. John S. Henderson, of Callaway county.

PALMER.—David Palmer, of New Jersey, married Ruth Davis, of Virginia, by whom he had—Joel, Harriet, John J., Lucinda, Thomas N., Adelaide and Marion. Joel, who is still living in

Callaway county, was born in Jefferson county, Va., in 1797. He volunteered in the war of 1812, and served under General Stansbury. He was in the battles of Bladdensburg and Baltimore. In 1821 he married Amy M. Yates, of Bedford county, Va., by whom he had—David, Harriet E., Sarah E., Burrell B., Marion, William B., Garret P., Martha I., Lucy C., John N., Amy M., and Cornelia H. Harriet, daughter of David Palmer, Sr., lived and died in St. Charles county, Mo. John J. is the present editor of the Richmond, Va., *Enquirer*. He has been married three times, and has but one child. Lucinda Palmer married John Potts, who settled in Callaway county in 1828. They had—Lydia, John, Joel, Susan and Caroline. Thomas N. Palmer disappeared in a very mysterious manner, and was never heard of again. Adelaide married and died in Texas. Marion died in his youth.

PATTON.—James Patton, Sr., had—Wilson, John, Thomas, James Jr., Margaret and Fanny. Wilson Married Polly Martins, and settled in Callaway county in 1826. John married Nancy Duncan, and settled in that county the same year. Thomas married Anna E. Duncan, and also settled in Callaway county in 1826. Margaret married Alexander Henderson, who settled in Kentucky. William married and settled in Callaway county in 1826.

POWELL. —Jonathan Powell, of Maryland, married Nancy Franklin, and they had—Sally, Miranda, Charlotte, and William. Mr. Powell died in 1815, and his widow afterward married Samuel Bowles, who came to Callaway county in 1836. Sally Powell married James Steel. Miranda married Judge Henry Nusum, of Callaway Co. Charlotte married Daniel Dunham, of Callaway Co.

PEMBERTON.—George Pemberton, of Virginia, had a son named John, who married Lucy Vivion, of Virginia, and settled in Scott county, Ky. They had—Fanny, Lewis, Vivion, Harvey, Lucinda, James, Tandy and Elizabeth, all of whom settled in Boone and Callaway counties in 1829.

RATEKIN.—John Ratekin, of Campbell county, Va., married Mary Smart, and settled in Montgomery county, Ky., from whence they emigrated to Callaway county, Mo., in 1828. Their children were—Anna E., Sarah, Eliza S., Edmund W., Mary S., Martha V., Legrand, Miranda, James C., and John G. Anna E. was married first to James D. Fisher, and second to Colonel Patrick Ewing. Sarah married James Crump, who built the penitentiary and court house at Jefferson City. Mary S. married Stephen Boulware. Martha V. married David H. C. Chratham. Miranda married Thomas Cress. Mr. Ratekin was a mechanic and a natural genius. He made all of his furniture, knives and forks, table ware, etc. He also built his own house. He once sold some mules to a man on credit, and the man stole one of his negroes and ran off with him and the mules to the South. Four years afterward the negro came back home, having run away from the man to whom he had been sold in the South.

RAMSEY.—Jonathan Ramsey was born in Livingston county, Ky. His father was Josiah Ramsey, who was captured by the Indians when he was seven years of age, and remained with them until he was thirty. He became a celebrated hunter, and settled in Callaway county, Mo., in 1819. Jonathan was married in Kentucky, to Hannah Lampkin, by whom he had—Allen, Ewell, Maria, and Jane. Mr. Ramsey was a delegate to the Constitutional Convention in 1820, and afterward represented Callaway county in the Legislature for several years. He was also one of the Commissioners selected to locate the Capital of the State. He strongly advocated Cotesansdessein as the place, but there was some dispute about the title to the land upon which the town was situated, and Jefferson City was selected as the future Capital. Mr. Ramsey was a shrewd business man, and accumulated a fortune before his death. Jane Ramsey married Robert Ewing, of Kentucky, and their son, Hon. Henry Clay Ewing, became Attorney-General of Missouri.

RILEY.—John Riley was born in Ireland. When he was fourteen years of age he came to America with his parents, and his uncle Charles Riley, and his aunts Elizabeth and Mary. They settled in Pennsylvania, and Charles Riley served as a soldier in the revolutionary war. John was married in Pennsylvania, to Mary Straham, and settled in Bourbon county, Ky., in 1793. His children were—Samuel, Elizabeth, Grizelda, Jane (who was a mute), Mary, Nancy, Sarah, and John, Jr. After the death of his first wife Mr. Ramsey married the widow Franks, by whom he had—Susan, Martha, and Charles. Samuel, now living in Callaway county, was in the war of 1812. After the war he made six trips to New Orleans in flatboats, and walked back to his home in Kentucky each time, a distance of nine hundred miles. In 1816 he was married to Jane Robertson, of Montgomery Co., Ky., and settled in Callaway county, Mo., in 1825. His children were—William C. (a physician), Mary G., Benjamin S., James M., Eliza J., John G., Samuel S., Jr., Julia A., George T., Joseph R. (also a physician), and Fielding S.

READ.—Robert Read, of Tennessee, married a daughter of Rev. William Coats, and settled on Coats' Prairie in 1817. He was a soldier in the war of 1812, and present at the battle of New Orleans. He was postmaster at Fulton for a number of years. He left no children; his widow is still living.

ROBINSON.—Henry Robinson, of Virginia, had two sons, Henry and Mitchell. The former married a Miss Scott, of Kentucky, and raised a large family. Mitchell married Nancy Waller, of Virginia, and they had a son named Henry, who married Nancy

A. Fisher, and settled in Pike county, Mo., where he died in 1860, leaving a widow and seven children. James, another son of Mitchell Robinson, married Nancy Alford, of Kentucky, and they had three children. Captain John Robinson, a third son of Mitchell Robinson, married Mary B. Walter, of Virginia, in 1824, and removed to Callaway county in 1826. He entered the land upon which the town of McCredie is now situated. His children were—Judith A., Agnes J., Walter A., Nancy W., John E., Mitchell W., Addison L., and Mary E.

RICE.—Shelton Rice, of Virginia, married Lucy Williams, and settled in Tennessee. In 1795 he removed to Mercer county, Ky. His children were—Absalom, Polly, Nancy, Joseph, Newton, Harvey, Lucy, and Kittura. Absalom married Ellen Hensley, of Kentucky, and settled in Callaway county, Mo., in 1831. His children were—Amanda, William, Mary and John. Mr. Rice is a minister of the Christian Church, and he organized the first church of that faith in Callaway county, in 1833. He and his wife have lived together fifty years, and a cross word has never passed between them.

ROBINSON.—Andrew Robinson and wife were born in Ireland, but came to America and settled in Pennsylvania previous to the revolutionary war. Their son James went to Bourbon county, Ky., during the early settlement of that State, and took part in the war against the Indians. He married the widow of Samuel Nesbit, whose maiden name was Elspy Watt. Her first husband was killed by the Indians. The children of James Robinson were—Andrew, James S., John, and Joseph. Andrew lives in Indiana. James and Joseph married and died in Kentucky. John married Barbara L. F. Willett, and settled in Callaway Co., Mo., in 1831. His children were—James E., William W., Eleanor P., Amanda, Elizabeth, and Viva M. Mr. Robinson is now in his 80th year, and has been an influential and useful citizen. He was Justice of the Peace in Callaway county for some time.

RANDOLPH.—The children of Obediah Randolph, of Virginia, were—William, Thomas, Edmund, James, Lucy A., and Martha. Edmund settled in Callaway county in 1828, and married Martha McClelland, by whom he had—Robert, James, Lucy, Sally, Elizabeth, and Thomas. William and Thomas, sons of Obediah Randolph, settled in Montgomery county, Mo.

REYNOLDS.—William and James Reynolds were sons of John Reynolds, of Halifax county, Va. William married Lucy E. Holt, daughter of Timothy Holt, Sr., and settled in Callaway county in 1828. His children were—Elizabeth, John, Martha, Anna, Bedford, Lucy, Ann, Fanny, and James.

RENO.—Francis Reno, was born in France, but came to America after he was grown, and settled in Prince William county, Va., where he married a Miss Bayliss. Their children were— Enoch, Frank, George, Bayliss, Millie, Fanny, Dolly, Jane, and Lydia. Bayliss married Jane Davis, and settled in Fleming county, Ky., in 1811. They had—Richard D., Matilda, Henry F., and Elizabeth. Mr. Reno settled in Callaway county in 1831. Richard D. was married twice; first to Mary Summers, and second to Jane H. Davis. He settled in Callaway county in 1826. Matilda married James R. Chalpant, who settled in Callaway county in 1829. Henry F. married Sarah Alexander, and settled in Callaway county in 1829. He served as Judge of the County Court several terms. Elizabeth married Felix G. Nichols, who settled in Callaway county in 1824.

ROBERTSON.—Benjamin Robertson, of North Carolina, married a Miss Allen, and settled in Montgomery county, Ky. They had— Polly, Jane, Margaret, Joseph, William, Benjamin, and John A. Jane married Samuel Riley, of Callaway county. William, who was a physician, settled in Pike county, Mo., and was drowned in Spencer's Creek. John A. settled in St. Charles in 1815, where he married Nancy Kerr, and removed to Callaway county in 1819.

RIDGEWAY.—Ninnian Ridgeway married Martha Redmon, of Kentucky, and settled in Callaway county in 1823. They had— John D , William, Zacharia, James R., A. D., Martin H., Mary, Thomas, Nancy, Martha, and Sarah. William married Paulina Rainfro, and they had eight children, all of whom live in Callaway county. The rest of the Ridgeway children married and settled in Callaway, Boone, and Montgomery counties, and are all living except Thomas, Martha, Nancy, and Sarah.

SMITH.—James Smith was born and raised in the northern part of Ireland. In 1783 he emigrated to America and settled in Berks county, Pa., where he married Jane Blakey, and removed to Madison county, Ky. Their children were—John, William, Polly, Elizabeth, Patsey, James, and David. John married Nancy Fowler, and died in 1857, leaving a widow and two children. William was born in Kentucky, in 1794, and was married in 1824 to Martha McMichel, daughter of John McMichel, of S . Louis county, Mo., by whom he had—James B., John M., Benjamin, William H., Oliver P., Warren A., Josephine, Martha O., and Fielding W. Mr. Smith represented Boone county in the Legislature one term. Polly, daughter of James Smith, Sr., married Henry Anderson, who died without issue. She is now living in Boone county, a widow. Elizabeth married John Mc-Calip, of Cooper county, and died without issue. Patsey married Thomas Taylor, who settled in Boone county in 1828. They both died, leaving four sons and two daughters. James, Jr., married Nancy Howard, of Kentucky, and settled in Howard county Mo. They had seven sons and two daughters. David Smith married Josephine McMichel, and settled in Boone county. They had eight sons and four daughters.

SMITH.—Hezekiah Smith, of Virginia, was married twice; first to the widow Dodson, by whom he had—Thomas, Patsey, and William. By his second wife he had—Hezekiah, Jr., James, and Joel. Thomas settled first in Kentucky, but in 1811 he came to Missouri, and brought with him in his saddle-bags the gun lock that was on Captain James Callaway's gun when he was killed. It was a waterproof flint-lock, of a superior pattern, and fitted so closely that water could not penetrate to the powder. Mr. Smith served as a ranger in one of Callaway's companies for some time. He was married first to Polly Darst, daughter of David Darst, Sr., by whom he had two children, Miles and Saily. After the death of his first wife Mr. Smith married her sister Elizabeth, by whom he had Burrell, Loyd, Lavinia, Mackey, David, Bethel, Polly, Cyrus C., Henry, and Zenaz. Mr. Smith was married the third time to the widow Craig, and after her death he was married the fourth time to Mary Hedderston. He settled in Callaway county in 1818, and established Smith's Landing, on the Missouri river, now called St. Aubert. Mr. Smith was a wealthy and highly respected citizen. He was a member of the Old Baptist Church forty-five years.

SMITH.—Thomas Smith, of England, came to America and settled in Virginia. His son, Thomas, Jr., married a Miss Davis, and settled in South Carolina. They had—John, Thomas, Charles, Moses, and several daughters. John was married first to Rebecca Jeffers, by whom he had—William, John, and Polly. He was married the second time to Sarah Moseley, by whom he had—Nimrod, Abel, Garland, James, Thomas, Edward, Susan, Nancy, and Lucretia. Nimrod married Celia Gunn, and settled in Callaway county in 1837. They had—Isaac, William, John, Thomas, Elizabeth, Sarah J., and Nancy. Mr Smith is still living, in his 73d year; his wife is in her 69th year, and blind.

SWAN.—John Swan, of England, came to America and settled first in Pennsylvania, from whence he removed to Virginia, then to Kentucky, and in 1815 he came to Missouri and settled on the St. Francois river, where he died. He was married in Virginia, to Margaret Coburn, by whom he had—Richard, Polly, John, Cynthia, Thomas, and Letitia, all of whom came to Missouri. Richard married Nancy Thompson of Kentucky, and settled in Missouri in 1834. He had four sons and six daughters.

SMITH.—Peter Smith was of German descent. He was born in Maryland, but settled in Montgomery county, Ky. He married Susan Millroy, and they had—Joseph, William, Margaret, John, Elizabeth, George L., James, and Polly. George L. was married in 1828 to Polly A. Scott, of Kentucky, the ceremony being performed by the celebrated Deacon Smith. Soon after their marriage Mr. Smith and his wife packed everything they possessed on three horses, and came to Missouri. When they stopped at the house of Mr. Thomas Harrison, on the Booneslick road, in Callaway county, they had just twenty-five cents as the total of their worldly wealth in cash. Mr. Smith has served both as Lieutenant and Captain of militia in Callaway county. James Smith, brother of John L., died in Ralls county, a bachelor.

SMITH.—James Smith, of Warren county, Va., married Catharine Webb. Their son Tarleton married Lucy Mallory, and settled in Callaway county in 1834. They had—Mary T., Permelia A., Sidney N., James H., Lucy, Tarleton, Frances E., Sarah N., Eliza, and Stephen I.

SCOTT.—John Scott, of Campbell county, Va., married the widow of Little Page, whose maiden name was Elizabeth Matthews. They had two children, Matthias and Martha. The latter died in Virginia, and the former was married in 1804 to Elizabeth Wayne, of Virginia. They settled in Montgomery county, Ky., where they lived twenty-five years, and then, in 1829, they came to Missouri and settled in Callaway county. They had thirteen children. After the death of his first wife Mr. Scott married Elizabeth Barnes, by whom he had one child. He died in 1852, but his widow still survives.

SNELL.—John Snell and his wife, whose maiden name was Elizabeth Watts, removed from Virginia to Scott county, Ky., at an early date. They had—John, Jr., Willis W., Robert, William, Joseph, Frank, and Anna. John married Polly Burton, of Virginia, and settled in Callaway county in 1825. He was married the second time to Barbara Roth, of Indiana, and by his two wives he had twenty-six children, thirteen of whom lived to be grown. The names of the latter were—Lucy, Frank, Greenup, William, Warfield, Garrett, Anna, Elijah, John R., Carroll, Polly, Maria, and Julia. Willis W., brother of John Snell, married Jane Herndon, of Kentucky, and settled in Callaway county in 1825. Their children were—Susan, William, James, Herndon, Edward, Willis, and Clay. Mr. Snell was Sheriff of Callaway county in 1828; he was also a member of the State Senate one term. Robert Snell married Polly Blanton, and settled in Callaway county. He was married the second time to the widow Simpson, by whom he had several children. William Snell settled in Howard county, Mo. Joseph was killed by his son-in-law, in Kentucky. Frank and Anna married and lived and died in Kentucky.

SCOTT.—The children of Reuben Scott, of Kentucky, were—

John, Martin, William, Reuben, Stephen, Elijah, Thomas, and Phœbe. Reuben married Jane Gilmore, and settled in Callaway county in 1827. Their children were—James, Nancy J., Stephen L., and Silas. Mrs. Scott died, and he afterwar l married the widow Allen, whose maiden name was Mary Steel, by whom he had—Martha, John A., Mary M., Sarah A., William, Samuel M., and Andrew Z. William Scott, son of Reuben, Sr., married Susan Tate, of Kentucky, by whom he had—Eliza, Elizabeth, William, and Margaret. Stephen Scott married a widow lady named Montgomery, by whom he had a son named William C., who settled in Mexico, Mo., in 1852.

SIMCO —In Albemarle county, Va., there lived a Mr. Simco who had three children—James, Brooks, and Catharine. The two latter married in Virginia, and lived and died there. James married Frances Kennedy, of Virginia, by whom he had—Mary, Elizabeth, Lucy, Judith, William, Reuben, Wharton, Samuel, and John. Mr. Simco was a soldier in the war of 1812, and settled in Callaway county in 1836. All of his children came with him to Missouri except Samuel. Mary married David Sheets, who died in Virginia. She then married William Hardin, who settled in Callaway county in 1836. Lucy married George Herron. Judith married John Fletcher. Reuben married Sarah Hill, and settled in Callaway county in 1834. Wharton married Julia A. Brockman, of Missouri. John was married twice; first to Mary Fletcher, and second to Frances Smith, both of Callaway county. William died in Mississippi, unmarried.

SCOTT.—William Scott and his wife, whose maiden name was Hawthorn, were natives of Pennsylvania, but removed to Lafayette county, Ky. Their son, William B., was married in 1806 to Lydia Metcalf, a niece of Governor Metcalf, of Kentucky. In 1819 they came in a keel-boat to Callaway county, and settled in the bottom on the Missouri river, six miles below Jefferson City, where Mr. Scott died, in 1840. Their children were— Charles M., Mary A., Angeline T., Eveline M., Alexander D., George W., Lydia, James M., and William V. Charles M. was married twice; first to Mary A. Hawkins, and second to Mrs. McLane. Mary A. Scott married Colonel John Boyd. Angeline married William H. McCamey. Eveline M. married Robert D. Irvin. Lydia married William C. Herron. Alexander married and removed to Texas. George W. married a widow lady named Daugherty. James M. married Jane Irvin. William V. was a soldier in the Mexican war, and died unmarried. Mrs. Scott widow of William B. Scott, Sr., is still living, in her 88th year, and keeps herself constantly employed making wax flowers and bed quilts of a superior pattern.

SCHOLL.—William Scholl, of England, married a Miss Morgan, and they had—Peter, Isaac, Aaron, Joseph, John, Sally, Elizabeth, and Rachel. Joseph was born in 1755, and died in 1835. He married Lavinia Boone, daughter of Daniel Boone, and settled in Clark county, Ky. They had eight children—Jesse B., Septimus, Marcus, Joseph, Selah, Marcia, Leah, and Daniel B. Jesse B. married Elizabeth Miller, of Kentucky, and settled in St. Charles county, Mo., in 1811. He died in 1839. Septimus married Sallie Miller, and came to Missouri. His children were —Nelson, Daniel B., Marcus, Joseph, Cyrus, Catharine, and Eliza. Marcus Scholl was married twice, and by his second wife had two sons, Marcus, Jr., and Joseph. Joseph, son of Joseph Scholl, Sr., married Rebecca V. G. Miller, and settled in Callaway county in 1820, where his wife died in 1829. Their children were—Oliver P., Cyrus R. M., and James R. Mr. Scholl was married the second time to Eliza A. Broughton, of Kentucky, by whom he had—Rebecca, Elizabeth, Catharine, Louisa, Eliza, Celia, Septimus, Jesse B., Joseph R., Nelson, and Sarah. Mr. Scholl was a Justice of the Peace in Callaway county for twenty-two years, and in early days was a great bear and deer hunter. His second wife, who is still living, often hunted with him, and has killed several deer. Mr. S. would frequently go into caves after bears, and was present when Robert Graham had the fight with the wolf in Loutre creek. He is now in his 76th year, and his eye sight is so good that he can see to read fine print through an awl hole in a pair of leather spectacles.—Peter, son of William Scholl, of England, married Mary Boone, daughter of George Boone, a brother of Daniel, by whom he had thirteen children. Two of his sons, John and Peter, came to Callaway county, the former in 1830, and the latter in 1826. John married Cenia Jones, and they had seven children. Peter married Elizabeth Hunter, and they had William M. and Mary. The former was Sheriff of Callaway county in 1875. He married Sallie Hughes, a daughter of Reese Hughes. Mary Scholl married Milton Jones, and died some time afterward.

SAYERS.—John T. Sayers was born in Virginia in 1758. He joined the patriot army during the revolutionary war and served with gallantry during that contest. He married Susan Crockett, and settled in Wythe county, Va., where they both died. Their children were—Robert, William, Samuel, John T., Margaret, Easter, Lucy, and Jane. Robert and John T. were in the war of 1812. Samuel married Elizabeth Goes, and settled in Callaway county in 1833. He died in 1855, leaving a widow, who still survives, and the following children—Susan C., Elizabeth J., Mary E., Lucy A. M., Helen C., Nancy V., John T., and George R.

SITTEN.—Joseph Sitten, of North Carolina, married Dinah Bick, and they had—John, Jeffrey, Philip, William, Thomas, Jesse, Lawrence, John, Lydia, Dinah, and Saland. Mr. Sitten and his family, with the exception of Thomas, who died in Tennessee, settled in Lincoln county, Mo., in 1816. Lawrence, the seventh son, had settled in St. Charles county in 1808. Jeffrey married Polly Bostick, of North Carolina, and settled in Callaway county in 1819. His children were—Joseph, John, Benjamin F., William M., Vincent R., Thomas B., Polly, Sally, Mahala, Lydia, and Maria. Joseph, son of Jeffrey Sitten, kept the first hotel in Fulton, in 1825.

SAMPSON.—Hugh Sampson, of Scotland, had a son named John, who came to America and settled in Madison county, Va. He married Elizabeth Major, by whom he had but one child, a son, named John. The latter married Frankie Medley, of Virginia, and they had one son, also named John. Mr. Sampson died, and his widow and her son came to Callaway county in 1837. The latter was married first to Mildred Tinsley, and after her death he married the widow of George Emerson, whose maiden name was Nancy Snell. Major Sampson is a very large man, measuring six feet six inches without his boots.

SIMMS.—Matthew Simms and his wife, who was a Miss Emory, removed from North Carolina to Madison county, Ky., in 1779. Their children were—Nancy, William, Elizabeth, Lucinda, and Josiah. William married Sally Barnes, of Kentucky, and settled in Howard county, Mo., in 1818. His children were—Elias, James, Tarleton, William, Irving, John, Elizabeth, Rebecca, Lucretia, Nancy, and Sally. Elias married Elizabeth Martin, and settled in Missouri in 1819. James settled in Callaway county in 1830. Tarleton married Permelia Bowlin, and settled in Boone county in 1819. William married Mary Gay, and settled in Audrain county in 1835. Irvin married Elizabeth Turner, and settled in Boone county in 1819. John married Martha Crews, and settled in Boone county the same year. Elizabeth married James Barnes, who settled in Boone county in 1816. Rebecca married Azal Barnes, who settled in Missouri in 1835. Lucretia married Benjamin Barnes, who settled in Boone county in 1816. Nancy married Ezekiel Hickman, who settled in Boone county in 1816. Sally married George Hickman, who settled in Boone county in 1835.

SELBY.—John Selby, of Maryland, was a Methodist preacher. He married Rebecca Jones, and settled in Bourbon county, Ky., in 1806. In 1824 he removed to Callaway county, Mo., where his wife died in 1828. Their children were—Isaiah, Jesse J., Assanith, William J., Anna, John M., James H., Louis V., Eliza, Lucinda, and Henry B. Isaiah married Sallie Bass, and settled in Callaway county in 1824. Jesse J. married Elizabeth Herreford. Assanith married Henry Swift, who settled in Boone county in 1823. William J. married Julia A. Turley. Ann married her cousin, Joseph Selby, who settled in Callaway county in 1824. John M. married Emily Dazey, James H. married

Louisa Dazey, and Louis V. married Milley Dazey. Eliza married Hawley Herreford. Lucinda married Samuel Hardin, who settled in Boone county. Henry B. married Mary Steele.

STEELE.—Colonel John Steele, of Virginia, married a widow lady named Sarah Holland, and settled in Callaway county in 1834. His children were—Isaac, Margaret, and Sarah. Colonel Steele served as Captain of militia for some time, and then as Colonel for a number of years.

SCOTT.—Captain Saybrook Scott lived in Georgetown, District of Columbia, and was a sea captain. He married Miss Canan Darne, by whom he had—Allen, Robert, and Elizabeth. Allen was also a sea captain. He married Mary Darne, by whom he had—James, John D., William A., Mary A., Melvina, Jeannette E., and Henry. Captain Scott settled in Callaway county in 1837. His son, John D., was captain of a steamboat on the Mississippi river for thirty years. He married Catharine Darne, of Virginia. James Scott married Maria Ellis, of Virginia, and settled in Callaway county in 1837. William A. married Margaret Brasher, and settled in Callaway county in 1837.

SMART.—John Smart, son of Elisha Smart and Amy Glover, of England, married Elizabeth Ford, of Kentucky, and they had —James, Edward, Enos, Ann, and Polly. James settled in Callaway county in 1828, and married Rachel Ewing, who died, and he afterward married Susan Glover. Edward married Matilda Glover, and settled in Callaway county in 1833. Enos was married three times, and settled in Callaway county in 1833. Polly, a daughter of John Smart, married Joseph Warner, who settled in Callaway county in 1835.—(Other children of Elisha Smart, Sr.)—Edward married Elizabeth Heath, and settled in Callaway county in 1833. William married Anna Glover, and settled in that county in 1828. David married Permelia Bledsoe, and settled in Callaway county in 1833. Thomas married Harriet Thompson, and settled in Callaway county in 1832. Glover Smart married Lou Moseley, and settled in Callaway county in 1832. Polly married John Ratekin, and settled Callaway county in 1828.

SHELEY.—John Sheley, Jr., of Virginia, married Mary Ridgeway, by whom he had—John, Benjamin, Harrow, Singleton, Van, George, Reason, Polly, Elizabeth, and Charlotte. Harrow married Sally Kelley. Benjamin married Elizabeth Boulware. Singleton was married first to Susan Oldham, and after her death he married Jane Creswell. Van was married first to Martha Woods, and second to Nancy Overton. All of the foregoing settled in Callaway county in 1831. George married Sally Brooker, and settled in Callaway county in 1834. Reason married Nancy J. White, and settled in Callaway county in 1833.

SUGGETT.—James Suggett, of Wales, came to America and settled in Baltimore, where he married Elizabeth Smith, by whom he had a son named John, who married Mildred Davis, of Virginia, and they had—James, William, John, Edgar, Milton, Elizabeth, Catharine, and Polly. James was a Hard-Shell Baptist preacher, and noted for his facility in telling yarns. He married Sally Ridden, of Virginia, and settled in Boone county, Mo., in 1822; but in 1833 he removed to Callaway county. His children were—Thomas S., James M., John, Edgcome, Joseph R., Henry, Benjamin, William W., Malinda, Nancy, Catharine, and Susan. Thomas served in the war of 1812. James M. is a bachelor, and, like his father, loves to tell amusing stories. John, a brother of Rev. James Suggett, married Winnifred Craig, and settled in Callaway county in 1835. His children were—Volney, Minter, John H., Garret, Frances, Araminta, and Martha.

STOKES.—Daniel Stokes, a German, who lived in Halifax county, Va., married a Miss Dupley, by whom he had—Thomas, Josiah, William, Young, Bartlett, Henry, and Polly. Thomas married Polly Wade, and they had Henry W. and Thomas, Jr. He was married the second time to a Mrs. Mundy, and they had—Singleton, Hamilton, Mumford, Armon, and Sarah. Henry W. Stokes settled in Callaway county in 1835. He married Polly Tatum, and they had nine children. He was married the second time to Eliza A. Bartley, by whom he had nineteen children. By his two wives he had twenty-eight children, fourteen sons and fourteen daughters.

SNEDICOR.—Christopher Snedicor emigrated to America from Holland, at an early date, and settled in Greenbriar Co., Va. He left two sons, Moses and Isaac. The former served seven, and the latter five years in the war of the revolution. Isaac was married in Greenbriar Co., Va., to Eleanor Story, a cousin of Chief Justice Story, and after the birth of three children they emigrated to and settled in Montgomery Co., Ky. The names of their children were—Abigail, James, Mary W., Rebecca B., Samuel, Parker, and Isaac. James and Isaac married in Kentucky and settled in Alabama. After the death of their father, the widow and the rest of the children came to Missouri in 1820, and settled in Boone county. In 1825 all except Abigail removed to Callaway county, and settled near Fulton. Abigail was married twice; first to a Mr. Emmons, and second to a Mr. Finley. Mary W. was married in Montgomery Co., Ky., to John Kelso, and they had—Joseph G., Elizabeth J., Harrison W., Hesteran R., William D., Isaac S., Maria S., Samuel P., John M., and Adam C. Of this large family, the mother, now in the 86th year of her age, and Harrison W. and John M. only survive. Harrison Kelso lives in Kansas City, and John M. lives in Callaway county, where he has always resided.—Eleanor Story, the grandmother of these children, was born in Greenbriar Co., Va., in 1758. Her parents were from Ireland.

SMITH.—Edward Smith, of Virginia, married a Miss Linnville, by whom he had Thomas, Edmund, and Nathan. Thomas married Margaret Zount, and settled in Howard county, Mo., in 1816. His children were—Jerry, Richard, Marion, Matilda, Malinda, Lusetta, John, Polly, and Boone. Richard married Elizabeth Wagoner, and after her death he married the widow Wagoner, whose maiden name was Susan Hart. He settled in Callaway county in 1836.

TATE.—Nathaniel Tate, of Bedford county, Va., had—Zachariah, Henry F., Nathaniel, Jr., Richard, and Polly. Zachariah married Polly Nichols, of Bedford county, and they had—John G., Nathaniel N., Jesse N., Henry M., Caleb W., Richard C., Susannah, and Mary J. John G. married Jeannette Hipinstall, and settled in Callaway county in 1837. Nathaniel N. was married first to Sarah Richardson, and second to Percy A. Hamlin. Jesse N. was married first to Julia L. Hipinstall, and second to Mary Carter. Caleb W. was married first to Emily Hamlin, and second to Orva Hamlin. Richard C. married Elizabeth Hamlin, and was killed in 1863 by the Federal soldiers. Susannah married Samuel Wilkes, who settled in Missouri in 1834. Henry M. died in Missouri, unmarried. The members of the Tate family are a reading, intelligent people, and excellent citizens.

TATE.—James Tate, of Augusta county, Va., was a Captain in the revolutionary war, and was killed at the battle of Guilford Court House, in North Carolina. His wife's maiden name was Sarah Hail, and at his death he left a widow and five children. The names of the latter were—Polly, Elizabeth,' Sarah, John and Isaac. John married Sarah Hall, of Kentucky, and settled in Callaway county, Mo., in 1829. His children were—Calvin, Milton, Isaac, James, Elijah, Sarah, Margaret, and Mary. Mr. Tate died in 1864, in his 83d year. Sarah Tate married William Scott, of Kentucky, who settled in Callaway county in 1837. Margaret married Major Daniel Nally, who settled in Callaway county in 1829. Mary married Robert R. Buckner, of Callaway county. James was married first to Clarinda P. Tate, and second to Sophia Lysle. He settled in Callaway county in 1823. The Auxvasse Presbyterian Church was organized at his house that year, and it was the first organization of that religious denomination west of St. Charles. Elijah Tate died in Kentucky. Milton married Rachel B. Granberry. Isaac was Colonel of militia for many years. He married Jane Henderson. Calvin was married first to Elizabeth Allen, and second to a widow lady named Miller. Mr. Tate went to California in 1849, and was engaged for some time in hauling with his six-horse wagon. During his sojourn in California he served on a case in which several Chinamen were witnesses, and they swore to everything but the truth, until the judge had a rooster brought into the court room and placed on a table, when a blank expression of dread came over the face of each Chinaman, and after that they swore to the truth.

THRAILKILL.—Hiram Thrailkill, of Scott county, Ky., married Nancy Craig, and settled in Callaway county, Mo., in 1835. His children were—Marcellus N., Elcina, James, John, Sisra, Mary, Eliza A., Ellen, and William. After the death of Mr. Thrailkill his widow married Creed Carter, of Callaway county.

TRIMBLE.—John Trimble, of Kentucky, married a Miss Turley, by whom he had seven children. His eldest son, James, was drowned by falling in a well. Mr. Trimble and the rest of his family settled in Callaway county at an early date, and he and his wife died in that county a number of years afterward. Mr. Trimble was a good-hearted man, and liked by all who knew him. He was very quiet, and rarely had anything to say, even at log-rollings, where it was customary to get tight and have a "high old time."

TODD.—John A. Todd and his wife, whose maiden name was Mary Howard, were raised in Warren county, Ky. They settled in Callaway county, Mo., in 1826, and had twenty-one children, ten of whom lived to be grown. The names of the latter were—Margaret, Robert L., Hugh A., Elizabeth S., Nancy J., Mary A., John A., Mildred F., Asa M., and Joseph H. Mr. Todd was married the second time to a widow lady, by whom he had William and Sarah J. He built a mill on Loutre creek, and the first Methodist preaching in that part of Callaway county was held in his house. He died in 1862.

TURNER.—Lewis Turner, of Scotland, was a soldier in the revolutionary war. He lived in Virginia, and his children were—Lewis, Edward, James, Mary, and Ann. Lewis married Sarah Martin, of Virginia, by whom he had—William, Martin, Casey, Graham, Henry S., Elizabeth, and Mary. In 1825 Mr. Turner removed to Missouri with his family, and settled in Callaway county, where he died in 1826. His son William was married first to Margaret McAdam, and second to Mary J. Scruggs. He lives in Platte county, Mo. Martin married Devolia Hornbuckle. Casey married Eliza Rawlings. Graham was married first to Cynthia A. Nuir, and second to her sister, Lucinda. Henry S. married Mary Houk, and settled in Callaway county in 1825. He was Justice of the Peace twelve years, Assessor of the county four years, and Judge of the County Court from 1865 to 1868. He also represented the county in the Legislature in 1855. Elizabeth Turner married Rufus Hornbuckle, and settled in Johnson county, Mo. Mary married Garret Nichols, who settled in Callaway county in 1824.

THOMAS.—Solomon Thomas, of East Tennessee, settled in Callaway county in 1817. He had no education, but was elected Justice of the Peace and performed his duties reasonably well. He was a great yarn teller, and could entertain a crowd as well as any other man.— Joel Tipton settled in Callaway county the same year that Mr. Thomas did, and near his place. He was a very large man and a good trapper, but no hunter.—William Thornton and his son James, also settled in Callaway county in 1817. They were great hunters and trappers.

TRUETT.—Samuel Truett, of Kentucky, married Ellen Parker, and they had — Thomas, William, Mary and Nancy. Thomas married Sally Kimbrough, of Kentucky, and settled in Callaway county in 1828. His children were—Nathaniel, Benjamin, Susan, Elizabeth, George, Mary, William, Sarah, John, Ellen, Martha and Thomas. William, son of Samuel Truett, married Ellen Brannon, and settled in Boone county, Mo. Mary married Berkley Estus, and settled in Boone county. Nancy married John Catonham, who settled in Monroe county, Mo.

THORNHILL.—Jesse Thornhill and his wife, Elizabeth Stephenson, of Buckingham county, Va., had a son named Thomas, who married Agnes Patterson, by whom he had—Samuel, Charles B., Nelson, Albert, Thomas, Jesse, Jemima, Hattie, Elvira, Susan and Mary. Samuel was married first to Susan Stevens; second to Agnes Robinson, and third to Margaret McCracken. He settled in Callaway county in 1838. Charles B. was married in Virginia, to Elizabeth Moseley, and settled in Callaway county in 1828. Nelson married his cousin, Elizabeth R. Thornhill, and settled in Callaway county in 1845.

TAYLOR.—Thomas T. Taylor, a revolutionary soldier, settled in Smith county, Tennessee. He had three sons—John, Thomas and Robert, and eight daughters. John married Peggy Smith, of Tennessee, by whom he had—Thomas, William, James, Wilson Y., Patsey, Elizabeth, Sally, Polly, Frances, Susan, Lucinda and Nancy. Thomas married Lydia V. Dearing, William married Lucy Ham, and James married Polly Dearing, all of whom settled in Callaway county from 1821 to 18_9. Wilson, Elizabeth and Polly also married and settled in Callaway county during the same period of time.

TAYLOR.—William Taylor, of Stokes Co., N. C., married Sarah Scruggs, and they had a son, Isaac, who married Catharine Vaughan, a sister of Martin Vaughan, of Audrain Co., Mo. Their children were—Carter, Fountain, and Mary. The mother died while they were young, and their father having married again to a widow lady of Indiana, they were adopted by their uncle Martin, who came to Missouri in 1830. Carter, the eldest, married Minerva Callock, and settled in Howard county, where they lived and died. Mary married James Duncan, who settled in Monroe county. Fountain settled in Callaway county. He married Anna Wilburn, and they had a large family of children. Mr. Taylor is a stone mason by trade, and once while blasting rock he was blown up and badly burnt with powder. The marks of the powder are still plainly visible on his hands and face.

THOMAS.—James Thomas, of Kentucky, married a Miss Hayden, by whom he had—William, James, Robert, Presley, George H., and Susan. George H. married Evelina Nichols, and settled in Callaway county in 1826. He was married the second time to Nancy P. Craighead Presley Thomas married Phœbe Mieur, and settled in Callaway county in 1831. He was married the second time to the widow Collier, and the third time to the widow Calbreath. James married Frances Vaughan, and settled in Callaway county in 1828. Susan married Jerry Mieur, and settled in Callaway county in 1830.

TARLETON.—Jerry Tarleton, of Maryland, married Mary Briscoe, by whom he had—Raphael B., Nancy, Alfred, Emily, John, Catharine, Meredith, Amanda, and Lewellen P. Emily married Samuel Moore, who settled in Callaway county in 1819. Meredith married Mary E. Lock, and settled in Callaway county in 1840.

WHITTINGTON.—Thomas Whittington, of London, England, came to America when he was twelve years of age, with his uncle, who was a sea captain. He settled in Virginia, and after he was grown married Elizabeth Brown, by whom he had—William, Thomas, Jr., James, Stark D., John, Edmund, Judith, Rhoda, Patsey, and Nancy. Stark D. married Elizabeth Loudon, and they had—James, Eliza, Martha, Emily, Anderson, George, Reuben, Frances, and Elmira. James married Harriet Gregory, and settled in Callaway county in 1841. He was married the second time to Lucy Burch. Reuben Whittington also settled in Callaway county.

WHITE.—John White, of Kentucky, was a soldier in the revolutionary war. He had a son named Archibald, who married a Miss Simpson, and they were the parents of Morgan B. and Archibald White, Jr. Morgan B. settled in Callaway county in 1826, and became a prominent and influential citizen. He has always been a staunch Democrat, basing his political faith upon the true Jeffersonian doctrine. He represented Callaway county in the Legislature in 1834-5, with credit to himself and to the satisfaction of his constituents. He is now past the age at which men participate in public affairs, but. he still feels an interest in the success of his beloved party, and the supremacy of honesty and good government. He reads a great deal, and keeps himself thoroughly posted in the events of the day: "Uncle Morgan's" opinions and ideas still carry weight in Callaway county, where he is respected as one of the few remaining actors in a better and more prosperous era of our government. The white haired pioneer is always given a prominent position at public meetings, and office-seekers can do no better than declare, as they point to him, that they will endeavor to perform their duty as faithfully and disinterestedly as he and his associates did. Mr. White tells an amusing anecdote on himself that occurred during his stay in Jefferson City, while attending the session of the Legislature of which he was a member. He boarded at a private house kept by a widow lady, who put him to sleep in a bed surrounded by heavy damask curtains. It was the first bed of the kind that he had ever seen, and for his life he could not tell how to get into the thing. He finally concluded that he would have to go in over the top; so drawing a table and chair to the side of the bed he mounted on to them, and rolled over, expecting to land on a nice, soft bed; but instead of that he was caught by the floor, and, like the Irishman, considerably hurt by the "sudden stopping." He learned the trick, however, and after that had no difficulty about getting into his bed. Mr. White was married first to Mary Ann Marmaduke, of Shelby county, Ky., by whom he had twelve children. His second wife was a widow lady named Hughes, whose maiden name was McMurtry. His children are intelligent and cultivated, and his sons are among the most enterprising men of the counties in which they live. One of his sons, Arch. H. White, is an ex-Sheriff of Montgomery county, and an influential citizen. Another of his sons, Morgan B., Jr., is a large stock raiser and successful farmer of Montgomery county. He also takes a great deal of interest in politics, and exercises considerable influence in his county.—Archibald White, brother of Morgan B., Sr., settled in Callaway county in 1832, and died two years later, leaving a widow and one child.

WRIGHT.—William Wright was a native of England. He had a son named John, who was Tobacco Inspector at Fredericksburg, Va., at a very early date. The latter married Rosamond Grant, daughter of Captain John Grant, by whom he had—Margaret, Rosamond, Elizabeth, William, John, and Winfield. The latter married Judith Tinsley, daughter of Edward Tinsley, of Madison county, Va., and settled in Franklin county, Ky., in 1817. They had—William, Henry T., James G., Rosamond, Elizabeth, Margaret P., Judith, and Polly. Henry T. married Rebecca Tinsley, of Kentucky, and settled in Callaway county, Mo., in 1837. They had—Henry, Jr., Winfield, Charles, and George. After the death of his wife Mr. Wright married Peachey Tinsley, and they had one child, a daughter. Mr. Wright was married the third time to Elizabeth Jameson. James G., son of Winfield Wright, married Rebecca Hawkins, of Franklin county, Ky., and settled in Audrain county, Mo. Elizabeth married Reuben Overton, who settled in Callaway county in 1824. Margaret P. married William R. Martin, who settled in Callaway county in 1827. Judith T. married Samuel P. Martin, who settled in Callaway county in 1824.

WILBURN.—John Wilburn married Mary Curtis, by whom he had—Caroline, Ann, Rebecca, St. Clair, William, Robert, and John. He settled in Callaway county in 1816.

WORD.—John Word, of England, settled in Goochland county, Va. He had two children, John and Mary. John married Lucy Rice, and settled in Kentucky in 1803. They had—William, Charles R., Matilda, and Nancy. Mr. Word removed to Missouri in 1817, and settled in Callaway county. William, his eldest son, married Polly Rives, who, after an affliction of seven years, went entirely blind. Charles R., now living, was a celebrated auger maker in his younger days. His augers were of such a superior quality that he could not make them fast enough to supply the demand. He married Jane McCormack, and they had— Nancy, John, Lucy, Martha, Charles W., James R., Margaret G., Mary E., Montezuma, and George W.

WILKERSON.—Moses and William Wilkerson were sons of Moses Wilkerson, of England, who came to America and settled in Virginia before the revolutionary war. He died some years afterward, and his widow married again. After their mother's second marriage, Moses and William went to Kentucky, and lived for some time in the fort at Boonesborough. Moses married Aletha Anderson, who had lived in the fort with her parents three years, and was there when Jemima Boone and the Callaway girls were captured by the Indians. They afterward settled in Montgomery county, Ky., and raised nine children, whose names were—John, William, Abraham, Henry, Hiram, Haley, Nimrod, Cenia, and Sally. Mrs. Wilkerson died in Kentucky in 1833. William, the second son, received a limited education, and after his father's death he was appointed executor of the estate and guardian for his brothers and sisters. The duties thus imposed upon him gave him a practical knowledge of business affairs, and the people of his county had so much confidence in his ability and integrity that they elected him a member of the County Court while he was quite young. The Court at that time was composed of twelve men, selected with reference to their ability and experience, and it was no small honor to be so chosen. Mr. Wilkerson enlisted in the war of 1812, and was chosen First Lieutenant of Captain George McArthur's company. They belonged to that portion of the army which operated in Canada, and Lieutenant W. assisted in capturing a fort in which several hundred of the enemy were garrisoned. After the close of the war he was elected Colonel of militia, and was subsequently chosen to represent his county in the Legislature. In 1830 he came to Missouri and settled in Callaway county. In 1836 he was elected a member of the Legislature, and afterward represented the county in the same body during a portion of two terms. He was also presiding Justice of the County Court for several years. He died in 1845; his wife died in 1839. Her maiden name was Elizabeth Clark, daughter of James Clark, who came from Ireland, married a Miss Arbuckle, and settled in Greenbriar county, Va. Colonel Wilkerson was a high-toned, honorable gentleman; moral and upright, but not a member of any church. He was highly respected in his community, and his counsel and advice were sought by all, which he gave without ostentation or display, and always for what he considered best. He was modest and unassuming in his manners, and possessed an excellent mind, which he diligently cultivated. He was temperate in his habits, and never used profane language. In his family circle he was kind and indulgent, but firm in requiring his children to do what was right. He was an honest politician, and no competitor could ever say that he took an unfair advantage of him. The names of his children were—Harrison, Achilles (a physician), William H., Narcissa, Martha C., Elizabeth, and Emily.

WREN.— James Wren of Fairfax county, Va., married Sarah M. Lee, daughter of Hancock Lee, and settled in Callaway county Mo., in 1833. His children were — Sarah E., James, Mary C., and John E. Mr. Wren was married the second time to the widow Williams, and died in Callaway county in 1875, aged 79 years. He was a soldier of the war of 1812.

WINN—Joseph Winn, of Kentucky, was married first to a Miss Bartley, and second to Peggy Turman. Mr. Winn settled first in Kentucky, and afterward removed to Clark county, Ohio, where he died. His children were—John, Charles, Martha, Jane, Susan, Myrtella and Douglass. The latter married Elizabeth Rawlings, and settled in Callaway county in 1838. His children were—Mary, Myrtella, John, Elizabeth, Thomas, Richard, Melvina Douglass, Jr., Martha, William, Susannah, and Ascenia.

WATSON.—John K. Watson was an early settler of Callaway county. He made his living by splitting rails and was known as the rail splitter of Callaway county.

WALKER.—Edward Walker settled in Callaway county in 1831. His children were—John, Edward, Griffin, Samuel, Elizabeth, Permelia, Patsey, Charlotte and Harriet.

WILLIAMS.—William Williams was a native of England, and was a soldier in the British army during the American revolution. He became so well pleased with the Americans and their country from what he saw of them during his soldier days, that when the war was over he remained, and settled in Virginia, where he soon after married Sally Martin. Their children were—William, Asa

T., Peyton, Robert, Richard, John, Joseph, Polly, Lucy, Sally, and Elizabeth, all of whom settled in Callaway county, Mo., from 1814 to 1824. Asa T. settled at Cotesansdessein in the spring of 1815, and was the first American settler in that part of the county. He afterward married Elizabeth Langley, and they had—John, Isaac, Henry B , Peyton T., Robert B , James M., Asa T., Jr., William G., Sally, Mary, Elizabeth J., Mordecai A., Matilda, and several others who died in childhood. William, brother of Asa T., Sr., married Elizabeth May, of Virginia, and settled in Callaway county in 1822. Peyton married Polly Langley, and settled in Callaway county in 1820. Robert married Frankie May, and settled in Callaway county the same year. John married Elizabeth Johnson, of Tennessee, and settled in Callaway county in 1824. Joseph settled in that county in 1817, and married Elizabeth Langley.

WAGONER.—Jacob Wagoner, of Roan county, N. C., married a Miss Zount, and they had a son named George, who married Alice Williams, of North Carolina, and settled in Tennessee. They had—Edward, Susan, Jane, and Martha. Mr. Wagoner was married again, after the death of his first wife, to Sarah Engle, by whom he had Catharine and Stokeley. All of this family settled in Callaway county from 1828 to 1831.

WINTERBOWER.—Jacob Winterbower, of Pennsylvania, married Polly Stone, and they had twenty children. One of their sons, named John, married Elizabeth Zumwalt, of Missouri, daughter of Jacob Zumwalt, who settled in Callaway county in 1817.

YATES.—Benjamin Yates was born in Virginia in 1767, and died in Shelby county, Ky., in 1558. He was married twice; first to Margaret Ford, of Kentucky, by whom he had—John, Edith, Gilson, Mary, Nancy, Milton, Benjamin F., Jeptha, and William F. His second wife was a Miss Sullivan, of Kentucky; they had no children. John Yates came to Missouri in 1816, when he was a young man, and began to learn the tailor's trade with Daniel Colgin, of St. Charles. But he soon grew tired of that business, and obtained a situation as porter in Collier & Co.'s store, at $12 per month. He had been in the store only a few days when Mr. George Collier wanted a legal paper drawn up for some purpose, and made inquiry among his employes to know if any of them could do it. Mr. Yates replied that he could, and the matter was entrusted to him. He performed the work so well and neatly that Mr. Collier was both pleased and surprised, and finding upon conversing with him that he was an educated man, he employed him as book-keeper, at good wages. A few years later he sent a stock of goods to Elizabeth, the first county seat of Callaway county, and sent Mr. Yates with it as superintendent. The goods were opened in the house of Mr. Henry Brite, which was also used as a tavern, court house, clerk's office, etc. This was the first store in Callaway county, except one at Cotesansdessein, owned by Daniel Colgin, Jr., of St. Charles. Mr. Yates soon became a partner in the store, and in 1825 he removed to Fulton, where he carried on the business for many years, and made a fortune. After his removal to Fulton the sales increased largely, and he ordered goods so often that Mr. Collier became uneasy and went to Fulton to see that all was right. Mr. Yates showed him the books to prove that the sales had been made as represented, and then handed him all the money due to date. This satisfied Mr. Collier, and he returned home. Soon after this Mr. Yates bought his interest in the store, and carried on the business himself. Mr. Yates was married first to Mary Nichols, by whom he had one son, George, who is now a druggist in Williamsburg. His second wife was Elizabeth Dawson, of Missouri, by whom he had—Benjamin D., William, Martha (Mrs. Samuel Grant), Thomas, John, and Martin. The latter is a physician. Edith, daughter of Benjamin Yates, Sr., married Theodore Drain, and they had—Stephen, Dulcinea, Emma, and Franklin. Gilson Yates married Catharine Ford, of Kentucky, and they had—James, John, and Frances. Mary Yates married William Guthrie, and they had six children. Nancy married H. Woods; they had four children. Benjamin F. died when he was sixteen years of age. Jeptha married Eliza J. Harrison, and they had— John, Mary, and Lucy J. William F. married Nancy Hopkins, and they had but one child.

YOUNG.—Sennett Young, of Bath county Ky., married Barsheba Catlet, and they had—Elizabeth, Polly, Original, Sennett, Jr., Edwin, Daniel and Willis. Original married Dorcas Moon, of Virginia, and they had—Hiram, Reuben, John A., Sally and Hannah. John A. was married twice, and settled in Callaway county in 1834.

HISTORIES OF FAMILIES.

AUDRAIN COUNTY.

THE county of Audrain was organized December 17, 1836, and named in honor of Colonel James H. Audrain, of St. Charles county, who was a man of considerable note, and a member of the Legislature in 1830. The seat of justice was located at Mexico at the same time the county was organized.

Mexico was founded in 1836 by Rev. Robert Mansfield and Mr. J. H. Smith, who donated twenty-five acres of their land to the embryo town. The place did not improve much until the opening of the North Missouri railroad, in 1857, when its growth became rapid and substantial. It is now one of the principal inland towns of Missouri, in point of location and trade, and numbers a population of more than 5,000. It commands a wholesale and retail trade that extends over several adjacent counties, and its public buildings, business houses and private residences are unsurpassed by those of any other inland town in the State. This is the home of Governor Charles H. Hardin, who has done much by his energy, influence and ample means to build up the town and give it a reputation abroad.

The early settlers of Audrain county were principally from Kentucky, Virginia, North Carolina and Tennessee. They built small cabins in the timber, on the water courses, and devoted themselves to hunting, trapping and fishing. Game was abundant, and hunting not only an exciting pastime, but a remunerative occupation, and pleasure and profit were combined in its pursuit. The game consisted of deer, elk, wolves, raccoons, wild turkeys, and a few bears and panthers. The buffaloes had already taken their departure to the prairies of the distant West. In fact the French and Spanish had, in a measure, driven them away before the Americans began to settle within the present limits of Missouri, and but few of those animals were to be found in this State after 1800. In early times there was a salt lick in Dog Prairie, St. Charles county, which was frequented by buffaloes as well as deer and other wild animals; but there is no authentic account of any buffaloes having been seen there after 1800, except an old one and its calf that were killed at that place about 1816. They had evidently strayed away from the herd and got lost.

Wolves were so numerous and daring that it was almost impossible to raise sheep or other domestic animals, and there being no inducements for any but hunters and trappers to locate in that region, the larger portion of the land in Audrain county remained unoccupied and in possession of the government until 1854, when it was rapidly entered at twelve and a half cents per acre, under the "Graduation Act." Citizens of other counties then flocked to Audrain, entered homesteads and erected cabins, many of which are still standing on the beautiful prairies, but most of them have given place to neat frame and brick farm houses.

The streams of this county are all small, and all except one or two head near its center. Salt river is the principal one, and is merely a prairie brook, distinguished by the title of river probably because of its association with streams of much smaller dimensions. The people supply themselves and their stock with water by digging cisterns and ponds, and except in extremely dry seasons they have all they require. The streams are fed by living springs, and flow during the entire year, affording abundant water for mills and manufacturing purposes.

Most of the creeks derived their names from the people who first settled upon them, and several incidents have been obtained in this connection sufficiently amusing and instructive to be presented here.

The creek called Littleby was named for Robert Littleby, an Englishman, who settled upon that stream, near where it empties into South Fork of Salt river, in 1816, and lived the life of a hermit for many years, his dogs being his only companions. He hunted and trapped extensively, and sold his furs and peltries in St. Charles. His food consisted of game, wild fruits, and the vegetable portion of the earth's natural productions. He cured his meat by soaking it a week in a strong concoction of lye.   Beaver, otter, muskrats, raccoons, etc., were there in abundance, and he reaped a rich harvest from their furs.   In 1822 he removed to Platte river, and died soon after.

The next settler in that part of the county was Benjamin Young, who located there in 1821; and Young's creek was named for him. He was a native of Stokes county, North Carolina; had been raised by the Indians, and married a squaw for his wife.   In the same county there lived a woman named Mary Ring, who was captivated by Benjamin's prepossessing appearance, and proposed matrimony to him.   He frankly told her that he was already married to the squaw, but had no desire to see her carried to an untimely grave from the effects of a broken heart, and if she would whip the squaw she might take him.   She accepted the proposition, "cleaned out" the squaw, and claimed her reward.   Young was not the man to " go back" on his word, so he dismissed the squaw and married the white woman.   The result proved good, for they lived pleasantly and happily together, and the devotion of his new wife to him increased as they passed down the stream of life together.   In 1809 Mr. Young placed his wife and worldly goods on a little pony, and started on a journey to Kentucky, which he performed on foot, with his rifle on his shoulder.   They lived in Kentucky two years, and then settled in Howard county, Mo., where they lived until 1821, when they removed to what is now Audrain county, and built their cabin on the bank of the stream since known as Young's creek.   For many years they were the only persons who lived in that part of the county, and they never saw the face of a fellow creature except when some traveler would get lost and wander that way, or a solitary hunter would stumble upon their humble habitation.

Colonel Thomas H. Benton used to stop at Mr. Young's house and pay him a visit whenever he was out on an electioneering tour, and the old hunter felt so much honored by the kind attentions of the great man that he named one of his sons Thomas Benton in honor of him.   Benton also sent him a great many public documents, which he could not read, but would place in prominent positions about the house as ornaments.

Mrs. Young, who was a very large woman, was almost as good a hunter as her husband, and would frequently go into the woods and camp for weeks at a time on hunting expeditions.   She was an excellent bee hunter, and always kept her family supplied with nice, fresh honey. One day she went into the woods accompanied by her son, Thomas B., on a bee hunt, and while they were wandering about Tom saw a nice, straight grape vine that he thought would make a good clothes line. So he mounted upon it some twenty feet, and cut the vine above his head, without stopping to consider the law of gravitation, or the effect of being suspended in the air with nothing to suspend upon. The natural result was that he got a fall which jolted him so severely that he never entirely recovered from it, and he did not make as great a man as his distinguished namesake.

When Mr. Young's eldest daughter was married, the wheat from which the bread and cakes for the festive occasion were to be composed, was ground on a hand mill, and the flour bolted through Mrs. Young's muslin cap. They had no sifter or bolting chest, but the muslin cap answered the purpose very well.

Mr. Young was killed in 1833, by a pet bull. His coffin was made by Rev. Mr. Hubbard, under directions from the widow, who stood by and told him to make it large and roomy, as her old man never did like to be crowded. It was accordingly made "large and roomy," and the old hunter was buried in a decent and comfortable manner. Let us hope that he sleeps well.

As the county began to settle up with enterprising farmers, schools and churches were established, mills and shops erected, and other branches of industry were inaugurated, so that to-day Audrain is fully abreast of the older and more populous counties by which it is surrounded.

FAMILIES OF AUDRIAN COUNTY.

ARMISTEAD.—Franklin Armistead was a soldier of the war of 1812. He married Hannah Rice, of Virginia, and they had— William, Franklin, Jr., Hannah, and Delpha. Franklin, Jr., married Martha Faulkner, and settled in Audrain county in 1833. They had—Franklin W., Martha, Lucy, Mary, Joseph, John, Virginia, James, and Eliza.

BYBEE.—James Bybee, of England, came to America and settled in Clark county, Ky. His children were—Alfred, James, Thomas, Louis, John, and two daughters. Alfred and John came to Missouri. The former settled in Cass county, and the latter in Howard. John was married six times: first to Polly Adams, of Kentucky, by whom he had six children; second to Nancy Adams—two children; third to Mary Myers—one child; fourth to Mary Kyle—four children; fifth to Nannette Creed—nine children; sixth to the widow McGee. He had twenty-two children in all. He settled in Audrain county in 1833, and two of his sons, Martellus and John, are still living there. One of his daughters, Mrs. Bloom, a widow, also lives in that county. Martellus is a great wit and humorist. He was the principal witness for the defence in the celebrated Boggs breach of promise suit that came off in Mexico, Mo., many years ago, and created a great deal of fun.

BROWN.—Coulborn Brown, of Pennsylvania, was killed in the revolutionary war. He had a son named Solomon, who settled in Bourbon county, Ky., when he was a boy. He married after he was grown, and had two sons, William and Coulborn. The former lived and died in Kentucky. Coulborn married Jane Taylor, who was of Irish descent, and they had—William, Samuel, Alexander, Clarissa, George, Laban I. T., Coulborn, Jr., Jane, Milton and Elijah, all of whom, except Alexander and Eliza, settled in Missouri.

BRADLEY.—Ichem Bradley, of Ireland, came to America and settled Virginia. His wife was a Miss McGee, by whom he had—John, Thomas, and William. John was a soldier in the revolutionary war. He married Martha Mosbey, and they had—David, Thomas, Edward, Ichem, Nancy, Sally, Polly, and Martha. David and Thomas were both soldiers in the war of 1812, the former serving in and near Norfolk, and the latter below Richmond. Thomas became tired of the smell of gun powder, and hired a substitute at $100 per day. He married Frankey Winler, and they had nine children. Mr. Bradley and his family settled in Audrain county in 1838.

BLUE.—Duncan Blue, of Scotland, married his cousin, Effie Blue, and came to America and settled in North Carolina before the revolution. He joined the American army when the war began, and served during the struggle for independence. After the war he removed to Christian county, Ky. His children were —Daniel, Neal, and Peggy. Neal was in the war of 1812. He married Elizabeth Galbreth, of North Carolina, and they had— Duncan, John, Sally, Effie A., Peggy, Flora, Eliza, Emeline, Caroline, and Charlotte E. Several of the children died young, and in 1831 Mr. Blue and the rest of his family came to Missouri and settled in Audrain county.

BYRNES.—John Byrnes and his wife were natives of Halifax county, Va. Their children were—William, John, Richard,

Rhoda, Martha, and Sarah. William married Catharine H. Thagmorton, and settled in Audrain county in 1830. They had—William H., John R., Sarah F., James T., Mary, Millie C., and Lucinda. Richard Byrnes married Patsey Barnes, of Virginia, and settled in Audrain county in 1832. His children were—John, Richard, Jr., William, George, Fielding, Sarah, Jane, and Ann. Rhoda Byrnes married George Bonar, and they had—Alexander, Catharine, Sarah, Rebecca, Elizabeth, and Georgiana. Martha Byrnes married Matthew Scott, who died, leaving her a widow with one child.

BOWEN.—Thomas Bowen, of Virginia, married Mary Stone, and removed to Kentucky, where they lived and died. Their children were—Benjamin, John, Reece, George, Lorenzo, Thomas, Sarah, Polly, Elizabeth, Anna, and Delilah. Thomas is a Baptist preacher, and lives in Mexico, Mo. He was born in Madison county, Ky., in 1796, and he and his brother Reece belonged to Nathan Boone's company of rangers during the Indian war in Missouri. Mr. Bowen married a daughter of Adam Zumwalt. He was very fond of dancing when he was a young man, and was present at Peter Yater's house warming, in Warren county, when the floor fell through. Mr. Bowen had the misfortune to get caught under Mrs. Yater in the fall, and she left an impression on him that he never forgot, for she weighed 250 pounds.

BEATTY.—James Beatty was born in Maryland, in 1742. He married Elizabeth Ramer, whose father fled from Germany to avoid religious persecution by Charles V. Mr. Beatty settled in Fayette county, Ky., among the first white people who sought homes in that State, and he experienced all the dangers and trials of the long and bloody Indian war that followed. After the return of peace he gave his assistance to the development of the country, and was one of the party who opened the first road to Ohio. His children were—Mary, Michael, James E., Lydia, Edward, Jonathan, Ann, Ruth, Amy, and Barbara. James E. married and lived in Mobile, Ala. Edward married Malinda Price, by whom he had—James E., John P., Elizabeth S., and William. He was married the second time to Anna S. Smith, and they had Joseph and Martha J. He was married the third time to Eliza J. Holmes, but they had no children. Mr. Beatty settled in Audrain county in 1837. John P. Beatty married Elizabeth J. Clark, and they had—Edward H., John W., Lycurgus, Mary E., Leonidas, Helen S., Lawrence, James, and Oliver, all of whom live in Missouri.

BARNETT.—John Barnett, of England, had a son named Hutchins, who married Polly Matthews, of Virginia, and settled in Boone county, Mo., in 1820. Their children were—John W., Thomas M., Jane W., Mildred A., and Sarah R. John W. married Arretta Willingham in 1822, and settled in Audrain county in 1831. They had—Sarah J., Mary M., Mildred A., Martha E., William J., Napoleon B., Sanders, Hutchins, Athanasis, John W., Thomas, and Jesse E. Thomas, son of Hutchins Barnett, Sr., settled in Audrain county in 1831. He never married. He possesses a remarkable memory, and can relate past events with great accuracy. Sarah R., daughter of Hutchins Barnett, Sr., married Daniel Ellington, of Boone county, Mo.

CROCKETT.—Hugh Crockett, of Virginia, was a Colonel in the revolutionary war, and was distinguished for gallantry. He married Rebecca Lorton, and they had—Samuel, Walter, Robert, Hugh, Nancy, Jane, Mary, and Rebecca. Samuel married Margaret Rayborn, of Virginia, by whom he had—Hugh, Rebecca, James, Joseph, Jane, William, Margaret, Walter, John D., Robert, and Randall. Mr. Crockett removed first to Williamson county, Tennessee, where he lived nine years, and then came to Missouri, and settled in Boone county. His eldest son, Hugh, now resides in Audrain county. He has been married three times; first to Mary A. Wright, second to Rhoda B. Finley, and third to the widow Turner, whose maiden name was Nancy Price. Rebecca married Judge James Harrison, of Audrain county. Jane married John B. Morrow, and Margaret married James G. Morrow. Joseph married Nancy Kright, and settled in Audrain county in 1840. John married Mary Pool, and settled in that county the same year. The members of the Crockett family are a jovial class of people, noted for their wit and humor and cheerful dispositions. They also love the sport of hunting.

CALHOUN.—Robert Calhoun, of Virginia, settled in Audrain county, Mo., in 1838. He married Elizabeth Bright, a sister of Judge Michael Bright, of Callaway county, and they had—Austin, Sarah, Margaret, Virginia, Samuel, and William. Mr. Calhoun was an industrious, energetic man, kind and affectionate in his family, and highly respected by his neighbors. Like all the early settlers, he was fond of hunting, and was one of the best marksmen in the county.

CLARK.—Daniel Clark and his wife, who was a Miss Shelton, were natives of Scotland. They emigrated to America and settled first in Lancaster county, Va., from whence they removed to Culpepper county, where they both died about 1799. They had six children—William, John, George, Robert, Elizabeth and Polly. William married Elizabeth Hudnall, and settled in Mason county, Va., where his wife died December 14, 1816, and he died at the same place July 4, 1826. Their children were—John H., Frances S., Jemima J., Elizabeth, Nancy, William M., and Polly A. William M. married Elizabeth H. McMullin, and settled in Audrain county in 1839. Mr. Clark is a good neighbor and citizen, hospitable, industrious, and persevering. He has a remarkable memory in regard to dates, and can remember the date of nearly every event that has occurred during his life.

CAWTHORN.—James Cawthorn, of England, came to America and settled in Virginia. He had but one child, a son named Charles, who served seven years in the America army during the revolutionary war. He was married first to Elizabeth Williams, and they had one son, whom they named Asa, and who was a soldier in the war of 1812. After the death of his first wife, Mr. Cawthorn married Mary Sanders, of Virginia, and they had seven sons and three daughters. Their names were—Asa, Jr., David, Paul, Silas, Richard, Stephen, Celia W., Elizabeth, and Martha. David and Paul married and settled in Andrew county, Mo. Peter married the widow of George Eubanks, and settled in Andrew county in 1835. Silas married Mary Jerman, and settled in Audrain county in 1835. Richard and Stephen and their three sisters settled in Indiana. Peter and Paul Cawthorn were twins, and very devoted to each other. They married widows of the same name (Eubanks), but who were not related in any way, and the brothers each had one daughter, which were of the same age.

CAUTHORN.—Richard Cauthorn, of Essex county, Va., was a school teacher and silversmith. He married a Miss Fisher, by whom he had—Vinson, James, Reuben, Leroy, Godfrey, Amos, and Patsey. James married Leah Allen, and they had—Allen, Carter, James, Jr., Ross, Alfred, Nancy, Henrietta, and Frances. Allen settled in Audrain Co., Mo., and married Elizabeth Harmon. At his death he left two sons and two daughters. Carter married Elizabeth Calvin, and settled in Audrain county in 1835. They had eleven sons and two daughters. James, Jr., married Frances Calvin, and settled in Audrain county in 1835. They had four sons and five daughters. Ross, Nancy, and Henrietta lived and died in Virginia. Alfred married Emily Brooks, and settled in Audrain county. They had seven sons and five daughters. Frances married William Garrett, who settled in Mexico, Mo. They had three sons and three daughters.

CHARLTON.—John Charlton, of Ireland, came to America and settled in Monroe county, Va. His children were—Joseph, Thomas, John, Isabella, Ella, Letitia, and Polly, all of whom, except John, lived and died in Virginia. John was a soldier of the war of 1812. He married Isabella Humphreys, and came to Missouri in 1820. The journey was made on a flatboat as far as Shawneetown, Illi., where they disembarked and came by land to St. Charles county. They settled first on Dardenne Prairie, and removed from there to Audrain county in 1830. Mr. Charlton built the first hewed log house in that county, and had to go twenty-five miles to get hands to assist in raising it. He was a very absent minded man, and a number of amusing anecdotes are related of him in that connection.   On a certain occasion when his wife was about to be confined, he started after the doctor, and did not return until the child was old enough to walk.   On another occasion he went to the store to get some salt, and was absent eighteen months.   When he came back he was carrying a broadax on his shoulder, but did not remember what he had been doing with it.   The names of his children were—James, Thomas, John H., and a daughter who died in childhood.   James died in Illinois in 1829.   Thomas died of small-pox in 1831, while returning home from New Orleans.   John H. was married first to Nancy Carter, and second to the widow of David Gloss.   He lives in Audrain county.   He had five children by his first wife, three sons and two daughters.

CARDWELL.—Thomas R. Cardwell, of England, came to America and settled in Richmond, Va.   His children were—John, Perrin and George.   John married Keziah Low, and they had—John, Jr., Thomas, William, James, Wiltshire, George, Elizabeth, Nancy, Martha, Lucy, and Mary.   George, son of Thomas Cardwell, Sr., married Anna Hamilton, and they had—John, Elizabeth, William, Keziah, Martha, Mary, George, Jr., Jane, Rebecca, Wyatt, and James.   George, Jr., married Ida Vansdoll, and settled in Missouri in 1832.   Martha married William Snelley.   Wyatt married May Woods, and settled in Audrain county in 1834.   Jane married William Woods.   William married Barbara Sanford, and settled in Audrain county in 1837.   He was married the second time to Elizabeth Watts.

CROUCH.—Jonathan Crouch, of Bath county, Ky., was of German descent.   He married Hannah Wells, and they had—Joseph, Isaac, Jonathan, Andrew, James, and Rebecca.   Joseph was drafted in the war of 1812, but obtained his exemption papers because he walked in his sleep.   He married Nancy Murie, of Kentucky, and they had—Thomas, Frank, Ellen, and William, all of whom came with their parents to Missouri in 1823, and settled in Ralls county, where they remained thirteen years and then removed to Montgomery county.   Thomas married Louisiana Fuget, and they had ten children.   He served as Justice of the Peace for sixteen years.   Frank married Nancy J. Johnson.   Ellen was married first to Hiram Fuget, and second to Samuel Davis.   William was married first to Phœbe A. McDaniel, and second to Sally Lovelace.   All of the above live in Audrain and Montgomery counties.

CANTERBERRY.—Gideon Canterberry, of Canterberry, England, emigrated to America and settled in North Carolina.   He served three years and a half in the revolutionary war, and afterward married Nancy Franklin, by whom he had—Reuben, John, Nimrod, and Benjamin.   Reuben and John settled first in Virginia, and afterward removed to Kentucky, where they died.   Nimrod married Mary Franklin, and settled in Monroe Co., Mo., in 1835. Benjamin married Susannah Hooser, of Tennessee, and settled in Audrain Co., Mo., in 1836.   His children were—Franklin P., Reuben M., John C., Benjamin F., Narcissa, Mary, Susan, Nancy J., and Eiizabeth.   Mrs. Canterberry died in August, 1875, in the 94th year of her age.

COPHER.—Thomas Copher was born in Pennsylvania, but settled in Virginia.   His children were—Josiah, Jacob, George, Reuben, and Jesse, all of whom settled in Kentucky.   George came to Missouri in 1820.   Jesse married Elizabeth Boone, daughter of George Boone, and settled in Boone Co., Mo., in 1819.   They had—Thomas, Samuel B., David N., Phœbe, Endecia, Jerusha, Sally, Hattie, and Millie.   Samuel B. lives in Audrain county.   He was married first to Anna Thompson, and second to Anna Maupin.   Thomas was a soldier in the war of 1812.   The rest of the children lived and died in Boone county.

CLARK.—James Clark, of Ireland, married Catharine Horne, of Scotland.   They came to America and settled in Winchester, Va., from whence they removed to Lincoln Co., N. C.   They had six sons—Alexander, William, James, Christopher, John, and David. Alexander, James and John lived and died in North Carolina. William and eleven other men were killed by the Indians in Kentucky.   They were in camp at night, and the savages came upon them and shot them by the light of the fire.   David came to Missouri on a visit in 1811.   After his return to North Carolina he married Margaret Douglass, and they had one son, named William.   Mr. Clark removed his family to Missouri in 1823, and settled in Lincoln county.   Captain Christopher Clark settled first in Lincoln county, Ky., where he married Elizabeth Adams, by whom he had—James, Sarah, Catharine, David, Hannah, and Elizabeth.   He was married the second time to Hattie Calvert, of Virginia, and they had—Raphael H. F., Julia, and William C. James and David came to Missouri among the early settlers, and the former was a ranger in Nathan Boone's company, while David served in Callaway's company.   They and two of their sisters, Sarah and Catharine, married and settled in Texas.   Hannah died single.   Elizabeth married Jesse Cox, who settled in Lincoln county, Mo.   Raphael H. F. was born in Green's Bottom, St. Charles county, while his mother was on a visit there.   He married Mary Murphy, of Kentucky, by whom he had two children. She died in 1839, and Mr. Clark afterward married Mary Atkinson, of Kentucky, by whom he had eight children.   His second wife is dead also, and he lives in Audrain county.   Captain Christopher Clark sent his stock to Missouri in 1799, and brought his family in a keel-boat to St. Charles county the following year.   He settled first at Gilmore Springs, where he remained one year, and

in 1801 he removed to Lincoln county, near where Troy stands.
He built a fort there during the Indian war, and was commissioned
captain of militia by Gen. Wm. H. Harrison. The musters took
place at Zumwalt's Springs, and most of the men would get drunk
on Adam Zumwalt's whisky. One day, after the drill was over,
the Captain treated his men to a wash-tub full of whisky, which
so elated them that they marched around it and fired a salute
with their guns, which were loaded with powder and toe wads.
One of the men was too drunk to hold his gun up when he fired,
and the wad entered Daniel McCoy's moccasin and cut off one of
his toes. Captain Clark commanded the company that went to
bury Price, Baldridge and Lewis, who were killed by the Indians
while hunting on Loutre Prairie. The bodies of Price and Baldridge were found and buried, but no trace of Lewis could be discovered. The Captain was a member of the Territorial Legislature when St. Charles county was reduced to its present dimensions, by the organization of Lincoln and Montgomery counties. A debate arose in regard to the boundary line, Mr. Cottle
advocating Peruque creek as the line between St. Charles and
Lincoln, and Captain Clark favoring Cuivre. The Captain at
length carried his point, and Cuivre became the line between the
two counties. He also secured the name for the county, by a
speech which brought tears to the eyes of the members, a number of whom were natives of Lincoln county, N. C., and Lincoln
county, Ky. He worked upon their feelings by bringing up tender recollections of their old homes, and then closed his speech
with a flight of eloquence that brought many of them to their
feet. Said he—"I was born in Lincoln county, North Carolina,
have lived in Lincoln county, Kentucky, and if God is willing I
want to die in Lincoln county, Missouri." His appeal could
not be withstood, and the county was named Lincoln without a
dissenting vote. Captain Clark was a most excellent citizen, and
his death was a great loss to the community.

CUNNINGHAM.—Jonathan and Delilah Cunningham were natives
of the State of Massachusetts. They had a son named Elliott
P. who came to Missouri in 1840, and settled in Audrain county.
He obtained the contract for building the State University at
Columbia, and was afterward elected a member of the County
Court of Audrain county. He married Cynthia Slocum, and
they had—Ellen, Clara, Russell S., Earle C., and Emmett R., all
of whom live in Audrain county.

DOAN.—Hezekiah J. M. Doan, of Harrison county, Ky., married Matilda Berry, and removed to Boone Co., Mo., in 1827,
from whence they removed to Audrain county in 1831. Mr.
Doan was appointed one of the first judges of the County Court
of that county, and was Justice of the Peace for many years.

He died in 1865, his wife having died in 1856. They had eight children, five daugthers and three sons.

DOUGLASS.—George Douglass, whose parents were Scotch, settled first in Amherst county, Va., and removed from there to Bedford county. He married Mary Tucker, and they had— Lucinda, David, John, Murphy, William, Polly, Susannah, and Sally. Lucinda, John, Polly and Susannah remained in Virginia, where they married and raised large families. Murphy married and settled in the northern part of Alabama. William married and settled in Byron Co., Ky. Sally married John Coward, who settled in Shelby Co. David was a soldier in the war of 1812. He married Sally White, a daughter of Jacob White and Rebecca Hollaway, by whom he had—Nancy, Elizabeth, William B., Louisa, Edward H., Mary A., Martha, Lumira, Sarah, Edith, Robert H., Edna, and Keren. William B., who is a minister, settled in Missouri in 1830. He was married in 1832, to Lucy Chick, the ceremony being performed by Esquire Enoch Fruite. They had six sons and two daughters. Mr. Douglass taught school for some time after he came to Missouri, and he had a great many grown pupils who did not know their letters. It was the fashion then to study out loud in the school-room, and each one would try to get his lesson in a louder tone than the others, and sometimes the noise would be so great that it could be heard half a mile. After Mr. Douglass began to preach he was frequently called upon to marry people. On one occasion he went seven miles to marry a couple, through a drenching rain, swimming several creeks that lay in his route, and returned the same day; for which he received the magnificent sum of fifty cents! He then had to go thirteen miles, on a cold, rainy day and pay that fifty cents to have the marriage recorded. Such were the trials of pioneer preachers. Edward H. Douglass settled in Audrain county in 1837. He married Mary J. Ogden, of Virginia, by whom he had two sons. He died in 1838. Sarah Douglass married her cousin, Robert Douglass, and settled in Johnson county, Mo.

DINGLE.—Edward Dingle, of Maryland, settled in Scott Co., Ky., where he married and had seven children. Three of them, Richard, Winder C., and Julia, settled in Marion Co., Mo. Mr. Dingle settled in Audrain county in 1840. He was married the second time to Frances Sallee, of Virginia, by whom he had— Samuel, Carter B., William S., John G., Polly S. Nancy C., and Mary A. Samuel was killed in Mexico, and left a widow and five children. Mary A. married Taswell Johnson. Carter B. married Nancy Ward, and died, leaving a widow and three children. His widow afterward married his brother, John G., and they had three children. William S. Dingle died in his youth.   Polly S. married Kinzey Hardister, and she is now a widow in California.   Nancy C. married a Mr. Landrum.

EUBANK.—John Eubank, of England, came to America and settled in the State of Maryland.   His children were—George, John, Thomas, Richard, William, Mary, Lamar, and Sophia. George married Rebecca Heringdon, of Maryland, and they had —David, Martha, George, Polly, Ellen, Rebecca, and Rhoda. David was a soldier of the war of 1812, and when the war was over he removed with his father to Kentucky, and from thence to Ohio.   He subsequently returned to Kentucky and married Anna Wyatt, and settled in Audrain Co., Mo., in 1837.   His children were—Cynthia, Julia, Lina, George, Rebecca, Jonathan, David, Loyd, and Ambrose.

ELLER.—Jacob, Joseph and Daniel Eller were born and raised in Maryland.   Jacob married Margaret Willard, and they had— Philip, George, Daniel, John, Sally, Susan, Margaret, Jacob, Jr., and Elias.   Jacob, Jr., married Elizabeth Grimes, and settled in Callaway county, Mo., in 1837.   His children were—Warner, Willard, John T., Ann M., Martha, and Elizabeth.   Elias Eller settled in Audrain county in 1838.   He married Mary Standerford, of Virginia, and they had—Abraham, Lizzie, Eleanor H., Margaret J., Mary A., Susan V., George E., Rachel, and Joseph.

FARCETT.—Edward Farcett, of North Carolina, settled in Audrain county in 1835.   He married Nancy McRay, and they had—John, Thomas, Nancy, and Sally.   Nancy married Josiah Gantt, of Audrain county.

FIKE.—John Fike, Sr., of Chatham Co., N. C., had—Aaron, James, John, Jr., and Nathan.   John, Jr., married Mary Rowe, and settled in Ralls Co., Mo., in 1817.   They had— Sally, Hasting, Elizabeth, Aussy H., Nelson, Dillard, Robert, Martha A., and Lucy.   Aussy H. married Mary Thompson, and they had a son named John, who married Virginia Fish.   Aussy H. Fike was married the second time to Mary Tipton.   Martha A. married William Powell, of Montgomery county, and after his death she married William H. Martin, of Audrain county.   Lucy married Caleb Martin, of that county.   Nelson, son of John Fike, Jr., married Mary J. Hughes, and settled in Montgomery county. Dillard, his brother, married the widow McConnell, whose maiden name was Ann Scott.   Robert married Mecha Holmes, and was afterward killed by lightning.

FUGET.—Josiah Fuget, of Virginia, settled first in Keutucky, and removed from there to Missouri in 1836.   He married Jane Musick, and they had—Jonathan, Sally, Josiah, Elizabeth, Ellen, Hiram, Polly, Hattie, James, Louisiana, Virginia and Nancy.

GILMER.—John Gilmer and Margaret Berry, his wife, settled in

Mercer Co., Ky. They had—Joseph, James, William, Alexander, Ann, and Jane. James was the only one who came to Missouri. He married Nancy Wilson, and settled in Monroe county in 1831, and in Audrain in 1842. His children were—Mary A., Margaret L., Eliza J., Sallie A., Harriet M., Emma C., and John J.

GANTT.—An English family named Gantt, and consisting of five brothers and two sisters, settled in North Carolina. Their names were—John, James, William, Zachariah, Ichem, Keziah, and Sally. William married Fannie Rippey, and settled in Ray county, Mo. Ichem married Sally Rippey, and they had—Jane, Levi, Josiah, Jesse, William, Thomas, and Ichem, Jr. Mr. Gantt died, and his widow afterward married his brother James, by whom she had James, Jr., and John. Josiah and Thomas, sons of Ichem Gantt, Sr., settled in Audrain county in 1835. The former married Nancy Farcett, and the latter married Cynthia Hurdell.

HEPLER.—Jacob Hepler was of German descent. He was born in Rockbridge county, Va., but married and settled in Ohio, where his wife died. Their children were—Obediah, John, Elizabeth, and Anna. Mr. Hepler was married the second time to Catharine Miller, of Ohio, by whom he had—Joseph, Edward, William H., Mitchell, Rebecca, Eliza, and Barbara. All of the children by his second wife settled in Audrain county.

HALL.—James Hall, of Nicholas county, Ky., had—Elizabeth, Polly, Cynthia, Melvina, James, John, Henry, Elihu, and Moses. John and Elihu came to Missouri in 1835. The former married Kitty Squires, and they had one son and ten daughters, viz.: Cynthia, Margaret, Mary, Amanda, Robert, Ruth, Liney, Mildred A., Judith A., Sally, and Caroline. Elihu Hall married Susan Bradshaw, and settled in Callaway county, Mo., in 1835, and in 1839 he settled in Audrain county. His children were—William, Rebecca, Elizabeth, Polly, Robert, John, David, and James. James, David and Amanda died in Indiana. Mr. Hall died in 1850, but his widow is still living, in her 77th year.

HENSON.—Francis Henson, of Virginia, married Elizabeth Hancock, a daughter of Stephen Hancock, and settled in Madison county, Ky., from whence he removed to Missouri in 1838. They had—Sarah, Elizabeth, William B., Zerelda, Polly A., Thomas H., and Frances. Sarah died single. Elizabeth married Archibald Cress, of Kentucky. William B. married a Miss Vaughan. Zerelda married James Horn. Polly A. married Burgoyne Bennett. Thomas H. was married first to Louisa J. Bybee, and second to the widow Green. Frances married Moses Baker.

HALL.—William Hall, of England settled in Pennsylvania, and

was killed by the Indians. His son John married Magdalene Smith, and they had—John, William, Matthew, Jesse, Hezekiah, Elisha, Tabitha, and Keziah. Elisha married Sarah Bent, and they had ten children. Two of their sons, John and Burkes B., settled in Missouri in 1832. John married Elizabeth Moon. She is dead, but he is still living.

HOOK.—Thomas Hook and Sally Long, his wife, were natives of Maryland. They removed first to Kentucky, and from there to Missouri in 1828. Their children were—Elizabeth, William, James, Samuel, Thomas. Patsey, Polly, Nancy, and Matilda. James married Cynthia Summit, and settled in Boone county, Mo., in 1826. Samuel married Mary Simms, and settled in Boone county in 1828. He died in 1829, and his widow married Thomas Hook, who died in 1850. The first husband's children were—Martha, Mary, and Samuel T., and the children of the second were—Graham, Robert S., Lucullus, William H., Joseph, and Martha E.

HUBBARD.—Thomas Hubbard was a Hard-Shell Baptist preacher. He bought a Bible that was published in London in 1708, for which he paid $100 in Continental money. The Bible is now in possession of his great-grandson and namesake, Thomas Hubbard, of Audrain county; and it contains the genealogy of the Hubbard family from 1718 to the present time. Thomas Hubbard had a son named Thomas, who also was a Baptist preacher. He was born in 1722, and learned the ship carpenter's trade. He married Anna Brent, of Pennsylvania, and they had one son, James. Mr. Hubbard was married the second time to Anna Yerby, and they had—Gilbert, Thomas, Hill, and Estell. He was married the third time to Anna Yarp, by whom he had— Jabez, Mary, Asap, Ebenezer, Nancy, Hulda. and Harriet. James, the eldest son, settled in Kentucky. Gilbert settled in Howard county, Mo., in 1807. Thomas settled in Washington county, Mo. Hill died while he was a boy. Estell married St. Clair Ledger, of Kentucky. Jabez was a member of the Legislature from St. Charles county in 1823–4. He died from the effects of intemperance. Asap settled in Howard county in 1808, and participated in the Indian war of 1812. He was a carpenter, and a Hard-Shell Baptist preacher. He married Mary Stephenson, who was living in New Madrid at the time of the great earthquakes. She was a granddaughter of Colonel Hugh Stephenson of revolutionary fame. The children of Asap Hubbard were— Henry C., Thomas J., Agnes E., and Fannie F. He settled in Audrain county in 1830.

JACKSON.—The parents of Zachariah Jackson, who were from Ireland, settled in Pamlico county, N. C. Zach was a soldier of the war of 1812, and was at the battle of New Orleans, where he was captured and held as a prisoner of war until peace was declared. He then settled in Williamson county, Tenn., where he married Malinda Slocum, by whom he had—Sarah A., James, Mary J., Zelpha, Slocum, Riley, Malinda, and Permelia. Mr. Jackson removed to Missouri with his family in 1819, and settled in Howard county, from whence he removed to Boone county in 1822. James, his eldest, married Asanith Turner, and settled in Audrian county in 1834. He was appointed first Sheriff of the county, but declined, and was elected the first Representative. He served two terms. The revenues of the county were so small at that time that his expenses had to be paid by the State. He was afterward clerk of the State Senate one term, and served as Judge of the County Court eight years. He is also a Baptist preacher of the Old School. Mr. Jackson says he was never "tight" but once in his life, and then he felt so good he tried to burn the grass on the prairie when the snow was a foot deep. He was very fond of hunting in early days, and one time while out on the prairie he came upon a rock about eight feet high, that had been split in the center, and the two halves were lying about eight feet apart. In 1860 he saw the same rock again, and the two pieces had grown fast together, and were only three feet high.

JESSE.—Rev. William M. Jesse, of Cumberland Co.. Va., was an Old School Baptist preacher. He married Polly A. Parker, and they had sixteen children—John P., Icham T., Mary A., Susan, Sally G., William J., Jesse S., Royal A., Paulina E., Cyrus S., Maria H., Alexander, and James M., several of whom died in childhood. John P., Icham T., William J. and Royal A. are all Baptist preachers, and live in Audrain county.

KILGORE.—Jonathan Kilgore, of Ireland, emigrated to America and settled in South Carolina. He removed from there to Caldwell Co., Ky., where he and his wife both died, the latter being 81 years of age at the time of her death. Their children were— John, David, William, Hugh, Jane, Samuel, Mary, and Jonathan. John and Hugh came to Missouri, the former in 1827 and the latter in 1837. John was married first to Polly Willingham, and they had—John, Samuel, Polly, Jane, Elizabeth, Nancy, and Margaret. He was married the second time to Phœbe Tart, of North Carolina, by whom he had Permelia, Amaretta, Lucinda, James B., Erretta, Nathan F., and Parthena. Nathan F. married Margaret J. Eller. Permelia married John H. Kilgore. Amaretta married Alfred Powell. Hugh, brother of John Kilgore, Sr., married Phœbe Bowlin, and they had several children, all of whom are dead.—John Hampton, Casana, and Isabella, children of David Kilgore, of Caldwell Co., Ky., settled in Missouri. John Hampton settled in Audrain county in 1830, and married Margaret Willingham, who died, and he afterward married Permelia Kilgore. He had eighteen children in all. Casana married

26

Icham Kilgore, who settled in Boone county in 1826, and in
Audrain in 1827. They had six sons and six daughters. Isabella
married William Wood, who settled in Callaway county in 1837,
and in Audrain in 1838. They had two sons and four daughters.

LEVAUGH.—Abraham Levaugh, of Woodford Co., Ky., was of
French descent. He had—Rebecca, Sally, Jane, William, Isaac,
James and Elizabeth. William married Polly Murphy, of North
Carolina, and settled in Montgomery Co., Mo., in 1823, and in
1832 he settled in Audrain county. He had but one child, a
son, who married Elizabeth Hall, by whom he had three sons.
He was married again to Minerva Jones, and they had three sons
and one daughter. Mr. Levaugh was a partner of the first merchant in Mexico, Mo.

LOCKRIDGE.—James Lockridge was born in Virginia, but
removed to and lived in Nicholson Co., Ky. His children were
—James, Jr., Robert, Andrew, William, and John. James and
John settled in Callaway Co., Mo., in 1828. The former married
Lavinia Hall, and they had—Margaret, Martha, James, Cynthia,
Elihu, John, Elizabeth, Perlissa A., Robert, and Melvina. John,
son of James Lockridge, Sr., married Mahala Brown, and they
had—John, Nancy, Martha, James, William, Robert, and Mary.
All of this family are now living in Audrain cou.ity.

McCLURE.—John McClure, of Scotland, settled in Virginia,
and afterward removed to Clark Co., Ky. He had—John,
Andrew, Samuel, and two daughters. John married Polly Redmon, and settled in Missouri in 1832. They had—John, William,
Louisa, Polly A., Lucinda, Sally, Mary, and Margaret. Samuel McClure married Emily Brown, and settled in Missouri in
1831. They had—James, David, John, Joseph, Clay, Elizabeth,
Mary, and Sallie.

McINTOSH.—Loyd McIntosh, of Logan Co., Ky., married
Catharine Harper, by whom he had—John, George L., Julia,
Rachel, and Jane. John married Elizabeth Gillum, and after his
death his widow settled in Missouri. George L. married Sarah
Harper, and settled in Missouri in 1838. Rachel married William
McIntire, of Fulton, Callaway county.

McDONNALD.—The parents of George and Jane McDonnald
were murdered by the Indians in the early settlement of Virginia.
George and his sister were in the lot, playing in a horse trough,
when the attack was made. They lay down in the trough and
were not discovered by the savages; but both of their parents,
who were in the house, were murdered. When George was
grown he married Mary Murdock, of Ireland, and they had—
John, Peter, Thomas, James, William, Elizabeth, and Ann. In
1795 they settled in Nicholas Co., Ky., where Mr. McDonnald
died, and his widow removed with her son William to Illinois,

where she died.   Thomas McDonnald married the widow Gray, whose maiden name was Sarah Franklin, and settled in Missouri in 1831.   They had—Malinda, William H., Zerelda, Arthur, Margaret, George, Elizabeth, Amanda, and Nancy, all of whom, except Zerelda, settled in Missouri.

MUNDY.—Samuel Mundy, of Albemarle Co., Va., married Mildred Croswhite.   Two of their sons, Logan and Isaac, settled in Missouri in 1836.   Isaac afterward removed to California, where he died.   Logan married Lucinda Creed, and lives in Audrain county.   He came to Missouri poor, but has prospered, and is now possessed of a goodly supply of worldly effects.

MARTIN.—John C. Martin, of Lincoln Co., N. C., married Phœbe Allen, and settled in Audrain Co., Mo., in 1830.   They had—Allen, Thomas, Rufus, Robert, Nelson, Polly, Nancy, Elizabeth, and Patsey.   Mr. Martin was a devout Methodist, and held family prayers regularly, night and morning; but no one could understand his prayers, as he used language which he alone could interpret.   It was his custom to give a corn shucking once every year, and wind up with a quilting, as he was very much opposed to dancing.   One of his daughters married Henry Williams, who at the time was so poor he could not pay the minister, but gave him an old spinning wheel for his trouble.   Mr. Williams afterward represented the county in the Legislature, and is now one of the leading merchants of Mexico.   He could pay several parson's fees now without any trouble.

MYERS.—Yosty Myers was of German descent, and lived in Maryland.   His children were—Louis, Jacob, John, Mike, Benjamin, Rebecca, and Mary.   Louis married Elizabeth McKay, of Virginia, and settled in Kentucky at a very early date.   His children were—Isaac M., Silas, William, Lewis, Elias B., Meredith, Harvey S., Abishai M., Mary A., Elizabeth, Sally, and Rebecca. Meredith married Nancy P. Jennings, a daughter of Gen. William Jennings, of the war of 1812, and settled in Audrain Co., Mo., where his wife died.   He afterward married Emeline Blue. By his first wife he had two sons and four daughters.   Louis Myers came to Missouri and bought land, intending to remove his family here, but he died on his way back to Kentucky.   His family came to Missouri after his death.

MURRAY.—William Murray, of Georgia, had five children— Nancy, Timothy, William, Douglass, and Samuel.   The latter volunteered as a soldier in the war of 1812, when he was only seventeen years of age.   After he was grown he married Mary A. Binns, and settled in Audrain Co., Mo., where he died in 1861, in the 65th year of his age, leaving a widow and five children.

MYERS.—Drury Myers, of Ireland, settled in Halifax Co., Va.

His children were—Drury, William, Gardner, and Beverly. Drury married Nancy Douglass, who had seven brothers in the American army during the revolutionary war.   They settled first in Tennessee, and removed from there to Kentucky, where Mr. Myers died in 1828.   He had six children, and his widow and five of the children settled in Boone Co., Mo., in 1832.   The names of the children were—Sally, Drury D., Nancy, Beverly S., and William M.   Sally married Marion Pate, who settled in Audrain county in 1835.   Drury D. married Mary A. Barnes, and settled in Audrain county in 1833.   Nancy married Hiram G. Miller, who also settled in Audrain county.   Beverly S. was married first to Martha Ridgeway, and settled in Audrain county in 1833.   He was married the second time to Emelia E. Bladus. William M. married Elizabeth H. Barnes, and settled in Audrain county in 1834.

McINTIRE.—Daniel McIntire and his wife, who was a Miss Weaver, were natives of Virginia, but removed to Kentucky, and settled near Lexington.   They had—Charles W., Roland, Duskin, William, Catharine, Frances, Jane, and Elizabeth.   Charles W. settled in Callaway Co., Mo., in 1819, and in Audrain in 1836. He was married in July, 1829, to Margaret Harrison, of Callaway county, and they had—Donald, Thomas, William, Eliza, Cynthia, and Nancy.   Mr. McIntire was very fond of a joke, and never let and opportunity pass to indulge in one; but he got badly sold on a certain occasion.   The people of Callaway county had been taunting the citizens of Audrain, and saying they had no money, and in order to convince them that there was some money in Audrain, he gave a man a $20 gold piece, and told him to go into Callaway and show it to everybody he could see, and tell them it was from Audrain.   The fellow took the money and departed, and is doubtless showing it around yet, as he never returned it to its owner.   On another occasion Mr. McIntire endeavored to borrow the entire revenue of the county from the Sheriff, who was conveying it to Jefferson City.   It consisted of $32 in money and six wolf scalps.   Roland McIntire was born in Fleming Co., Ky., in 1800.   He married Maria Hunter, of Ohio, and settled in Audrain county, Mo., in 1831.   He hewed the logs to build his house, and while they were lying in the woods some Indians set the woods on fire, and the logs were burnt black, rendering them unfit, in that condition, for use.   Mr. McIntire and a party of his neighbors pursued the Indians, and caught and whipped them, to learn them not to do so another time.   He then hewed his logs again and built his house.   He had eight children— Roland, Jr., Marvin, Amanda, Laura, Mary, Fleming, Catharine, and Redmon.   Duskin and William McIntire remained in Kentucky.   Catharine married Lewis Day, who settled in Audrain county in 1830.   The widow of Frank McIntire lives in Fulton,

Mo. Jane married James McClannahan, of Callaway county. Elizabeth married Wiley Reynolds, of the same county.

Musick.—About the last of the seventeenth century, a small boy was found in Wales who could give no account of his parents or himself, except that his first name was George. George manifested a fondness for music, and his friends surnamed him Musick, as the word was then spelled. He emigrated to Virginia in the beginning of the eighteenth century, where he raised five sons, viz: Daniel, George, Alexis, Ephraim, and Abraham. He also raised some daughters, but of these we know neither the number nor names. Ephraim married a Miss Roy, and raised a family in Spottsylvania county. He raised two daughters, one of whom married a Jenkins, and one a Cauthorn. He raised four sons, viz: Abraham, John, Thomas R., and Ephraim. Thomas R. Musick was born October 10, 1757. He joined the Baptist Church, and commenced preaching at about seventeen years of age. He went to North Carolina during the revolutionary war, where he married Mary Nevel. Thomas served a part of the time in the American army. He removed to South Carolina in the year 1789, and in 1794, he removed to Barren county. He visited Missouri several times while it was under the Spanish Government, and preached in St. Louis county as early as the year 1797. While preaching there he was frequently threatened with violence. In the spring of 1804 he removed with his family to Missouri and settled in St. Louis county, one mile north of the present town of Bridgeton. Shortly afterward he instituted Fefee Creek Baptist Church, which was doubtless the first Baptist Church west of the Mississippi river, of which he was pastor for many years. In the year of 1823 or 1824 his wife Mary died at home in St. Louis county. After the death of his wife, he made his home at the house of his nephew, Ury Musick, a son of Abraham Musick. He continued to preach in various parts of Missouri and Illinois until a short time previous to his death, which occurred on the 2d of December, 1842, at the house of Ury Musick. The family of Thomas consisted of three sons and six daughters, viz: William, Nancy, Lewis, Mary, Charlotte, Sarah, Drucilla, Joyce, and Thomas. William died at seven or eight years of age, and Thomas at sixteen; all the others lived to be grown and married. Lewis Musick was born the 1st day of February, 1784. He came with his father to Missouri in 1804, and married Nancy Martin, who died some years afterward, after which he married Mary Fitzwater. Lewis removed to Pike county in the fall of 1819, and from there to Audrain county in the spring of 1839. From Missouri he went to California, starting on the 15th of April, 1849. He died in Sacramento Valley, October 27, 1849. He was engaged in trading in live stock during the greater part of his life, and in the course of his business was occupied in driving horses and cattle in various directions all the way from Texas to Selkirk's Colony on North Red river, the country over which he had to pass for the most part a savage wilderness. Lewis raised ten children, viz: Lawson T., Elvira, Lafrenier C., Mary Ann, Charlotte M., Sarah T., Thomas R., Ephraim L., James J., and Mandana A. Lafrenier was born in St. Louis county on the 29th day of July, 1815, and married Jane D. Hayden. He joined the Baptist Church in March, 1833, commenced preaching immediately afterward, and was ordained in October, 1835. His present residence is in Audrain county.

MANSFIELD.—Robert Mansfield and Mourning Clark, his wife, of Virginia, had—William H., James W., Thomas M., Robert C., Joseph, Mildred, Elizabeth, Nancy H., Mary, Sarah, and Susannah. William H., James W. and Joseph were Baptist preachers, Thomas M. was a Methodist preacher, and Robert was a Presbyterian preacher. The latter settled in Audrain county in 1836, and he and Mr. J. H. Smith entered the land on which the city of Mexico stands. They donated 25 acres to the city the same year. Robert C. Mansfield married Elizabeth S. Beatty, and they had—Malinda, Mary, William, Edward, Charles and Lelia. Mildred, Elizabeth, Nancy H. and Sarah, daughters of Robert Mansfield, Sr., remained in Virginia. Mary married and settled in Illinois. Susannah married and settled in Monroe Co., Missouri.

PETLEY.—Joseph Petley, of Warren Co., Ky., married Nancy Hamilton, and they had—Alfred, Allen, Alexander, John, George, Mary, Margaret, Rachel, and Nancy. Alfred settled in Audrain county in 1828. He was married first to Malinda Meigs, by whom he had three children. He was married the second time to Cynthia Howard, by whom he had nine children. Mr. Petley was the greatest hunter and trapper of his day. It is said by those who had opportunities of knowing, that he killed more bears, deer, panthers, wild cats, raccoons, and wild turkeys than any two men in Missouri. He was very stout, and was often seen carrying two deer, one strapped on each shoulder, and his gun at the same time. He would carry such a load as this for miles without seeming to grow weary. He lived to a very old age, and died in 1874. While he was lying on his death-bed he had his gun and powder horn, a set of bucks' antlers, and the skins of a wild cat, raccoon and bear hung where he could see them, and they were the last objects that his gaze rested upon as his soul took its flight to the spirit land. Allen Petley settled in Montgomery county, and married Ellen Bishop. Alexander also settled in Montgomery county. One day during harvest he cut seven acres of wheat with a cradle, and drank a large quantity of cold water while he was heated, from the effects of which he died that night.. Margaret married Taliaferro Reed, who settled in Montgomery county in 1834. Rachel married William Williams, who settled in that county the same year.

PULIS.—The parents of John Pulis, of New York City, were Irish. John was married twice, and by his first wife he had David and Conrad. His second wife was a Miss Plunkett, by whom he had Peter and John. David was married in the city of New York, to Phœbe Taylor, by whom he had—Elizabeth, William, John, Reuben, Conrad, and Samuel E. Mr. Pulis removed to Kentucky, where he lost his wife, and was married again to Mary N. Gardner, by whom he had—Thomas M., Stephen M., George, and Joseph. He then removed to Warren Co., Mo., where he died in 1848. William and John Pulis married and settled in Missouri in 1829 and 1830. Reuben ran away from home when he was sixteen years old, and came to Missouri. He landed at Hannibal, which at that time consisted of one house. There he made a bark canoe and went down the Mississippi river to St. Louis, from whence he worked his way back to Kentucky on a steamboat. He then learned the trade of a blacksmith, and married the widow Hutson. Her property consisted of a feather bed, a gun, a cradle, two chairs and a pair of scissors; while he had $25 in money and a set of blacksmith's tools. He paid the $25 to a man to haul himself and wife and their property to Missouri. They settled first in Audrain county, removed from there to Callaway, and returned to Audrain again, where Mrs. Pulis died, and he afterward married Nancy McDonald. Mr. Pulis was a Justice of the Peace in Audrain county for six years. Conrad, Samuel, Thomas and Stephen Pulis married and settled in Missouri, Thomas in Audrain county.

PEERY.—James Peery and his wife, who was a Miss Jameson, were natives of Ireland. They settled in Tazewell Co., Va., and had—Thomas, James, John, William, and Samuel. Mr. Peery and his son Thomas were both soldiers in the revolutionary war. The former was wounded severely, and the latter was killed. Samuel Peery married Sarah Cartman, by whom he had—John, William, Joseph, Thomas, Martha, Elizabeth, Althamira, and Matilda. Thomas married Narcissa Canterberry, and split rails at 50 cents per 100 to get money to pay the parson. He paid his first taxes in Audrain county in 1837, to Jack Willingham, who was the first Sheriff. His taxes amounted to two wolf scalps and half-a-pound of powder. Mr. Peery is a devoted Methodist, and loves to attend camp-meetings. He was present at a camp-meeting, a good many years ago, when a violent rain and wind storm came up and broke the ridge pole of the large tent, which let the canvas sink down in the shape of a funnel, into which a large quantity of water gathered, when some one cut a hole in the canvas and the water rushed out with such violence that the preachers were washed out of the pulpit and the women away from the altar.

PEARSON.—Stephen Pearson, of Burch county, N. C., married Mary Potts, and they had twd sons, John A. and Joseph, both of whom settled in Audrain county, Mo., where the city of Mexico now stands, in 1835. When the town was laid off the following year, Joseph donated three acres of land to help it along. John A. married Nancy Carlton, of North Carolina, by whom he had— Rufus S., Leander P., John V., Marschall C., Joseph W., Clinton P., Julia A., Mary E., Emily L., and Elizabeth L. In addition to his own family Mr. Pearson had eight negro slaves, and they all lived in two small cabins for a number of years. He served eight years as a member of the County Court, and was an esteemed and influential citizen.

POWELL.—Thomas Powell and Nancy Chaney, his wife, were natives of Maryland, but settled in Nicholas county, Ky., in 1796. They had eleven children, nine of whom lived to be grown, viz.: John, Charles, Jerry, Thomas, Isaac, William, Robert, Polly, and Nancy. John, Isaac, and Nancy settled in Indiana. Charles, Thomas, and William lived in Kentucky. Polly married, and she and her husband lived in Ohio. Jerry settled in Illinois. Robert was a soldier of the war of 1812, and became an early settler of Audrain county, where he still lives in his 83d year. He was married first to Celia Murphy, of Kentucky, by whom he had—Alvin, Alfred, Monroe, Jefferson, Jameson, Columbus, Jackson, Robert T., Julia A., Nancy, and Grezella. Mr. Powell was married two other times, his last wife being the widow Hunt. All of his children live in Audrain county.

RODGERS.—Charles Rodgers and his wife, Elizabeth Harris, of Halifax county, Va., had one son, Charles B., who was a Lieutenant in the war of 1812. He settled in Callaway county, Mo., in 1829, and at the commencement of the war with Mexico he raised a company in Callaway and Audrain counties, and served as Captain of his company during the war. His wife was Aletha Overfelt, of Bedford county, Va., and their children were—Richmond H., Charles A., Andrew J., James C., John L., Elizabeth J., Sarah H., Virginia C., Thomas R., Isaac C., William G., and Aletha J. Charles A. was a private in his father's company during the Mexican war.

REED.—Zachariah Reed, of Richmond, Va., married Margaret Cockrell, by whom he had five sons and five daughters. They left Virginia and settled in Kentucky, where they lived for many years. Their son James, who was a coppersmith, married Susan Williford, and settled in Boone county, Mo., in 1826, and in Audrain county in 1834, where he still lives, in his 87th year. He served in the war of 1812, under Isaac Shelby, in Canada. He had two sons and seven daughters.

REYNOLDS.—John Reynolds, of South Carolina, married Nancy Griggs, by whom he had—Allen, John, Sarah, Shadrach, Emily, William, Wiley, Judith, Joseph, and Durham. Mr. Reynolds settled in Boone county, Mo., in 1829, and in Audrain county in 1832.

ROSE.—George Rose and his wife, of Germany had three children—Louis, Martin, and Matthias. Louis was Colonel of a regiment in the battle of Blue Licks, Ky., and was captured and taken to Detroit, where he was exchanged, and returned home in August, 1783. Matthias married Nancy Hickman, of Loudon county, Va., and settled in St. Louis Co., Mo., in 1818. His children were—Louis, Elga H., Rolley F., Elizabeth, Sarah, and Angeline. Louis married Elizabeth Massey, and they had one son, Frank E., who lives in St. Louis county. Elga H., better known as Judge Rose, lives in Mexico, Mo. He married Ellen B. Sullivan, and they had Matthias D. and Lucy E. Rolley F. was married first to Mary Clark, by whom he had—Louis, William, Franklin, and Nancy. He was married the second time to Adeline DeHare, a French lady. Elizabeth married James McClure. Sarah married Nicholas S. Burkhart. Angeline married Benjamin D. Ray.

RUSSELL.—Mr. Russell, of North Carolina, was a soldier of the revolutionary war. He married in North Carolina, and settled in Campbell county, Va. His children were—Mark, Henry, Daniel, and Louis. Daniel married Lucy Lane, and settled in Carroll county, Mo., 1836. Louis married Jane Davidson, and they had—Frank, David, William, Eliza, Henry, John, and three others. Mr. Russell lived for many years on the Ohio river, in West Virginia, and made regular trips to New Orleans with flatboats. He was fond of hunting and trapping, and devoted a great deal of time to those occupations. He settled in Audrain county, Mo., in 1835, and died in 1872, in the 84th year of his age.

SPENCER.—Barnard Spencer and his wife, Mary Hampton, of Gallatin Co., Ky., had—Preston H., Sarah A., Joseph D., James H., Eliza, Rosa, Susannah, Henry H., and Barnard H. Joseph D. married Elizabeth Bishop, and settled in Audrain county in 1839. Henry H. was married twice, and settled in Audrain county. Barnard H., Eliza and Susannah also settled in Audrain county.

STRAHAN.—John Strahan was the son of Robert Strahan and Nancy Scott, of Doun Co , Ireland. When John was three years old his mother died, and in 1812 his father came to America, bringing his son with him, and settled in Beaver Co., Pa. His brother William and sister Nancy also came with them. John lost his father when he was only eleven years of age, and he was bound out to learn the carpenter's trade. But that trade did not suit him, and he left the man he was bound to and learned the boot and shoe business. He also procured books and acquired such an education as he could by his own efforts. He was naturalized in 1824, and settled in Lincoln Co., Ky., in 1832, where he married Celia Canterberry, by whom he had four sons and four daughters. He came to Missouri in 1841, and settled first in Platte county, but removed from there to Audrain county in 1844. In 1849 he went to California, and during his absence his wife died. He returned home in 1854, and married Cynthia Eubank. He was elected Justice of the Peace in 1846, but resigned his office when he went to California. He was re-elected upon his return, and continued to hold the office for many years. He has been a great friend of public improvements, and when the North Missouri Railroad was built he subscribed largely to the capital stock, saying that if he could not pay his railroad tax when it was due, he would take his spade and work it out. The Esquire is now living on his farm in Audrain county, and is a worthy and respectable citizen.

SHOCK.—Henry Shock, of Germany, emigrated to America and settled first in Pennsylvania, from whence he removed to Greenbriar Co., Va. His children were—Henry, John, Jacob, Rayner, Christina, and Sally. John married Polly Shiley, and they had— Milley, David, Henry, Hector P. L., Eliza, Polly, William, Rebecca, Peggy, and Sarah. Mr. Shock settled in Boone Co., Mo., in 1816, and built a horse-mill. His son Henry was married first to Mary Jackson, and second to Hannah L. Cox, and by his two wives he had sixteen children. He settled in Audrain county in 1831, and bought out Richard Willingham, "stock, lock and barrel," for $80. He afterward purchased the property of Colonel Robert Fulkerson, whose land adjoined his, and the latter removed to Montgomery county. Mr. Shock is called the "fat man" of Audrain, county and we give his portrait on page 228. David Shock married Cynthia Gibson, of Boone county. Hector P. L. married Sarah A. Jackson, and settled in Bates county, where he died. Eliza married Thomas Strickland, the first stage contractor on the Booneslick road. Polly married William Brewer. William married the widow Evans. Margaret married Perry Cox. Sarah A. married Milton Blythe. Richard died in childhood.

STEPHENSON.—Hugh Stephenson, of Ireland, settled in Pennsylvania, and fought under Washington during the revolutionary war. His children were—John, Hugh, Richard, and Marcus. The three latter also served in the revolutionary war. Marcus married Agnes Hinkson, and they had—Polly, Elizabeth, Hugh, Nancy, Marcus, Peggy, and Garret. Mr. Stephenson removed to Missouri in 1807, and died in 1814, while on his way to Howard county. His widow afterward married Thomas Reynolds, of

Kentucky, and died in 1865. Garret, son of Marcus Stephenson, married Effie A. Blue, and lives in Audrain county.

SLOCUM.—Joseph Slocum, of England, settled in North Carolina, where he married Mary Riley, and they had—Riley, Nancy, Robert, and Cynthia. Riley married the widow Potts, whose maiden name was Nancy Crockett, of Tennessee, and settled in Boone Co., Mo., in 1819. They had—Nancy, Robert and Cynthia. Nancy, daughter of Riley Slocum, married Joseph M. Gray, and they had two children. Cynthia married Elliott P. Cunningham. Robert is a bachelor, and lives in Audrain county. Riley Slocum was married the second time to Annie Herring, by whom he had—William, Alfred, Joseph, Susan, John C., and Amanda J. The first four died young. Amanda J. was married first to Charles V. McWilliams, and second to Oliver C. Cunningham. She had two children by her second husband, Charles and Price.

THOMAS.—Jackson Thomas was born and raised in Mercer Co., Ky., but removed to Monroe Co., Mo., in 1834, and to Audrain county in 1838. He married Sarah D. McGee, and they had—Ida C., James S., Mary J., Louisa A., Sarah E., Susan F., Martha E., and William J.

TINSLEY.—The father of Edward Tinsley came from Scotland and settled on James river, in Virginia, before the revolutionary war. Edward married Elizabeth Buford, who was a sister of Colonel William Buford of the revolutionary war. They had—Caleb, Henry, Joshua, William, Abraham, Judith, Elizabeth, Rachel, and Frances. Caleb married Elizabeth Medley, of Virginia, and they had—Ann, Mildred, Peachey, Frances E., and Abraham B. Mr. Tinsley removed to Kentucky in 1816, and settled in Callaway Co., Mo., in 1837. Abraham B. married Rachel Jains, and settled in Audrain county in 1837. He was Sheriff of that county three terms, and represented it in the Legislature two terms.

TALLEY.—George, Abraham, Richard, and William Talley were born and raised in England, but settled in Halifax Co., Va., at a very early date. George and William came to Missouri in 1817, and settled in Howard county, where they remained two years and then removed to Boone county. William settled in Audrain county in 1829, and George in 1831. The latter married Martha Wilson, and they had—William, Jr., Sally, James, Martha, Harriet, George, Boswell W., Wiley, and Judith. William Talley, Sr., married Judith Wilson, of Virginia, and they had—Elizabeth, John, Daniel, Wiley, Berry, Jennie, George, William and Lethe.

TURNER.—Thomas Turner, of Virginia, married Catharine Smith, of the same State, and settled on the Yadkin river, in North Carolina. They had a son named William, who was born

in January, 1778, and is now living in Audrain Co., Mo.   He has
been a member of the Old Baptist Church for seventy-six years.
He went to Kentucky with his parents in 1790, where he married
Elizabeth Crooks, and in 1837 he settled in Boone Co., Mo.,
where he resided until 1869, when he settled in Audrain county.
His children were—Thomas, James, Clinton, John, Samuel,
Silas, Mary, Lucinda, Nellie, Sarah, Margaret, Narcissa, Eliza-
beth, and Catharine.   Four of Mr. Turner's brothers, Smithton,
James, John, and Thomas, settled in Boone Co., Mo.

VAUGHAN.—Frederick Vaughan was a soldier of the revolution,
and lived in Henry Co., Va.   He married Nancy Boulware,
and they had—Catharine, Polly, Nancy, Fannie, Patsey,
Robertson, Frederick, and Martin, all of whom settled in Shelby
Co., Ky.   Martin, Frederick, Polly, Fannie, and Patsy came to
Missouri with their parents.   Martin was married three times;
first to Rebecca Taylor, second to Susannah Proffit, and third to
Coroline Wilborn.   He had only three children, and is now a
widower in his 80th year.

WAYNE.—John Wayne, of Virginia, had a son named Temple,
who was of a roving disposition and passionately fond of hunting.
He settled in Audrain Co., Mo., in 1827, and killed six deer the
first day he stopped there.   During the hunting seasons no one
killed more deer and wolves than he did, and he lived for years
entirely on wild game.   He was never satisfied except when he
was in the woods, where he spent nearly all of his time, night
and day—Sunday being like any other day to him.   He was married first to Lorinda Peyton, by whom he had—William, Mary,
Temple, Jr., Joseph, Lorinda, Jane, and James.   He was married the second time to Elizabeth Griggs, and they had—Lucy
A., George, Elizabeth, Emily, Alfred, and Franklin.

WILSON.—Moses Wilson married Mary Russell, of Virginia,
and settled in Boone Co., Ky.   They had—John H., Sarah,
Martha, William, Elizabeth, Samuel, Susan, and Chrine.   John
H. was a soldier in the war of 1812.   He married Susan Sim-
mons, and settled in Audrain Co., Mo., in 1834.   They had—
Sally, Martha A., Esther, William W., Mary, Joseph R., Susan
C., and Samuel M.

WILLIAMS.—Cobb Williams was a native of Virginia, but settled in Lincoln Co., N. C., where he married Patsey Brown.   He
settled in Audrain Co., Mo., in 1830.   His children were—Polly,
Patsey, Delilah, Granderson, Caleb, John, William L., Gideon,
and Absalom.   John and Delilah died in North Carolina.   Polly
married John Allen.   Patsey married John Kilgore.   Granderson
and Abraham live in Monroe county.   Caleb is in California.
William L. was married first to Cordelia Kilgore, and second to
Mary E. Evans.   Gideon married Elizabeth Gulley.   Caleb Will-

iams, Sr., died in 1832, and his funeral was the first preached in Audrain county. The services were conducted by Rev. Robert Younger, a Methodist minister of Boone county.

WEATHERFORD. — John Weatherford, of Ireland, settled in Virginia at an early date. His children were—George, Joel, Archibald, Harden, Lindsley, and Milley. Joel married Catharine Dry, and settled first in Kentucky, from whence he removed to Pike Co., Mo., in 1829. They had one child, Polly, when Mrs. Weatherford died, and he married Margaret Dry, by whom he had—Catharine, George J., Joel M., Caroline, Margaret, Jane, Frank, and Jacob. Joel M. married Mary B. Stanford. Polly married Frank McCord. Catharine married John Pardon. George J. married Susan Johnson. Caroline married S. T. Love. Margaret married William Hoard. Jane married George Walker. Frank married Anna Atkins, and Jacob married a Miss Ferrell.

WILLINGHAM.—Many years before the revolutionary war, a family of Willinghams lived in North Carolina. About 1800 two brothers of the family, named John and William, settled in Kentucky, and in 1816 they came to Missouri and settled on Rocky Fork creek, within the present limits of Boone county, from whence they removed to what is now Audrain county in 1825. John Willingham had a son named Jack, who was the first Sheriff of Audrain county. He collected the revenues in 1837, which amounted to $32 in money and six wolf scalps.

WATTS.—Samuel Watts, of Halifax Co., Va., was born in England. He married Sally Burchett, and they had—Rebecca, Daniel, Lizzie, Gillum, John, Roland, Joseph, Berry, Brackett, and Sally. Roland married Polly Lane, and settled in Audrain county in 1833. Joseph was married first to Dorothea Conner, of Virginia, and second to the widow of Henry Burnes, whose maiden name was Arsissa Johnson, daughter of Richard Johnson and Ann Withens, who came from Bourbon Co., Ky., to Callaway Co., Mo., in 1824.

WOODS.—Andrew Woods, of Mercer Co., Ky., married Mary McGee, and they had—John, James, and William. John and James settled in Monroe Co., Mo. William married Jane Cardwell, and settled in Audrain county in 1837. They had—George A., David, James, William, Mary A., Joseph, John, Albert, Olivia, Martha J., and Susan.

WOODS.—The parents of Archibald Woods were Irish. He was married in Virginia, and removed to Kentucky during the early settlement of that State, where he was killed by the Indians during one of their attacks upon the fort where he and his family were staying. He left a widow and four children—William, Franklin, Nancy, and Archibald. William was married in Ken-

tucky, and settled in Missouri in 1820.   Frank died unmarried in
Boone Co., Mo.   Nancy married William Mullins, who settled in
Howard county in 1820.   Archibald married Fannie Hill, and
settled in Callaway county in 1826.   His children were—David
H., Elizabeth, John, Nellie, Nancy, and Patsey.   David H. mar-
ried Sarah Reynolds, and lives in Audrain county.

WEST.—William West married a Miss Bybee, and removed
from Virginia to North Carolina, and in 1800 he settled in East
Tennessee.   Mr. West was a soldier of the revolutionary war,
and while he was in the army his wife kept all the pewter ware,
of which she had quite an amount, buried to keep the soldiers
from moulding it into bullets.   Their eldest son, Jolley H., married Nancy Williams, of North Carolina, by whom he had—
James, John, Emily, William, Elizabeth, Jeremiah J., and
Louisa.   After the death of Mr. West his widow came to Missouri with three of her children, Jeremiah J., William and
Elizabeth, and settled in Audrain county in 1834.   Mrs. West
afterward married Elias Gilpin, who removed to Texas.   William
West married Polly Mullins, of Tennesse.   Jeremiah J. married
Zelpha Hatton, of Kentucky, by whom he had ten children,
nearly all of whom are named for Methodist preachers.   Louisa
West married B. A. Fields, and died in 1856, leaving seven
children.

PART IV

BIOGRAPHIES AND SKETCHES.

The reader will find in the following pages the biographies of a few leading men and pioneers of the region of country embraced in the plan of this work, with several sketches of an interesting character. Also a life of the celebrated Indian Chief Black Hawk, with an account of his exploits as a warrior in Lincoln and St. Charles counties, taken from his autobiography as published in 1836, by Antoine Leclair, at that time U. S. Interpreter for the Sac and Fox Indians, and to whom Black Hawk dictated the matter contained in the book. A history of the Black Hawk war, so often referred to in these pages, is also given in that connection.

BISHOP ENOCH M. MARVIN.

The Marvin family is a very old one, dating back in this country to about 1635. Like most of our American families, it originated in England, but we have no account of it previous to its advent into this country.

Reinold Marvin came from England to America with his family about the year 1635. He settled first in Hartford, Ct., but soon removed from there to the town of Lyme, in the same State. Mr. Marvin was an intelligent man, and fully appreciating the value and power of knowledge, he educated his children as well as he could in those early times, when schools, books and teachers were not so abundant as they are now. The result was that his children occupied leading positions in the community where they lived, and were distinguished for their intelligence, fine social qualities, and good characteristics as citizens.

Lieutenant Reinold Marvin, a son of Reinold Marvin, Sr., was born (probably in England) in 1634, and died in Lyme, Ct., in 1676. He was a prominent and influential citizen, and in addition to his services as a soldier, in assisting to defend his country against the attacks of a savage foe, he occupied a high position in civil affairs, and represented the Colony in the General Court, a body similar to our modern Legislatures. His son, Captain Reinold Marvin, was born in Lyme, Ct., in 1669, and died in 1737. He represented his native town in the General Court from 1721 to 1728, and was also an officer in the colonial army.

Elisha, son of Captain Reinold Marvin, was born in Lyme, March 8, 1717, and died December 3, 1801. He married Catharine Mather, daughter of Timothy Mather, who was a member of the celebrated Cotton Mather family.*

Enoch, son of Elisha Marvin, was born in Lyme, Ct., in 1747. He married Ruth Ely, and removed to Berkshire county, Mass., where his son, Wells Ely, was born. Soon after that event Mr. Marvin removed to Shenango county, N. Y., where his family was principally reared. In 1817 he came to Missouri with his son, and died December 24, 1841.

Wells Ely Marvin was born in Berkshire county, Mass., as above stated. He married Polly Davis, whose ancestors were

---

* Increase, the father of Cotton Mather, was born at Dorchester, Mass., June 21, 1639. He graduated at Harvard College in 1656, and in June 1685 he became President of that institution of learning, which position he occupied until 1701. He was ordained a minister of the gospel in 1661, but had preached before with great success in Boston. He also distinguished himself as a skillful statesman, and among other public services rendered to his county, he prevented the Charter of Massachusetts from being surrendered to the King, Charles II., for which he received the thanks of the General Court. He died at Boston, August 23, 1723, in the 85th year of his age, having been a preacher sixty-six years. It is said that he usually spent sixteen hours a day in his study, and his sermons and other publications were proportionably numerous. During the witchcraft delusion he exerted all his influence to allay the excitement, and thereby saved many persons from a violent death at the hands of an ignorant and superstitious mob.

Cotton Mather, D. D., son of Increase Mather, surpassed even his father in learning, influence, and the variety and multitude of his productions. In one year he preached 72 sermons, kept 60 fasts and 20 vigils, and wrote 14 books. His publications amount to 382, some of them being of huge dimensions. His largest and most celebrated work is his *Magnalia Christi Americana*, or the Ecclesiastical History of New England, from 1625 to 1698, folio. He was born in Boston, February 12, 1663, graduated at Harvard College in 1678, and was ordained a minister in 1684. He died in 1728, aged 65 years, with the reputation of having been the greatest scholar and author that America had then produced.

Welch, and came to Missouri in 1817. He settled on Dardenne creek, in the eastern part of Howell's Prairie, where he remained one year, and then removed to now Warren county, and settled two and a half miles southwest of the present town of Wright City, on a small stream called Barrett's creek. There he built a double-log cabin, and covered it with rough clapboards, which were kept in their places by heavy poles laid transversely across the boards. A wooden chimney stood at each end of the house, and between the two rooms there was a passage or hall. Each room was lighted by a single small, square window, containing but one sash. In this house Bishop Marvin was born, but was principally raised in a new hewed log house which his father built after his birth. The latter is still standing, and is what is known as a story and a half house; that is, the second story is only half as high as the first, and so low that a grown person can stand upright only in the middle of the room, under the cone of the roof. The Bishop and his brothers slept in this low upper-story, which they entered through a door in the gable end of the house, which was reached by a ladder on the outside. If a storm or an accident overthrew the ladder, they were prisoners until some one came to their relief and hoisted it up again, for there was no other mode of egress or ingress. As they lay in their beds they could plainly hear the pattering of the rain upon the roof, and in the morning they were aroused by the singing of birds in the branches of the trees over their heads. Two little windows in their humble chamber looked out upon a rolling, hilly country, covered with oak, hickory and walnut trees, among the branches of which squirrels played and frolicked in undisturbed merriment. Beautiful green cedars fastened their roots in the sides of the rocky hills, and gave an emerald tinge to the solemn forest shade. Little rivulets, warbling down the sides of the hills, mingled their sparkling waters with the more pretentious brook in the valley below, and murmuring a quiet salutation, flowed on together to the river and the ocean. Raised in the midst of such surroundings, the embryo Bishop necessarily acquired a poetic nature as he grew up, and much of the beautiful imagery of his incomparable sermons, which flow from his lips in streams of sparkling metaphors, can be traced to his early associations.

Wells E. Marvin and wife had four children, all of whom were born in Warren county, viz.: Elisha, born April 19, 1818, married in 1845 to Margaret Faulkner, and died about 1850; Nathaniel

27

Davis, born August 13, 1821; Enoch Mather, born June 12, 1823; Maria, born September 1, 1831, and died about 1851. Nathaniel D. lives in Pike county, Mo., is married and has a family.

Mr. Marvin was not a member of any church, and made no pretensions to religion; but he never threw any obstacles in the way of the religious training of his children. He died December 30, 1856, and was buried in the family graveyard on the home place.

Mrs. Marvin was a member of the Baptist Church, and a devoutly religious woman. She instructed her children in the principles of Christianity from the earliest moment that they could comprehend her words, and they grew up with a firm faith in its truths and divine origin. Bishop Marvin stated in his farewell sermon in St. Louis, before starting on his journey to China and the East, that the first distinct recollection of his life was sitting on his mother's knee and listening to her sing—

"Alas! and did my Saviour bleed,"

while the tears rolled down her cheeks and fell upon his upturned face. She was a superior woman, intelligent and refined, and so gentle and kind in her disposition that no one could know her without loving her. The devotion of her children amounted almost to idolatry, and the two who are still living never pass near the old home without making a pilgrimage to her humble grave. Her teachings are manifest in their lives and characters, and the good seed which she sowed, with apparently but little prospect of its fruition, has brought forth a thousand fold, in the spread of the truths which she inculcated around the globe. She taught school a considerable length of time in a small house that was built for that purpose in the yard, and there she imparted to her own children and the youth of the neighborhood the elements of an English education. This house, we believe, is still standing. She died January 1, 1858, and was buried by the side of her husband.

Bishop Marvin began to exhibit evidences of his oratorical talents at a very early age. Frequently he would gather his youthful playmates around him, mount upon a stump in the woods or fields, and astonish them with a speech or sermon replete with beautiful thoughts, clothed in the language of natural eloquence. In their neighborhood debating societies he stood higher than all the others, and no one could compete with him. If he had the weak side of a question he would present it so plausibly, and with so much eloquence, force and wit, that the judges would forget the merits of the case and unanimously declare him the victor.

It was customary in their societies for the opposing speakers to announce themselves as candidates for some office, and then present their claims to their constituents in the best manner they could. After the speakers were all done, an election would be held, and the candidates who had presented their claims in the most favorable light would be elected.

One evening young Marvin and Royal Kennedy, both about sixteen years of age, and classmates in school, were opposing candidates for the office of constable, in the debating society. Kennedy made the first speech, in which he announced his candidature, and made an earnest appeal for the support of his friends. He promised to bring all transgressors of the law to condign punishment, and to employ his best efforts to collect all accounts placed in his hands; but if he failed to collect them he would return the accounts to their rightful owners. He would discharge all the duties of his office in an honorable and satisfactory manner, and, believing himself better qualified for the position than his opponent, he hoped to receive the unanimous vote of the audience. He took his seat in the midst of great applause, and his election seemed sure.

Marvin then arose, straightened his tall figure, brushed the drooping hair from his brow, and began his speech. He referred to the speech of his opponent, repeated its principal points, and then throwing his head back, and casting one of his peculiarly searching glances around the room, he said—"Now, my friends, I will do all that my opponent has promised, and much more besides. I will not only bring all transgressors to justice, but if I fail to collect accounts that are entrusted to me, I will run my hand down into my pocket (illustrating his words by the action), pull out the money and pay them myself!"

This speech, so ludicrous in its application (for Marvin's pockets were always empty), and so dramatically uttered, "brought the house down," and he was elected on the spot, without a dissenting vote.

Young Marvin joined the Methodist Church in August, 1839, and was converted in December, 1840, being then in his 18th year. He does not remember that any minister was specially instrumental in his conversion, but attributes it more to the religious influence of his mother than any other agency. He began to preach in 1841, being admitted by the Conference that met in Palmyra that year. He did not attend that Conference, but was admitted upon the recommendation of his pastor and class; for at that time the rules of the Church did not require a young minister to be present at Conference in order to be admitted. The first Conference which he attended was held in Jefferson City, and it is said—though we do not vouch for the truth of the statement—that the suit of clothes which he wore on that occasion was made of calico and presented to him by some of the sisters of the Church.   They had no opportunity to take his measure, and the clothes being made "by guess," proved to be too short by several inches, and he presented the appearance of having run to seed below his elbows and knees.

He preached his first sermon in old Bethlehem Church, near Flint Hill, in St. Charles county, taking for his text the 10th and 11th verses of the third chapter of Isaiah.   "Say ye to the righteous, that it shall be well with him: for they shall eat the fruit of their doings.   Woe unto the wicked! it shall be ill with him: for the reward of his hands shall be given him."

This sermon was preached at the request of Rev. D. T. Sherman, well known among the Methodists of Missouri, and who is still connected with the itinerant ministry in this State. He was at that time a local preacher, and had an appointment to preach at Bethlehem on that day, but being unable to attend, he requested Marvin to fill the appointment for him.   An account of that sermon and various incidents connected with it was written by Rev. J. W. Cunningham, at present of St. Louis, and published in the St. Charles *News* about a year ago.   From that account we make the following extracts:

"It was young Marvin's first sermon. People who were present say his appearance was that of an awkward country boy, dressed in home-spun, home-cut, home-made and well-worn clothes. The Bishop says his pantaloons were of blue cotton, when new, but many washings had largely relieved them of the original indigo color.   They were sadly faded, and worn into holes at the knees, and, to hide the openings, a tender mother's hands had placed patches over them, with pieces of the original blue.   Said he: 'The pale was very pale, and the blue was very blue.'   With little or no thought of his parti-colored pantaloons and other faded and worn apparel, the young preacher entered the church and pulpit, and did as best he could.   Mr. Ben Pierce remembers that he said: 'When man came from the plastic hand of his Creator.'

That is all he recollects of that ' first sermon,' and it is proba
bly the only relic of it that survives in the neighborhood in which
it was preached.   The preacher was neither greatly embarrassed
nor over-confident.   He was earnest and boisterous, without
much of the emotional.   As the service closed, John P. Allen
took John B. Allen by the arm, and gave it a severe grip by way
of emphasizing his whispered words, as he said : ' That youth
had better quit preaching and continue to work on the farm.   He
will never make a preacher.'   John B. replied : ' He may be a
Bishop yet.'

"The service ended, the people retired, and no one was thoughtful enough to invite the young stranger to dinner.   He mounted
his horse and started homeward.   He had left home early in the
morning, had eaten but little, '*was very hungry*,' and was determined not to stand on formalities.   If no one would invite him,
he would invite himself.   He soon rode up beside Warren Walker,
who was traveling the same road, and said to him : ' Brother, how
far do you live from here?'   On being told the distance, he said :
' Well, I am going home with you to get my dinner.'   ' Certainly,'
said Mr. Walker, ' I will be glad to have you do so.'   And to Mr.
Walker's he went and was cordially entertained."

The people who lived in the vicinity of Bethlehem Church were
noted for their hospitality, and there were none present on that
occasion who would not gladly have had the young minister go
home with them and appease his hunger ; but he had come to the
church in company with Mr. Walker, and most of them supposed
he was his guest and would be entertained by him.   The failure
to invite him to dinner was not an intentional slight, but simply
an oversight resulting from thoughtlessness, and was so regarded
by the young preacher himself.

After his marriage, and after he had become distinguished as a
minister, he preached at Bethlehem again, attended by his wife.
When the services were over, quite a number of persons crowded
around and invited the minister and his wife to dinner, and among
them were several who had heard his first sermon.   He recognized them, and a merry twinkle came into his eyes as he said :
"The first time I came here I got no invitation to dinner, but now
I have the pick and choice of the neighborhood, and am going to
the nearest place where they have plenty to eat ; where is that?"
To this question Uncle Ben Pierce quickly replied : "That's my
house—right over there," pointing to his elegant residence only
a short distance from the church.   "We have plenty to eat, and
know how to cook it."   "Very well," said Marvin, "I will go
with you," and there he went.

Some years after this event, Marvin, who was then a Bishop, repeated the incidents of his first and second visits to Bethlehem Church, in a spirit of pleasantry, to a circle of friends in St. Charles, Uncle Ben Pierce being present at the time. When he had concluded, he turned to the latter and said: "Uncle Ben, I discovered by my visits to your neighborhood, that you don't think much of a man that wears patched clothes." To which Pierce dryly replied: "Well, Marvin, the fact is, you were not much of a preacher, then, no how, and that was not much of a sermon, either."

Marvin was ordained deacon in 1843, and elder in 1845. In 1852 he was appointed presiding elder of St. Charles District, and acted as agent for St. Charles College in 1854–5. He was then transferred to St. Louis Conference, and stationed in the city of St. Louis until 1861, having charge of the church on the corner of Washington Avenue and Eighth street during the greater portion of that time.

In February, 1862, he ran the guantlet of the Union armies and went South as a missionary to the soldiers. He continued in the South during the remainder of the war, preaching to the soldiers and administering to their spiritual and physical wants. Many conversions took place under his preaching among the soldiers, and many parched lips on bloody battle fields opened in thanks for the cup of cold water placed to them by the hands of the devoted follower of the Nazarene. Neither the vicious whistle of the minnie ball nor the roar of cannons and muskets could drive him from his duty, or prevent him from ministering to the wants of his suffering fellow-creatures.

Among the other duties of the General Conference of the M. E. Church, South, which met in New Orleans in 1866, was the election of a new Bishop, and the choice fell upon Enoch M. Marvin, than whom a more worthy selection could not have been made. The action of the Conference met with universal approval throughout the limits of the Church, and the young Bishop at once took a high position in the love and esteem of his brethren.

In connection with the life of Bishop Marvin, we present a history of the church over which he presided, as embraced in the region of country to which this book relates. This history was prepared especially for this work, by Rev. J. W. Cunningham, of

St. Louis, who has taken great pains to have it correct, and it may be relied upon as authentic. In some of its statements it differs slightly from that given elsewhere in the book, but as Mr. Cunningham's opportunities for obtaining correct information in regard to matters pertaining to his church are excellent, his statements should be considered correct in preference to the others.

HISTORY OF THE METHODIST CHURCH.

ITINERANT AND LOCAL MINISTRY.—In the Methodist Episcopal Church there are local and itinerant preachers. The local are those who have no pastoral work, are engaged in secular pursuits, and preach when and where they choose, without compensation. The itinerants are engaged in the ministerial work, and look to the Church for a support.

The itinerants are called station and circuit preachers, presiding elders and bishops. A station preacher is the pastor of a single church, called a station; a circuit preacher ministers to several churches, forming a circuit; a presiding elder has the charge of a district, comprising several circuits, or circuits and stations, and their pastors, whom he visits quarterly; a bishop is a general superintendent, having the oversight of all the churches, pastors and presiding elders, in the bounds of several annual conferences committed to his care for a year, and who annually appoints pastors and presiding elders to their respective fields of labor.

THE FIRST LOCAL PREACHER IN MISSOURI.—In the days of the Spanish rule the Rev. John Clark occasionally visited Missouri from Illinois, and preached in the neighborhood of Spanish Pond in St. Louis county. Some old people who knew him in their childhood think he was a Methodist local preacher when he first visited Missouri, but he subsequently became a Baptist. He died in St. Louis county in 1833.

FIRST LOCAL PREACHERS IN NORTH MISSOURI.—One of the first Protestant preachers in North Missouri was a Dutch Tunker—Hostetter—who occasionally preached in "Dutch," in the region of Flint Hill, to his American neighbors, who sat quietly under his ministry of which they understood not a word—drinking in the gospel in an unknown tongue, and he as rigorously supplied it as if they understood it all. As early as 1810 a Methodist local preacher named Edwards lived in Darst's Bottom, and preached in the western part of St. Charles county. He subsequently removed to Illinois, and died there in 1833.

THE FIRST ITINERANT PREACHERS IN NORTH MISSOURI.—The first itinerant preachers sent to Missouri were John Travis and Wm. McKendree, the first a circuit preacher, and the latter a presiding elder. Mr. Travis was a young Kentuckian appointed to "Missourie Circuit" in September, 1806. He remained a year, preaching to the American settlements on both sides of the Missouri river. After several years of itinerant life he located, studied medicine, and lived till 1852—serving his neighbors in Crittenden county, Ky., as a physician and local preacher. When Mr. Travis preached in Missouri, there was not a Methodist preacher in Indiana, and only one—Jesse Walker—in Illinois.

FIRST CAMP MEETING IN MISSOURI.—Mr. McKendree's district—the Cumberland—embraced nine circuits, including half of Tennessee, a third of Kentucky, and the pioneer settlements of Illinois and Missouri. He visited only once in the year the remote circuits of Walker and Travis. In the summer of 1807, accompanied by Revs. James Gwinn and Abbott Goddard, he crossed the Ohio river near Shawneetown, and traversed the wilderness of Illinois to Kaskaskia. Leaving their horses in Illinois they crossed into Missouri, and walked forty miles to a camp meeting, supposed to have been somewhere between the Meramec and the Missouri rivers. The preachers present were McKendree, Gwinn, Goddard, Travis, and Walker.

McKendree spent nearly two months in Illinois and Missouri, but did not cross the Missouri river.

A WESTERN BISHOP.—In 1807 McKendree was returned to the "district," with two circuits in Missouri—Missouri circuit above, and Meramec circuit below the Missouri river, with Jesse Walker supplying the first and Edmund Wilcox the other.

In May Mr. McKendree attended the General Conference in Baltimore as a delegate from the West. On the first Sabbath he preached before the multitude, "clothed in very coarse and homely garments, which he had worn in the woods of the West." His appearance led the great Dr. Bangs, of New York, to mentally to exclaim, "I wonder what awkward backwoodsman they have put in the pulpit this morning, to disgrace us with his mawkish and uncouth phraseology." But the sermon which followed was one of great power. "That sermon," said Bishop Asbury, "will make him a bishop," and on the Thursday following he *was* elected bishop by an overwhelming majority. He filled the office of bishop twenty-seven years, and died in 1835.

FIRST CAMP MEETING IN NORTH MISSOURI.—James Ward took the place of Bishop McKendree as presiding elder of the Cumberland district in June, 1808, and in company with the Bishop and others visited Missouri in July. On the 30th they commenced a camp meeting on the Peruque, near the railroad trestle work west of O'Fallon. Mrs. Mary Kent, of Warren county, who joined the church that year, and is the oldest Missouri Methodist now living, was at that meeting and heard the "Bishop preach." The Bishop's tent was made by sewing the preachers' saddle-blankets together and spreading them over a pole, supported by forks placed in the ground, like soldiers' tents; one end of the tent was closed with green boughs; the other was left open, and in front of it a fire was made. His food was bread, and flesh broiled on the ends of sticks. That was the first camp meeting in North Missouri, and at that camp ground, the same year, a rude round log church was built, but never completed, and was used only for a few years for summer services. It was the first church north of the Missouri river.

JAMES WARD AND JESSE WALKER.—James Ward had an afflicted hand, around which he always wore a large silk handkerchief. Under his preaching sinners sometimes fell and cried for mercy. Objectors were accustomed to say that he had concealed in his handkerchief powders which he scattered on the people and by which they were overcome, as described. Mr. Ward spent most of his life in Kentucky, and died there at a good old age.

Jesse Walker spent several years in Missouri as circuit preacher and presiding elder. In 1821 he organized the church in St. Louis, and was instrumental in the erection of the first house of worship there. He spent several years as missionary to the Indians, organized the church in Chicago, and died not far from that city in 1835.

SAMUEL PARKER AND OTHERS.—In 1808 the Indiana District was formed, including Indiana, Illinois, and Missouri, with two circuits in Missouri. Samuel Parker was Presiding elder that year, and for four years continuously. Parker was a great preacher, an accomplished man and almost unequaled as a singer. He died in 1819, while presiding elder of a district embracing the State of Mississippi and part of Louisiana.

The preachers who served the church in North Missouri under Parker, from 1808 to 1812, were Abram Ames, John Crane, Thos. Wright, and John Cord. Ames was a few years an itinerant preacher, and then a local preacher. Crane preached two years in North Missouri, and the second year also supplied Cold Water circuit in South Missouri, and frequently swam the Missouri river to reach his appointments. He was a popular and successful preacher, and died in young manhood in Tennessee. Thos. Wright was fourteen years a preacher in Missouri, all but one in South Missouri; was several years a presiding elder, and died in 1826. John Cord spent most of his minsitry in Indiana and Illinois, and died in Indiana in 1827.

Jesse Walker was presiding elder of Illinois District, including Missouri, from 1812 to 1814, and Jesse Haile served the Church north of the Missouri river during that period. In 1814 Samuel H. Thompson became presiding elder of the Missouri district, and served it two years. Wm. Stribling was the preacher on Missouri circuit one year, and Jacob Whitesides the next, under Thompson. These three men spent most of their lives in Illinois, where they died with good names in the Church. In 1815 Booneslick circuit was organized. It extended up the Missouri river, above St. Charles county. Joseph Piggott, its first preacher, was a son of Captain Piggott, of Piggott's Fort, in Illinois, who established the first ferry across the Mississippi river at St. Louis.

PIONEER PREACHING PLACES.—The house of Jacob Zumwalt (now D. Heald's), near O'Fallon, was one of the pioneer preaching places for the Methodists. John Travis preached there, and organized a society in 1807, out of which Mount Zion Church grew. Another pioneer society was near Flint Hill, from which Bethlehem Church sprang, between Flint Hill and Wentzville, which subsequently gave place to Flint Hill Church; a third was on the Femme Osage, not far from the home of Daniel Boone; a fourth in Darst's Bottom, at the house of Mr. Crow, from which the Pleasant Hill Church descended; and a fifth at Marthasville, where a good church exists. In those times private houses were the preaching places.

Sometimes the "meeting day" was an occasion of social, as well as religious enjoyment. A big dinner was prepared and a general invitation to the people was given to stay and eat the dinner prepared, and many accepted it. An old lady with a good experience in entertaining the preacher and his congregation, meekly suggested that "the meeting" become an itinerant one. Said she, "if the meeting's a *burden*, I think some of you ought to *bear* it with me, and if it's a *blessing* I am willing for you to *share* it with me."• For this or some sufficient reason the preaching was in some neighborhoods, changed from house to house. Many esteemed it a blessing, extemporised seats for the occasion, and joyfully bade preacher and people welcome to their houses and their tables. Some houses were permanent preaching places: This was true of Jacob Zumwalt's. David K. Pitman's father selected his land in 1809, because of the preaching there, and he—D. K. P.—remembers to have attended a service in it conducted of J. Whitesides in 1816.

When Methodism was introduced into Missouri, in 1807, there was only one conference, called the "Western Conference," west of the Allegheny Mountains. In 1812 the Tennessee Conference was organized, including Missouri. In 1816 the Missouri Conference was formed, including Missouri, Indiana, Illinois, and Arkansas, and so remained till 1824, when the territory of the Missouri Conference was reduced to the State of Missouri. To this point, 1816, our recital of facts comes. From this date the Church gradually extended with the increase of population. Till 1832 the territory included in St. Charles couny bore the original name, "Missouri Circuit;" after that it was for several years called the St. Charles Circuit, and was subsequently divided into other pastoral charges.

The preachers on Missouri Circuit from 1816 to 1830 were: John

Schrader, Philip Davis, Wm. Townsend, A. McAllister, Wm. L. Hawley, W. W. Redmond, Thomas Randle, John Glanville, Cassell Harrison, John Bassdel, R. I. Dungan, Wm. Heath, A. H. Stemmons, E. T. Peery, N. M. Talbott, J. P. Burks, and Benj. Babbitt. Up to this time Missouri Circuit embraced the settlements in the counties of St. Charles, Warren, Lincoln, Montgomery, Audrain and Pike. In 1830 Palmyra Circuit and Salt River Mission were organized, with Wm. Kitron on the former, and E. T. Peery on the latter. In 1831 Bowling Green Circuit appeared under F. B. Leach and J. Lamins. In 1833 Paris Circuit, under J. Lamins. In 1835 Danville Circuit, with J. M. Jamison as preacher. In 1840 Warrenton Circuit, under G. W. Bowman.

During the period indicated, the following served as presiding elders of the Missouri District: Jesse Walker, Jesse Haile, S. H. Thompson, David Sharp, Jesse Haile, John Dew, Andrew Monroe, Jesse Green, A. McAllister, J. Edmunson, Jesse Green, G. C. Light, Richard Bond, A. Monroe, W. W. Redmond, Geo. Smith, Wm. Patton, E. M. Marvin—which brings us to 1852. To introduce all the names of circuits subsequently organized, and the names of preachers serving them, would make the list too lengthy for our space.

In 1820 Mrs. Catharine Collier erected a house of worship in St. Charles for the Methodists, but for several years thereafter there was no regular preaching there. In 1829 she erected a larger church on Main street—yet standing—where Methodism was established. It is supposed to be the oldest church building in Missouri. The church now occupied was built in 1853. To Mrs. Collier and her son George the Methodists are indebted for the building and partial endowment of St. Charles College—the oldest college in the West.

COLONEL J. F. JONES.

THERE are but few persons in Missouri who have not heard of Colonel Jeff. Jones, of Calaway county—the "Kingdom of Callaway," as he appropriately named it during the " late unpleasantness." He is one of the leading thinkers of our State, and has only failed to gain a national reputation by his honest repugnance to mingling in the dirty politics of the day. He is firm in his convictions of right and justice, and would not yield an iota of his principles for the highest place in the gift of his fellow-countrymen. He has never hesitated to denounce wrong and the authors of it in the boldest and most unequivocal language, and hence he has frequently incurred the enmity of men in high places, but on the other hand has gained the respect and confidence of hosts of frends and honest men wherever he is known.

He belongs to one of our old American families which dates back beyond the revolutionary war, and which has numbered among its members heroes and patriots.

William Jones, the founder of the family, in this country, was born of Welch parents, in the city of London, England. He died on his way to America, leaving a young widow, who, soon after landing in Virginia, gave birth to a son whom she named Mosias. She afterward married a man named Webb, of Albemarle county, and they soon removed to Greenbriar county, Va., where Mosias was raised, and married. After his marriage he removed to Kentucky, and settled on the head waters of Caney fork of Otter creek, in Madison county, four miles east of Richmond. His children were—Mosias, Foster, George, William, Roger, John, Thomas, Rebecca, and one other daughter, who married a gentleman from Virginia named Garrison. Rebecca married Henry Burnham, a Hard-Shell Baptist preacher. All the boys served in the revolutionary war, and most of them through the entire struggle.

William married Lucy Harris, who was also a native of Greenbriar county, Va., and they had—Levi, Thomas G., Elizabeth, Robert H., Nancy, John B., Ransom P., William, Milton and Rebecca. Elizabeth married Joel Hern. Nancy married Tyro Harris. Rebecca married Irvin Ogan.

Thomas G., the second son of William Jones, was married in Montgomery county, Ky., to Rebecca B. Snedicor, and removed with his father to Boone county, Mo., 1824 and in 1848, he settled in Callaway county. His children were—JEFFERSON F., Pamelia A., William D., Caroline M., Sidney F., William H., Miranda J., Mary E., and George W. Pamelia A. was married first to S. B. Ham, and second to Joseph Young, now of Johnson county, Mo. Caroline M. married Dr. B. B. Thornton, of Johnson county. Miranda J. married William S. Foster, of Johnson county, and Mary E. married Joseph L. Craig, of Callaway county.

Colonel Jefferson F. Jones was married on the 6th of March, 1844, to Sally Ann Jameson, by whom he had sixteen children, ten of whom are living. The Colonel began the practice of law at Fulton, where he was raised, in 1843, and soon gained a large and lucrative business, his superior talents placing him at the start among the leaders of the bar in his county. His powers as a debater were soon recognized by the party to which he belonged (the Whig), and in 1844 he was appointed to canvass the county against his wife's uncle, Hon. John Jameson. In 1848 he was appointed Whig Elector for the State of Missouri; and in 1852 he was nominated by his party as a candidate for the Legislature, but declined to run. In 1856 he was again nominated for the same position, and although he again declined, he was elected by a large majority, and served his county to the entire satisfaction of his constituents. In 1860, after his removal to his farm, he was again nominated for the Legislature, but declined positively. In 1875 he was again elected a member of that body, on the Democratic ticket, and became one of the leaders of the House immediately upon assuming his seat. Since the close of the war he has been sent as a delegate to every Democratic State Convention except one, and so great is the confidence of the people of his county in his ability and integrity that they would readily entrust him with any office in their gift.

Colonel Jones was for many years a manager of the State Lunatic Asylum at Fulton, the duties of which position he discharged in the most faithful and conscientious manner. When the North Missouri Railroad Co. was organized he became a member of the incorporating board of directors, and did much toward the construction and progress of the road.

In all his public services he has regarded himself as a servant of the people, and endeavored to perform his duties in such a manner that their interests would be protected and advanced. Fidelity and energy have marked his entire career, and if our affairs of State could always rest in hands as true as his, they would be safe.

FRANCIS SKINNER.

AMONG the few old pioneers of Missouri who are still left to bring up memories of the past, is Mr. Francis Skinner, of Jonesburg, Montgomery county. (See portrait on frontispiece. He was born in 1794, and is now more than 82 years old, but still vigorous and active. It has not been very long since he was seen, while riding at full gallop, to stoop and pick his hat up from the ground, a feat which very few young men of the present day can accomplish.

John Skinner, the father of Francis, was born in the Highlands of Scotland, in 1757. He remained among the hills and mountains of his native country until he was twenty years of age, and then (in 1777) he came to America, which at that time was rent and torn by civil war and seemed to be in the death struggle of its national existence.

The young Scotchman settled in Virginia, where he witnessed the final dawn of peace after the dark and bloody night of war, and lived to see the new republic in its grandest and purest era. He was married in 1785, in Culpepper county, Va., to a daughter of John and Nancy Story, who were among the first English families to come to America after the revolution. Mr. Skinner and his wife had ten children, eight sons and two daughters, all of whom lived to be grown, and all but one, the eldest, who died in Virginia, came to Missouri.

Two of the sons, Francis and Hugh, married sisters, daughters of Robert Jasper, and came to Missouri in 1820, their object being to obtain cheap lands for their rising families. They came by land and water to St. Louis, crossing the river at the latter place on a ferryboat propelled by horse power. They found the place to be nothing more than a French village, built principally along one street, called Main street. They camped near the old market on Broadway, which at that time was a forest of young timber. About one hundred Indians were camped near them, and as they had never seen any red men before, they slept but little that night. Just north of the old market there was a steep, rocky bluff, with a cabin built of cedar logs on the summit. The cabin remained there until about twenty years afterward, when the bluff was quarried away, and the stone used in building warehouses.

After leaving St. Louis they proceeded to St. Charles, and found the river so covered with driftwood, on account of the June rise, that they were afraid to attempt to cross it. They delayed several days, and then having become more accustomed to the river, and less afraid of its angry appearance, they crossed their families and horses over on a boat made by lashing a platform on the top of two canoes, which ran parallel with each other, at the distance of several feet apart. Their wagons had to be conveyed across in a large flat-boat, which was so clumsy and unwieldy that it floated down the river about four hundred yards while they were pushing it across the stream.

They all crossed in safety, and resumed their march westward until they reached Camp Branch in Montgomery county, where they located. In St. Louis they had met with an old friend, Colonel George Strother, who was receiver at the land office, and he introduced them to Mr. Thomas Rector, who had surveyed a great deal of land in the region of country north of the river, and who gave them much valuable information in regard to surveys, etc. They bought their first land under his instructions, and did well by so doing. Government lands were sold then at $2 per acre, one-fourth of which was paid at the time of purchase, and the balance in three equal installments, with interest. Many of the early settlers burdened themselves with heavy debts in endeavoring to buy large tracts of land, and at the session of Congress of 1820-21 a law was passed for their relief, which permitted them to hold in fee simple the one-fourth for which they had paid, and relinquish the rest. These relinquished lands were placed in the market again at the end of five years, and rapidly sold. Mr. Skinner bought all he could, and he still owns the first eighty acres that he ever purchased. Since then he and his children have bought, and still own 2,600 acres, being the most choice land in the region of country where they live, as it was purchased when there was no competition. Mr. Skinner holds in own name 892 acres, divided into three farms, which aggregate 500 acres in cultivation. He now lives in Jonesburg, a town of five hundred inhabitants, the site of which, for years after he came to Montgomery county, was an uninhabited waste.

When he first settled in Montgomery county, the population was so thin that they frequently had to go ten to fourteen miles to help their neighbors raise their cabins. A great many built cabins and "squatted" on government lands, without making any effort to obtain titles to them; and they were generally unmolested by land hunters, who could obtain plenty of the best without disturbing them.

Wolves and other wild animals abounded in those days, and it required the most careful attention to protect sheep, pigs and poultry from their ravages. Mr. Skinner still has a trap from which he and his sons have taken sixty-three wolves, and they killed many more with their rifles.

On the 15th day of November, 1820, snow fell to the depth of about ten inches, rendering it an excellent season for hunting. Mr. Skinner and one of his brothers shouldered their rifles and started out on a deer hunt, but found the deer scarce. They soon, however, heard some heavy animal running through the brush, and hastening forward they discovered the fresh tracks of a huge bear. Knowing it would be useless to pursue him on foot, and being inexperienced hunters, they repaired to the house of a neighbor for instructions. Acting under his advice, they procured horses and dogs and started in pursuit. The excitement was so great that Mr. Skinner s aged father, who was 82 years old, determined to go with them. They obtained the services of a youth as a guide, and followed rapidly on in the direction the bear had taken, the youth constantly cautioning them not to make a noise, lest the bear should get frightened and run away. But they soon came up with him, and upon the first sight of his shaggy hide all the dogs but one took to their heels and scampered away. The one that was brave enough to remain ran to the bear and snapped him first on one side and then on the other, making him jump about and break the brush and young sapplings, which were loaded down with snow. Seeing that he could make no progress in the timber, he started for the prairie, which was only a short distance away. Mr. Skinner observed his tactics, and hastily examining the flint and priming of his gun, he spurred his horse to the edge of the prairie, where he dismounted and made ready; and as the bear came crashing out of the brush, still pursued by the faithful dog, he sent a ball through his heart and killed him in his tracks. At the sound of the gun the other dogs all came running up as bold as lions, and seemed brave enough to eat poor bruin on the spot.

The hunters were highly elated with their success, and made the woods ring with their cheers. The bear proved to be a fine one, weighing 400 pounds net, with four inches of fat on his ribs, and they had bear bacon in abundance for sometime afterward.

Having trained their dogs, they started on another hunt among the mountains that border on Loutre creek, in the southern part of Montgomery county. Soon after reaching the hunting grounds they came upon a large bear track that measured nearly seven inches broad at the toe, and observing the course of the trail, they started around through the woods to head it off. They had not gone far when, looking up at the top of a bluff under which they were riding, they observed a large bear reared up on his haunches and quietly looking down at them. Mr. Skinner, Miles Price and John Ferguson immediately turned their horses into a ravine that led to the top of the bluff, and started in pursuit of the bear, making as little noise as possible. When they reached the place where they had seen the bear he had fled, but the dogs struck the trail and started in hot pursuit. They came up with

him about half a mile distant, and a battle ensued between them.
When the hunters came up they found one of their best dogs
badly wounded, and the others fighting with great fury. The
bear observing their approach, started again to run, but they
overhauled him as he began to ascend the next hill.   He had
mounted upon a log that lay along the side of the hill, for the
purpose of facilitating his progress, and Mr. Skinner, riding to
the opposite end of the log, discharged his gun at him, and gave
him a desperate wound in the hip, the ball passing nearly through
his body.   The dogs now closed in upon him and fought with increased courage, the bear resisting their attacks as well as he
could in his wounded condition.   One of the dogs got a slap
from his jaw and started to run, and at the same instant one of
the hunters discharged his gun and accidentally killed the dog.
The bear now made off up the side of the hill, regardless of the
dogs, but fell dead in about four hundred yards.   He weighed
500 pounds and had four inches of fat on his ribs.

The hunters had neglected to bring their tomahawks with them,
and consequently had some trouble in getting the meat divided
so they could carry it conveniently.   But they succeeded finally
in dividing it with their knives and a sharp rock.   They obtained
half a bushel of fat, and were at a loss how to carry it to their
camp, until a happy thought struck Mr. Skinner.   Removing his
buckskin drawers he tied up the bottoms of the legs with stout
strings, and loading the fat into them he had no difficulty in
carrying it to camp thrown across his horse.   When they arrived
in camp he and his horse and saddle were well greased with
bear's oil.

About the middle of February, 1828, Mr. Skinner and several
of his neighbors went on another bear hunt among the Loutre
hills, and soon after they had arrived on the hunting grounds they
observed a large bear on the opposite side of a creek.   Bruin
discovered them about the same time, and made off as fast as
his legs could carry him.

The hunters had to descend a hill, cross the creek and climb a
high bluff on the opposite side, by which time the bear had
obtained a good start.   But the dogs caught the scent of the trail
and sped away like lightning, with Mr. Skinner, Miles Price, John
Ferguson and Sam Grubbs after them as fast as they could ride.
Now and then they could see the bear through an opening in the
trees or rocks, and away they would go with wild shouts and

renewed energy. After running about five miles the bear came to his den, and disappeared in it, followed by one of the boldest dogs, which was soon crushed to death in the embrace of his huge antagonist.

When the hunters came up they built a fire at the mouth of the cave and kept it burning until they felt confident that the bear was suffocated by the smoke, when, night being near at hand and the weather having grown very cold, they started in the direction of a sugar camp, not far distant, to find comfortable quarters for the night. They found the camp without much difficulty, received a hearty welcome from the sugar makers, and early next morning they started in quest of their game. As they were descending a steep bluff on the way to the cave, they arrived suddenly on the verge of a precipice some twelve feet high, and which was rendered more precipitous by the steep slant of the bluff below its base. To retreat was impossible, for their horses could not climb the hill that lay behind them, and their only recourse was to go over the precipice and trust to luck. So seating themselves firmly in their saddles they spurred their horses forward and landed safely at the bottom, the earth giving away some distance around them and breaking the force of their fall.

Upon arriving at the cave where the bear lay, a discussion arose as to which of them should go in, for it was a dangerous venture and no one was anxious to undertake it. It finally fell to Mr. Skinner's lot to perform the dangerous duty, and preparing himself with a torch, and carefully examining his gun, he cautiously made his way into the depths of the cavern. He soon reached the bear, which lay dead and cold, with their dead dog lying under him. Attaching a rope around the carcass, Mr. Skinner called to his comrades on the outside, and they quickly drew both him and the bear out of the cave. They divided their game with the sugar makers who had entertained them so hospitably the previous night, and then returned home, having had fun enough for one time.

Some time after this, Mr. Skinner and another party went on a deer hunt. One morning he had fine luck and killed two fat deer, which he conveyed to camp, and there found his brother awaiting his arrival to go with him after a large buck that he had wounded. They started immediately, and arriving upon the ground soon found traces of blood, which were pointed out to the dogs, and they started in pursuit. The trail was cold, and they
28

followed slowly, but finally came upon the buck where he was
lying down in a thicket.   As soon as he discovered them he
sprang up and started toward them with a vicious look in his
eyes.   One of the dogs ran up and caught hold of him, but the
buck, turning a somersault, broke his hold and then pinned him
to the earth with his horns.   In the meantime Mr. Skinner had
run up and caught the buck by the hind-legs, but having his
gloves on he could not hold tight, and the deer kicked loose.   He
took one jump away, and then turning sharply around darted
upon the now helpless hunter, with his horns lowered and fire flash-
ing from his eyes.   The prongs of his horns passed on either side
of Mr. Skinner's thigh, ripping his buckskin pants and graining
the skin on both sides, but doing no other damage.   Quickly
stooping he caught the infuriated animal by the fore-legs, and
held him tight, while the dogs worried him behind.   He also
called to his brother to draw his knife from its scabbard and stab
the deer, but he was so excited that it took him some time to do
so.   He finally succeeded in getting the knife, and stabbed the
buck to the heart.   The fight was soon over then, and after resting a while they shouldered their game and returned to camp,
with something more than an ordinary hunting adventure to
relate to their comrades.

This closes the account of the hunting experiences of "Uncle
Frank" Skinner, as he is familiarly called.   He had many others,
but those just related were the most important, and we have no
room for more.

Uncle Frank is a stone and brick mason by trade, and all the
work that he ever did stood firm without cracking or breaking.   He
built the cellar wall and foundation of the first brick house erected
in Danville, which is now occupied by Mr. Samuel A. Wheeler,
and though it has stood forty years, there is not a crack or flaw
in the wall.

Mr. Skinner's father was a Baptist preacher, but he never gave
much thought to religious matters until his children were all
about grown.   Then through the illness of one of his sons, whom
he loved dearly, he was led to seek religion, and united with the
Christian Church, since which time he has been a faithful and
consistent member.   He and his son, with a little aid from their
neighbors, built the brick church at Jonesburg, which is occupied
by the Christian congregation.

And now, having passed beyond the allotted time of man's

duration upon the earth, and having performed his life's work well, he quietly and serenely awaits the summons to "come up higher," and enjoy the rewards that are in store for the faithful servant.

FRANCIS DUQUETTE.

THERE lived many years ago, in St. Charles, a Canadian Frenchman, named Francis Duquette, who occupied a prominent and influential position in that town during the close of the last and the beginning of the present century. It was he who transformed the old round fort into a wind-mill, and thereby converted an establishment of war into one of the most useful implements of peace. He was also the father of the Catholic Church in St. Charles, for although he was not a priest, and did not organize the Church, yet he built it up from a small beginning and sustained and cultivated it for many years; and his memory is held in affectionate regard by the Catholics of St. Charles.

Francis Duquette was born in Quebec, Canada, in 1774. When quite a young man he came West, and landed first at Ste. Genevieve, then the principal town west of the Mississippi river.

While there he had the funeral rites of the Catholic Church performed over the remains of a deceased friend, and the mystery connected therewith caused universal comment and has never yet been solved. Twelve years before a young Canadian made his appearance in Ste. Genevieve and engaged in the then common occupation of hunting. No one knew him, and he took no pains to enlighten the citizens in regard to himself. In fact his presence created very little comment in the community, for it was no unusual thing for strange hunters to make their appearance there, remain a short time, and disappear as mysteriously as they came. He gave his name as Pierre Gladu, and stated that he was from Canada. One day he went out to hunt, and was killed by some Indians, in a little prairie near the town. His remains were subsequently found and buried where he had fallen, and the incident soon ceased to be a subject of comment among the citizens of the town.

Twelve years afterward another young Canadian made his appearance in Ste. Genevieve, gave his name as Francis Duquette, and immediately sought out the lone grave on the little prairie. He then caused the remains to be disinterred, and buried in the grave-yard of the town with all the solemnities and ceremonies of the Catholic Church. Curiosity attracted numerous visitors, and a large procession marched from the grave to the cemetery, Duquette walking near the coffin, bareheaded, with a lighted taper in his hand. After the reinterment he caused to be placed at the head of the grave a large cross, bearing the name of the deceased. He then disappeared from the country, leaving his conduct an unexplained mystery, which the inhabitants never could solve.

Duquette proceeded to St. Charles, where he purchased property and located. For a number of years he carried on business as a trader, dealing in furs, peltries, goods, etc. He also invested largely in lands, and thereby became involved in his mercantile business. His goods had been purchased in Canada, and his creditors there sent an agent to Missouri who levied on most of his property and sold it under execution. He saved enough, however, to leave him in comfortable circumstances.

He was married in 1736 to Miss Mary Louisa Bauvis, of Ste. Genevieve, but they had no children.

Mr. Duquette's house stood on the same square where the stone church was afterward erected, and the members of his church used to gather there during the Lenten season for devotional services. He planted some fruit trees near his house soon after his arrival in St. Charles, and two of these were bearing not more than three years since, and they may be still for aught we know.

Duquette died February 2, 1816, and was buried in the old cemetery on Jackson and Second streets. His remains were afterward taken up and removed to the Catholic grave-yard where the church of St. Charles Borromeo now stands, and there they rested for many years. But eventually the growth of the city required the removal of the cemetery, and about twenty years ago a new one was established beyond the limits of the corporation. Duquette's remains were again disinterred and deposited in the new cemetery, where a massive, old-fashioned monument marks his grave. It was erected nearly sixty years ago, and the sculptured work upon it is partially obliterated by the ravages of time and its frequent removals.

Mrs. Duquette died April 2, 1841. Previous to 'and at the time of her decease, she lived in the house now occupied by Mrs. Walton, on Clay street. She was highly respected by the citizens of the town and vicinity, and the funeral procession that followed her remains to the grave was the largest that had ever been seen in St. Charles at that time. The bells of the various churches, irrespective of creed, were tolled in honor of the beloved dead as the hearse bore her remains to their last resting place.

In connection with the lives of these two pioneers of the Catholic religion in St. Charles, it will be appropriate to present the histories of the Academy of the Sacred Heart and Church of St. Charles Borromeo, which were prepared expressly for this work, the first by the Secretary of the Academy, and the second by Rev. John Roes, pastor of the church. These histories will be the more interesting because the two institutions to which they relate date back to the very infancy of the town in which they are situated, and no public history of them has ever been published before.

ACADEMY OF THE SACRED HEART.

THIS was the first foundation made by the religious of the Society of the Sacred Heart of Jesus in America. On the Feast of the Sacred Heart, in the year 1818, after a perilous voyage of one hundred days, Madame Duchesne, one of the first companions of the Venerated Mother Madeline Sophie Barrat, founder of the Society, landed in New Orleans. For long years Madame Duchesne burned with the desire of devoting her life for the salvation of the Indians. Now she had the realization of all her hopes; a wide field lay opened before her, but one thickly strewn with difficulties. A severe illness compelled her to prolong her stay in New Orleans, yet her ardent soul sighed to begin the work. Scarcely convalescent, she proceeded with her co-laborers, Madames Eugenie Ande, Octavie Berthold and two co-adjuting sisters, Catharine and Margaret, and arrived at St. Louis the same year. While remaining in this city, Madame Duchesne received the approbation of the Right Reverend Bishop Dubourg, whose pastoral cares extended over the two Louisianas, to lay the foundation. The present site, at St. Charles, was selected as the most desirable spot. The Cure of the village, the celebrated and Reverend Gabriel Richard, who was also elected member of Congress, installed the little colony in their humble dwelling, a log hut, containing two rooms; it stood in the midst of two acres of barren soil. Here and there might be seen the cabin of the Sioux. By an authentic act, the Bishop renewed his approbation, and the Sovereign Pontiff blessed, from afar, the new mission of the Sacred Heart. Too soon their little resources failed them, and extreme poverty menaced them on all sides. Incapable of supporting so rude a trial, sufficient to cause the stoutest heart to recoil, the little colony returned to St. Louis in September, 1819; but their destined home was St. Ferdinand, Florissant. On Christmas eve they took possession of their new residence, and at midnight they had the happiness of assisting at mass, with the five pupils who had followed them from St. Charles.

At St. Ferdinand the prospects were very favorable, and brightened each year. Auxiliaries were received from the Mother House in France; new colonies were sent out, and houses established at St. Louis, Grand Couteau, and St. Michael. Madame Duchesne governed all, in quality of Provincial, but made St. Louis her home.

Since the departure from St. Charles all hopes were not extinguished in renewing their efforts to plant the standard of the Sacred Heart in that city. Encouraged by their success at St. Ferdinand, Madame Duchesne once more looked toward St. Charles to recommence the foundation. So on the morning of October 10, 1828, the little caravan, consisting of Madames Duchesne, Octavie, Lucille and O'Connor, set out from St. Ferdinand. The Right Reverend Bishop Rosatti, nine Jesuit Fathers, and three secular priests accompanied them. His lordship was mounted on a humble courser, while the fathers walked at his side; the ladies occupied a carriage, and consequently arrived sooner. Their presence was announced and the inhabitants, who were now increased by one-half, testified their joy on the return of the religious. They were conducted to their house, which consisted of boards; underneath was a cellar, the receptacle for all the animals of the village; the odor arising from this assemblage of sheep, pigs and rats was almost intolerable, but in a short time they were freed from these interlopers. A chapel adjoining the house was hastily constructed, and here nine masses were celebrated in one day.

On the 14th Madames Lucille and O'Connor were left the sole occupants. Before departing to St. Ferdinand, Madame Duchesne installed Madame Lucille as Superior of the household, assisted by Madame O'Connor. They immediately went to work to fulfill the functions of carpenters, painters, masons, etc., and by dint of industry in fifteen days the house was beyond recognition.

The 29th of October the classes of the day school were opened, composed of five pupils; in November there was twelve; in December, sixteen; and in a few months more the number amounted to fifty. During the first six years one hundred and twenty pupils received instructions, and many of them became excellent mothers of families.

In March of 1829 reinforcements arrived; among them was Sister Mary Layton, the first American novice. In 1832 Sister Ann Egarty, and in 1833 Madame Guillot were sent to give their assistance. Amid this seeming prosperity privations were gathering, and soon pecuniary want was on the point of forcing them to abandon once more the work; but a divine Providence, who never forsakes those who place their confidence in him, rescued them in this painful dilemma; and in 1838 they were enabled to begin and complete the new building, contiguous to the church belonging to the Jesuit Fathers. Madame Lucille retained her office until 1840. About this time Bishop Rosati demanded a colony of the religious of the Sacred Heart for Sugar Creek, which was peopled by the Potowotamies. Obedience called Madame Lucille to take charge of the new mission. Here she endeared herself to the hearts of the Indians by her unwearied cares, making herself their common mother. It was the ardent desire of this devoted soul to live and die among her savage children. St. Mary's also witnessed her labors and there she passed the remainder of her days accomplishing the wish of her heart. It was only in January of 1875 that this admirable religious went to receive her reward, at the advanced age of 81 years.

For some years previous to the foundation at Sugar Creek Madame Duchesne had been released from the burden of Superiority; her declining years requiring rest, she withdrew into her solitude at St. Charles, where she continued her prayers and sufferings for her dear Indians.

In 1840 Madame Regis Hamilton, now assistant superior in Chicago, replaced Madame L ucille; she was succeeded in 1844 by Madame St. Cyr, who governed seven years. During this time a purchase was made from Reverend Father Verhægen, pastor of the church, and the grounds were considerably enlarged.

In 1851 Madame Hamilton resumed the charge for the space of one year. Her presence was a solace to the Worthy Mother Duchesne, whom Providence had preserved until this time; but now her days were numbered, and soon her holy soul was to wing its flight toward its eternal home. Until her last she submissively obeyed the most trivial order with child-like simplicity and resignation. It was at 10 o'clock on the morning of the 18th of November, 1852, that this venerated Mother, surrounded by her sorrowing family, passed from a sweet slumber to the presence of the Master, whom she had so long and so generously served. She was aged eighty-four years, thirty-four of which were passed in the missions of America.

Madame Aloysia Jacquet relieved Madame Hamilton for a few months. She was then recalled to superintend the Community at St. Louis. In 1853 Madame Boullion was appointed Superior, but in December of the same year she was sent to the Southern province, and Madame Aloysia returned to her former charge.

In 1854 the increase of the pupils was so rapid that extensive alterations were obliged to be made in the building. The new addition consisted of a large and commodious study hall, 45x35 feet, a class room, a refectory and play room beneath, with a dormitory and an infirmary above, and a spacious upper division. In 1855 the Parish School was built upon the Convent grounds. Here yearly about fifty or sixty children, mostly of the poorer class, are instructed in their religion and in the principles of education fitted to their station.

Madame Aloysia had made a vow to erect a shrine in honor of "Our Lady of the Pillar," if a favor she so earnestly sought for would be granted her. Heaven being propitious to her request, the chapel was constructed and the statue placed upon a pedestal over the altar. The Reverend Father De Smet blessed the first stone. This little sanctuary, now hallowed by the souvenirs connected with it, stands in the front yard, facing the right of the Convent. Immediately after the completion of the work the precious remains of the beloved founder of the society in America were transferred from their former resting place and deposited in the vault. The base of the altar bears this inscription: "Pray for the Conversion of the Indians."

In 1856 Madame Tucker directed the Community, but in 1858 she was summoned to St. Louis to receive again the charge of Superiority. Since then she has governed some of the houses of the East. In 1870 she was named Superior Vicar of the Western Province, which comprised the houses of St. Charles, St. Louis, St. Joseph, Chicago, St. Mary's Mission and Maryville.

In 1858 Madames Jouve and Ludovica Boudreaux successively governed, and in 1860 Madame Miller was appointed Superior. She endeared herself, like her predecessors, to all hearts by her devotedness to her Community.

In 1865 Madame Wall attached herself, with untiring zeal, to the new charge which was placed upon her; but in 1868 obedience called her to St. Joseph.

Then Madame Bourke assumed the care of government; she held her office five years. At the expiration of this time she was removed to Chicago, to continue her labors as Superior.

In the spring of 1870 the church of the Jesuits, adjacent to the Convent, was torn down, and the land on which it was built was purchased from the Fathers; it now forms part of the garden which surrounds the house.

In September of 1873 Madame Niederkorn, the present Superior, was nominated. Since that period many improvements have been made on the Convent and its surroundings. But in November, 1875, a fire, originated by a spark from the flue, broke out in the upper story of the middle building, and threatened destruction to the entire place. Evidently the flames had been playing for some hours between the roof and the timbers before the inmates were aware of their danger, but as soon as the alarm was made public, the kind-hearted citizens of St. Charles flocked to their assistance. To their indefatigable efforts and the interposition of a divine providence may be attributed the saving of the house, at a moment when all hopes were renounced. Unable to make the necessary repairs during the winter season, the religious waited for the coming spring; but a temporary roof prevented their being exposed to the inclemency of the weather. In February, 1876, the fearful tornado, which almost devastated the city, augmented the damages caused by the fire. Nearly every pane of glass on the east side of the house was shattered into fragments; the fences and grape arbors were thrown down, trees uprooted and transported with the wind, and immense rocks which supported the lower wall facing the street were hurled from their places—thus adding an expense of several hundred dollars.

In March the carpenters began their work, and notwithstanding the many interruptions, the results of the heavy rain and snow storms, in a few weeks the burnt-out attic was transformed into large and elegant apartments.

CHURCH OF ST. CHARLES BORROMEO.

The first church in the town of St. Charles was built by the Roman Catholics, the year and day not known by the people now living. Pioneer French priests visited these Western wilds at a very early day. The church was a humble log house, with its timbers standing upright, which consequently soon rotted down. Governor Blanchette replaced it by a neat frame building on Second, near Jackson street, on the northwestern part of Block 28. This must have been before 1793, as Governor Blanchette is reported to have died that year, as we gather from tradition, and to have been interred along the walls of the church. The records kept at the church of St. Charles Borromeo date from 1792, and indicate sufficiently the approximate date of the erection of the latter building. The first baptism recorded is that of Peter Beland, on the 21st of July, 1792; it was administered by Rev. Peter Joseph Didier, a Benedictine of the Congregation of St. Maus, of the Royal Abbey of St. Dennis, at Paris, then the acting, although not resident Pastor. Father Didier was succeeded in 1798 by Rev. Father L. Lusson, a Recollect Priest. Father Lusson's name disappears from the records after October, 1804, and after that time several priests, some of whom were Trappists, ministered to the spiritual wants of the Congregation; some for a longer, others for a shorter period of time. These came either from St. Louis or Portage, where priests resided at a much earlier date than at St. Charles. One of these, long remembered was the Rev. Joseph Mary Dunand, a trappist, who acted as pastor at St. Charles from the year 1809 to the year 1815. In 1814 Bishop Flaget, of Louisville, is reported to have visited St. Charles, while Father Dunand was pastor.

In 1823 the Jesuits settled in the Florissant Valley, on what is now generally known as the Priest's Farm. Solicited by Bishop Dubourg, they undertook the care of the Missionary Stations across the Missouri in St. Charles county, but had for some time no permanent residence in any of them. The first Jesuits who visited St. Charles were Father Van Quickenborn, the Superior of the Missions, and Father Timmermans.

In 1827 Father Van Quickenborn bought a new frame building on Main street, near Lewis, and the Fathers took up their residence there. In 1827, also, they began the building of the stone church, corner of Second and Decatur. Completed in the fall of 1827, by the indomitable energy of the pastors, and the corresponding courage of the parishoners, it was solemnly consecrated by Bishop Rosatti on the 12th of October. On that grand occasion, Father Van Quickenborn acted as assistant priest, Fathers DeTheux and Dusosey as Deacons of Honors, and Fathers Smedts and DeSmet as Deacon and sub-Deacon. Gladly would we give here a short sketch of the Fathers who in turn acted as Superiors of the St. Charles Residence and as pastors of the congregation, but this would exceed the limits of the intended sketch, and would be difficult to do, for one who has not the necessary dates at command; thus, however, we must say that they were all men who knew how to make generous sacrifices for the interest of religion and education; nay, even for the temporal welfare of St. Charles. They were all men of zeal and of indomitable energy, most of them too, were men of talent and superior education.

Before passing on there is one name, however, which is so familiar still to all the people of St. Charles that we cannot pass it over in silence; it may seem invidious, but we cannot withstand giving it with a brief sketch of his life. We mean the Rev. P. J. Verhægen, whose name has left a deep impression on the Protestants as well as on the Catholics:

Born in Belgium on the 21st of June, 1800. He came to Missouri in 1821, as one of the little band of Jesuit missionaries, whom Bishop Dubourg had succeeded in drawing to his vast diocese which stood so sadly in need of clergymen to break the word of life to them. Before his ordination he had already visited St. Charles to instruct the people and to gather them together on Sunday. Ordained in 1826 he became the regular Pastor and Superior, and remained until August, 1828. Incredibly hard and laborious was his position, especially during the building of the stone church, at which he worked almost as a day laborer. In 1828 he was succeeded by Father J. B. Smedts as Pastor and Superior of St. Charles, and Father Felix Verreydt as Missionary to the surrounding country.

Father Verhægen, transferred to the St. Louis University, acted there as its President, later as Superior of the missions, and later again as Vicar General and Administrator of the diocese of St. Louis. Relieved of these arduous duties he returned to St. Charles in 1843, to leave it again in 1844 to become Provincial of the Jesuits in Maryland. Having there completed his term of office he returned to the West and became the first President of the College of St. Joseph at Bardstown, which the Bishop of Louisville confided to the Society in 1848. In 1851 he returned once more to St. Charles to leave it only for one year, that is the year 1857-58, which he spent at the St. Louis University to teach Theology to the young scholastics, and to give the Sunday evening lectures at St. Xavier's Church; returned to St. Charles, which was the place of his choice, he acted as Superior of the residence, and as first pastor until his death, and in that double capacity, he endeared himself more and more with the people of the city. In 1808 his health began visibly to give way, and after a few days of serious illness he died at the pastoral residence on Third street, on the 21st of July, regretted by all; on the 28th his mortal remains were followed to their last resting place at the Novitiate near Florissant, by many of his sorrowing spiritual children.

Father Verhægen was a man of superior mind, of profound knowledge and of genial manners; he was the friend of all who knew him, ever cheerful, and with a kind word for all who came near him. During his long career of usefulness in the high positions he so successfully filled as Rector of Colleges, as Superior of the Missions, as Provincial of Order and as Administrator of the Diocese of St. Louis, he gained what he did not seek, a great name, and an extensive popularity, and promoted what was the sole object of his ambition, the good of religion and education and the greater glory of God.

On the 29th of July, 1868, he was succeeded by the Rev. J. Roes as Superior of the residence and as first pastor, who holds the same office still.

A month after his appointment it was found necessary, on account of the constantly increasing number of the parishoners, to secure as soon as possible, a larger church edifice, and on the last Sunday of August, a spirited meeting of the congregation was held in the old school-house on Third street, now known as the Franklin School, at which it was determined to begin at once the new church. Permission was obtained from his grace Archbishop Kenrick and from the Provincial of the Society, and soon several thousand dollars were subscribed; the foundations were begun in October, the corner stone however was only laid on the 9th of May, 1869, by his grace the Archbishop, in the midst of an immense concourse of people who had flocked together from St. Louis and from the neighborhood; they were addressed by Rev. Father Tschieder of St. Joseph's in St. Louis, their former pastor, in German, and Rev. Father O'Reilly, now as then pastor of the Immaculate Conception, St. Louis, in English. After four years of persevering sacrifices, on the part of the people, and of struggle and toil on the part of the pastors, the splendid edifice was completed. In the beginning of October, 1872, and on the 13th of that month it was solemnly consecrated by Rt. Rev. P. J. Ryan, Coadjutor Bishop of St. Louis, assisted by a great number of clergymen from St. Louis and St. Charles counties. The crowd assisting at the beautiful and grand ceremony of consecration was very large; it was addressed by Rev. J. DeBleick, S. J., of the St. Louis University, in English, and by Rev. P. J. Tschieder of St. Joseph's, in German; both sermons were masterly pieces. The consecration was followed by a solemn high mass, Father Van Assche, of Florissant, one of the original founders of the Missouri Province was the celebrant, and was assisted by Fathers J. Van Mierlo and Van Leert as Deacon and sub-Deacon. On the 29th of March, 1873, the church was permanently opened for divine service by a very successful mission preached by Rev. J. Coghlan, S. J., from St. Mary's, Kansas, assisted by Rev. Kuhlman, S. J., from the Novitiate. The present pastors are Father J. Roes assisted by Fathers W. B. V. Heyden and H. Van Mierlo.

The financial crash of 1872 has put the congregation to great trouble and sacrifice; but it is to be hoped this will now soon end, and with the available property sold on even reasonably low figures, the congregation will find an end to their troubles and will be able to boast of their fine church and school and pastoral residence, and leave a glorious legacy to their children.

MAJ. GEORGE BAUGHMAN, THE MONTGOMERY COUNTY HERMIT.

In a lonely, desolate hillside, a short distance from Danville, there lives a singular being known as the Montgomery county hermit. His place of abode is in a small cavern, formed by a shelving rock in the side of the hill, on one side of which he has built a wall of stone and formed a rough doorway, which is closed by some boards clumsily fastened together. The sides of the cave are smoky and dirty, and a more gloomy, desolate place could hardly be found. Here this singular man has resided since about 1852, twenty-four years, and he will doubtless remain there until death removes him to a more pleasant habitation. He subsists upon charity, public and private, and the fruits of his gun and fishing tackle. He also raises a small crop of corn each year, and has a a few peach trees near his cave, which yield him a small amount of that delicious fruit each season. His gun is of the most antique pattern, long and ungainly, like himself, and shows the effects of age and constant use, being held together by numerous strings and bands. He dresses in a style peculiar to himself, as will be observed by referring to his portrait on the frontispiece, which is copied from a photograph taken expressly for this work, the sitting being secured just after he had return from a fishing excursion. His shoes, which do not show in the picture, are composed of rough leather, tied with strings to a sole composed of a piece of a clapboard; he discards socks entirely.

In the side of the hill near his den he has dug two large wells, twenty-five or thirty feet deep, in quest of golden treasures which he imagines are hid there. The greater portion of the excavations has been made through solid rock, without the aid of powder or blasting tools, and he has carried the *debris* to the top in his pockets and shirt bosom, ascending and descending by means of a ladder of the most primitive construction. Some idea, therefore, may be formed of the patience and perseverance that have been employed in the prosecution of his work.

We have obtained a history of this singular person, which we present below, and from it may be gleaned the cause of his hallucination and peculiar mode of life.

Henry Baughman, the grandfather of the subject of this sketch, was a native of Holland, but desiring to better his prospects in life, he came to America, and settled in Pennsylvania. When the revolutionary war began he enlisted in the American army and served his adopted country during its struggle for independence. After the close of the war he removed to Stark county, Ohio, where he settled and lived. He had a son named George, who married Mary McIntire, and settled in Carroll county, Ohio. They had ten children, viz.: Jacob, Joseph, Emanuel, William, James, Henry, GEORGE, Polly, Esther, and Rachel.

George was born December 3, 1814, and is now nearly 62 years of age. He received a good common school education, having attended the public schools in the vicinity of his father's house during the winter months from the time he was eight years old until he was nearly grown.

In 1836 he came to St. Louis, Mo., where he remained one month, and then went to Washington county, Illinois, and settled on 80 acres of land that his father had given him. He remained there until 1847, when he traded his farm for one in Christian county, Mo., where he settled and resided five years. At the end of that time he paid a visit to his father in Ohio, remaining only a short time. He then purchased a cart and a yoke of oxen, and accompanied by his little nephew, started on his return to Missouri. His route lay through Montgomery county, and he camped one night at Loutre Lick, where he lost one of his oxen, and spent a month in looking for him, without success.

In the meantime his mind became deranged on the subject of gold, and he located at the place where he has since lived, and began to dig for hidden treasure. His nephew remained with him several years, but being in destitute circumstances he was finally sent home by some of the citizens of the community.

Baughman says that many years ago the French concealed large quantities of gold where he has dug his wells; that he has now found the treasure and is waiting for France to send an army to stand guard while he takes it out. He declares that he has written several letters to the *Boss of Paris* in regard to the matter, and thinks the army will be here soon. He will converse in a perfectly sane manner on any subject except that of gold, but the moment that is mentioned he forgets everything else and will talk about nothing but his hidden treasures.

He has an old horse with which he cultivates a small patch of government land, and the County Court appropriates $25 a year to his support. This money is placed in the hands of Mr. Dock Graham, who expends it to the best advantage, and in such a way that Baughman imagines he earns it, for if he had the slightest intimation that it was a public charity he would not accept it under any circumstances. He catches fish and shoots squirrels, rabbits, turkeys and other game, which he sells or trades for groceries and other necessary articles; so that he does not suffer for something to subsist upon. Mr. Graham and other citizens of the vicinity extend a helping hand to him when he needs assistance, and are careful to see that he does not suffer for anything. He grinds his meal on a mill of his own construction, and does his own cooking and washing—though from his usual appearance one might infer that he did very little of the latter. He is a gentleman in his manners, quiet and inoffensive, and his cave is often visited by children, of whom he is quite fond. He is liked and respected by the people of the vicinity, who are careful not to offend him or wound his feelings by making light of his singular hallucination and mode of living; and notwithstanding his seclusion and eccentricities he will be sincerely mourned when the hand of death is laid upon him.

THE SLICKER WAR.

Only a few of the older citizens of Lincoln and St. Charles counties remember anything about the "Slicker War," as it was called, that occurred between rival organizations in the two counties, beginning about 1844, and closing about three years afterward. It was a civil war of considerable dimensions, and well deserves a place in this history.

The organizantion known as Slickers originated in Benton county about 1841. The name came from their mode of inflicting punishment, which was to tie the culprit to a tree and "slick" or whip him with hickory withes, and then give him notice to leave the country in a designated time. The Slickers were organized for the purpose of breaking up a band of horse thieves and counterfeiters, who had their headquarters among the hills and mountains of Benton county. Similar organizations were formed in various parts of the State for like purposes, and were known by the same general appellation of Slickers. In some instances bad men, and even the very thieves and counterfeiters against whom they were warring, contrived to become members of these societies and through their evil influence and false and malicious representations innocent and unoffending persons were severely and cruelly punished. This led to the organization of anti-Slicker companies, and in some parts of the State actual war raged between the opposing factions, and many persons were killed, wounded, or maltreated.

During the high water in June, 1844, several small steamers ascended Cuivre river to Chain-of-Rocks, in Lincoln county, where there was a small village consisting of several stores, a mill, one or two shops, etc. One of these boats, called the *Bee*, made several trips between St. Louis and that place, and on one of her trips landed a man at the Chain-of-Rocks who gave his name as Hal Grammar, and who proved to be a counterfeiter, horse thief, and bad character generally.

The next time the *Bee* came up she brought a peddler, who landed from the boat and proceeded to the hotel to get his dinner. He left his pack in the office of the hotel and passed into the dining room, and while engaged in eating his dinner Hal Grammar and his confederates, who at that time were unknown, stole the goods and left. Grammar was captured soon after, but had disposed of the goods, which were never found. He escaped from his captors, and it soon became evident to the citizens that there was a regular organization of thieves and counterfeiters in their county, and that Grammar was doubtless the originator and chief of the band.

The county became flooded with counterfeit money; horses, cattle and hogs were stolen and run out of the country; and the thieves finally became so bold that they butchered beef cattle on the farms of their owners, and shipped the meat to St. Louis in boats prepared for the purpose.

The evil having become unendurable, the citizens organized a company of Slickers for the purpose of ridding themselves of their grievance. Many of the best men of the county joined the organization, and Mr. James Stallard, of Hurricane township, was elected captain. In the company were such men as Ira T. Nelson, Rolla Mayes, Abraham and Joshua King, Rufus Gibson, Mitchell Bosman, John and Malachi Davis, Washington Noel, Lewis G. Martin, Sebran Wallace, Littleton Dryden, William and Benjamin Cooper, William Wilson, Thomas Wallace, James Bedows, Abraham Burkhead, Dr. William Wise, James Day, John

Argent, George Smith, John W. McKee, John Dalton, Joseph
Wright, James Oliver, James and John Lindsay, Kinchen Robinson, Jacob Boone, Levi Bailey, Jacob Groshong, George Pol-
lard, Elihu Jones, Taylor Crumes, Willis Hutton, Samuel and
James Alexander, Andrew Hill, Jacob Conn, John Loving,
Charles McIntosh, Charles W. Martin, Lawrence B. Sitten, Tandy
K. Nichols, James Blademore, Harrison Anderson, Joseph Woodson, Carroll Sitten, Zoar Perkins, M. Martin, Vincent Shields,
and others, among whom, as was afterward ascertained, were several of the counterfeiters and thieves. All of those whose names
are given were good, honest, law-abiding citizens, who went into
the organization from the best of motives. Only seven of the
entire number are now living.

The thieves and counterfeiters were hunted out and tried, and
most of them were whipped and ordered to leave the country,
which they were glad to do; but a few of the ring leaders were
executed.

These vigorous measures soon restored peace and security to
the honest people of the county, and the Slickers ought then to
have disbanded, but they kept up their organization, and, as usual
with such bodies, soon began to punish some that were innocent
along with the guilty.

In the spring of 1845 reports came to the Slickers that the sons
of Mr. James Trumbull were in sympathy with counterfeiters,
and were encouraging and abetting them in their unlawful business. The reports were not true, but were made by malicious and
evil minded persons, and led to a serious and deadly affray. The
boys were ordered to leave the country, which they positively
refused to do. The Slickers therefore determined to enforce their
order, and one day about the middle of April, 1845, a party of
them went to Trumbull's house for that purpose. They arrived
about noon, and found the family, who had expected an attack,
armed and barricaded in their house. Mr. Trumbull and his
daughter Sarah came out to expostulate with the Slickers and
entreat them to go away, declaring that they and their relatives
were entirely innocent of the charges made against them. But
their appeals were unavailing, and they were told that they must
immediately leave the county.

The slickers at once attacked the house, and John and Malachi Davis endeavored to enter together. The former was
wounded on the head by a corn knife in the hands of one of the

Trumbull girls, and the latter received two gunshot wounds from one of the boys, named Squire, from the effects of which he died next day. John Davis, though suffering severely from his wound, shot both Squire Trumbull and his brother James, shattering the thigh bone of the former with a rifle ball, from the effects of which he died several weeks later. James Trumbull was shot through the mouth and neck, and fell apparently dead, but finally recovered from his wounds, though he remained paralyzed the rest of his life. He died several years afterward, in Arkansas. Several Slickers were wounded, but not seriously, and they finally withdrew without having accomplished their purpose.

Among the Slickers engaged in this affair was Kinchen Robinson, who was a great gasser, and who styled himself the "lamplighter of the twelve apostles." When the fight was over he retreated with considerable haste, and just as he sprang over the yard fence one of the Trumbull girls cut the tail of his coat off with a corn knife. His acquaintances enjoyed a good deal of fun at his expense after that adventure.

This unfortunate affair became noised over the entire country, and opposition at once began to manifest itself against the Slickers. Many who had previously been in full sympathy with them now denounced them without stint, and demanded that their organization should be broken up, as they had accomplished their object and were now going beyond the bounds of reason, and even becoming outlaws themselves.

A company of anti-Slickers was organized in St. Charles county, in the vicinity of Flint Hill, with the avowed determination of dispersing the Slickers of Lincoln county. They stationed a guard at Trumbull's house, to prevent further bloodshed, and warned the Slickers not to cause any more trouble. Mr. James Shelton was elected captain of this company, and among his men were David McFarlane, Robert Sheley, Bob Woolfolk, Joseph Allen, Perry Custer, George W. Wright, Sam Carter, Scott Evans, Sam Newland, Benjamin and Oliver Pitts, George M. Coats, Jeff. Dyer, George McGregor, Archibald M. Wade, John T. Daniels, Elliot Lusby, Lewis and Peter Daniels, Dr. William Coleman, S. L. Barker, Thomas, Amos and Joseph Dyer, William A. Abington, John P. Allen, and many other leading men of that part of the county. They were all citizens of St. Charles county, while the Slickers were all citizens of Lincoln, and on that account considerable enmity arose between the people of the two counties. Both organizations were composed of good men actuated by honest motives, but through misrepresentations and the excitement of the times they were brought into antagonism, and several fights and skirmishes ensued, in which a number were wounded, others were whipped, and one or two lives were lost.

But the excitement finally died away, and both companies were eventually disbanded.

About two years afterward Captain Shelton, while crossing Cuivre river in a skiff, was fired upon by some person concealed in the brush on the Lincoln county side, and his arm was broken. One Jacob Boone, who had been a Slicker during the late trouble, was accused of the crime, arrested, and taken to Troy for trial. When his trial came off he was acquitted, as there was no direct evidence against him. But the friends of Shelton, a few of whom had attended the trial, declared that he had escaped justice through the connivance and influence of his friends in Lincoln county, who had been his companions in the Slicker war; and an angry discussion arose in regard to the matter, during which the old Slicker and anti-Slicker difficulties were revived, and much bitterness was manifested on both sides. That night as Shelton's friends were returning home, several of them were waylaid and fired upon but fortunately none were hurt. The same evening, about dusk, two young men, nephews of Mr. Levi Bailey, who had expressed anti-Slicker sentiments, were fired upon by parties in ambush just as they were entering the outer gate that led to their uncle's house, where they were going on a visit. One of their horses was shot through the jaw, and several buckshot passed through a shawl that one of the boys wore.

These events again aroused the old excitement, which ran high for some time; and several years elapsed before the matter was forgotten and friendly feelings restored.

And such was the great Slicker war, which threatened for some time to array the citizens of two populous counties in deadly hostility against each other, to bathe their hearth-stones in blood, and lay waste their farms and homes. It teaches a practical lesson that should not be forgotten, ·viz.: that good men, with the best intentions, may be led into the commission of unjust, unlawful and cruels deeds when they take the law into their own hands and attempt to punish criminals and allay crime by summary proceedings.

29

THE GERMAN IMMIGRATION.

In 1824–25 an educated and intelligent German named Gottfried Duden, came to America and traveled extensively over our country, observing our climate, soil and productions, and taking notes of our manners, customs, laws, etc. He spent nearly a year in the region of country embraced in the counties of St. Charles, Warren and Montgomery, traveling under the guidance of Daniel M. Boone and others, whom he paid liberally for their services.

He was highly pleased with the country and the people whom he found here, and upon his return to Germany wrote and published a book of 350 pages, giving a complete history of our laws, forms of government, etc., with a thorough description of the portions of country that he had visited. The book had an immense sale, and he became wealthy from the proceeds.

In a few years the effect of his writings began to be manifest by the arrival of German immigrants, preceded by a few educated and wealthy men who came in advance to prepare the way for them. Each family had a copy of Duden's book, and so accurate were his descriptions of place's and names that they knew the farms and the names of their owners as they came to them.

They expected not only to find an abundance of game and wild animals of all kinds—in which they were not disappointed—but also to be under the necessity of defending their homes against the attacks of the savages; and hence they came prepared with swords, muskets, pistols, etc. It was no uncommon thing to see a stout burgher marching at the head of his family with an immense sabre buckled around his portly form and a musket or portentious yager resting upon his broad shoulders. But they soon beat their swords into plowshares and used their fire-arms to kill squirrels, turkeys, deer and other game with which the country abounded.

The Americans rejoiced at their coming, and extended to them a hearty welcome, for they brought with them money, which the country greatly needed just at that time, bought lands, and proved to be honest, industrious, thrifty citizens. They also introduced the mechanical arts of an older country, and manufactured many useful articles that had before been unknown to the Americans.

Louis Eversman came with Duden, traveled with him, and

remained when the latter returned to Europe; so that he was the first German settler in that part of Missouri. He married a Miss McLane, bought a farm in Warren county, raised an intelligent family, and became a prominent and influential citizen.

Most of the first immigrants were from Hespers, Germany, and they arrived in 1833. They came in societies or companies, which bore the names of their native places in Germany. The Berlin Society was composed of the following families: Charles Madler, Charles A. Miller, William and Ferdinand Roch, Henry Walks, Henry Seitz, Louis, William, and Conrad Haspes, August Rixrath, Jerry Schieper, Daniel Renner, Justus Muhnn and his two brothers, Charles Lipross, Philip Renner, Jacob Sack, Henry Schaa, Harmon Stuckhoff, and Charles V. Spankern. Most of these settled in the western part of St. Charles county, in the vicinity of Augusta. Other families came about the same time, amongst whom were, Charles Wincker, George H. Mindrup (who served as Judge of the County Court of St. Charles county four years), Frederick Wincker (who was postmaster at Augusta for sometime), Bernhard and Henry Stuckhoff, Arnold Vaelkerding, William, August, and Julius Sehart, Francis Krekel (father of Judge Arnold Krekel), and Julius, Emile, Herman, and Conrad Mallinckrodt. The Mallinckrodts were all well educated, and became influential citizens in the communities where they settled. They studied the English language before they came to America, but the pronunciation was incorrect, and when they arrived in this country they were mortified to find that they could not converse with our people until they had unlearned the English which had been taught them in Germany. When Julius Mallinckrodt arrived in St. Louis, he met a man in the street, and desiring to make some inquiries of him, he addressed him in what he supposed to be the English language, but the man could not understand him. He then addressed him in German, and then in Latin, but he still could not understand. By this time they were both excited and beginning to grow angry, when Mallinckrodt exclaimed in a fit of desperation, "*Parlez-vous Francais, Monsieur?*" Instantly the man threw his arms around his neck and embraced him, while tears of joy ran down his cheeks. He proved to be a Frenchman who had just arrived in the city, and, like Mallinckrodt, could not find any one with whom he could converse. The latter spoke French almost as fluently as he did his mother tongue, and a warm friendship, which lasted for years, at once sprang up between the two strangers in a strange land.

In 1834 the Gissen Society arrived. It was under charge of Hon. Frederick Munch, who still resides in Warren county, and besides being a man of great local influence, is a writer and author of some renown. He has been a member of the Legislature and State Senate several times, and is everywhere recognized as a man of ability and a profound thinker and philosopher. He was born and raised in the province of Upper Hesse, in Prussia, and educated for the ministry. He was pastor of a Protestant Liberal church in Germany thirteen years, and in 1834 he organized the Gissen Society from among the members of his congregation, and came to America. In the Society were the following families: Gotlieb Beng, John Kessler, Jacob Jeude, Frederick Reck, Dr. Frederick Kruge, Henry Becker, Charles Kesel, Jonathan Kunze, Mr. Guhlemann, Frederick Feach, Andrew and Louis Klug, Pressner Goepel (whose son Gelt afterward represented Franklin county in both Houses of the Legislature), Frederick Bruche (whose son Henry represented Cape Girardeau county in the Legislature), and Augustus Kroell, who was pastor of a German Protestant church in Cincinnati at the time of his death. The above families settled in the eastern part of Warren and western portion of St. Charles counties, where they and their descendants still reside. Their religious belief is *rational*. They discard all miracles and the doctrine of atonement through the blood of Christ, believing that we make our own future condition by the life we live here, receiving punishment for our evil deeds and rewards for our good ones. They accept Christ as a good man and a great teacher, but do not believe that he was divine.

Some time after the arrival of the Gissen Society, the following families came: Jacob and Frederick Ahmann, Charles Winkelmeir, Frederick and Erasmus Hieronymus, Ulmfers and Frederick Blantink, Erastus Grabbs (who became a merchant, postmaster, and Justice of the Peace in Marthasville, Warren county), William Barez, (who was a banker in Berlin and a very intelligent man), George Munch, Henry and George Berg, Mr. Fuhr and his five sons, John Miller, Henry Dickhouse, Harmon Lucas and his brother, Henry and Luke Hurmann, Mr. Tuepperts, and Mr. Oberhellmann.

In 1833 the following families settled in St. Charles county, in and near Dog Prairie, all of whom were from Prussia: Antone

Arens (whose wife was Amelia Ostoman, and the names of their children were Joseph, Sophia, Antone, Amelia, and Theodore), Joseph Floar, Joseph and John Shoane, Francis Moledor and his two sons Frank and Casper, Anton Stahlsmidth, John Freymuth, Mr. Mescheda (who came in 1837), Alexander Arens, Joseph Stahlsmidth, John Heidelmann, Frederick Lœbecke, Andrew Sali, and Baltasar Vetsch, who came from the province of Alsace.

Most of the Germans who came to America with money, lost it by injudicious speculations in lands, but those who came poor generally prospered on their small beginnings, and soon became money-loaners and land-owners. Many of them became wealthy, and left large families in affluent circumstances. No other race of people ever did more for the development of a country, or made better or more thrifty citizens. They caused barren hillsides to blossom with grape-vines and fruit trees, and opened large farms in the midst of dense forests. Swamps and marshes were drained, and fertile fields took the place of stagnant ponds that for years had sent out their miasmas to poison the atmosphere of the surrounding country and breed fevers, chills, and pestilence. Villages and towns sprang up where solitude had previously reigned, and the liberal arts began to flourish. The country received a new impetus, and prosperity smiled upon the people.

Many of the descendants of those early German families have become influential and leading men, in politics, letters, sciences, arts and commerce. Among this class may be mentioned the children of Francis Krekel, several of whom have become distinguished through their own efforts and perseverance. Judge Arnold Krekel, of the United States District Court, has gained a reputation that is national, and when we consider the difficulties that he had to contend against, we can not do otherwise than accord to him an unusual degree of talent and energy.

He was about sixteen years of age when his father arrived in Missouri, his mother having died of cholera on the route. He could neither speak nor understand a word of the English language, but at once began the study of it, and was soon able to converse intelligibly with his American neighbors. He worked as a farm hand, and made rails at twenty-five cents per 100, until he obtained money enough to pay his expenses at school, when he went to St. Charles and became a student in St. Charles College. He graduated at that institution, studied law, and began to practice in the city of St. Charles. He was successful from the start and soon gained both distinction and wealth. His subsequent history is familiar to the people of the State, and need not be given here.

His father was a devout Catholic, and several of his brothers are members of that Church, but he embraced liberal views in religious matters at a very early age, and though perhaps not an infidel in the real meaning of that word, he does not believe in the divine origin of the Bible or the biblical account of creation.

His early views with regard to the origin of man were somewhat peculiar, but we cannot say whether he still entertains the same opinions or not. Being asked one day how he would account for the existence of man if he discarded the biblical theory, he replied that he supposed there was a place in some remote country where, the soil and elements being favorable, man germinated and grew like the vegetable productions of the earth, and afterward developed from that imperfect state into his present condition. The Judge would hardly advance such an idea now, but he doubtless still believes in the natural and scientific theory of the creation of man rather than the scriptural.

THE TOWN OF TROY, LINCOLN COUNTY.

THIS town was named from Troy, N. Y., by Mr. Joshua N. Robbins, a native of that city, and who was the first merchant of Troy, Mo. The latter place was founded in 1802, on two Spanish grants, made respectively to Joseph Cottle and Zadock Woods. The dividing line ran through the big spring, giving one-half of it to each of the parties, Woods getting the north and Cottle the south half. During the Indian war a fort was built on Woods' land, and called Woods' Fort, and during the winter of 1813–14 Lieut. Zachary Taylor, who subsequently became a Major-General and then President of the United States, had his headquarters in this fort.

In 1824 Mr. Woods sold his land and removed to Austin, Texas, where he and several of his sons were killed during the war between Mexico and the Lone Star Republic.

In 1827 there were four stores in Troy, owned by the following gentlemen, viz.: Joshua N. Robbins, Emanuel Block, R. J. Peers and H. C. Draper. The place contained one hotel, kept by Rev. Andrew Monroe, and thirty families, none of whom are there now. Troy was not made the county-seat until 1829, when it was removed from Old Alexandria and located there.

Many exciting events occurred at and near Troy, then called Woods' Fort, during the Indian war, but as they are given elsewhere we will not repeat them here.

During early days a physician named Linn lived at Troy, and one day he was sent for to see a negro woman named Sall, who belonged to Mr. John Carty. The woman had had a chill, an the doctor inquired what time the chill came on. She replied, "Jes as Isaac cum from de mill." "Well, Isaac," said the doctor, "when did you come from the mill?" "Jes 'fore John cum wid de wood," was the reply. "Well, John, when did you come with the wood?" "Jes 'fore Bill cum home." "And when did Bill come home?" sharply inquired the doctor, whose ire was beginning to rise. "I golly!" said Bill, "jes 'fore Sall had de chill." "And how in thunder am I to find out from you blamed fools when the woman had the chill?" exclaimed the now furious doctor. Bill sighed a melancholy sigh, and replied, "God knows; *I* want dar."

THE BLACK HAWK WAR.

DURING the winter of 1831-2, several tribes of Indians whose country lay within the present limits of Illinois, Iowa and Wisconsin, began to manifest warlike intentions. They were led by the celebrated Black Hawk, a chief of the Sac Nation, who proved himself to be, by nature, both a soldier and a statesman; and had he possessed the advantages of civilization and education he would have made one of the most celebrated characters of history. He possessed an implacable hatred against the Americans, probably with good cause, if we may believe the statements made in his autobiography published in the following pages, and nearly his entire life was spent in fighting against them. During the war of 1812 he received a commission as Brigadier General from the British government, and commanded an army of Indians who served one campaign with the British regu-

lars in the lake region. They were defeated in several engagements, when Black Hawk and his warriors returned in disgust
to their own country, where they resumed operations against the
American settlements lying between the Mississippi and Missouri
rivers.   Black Hawk was the leading spirit in all the attacks made
upon those settlements, several of which he led in person.   (For
a full account of these events, see Indian War, and Life of Black
Hawk.)

The troubles of 1831–2 arose out of a refusal of the Sac Indians,
or a portion of them, to leave their country in Illinois, which they
had previously ceded to the United States government. A portion
of the tribe, led by a chief named Keokuk, acquiesced in the
terms of the treaty, and peacefully removed to the western bank
of the Mississippi; but Black Hawk claimed that the treaty was
a fraud, and refused to leave his village.   In the summer of 1831
several American families settled in the Sac village, and were
ordered away by Black Hawk and his warriors.   They appealed
to the government for protection, and refused to leave.   Black
Hawk raised a band of several hundred warriors from among the
Sacs, Foxes and Winnebagoes, and assumed a warlike attitude.
The Sacs and Foxes had for ages been in close alliance with each
other, and always made common cause against any nation with
whom they were at war.

The white families that had settled in the Sac country now became alarmed, and fled for safety to the adjacent forts, while an
army of United States regulars and Illinois and Missouri militia,
under the command of Gens. Scott and Atkinson, advanced
agaist the hostile Indians.   The latter retired northward expecting
assistance from the British in Canada, in which they were, of
course, disappointed.   Several skirmishes and one principal battle
took place, in which the Indians were defeated and scattered.
They eventually came within the American lines and surrendered,
and were removed to their reservation west of the Mississippi.

Black Hawk, being deserted by his warriors after their defeat,
wandered about for some time, endeavoring to evade the American forces, but finally came within the lines and surrendered un-
conditionally.   He was treated with marked distinction by the
American officers, and after a short confinement in Jefferson Barracks, below St. Louis, he was taken on a tour through the eastern cities of the United States, where immense crowds of people
flocked to see the distinguished warrior.   He was finally returned

to his people with a much better opinion of the Americans than he had previously entertained, and from that time until his death he went no more upon the war-path.

LIFE OF BLACK HAWK.

The Indian name for Black Hawk is Ma-ka-tai-me-she-kia-kiak, which we presume very few Americans can pronounce.

The following autobiography was dictated by Black Hawk to Mr. Antoine Leclair, United States Interpreter for the Sac and Fox Indians, in August, 1833, and published by him in October of the same year. It is Black Hawk's own account of his life, given in his own words, as translated into English, and it is deeply interesting from the beginning to the end. Of course it will not do to accept all his statements as true, for many of them are, no doubt, highly colored in his favor, but in general the history is correct, and agrees in the main with our own histories, made from official reports, etc. This autobiography shows Black Hawk to have been a strong and original thinker, a keen observer of the ways of men, and a shrewd leader among his own people. He also represents himself as a man of humane and generous feelings, in such a straightforward, unostentatious manner that we cannot accuse him of egotism, but on the contrary, are led to believe that he spoke the truth, as he understood it, at least; and, in fact, the accounts which have been given of his generosity and humanity, by white men, correspond with what he says in regard to himself.

We are indebted for the privilege of copying this little book, to the Librarian of the St. Louis Mercantile Library, where it has been on exhibition since the death of Rev. Wm. M. Peck, by whom it was willed to the Library. It has been out of print many years, and being a very rare and entertaining work, will no doubt be highly prized by the readers of this book.

CERTIFICATE.

INDIAN AGENCY, ROCK ISLAND, }
October 16th, 1833.   }

I do hereby certify that Ma-ka-tai-me-she-kia-kiak, or Black Hawk, did call upon me, on his return to his people in August last, and express a great desire to have a history of his life written and published, in order (as he said) that the people of the United States might know the causes that had impelled him to act as he had done, and the principles by which he was governed. In accordance with his request I acted as Interpreter; and was particularly cautious to understand distinctly the narrative of Black Hawk throughout, and have examined the work carefully, since its completion, and have no hesitation in pronouncing it strictly correct in all its particulars.

Given under my hand, at the Sac and Fox Agency, the day and date above written. ANTOINE LECLAIR,

U. S. Interpreter for the Sacs and Foxes.

DEDICATION.

TO BRIGADIER-GENERAL H. ATKINSON.:

SIR—The changes of fortune and vicissitudes of war made you my conqueror. When my last resources were exhausted, my warriors worn down with long and toilsome marches, we yielded, and I became your prisoner. The story of my life is told in the following pages; it is intimately connected, and in some measure, identified with a part of the history of your own; I have, therefore, dedicated it to you.

The changes of many summers have brought old age upon me, and I cannot expect to survive many more. Before I set out on my journey to the land of my fathers, I have determined to give my motives and reasons for my former hostilities to the whites, and to vindicate my character from misrepresentation. The kindness I received from you while a prisoner of war, assures me that you will vouch for the facts contained in my narrative, so far as they came under your observation.

I am now an obscure member of a nation that formerly honored and respected my opinion. The path to glory is rough, and many gloomy hours obscure it.

May the Great Spirit shed light on yours, and that you may never experience the humility that the power of the American Government has reduced me to, is the wish of him, who, in his native forests, was once as proud and bold as yourself. BLACK HAWK.

10th moon, 1833.

I was born at the Sac Village, on Rock River, in the year 1767, and am now in my 67th year. My great-grandfather Na-na-ma-kee, or Thunder, was born in the vicinity of Montreal, where the Great Spirit first placed the Sac nation, and inspired him with the belief that, at the end of four years, he should see a *white man*, who would be to him a father. Consequently, he blacked his face, and eat but once a day (just as the sun was going down,) for three years, and continued dreaming throughout all this time whenever he slept; when the Great Spirit again appeared to him, and told him that, at the end of one year more, he should meet his father, and directed him to start seven days before its expiration, and take with him his two brothers, Nah-ma or Sturgeon, and Pan-ka-hum-ma-wa or Sun-fish, and travel in a direction to the left of sun-rising. After pursuing this course five days, he sent out his two brothers to listen if they could hear a noise, and, if so, to fasten some grass to the end of a pole, erect it, pointing in the direction of the sound, and then return to him.

Early next morning they returned and reported that they had heard sounds which appeared near at hand, and that they had fulfilled his order. They all then started for the place where the pole had been erected; when, on reaching it, Na-na-ma-kee left his party and went alone to the place from whence the sounds proceeded, and found that the white man had arrived and pitched his tent. When he came in sight, his father came out to meet him. He took him by the hand, and welcomed him into his tent. He told him that he was the son of the King of France—that he had been dreaming for four years—that the Great Spirit had directed him to come here, where he should meet a nation of people who had never yet seen a white man—that they should be his children, and he should be their father—that he had communicated these things to the King, his father, who laughed at him, and called him a Ma-she-na, but he insisted on coming here to meet his children, where the Great Spirit had directed him. The King told him that he would neither find land nor people—that this was an uninhabitable region of lakes and mountains; but finding that he would have no peace without it, fitted out a na-pe-qua, manned it, and gave it to him in charge, when he immediately loaded it, set sail and had now landed at the very place that the Great Spirit had told him, in his dreams, he should meet his children. He had now met the man who should, in future, have charge of all the nation. He then presented him with a medal, which he hung round his neck. Na-na-ma-kee informed him of *his* dreaming and told him that his two brothers remained a little way behind. His father gave him a shirt, blanket, and handkerchief, besides a variety of presents, and told him to go and bring his brothers. Having laid aside his buffalo robe, and dressed himself in his new dress, he started to meet his brethren. When they met he explained to them his meeting with the white man, and exhibited to their view the presents that he had made him, took off his medal, and placed it upon Nah-ma, his eldest brother, and requested them both to go with him to his father. They proceeded thither, were ushered into the tent, and after some brief ceremony his father opened his chest and took presents therefrom for the newcomers. He discovered that Na-na-ma-kee had given his medal to Nah-ma. He told him that he had done wrong—he should wear that medal himself, as he had others for his brethren. That which he had given him was a type of the rank he should hold in the nation. That his brethren could only rank as *civil* chiefs, and their duties should consist of taking care of the village, and attending to its civil concerns, whilst his rank, from his superior knowledge, placed him over them all. If the nation got into any difficulty with another, then his puc-co-ha-wa-ma or sovereign decree, must be obeyed. If he declared war, he must lead them on to battle. That the Great Spirit had made him a great and brave general, and had sent him here to give him that medal, and make presents to him for his people. His father remained four days, during which time he gave him guns, powder and lead, spears and lances, and showed him their use, so that in war he could chastise his enemies, and in peace they could kill buffalo, deer, and other game necessary for the comforts and luxuries of life. He then presented the others with various kinds of cooking utensils, and learned them their uses, and having given them a large quantity of goods, as presents, and every other thing necessary for their comfort, he set sail for France, after promising to meet them again, at the same place, after the twelfth moon. The three newly made chiefs returned to their village and explained to Muk-a-ta-quet, their father—who was the principle chief of the nation—what had been said and done.

The old chief had some dogs killed and made a feast preparatory to resigning his sceptre, to which all the nation were invited. Great anxiety prevailed among them to know what the three brothers had seen and heard, when the old chief rose and related to them the sayings and doings of his three sons; and concluded by observing that the Great Spirit had directed that these, his three children, should take the rank and power that had been his, and that he yielded these honors and duties willingly to them, because it was the wish of the Great Spirit, and he could never consent to make him angry. He now presented the great medicine bag to Na-na-ma-kee, and told him that he cheerfully resigned it to him —it is the soul of our nation—it has never yet been disgraced, and I will expect you to keep it unsullied. Some dissension arose among some of them, in consequence of so much power being given to Na-na-ma-kee, he being so young a man. To quiet this, Na-na-ma-kee, during a violent thunder storm, told them that he had caused it and that it was an exemplification of the name the Great Spirit had given him. During the storm the lightning struck, and set fire to a tree close by (a sight they had never witnessed before). He went to it and brought away some of its burning branches, made a fire in the lodge, and seated his brothers thereby, opposite to each other, whilst he stood and addressed his people as follows: "I am yet young, but the Great Spirit has called me to the rank I now hold among you. I have never sought to be any thing more than my birth entitled me. I have not been ambitious, nor was it ever my wish whilst my father lives to have taken his place, nor have I now usurped his power. The Great Spirit caused me to dream for four years; he told me where to go and meet the white man, who would be a kind father to us all. I obeyed his order. I went and have seen our new father. You have all heard what was said and done. The Great Spirit directed him to come and meet me, and it is his order that places me at the head of my nation, the place which my father has willingly resigned. You have all witnessed the power which has been given to me by the Great Spirit, in making that fire, and all that I now ask is, that these, my two chiefs, may never let it go out, that I may preserve peace among you, and administer to the wants of the needy. And should an enemy invade our country, I will then, but not until then, assume command and go forth with my band of brave warriors and endeavor to chastise them.''

At the conclusion of this speech every voice cried out for Na-na-ma-kee—all were satisfied when they found that the Great Spirit had done what they suspected was the work of Na-na-ma-kee, he being a very shrewd young man.

The next spring, according to promise, their French father returned, with his na-pe-qua richly laden with goods, which were distributed among them. He continued for a long time to keep up a regular trade with them, they giving him in exchange for his goods, furs and peltries. After a long time the British overpowered the French, (the two nations being at war) drove them away from Quebec, and took possession of it themselves. The different tribes of Indians around our nation, envying our people, united their forces against him, and succeeded, by their great strength, in driving them to Montreal, and from thence to Mackinac. Here our people first met our British father, who furnished them with goods. Their enemies still pursued them, and drove them to different places on the lake, until they made a village near Green Bay, on what is now called Sac river, having derived its name from this circumstance. Here they held a council with the Foxes, and a national treaty of friendship and alliance was concluded upon. The Foxes abandoned their village and joined the Sacs. This arrangement being mutually obligatory upon both parties, as neither was sufficiently strong to meet their enemies with any hope of success, they soon became as one band or nation of people. They were driven, however, by the combined forces of their enemies, to Wisconsin. They remained here for some time, until a party of their young men, (who had descended Rock river to its mouth) returned and made a favorable report of the country. They all descended to Rock river, drove the Kas-kas-kias from the country, and commenced the erection of their village, determined never to leave it. At this village I was born, being a regular descendant of the first chief, Na-na-ma-kee, or Thunder. Few, if any, events of note transpired within my recollection, until about my fifteenth year, I was not allowed to paint, or wear feathers; but distinguished myself at that early age, by wounding an enemy; consequently I was placed in the ranks of the braves.

Soon after this, a trading chief of the Muscow nation, came to our village for recruits to go to war against the Osages, our common enemy. I volunteered my services to go, as my father had joined him; and was proud to have an opportunity to prove to him that I was not an unworthy son, and that I had courage and bravery. It was not long before we met the enemy, when a battle immediately ensued. Standing by my father's side I saw him kill his antagonist, and tear the scalp from his head. Fired with valor and ambition, I rushed furiously upon another, smote him to the earth with my tomahawk, ran my lance through his body, took off his scalp, and returned in triumph to my father. He said nothing, but looked pleased. This was the first man I killed. The enemy's loss in this engagement having been great, they immediately retreated, which put an end to the war for the present. Our party then returned to our village and danced over the scalps we had taken. This was the first time I was permitted to join in a scalp dance.

After a few moons had passed, I led a party of seven, and attacked one hundred Osages. I killed one man, and left him for my comrades to scalp, whilst I was taking an observation of the strength and preparations of the enemy; and finding they were all equally well armed with ourselves, I ordered a retreat, and came off without losing a man. This excursion gained for me great applause, and enabled me, before a great while, to raise a party of one hundred and eighty, to go against the Osages. We left our village in high spirits, and marched over a rugged country, until we reached that of the Osages on the Missouri. We followed their trail until we arrived at their village, which we approached with great caution, expecting that they were all there, but found to our sorrow that they had deserted it. The party became dissatisfied, in consequence of this disappointment, and and all with the exception of five dispersed and returned home. I then placed myself at the head of this brave little band, and thanked the Great Spirit that *so many* remained, and took up the trail of our enemies, with a full determination never to return without some trophy of victory. We followed on for several days, killed one man and a boy, and then returned with their scalps. In consequence of this munity in my camp I was not again enabled to raise a sufficient party to go against the Osages, until about my nineteenth year. During this interim, they committed many outrages on our nation and people. I succeeded at length, in recruiting two hundred efficient warriors, and took up the line of march early in the morning. In a few days we were in the enemy's country, and had not traveled far before we met an equal force to contend with. A general battle immediately commenced, although my braves were considerably fatigued by forced marches. Each party fought desperately. The enemy seemed unwilling to yield the ground, and we were determined to conquer or die. A large number of the Osages were killed, and many wounded, before they commenced retreating. A band of warriors more brave, skillful, and efficient than mine, could not be found. In this engagement I killed five men and one squaw, and had the good fortune to take the scalps of all I struck, except one. The enemy's loss in this engagement was about one hundred men. ours nineteen. We now returned to our village, well pleased with our success, and danced over the scalps we had taken. The Osages in consequence of their great loss in this battle, became satisfied to remain on their own lands, and ceased, for awhile, their depredations on our nation. Our attention, therefore, was directed towards an ancient enemy, who had decoyed and murdered some of our helpless women and children. I started with my father, who took command of a small party, and proceeded against the enemy. We met near Meramec, and an action ensued; the Cherokees having greatly the advantage in numbers. Early in this engagement my father was wounded in the thigh, but had the pleasure of killing his antagonist before he fell. Seeing that he had fallen, I assumed command, and fought desperately until the enemy commenced retreating before us. I returned to my father to administer to his necessities, but nothing could be done for him. The *medicine man* said the wound was mortal, and from which he soon after died.

In this battle I killed three men, and wounded several, the enemy's loss being twenty-eight and ours seven. I now fell heir to the great medicine bag of my forefathers which had belonged to my father. I took it, buried our dead, and returned with my party, all sad and sorrowful, to our village in consequence of the loss of my father. Owing to this misfortune, I blacked my face, fasted, and prayed to the Great Spirit for five years, during which time I remained in a civil capacity, hunting and fishing.

The Osages having commenced aggressions on our people, and the Great Spirit having taken pity on me, I took a small party and went against the enemy, but could only find six men. Their forces being so weak, I thought it cowardly to kill them, but took them prisoners, and carried them to our Spanish father at St. Louis, and gave them up to him; and then returned to our village. Determined on the final extermination of the Osages, for the injuries our nation and people had received from them, I commenced recruiting a strong force, immediately on my return, and started in the third moon with five hundred Sacs and Foxes, and one hundred Ioways, and marched against the enemy. We continued our march several days before we came upon their trail, which was discovered late in the day. We encamped for the night, made an early start next morning, and before sundown fell upon forty lodges, and killed all their inhabitants, except two squaws, whom I captured and made prisoners. During the attack I killed seven men and two boys, with my own hand.

In the engagement many of the bravest warriors among the Osages were killed, which caused the balance of their nation to remain on their own lands, and cease their aggressions upon our hunting grounds. The loss of my father by the Cherokees made me anxious to avenge his death, by the annihilation, if possible, of all their race. I accordingly commenced recruiting another party to go against them.

Having succeeded in this, I started with my party, and went into their country, but only found five of their people, whom I took prisoners. I afterward released four men, the other, a young squaw, we brought home. Great as was my hatred for this people, I could not kill so small a party. During the close of the ninth moon, I led a large party against the Chippewas, Kaskaskias and Osages. This was the commencement of a long and arduous campaign, which terminated in my thirty-fifth year, having had seven regular engagements, and a number of small skirmishes. During this campain several hundred of the enemy were slain. I killed thirteen of their bravest warriors with my own hand.

Our enemies having now been driven from our hunting grounds, with so great a loss as they sustained, we returned in peace to our villages; and after the season of mourning and burying our dead relatives, and of feast dancing had passed, we commenced preparations for our winter's hunt. in which we were very successful. We generally paid a visit to St. Louis every summer; but in consequence of the protracted war in which we had been engaged. I had not been there for some years. Our difficulties having all been settled, I concluded to take a small party that summer, and go down to see our Spanish father. We went, and on our arrival put up our lodges where the Market House now stands. After painting and dressing, we called to see our Spanish father, and were well received. He gave us a variety of presents and plenty of provisions. We danced through the town as usual, and the inhabitants all seemed to be well pleased. They appeared to us like brothers, and always gave us good advice. On my next and last visit to my Spanish father, I discovered, on landing, that all was not right; every countenance seemed sad and gloomy; I imagined the cause, and was informed the Americans were coming to take possession of the town and country, and then we should lose our Spanish father. This news made myself and band sad, because we had always heard bad accounts of the Americans from Indians who had lived near them, and we were sorry to lose our Spanish father, who had always treated us with great friendship.

A few days afterwards the Americans arrived. I took my band, and went to take leave for the last time, of our father. The Americans came to see him also. Seeing them approach, we passed out at one door as they entered another, and immediately started in our canoes for our village on Rock river, not liking the change any more than our friends at St. Louis appeared to.

On arriving at our village we gave the news that strange people had taken St. Louis, and that we should never see our Spanish father again. This information made all our people sorry.

Some time afterwards a boat came up the river with a young American chief [Lieutenant (afterwards General) Pike] and a small party of soldiers. We heard of him some time after he had passed Salt river. Some of our young braves watched him every day, to see what sort of people he had on board.

The boat at length arrived at Rock river, and the young chief came on shore with his interpreter, made a speech, and gave us some presents. We, in return, presented him with some meat and such provisions as we could spare. We were all well pleased with the speech of the young chief. He gave us good advice; said our American father would treat us well. He presented us an American flag, which was hoisted. He then requested us to pull down our British flags and give him our British medals, promising to send us others on his return to St. Louis. This we declined, as we wished to have two fathers. When the young chief started, we sent runners to the Fox village, some miles distant, to direct them to treat him well as he passed, which they did. He went to the head of the Mississippi and then returned to St. Louis. We did not see any Americans again for sometime, being supplied with goods by British traders.

We were fortunate in not giving up our medals, for we learned afterwards from our traders, that the chiefs high up on the Mississippi who gave theirs, never received any in exchange for them. But the fault was not with the young American chief. He was a good man, and a great brave, and died in his country's service.

Some moons after this young chief descended the Mississippi one of our people killed an American, and was confined in the prison at St. Louis for the offence. We held a council at our village to see what could be done for him, which determined that Quash-qua-me, Pa-she-pa-ho, Ou-che-qua-ka and Ha-she-quar-hi-qua should go down to St. Louis, see our American father, and do all they could to have our friend released, by paying for the person killed, thus covering the blood, and satisfying the relatives of the man murdered. This being the only means with us for saving a person who had killed another, and we then though it was the same way with the whites.

The party started with the good wishes of the whole nation, hoping they would accomplish the object of their mission. The relatives of the prisoner blacked their faces and fasted, hoping the Great Spirit would take pity on them, and return the husband and father to his wife and children. Quash-qua-me and party

30

remained a long time absent. They at length returned and encamped a short distance below the village, but did not come up that day, nor did any person approach their camp. They appeared to be dressed in *fine coats* and had medals.

From these circumstances, we were in hopes that they had brought good news. Early the next morning the Council Lodge was crowded. Quash-que-me and party came up and gave us the following account of their mission:

On their arrival at St. Louis, they met their American father, and explained to him their business, and urged the release of their friend. The American chief told them he wanted land, and they agreed to give him some on the west side of the Mississippi, and some on the Illinois side, opposite the Jeffreon. When the business was all arranged, they expected to have their friend released to come home with them. But about the time they were ready to start, their friend was let out of prison, who ran a short distance and was shot dead. This was all they could recollect of what was said and done. They had been drunk the greater part of the time they were in St. Louis.

This is all myself and nation knew of the treaty of 1804. It has been explained to me since. I find by that treaty all our country east of the Mississippi, and south of the Jeffreon, was ceded to the United States for *one thousand dollars* a year. I will leave it to the people of the United States to say whether our nation was properly represented in this treaty, or whether we received a fair compensation for the extent of country ceded by those four individuals. I could say much about this treaty, but I will not at this time. It has been the origin of all our difficulties.

Some time after this treaty was made, a war chief with a party of soldiers came up in keel boats and encamped a short distance above the head of the Des Moines rapids, and commenced cutting timber and building houses. The news of their arrival was soon carried to all the villages, where council after council was held.

We could not understand the intention, or reason, why the Americans wanted to build houses at that place, but were told that they were a party of soldiers, who had brought great guns with them, and looked like a war party of whites. A number of our people immediately went down to see what was doing, myself among them. On our arrival we found they were building a fort. The soldiers were busily engaged in cutting timber, and I observed that they took their arms with them when they went to the woods, and the whole party acted as they would do in an enemy's county. The chiefs held a council with the officers, or head men, of the party, which I did not attend, but understood from them that the war chief had said that they were building houses for a trader who was coming there to live, and would sell us goods very cheap, and that these soldiers were to remain to keep him company! We were pleased at this information, and hoped it was all true, but we could not believe that all these buildings were intended merely for the accommodation of a trader. Being distrustful of their intention, we were anxious for them to leave off building, and go down the river again. By this time a considerable number of Indians had arrived to see what was doing. I discovered that the whites were alarmed.

Some of our men watched a party of soldiers, who went out to work, carrying their arms, which were laid aside before they commenced. Having stolen up quietly to the spot, they seized the guns and gave a yell!

The party threw down their axes and ran for their arms, but found them gone, and themselves surrounded. Our young men laughed at them, and returned them their guns. When this party came to the fort they reported what had been done, and the war chief made a serious affair of it. He called our chiefs to council inside of his fort. This created considerable excitement in our camp; every one wanted to know what was going to be done, and the picketing which had been put up, being low, every Indian crowded around the fort, and got upon blocks of wood and old barrels, that they might see what was going on inside. Some were armed with guns, and others with bows and arrows. We used this precaution, seeing that the soldiers had their guns loaded, and having seen them load their *big gun* that morning.

A party of our braves commenced dancing and proceeded up to the gate, with an intention of going in, but were stopped.

The council immediately broke up; the soldiers with their arms in their hands, rushed out of their rooms where they had been concealed, the cannon was hauled in front of the gateway, and a soldier came running with fire in his hand, ready to apply the match. Our braves gave way, and all retired to the camp.

There was no preconcerted plan to attack the whites at that time, but I am of the opinion now, had our party got into the fort, all the whites would have been killed, as the British soldiers had been at Mackinaw many years before.

We broke up our camp and returned to Rock river. A short time afterwards, the first party received a reinforcement, among whom we observed some of our old friends from St. Louis.

Soon after our return from Fort Madison, runners came to our village from the Shawnee Prophet* with invitations for us to meet him on the Wabash. Accordingly a party went from each village. All of our party returned, among whom came a Prophet, who explained to us the bad treatment the different nations of Indians had received from the Americans, by giving them a few presents, and taking their land from them. I remember well his saying, *If*

---

* Tecumseh's brother.

you do not join your friends on the Wabash, the Americans will take this very village from you. I little thought then that his words would come true, supposing that he used these arguments merely to encourage us to join him; we agreed that we would not. He then returned to the Wabash, where a party of Winnebagoes had arrived, and preparations were making for war. A battle soon ensued, in which several Winnebagoes were killed. As soon as their nation heard of this battle, and that some of their people had been killed, they started war parties in different directions. One to the mining country, one to Prairie du Chein, and another to Fort Madison. This last returned by our village, and exhibited several scalps which they had taken. Their success induced several other parties to go against the fort. Myself and several of my band joined the last party, and were determined to take the fort. We arrived in the vicinity during the night.

The spies that we had sent out several days before, to watch the movements of those at the garrison, and ascertain their numbers, came to us and gave the following information: That a keelboat had arrived from below that evening with seventeen men; that there were about fifty men in the fort, and that they marched out every morning at sun-rise to exercise. It was immediately determined that we should take a position as near as we could (to conceal ourselves) to the place where the soldiers would come; and when the signal was given each man to fire and then rush into the fort.

I dug a hole with my knife deep enough (by placing a few weeds around it) to conceal myself. I was so near the fort that I could hear the sentinel walking. By daybreak I had finished my work, and was anxiously awaiting the rising of the sun. The drum beat; I examined the priming of my gun, and eagerly watched for the gate to open. It did open, but instead of the troops marching out, a young man came alone. The gate closed after him. He passed close by me, so near that I could have killed him with my knife, but I let him pass. He kept the path towards the river; and had he had gone one step out of it, he must have come upon us, and would have been killed. He returned immediately and entered the gate. I would now have rushed for the gate and entered it with him, but I feared our party was not prepared to follow me.

The gate opened again; four men came out, and went down to the river after wood. Whilst they were gone another man came out, walked towards the river, and was fired upon and killed by a Winnebago. The others immediately ran for the fort, and two of them were killed. We then took shelter under the bank, out of reach of fire from the fort.

The firing now commenced from both parties, and continued all day. I advised our party to set fire to the fort, and commenced preparing arrows for that purpose. At night we made the attempt, and succeeded in firing the buildings several times, but without effect, as the fire was always extinguished. The next day I took my rifle, and shot in two the cord by which they hoisted their flag, and prevented them from raising it again. We continued firing until all of our ammunition was expended; and finding that we could not take the fort, returned home, having had one Winnebago killed, and one wounded during the siege. I have since learned that the trader, who lived in the fort, wounded the Winnebago when he was scalping the first man that was killed. The Winnebago recovered, is now living, and is very friendly disposed towards the trader, believing him to be a *great brave*.

Soon after our return home, news reached us that war was going to take place between the British and the Americans. Runners continued to arrive from different tribes, all confirming the report of the expected war. The British agent, Col. Dixon, was holding talks with, and making presents to, the different tribes. I had not made up my mind whether to join the British or remain neutral. *I had not discovered one good trait in the character of the Americans that had come to the country.* They made *fair promises* but *never fulfilled them.* Whilst the British made but few, but we could always rely upon their word. One of our people having killed a Frenchman at Prairie du Chien the British took him prisoner, and said they would shoot him the next day. His family were encamped a short distance below the mouth of the Wisconsin. He begged permission to go and see them that night, as he was to die the next day. They permitted him to go, after promising to return the next morning by sunrise. He visited his family, which consisted of a wife and six children. I cannot describe their meeting and parting, to be understood by the whites; as it appears that their feelings are acted upon by certain rules laid down by their preachers, whilst ours are governed only by the monitor within us. He parted from his wife and children, hurried through the prairie to the fort, and arrived in time. The soldiers were ready, and immediately marched out and shot him down. I visited his family, and by hunting and fishing, provided for them until they reached their relatives. Why did the Great Spirit ever send the whites to this island, to drive us from our homes, and introduce among us poisonous liquors, disease, and death? They should have remained on the island where the Great Spirit first placed them.

But I will proceed with my story; my memory however is not very good. Since my late visit to the white people, I have still a buzzing in my ears, from the noise, and may give some parts of my story out of place, but I will endeavor to be correct. Several of our chiefs and head men were called upon to go to Washington, to see their Great Father. They started; and during their absence, I went to Peoria, on the Illinois river, to see an old friend, a trader, to get his advice. He was a man that always told us the truth, and knew everything that was going on. When I arrived at Peoria, he was not there, but had gone to Chicago. I visited the Pottawatomie villages, and then returned to Rock river. Soon after which, our friends returned from their visit to our Great Father and related what had been said and done. Their Great Father (they said) wished us, in the event of a war taking place with England, not to interfere on either side, but to remain neutral. He did not want our help, but wished us to hunt and support our families and live in peace. He said that British traders would not be permitted to come on the Mississippi, to furnish us with goods, but we would be well supplied by an American trader. Our chiefs then told him that the British traders always gave us credits in the fall, for guns, powder, and goods, to enable us to hunt and clothe our families. He replied that the trader at Fort Madison would have plenty of goods, that we should go there in the fall, and he would supply us on credit, as the British trader had done. The party gave a good account of what they had seen, and the kind treatment they received.

This information pleased us all very much. We all agreed to follow our Great Father's advice, and not interfere with the war. Our women were much pleased at this good news. Everything went on cheerfully in our village. We resumed our pastimes of playing ball, horse racing, and dancing, which had been laid aside when this great war was first taiked about. We had fine crops of corn, which was now ripe, and our women were engaged in gathering it, and making *caches* to contain it. In a short time we were ready to start to Fort Madison to get our supply of goods, that we might proceed to our hunting grounds. We passed merrily down the river, all in high spirits. I had determined to spend the winter at my old favorite hunting grounds, on Skunk river, and left part of my corn and meal at its mouth, to take up when I returned. Others did the same. Next morning we arrived at the fort, and made our encampment. Myself and principal men paid a visit to the war chief at the fort.

He received us kindly, and gave us some tobacco, pipes and provisions. The trader came in, and we all arose and shook hands with him, for on him all our dependence was placed, to enable us to hunt, and thereby support our families. We waited a long time, expecting the trader would tell us that he had orders from our Great Father to supply us with goods, but he said nothing on the subject. I got up and told him, in a short speech, what we had come for, and hoped he had plenty of goods to supply us, and told him that he should be well paid in the spring, and concluded by informing him that we had determined to follow our Great Father's advice and not go to war.

He said that he was happy to hear that we intended to remain at peace; that he had a large quantity of goods, and that if we made a good hunt we would be well supplied, but remarked that he had received no instructions to furnish us anything on credit, nor could he give us any without receiving the pay for them on the spot. We informed him what our Great Father had told our chiefs at Washington, and contended that he could supply us if would, believing that our Great Father always spoke the truth. But the war chief said that the trader could not furnish us on credit, and that he had received no instructions from our Great Father at Washington. We left the fort dissatisfied, and went to our camp.

What was now to be done we knew not. We questioned the party that brought us the news from our Great Father that we could get credit for our winter's supplies at this place. They still told the same story, and insisted upon its truth. Few of us slept that night; all was gloom and discontent. In the morning a canoe was seen descending the river; it soon arrived, bearing an express, who brought intelligence that La Gutrie, a British trader, had landed at Rock Island, with two boats loaded with goods, and requested us to come up immediately because he had good news for us, and a variety of presents. The express presented us with tobacco, pipes and wampum. The news ran through our camp like fire in the prairie. Our lodges were soon taken down, and all started for Rock Island. Here ended all hopes of our remaining at peace, having been forced into war by being deceived. Our party was not long in getting to Rock Island. When we came in sight and saw tents pitched we yelled, fired our guns, and commenced beating our drums. Guns were immediately fired at the island, returning our salute, and a British flag hoisted. We landed and were cordially received by La Gutrie, and then smoked the pipe with him, after which he made a speech to us, that had been sent by Col. Dixon, and gave us a number of handsome presents, a large silk flag and a keg of rum, and told us to retire, take some refreshments and rest ourselves, as he would have more to say to us the next day. We accordingly retired to our lodges and spent the night. The next morning we called upon him and told him that we wanted his two boat loads of goods to divide among our people, for which he should be well paid in the spring with furs and peltries. He consented, told us to take them and do as we pleased with them.

Whilst our people were dividing the goods, he took me aside, and informed me that Col. Dixon was at Green Bay with twelve boats loaded with goods, guns and ammunition, and wished me to raise a party immediately and go to him. He said that our friend, the trader at Peoria, was collecting the Pottowatomies, and would be there before us. I communicated this information to my braves, and a party of two hundred warriors was soon collected and ready to depart.

I paid a visit to the lodge of an old friend, who had been the comrade of my youth, and had been on many war paths with me, but was now crippled and no longer able to travel. He had a son that I had adopted as my own, who had hunted with me the two preceding winters. I wished my old friend to let him go with me. He objected, saying that he could not get his support if his son left him; that I would be gone, and he had no other dependence than his son. I offered to leave my son in his place, but he still refused. He said he did not like the war; he had been down the river and had been well treated by the Americans, and could not fight against them. He had promised to winter near a white settler, above Salt River, and must take his son with him. We parted. I soon concluded my arrangements, and started with my party to Green Bay. On our arrival there we found a large encampment and were well received by Dixon and the war chiefs that were with him. He gave us plenty of provisons, tobacco and pipes, and said he would hold a council with us the next day.

In the encampment I found a large number of Pottowatomies, Kickapoos, Ottawas, and Winnebagoes. I visited all their camps and found them all in high spirits. They had all received new guns, ammunition, and a variety of clothing. In the evening a messenger came to me to visit Col. Dixon. I went to his tent, in which were two other war chiefs and an interpreter. He received me with a hearty shake of the hand and presented me to the other chiefs, who shook my hand cordially and seemed much pleased to see me. After I was seated, Col. Dixon said: "Gen. Black Hawk, I sent for you to explain to you what we are going to do, and the reasons that have brought us here. Our friend, La Gutrie, informs us, in the letter you brought from him, what has lately taken place. You will now have to hold us fast by the hand. Your English father has found out that the Americans want to take your country from you, and has sent me and his braves to drive them back to their own country. He has likewise sent a large quantity of arms and ammunition, and we want all your warriors to join us." He then placed a medal around my neck, and gave me a paper and a silk flag, saying: "You are to command all the braves that leave here day after to-morrow, to join our braves near Detroit." I told him that I was very much disappointed, as I wanted to descend the Mississippi and make war upon the settlements. He said he had been ordered to lay the country waste around St. Louis; that he had been a trader on the Mississippi many years and had always been kindly treated, and could not consent to send brave men to murder women and children. That there were no soldiers there to fight; but where he was going to send us there were a number of soldiers; and, if we defeated them, the Mississippi country should be ours. I was pleased with this speech; it was spoken by a *brave*. I inquired about my old friend, the trader at Peoria, and observed that I expected he would have been here before me. He shook his head, and said he had sent express after express to him, and had offered him large sums of money to come and bring all the Pottowotamies and Kickapoos with him; but he refused, saying your British father had not money enough to induce him to join us. I have now laid a trap for him. I have sent *Gomo* and a party of Indians to take him prisoner and bring him here alive. I expect him in a few days. The next day, arms, ammunition, tomahawks, knives and clothing were given to my band. We had a great feast in the evening, and in the morning following I started with about five hundred braves to join the British army. The British war chief accompanied us. We passed Chicago. The fort had been evacuated by the American soldiers, who had marched for Fort Wayne. They were attacked a short distance from that fort and defeated. They had a considerable quantity of powder in the fort at Chicago, which they had promised to the Indians; but the night before they marched they destroyed it. I think it was thrown into the well. If they had fulfilled their word to the Indians I think they would have gone safe. On our arrival, I found that the Indians had several prisoners. I advised them to treat them well. We continued our march and joined the British army below Detroit; and soon after had a fight. The Americans fought well, and drove us back with considerable loss. I was surprised at this, as I had been told that the Americans could not fight.

Our next movement was against a fortified place. I was stationed with my braves, to prevent any person going to, or coming from the fort. I found two men taking care of cattle, and took them prisoners. I would not kill them, but delivered them to the British war chief. Soon after several boats came down the river full of American soldiers. They landed on the opposite side, took the British batteries, and pursued the soldiers that had left them. They went too far without knowing the forces of the British, and were defeated. I hurried across the river, anxious for an opportunity to show the courage of my braves; but before we reached the ground all was over. The British had taken many prisioners, and the Indians were killing them. I immediately put a stop to it, as I never thought it brave, but cowardly, to kill an unarmed and helpless enemy. We remained here some time. I cannot detail what took place, as I was stationed with my braves in the woods. It appeared, however, that the British could not take this fort, for we were marched to another some distance off. When we approached it, I found it a small stockade, and concluded that there were not many men in it. The British war chief sent a flag; Col. Dixon carried it, and returned. He said a young war chief commanded, and would not give up without fighting. Dixon came to me and said, "You will see to-morrow how easily we will take that fort." I was of opinion that they would take it; but when the morning came I was disappointed. The British advanced, commenced an attack, and fought like braves, but by braves in the fort were defeated, and a great number killed. The British army were making preparations to retreat. I was now tired of being with them; our success being bad, and having got no plunder, I determined on leaving them and returning to Rock river, to see what had become of my wife and children, as I had not heard from them since I started. That night I took about twenty of my braves and left the British camp for home. We met no person on our journey until we reached the Illinois river. Here we found two lodges of Pottowotamies. They received us very friendly, and gave us something to eat; and inquired about their friends that were with the British. They said that there had been some fighting on the Illinois, and that my old friend, the trader at Peoria, had been taken prisoner. "By Gomo and his party?" I immediately inquired. They said no, but by the Americans, who came up with two boats. They took him and the French settlers, and then burnt the village of Peoria. They could give us no news respecting our people on Rock river. In three days more we were in the vicinity of our village, where I discovered a smoke ascending from a hollow in the bluffs. I directed my party to proceed to the village, as I wished to go alone to the place from whence the smoke proceeded, to see who was there. I approached the spot, and when I came in view of the fire, saw a mat stretched and an old man sitting upon it in sorrow. At any other time I would have turned away without disturbing him, knowing that he had come there to be alone to humble himself before the Great Spirit that he might take pity on him. I approached and seated myself beside him. He gave one look at me, and then fixed his eyes on the ground. *It was my old friend.* I anxiously inquired for his son, and what had befallen our people. My old comrade seemed scarcely alive; he must have fasted a long time. I lighted my pipe and put it in his mouth. He eagerly drew a few puffs, cast up his eyes which met mine, and recognized me. His eyes were glassy! He would again have fallen off into forgetfulness, had I not given him some water, which revived him. I again inquired what had befallen our people, and what had become of our son? In a feeble voice he said: "Soon after your departure to join the British, I descended the river with a small party, to winter at the place I told you the white man had requested me to come to. When we arrived I found a fort built, and the white family that had invited me to come and hunt near them had removed to it. I then paid a visit to the fort, to tell the white people that myself and little band were friendly, and that we wished to hunt in the vicinity of their fort. The war chief who commanded it told me that we might hunt on the Illinois side of the Mississippi, and no person would trouble us; that the horsemen only ranged on the Missouri side, and he had directed them not to cross the river. I was pleased with this assurance of safety, and immediately crossed over and made my winter's camp.

"Game was plenty; we lived happy, and often talked of you. My boy regretted your absence, and the hardships you would have to undergo.

"We had been here about two moons, when my boy went out as usual, to hunt. Night came on and he did not return; I was alarmed for his safety, and passed a sleepless night. In the morning my old woman went to the other lodges and gave the alarm, and all turned out in pursuit. There being snow on the ground, they soon came upon the track, and after pursuing it some distance, found he was on the trail of a deer, that led towards the river. They soon came to the place where he had stood and fired, and found a deer hanging upon the branch of a tree, which had been skinned. But here were found the tracks of white men. They had taken my boy prisoner. These tracks led across the river and then down towards the fort. My friends followed them and soon found my boy lying dead. He had been most cruelly murdered! His face was shot to pieces, his body stabbed in several places, and his head scalped. His arms were tied behind him."

The old man paused for some time, and then told me that his wife had died on her way up the Mississippi. I took the hand of my old friend in mine, and pledged myself to avenge the death of his son. It was now dark, a terrible storm commenced raging, with heavy torrents of rain, thunder, and lightning. I had taken my blanket off and wrapped around the old man. When the storm abated, I kindled a fire, and took hold of my old friend to remove him near it, but *he was dead.*

I remained with him the balance of the night. Some of my party came early in the morning to look for me, and assisted me in burying him on the peak of the bluff. I then returned to the village with my friends. I visited the grave of my old friend for the last time, as I ascended Rock river. On my arrival at the village, I was met by the chiefs and braves, and conducted to a lodge that had been prepared to receive me. After eating, I gave an account of what I had seen and done. I explained to them the manner the British and Americans fought. Instead of stealing upon each other, and taking every advantage to kill the enemy and save their own people, as we do, they march out in open day light, and fight, regardless of the number of warriors they may lose. After the battle is over they retire to feast and drink wine, as if nothing had happend; after which, they make a statement in writing of what they have done, each party claiming the victory and neither giving an account of half the number that have been killed on their own side.   They all fought like braves, but would not do to lead a war party with us.   Our maxim is to kill the enemy and save our own men.   Those chiefs would do to paddle a canoe, but not to steer it.   The Americans shoot better than the British, but their soldiers are not so well clothed, or provided for.   The village chief informed me that after I started with my braves, and the parties who followed, the nation was reduced to so small a party of fighting men, that they would have been unable to defend themselves, if the Americans had attacked them; that all the women and children, and old men, belonging to the warriors who had joined the British, were left with them to provide for; and that a council was held, which agreed that Quash-qua-me, the Lance, and other chiefs, with the old men, women and children, and such others as chose to accompany them, should descend the Mississippi and go to St. Louis, and place themselves under the protection of the American chief stationed there.   They accordingly went down to St. Louis, and were received as the friendly band of our nation—sent up the Missouri and provided for, whilst their friends were assisting the British.   Ke-o-Kuck was then introduced to me as the war chief of the braves then in the village.   I inquired how he had become a chief.   They said that a large armed force was seen by their spies going towards Peoria; that fears were entertained that they would come upon and attack our village, and that a council had been convened to decide upon the best course to be adopted, which concluded upon leaving the village and going on the west side of the Mississippi, to get out of the way.   Ke-o-Kuck during the sitting of the council had been sitting at the door of the lodge, where he remained until old Wa-co-me came out.   He then told him that he had heard what they had decided upon, and was anxious to go in and be permitted to speak before the council adjourned.   Wa-co-me returned and asked leave for Ke-o-Kuck to come in and make a speech.   His request was granted, Ke-o-Kuck entered and addressed the chiefs.   He said: "I have heard with sorrow, that you have determined to leave our vallage, and cross the Mississippi, merely because you have been told that the Americans were seen coming in this direction.   Would you leave our village, desert our homes, and fly before an enemy approaches?   Would you leave al.—even the graves of our fathers, to the mercy of our enemy, without trying to defend them?   Give me charge of your warriors; I'll defend the village, and you may sleep in safety."   The council consented that Ke-o-Kuck should be a war chief.   He marshalled his braves, sent out spies, and advanced himself on the trail leading to Peoria. They returned without seeing an enemy. The Americans did not come by our village. All were well satisfied with the appointment of Ke-o-Kuck. He used every precaution that our people should not be surprised. This is the manner in which, and the cause of receiving the appointment. I was satisfied, and then started to visit my wife and children. I found them, and my boys were growing finely. It is not customary for us to say much about our women, as they generally perform their part cheerfully, and never interfere with business belonging to the men. This is the only wife I ever had, or ever will have. She is a good woman, and teaches my boys to be brave.

Here I would have rested myself, and enjoyed the comforts of my lodge, but I could not; I had promised to avenge the death of my adopted son. I immediately collected a party of thirty braves, and explained to them my object in making this war party—it being to avenge the death of my adopted son, who had been cruelly and wantonly murdered by the whites. I had explained to them the pledge I had made his father, and told them that they were the last words he had heard spoken. All were willing to go with me, to fulfill my word. We started in canoes and descended the Mississippi until we arrived near the place where Fort Madison had stood. It had been abandoned by the whites and burnt, nothing remained but the chimneys. We were pleased to see that the white people had retired from our country. We proceeded down the river again. I landed with one brave, near Cap au Gris; the remainder of the party went to the mouth of the Cuivre. I hurried across the trail that led to the mouth of the Cuivre to a fort, and soon after heard firing at the mouth of the creek. Myself and brave concealed ourselves on the side of the road. We had not remained here long before two men riding one horse came in full speed from the direction of the firing. When they came sufficiently near we fired; the horse jumped and both men fell. We rushed towards them—one rose and ran. I followed him, and was gaining on him, when he ran over a pile of rails that had lately been made, seized a stick and struck at me. I now had an opportunity to see his face—I knew him! He had been at Quash-qua-me's village, to learn his people how to plow. We looked upon him as a good man. I did not wish to kill him, and pursued him no further. I returned and met my brave; he said he had killed the other man and had his scalp in his hand. We had not proceeded far before we met the man, staggering like a drunken man, all covered with blood. This was the most terrible sight that I had ever seen. I told my comrade to kill him, to put him out of his misery; I could not look at him. I passed on and heard a rustling in the bushes, and distinctly saw two little boys concealing themselves. I thought of my own children, and passed on without noticing them. My comrade here joined me, and in a little while we met the balance of our party. I told them that we would be pursued, and directed them to follow me. We crossed the creek and formed ourselves in the timber. We had not been here long before a party of mounted men rushed at full speed upon us. I took deliberate aim and shot the man leading the party. He fell from his horse lifeless. All my people fired, but without effect. The enemy rushed upon us without giving us time to reload. They surrounded us and forced us to run into a deep sink hole, at the bottom of which there were some bushes. We loaded our guns, and awaited the appearance of the enemy. They rushed to the edge of the hole and fired, killing one of our men. We returned the fire instantly and killed one of their men. We reloaded and commenced digging holes in the side of the bank to protect ourselves, whilst a party watched the movements of the enemy, expecting that their whole force would be upon us immediately. Some of my warriors commenced singing their death songs. I heard the whites talking, and called to them to come out and fight. I did not like my situation, and wished the matter settled. I soon heard chopping and knocking; I could not imagine what they were doing. Soon after they ran up wheels with a battery on it, and fired down without hurting any of us. I called to them again and told them if they were brave men to come down and fight us. They gave up the seige and returned to their fort about dusk. There were eighteen in this trap with me. We all got out safe and found one white man dead on the edge of the sink hole. They did not remove him for fear of our fire. We scalped him and placed our dead man upon him. We could not have left him in a better situation than on an enemy.

We had now effected our purpose, and started back by land, thinking it unsafe to return in our canoes. I found my wife and children and the greater part of our people at the mouth of the Iowa river. I now determined to remain with my family, and hunt for them, and humble myself before the Great Spirit and return thanks to him for preserving me through the war. I made my hunting camp on English river, (a branch of the Iowa). During the winter a party Pottowatomies came from the Illinois to pay me a visit; among them was Wash-e-own, an old man, that had formally lived in our village. He informed us that in the fall the Americans had built a fort at Peoria, and prevented them from going down the Sangomon to hunt.

He said they were very much distressed, that Gomo had returned from the British army, and brought news of their defeat near Malden, and told us he went to the American chief with a flag, gave up fighting, and told the chief that he wished to make peace for his nation. The American chief gave him a paper for the war chief at the fort at Peoria, and I visited that fort with Gomo. It was then agreed that there should be no more fighting between the Americans and Pottowatomies; and that two of their chiefs and eight braves, with five Americans, had gone down to St. Louis to have the peace confirmed. "This." said Wash-e-own, "is good news; for we can now go to our hunting grounds, and, for my part, I never had anything to do with this war. The Americans never killed any of our people before the war, nor interfered with our hunting grounds; and I resolved to do nothing against them." I made no reply to these remarks, as the speaker was old, and talked like a child. We gave the Pottowatomies a feast. I presented Wash-e-own with a good horse, my braves gave one to each of his party, and at parting they said they wished us to make peace; which we did not promise, but told them that we would not send out war parties against the settlements. A short time after the Pottowatomies left, a party of thirty braves belonging to our nation, from the peace camp on the Missouri, paid us a visit. They exhibited five scalps which they had taken on the Missouri, and wished us to dance over them, which we willingly joined in. They related the maner in which they had taken these scalps. Myself and braves then showed them the two we had taken near the Cuivre, and told them the reason that induced that war party to go out; as well as the manner and difficulty we had in obtaining these scalps. They recounted to us all that had taken place; the number that had been killed by the peace party as they were called and recognized, which far surpassed what our own warriors who had joined the British had done. This party came for the purpose of joining the British. I advised them to return to the peace party, and told them the news the Pottowatomies had brought. They returned to Missouri, accompanied by some of my braves, whose families were with the peace party.

After sugar-making was over, in the spring, I visited the Fox village at the lead mines. They had nothing to do with the war and were not in mourning. I remained there some days, and spent my time pleasantly with them, in dancing and feasting. I then paid a visit to the Pottowatomie village on the Illinois river, and learned that Sa-na-tu-wa and Ta-ta-puc-key had been to St. Louis. Gomo told me that peace had been made between his people and the Americans, and that seven of his party remained with the war chief to make the peace stronger. He then told me that Wash-e-own was dead. That he had been to the fort to carry some wild fowls to exchange for tobacco, pipes, etc. That he had got some tobacco and a little flour, and left the fort before sundown, but had not proceeded far before he was ‚shot dead by a war chief who had concealed himself near the path for that purpose, and then dragged him to the lake and threw him in where I afterwards found him. I have since given two horses and my rifle to his relations, not to break peace; which they had agreed to. I remained some at the village with Gomo, and went went with him to the fort to pay a visit to the war chief. I spoke the Pottowatomie tongue well, and was taken for one of their people by the chief. He treated us very friendly, and said he was very much displeased about the murder of Wash-e-own, and would find out and punish the person that killed him. He made some inquiries about the Sacs, which I answered. On my return to Rock river, I was informed that a party of soldiers had gone up the Mississippi to build a fort at Prairie du Chein. They had stopped near our village, and appeared to be friendly, and were kindly treated by our people. We commenced repairing our lodges, putting our village in order, and clearing our corn fields. We divided the fields of the party on the Missouri, among those that wanted, on condition that they should be relinquished to the owners when they returned from the peace establishment. We were again happy in our village; our women went cheerfully to work, and all moved on harmoniously. Sometime afterwards five or six boats arrived, loaded with soldiers going to Prairie du Chein to reinforce the garrison. They appeared friendly, and were well received. We held a council with the war chief. We had no intention of hurting him, or any of his party, or we could easily have defeated them. They remained with us all day, and used, and gave us plenty of whiskey. During the night a party arrived and brought us six kegs of powder. They told us that the British had gone to Prairie du Chein and taken the fort, and wished us to join them again in the war, which we agreed to. I collected my warriors, and determined to pursue the boats, which had sailed with a fair wind. If we had known the day before, we could easily have taken them all, as the war chief used no precautions to prevent it. I immediately started with my party, by land, in pursuit, thinking that some of their boats might get aground, or that the Great Spirit might put them in our power if he wished them taken and their people killed.

About half-way up the rapids I had a full view of the boats, all sailing with a strong wind. I soon discovered that one boat was badly managed, and was suffered to be driven ashore by the wind. They landed by running hard aground, and lowered their sail. The others passed on. This boat the Great Spirit gave us. We approached it cautiously, and fired upon the men on shore. All that could, hurried aboard, but they were unable to push off, being fast aground. We advanced to the river's bank, under cover, and commenced firing at the boat. Our balls passed through the plank and did execution, as I could hear them screaming in the boat. I encouraged my braves to continue firing. Several guns were fired from the boat without effect. I prepared my bow and arrows to throw fire to the sail, which was lying on the boat, and after two or three attempts, succeeded in setting the sail on fire. The boat was soon in flames. About this time one of the boats that had passed returned, dropped anchor and swung in close to the boat on fire, and took off all the people, except those killed and badly wounded. We could distinctly see them passing from one boat to the other, and fired on them with good aim. We wounded the war chief in this way. Another boat now came down, dropped her anchor, which did not take hold, and was drifted ashore. The other boat cut her cable and drifted down the river, leaving their comrades without attempting to assist them. We then commenced an attack upon this boat, and fired several rounds. They did not return the fire. We thought they were afraid, or had but a small number on board. I therefore ordered a rush to the boat. When we got near they fired and killed two of our people, being all that we lost in the engagement. Some of their men jumped out and pushed off the boat, and thus got away without losing a man. I had a good opinion of this war chief, he managed so much better than the others. It would give me pleasure to shake him by the hand. We now put out the fire on the captured boat, to save the cargo, when a skiff was discovered coming down the river. Some of our people cried out, here comes an express from Prairie du Chien. We hoisted the British flag, but they would not land. They turned their little boat around and rowed up the river. We directed a few shots at them, in order to bring them to, but they were so far off that we could not hurt them. I found several barrels of whisky on the captured boat, and knocked in their heads and emptied out the *bad medicine*.

I next found a box full of small bottles and packages, which appeared to be medicine also; such as the medicine men kill the white people with when they get sick. This I threw into the river; and, continuing my search for plunder, found several guns, large barrels full of clothing, and some cloth lodges, all of which I distributed among my warriors. We now disposed of the dead, and returned to the Fox village, opposite the lower end of Rock, Island, where we put up our new lodges and hoisted the British flag. A great many of our braves were dressed in the uniform clothing which we had taken, which gave our encampment the appearance of a regular camp of soldiers. We placed our sentinels and commenced dancing over the scalps we had taken. Soon after several boats passed down, among them a large boat carrying *big guns*. Our young men followed them some distance, firing at them, but could not do much damage, more than to frighten them. We were now certain that the fort at Prairie du Chien had been taken, as this large boat went up with the first party who built the fort. In the course of the day some of the British came down in a small boat; they had followed the large

31

one, thinking she would get fast in the rapids, in which case they were certain of taking her. They had summoned her on the way down to surrender, but she refused, and now, that she had passed over the rapids in safety, all hope of taking her had vanished. The British landed a big gun and gave us three soldiers to manage it. They complimented us for our bravery in taking the boat, and told us what they had done at Prairie du Chien; gave us a keg of rum, and joined with us in our dancing and feasting. We gave them some things which we had taken from the boat, particularly books and papers. They started the next morning, after promising to return in a few days with a large body of soldiers. We went to work under the direction of the men left with us, and dug up the ground in two places, to put the big gun in, that the men might remain in with it, and be safe. We then sent spies down the river to reconnoitre, who sent word by a runner that several boats were coming up filled with men. I marshalled my forces, and was soon ready for their arrival, and resolved to fight, as we had not yet had a fair fight with the Americans during the war.

The boats arrived in the evening, and stopped at a small willow island nearly opposite to us. During the night we removed our big gun further down, and at day-light next morning commenced firing. We were pleased to see that almost every fire took effect, striking the boats nearly every shot. They pushed off as quickly as possible, and I expected would land and give a fight. I was prepared to meet them, but was soon sadly disappointed, the boats having all started down the river. A party of braves followed to watch where they landed; but they did not stop until they got below the Des Moines rapids, when they landed and commenced building a fort. I collected a few braves and started to the place where it was reported they were building a fort. I did not want a fort in our country, as we wished to go down in the fall to the Two-river country, to hunt—it being our best hunting-ground; and we concluded that if the fort was established, we should be prevented from going to our hunting-ground. I arrived in the vicinity of the fort in the evening, and stopped for the night, on the peak of a high bluff. We made no fire for fear of being observed. Our young men kept watch by turns, whilst the others slept. I was very tired and soon went to sleep. The Great Spirit, during my slumber, told me to go down the bluff to the creek, where I would find a hollow tree cut down; to look into the top of it and I would see a large snake, to observe the direction he was looking, and I would see the enemy close by and unarmed. In the morning I communicated to my braves what the Great Spirit had told me, and took one of them and went down a hollow that led to the creek, and soon came in sight of the place on an opposite hill, where they were building the fort. I saw a great many men. We crawled cautiously on our hands and knees until we got into the bottom, then through the grass and weeds, until we reached the bank of the creek. Here I found a tree that had been cut down. I looked in the top of it and saw a large snake, with his head raised, looking across the creek. I raised myself cautiously and discovered, nearly opposite to me, two war chiefs, walking arm-in-arm, without guns. They turned and walked back towards the place where the men were working at the fort. In a little while they returned, walking immediately towards the spot where we lay concealed, but did not come as near as before. If they had, they would have been killed, for each of us had a good rifle. We crossed the creek and crawled to a bunch of bushes. I again raised myself a little, to see if they were coming, but they went into the fort. By this they saved their lives. We recrossed the creek, and I returned alone, going up the hollow we came down. My brave went down the creek, and, on rising the hill to the left of the one we came down, I could plainly see the men at work, and discovered, in the bottom near the mouth of the creek, a sentinel walking. I watched him attentively, to see if he preceived my companion, who had gone towards him. The sentinel first walked one way and then back again. I observed my brave creeping towards him. The sentinel stopped for some time, and looked in the direction where my brave was concealed. He lay still and did not move the grass, and as the sentinel turned to walk, my brave fired and he fell. I looked towards the fort and saw they were all in confusion, running in every direction, some down a steep bank to the boat. My comrade joined me and we returned to the rest of our party, and all hurried back to Rock river, where we arrived in safety at our village.

I hung up my medicine bag, put away my rifle and spear, and felt as if I should not want them again, as I had no wish to raise any more war parties against the whites without new provocation. Nothing particular happened from this time until spring, except news that the fort below the rapids had been abandoned and burnt. Soon after I returned from my wintering ground we received the information that peace had been made between the British and Americans, and that we were required to make peace also, and were invited to go down to Portage des Sioux for that purpose. Some advised that we should go down, others that we should not. No-mite, our principal civil chief, said he would go as soon as the Foxes came down from the mines. They came, and we all started from Rock river. We had not gone far before our chief was taken sick. We stopped with him at the village on Henderson river. The Foxes went on, and we were to follow as soon as our chief got better; but he continued to get worse, and died. His brother now became the principal chief. He refused to go down, saying that if he started he would be taken sick and die, as his brother had done, which was reasonable. We all concluded that none of us would go at this time. The Foxes returned. They said they had smoked the pipe of peace with the Americans, and' expected a war party would be sent against us because we did not go down. This I did not believe, as the Americans had always lost by their war parties that came against us.

La Gutrie and other British traders arrived at our village in the fall. La Gutrie told us that we must go down and make peace, that it was the wish of our English father. He said he wished us to go down to the Two-river country to winter, where game was plenty, as there had been no hunting there for several years. Having heard that a principal war chief, with troops, had come up, and had commenced to build a fort near Rapids des Moines, we consented to go down with the traders to see the American chief, and tell him the reason why we had not been down sooner. We arrived at the head of the rapids. Here the traders left their boats except one, in which they accompanied us to the Americans. We visited the war chief and told him what we had to say, explaining the reason we had not been down sooner. He appeared angry, and talked to La Gutrie for some time. I inquired of him what the war chief said. He told me that he was threatening to hang him up on the yard-arm of his boat. But said he: "I am not afraid of what he says. He dare not put his threats into execution. I have done no more than I had a right to do, as a British subject." I then addressed the chief, asking permission for ourselves and some Menomonees to go down to the Two-river country to hunt. He said we might go down, but must return before the ice made, as he did not intend we should winter below the fort. "But," said he, "what do you want the Menomonees to go with you for?" I did not know at first what reply to make, but told him that they had a great many pretty squaws with them, and we wished them to go with us on that account. He consented. We all started down the river, and remained all winter, as we had no intention of returning before spring when we asked leave to go.

We made a good hunt. Having loaded our traders' boats with furs and peltries, they started to Mackinaw, and we returned to our village.

There is one circumstance which I forgot to mention in its proper place. It does not relate to myself or people, but to my friend Gomo, the Pottowatomie chief. He came to Rock river to pay me a visit. During his stay, he related to me the following story: "The war chief at Peoria is a very good man; he always speaks the truth and treats our people well. He sent for me one day and told me that he was nearly out of provisions, and wished me to send my young men out to hunt, to supply his fort. I promised to do so; and immediately returned to my camp and told the young men the wishes and wants of the war chief. They readily agreed to go and hunt for our friend; and soon returned with about twenty deer. They carried them to the fort, laid them down at the gate, and returned to our camp. A few days afterwards I went again to the fort to see if they wanted more meat. The chief gave me some powder and lead and said he wished me to send my hunters out again. When I returned to my camp I told my young men the chief wanted more meat. Ma-ta-tah, one of my principal braves, said he would take a party and go across the Illinois, about one day's travel, where game was plenty, and make a good hunt for our friend the war chief. He took eight hunters with him; his wife and several other squaws accompanied them. They had traveled about a day in the prairie when they discovered a party of white men coming towards them with a drove of cattle. Our hunters apprehended no danger, or they would have kept out of the way of the whites (who had not yet perceived them). Ma-ta-tah changed his course, as he wished to meet and speak to the whites. As soon as the whites saw our party some of them put off at full speed and came up to our hunters. Ma-ta-tah gave up his gun to them and endeavored to explain to them that he was friendly, and was hunting for the war chief. They were not satisfied with this, but fired at and wounded him. He got into the branch of a tree that had been blown down, to keep the horses from running over him. He was again fired on by several guns and badly wounded. He found he would be murdered, and sprang at the nearest man to him, seized his gun, and shot him from his horse. He then fell, covered with blood from his wounds, and almost instantly expired. The other hunters, being in the rear of Ma-ta-tah, seeing that the whites had killed him, endeavored to make their escape. They were pursued and nearly all the party murdered. My youngest brother brought me the news in the night, he having been with the hunters and but slightly wounded. He said the whites had abandoned their cattle and gone back towards the settlement. The remainder of the night was spent in lamenting for the death of our friends. At day-light I blacked my face and started to the fort to see the war chief. I met him at the gate and told him what had happened. His countenance changed; I could see sorrow depicted in it for the death of my people. He tried to persuade me that I was mistaken, as he could not believe that the whites would act so cruelly. But when I convinced him, he told me that those cowards who had murdered my people should be punished. I told him that my people would have revenge; that they would not trouble any of his people of the fort, as we did not blame him or any of his soldiers, but that a party of my braves would go towards the

Wabash to avenge the death of their friends and relatives. The next day I took a party of hunters and killed several deer, and left them at the fort gate as I passed." Here Gomo ended his story. I could relate many similar ones that have come within my own knowledge and observation; but I dislike to look back and bring on sorrow afresh.

I will resume my narrative. The great chief at St. Louis having sent word for us to go down and confirm the treaty of peace, we did not hesitate, but started immediately, that we might smoke the peace pipe with him. On our arrival we met the great chiefs in council. They explained to us the words of our Great Father at Washington, accusing us of heinous crimes, and divers misdemeanors, particularly in not coming down when first invited. We knew very well that our Great Father had deceived us and thereby forced us to join the British, and could not believe that he had put this speech into the mouths of these chiefs to deliver to us. I was not a civil chief, and consequently made no reply; but our chiefs told the commissioners that what they had said was a lie. That our Great Father had sent no such speech; he knowing the situation in which we had been placed had been caused by him. The white chiefs appeared very angry at this reply, and said they would break off the treaty with us, and go to war, as they would not be insulted. Our chiefs had no intention of insulting them, and told them so; that they merely wished to explain to them that they had told a lie without making them angry, in the same manner that the whites do when they do not believe what is told them.* The council then proceeded, and

*An account of this council was given by Rev. Timothy Flint, who witnessed it, in the following language: At the grand council at St. Louis, where all the American commissioners were present, and a vast concourse of Indians and Americans,—that portion of the Sacs that had been hostile to us during the war, was engaged in the debates of the council. Some noble-looking chiefs spoke on the occasion. They fully exemplified all that I had ever heard of energy, gracefulness, and dignity of action and manner. The blanket was thrown round the body in graceful folds. The right arm, muscular and brawny, was bare quite to the shoulder. And the movement of the arm, and the inclinations of the body, might have afforded a study to a youthful orator. I observed a peculiarity of their posture, which I have not seen elsewhere noticed. When they closed an earnest and emphatic sentence, they regularly raised the weight of the body from the heel, to poise it on the toes and the fore part of the foot. The rest looked on the speaker eagerly, and with intense interest. When he uttered a sentence of strong meaning, or involving some interesting point to be gained, they cheered him with a deep grunt of acquiescence. A favorite chief, of singular mildness of contenance and manner, had spoken two or three times, in a very insinuating style. He was, in fact, the "Master Plausible" of his tribe. I remarked to the govenor, that he was the only Indian I had ever seen, who appeared to have mildness and mercy in his countenance. He replied, that under this mild and insinuating exterior, were concealed uncommon degrees of cunning, courage, revenge, and cruelty; that in fact he had been the most bloody and troublesome partisan against us, during the war, of the whole tribe. The grand speech of this man as translated, was no mean attempt to apply to the ladies and gentlemen present, the delightful unction of flattery. Some reports had got in circulation among them, which inspired them with arrogant expectations of obtaining permission to retain the

the pipe of peace was smoked. Here, for the first time, I touched the goose quill to the treaty, not knowing, however, that by that act I consented to give away my village. Had that been explained to me, I should have opposed it, and never would have signed their treaty, as my recent conduct will clearly prove.

What do we know of the laws and customs of the white people? They might buy our bodies for dissection, and we would touch the goose quill to confirm it, without knowing what we are doing. This was the case with myself and people in touching the goose quill the first time. We can only judge what is proper and right by our standard of what is right and wrong, which differs widely from the whites, if I have been correctly informed.

The whites *may do bad* all their lives, and then if they are *sorry for it when about to die, all is well!* But with us it is different. We must continue throughout our lives to do what we conceive to be good. If we have corn and meat, and know of a family that have none, we divide with them. If we have more blankets than sufficient, and others have not enough, we must give to them that want. We were friendly treated by the white chiefs, and started back to our village on Rock river. Here we found that troops had arrived to build a fort at Rock Island. This, in our opinion, was a contradiction to what we had done—to prepare for war in time of peace. We did not, however, object to their building the fort on the island, but we were very sorry, as this was the best island on the Mississippi, and had long been the resort of our young people during the summer. It was our garden which supplied us with strawberries, blackberries, gooseberries, plums, apples, and nuts of different kinds; and its waters supplied us with fine fish,

---

British traders among them, for whom, it seems, they had contracted a great fondness. The govenor replied with great firmness, that these expectations were wholly inadmissible. His answer was received with a general grunt of anger. A speaker of very different aspect from the former arose, and with high dudgeon in his countenance, observed, that he had understood that the thing which they wished, had been promised; but that "the American people had two tongues." Mr. Clarke, who perfectly understood the import of their figures, explained the remark to mean, that we were a perfidious and double-tongued people. Justly indignant to be addressed by a principal chief in this way, and to notice that the remark was cheered by the grunt of acquiescence on the part of the tribe, he broke off the council with visible displeasure. In the afternoon of that day, a detachment of United States artillery arrived on the shore of the river opposite the Indian camp. This detachment was ordered to the Sac country. The men paraded and fired their pieces. The terror of the savages at artillery is well known. The courage of these fierce men was awed at once in the prospect of this imposing force, which they had understood was bound to their country. The next morning the Sac chiefs, rather submissively, requested the renewal of the conference which had been broken off. We all attended the council to hear how they would apologize for their insolence the day before. The same chief who had used the offensive language came forward and observed that the father had misunderstood the meaning of the poor ignorant Indians; that he had intended only to say, that he had always understood from his fathers, that the Americans used two languages, viz.: French and English; and that they had two ways to express all that they had to say to the Indians.

being situated in the rapids of the river. In my early life I spent many happy days on this island. A good spirit had care of it, who lived in a cave in the rocks immediately under the place where the fort now s tands, and has often been seen by our people. He was white, with large wings like a swan's, but ten times larger. We were particular not to make much noise in that part of the island which he inhabited, for fear of disturbing him. But the noise of the fort has since driven him away, and no doubt a bad spirit has taken his place. Our village was situated on the north side of Rock river, at the foot of its rapids, and on the point of land between Rock river and the Mississippi; and in our rear, a continued bluff, gently ascending from the prairie. On the side this bluff we had our corn fields, extending about two miles up, running parallel with the Mississippi; where we joined those of the Foxes whose village was on the bank of the Mississippi, opposite the lower end of Rock Island, and three miles distant from ours. We had about eight hundred acres in cultivation, including what we had on the islands of Rock river. The land around our village, uncultivated, was covered with blue grass, which made excellent pasture for our horses. Several fine springs broke out of the bluff near by, from which we were supplied with good water. The rapids of Rock river furnished us with abundance of excellent fish, and the land being good, never failed to produce good crops of corn, beans, pumpkins, and squashes. We always had plenty; our children never cried with hunger, and our people were never in want. Here our village had stood for more than a hundred years, during all of which time we were the undisputed possessors of the valley of the Mississippi from the Wisconsin to the Portage des Sioux near the mouth of the Missouri, being about seven hundred miles in length. At this time we had very little intercourse with the whites, except our traders. Our village was healthy, and there was no place in the country possessing such advantages, nor no hunting grounds better than those we had in possession. If another prophet had come to our village in those days and told us what has since taken place, none of our people would have believed him. What! to be driven from our village and hunting grounds, and not even permitted to visit the graves of our forefathers, our relations and friends?

This hardship is not known to the whites. With us it is a custom to visit the graves of our friends, and keep them in repair for many years. The mother will go alone to weep over the grave of her child. The brave, with pleasure, visits the grave of his father after he has been successful in war, and repaints the post that shows where he lies. There is no place like that where the bones of our forefathers lie, to go to when in grief. Here the Great Spirit will take pity on us. But how different is our situation now from what it was in those days. Then we were as happy as the buffalo on the plain, but now, we are as miserable as the hungry, howling wolf in the prairie. But I am digressing from my story. Bitter reflection crowds upon my mind, and must find utterance. When we returned to our village in the spring, from our wintering grounds, we would finish trading with our traders, who always followed us to our village. We purposely kept some of our fine furs for this trade; and, as there was great opposition among them who should get these skins, we always got our goods cheap. After this trade was over, the traders would give us a few kegs of rum, which was generally promised in the fall, to encourage us to make a good hunt and not go to war. They would then start with their furs and peltries for thier homes. Our old men would take a frolic, (at this time our young men never drank). When this was ended the next thing to be done was to bury our dead (such as had died during the year). This is a great medicine feast. The relations of those who have died, give all the goods they have purchased, as presents to their friends, thereby reducing themselves to poverty, to show the Great Spirit they are humble, so that he will take pity on them. We would next open the caches, and take out corn and other provisions, which had been put up in the fall, and then commence repairing our lodges. As soon as this is accomplished, we repair the fences around our fields, and clean them off ready for planting corn. This work is done by our women. The men, during this time, are feasting on dried venison, bear's meat, wild fowl, and corn prepared in different ways; and recounting to each other what took place during the winter.

Our women plant the corn, and as soon as they get done we make a feast, and dance the *crane dance*, in which they join us, dressed in their best and decorated with feathers. At this feast our young braves select the young woman they wish to have for a wife. He then informs his mother, who calls on the mother of the girl, when the arrangement is made, and the time appointed for him to come. He goes to the lodge when they are asleep (or pretend to be), lights his matches, which have been provided for the purpose, and soon finds where his intended sleeps. He then awakens her, and holds the light to his face that she may know him, after which he places the light close to her. If she blows it out the ceremony is ended, and he appears in the lodge the next morning as one of the family. If she does not blow out the light but leaves it to burn out, he retires from the lodge. The next day he places himself in full view of it, and, plays his flute. The young women go out, one by one, to see who he is playing for. The tune changes to let them know he is not playing for them. When his intended makes her appearance at the door, he continues his courting tune until she retires to the lodge. He then gives over playing, and makes another trial at night, which generally turns out favorable. During the first year they ascertain whether they can agree with each other, and can be happy; if not, they part, and each looks out again. If we were to live together and disagree, we should be as foolish as the whites. No indiscretion can banish a woman from her parental lodge; no difference how many children she may bring home she is always welcome, the kettle is over the fire to feed them. The crane dance often lasts two or three days. When this is over we feast again, and have our national dance. The large square in the village is swept and prepared for the purpose. The chiefs and old warriors take seats which have been spread at the upper end of the square, the drummers and singers come next, and the braves and women form the side, leaving a large square in the middle. The drums beat and the singers commence. A warrior enters the square, keeping time with the music. He shows the manner he started on a war party, how he approached the enemy; he strikes and describes the way he killed him. All join in applause. He then leaves the square, and another enters and takes his place. Such of our young men as have not been out in war parties, and killed an enemy, stand back ashamed, not being able to enter the square. I remember I was ashamed to look where our young women stood before I could take my stand in the square as a warrior. What pleasure it is to an old warrior to see his son come forward and relate his exploits; it makes him feel young, and induces him to enter the square and fight his battles over again. This national dance makes our warriors. When I was travelling last summer, on a steamboat, on a large river going from New York to Albany I was shown the place where the Americans dance their national dance [West Point], where the old warriors recount to their young men what they have done, to stimulate them to go and do likewise. This surprised me, as I did not think the whites understood our way of making braves.

When our national dance is over, our cornfields hoed, and every weed dug up, and our corn about knee high, all our young men would start in a direction towards sun down, to hunt deer and buffalo, being prepared also to kill Sioux if any are found on our hunting grounds; a part of our old men and women to the lead mines to make lead; and the remainder of our people start to fish and get mat stuff. Every one leaves the village and remains about forty days. They then return, the hunting party bringing in dried buffalo and deer meat, and sometimes Sioux scalps, when they are found trespassing on our hunting grounds. At other times they are met by a party of Sioux too strong for them, and are driven in. If the Sioux have killed the Sacs last, they expect to be retaliated upon, and will fly before them, and *vice versa.* Each party knows that the other has a right to retaliate, which induces those who have killed last to give way before their enemy, as neither wishes to strike except to avenge the death of their relatives. All our wars are predicated by the relatives of those killed, or by aggression upon our hunting grounds. The party from the lead mines brings lead, and the others dried fish and mats for our winter lodges. Presents are now made by each party, the first giving to the others dried buffalo and deer, and they, in exchange, presenting them lead, dried fish, and mats.

This is a happy season of the year, having plenty of provisions, such as beans, squashes, and other produce. With our dried meat and fish we continue to make feasts, and visit each other, until our corn is ripe. Some lodge in the village makes a feast daily to the Great Spirit. I cannot explain this so the whites would comprehend, as we have no regular standard among us. Every one makes his feast as he thinks best, to please the Great Spirit, who has the care of all beings created. Others believe in two Spirits, one good and one bad, and make feasts for the bad Spirit *to keep him quiet.* If they can make peace with him, the good Spirit will not hurt them. For my part I am of opinion that so far as we have reason we have a right to use it in determining what is right or wrong, and should pursue that path which we believe to be right, believing that whatever is, is right. If the Great and Good Spirit wished us to believe and do as the whites, he could easily change our opinion so that we could see and think and act as they do. We are nothing compared to His power, and we feel and know it. We have men among us, like the whites, who pretend to know the right path, but will not consent to show it without *pay.* I have no faith in their paths, but believe that every man must make his own path. When our corn is getting ripe, our young people watch with anxiety for the signal to pull roasting ears, as none dare touch them until the proper time. When the corn is fit to use another great ceremony takes place, with feasting and returning thanks to the Great Spirit for giving us corn. I will here relate the manner in which corn first came. According to tradition, handed down to our people, a beautiful woman was seen to descend from the clouds, and alight upon the earth, by two of our ancestors, who had killed a deer, and were sitting by a fire roasting a part of it to eat. They were astonished at seeing her, and concluded that she must be hungry and had smelt the meat, and immediately went to her, taking with them a piece of the roasted venison. They presented it to her and she ate, and told them to return to the spot where she was sitting, at the end of one year, and they would find a reward for their kindness and generosity. She then ascended to the clouds and disappeared. The two men returned to their village, and explained to their nation what they had seen, done and heard; but were laughed at by their people. When the period arrived for them to visit this consecrated ground, where they were to find a reward for attention to the beautiful woman of the clouds, they went with a large party, and found where her right hand rested on the ground *corn* growing, and where the left hand rested *beans* growing, and immediately where she had been seated *tobacco*. The two first have ever since been cultivated by our people as our principal provisions, and the last used for smoking. The white people have since found out the latter, and seem to relish it as much as we do, as they use it in different ways, viz.: smoking, snuffing and eating.

We thank the Great Spirit for all the benefits he has conferred upon us. For myself, I never take a drink of water from a spring without being mindful of his goodness. We next have our great ball play; from three to five hundred on a side play the game. We play for horses, guns, blankets, or any other kind of property we have. The successful party takes the stakes, and all retire to our lodges in peace and friendship. We next commence horse racing, and continue our sport and feasting until the corn is all secured. We then prepare to leave our village for our hunting-grounds. The traders arrive and give us credit for such articles as we want to clothe our families and enable us to hunt. We first, however, hold a council with them, to ascertain the price they will give us for our skins, and what they will charge us for goods. We inform them where we intend hunting and tell them where to build their houses. At this place we deposit part of our corn and leave our old people. The traders have always been kind to them and relieved them when in want. They were always much respected by our people, and never, since we have been a nation, have one of them been killed by one of our people. We disperse in small parties to make our hunt, and as soon as it is over we return to our traders' establishment with our skins, and remain feasting, playing cards, and other pastimes, until near the close of the winter. Our young men then start on the beaver hunt; others to hunt raccoons and muskrats, and the remainder of our people go to the sugar camp to make sugar. All leave our encampment and appoint a place to meet on the Mississippi, so that we may return to our village together in the spring. We always spent our time pleasantly at the sugar camp. It being the season for wild fowl, we lived well and always had plenty when the hunters came in, that we might make a feast for them. After this is over we return to our village, accompanied sometimes by our traders. In this way the year rolled round happily. But these are times that were!

The remainder of Black Hawk's narrative is principally made up of an *exparte* argument in regard to the purchase and occupation of the Sac and Fox country by the United States government, with a detailed and uninteresting account of the campaign between his forces and the army under Gen. Atkinson, all of which is familiar to every person who has read the history of our country, and it would be a work of supererogation to repeat it here.

After Black Hawk's defeat and capture he was taken on a tour through the Eastern cities, in order that he might see the greatness of the American nation and learn how futile would be his feeble efforts to war against such a people. He was treated kindly everywhere, and upon his return recorded his impressions of the trip and what he saw and heard, in his book, in his own peculiar fashion. His account of the trip is given in the following words:

On our way up the Ohio we passed several large villages, the names of which were explained to me. The first is called Louisville, and is a very pretty village, situated on the bank of the Ohio river. The next is Cincinnati, which stands on the bank of the same river. This is a large and beautiful village, and seemed to be in a thriving condition. The people gathered on the bank as we passed, in great crowds, apparently anxious to see us. On our arrival at Wheeling, the streets and river banks were crowded with people, who flocked from every direction to see us. While we remained here many called upon us and treated us with kindness—no one offering to molest or misuse us. This village is not so large as either of those before mentioned, but is quite a pretty village. We left the steam boat here, having traveled a long distance on the prettiest river (except our Mississippi) I ever saw, and took the stage. Being unaccustomed to this made of traveling, we soon got tired and wished ourselves in a canoe on one of our own rivers, that we might return to our friends. We had traveled but a short distance before our carriage turned over, from which I received a slight injury and the soldier had one arm broken. I was sorry for this accident, as the young man had behaved well. We had a rough and mountainous country for several days, but had a good trail for our carriage. It is astonishing to see what labor and pains the white people have had to make this road, as it passes over an immense number of mountains, which are generally covered with rocks and timber; yet it has been made smooth and easy to travel upon. Rough and mountainous as is the country, there are many wigwams and small villages standing on the road side. I could see nothing in the country to induce the people to live in it; and was astonished to find so many whites living on the hills. I have often thought of them since my return to my own people; and am happy to think they prefer living in their own country to coming out to ours and driving us

from it, that they might live upon and enjoy it—as many of the
whites have already done.   I think, with them, that wherever the
Great Spirit places his people they ought to be satisfied to remain,
and thankful for what he has given them; and not drive others
from the country he has given them, because it happens to be
better than theirs.   This is contrary to our way of thinking; and
from my intercourse with the whites, I have learned that one great
principle of their *religion* is to do unto others as you wish them
to do unto you.   Those people in the mountains seem to act upon
this principle; but the settlers upon our frontiers, and on our
lands, seem never to think of it, if we are to judge by their
actions.

The first village of importance that we came to, after leaving
the mountains, is called Hagerstown.   It is a large village to be
so far from a river, and is very pretty.   The people appear to
live well, and enjoy themselves much.

We passed through several small villages on the way to Fred-
ericktown, but I have forgotten their names.   This last is a large
and beautiful village.   The people treated us well, as they did at
all other villages where we stopped.   Here we came to another
road, much more wonderful than that through the mountains.
They call it a *railroad.*   I examined it carefully, but need not
describe it, as the whites know all about it.   It is the most astonishing sight I ever saw.   The great road over the mountains will
bear no comparison to it, although it has given the white people
much trouble to make.   I was surprised to see so much labor and
money expended to make a good road for easy traveling.   I prefer riding on horseback, however, to any other way; but suppose
these people would not have gone to so much trouble and
expense to make a road, if they did not prefer riding in their new
fashioned carriages, which seem to run without any trouble.
They certainly deserve great praise for their industry.   On our
arrival at Washington, we called to see our Great Father, the President.   He looks as if he had seen as many winters as I have, and
seems to be a great brave.   I had very little talk with him, as
he appeared to be busy, and did not seem much disposed to talk.
I think he is a good man; and although he talked but little, he
treated us very well.   His wigwam is well furnished with every
thing good and pretty, and is very strongly built.   He said he
wished to know the cause of my going to war with his white children.   I thought he ought to have known this before; and consequently said little to him about it, as I expected he knew as well
as I could tell him.   He said he wanted us to go to Fortress Monroe, and stay awhile with the war chief who commanded it.   But
having been so long from my people, I told him that I would
rather return to my nation, that Ke-o-kuck had come here once
on a visit to see him, as we had done, and he let him return again

as soon as he wished; and that I expected to be treated in the same way. He insisted, however, on our going to Fortress Monroe; and as our interpreter could not understand enough of our language to interpret a speech, I concluded it was best to obey our Great Father, and say nothing contrary to his wishes. During our stay at the city, we were called upon by many people, who treated us well, particularly the squaws. We visited the great *council house* of the Americans—the place where they keep their *big guns*—and all the public buildings, and then started to Fortress Monroe. The war chief met us on our arrival, and shook hands, and appeared glad to see me. He treated us with great friendship, and talked to me frequently. Previous to our leaving this fort, he gave us a feast, and made us some presents, which I intend to keep for his sake. He is a very good man, and a great brave. I was sorry to leave him, although I was going to return to my people, because he treated me like a brother, during all the time I remained with him.

Having got a new guide, a war chief (Maj. Garland) we started for our own country, taking a circuitous route. Our Great Father being about to pay a visit to his children in the *big towns* towards sunrising, and being desirous that we should have an opportunity of seeing them, directed our guide to take us through. On our arrival at Baltimore, we were astonished to see so large a village; but the war chief told us that we would soon see a larger one. This surprised us more. During our stay here, we visited all the public buildings and places of amusement, saw much to admire, and were well entertained by the people, who crowded to see us. Our Great Father was there at the same time, and seemed to be much liked by his white children, who flocked around him, to shake him by the hand. He did not remain long—having left the city before us. We left Baltimore in a steamboat, and traveled in this way to the big village, where they make *medals* and *money* (Philadelphia). We again expressed surprise at finding this village so much larger than the one we had left; but the war chief again told us, that we would soon see another, much larger than this. I had no idea that the white people had such large villages, and so many people. They were very kind to us—showed us all their great public works, their ships and steamboats. We visited the place where they make money and saw the men engaged at it. They presented each of us with a number of pieces of the coin as they fell from the mint, which are very handsome. I witnessed a militia training in this city, in which were performed a number of singular military feats. The chiefs and men were well dressed, and exhibited quite a war-like appearance. I think our system of parade far better than that of the whites, but, as I am now done going to war, I will not describe it, or say anything more about war, or the preparations necessary for it. We next started to New York, and on our arrival near the wharf, saw a large collection of people gathering at Castle Garden. We had seen many wonderful sights in our way—large villages, the great national road over mountains, the railroads, steam carriages, ships, steamboats, and many other things; but we were now about to witness a sight more surprising than any of these. We were told that a man was going up into the air in a balloon. We watched with anxiety if it could be true; and to our utter astonishment, saw him ascend in the air until the eye could no longer perceive him. Our people were all surprised, and one of our young men asked the Prophet if he was going up to see the Great Spirit.

After the ascension of the balloon, we landed, and got into a carriage, to go to the house that had been provided for our reception. We had proceeded but a short distance before the street was so crowded that it was impossible for the carriage to pass. The war chief then directed the coachman to take another street and stop at a different house from the one he had intended. On our arrival there, we were waited upon by a number of gentlemen, who seemed much pleased to see us. We were furnished with good rooms, good provisions, and everything necessary for our comfort. The chiefs of their big village, being desirious that all their people should have an opportunity to see us, fitted up their great council house for this purpose, where we saw an immense number of people; all of whom treated us with friendship, and many with great generosity. The chiefs were particular in showing us every thing that they thought would be pleasing or gratifying to us. We went with them to Castle Garden to see the fireworks, which was quite an agreeable entertainment, to the whites who witnessed it, but less magnificent than the sight of one of our large prairies would be when on fire. We visited all the public buildings and places of amusement, which, to us, were truly astonishing, yet very gratifying. Every body treated us with friendship, and many with great liberality. The squaws presented us many handsome little presents, that are said to be valuable. They were very kind, very good, and very pretty—*for pale-faces.*

Having seen all the wonders of the big village, and being anxious to return to our people, our guide started with us for our own country. On arriving at Albany, the people were so anxious to see us that they crowded the streets and wharves, where the steamboats landed, so much that it was almost impossible for us to pass to the hotel which had been provided for our reception. We remained here but a short time, and then started for Detroit. I had spent many pleasant days at this place, and anticipated on my arrival to meet many of my old friends, but in this I was disappointed. What could be the cause of this? Are they all dead? Or what has become of them? I did not see our old father there, who had always given me good advice and treated me with friendship. After leaving Detroit, it was but a few days before we landed at Prairie du Chien. The war chief at the fort treated us very kindly, as did the people generally. I called on the father of the Winnebagoes (Gen. J. M. Street) to whom I had surrendered myself after the battle at the Bad Axe, who received me very friendly. I told him that I had left my great medicine bag with his chief before I gave myself up; and now that I was to enjoy my liberty again, I was anxious to get it, that I might hand it down to my nation unsullied. He said it was safe; he had heard his chiefs speak of it, and would get it and send it to me. I hope he will not forget his promise, as the whites generally do, because I have always heard he was a good man, and a good father—and made no promises that he did not fulfill.

PART V

ANECDOTES *&* ADVENTURES.

In the summer of 1812 James Murdock, Temple and Stephen Cole, James Patton and John Gooch, left the settlements on Loutre Island and went in pursuit of a party of Indians who had stolen some horses from them and other settlers. They followed their trail to Grand Prairie, now in Audrain county, and night coming on they camped on the bank of a small stream. It appears that the savages were in the vicinity and watching them, for soon after they had fallen asleep they were fired upon, and three of their number, Patton, Gooch and Stephen Cole, were instantly killed. Temple Cole engaged in a desperate hand-to-hand contest with one of the Indians, and was wounded, but succeeded in making his escape. Murdock escaped unhurt. Many years afterward the skulls of the murdered men were found near where they fell, and the stream upon the bank of which they had camped was named Skull Lick, the latter part of the name being derived from a deer lick not far distant on the same stream.

MR. WILLIAM KEITHLEY, of St. Charles county, served as a ranger during the entire Indian war, part of the time under Capt. James Callaway and part under Nathan Boone. He was one of the party of rangers that was sent with Lieutenant Campbell in 1814 to the relief of the garrison at Prairie Du Chien (see pages 92-94), and was wounded in the engagement which took place in the rapids above Rock river. He was under Lieutenant Riggs at the time, but was with Campbell's men when the attack was made.

They reached Rock river on the 12th of June, 1814, and the next day they met a party of Indians who pretended to be friendly, and proposed a treaty. These Indians were under Black Hawk himself, who tells a different story from that of the rangers, and entirely in his own favor. (See page 480.) While the treaty was progressing, the Indians proposed a foot-race between one of their crack runners and a white soldier, the latter to be selected by his companions. The soldiers, desiring to manifest as friendly a spirit as the red men, accepted the challenge, and the wager, consisting of blankets and moccasins, was hoisted on a pole near the race ground. The soldiers selected as their champion a little man named Peter Harpool, who was so small that the Indians laughed at him, and thought they would have an easy conquest; but when the race came off he beat their champion very badly. They were greatly surprised at the result, and gathering around Harpool they looked and pointed at him in astonishment, and jabbered and made signs among themselves to indicate their state of feelings.

Early the next morning Lieutenant Campbell's boat was attacked by a large body of Indians, and a number of his men were killed, Harpool being among the first. Keithley and several others were in the water bathing when the attack was made, and the former received a severe wound in the hip, but escaped to the boat. They fought about an hour, when the Indians shot blazing arrows into their boat and set it on fire. Lieutenant Rector then came alongside and took their men on board; and they all dropped down the river to Cap-au-Gris. The men who were bathing when the fight began lost their clothing, which they left on the shore, and they had to go as far as Cap-au-Gris in the dress that Adam wore. Among the rangers killed in this engagement, besides Peter Harpool, were Samuel Brumfield and Berry Pitman. Several weeks later Captain Callaway marched his company into the Indian country, and came upon a large force of British and Indians entrenched at Rock Island. Callaway attacked them with his usual impetuosity, nothwithstanding they outnumbered him ten to one; but having lost several men, and seeing that he could make no impression against the enemy with his small force, he retreated to Cap-au-Gris.

Mr. Keithley was not with Callaway when he was killed, but he was present when his body was found and buried. This took place late in the afternoon, and the party rode to Loutre Island that night. They swam Loutre slough, which was very high at the time. One of the rangers, named Robert Baldridge, rode a horse that was not accustomed to swimming, and when he got to deep water he began to struggle, and sank, carrying his rider with him. Baldridge prayed for help like a good fellow, and finally got safe to shore.

CAPTURED BY THE INDIANS.—A short time before the commencement of the war of 1812 Captain Nathaniel Heald, whose history is given on page 153, was stationed at Fort Dearborn, where Chicago now stands; and during the time that he was there, the fort was visited by a beautiful and accomplished young lady from Louisville, Ky., whose name was Rebecca Wells. She came in company with her uncle, Major William Wells, of the U. S. army, who had been captured by the Indians when he was eight years of age and remained with them until he was thirty. He then joined the army and was commissioned major for gallantry and good conduct. The father of the young lady, Colonel Samuel Wells, was also an officer of the war of 1812, and distinguished for gallantry on the battle field.

The charms and graces of the young lady soon won the heart of Captain Heald, and led to an avowal of his affection and an offer of his hand. He was rejoiced to find that his sentiments were reciprocated, and on the 23d of May, 1811, they were married at the residence of the bride's father, in Louisville. The Captain immediately returned to his post of duty, accompanied by his young bride.

On the 15th of August, 1812, Fort Dearborn was evacuated, and shortly after the troops left the fort they fell into an Indian ambuscade, and were nearly all massacred. A few were saved, among whom were Captain Heald and his gallant wife, but they were both severely wounded, the Captain having been shot through the hips and his wife through the body and both arms. They and the other survivors were all taken prisoners by the Indians. Mrs. Heald was finely mounted on a spirited young mare, and notwithstanding her severe and painful wounds she maintained her seat in the saddle, and became an unwilling witness of the horrible atrocities that were perpetrated upon the bodies of her murdered friends. She saw an Indian cut out the heart of her uncle, Major William Wells, and after having flourished it in triumph over his head, on the end of a ramrod, he took it down and ate it.   This and other sickening spectacles of a like character made an impression upon her young mind which time has never effaced; and even now, since so many years and changes have intervened, she cannot speak of them without a shudder.

While Mrs. Heald was sitting on her horse, a horrified observer of the barbarities that were taking place around her, a squaw approached and attempted to snatch a beautiful red blanket that was folded over her saddle, but, reckless of the consequences, she drew her riding whip, and gave the squaw several sharp cuts over the shoulders and face, which made her glad to retire without the coveted blanket.   The Indians observed the incident, and yelled and shouted with laughter, for they richly enjoyed the discomfiture of the squaw and the spirit of the white woman.   Mrs. H. was afterward informed, by one of the chiefs, that this exhibition of bravery on her part saved the lives of both herself and husband; but it did not prevent her from being deprived of her horse, the greater portion of her clothing and all her jewelry.   The latter she prized very highly, as most of it had been presented to her by her father, husband and friends, and she deeply regretted its loss; but on arriving at home, after she and her husband had escaped from the Indians, she was rejoiced to find her jewelry all safe.   It had been traded by one of the savages engaged in the massacre to John O'Fallon, an Indian trader at St. Louis, who recognized the name engraved upon the several pieces, and restored it to her father in Louisville.

After the massacre Captain Heald and his wife were separated and taken by different tribes into their country on the northern lakes; but Shandarry, the chief of the tribe that held the Captain, proved to be their friend, and in order that they might be together he purchased Mrs. Heald from her captors, giving in exchange an old mule and a bottle of whisky.   The husband and wife were deeply thankful to Shandarry for this generous act of kindness; but he proved himself to be more generous still, for soon afterward he hired a young Indian, named Robinson, to assist the prisoners in making their escape.   He conveyed them in a birch bark canoe along the shore of Lake Michigan to Mackinaw, a distance of two hundred miles, traveling only at night.   Two weeks were consumed in making the dangerous voyage, and during that time the young Indian kept them supplied with game with a little single-barreled gun that belonged to the Captain, and which had been returned to him by Shandarry when they started on the trip.   During the day they would hide their canoe in the woods on the shore, while they slept and refreshed themselves, and at night resume their journey again.   Frequently when they attempted to land they found the water very shallow, and were compelled to wade to the shore.   This was the most trying part of the voyage, for the Captain had one leg broken, and being without crutches he had to be supported to shore by his wife, who also suffered greatly from her wounds.

Upon arriving at Mackinaw the Captain paid the young Indian $100 for his services, and discharged him with many expressions of gratitude for his kindness and devotion.   The Captain had saved this money, and $200 besides, by keeping it concealed in a pocket in his undershirt during the time they were with the Indians.   He also retained his little gun, which remained in the family as a relic until the late war between the North and South, when the St. Charles militia took it and kept it.

The British officer in command of the fort at Mackinaw proved to be a true friend, and did everything he could to render the prisoners comfortable.   He assured them that as soon as their wounds were better and they had recovered from the fatigue of their journey he would send them to Detroit, where they would be exchanged and returned to their friends. He and Captain Heald were both Masons, and the mystic link of brotherhood greatly strengthened their friendship.

They had been at Mackinaw only a few days when a party of their old captors, who had followed them, arrived at the fort and demanded the restoration of their prisoners. Under the conditions of the treaty between his government and the savages, the officer was bound to accede to their demand, but being loth to deliver them up to savage cruelty, he secretly transferred them to a sailing vessel that was lying in the harbor, and they escaped to Detroit, where they were exchanged and returned to Louisville. Upon arriving there Capt. H. found a commission of Major in the regular army awaiting him; but having grown tired of military life he resigned his commission at the end of the war and removed with his family to Missouri, where he spent the rest of his life engaged in the peaceful pursuit of agriculture.

Before his death he received a visit from Shandarry and his son. They remained about two weeks, and were treated with the greatest kindness and hospitality. At the end of their visit they took their departure for the distant West, and never returned again.

Robinson, the young Indian who conveyed them to Mackinaw, settled, at the close of the war, in Illinois, about fifteen miles northwest of Chicago, where he became wealthy and raised a large family. In 1856 Mr. Darius Heald, a son of Major Nathaniel Heald, paid him a visit, for the purpose of expressing his gratitude for his kindness to his father and mother during their captivity. He was an old man then, with gray hair and venerable appearance, and Mr. Heald found him living in a wigwam near the house where his family resided. The house was well built and handsomely furnished, and the old Indian's daughters were educated and accomplished; but he preferred to live in a wigwam and sleep on skins and blankets, as his people had done for ages before. He could not speak a word of English, and at first regarded Mr. Heald with distrust, supposing him to be merely an intruder or curiosity-hunter. But when his daughters explained to him the purpose of Mr. Heald's visit, and who he was, he received him with great cordiality and treated him to the best he had. He tapped a keg of whisky that was twenty years old, brought out some wine of the same age, and pressed Mr. Heald to drink of both; but he was compelled to refuse, owing to the fact that he had just taken a pledge of total abstinence. The old Indian then took down some dried buffalo meat that he had suspended from the roof of his wigwam, and they both ate of that. His mode of presenting the meat to his visitor was rather peculiar. He would jump up and cut off a piece several inches in length, and then gravely seat himself again and place one end of the piece of meat in Mr. Heald's hand. He would then divide it in the middle between them with his knife, and each would keep a half. When that was disposed of he would repeat the same thing, and kept it up until they were satified. Mr. Heald remained with him several days, and when he took his departure the old Indian expressed heartfelt regret.

THE following directions were recently given by our friend, Mr. James L. Pegram, of Montgomery City, to a deaf old gentleman from Callaway county, who was in search of some stray horses which he understood were in a pasture near that town. Observing that he was deaf, Mr. P. gave his directions in a very loud voice, as follows: "You go by that house you see yonder where that yellow dog is, and go a little lower on the other side of the railroad, and you will see another road, *you know*. Take that end until you come to a lane running *so* (throwing both hands up), with one of the fences gone, *you know*, and you will see a gate, but don't go through it, *you know*, but keep straight on to the left and cross another branch, *you know*, and you will see another lane *with both fences gone.* Go through that, and go on and go through another gate, *you know*, and take a corn row; and see if the fence is up, *you know*, (the gap was down last year ·when I was out there), but if it is up, come back, *you know*, and take up the main big road, which runs straight on so, *you know*, and you will see a hay stack that was cut last year, for I helped to cut it, *you know.* Then you will see a ditch; go across that and you will see a pasture with some horses in it, *you know*, and may be your horse is there. If he ain't there, *you know*, you had better ask somebody else, for I have n't been out there for ten years, *you know.*" By this time a crowd had gathered around the two, and when Mr. Pegram ceased speaking there was a general roar of laughter, in which he joined heartily, for he appreciated the joke as well as any of them. The deaf man had listened very attentively all the way through, and he now leaned over his horse's neck to inquire what Mr. Pegram had said about the hay stack. This created ·another explosion of mirth, during which Mr. P. repeated his directions in a louder tone of voice than before, whereupon the old gentleman thanked him and rode off in the direction of the house where the yellow dog was, and late that evening he was seen on the top of a hay stack *smelling* and looking around to see if it was the one Mr. Pegram had mentioned in his directions, and had helped to cut.

One day Mr. Pegram yoked his oxen to his wagon and, accompanied by his eldest son and one of his nephews, went down to what is called the "devil's back-bone," in the southern part of Montgomery county, to get some flat rocks for hearth-stones. The first rock they prized up had a yellow jacket's nest under it, and the vicious little insects stung the oxen so that they ran away. They brought the oxen back and prized up another rock, under which there was a bumble-bee's nest, and all hands got badly stung. They then tried another rock, and found another bumble-bee's nest, and got stung again. By this time they began to be discouraged, and felt like they wanted to go home; but finally decided to try another rock. They did so, and found five large rattle-snakes, but fortunately escaped being bitten. They killed all the snakes, and skinned the largest one, which measured five feet in length and four inches in diameter. They were now so disheartened that they decided to go home without any rocks at all, and got on the wagon and started. They had not gone far when they ran over a hornet's nest, and the hornets stung the oxen so that they ran away and tore the wagon all to pieces. They finally reached home, almost starved, having had nothing to eat all day, and half dead from their stings and other misfortunes. After that they always gave the "devil's back-bone" a wide berth.

ONE among the most original characters of early days in Missouri—and there were some very original ones about that time—was Hon. Jacob Groom, of Montgomery county, who was a member of the first State Legislature. During the sitting of that body in St. Charles, Mr. Groom and other members were invited one evening, by Dr..Young, to take tea at his house. Mrs. Young, who was a highly cultivated lady, had a piano and played well upon it. A piano at that time was a great curiosity, for there were none in the country until Mrs. Young brought hers, and people traveled thirty and forty miles just to see the wonderful instrument and hear its music. Mr. Groom possessed an ardent desire to see the piano, and he kept his eyes open from the time he entered the house. They were ushered into a room which contained, among other things, a large, old-fashioned curtained bedstead, which Groom at once concluded must be the much talked of piano. He eyed it curiously, and cautiously felt of the curtains, longing for the appearance of the hostess. He was not kept long in suspense, for she soon entered and welcomed her guests. As soon as an opportunity presented itself, Groom addressed her and said that he was passionately fond of music, that he had heard of her wonderful piano and the elegant manner in which she played upon it; "and now, Madam," said he, "I would like the best in the world to see you *perform on that instrument*," pointing to the bed. Mrs. Young blushed and left the room in great confusion, while the rest of the company roared with laughter at Groom's expense.

During that session of the Legislature he made a speech, which created so much amusement that it was taken down and published, with suitable caricatures, in one of the newspapers of that time. We have obtained a copy of the speech, which is as follows:

"*Members of this Meeting:*

"You don't know me I 'spose; well, it's no matter. I tell you my name is Jacob Groom—live at the Big Spring Post-office, Montgomery county (I air the postmaster), and bein' a Jackson Dimocrat of the upright principle. You see I am a big man—can eat a heap—can eat green persimmons without puckerin'. Salt don't keep me, nor liquor injure me. I am a tearin' critter of the catamount school, and a most decided and total porker in pollyticks. In religion I am neutral, and am decidedly masculine on the upright principle.

"Gentlemen Jacksonians and fellows of the conflicacious community in this land of con-

MR. GROOM ARISES TO A POINT OF ORDER.

cussence and supernaciousness, Jacksonians, I say, exaggerate yourselves and support the insufficiousnes of the oracle of Jackson. Friends, the cause of the veto on the veloniousness of the United States Bank was the purlicution of the Clay party, and when Jackson has spyfi-cated the confidence of the present Congress, he will rise to his super-cillious majesty and crush the growing powers of these illusible States. The gentleman, Jacksonians, was adequate to the circumference of Jacksonianism. And now I previse you to exaggerate yourselves, and let them that you left behind see the doings of this 'sembly, the first that has ever met in this town of St. Charles. Just before we all got to this place we stayed all night at our friend John Pitman's, on the road, where we enjoyed the good eating, drinking and dancing of the hospeculities of our old friend Pitman.

"I am no book larnt man, but there is few who can beat me swapping horses or guessing at the weight of a bar. I have come here because my people voted for me, knowing I was a honest man, and could make as good whisky and apple brandy at my still as any man. I want you all to commit the same like feeling, and finish the whole job on the Jacksonian principle, and if you don't do as I previse you will come short, and it will be harder for you to git to this place again than it would be for you to ride down from the clouds on a thunderbolt through a crab apple tree and not git scratched."

Mr. Groom resumed his seat amidst deafening applause.

ADVENTURES OF LEWIS JONES.—Lewis Jones was a noted hunter, trapper and surveyor of early times in Missouri. His father was an Englishman, who settled in Virginia at an early date, and had two sons, Lewis and Benjamin. The latter ran away from home when he was sixteen years of age, and came to St. Louis, where he joined the Indians and engaged in hunting and trapping, until Lewis and Clark started on their expedition, when he joined their party in the capacity of a scout. Before the expedition reached the Pacific Ocean, he and one or two others were sent back to St. Louis with dispatches. They fell into an Indian ambuscade, lost their horses, and had to perform the journey on foot, which occupied six months, but they arrived safe and delivered the dispatches. Jones afterward married and settled in St. Louis county, on the Mississippi river, just below the mouth of the Missouri. He subsequently went on an expedition to Santa Fe, and was absent four years. On his return he removed his family below St. Louis and settled on the Mississippi, where he resided until his death.

Lewis Jones also ran away from his parents, and came to Missouri in 1802, a mere boy. He engaged at first in hunting and trapping, and soon became famous among the old pioneers. He married Susannah Hays, a grand-daughter of Daniel Boone.

When Lewis and Clark passed up the river on their westward march, they came upon Lewis Jones and John Davis—a noted hunter of early times—engaged in sawing lumber with a whip-saw. They endeavored to persuade them to go along, but they refused unless they could go as independent scouts, without being subject to the commands of the officers. The commanders would not consent to this arrangement, and they resumed their sawing.

Some time after this, Jones and Davis went on a hunting expedition up into the Platte river country and were captured by the Indians, who stripped them of their clothing, gave them an old musket with six loads of ammunition, and started them back home. The weather was very cold, and being naked, they suffered severely. But before they started Davis stole a blanket from one of the squaws, and with that they managed to keep themselves from freezing the first day. That night they came upon an old Indian camp, and upon stealthily approaching it, they discovered a large panther stretched out in the ashes of the smouldering fire. They shot him with their old musket, and removed his hide with sharp stones. Jones then turned the hide and drew it on over his body, with the fur next to his flesh, and had a warm, comfortable suit. They made their supper from a portion of the carcass of the panther, and when they resumed their journey in the morning they took several pounds of the meat along with them for future use. During the trip they killed a turkey and squirrel, which, with their panther meat, sustained them until they reached home, where they arrived in ten days. In the meantime Jones' panther skin had become hard and dry, and he had to cut it off with a knife before he could resume his usual dress. He often said, afterward, that it was the most comfortable suit he had ever worn.

Jones subsequently made several trips to the mountains as guide to a party of fur traders, and while on one of these expeditions a grizzly bear attacked his little white pony, which he thought a great deal of, while it was grazing on the prairie, and killed and ate it. He was very much enraged when he discovered the remains of his pony, and asked the traders if any of them would go with him to kill the bear. Only one of them was brave enough to volunteer, and the two immediately left the camp in pursuit of old grizzly. They had not gone far when they saw the bear coming toward them, and Jones stationed himself in front with the understanding that he would fire first, and if he did not kill the bear then his companion was to give him the contents of his gun. Jones waited until the bear came within one hundred yards of him, and then fired and killed him in his tracks, the ball passing through his brain. He then turned toward his companion and was surprised to see him two hundred yards in the rear, running as fast as his heels could carry him in the direction of the camp. "Hallo! you blockhead," shouted Jones, "why in the mischief are you running from a dead bear?" The man returned, very much crestfallen, and begged Jones not to say anything about the affair to the rest of the party.

When game became scarce, and hunting was no longer a paying occupation, Jones studied surveying under Prospect K. Robbins, and became one of the most efficient and correct surveyors in North Missouri. If any of the land owners had a dispute about a line, Jones would be sent for to decide the matter, and wherever he said the line ought to go, there it went, because they all knew he understood his business and would not make a false or incorrect survey.

One day he was running a line for Mr. Benjamin Sisk, who had built his house before his land was surveyed, and unfortunately the house extend'd over upon another man's land. As they were running the line, Sisk, who felt anxious about the matter, looked through the sights of the compass and saw that it would go through the middle of his house. Greatly agitated, he led Jones to one side, where the chain bearers could not overhear him, and said, "For God's sake, Jones, alter the course of your compass, or it will ruin me!" "No," said Jones, "I'll follow the compass if it goes to h—l!" and he kept his word.

Jones was a great reader, and a close student of the Bible, but notwithstanding he was an avowed infidel, and made no effort to conceal or modify his views. One day he was surveying a piece of land in the presence of Revs. Jabez Ham and William Stevens, who entered into conversation about the Bible, and in the course of their remarks they eulogized Moses in the highest terms, as an honest, humble follower of the Lord, and a man in whom there was no guile. Jones attentively observed his compass for some time, but presently he looked up, lifted his spectacles from his nose to the top of his head, and remarked, " Yes, I guess Moses was a pretty good sort of an old fellow; but he was an awful liar." " How so?" inquired one of the ministers. " Why, he said he saw God, and he never saw him any more than I have seen him."

On another occasion he had a dispute with Rev. Mr. Nowlin about a place of future punishment, Nowlin affirming that there was such a place and Jones denying it. At last Nowlin said, "Now, Jones, if there is no hell, how are such fellows as old S. and his sons (naming some very bad characters who lived in that vicinity) going to get their dues after they are dead?" Jones studied a little while, and then replied, "Well, parson, that's a fact. I never thought of that before; and darn it, if there is no hell for those fellows, I'll give five hundred dollars to help build one for them."

HISTORY OF MAJOR JACK A. S. ANDERSON.—One among the most eccentric characters of early times in Missouri was Major Jack A. S. Anderson, well known to the older settlers of North Missouri. He was born in North Carolina, but removed with his parents to Kentucky in 1770. His father died in that State, and his mother and her children afterward emigrated to Missouri. Jack received a good education, and became a fine mathematician, surveyor and scribe. During the war of 1812 he served as a Major in Colonel Dick Johnson's regiment, and was present in the battle of the Thames when his leader killed the celebrated Tecumseh.

After his removal to Missouri he was employed by the government to assist in surveying the Territorial county of St. Charles, and in that capacity became well known to the older settlers. His compass, a bottle of whisky and his dogs were his inseparable and most beloved companions. He dressed entirely in buckskin, and his hunting shirt was filled with pockets, inside and out, in which he carried his papers and other worldly possessions. He would often carry young puppies in his pockets or the bosom of his shirt, while their mother trotted behind or hunted game for her master to shoot. He paid no attention to roads or paths, but always traveled in a direct line to the place where he was going, across creeks, hills, valleys, and through thick woods. He was never known to sleep in a bed, preferring to lie on the ground or a puncheon floor, covered with a blanket or buffalo robe. No one ever saw him smile, and his countenance always bore a sad and melancholy expression. He was never married, and died in old age, in destitute circumstances, in an old out-house two and a half miles south of Fulton. He was buried in Mr. Craighead's family graveyard.

A number of amusing anecdotes are related of this singular character, a few of which we give in this connection.

One day Mr. Thomas Glenn, of Montgomery county, went to Flanders Callaway's mill, on Teuque creek, with a sack of corn to be ground into meal, and on his return home he met Jack Anderson, who accompanied him as far as Cuivre creek, which they found to be frozen over. The ice was not strong enough to bear the weight of the horse, so they slid the sack of meal over, and then started up the stream, intending to cross higher up where the water was so swift that it had not frozen; but Anderson purposely wandered around with his companion until he had confused and bewildered him, and then took him on a long jaunt into Boone and Callaway counties, where they remained about three weeks engaged in hunting, and when they returned they were loaded down with game. They stopped one night at the house of Mr. Thomas Harrison, who treated them in a very hospitable manner and gave them the best room in his house. During the night Anderson got up and skinned several raccoons, and after having roasted them he called his dogs in and fed the carcasses to them on the floor, which of course ruined the carpet and greatly damaged the furniture. Mr. Harrison, who felt outraged at the affair, charged them for the damages, and as Anderson had no money Glenn had to pay the bill.

During his wanderings Anderson frequently stopped at the house of Major Isaac VanBibber, where he was always treated well and fared sumptuously; but on one occasion he stopped there late at night when they happened to be out of meal, and he had to go to bed without his supper. He lay down on the floor and pretended to be asleep. Soon after a son-in-law of VanBibber's, named Hickerson, who was living there, came in from a day's hunt, almost famished, having had nothing to eat during the day. He begged his wife to sift the bran and see if she could get meal enough to bake him a hoe cake. She did as requested, made the cake and put it to bake in the ashes of the fire. Anderson, who had observed the proceedings, now arose, complaining that he couldn't sleep, owing to the disturbed condition of his mind in regard to a survey he had made that day, in which he could not find the corners. Pretending to illustrate the matter, he took the Jacob staff of his compass and began to mark in the ashes, first cutting the cake into four equal parts, and then stirring it round and round until it was thoroughly mixed with the ashes. Hickerson watched the operation with tears in eyes, for he was nearly starved, and when Anderson had retired again, he begged his wife to go out and milk the cows and get him some milk to drink. She did so, but on her return Anderson met her at the door, and it being very dark, she supposed he was her husband, and gave him the milk, which he drank, and went back to bed. This exhausted Hickerson's patience, and calling up his dogs he went into the woods and caught a raccoon and roasted and ate it before he returned to the house, swearing that old Jack Anderson should not beat him out of his supper again.

*THOMAS MASSEY, JR., of Montgomery county, was a ranger under Nathan Boone during the Indian war, and one day while he and a party of rangers were scouting in the Indian country on the east side of the Mississippi river, they came upon an old Indian and his son, who professed to be friendly. They let the old man go, but took the boy with them, and after they had crossed the river on the ice they killed him in cold blood and without provocation. In order to avenge the wrong, a party of Sac warriors, to which tribe the young Indian belonged, went to the house of Mr. Massey's father, at Loutre Lick, in Montgomery county, and killed his brother Harris, who was plowing in a field near the house. His sister, who was standing in the door at the time, and witnessed the killing of her brother, blew a trumpet which they kept in the house for that purpose, and the Indians became frightened and fled without committing further outrages. There are a number of instances on record, similar to this, where the Indians murdered white people solely in revenge for wrongs inflicted upon themselves; and if the whites had always acted fairly and justly toward them, much trouble would have been averted.

THE late Thomas Howell, of St. Charles county, was a very active man in his youth, and became the champion runner and jumper of his locality. He belonged to Captain Callaway's company of rangers during the Indian war, and married the Captain's sister, who is still living: (See portrait on frontispiece.) The Captain also married Howell's sister, previous to the commencement of the war; and Howell's sweetheart was present at the wedding festivities. He naturally wanted to make a good impression and was dressed in his best and put on his best behavior. On the same occasion there was another young man present named Lewis, who was the champion jumper of his community. He presently challenged Howell for a trial of their skill, but the latter knew Lewis' reputation as a jumper, and dreading the shame of a defeat in the presence of his sweetheart, he held back for some time and tried to evade the challenge. But Lewis persisted; and finally walking up to the table, which was spread in the yard under some trees, and loaded down with good things for the wedding dinner, he stood for a moment, and then sprang clear over the table, dinner and all, and alighted several feet beyond it. "There now," said he, "beat that if you can!" It was a tremendous leap, and Howell's heart sank within him; but it would never do to have his championship taken from him without a trial. He was determined to make the effort if he smashed the table and ruined the dinner. So straining every nerve in his body he made a desperate leap, cleared the table, and alighted several inches beyond Lewis. This gave him the championship for all that part of the country, and made him the lion of the occasion. His sweetheart thought he looked ten times more handsome than ever, and after that he had no difficulty in winning her affections.

HUGH LOGAN, of Montgomery county, suffered severely from rheumatism for several years, being confined to the house the greater part of the time. At last he got a little better, and hobbled out into the woods near his house, one pleasant day, to feed a sow and some young pigs that he thought a great deal of. As he was returning he met an old bear that was teaching her young cubs how to climb a tree. When she saw Mr. Logan she left the cubs, reared up on her hind feet and came at him with extended paws and open mouth. Mr. Logan stood still until she came

---

*This incident is given by Black Hawk, though in a different manner, on page 474.

nearly to him, and then flung his hat into her open mouth, and throwing away his crutches he started for the house at full speed, followed closely by the old bear. He said he could feel her hot breath on his legs every step he took; but he beat her to the fence, when she turned back. That adventure cured him of the rheumatism.

MR. TATE, of Callaway county, owned a little negro boy named Skilt, who was so deaf that he could hardly hear it thunder. One morning Skilt got up much earlier than usual, and saw some wild turkeys eating corn out of the crib near the house. He determined to have one of those turkeys or do something desperate in the attempt to catch them; so he cautiously made his way to the opposite side of the crib, crawled under it, and seized two old goblers by the feet. But they proved too much for him, and flew away with him hanging to their legs. Skilt's mother witnessed the adventure and began to scream, and Mr. Tate ran out of the house to see what was the matter. He looked up and saw Skilt and the turkeys just go-

SKILT AND THE TURKEYS.

ing into the clouds, with no apparent intention of coming back again. He called to the little darkey to let one of the turkeys go and the other would bring him down safely. Skilt, notwithstanding his deafness, heard what his master said, and obeying his directions he brought one of the turkeys down in triumph.

ABOUT 1820 a man named Brazzleton came from Virginia to Missouri to look for land, and while here he thought he would have a hunt. So a party was made up and went to what is now Johnson county, in the western part of the State, where they found plenty of bears, deer, elk, etc. One day Brazzleton went out by himself, and wounded a cub bear, which he caught and began to tease by pulling its ears. He was not enough of a hunter to know that he was getting himself into trouble by so doing, but he soon became aware of that fact. The cub set up a piteous squalling, and directly he heard a dreadful snorting and cracking of brush near him, and looking up the side of a hill he saw the old bear coming toward him as fast as she could run, with her bristles elevated and furious growls issuing from her distended jaws. It occurred to him about that time that he could find other portions of the country equally as desirable as that which he was then occupying, and he lost no time in putting his ideas into execution. He arose and departed in the direction of a small prairie about two hundred yards distant. He felt as if he wanted to see that prairie immediately, so he ran. But the old bear was in a hurry too, and he could feel her hot breath on his back; so he accelerated his pace and got along a little faster than he ever did at any other period of his life. He came out into the prairie about two inches ahead of the old bear, and felt very proud because he had won the race. The old bear went back to her young one then, but Brazzleton never looked back to ask her how she felt. He kept straight on to the camp, and remarked when he got there that he believed he would never pull another cub bear's ears; he didn't like the noise they made.

BUT even old hunters sometimes got caught as Brazzleton did. William Ramsey, a pioneer of Warren county, wounded a cub bear one day, and sat down to amuse himself with it. Presently he heard a rustling of the bushes behind him, and before he could look around he was in the embrace of the old bear. She hugged him until she made his ribs crack, and gnawed the back of his head with her teeth until he thought she would certainly pull his scalp off. He felt as if his time had come, but made a desperate effort to save his life, and succeeded in drawing his knife from his belt. The next instant he plunged it into the bowels of the ferocious brute, when her grip began to slacken and she soon sank down lifeless at his feet. This adventure took place in the woods near Marthasville. Ramsey was an old hunter, and had killed scores of bears, but that affair taught him a lesson he had not learned before, and he never afterward sat down to play with a cub bear without having his gun in a convenient position to shoot the old one if she came upon him.

Boss LOGAN, of Montgomery county, had a donkey that he thought a great deal of, and was considerably worried because some rascal was in the habit of taking him out at night and riding him. Being unable to endure the outrage any longer, he wrote the following notice and posted it over the stable door: "Whereas, some no account fellow has been riding my ass at night when I am asleep, now lest any accident happen, I, Henry Logan, take this method of letting the people know that I am determined to shoot the ass, and warn any one who may be riding him at the time to take care of himself, for by mistake I may shoot the wrong ass." His donkey was not disturbed any more after that.

OLD Isaac Van Bibber, of Montgomery county, believed in the transmigration of souls. He advocated the doctrine that there was a complete revolution of nature every six thousand years, and at the end of each of these periods everything would return exactly where it had been six thousand years before. He kept hotel at Louter Lick, and took great delight in explaining his belief to his guests. A party of Kentuckians stopped with him one night, and after supper, while they were seated around the roaring log fire, he broached the subject of his religious faith. They listened attentively, and seemed interested; and after they had retired to bed he told his wife that he believed he had converted those men. He felt so good over his fancied conquest that he lay awake nearly all night thinking about it. Next morning, when the men were ready to start, one of them said to Mr. Van Bibber: "We were very much impressed with your argument last night, and believing that there may be some truth in your doctrine, and being short of cash just now, we have decided to wait until we come around again at the end of six thousand years, to settle our bills." The old Major saw the point at once, and was considerably nonplused as to how he would get over it without losing the value of their night's lodging or exhibiting a practical unbelief in his own doctrine. But a happy thought struck him. "No," said he, "you are the same d—d rascals who were here six thousand years ago, and went away without paying your bills, and now you have got to pay before you leave." They laughed, paid their bills and took their departure; but the old Major was never again heard to brag about his converting powers.

Isaac Van Bibber, Jr., a son of the Major, once wrote a business letter to a commission merchant in New Orleans, which created a national sensation. It was published first in the New Orleans *Picayune*, copied from that into the New York *Tribune*, and then took the rounds of the press. We have obtained a copy of the letter, which is given below. The *Picayune* published it under the following introduction:

"A BUSINESS LETTER.—The following is a verbatim copy of a business letter, lately received by a commission house of this city. It is in reply to a letter from the firm announcing the non-reception of a letter said to contain a draft from California on New Orleans. The writer gives a very interesting account of the trouble he underwent about the time his letter should have been deposited, whereby he was made to forget what he did with it. We think he has made out a pretty good case of a confused mind."

THE LETTER.

"JOHNSTOWN, Bates Co., July 13, 1851.

" I receved your leter which you cent Mr. Elias House, of June 8th, and I examined the post office where I should have maled mi leter, which was Johnstown, and I supose that I never put sayed leter in the box, tho' I rote the leter and inclosed the sayd Bill and went to Johnstown for the expres purpose to male sayd leter, on the 6th of February last. When I got to Johnstown, which was 9 miles from mi residence, Samuel C. Van Bibber, mi nefue, a uthe 18 years old, and the only sun of mi bruther Ewing A. Van Bibber, ho lives in California, and the man that sent me that draft. Samuel C., mi nefue, has been with me 12 years, and a good boy he is. Upon him coming up covered with a *Gore* of Blud, having recd a blow on the left cide of the head from Elihue Ashcrof, ho had come to mi house a few minits after I left home, for the purpose of whipping mi nefue, Samuel C. Van Bibber aforesayed, the only son of my bruther Ewing A. Van Bibber of California, having with him his two suns, John and Gronnel, one 15 years old and the other 18 years old, all attacking Samuel C. mi nefeu in the most furrious and friteful manner. The old man Ashcrof striking Samuel C. with the spike end of a big hickory stick, which I heard him brag that his father nocked Jim Sullivan's brains out in an affray in the expedition against the Mormons, in an affray that took place or that arose after the defeat of the Mormons. Elihue Ashcrof payed $10 for the stick at his father's sale 12 months before the affray with mi nefue, Samuel C. Van Bibber, took place, which the sayed Ashcrof wanted to regain the renown of his ded father by nocking out Samuel C. mi nefue's brains with the same stick. In the fury Samuel C. mi nefue renched the stick out of Ashcrof's hands, and turned the spike end which he punched Ashcrof twice in the belly just above the nable, and he fell on the floor, upon which his boys became intimidated and exclaimed, *O, dady is dead*, whereupon Samuel C. mi nefue, being as much alarmed as the Ashcrof boys, cort a horse and came after me ful tilt, and overtook me just as I was going into Johnstown to male the aforesayed leter, and made his statement, which throwed me into a confusion, I being a non-resident of the place, and never having had anything to do with the fury between Samuel C. mi nefeu and old Ashcrof. Old Major Cummings advised Samuel C. to take them with a peace warrant, which Samuel C. dun, and Ashcrof was 3 dais getting a councellor to trie the case, which lasted 8 dais, during which time I never thought about what took me to Johnstown, and all the time at mi house and his phisician saiing he, Ashcrof, would dy to-nite.

" I miself pleaded mi nefue Samuel C.'s case before 3 squires, ho after 8 day's deliberation pronounced it a case of man slarter in the fifth degree, which was for Samuel C. to pay $20 and leve the county, which he dun. All the time old Ashcrof's second wife and sun and a fue of his knaighbors attending him, he expressed a wish to get well and a great determination of revenge, when on the 10 day I became afraid that the prairs of his second wife and knaighbors, and which I miself hartily concurred in, would not be ansured, which was, mite God increse his paine and lay it close to his sinful hart, that his moments mite be fue. I made them haul him home, where he linguered until the first of March, when to the gratification of his second wife and to his naighbors and I miself also we buryed him.

"I have ritten mi bruther Ewing A. Van Bibber, of California, making a statement of the matter to him, and I must now wate the result of mi mismanagement, as I may be mistaken as to the house I rote to in New Orleans, as I only had his leter to refur to, which only said I send you a draf on New Orleans. You must excuse the length of mi unimportant and almost unconsiderate leter, and consider me most considerately your friend, "ISAAC VAN BIBBER."

Samuel C. VanBibber, the "nefue" who gave the old gentleman such a turn, joined the Confederate army during the late war, and was captured and taken to Fort Delaware, where he died of measles soon after.

VanBibber went on an expedition to the Rocky Mountains in the employ of the government, previous to his removal to California, and upon his return to Montgomery county he raised a company to go back with him. The following is a copy of one of his speeches, delivered at Loutre Lick, to an audience of attentive listeners, from among whom he was seeking volunteers:

"Westward! Westward! my friends, I am bound. I call on you to-day to answer, or hereafter hold your tongues.

"Who will join in the march to the Rocky Mountains with me, a sort of high-pressure-double-cylinder-go-it-ahead-forty-wild-cats-tearing sort of a feller? Westward bound! Come on, boys; let's streak it like a rainbow, and feast it like a wolf's eye to the West, to the Rocky Mountains, where you may learn to sing rockaby baby up in a tree top to all creation, with a wolf's howl and a bear's growl just by way of echo. Wake up, ye sleepy heads! Kick your eyes open and git out of this place. Git out of this brick kiln—these mortality turners and murder mills, where they render all the lard out of a feller until he is too lean to sweat. Git out of this warming-pan, ye holly hocks, and go out to the West where you may be seen. You can't make a shadow where you are nor see how to breathe. Why, I could cram a dozen such nations into a rifle barrel like buckshot; and I have a kind of a creeping calculation that about the time you smelt powder there would be little of you left. I guess if all of you chicken-hearted fellers were melted and run into one, you might make a shadow.

"Come, come, jump on behind, boys, and I will gallop you to the West, and I will show you such things that all natur nor a brace of earthquakes couldn't break. Fine people, lots of land—and *such* land, too! Why, you can plant a punkin over night, and next morning it will sprout pies! Such good things, such land, such deer—plenty to eat—oceans of Injuns, wild cats, rattlesnakes—and snappers as thick as onions on a rope. So hitch on, boys; there is room for a hog pen full of you, baggage and all. I have got one pocket as is not engaged, besides I guess I might stow away a ton of you aboard of my hat, taking inside and outside seats in the count, and when you find the craft too full, why jump into the hole. This is the only regilar United States craft that runs by land, chartered to the Rocky Mountains, as swift as a rocket and as safe as a possum in a pie. And those mountain gals will scramble for you like pigs after a punkin. Such gals! You never saw any like them. They are like young hurricanes! And I guess some of them are full grown storms, rainbow and all. Some of you would think you had run afoul of an earthquake. What are you sniggering at. I guess if you would sink in a basket full of our Western breezes it would crack the drawing string and take all the puckers out of your mouth.

"So come along, boys; what is the use of staying here. Come out and pasture awhile in the West, and I will bet a dozen raccoons and throw in a possum, if you will get aboard this dry land ship of Uncle Sam's, that before the year 1840 comes jumping over the stile you will spread out, scatter your limbs, overrun the country with your branches and breed a famine.''

We can readily believe that after this famous speech, he had but little difficulty in enlisting all the men he wanted.

AMONG the queer geniuses of early times was old 'Squire Colgin, of St. Charles. He was a Justice of the Peace, and usually rendered his decisions in a manner peculiar to himself, and the way he considered right, without descending from his lofty prerogative to consult the law. A man named Miller once sued a neighbor named Kirkpatrick on an open account in Colgin's court. Colgin rendered judgment in favor of the plaintiff, and after the decision was given, Miller thought of a buffalo robe he had sold Kirkpatrick, but which he had forgotten to include in the bill. So he whispered to Colgin to make an entry of it on the back of the judgment, which he did in the following words: ''Mr. Miller says that Kirk (as he wrote it) got a buffalo skin for $8, that he forgot to charge in the account, therefore I, Daniel Colgin, Justice of the Peace of this court, believe that Miller tells the truth about the skin, and I do hereby put it down on the back of the judgment, for to be collected at the same time the balance is paid. "DANIEL COLGIN, J. P."

Kirkpatrick very naturally got mad at the decision, and said if he were going to heaven and should see Miller coming too, he would change his course and go to—the other place. Colgin considered this contempt of his court, and fined him one dollar.

Another case that was entered upon Colgin's docket still further manifested his peculiar sense of justice. Two citizens of St. Charles had a quarrel about a piece of ice which one had sold to the other, and which fell short half a pound. While they were quarrelling the ice all melted, and the dealer went to Colgin and sued the other man for the price of the ice, which was six and one-fourth cents. Colgin gave judgment in his favor, but made him pay half the costs (seventy-five cents), because he thought it was right that the costs should be divided between them for being ''such blamed fools as to quarrel about a little piece of ice that he could eat in five minutes any warm day.''

Colgin afterward removed to Cotesansdessein, in Callaway county, where he and his son opened a store, which was the first store kept by Americans in that county.

A FOURTH OF JULY ORATION.—Adam Cobb, of Montgomery county, was a great admirer of Gen. Washington and the heroes who fought with him. He had a speech which he used to deliver at every Fourth of July celebration that he could attend, and the people would ride a great many miles to hear it. When he was delivering his oration he would walk to and fro on the rostrum, flourish his large bandana handkerchief, and weep. The following is a literal copy of his speech:

"GENTLEMEN AND LADIES, FRIENDS AND ENEMIES:

"I appear before you, at this time, in behalf of our beloved Washington and our forefathers. I have come to speak their praises, for it was them that bore the *brunt* of our sorrows and made us a free and a happy people.

"Yes, my friends and enemies, it was my forefathers and anchestors as well as yours that fit with our beloved Washington when he whipped the great battle of the cow pens in the State of old North Carolina. When the Red Jackets came to beguile us from our homes, besides the Red Man of our native land. Our forefathers and our *anchestors* had to work their *craps* the best they could, with the rifle in one hand and the Brazin seikle in the other, and the hot briling sun shining down on their backs.

" But our glorious, beloved Washington is no more, for he is buried way down on old Faginia shore. Whar the willows wave over his grave. and we see him no more, for he is buried way down on old *Faginia* shore, where the willows wave over his grave, and we see him no more. So *Sweet-Li* let him Lye, and sleep for ever more.

For I don't expect to detain this large, highly *larnt ordinance*, that is spread out before me, this day, but I do expect to *spificate* the great doctrine of our Great and Glorious Country that spreads from the rivers to the great Oceans of the East and the West, and should I fail to do it, I hope the memory of our forefathers and our beloved Washington will make up.all I lack.

"You, my friends and enemies, I tell you this day with tears in my eyes, that it was our beloved Washington, with General Green and our forefathers that *fit* the Battle of Bunkers Hill, a way down in North Carolina. It was there the Brazen Mouth Cannon belched forth her thunder and Spit Lightning at the same time.

"Yes, my friends, them was trying times with our beloved Washington, and our forefathers, for they had to leave their poor wives and little children at home, and fight in their bare feet with their toes bleeding as they marched down Lundy's Lane, in the State of Georgia, whar our great and good General Montgomery was killed. Yes, you ought to think a heap of that great man, for they tell me this county is named after him, and there is one on the other side of the river is named after our beloved Washington.

"I never felt better in my life as I do to-day, it makes me happy, my friends to talk to such a well *manners ordinance* as this, for our beloved Washington for seven long years, he sat in his saddle on his white horse, and fit the Red Jackets, with sword and pistol, and never got a scratch, for our forefathers and our beloved Washington sat upon their mother's knees, when they was babies, and rocked to sleep, and they have grown from small children to be great men to save the people of this great land, that reaches from North to South, from East to West, has hearn of his death, and we this day, as I was going to say, all things happens for the best. This great *Americanas* with her wide and long·rivers, and high mountings is left us, and our *prosperity* to be enjoyed by us, by our beloved Washington, for at Braddock's defeat in old Faginia our forefathers bled and died while the Red Jackets and the Red Man was made to run away.

"Our father Washington was too small then to do much good, but the military was in him, for he was chock brim full of the *gredience* that makes the warrior. Yes, my friends, this is a glorious day, with us all, I am proud of having the liberty of sending forth my feelings as old father Noah sent forth the dove from his ark.

SOON after David Darst settled in Darst's Bottom, he built a still-house, and made some splendid apple brandy, which was so good that it soon became celebrated all over the country. All the family drank of it freely, and when visitors came it was set out for them to drink, as the custom was in those times. They had but few cups then, and in their places they used gourds, wild cimblings, horns, tin cups, etc., the favorite vessel being a horn; and no one ever called without "taking a horn" before he departed. Old Brother Clark, an Ironside Baptist preacher, called at Mr. Darst's one morning to get his breakfast, and a tin cup full of apple brandy was warmed and set by his plate. He viewed it with delight, took a sip and smacked his lips over its fragrance, and then holding it up in his hand, he said the following grace: " May the good Lord bless this cup of spirits, and may we all drink of it, or of the same spirits, to the salvation of our souls, and to our coming posterity."

After the grace he drank the brandy with great relish, and it no doubt did his body and soul both good.

Mr. Darst had several neighbors who were not very fond of work, and depended principally upon their neighbors' cribs and smoke-houses for a support. Mr. Darst suffered severely from their depredations, and finally growing tired of feeding several families besides his own, he put a lock on his corn crib. Such a thing had never been heard of before in that part of the country, and it aroused the indignation of those who had been in the habit of helping themselves. Among the latter was a man named Smith, an idle, good-for-nothing sort of a fellow, whom Mr. Darst had long suspected. Locks did not prevent him from slipping corn out at the cracks of the crib, and Mr. Darst finally determined to catch him. So he sent for him one day to come and show him how to set a steel trap. Smith considered it quite an honor to be requested by so prominent, a man as Mr. Darst to show him how to do anything, and he came very readily. Mr. Darst explained that some person had been stealing corn out of his crib, and he wanted to set a trap by a certain crack in order to catch the thief. The trap was accordingly fixed, and Smith took his departure, laughing in his sleeve as to how he would fool the old man; but as soon as he was out of sight Darst removed the trap and set it by another crack, on the other side of the crib. The next morning being Sunday he walked out early to observe the situation, and was *surprised* to see his friend Smith hugging close up to the corn crib, with his right hand fast in the steel trap. "Good morning, Mr. Smith," said Mr. Darst, "you are up early this morning. Won't you come in?" Smith excused himself by saying that he could not just then, as his hand was hurting him very much. And then he begged Darst not to say anything about it, and said if he would keep it still he might take his shirt off and give him thirty-nine lashes. Darst accepted the proposition, and gave him the whipping; but the affair leaked out, and Smith left the country.

CHRISTOPHER SANDERS, of Montgomery county, was very fond of hunting, but did not like the trouble of carrying a gun, so he generally depended upon borrowing one after he found his game. He borrowed so often of the VanBibber boys, who lived near Loutre Lick, that they finally became tired of it, and determined to give him a dose that would cure him. So the next time he called for a gun, they loaded an old musket about half full of powder and bullets and gave it to him; but he suspected that something was wrong, from the peculiar manner in which the boys winked at one another, and he returned the gun with the load still in it. The boys were now greatly troubled to devise some means to get the load out of the gun, for they were afraid to shoot it, and there was no other way to get it out. A few days afterward an Irishman came along, who had seen several deer at the side of the road, and wanted to borrow a gun to shoot them with. The boys very readily loaned him the old musket, and he took his departure in quest of the game. Pretty soon they heard a roaring in that direction, which sounded like several small earthquakes had broken loose; and they waited with some degree of anxiety for Pat to put in an appearance. Presently he returned, having killed three deer and wounded a fourth; but the old musket had kicked him heels over head, dislocated his arm and mashed his nose. He was delighted, however, with his success, and exclaimed, "Faith, an' I kilt three of the buggers, and would have got another if the blamed ould gun had had a good load in her!"

A CHURCH meeting was once held in Danville, over which the celebrated Dr. Bond presided, to decide where they should hang their new church bell. One of the members suggested that they should hang it on the *parapet* of the church, but Dr. Bond objected, saying that it would shake the walls down. After a good deal of discussion, without arriving at anything definite, Dr. Adams, who was not a member of the church but merely a spectator, suggested that they plant a forked tree, and hang the bell in that. Bond jumped at this proposition as the very thing they wanted, thanked the doctor for his kindness, put the suggestion in the form of a motion to the meeting, and it was carried. This aroused the ire of the brother who had suggested the parapet of the church, and arising from his seat he addressed the chair and said he was more than surprised at such a foolish thing. "Why," said he, "do you let a mere outsider, *and a fool at that,* come in here and make such a silly suggestion? The idea of planting a forked tree and waiting for it to grow large enough to hold a bell that will weigh five hundred pounds, is the most absurd thing I ever heard of in my life." He took his seat in the midst of a universal titter, and for years afterward it would make him as mad as a hornet to say anything about planting a forked tree in his presence.

JAMES RIPPER, of Callaway county, went on a hunt, one day, with several of his neighbors, and while they were in the woods they caught two cub bears. Ripper wanted to save them alive for pets, and the rest of the party agreed to let him have them if he would carry them home alive. So he tied their legs together, slung them across a stick and shouldered them. He had proceeded only a short distance on his way home when each of the bears caught him by one of the ears, and bit them off. That worried him, and he threw the bears down and killed them on the spot.

In early days a disease called the hollow horn was very bad among the cattle of Callaway county, and many of them died. Ripper thought he could fool the hollow horn and give it something to think about; so he sold all of his horned cattle and bought muleys instead. But pretty soon the muleys had the hollow horn too, and when Ripper went in great distress to his neighbors to inquire what he should do, they advised him to take a gimlet and bore holes into the heads of his cattle. He did so, and killed them as dead as the hollow horn could have done.

GATHERING FODDER IN CALLA-
WAY COUNTY.

Ripper used to farm in partnership with a neighbor named Hamlin. The latter was low, but large and fat, while Ripper was low and lean as a lucifer match. In the fall they would gather the fodder and the tops of the stalks of their corn while it was green and sweet, and bundle it up for winter food for their stock. But the corn grew very tall, and they were both so low that they could not reach to the tops, so they had to invent some plan to increase their stature. They finally decided to splice themselves, and upon trying it they found that the plan worked admirably. Ripper would stand on Hamlin's shoulders and pull the top blades while his fellow-laborer pulled those lower down; and thus they gathered their crop in peace and harmony.

BENJAMIN ELLIS, of Callaway county, was a great bear hunter when bears were plentiful in Missouri. He wore a suit of buckskin, the pants being very stout and thick, and when he came to a steep hill, in pursuit of a bear, he would sit down and slide to the bottom on the seat of his pants, keeping his legs crossed so they could not divide on the saplings and bushes that came in his way. By this means he would reach the foot of the hill much sooner than he could walk or run down; and, besides, he could take a little rest while he was sliding along.

Mr. JAMES SUGGETT, of Callaway county, heard a peculiar noise in his stable, one day, and upon going out to ascertain what caused it, he found a large buck quietly feeding himself from the horse-trough. Mr. S. hastily slammed the door shut, intending to fasten the deer in; but he was not quick enough, and the frightened animal plunged against the door and carried it off the hinges. It remained fast on his horns, and while he was struggling with it Mr. Suggett laid hold of him, thinking he could hold him down; but the deer proved to be the stronger of the two, and

SUGGETT AND THE BUCK.

dragged him and the door to the lot fence. Seeing that he was going to jump over, Mr. S. let go, having no desire to perform such a feat of gymnastics, and the deer went over the fence as light as a bird, the door still hanging to his horns. He soon disappeared in the woods, and that was the last Mr. Suggett ever saw of the deer or his stable door.

HER "EXPERIENCE."—Mrs. P., a pioneer of Montgomery county, applied for membership in the Baptist Church at New Providence, of which Rev. Jabez Ham was pastor. Brother Ham said:

"Sister P., have you had an experience?"

"Oh, yes," she replied; "I heard some beautiful music down in the creek bottom near my house, the other night; it was mighty pretty music."

"Sing it for us, sister," said Mr. Ham, "and if you can't sing it, just try and hum it a little."

"Well, I reckon I can," said Mrs. P., "but I'm afraid."

"Afraid of what?" inquired Mr. Ham.

"Why, I'm afraid to mock the angels," she replied.

"Don't be afraid of that," exclaimed the minister; "mock them if you can; I'll be responsible."

So she settled herself in her seat, cleared her throat, and rolled her eyes up toward the ceiling, in the direction where it is popularly supposed heaven is located, while they all gathered around her to hear her "mock the angels." Presently she broke out on the C sharp note with the refrain—

"The camels are coming,
The camels are coming,
Hi ho! Hi ho!"

winding up with a shriek and a demi-semi-quaver that made the rafters of the old church quake with terror.

"Stop! Stop!" cried Brother Ham, with his fingers in his ears, "for the love of mercy don't give us any more of that." Then in a milder tone he added, "your experience won't do, sister—you must try again," and without further ceremony he dismissed the meeting.

JOHN CROCKETT and his sister Lucy, who settled on Loutre Island at a very early date, were both splendid shots with the rifle, and could bring down a turkey or a deer at long range every fire. One day John bought an ox from Stephen Patton, which Patton represented as being a good riding ox. So John mounted on his back and started home, when the steer became frightened and ran away. He took his course through the thick woods, and in addition to ruining John's clothes came very near killing him. He had life enough left in him, however, to crawl home, where he and his sister nursed his wound until they were well, vowing all the time that they would have revenge. The opportunity soon came. Patton was passing through the woods, one day, without his gun, when he discovered a large, fat deer, and Crockett's house being near, he went there to borrow a gun. John was away, but his sister remembered the adventure with the ox, and rejoiced that the time had come when she could pay Patton back. They had an old musket in the house which she loaded half full of powder and shot, and gave it to Patton with the re- mark that she guessed it would "bring something down." Patton took the gun, found his deer and blazed away. But the moment he touched the trigger he imagined that an earthquake had sprung up around him. The old musket dislocated his shoulder, cut off one of his ears, mashed his nose, nearly burnt his eyes out, and left him flat on his back on the ground, a hopeless wreck; and then to add insult to injury, the old gun got up on its breech and danced around him and whooped and yelled like a wild Indian. But it killed the deer! After lying on the ground several hours Patton recovered sufficiently to make his way home, but it was several weeks before his wounds and bruises were cured.

HOW TO BREAK A COLT.—Old Fred Sluggs, a Dutch pioneer of Audrain county, had a two-year old colt that he wanted to break and make gentle. So he said to his son Jake, "Now Jake, you go up into the lane, and vhen I cum along on the colt you shump oud and say boo! mit your mout." Jake did as he was told, and directly he saw his father cantering along on the colt in a very agreeable and pleasant manner. Just as they came oppo- site to where he was concealed Jake sprang out on his all fours and shouted "*Boo! Boo! Boo!*" as loud as he could yell. The colt was frightened out of its wits, and threw the old man on his head, breaking his arm and knocking the breath out of him. Jake thought his father was dead, and ran to him and began to blow his breath into his mouth. Presently the old man came to, and looking up at his son with a rueful countenance, and groaning with pain, he said, "Ah, Jake, Jake, you boo'd too dam much!"

AMONG the first settlers of Audrain county were two neighbors, shout- ing Methodists, who made a rule of "getting happy" on all occasions, especially at camp-meetings, and manifesting their joy by shouting, clap- ping their hands, and performing various grotesque maneuvers. They both became exceedingly happy at a camp-meeting, one day, and in order to give free vent to their exuberant feelings, they climbed into the top of a tall tree, in the camp ground, and shouted and sang, and bade farewell to all below, saying that they could see their Jesus on a white horse and were on their way to meet him. Presently one of those rapid little August thunder clouds came up and overshadowed the heavens, and its bright flashes of lightning were followed by keen, sharp bursts of thun- der, which caused the women and children to scream and the men to shrink and dodge like raw recruits on their first battlefield. In a few minutes a tall tree near the camp was struck by lightning and shivered into splinters, the flash being followed by a crash of thunder that seemed to rend the very bowels of the earth. Things were getting too hot for the two old fellows in the tree top, and they came down to the ground as nimbly as squirrels, and complained that the storm had bothered them and prevented them from having a fair chance.

ADVENTURES OF GENERAL BURDINE.—The older citizens of St. Charles county will remember a rich character known as General Burdine, who resided in Dog Prairie at an early date. He made his living by hunting and fishing, and was distinguished for his eccentricities and the marvelous yarns he could tell about his adventures in the woods. A few of these we give below, as the General told them:

He shot a buck, one day, and killed him so dead that he did not fall, but remained standing until the General went up to him and pulled him over by the ear. On another occasion he was hunting on Cuivre river, when he discovered a large, fat buck standing on the opposite side, and on looking up into a tree just over him he saw a fine large turkey. He desired to kill both, but had only a single-barreled gun, and knew that as soon as he shot one the other would leave. But a happy thought struck him. He put another ball down on top of the one that was already in his gun, and with that he shot the turkey; then dropping the muzzle of his gun in the twinkling of an eye he killed the buck with the other ball. He now had to wade the river to get his game, and in doing so caught the seat of his buckskin pants full of fine fish, which he carried home along with his turkey and deer.

Another time while the General was hunting, he shot all his bullets away, but happening to have a lot of shoemaker's awls in his pocket, he loaded his gun with them. Presently he saw three deer in a group, and fired at them and killed two. The third one was pegged fast to a tree by one of the awls, where he swung and kicked until the General let him loose and took him home alive.

Late one very cold afternoon the General shot a buffalo on the bank of a creek, and removing the skin he rolled himself up in it and lay down and slept all night. Next morning the skin was frozen so hard that he could not unroll himself or even get on his feet, and he began to think he would have to lie there and starve to death. But finally he rolled himself down the bank of the creek and landed in a warm spring, which soon thawed the skin until it was soft, and he unrolled himself and went home rejoicing.

One day, before he was grown, the General saw a wood-pecker fly into his hole in a tree, and he climbed up to catch him. When he put his hand into the hole he caught a black snake, which frightened him so badly that he let go his hold and fell into the forks of the tree, where he became wedged in so tight that he could not get out. He began to call for help, and pretty soon a boy came along, whom he sent to get an axe to cut the tree down. The boy did as he was directed, and cut the tree so that it fell right side up, and the General was saved.

He had a pony named Ned, that he rode on all his hunting expeditions; and Ned was as smart a horse as any one could desire to see. One day they came to a deep creek, with steep banks, across which the General felled a small sapling with his tomahawk, intending to walk over, and let Ned swim. But Ned winked one eye and smiled in his peculiarly sly manner, as much as to say, "Never mind, old fellow, I'll show you a trick worth knowing." The General started across, holding the bridle in his hand, but when he reached the middle of the creek, he stopped and looked back to see how Ned was getting along, when, to his amazement, he saw the pony walking the sapling after him! Ned shook his head and motioned for his master to go on; and so they passed over in safety, without either of them getting wet. Ned was a native of Kentucky, and his master had owned him so long that they felt like brothers. The pony was thoroughly trained in hunting, and was exceedingly fond of the sport. Whenever his master killed a deer, he always insisted upon licking the blood, of which he was very fond.

The General once undertook to explain to a party of gentlemen the manner in which the distance across Cuivre river could be measured by an engineer. Said he, "You see, gentlemen, the surveyor first gits a *obligation* across the stream, and sticks down his compass. Then he *leanders* up or down the river, as the case may be, and gits a nuther *obligation* from that; then he leanders back to the first obligation and works it out by figgers. It's simple enough," added the old General, "and I could do it myself, although I don't know a darned thing about figgers."

His children were about as eccentric as himself. One of his sons, whom he called Jim, was particularly noted for his oddities and the number of singular scrapes that he managed to get himself into. In early days the people sometimes amused themselves at an entertainment called a "gander pulling," which which was something like the more modern "tournaments." A suitable track having been cleared off, an old gander would be hung on a cross-bar, with his head down, and just low enough so that a man on horseback could reach his outstretched neck. Then the contestants would ride at full gallop under the cross-bar, and the one who succeeded in pulling the gander's head off, without losing his seat in his saddle, was declared the victor and crowned accordingly. Jim went to one of these gander-pullings one day, on board of an old mule, which was so extremely lazy and slow that he felt confident he would have plenty of time to "pull the gander." When his turn came he started in at a gait that was slow enough to satisfy his brightest anticipations, and when he came under the gander he laid hold of his head with a full determination never to let go until victory crowned his efforts. But just at that moment somebody gave the old mule a sharp cut with a whip, and he made a lunge forward and left Jim hanging in the air by the gander's neck. The old gander proved to be a tough one, and Jim had to let go without wringing his coveted neck.

During the Slicker war Jim fell in with a party of Slickers, one day, who were on their way to lynch a horse theif, and falling into the rear he followed after them "just to see the fun." He had two bottles of whisky in his pockets, and presently he drew one out and took a long pull at it. One of the rules of the Slicker organization was that none of their members, nor any one who accompanied them, should drink any intoxicating liquors while they were on an expedition; and the Captain of the company, observing Jim thus impudently breaking one of their strictest rules, rode back to his side and broke the bottles over his head. Jim left in a hurry then, saying he had seen all the fun he wanted to that day.

ANOTHER HARD-SHELL SERMON.—Rev. Mr. Green, of Callaway county, preached the following sermon in Mr. Henry Logan's house, on Bear creek, one Sunday night, after having eaten a hearty supper of onions, etc. He read his text as follows:

"And my sheep will know my voice, and when I call they will come; and a stranger's voice they know not, therefore they won't come, ah."

"Now, my brethering," he continued, "my sheep is likened unto a little goat, named Cato, that my daddy had in North Carolina, ah, that come up missing one day, ah, and the thunder and lightning and the wind was coming on at a mighty rate, ah, and we children went out and called Cato, ah, and no Cato answered we children, ah. But daddy just poked his head out of the winder, ah, and called Cato one time, ah, and poor Cato said Baa, ah. So you see, my brethering, ah, poor Cato knowed daddy's voice, ah, and as soon as he called him he answered, ah. Just so it will be with us at the great day of judgment, ah. When the Master shall call his sheeps, ah, they will answer; and a heap of them will answer, ah, that he did not call, ah; and a heap of them will have on wolves' skins, ah, and pretend they are sheep, ah, but the Great Shepherd will know which of them wears the wool, ah. So daddy called poor

Cato, and he said Baa, ah. Yes, my brethering, when Gabriel shall stand with one foot on the ground and the other foot in the water, ah, and blow that long trumpet, ah, that will wake up the dead, ah, and the living will start a-running, ah, and calling on you, brother Ham, ah, to save them from the blue blazes of hell, ah.

"I think I hear somebody say over in that corner, ah, that brother Green can't preach, ah, and I think I hear somebody in that corner say that brother Green can preach, ah; but if you will wait a while Brother Green will lumber, ah. And when daddy called poor Cato he said Baa, ah.

"We are told, my brethering, ah, that we must not put new wine into old bottles, ah, nor old wine into new bottles, ah; and it becometh us to *fill full* all righteousness, ah, and not to back bite our neighbors, ah, nor our neighbor's a**s, ah, nor anything that is his, ah; and the Bible says, wives do good to your husbands, ah, and husbands do good to your wives, ah, and children obey your father and mother, ah. Now, I want to know to-night, ah, how many of you have done any of these things, ah. And daddy called poor Cato, and he said Baa, ah.

"Now, in conclusion, I want to say to you my brethering, ah, that if any of you get to heaven, ah, before brother Ham or brother Green, ah, just keep yourselves ready to meet us, for we are coming too, ah And while I have been preaching this night, ah, some of my sheep have gone to sleep, ah; and I will get you, brother Logan to just say to that man talking at the door, ah, not to talk so loud, ah, or he will wake up my old sister Cobb, ah, who is sitting there in the corner asleep, ah.

"And my sheep will know my voice, ah, and when I call they will come, ah, and a stranger's voice they don't know, ah, neither do they come, ah. And daddy called poor Cato, ah, and Cato said Baa, ah."

THE first piano was brought to North Missouri in 1816, by Mrs Dr. Young, whose husband laid off the town of Marthasville, in Warren county. It excited a great deal of wonder, and people performed long journeys to see it and hear Mrs. Young play upon it. A number of old ladies walked from Callaway, Montgomery, Lincoln and St. Charles counties, and carried their shoes and babies in their arms, just to see the wonderful instrument.

AT a camp-meeting in Warren county, many years ago, an old style Baptist preacher from Illinois was invited to preach. He read his text as follows: "And Joseph is not, and Benjamin is not, and Simon was not also," from which he preached the following short sermon: "My brethering and sisters, I am all the way from Elinois, ah. And we read in the scriptures, ah, where our blessed Savior, ah, held the man and let him go at the same time, ah—held him, my brethering, ah, and let him go at the same time, ah. I can't see how he done it, ah, nor understand it, ah; and I venture to say, ah, that there is no man on this ground that could do it, ah." And with that he closed his sermon.

AN old pioneer of South Bear Creek had a "log-rolling," which, as usual, wound up with a dance. During the night one of his guests became very warm from the exercise of dancing, and pulling off his pants he continued to dance in the airy costume of a buckskin hunting shirt. The old pioneer became offended at his free and easy manner, and led him out of the house by the ear, remarking that he "didn't allow any such exhibitions in his house." But his guest argued the question with him, and finally convinced him that there was nothing so neat and elegant to dance in as a buckskin hunting shirt. So the old pioneer pulled his pants off too, and both went back and danced in that "light fantastic costume" until morning.

In early times a youth named Jim Stewart, of Montgomery county, concluded he would try a new plan for hunting wild turkeys. So he dug a trench near his father's house, and baited it with corn. Then he put a tremendous load of shot and powder into his gun, and seating himself at one end of the trench, he quietly awaited coming events. He watched patiently all night, and when day light came the next morning' the trench was filled with wild turkeys, squirrels and hogs. Jim blazed away and brought down sixteen turkeys, one squirrel and an old sow.

Poetry by a Pioneer.—Many years ago an old pioneer, while wandering through the then wilderness of what is now Montgomery county, found a family of "squatters" who were originally from the State of Indiana. He was hospitably entertained by them, and his feelings found vent in the following effusion, which is well seasoned with truth, even if it does not contain much genuine poetry :

> "As a stranger traveling through the West,
>   I came upon a Hoosier nest—
>   Or, in other words, a Buckeye cabin,
>   Just big enough to hold Queen Mabin.
>   Its situation, low, but airy,
>   On the border of the prairie.
>   Fearing he might be benighted,
>   He hail'd the house, and then alighted.
>   The Hoosier met him at the door—
>   The salutations soon were o'er;
>   He took the stranger's horse aside,
>   And to a sapling tied;
>   Having taken the saddle off,
>   He fed him in the sugar trough.
>   The stranger stooped to enter in,
>   The entrance closing with a pin;
>   He manifested strong desire
>   To sit himself by the log-heap fire,
>   Where half a dozen Hoosier-roons,
>   With mush and milk, tin cups and spoons,
>   White heads, bare feet, and dirty faces,
>   Seemed much inclined to keep their places.
>   The Madam, anxious to display
>   Her rough and undisputed sway,
>   Her offspring to the ladder led,
>   And cuff'd the youngsters up to bed,
>   Inviting the stranger to partake
>   Of venison, milk and Johnny cake.
>   The stranger ate a hearty meal;
>   A glance around the room would steal;
>   One side was hung with divers garments,
>   The other strung with skins of varments—
>   Two rifles placed above the door,
>   Three dogs stretched upon the floor—
>   In short, the domicile was rife,
>   With specimens of Hoosier life."

Mr. David Kennedy, of Callaway county, poured some slop into his hog trough, one day, and a little bull calf came along and drank it all. It filled him as full as a tick, and resulted in a serious catastrophe immediately afterward. As he turned to go out of the lot his belly struck against the end of a fence rail, and he was stuffed so tight that he bursted open on the back and the slop flew ten feet high.

PIGEONS.—Mr. Calvin Tate, of Callaway county, says that the wild pigeons were so plentiful one summer that frequently when they would alight on a tree it would bend down to the ground with their weight. He went hunting one day, and seeing a fine lot of pigeons in a tree, he hitched his horse to one of the limbs and fired and killed three hundred at one shot. The rest flew away, and as soon as the tree was relieved of their weight it straightened up, carrying his horse with it, and the poor brute had to hang there until he could go home and get an ax and cut the tree down.

THREE old pioneers of Montgomery county became insulted because one of their neighbors did not invite them to his daughter's wedding. So they went to his house after night, built a large log fire in the yard, then caught his old yellow dog and cut his tail off, roasted and ate it, and returned home happy and contented.

UNCLE BILLY GRANT, of Callaway county, was not much of a hunter, but one time a friend of his from Kentucky, who was exceedingly fond of the sport, paid him a visit, and Uncle Billy thought it would never do to let him go back home without taking a hunt in our Missouri woods. He remembered where he had seen a deer about three years before, and he thought now would be a good time to show his skill as a hunter and get the deer too. So one morning he proposed to his friend that they should take a hunt, and the friend readily consented. They started, and having arrived on the ground near where Uncle Billy had seen the deer, they dismounted and cautiously crept up to a large log that lay in front of them. When they reached it Uncle Billy slowly raised his head above it, and having taken a long look into the woods, he said in a loud whisper: "Now, just here, three years ago, I saw a *buster!*" His friend at first looked as if he was badly sold, but seeing that Uncle Billy was in dead earnest, he burst into a laugh, in which his companion joined, and they soon after returned home without the deer.

MR. BENJAMIN BARNES, a pioneer of Boone and Callaway counties, went to school to his brother James, in Cooper's Fort, during the Indian war. One day he and several other boys climbed over the pickets and went to the river to bathe. Benjamin being small, was left on the bank to guard their clothes while the other boys were in the water, and he keenly felt the slight thus put upon him because he was not a "big boy." He determined to pay them back, and as soon as they were all in the water he yelled, "Indians! Indians!" and ran toward the fort. The other boys followed as fast as their feet could carry them, naked and scared half to death. They tumbled over the picketing like frightened sheep, and for a while there was great excitement in the fort, everybody expecting an immediate attack. But finally young Barnes had to explain, and then he was locked up in the guard house and kept there for a week —which was not half so funny as scaring the boys.

Mr. Barnes had a cousin named Azel, who was a blacksmith, and distinguished for his ability to spin yarns. He said he made a scythe, once, seven feet in length—beat it out on his anvil. Then he put a handle to it, and cut seven acres of grass in one day, without whetting or grinding his blade. As he was going home that evening he saw a sheep skin lying on a pond of water, with the wool side up, and with one sweep of his scythe he shaved the wool off clean without making a riffle on the water. He raised five acres of corn, one summer, and when it was nearly ripe a very large turkey gobbler (he must have been very large indeed) stood on the outside of the fence and picked off nearly all the ears! He afterward killed the gobbler, and he weighed 150 pounds to the quarter, or 600 pounds in all, and yielded 29 pounds of good feathers.

ADVENTURE WITH A BULL.—Mr. John Hudson lived in Montgomery county, near the line of Lincoln, and one day he rode his little pony down to Dr. Brandt's, in Warren county, to get some medicine for his family. On his way back a vicious bull attacked the pony, which threw his rider into a branch and then ran home with the bull after him. John was so frightened that he crawled out of the branch and climbed up into a tree, where he tied himself fast with his suspenders and remained until morning. When the first gray streaks of dawn began to appear, he cautiously made his way to the ground and started home, but had not gone far when he met the same bull returning from his chase after the pony. John "skinned" another tree in a twinkling, and the bull charged up to him just in time to be too late to give him a lift with his horns. John thanked him for his kind intentions, but said he preferred to climb his own way—it was slower, but more comfortable. The bull sat down and crossed his legs and watched him all that day and night, but just at day light the next morning he fell into a doze, when John tremblingly slipped down to the ground and walked home (he walked pretty fast too.) The distance was twelve miles, and when he arrived at home he was nearly dead from starvation and loss of sleep.

MR. MICAJAH HARRISON of Callaway county, was passionately fond of hunting, and would frequently go out with hunting parties and camp for weeks at a time. On one occasion Hon. Wm. H. Russell, of Boone county, was a member of the party. Mr. Russell was a candidate for the Legislature at the time, and never lost an opportunity to advocate his claims where he thought he could do the most good. One day he became separated from the party and got lost in the woods. There was snow on the ground, and in trying to find his way back to the camp he became so confused that he wandered in a circle instead of pursuing a direct course. At last he completed the circle and came upon his own tracks. "Hallo!" he exclaimed, "here's one of the fellows," and away he went to overtake him. He soon performed the circle again and came upon two tracks, which he imagined were made by two of the hunters; and away he went after them as hard as he could go. He kept this up until he had gone around four times, when an old owl in the woods called out, "Who-who-who-a-e-i-u?" Russell immediately replied, "I am William H. Russell, sir, formerly of Kentucky, but now of Missouri, and a candidate for the Legislature." About this time Mr. Harrison and the rest of the party came up, and had a hearty laugh over Russell's morning adventures and his address to the owl. The joke was so good that it got into the papers, and was related at every public speaking during the canvass by Mr. Russell's opponent.

MR. ALECK WEANT, a pioneer of Callaway county, was a blacksmith by trade, and he used his arms so much that the blood stopped circulating in them. He says that for nine months he had to have them lanced nine times every morning before sun rise, and had to carry his hands tied up over his head, while his heels were stretched over a bench seven feet high. This heroic mode of treatment finally restored the circulation, and he got well. Mr. Weant went hunting in Kentucky, one day, before his removal to Missouri, and wounded a buck, which first jumped upon him and then went over a precipice forty feet high, and escaped. Soon afterward he shot a turkey, which fell over the same precipice, and while he was trying to get it a panther came along and picked the turkey up, and then sprang on him and scared him nearly to death; after which it trotted away and ate the turkey. Mr. Weant saw a cannon, captured from the British at the battle of New Orleans, which was so large that the ball had to be drawn into it with a yoke of oxen, and then the oxen were driven out at the touch hole. Mr. Weant was standing near the gun when it was discharged, and the concussion was so great that it made him deaf for a month. That was a very large cannon.

MR. PETER BRATTON, of Montgomery county, has met with some very ren arkable adventures during his life; so many in fact that we can notice only a very small number of them. He formerly lived in Iowa, where it was very cold, and they had good skating almost the year round. They would frequently get up skating parties, and spend an entire day at this exciting amusement. In one of their parties there was a young man who was such an adapt in the use of his skates that he never thought of going around air-holes, but would jump right over them. Some of the air-holes were thirty feet across, but he went over them without any difficulty whatever.—Mr. Bratton was hauling a load of iron, one day, while he lived in Iowa, when a violent thunder storm came up. The lightning bolts fell thick and fast around him, but he escaped unharmed, as they passed under him and struck the iron. On another occasion Mr. Bratton went on a sea voyage, and one day they discoverad an immense whale. It was so large that an entire day was consumed in sailing from one end of the whale to the other. But perhaps the greatest feat that Mr. Bratton ever accomplished was when he got six fox skins off of five foxes. They were very large, fine foxes, however, and that may account for it. Mr. B. and one of his friends have frequently jumped from the roof of a four-story mill into a creek, when they were bathing, without getting hurt in the least. They did it just for fun.

CAPT. WM. OXLEY, of Montgomery county, obtained his title at the battle of New Orleans, where he cammanded a flat-boat in the service of General Jackson. After the General was elected President he appointed Capt. Oxley to the position of postmaster of a small town in Kentucky, which yielded him the enormous salary of $6.50 a year. He was a farmer as well as postmaster, and desiring to devote as much time as possible to his work, he carried all the letters that came to the office in his hat, so he could deliver them without stopping his work when the persons to whom they were addressed called for them. The Captain says he was a very strong man when he was younger, and one day he shouldered one thousand green shingles and started to carry them up a ladder to the roof of a house. Every round of the ladder broke as he went up, and when the last one broke he was just high enough so that he could catch the eave of the roof with his teeth, and he held on there until the workmen came to his relief. Some time afterward he met with an accident and lost his teeth, which had so opportunely saved his life on the occasion referred to. The accident happened in this way: He had shouldered a large beech log, and started to carry it into the house for a back-log to his fire, but just as he reached the door he stumbled and fell, and the log came down on the back of his head with so much force that it drove his teeth several inches into the door sill, where they remained fast and were drawn out of his mouth when he arose. He afterward chopped them out of the door-sill with an ax.—The Captain was out hunting, one day, and heard a sound like some one mauling rails at a distance. His curiosity was excited, and he hurried on in the direction of the sound to see what caused it. He soon came in sight of a hollow stump, which was "chuck" full of 'coons, and there was just one 'coon more than the stump would hold. This extra 'coon cavorted around on the outside awhile, and then snapped and bit his way into the stump through a hole at the bottom. This crowded out another one at the top, which fell to the ground with a loud thump. This one then made his way in at the bottom, as the other had done, when another was crowded out at the top; and they kept this up for several hours, the extra 'coons falling to the ground with so much regularity that the noise sounded like a man mauling rails.

JONATHAN BRYAN built the first water mill in Missouri, in 1801. It was situated on a small spring branch, that empties into the Femme Osage creek, in St. Charles county. The mill would grind from six to ten bushels of grain in twenty-four hours, and for several years it supplied the settlements from St. Charles to Loutre Island with meal and flour, the same stones* grinding both wheat and corn. The flour was bolted in a box, by hand, and they made pretty good flour that way. Mr. Bryan would fill the hopper with grain in the morning, and the mill would grind on that until noon, when the hopper would again be filled. The meal ran into a large pewter basin which sat on the floor at the bottom of the stones. Daniel Boone was living at that time with his son Nathan, about a mile from the mill, and he had an old dog named Cuff that used to go to the mill in Mr. Bryan's absence and lick the meal out of the basin as fast as it ran from the spout. When it did not run fast enough to suit him he would sit down and howl and bark, and one day Mr. Bryan heard him and hastened to the mill to see what was the matter. He soon discovered where his meal had been going, and after that he exchanged the pewter basin for a tin coffee pot, which was too small at the top for Cuff to get his head into it. But he made the attempt one day, and got the coffee pot fast on his head and ran away with it. Mr. Bryan subsequently built a larger mill, and sold the stones of the old one to Mr. Aleck Logan, of Montgomery county, who tied them together with a hickory withe and carried them to his home on Bear creek. The same stones are now in the possession of Mr. Aleck Logan, Jr., who uses them to set his bee stands on.

WM. STRODE, a scout and Indian fighter of early days in Kentucky, was captured on one occasion by a large party of Indians, and as they knew him well he expected immediate death or future torture at the stake. But he determined to make the best of his misfortune, and show his captors that he was not afraid of them; so he jumped on to a log and crowed like a chicken, at the same time moving his arms like a chicken flapping its wings. The Indians were highly amused and laughed heartily, and from that time forward they treated him as a friend rather than an enemy, suffering him to remain in their camp unguarded and to do nearly as he pleased. He finally made his escape and returned to his friends.

MANY remarkable feats were performed by the old pioneers, and occasionally it is hard to avoid the belief that they sometimes "stretched the blanket." For instance, a pioneer of Callaway county, who was a native of Tennessee, says that he swam the Tennessee river, one day, with his head through the hole of a millstone; and on another occasion he dived to the bottom of a deep spring, where his head got fast under a root, which he had to gnaw in two with his teeth before he could rise to the surface again. Wonder how he got his breath while he was gnawing that root?

WHEN Mr. Samuel Cobb first settled in Montgomery county, rattlesnakes were numerous, and he says they used to gather around his house and sing all night. One morning he found a large rattlsnake coiled up in his oven. He was not a very tempting piece of meat to roast, but Mr. Cobb determined to give him a trial; so he quickly placed the lid on the oven, built a fire under it, and roasted the snake brown.

MR. IRA COTTLE, of St. Charles county once had a difficulty with Hon. Benjamin Emmons, Sr., about a calf, each claiming it as his property. They

---

* It is stated on page 133 that these stones were brought from Kentucky to Missouri on a pack-horse, but this is an error, as they were made by Mr. Bryan's father, from stones taken from the hill near where the mill stood.

finally concluded to try Solomon on the calf, and let it decide which cow was its mother. So it was turned into a lot with the two cows, and at first it ran to the one owned by Cottle. "Aha!" he exclaimed, greatly elated, "I told you it was my calf—see how it runs to its mother." But about this time the calf discovered its mistake and ran to the other cow, and remained with her. "Confound the calf," said Cottle, "it don't know its own mother." But it had decided against him, and according to the terms of the agreement he was bound to submit, which he did with as good grace as he could command.

THE HEN-EGG REVIVAL.—During early days in Kentucky there was a great revival of religion, known as the "hen-egg revival," which occurred in this way: Some one had found an egg, upon which was legibly inscribed the portentious words—" *The day of judgment is close at hand.*" The inscription had been made after the egg was laid, by some one who was "up to snuff," but it answered the purpose just as well as if it had been there from the first, and great excitement prevailed in that community. People who had not read their Bibles or prayed for years now did both with great fervor, and nothing was thought or alked of but religion and the end of the world. A Baptist preacher got possession of the egg and read the ominous inscription from his pulpit, after which he preached a sermon that fairly glowed with the blazing brimstone of future punishment. He dwelt upon the horrors of hell and the terrors of the judgment day until women shrieked with fright, and strong men fell upon their knees and begged aloud for mercy. The minister then called for penitents, and the altar was filled to overflowing. A great revival immediately took place, and among the converts was a young man named Theodoric Boulware, who subsequently became a minister in the Baptist Church, and located in Callaway county, Mo. His conversion proved to be genuine, and he made an able and efficient worker in the cause of Christianity. But in after years he often related with great relish the amusing incidents of the "hen-egg revival." Previous to Mr. Boulware's removal to Missouri he preached a sermon from the text, "And Peter's wife's mother lay sick of a fever." There was a backwoodsman in the congregation who seemed deeply interested in the sermon, and gave his undivided attention to it. About forty years afterward Mr. Boulware visited that neighborhood, and preached again from the same text. The same backwoodsman was present again on this occasion, having grown to be an old man, and he seemed more deeply interested than before. When the services were over he led the minister aside, and with genuine anxiety and distress depicted upon his features, he said: "For the Lord's sake, ain't that old woman dead yet? How long do you think she will live? Poor old critter! what a lot she must have suffered these forty years. I'll warrant she's needy, and really the people ought to send her something to help her along." Mr. Boulware explained the situation as well as he could, but had to leave the old man not more than half satisfied.

HOW DOG PRAIRIE GOT ITS NAME.—Dog Prairie, in the northeastern part of St. Charles county, was originally called White's Prairie, in honor of Capt. James White, of Ohio, who was the first settler upon it; and during the Indian war he built a fort which also bore his name. Some years after this Mr. Comegis built a mill on the prairie, and the name was subsequently changed to Comegis' Prairie, which it retained until 1830, when it received the name it has since borne from a celebrated dog fight which took place at the mill. An election was being held there for some purpose, and nearly everybody in the vicinity was present. Among the rest were two brothers named George and Sam Wells. The latter had a dog that he thought a great deal of, and he bet fifty cents that he could whip any other dog on the ground. Bob Pruett took up the bet, but having no dog of his own, he borrowed one, named Bulger, from Mr. Absalom Keithley. Bulger whipped Wells' dog, and two others besides, which so enraged the Wells boys that they jumped on to Pruett to whip him, when a general fight ensued. Felix Scott knocked the two Wells boys down, and Pruett bit Sam's chin off. During the row, Mr. Robert Guthrie, who was a very small man, became badly frightened, and ran and hid himself in the meal chest of the mill, where he was found several hours afterward, still trembling with apprehension. When they found him he sprang out of the chest, all covered with meal, and wanted to know if the fight was over. So many were engaged in this fight, and it became so widely known, that the prairie was at once named "Dog Prairie," which title it has borne ever since.

EARLY one morning, in the year 1814, Abraham Keithley went into the woods to hunt his horses. He crossed Cuivre river at Chain-of-Rocks, and was soon afterward killed and scalped by a party of Indians. His body was found by his friends a few days afterward, and buried where he fell.

CALLAWAY county is distinguished in many ways, and no matter what the "Kingdom" undertakes it generally makes the best of it. Among its other remarkable productions is the tall man—a descendant of Daniel Boone—who is so tall that nobody knows what his height really is. During harvest seasons the farmers employ him to stack their oats and hay, and he has to sit on the ground to make himself low enough to reach down to the top of a stack. He hangs his lunch basket in the tops of the tallest trees, and when he wants a drink he reaches up and squeezes a cloud into his mouth.

This description of the tall man may be somewhat exaggerated, and we believe it is, but if any of the readers of this book want to believe that it is true, we shall not get mad about it.

THE TALL MAN OF CALLAWAY COUNTY.

CHASED BY INDIANS. — The horses belonging to the rangers who were stationed at Fort Madison during the Indian war, were allowed to graze upon the prairie, several of the men being detailed every morning to watch them and prevent them from straying away or being stolen or killed by the Indians. One morning three of the men—Morgan Bryan, Towning and Bays—were detailed to guard the horses. They left the fort about sunrise, and proceeded to the place where the horses were grazing, which was about five miles distant. That evening as they were returning to the fort they were fired upon at a distance of not over ten feet, by a party of Indians who were concealed behind a large log. Fortunately none of them were touched, and they at once started on a run for the fort. Bryan and Towning wore heavy boots, which greatly hindered them in running, but Bays had on a pair of buckskin moccasins and could run with the fleetness of a deer. Observing that his companions were falling behind, he sprang behind a tree and presented his gun at the pursuing Indians, who at once took shelter behind trees and began to reload their guns. It is proverbial that an Indian will never run upon a loaded gun, and knowing this Bays determined to save his two companions if possible. He held the Indians in check until they had passed him some distance, and then he ran ahead of them again, and stationed himself behind another tree until they came up and passed on, when he repeated the same maneuver, and kept it up until they all escaped to the fort, never allowing the Indians time enough to reload their guns. After having run some distance Bryan and Towning threw off their heavy boots and ran in their stockings, after which they had no difficulty in keeping up with Bays. The Indians followed them within half a mile of the fort, and then turned and fled.

JOSEPH LAMB, a pedagogue of early days in Warren and St. Charles counties, had an old brass watch that he thought a great deal of, but one day while binding wheat for Mr. Isaac Fulkerson he lost it, and it could not be found. About twelve months afterward Mr. Fulkerson was plowing in the same field, when suddenly he heard something go *tick, tick, tick,* in the furrow behind him. Thinking it might be a snake, he sprang to one side of his plow, very much frightened; but on looking back he saw Lamb's old brass watch ticking away as merrily as ever. It had never stopped running during the twelve months.

THE names of Revs. Jesse Walker and David Clark, the former a Methodist and the latter a Baptist preacher, are already familiar to the readers of this book. These two old fashioned ministers affiliated together, notwithstanding the wide difference between the two sects which they represented, and they would often travel together on foot through the settlements and hold religious services in the cabins of the pioneers. One day they were traveling from the settlements on the Femme Osage to the house of Mr. Flanders Callaway, near the present town of Marthasville, where they intended to hold a meeting. As they were crossing Femme Osage creek they were fired upon by some Indians, and one of the balls passed through Mr. Walker's hat, just grazing the scalp. They both ran, and were soon out of danger, as the Indians did not follow or fire at them again. Previous to that time, Mr. Walker had always declared that he was not afraid of Indians, but after that adventure he changed his mind, and was careful not to give them an opportunity to try their aim on him again.

THE END.

GENEALOGICAL INDEX

A

ABINGTON, HENRY . . . 185
" JOHN . . . 127
" SAMUEL . . . 215
ADAMS, EDMOND F. . . 256
" ELIZABETH . . . 395
" JAMES . . . 238
" JOHN . . . 304
" MARGARET . . . 281
" NANCY . . . 390
" POLLY . . . 390
" SALLY . . . 350
" WILLIAM . . . 252
ADAIR, JOSEPH . . . 303
" SALLY . . . 325
ADCOCK, JOHN . . . 303
" SARAH . . . 303
AGEE, MATTHEW . . . 302
" TILMAN . . . 302
AIKEN, J. H. . . . 200
AIKENS, POLLY . . . 365
ALDERSON, B. H. . . . 161
ALEXANDER, JAMES . . 171
" JOHN . . 197
" SALLY . . 138
" WILLIAM H. . 271
ALFORD, NANCY . . . 368
ALKIRE, BARBARA . . . 159
ALLEN, ANNA M. . . . 304
" ARCHIBALD . . 301
" CHARLES . . . 237
" DANIEL . . . 302
" DAVID . . . 302
" ELIZABETH . 311, 332, 377
" ELLEN N. . . . 302
" ELVIRAH . . . 304
" FRANCES . . . 184
" HARRIETT . . 238, 352
" JANE . . . 270, 320
" JOHN . . . 365, 412
" JOSEPH . . . 351
" LEAH . . . 393
" MARTHA L. . . 126
" MARY J. . . . 207
" MARY S. . . . 372
" NANCY . . . 365

ALLEN, PHOEBE . . . 403
" RUTH . . . 136
" SALLY E. . . . 304
" WILLIAM . . . 126
" WILLIAM M. . . 185
" ———— . . 369
ALLNUT, REBECCAH . . 326
AMBROSE, SALLIE . . . 291
AMOS, ELIZABETH . . . 356
ANDERSON, ALETHA . . 382
" ANNA . . . 281
" ELIZA . . . 335
" ELLEN . . 339
" HARRIETT J. . 203
" HENRY . . 369
" JAMES . . 267
" JANE . . 150
" JEMIMA . . 225
" JOHN . . . 239
" MARY . . . 239
" PATSEY . . 335
" PRESLEY . 238, 260
" REBECCAH . . 208
" ROBERT A. . . 197
" WILLIAM
225, 239, 243, 302
ANSEL, ROBERT . . . 306
APPLEBERRY, ELIZABETH . . 267
ARBUCKLE, KITTY . . . 351
ARCHER, CREED . . . 188
" CHARLES C. . . 206
ARLINGTON, REBECCAH . . 288
ARM, ROBERT . . . 357
ARMISTEAD, FRANKLIN . . 389
ARMSTRONG, ELIZABETH . 212
ARMSTRONG, THOMAS . . 302
ARNOLD, WILLIAM . . . 303
ARNOTT, ———— . . . 358
ASHBROOK, RACHEL . . 344
ASHLEY, MARY D. . . . 153
ASHWORTH, ELIZABETH . 334
ASKRENS, DENNIS . . . 332
ATKINS, ANNA . . . 413
ATKINSON, JOHN . . . 198
" MARY . . . 395

(529)

E

G

GREENWELL, JOHN . . . 263
GREGORY, GRANVILLE L. . . . 283
   "   HARRIET . . . 380
   "   R. F. 364
   "   WILLIAM . . . 336
GRESHAM, NANCY . . . 246
GRIFFITH, ASA 161
   "   ELIZABETH . . 319
   "   GREENBERRY . . 245
   "   MARY . . 176, 361
   "   SAMUEL . . . 152
GRIFFIN, GEORGE W. . . . 190
   "   JOHN 190
   "   SALLIE A. . . . 317
GRIGG, OBEDIENCE 242
GRIGGS, ELIZABETH . . . 412
   "   LOUISA 159
   "   RUTH A. . . . 219
   "   SARAH 262
   "   ———— . . . 213
   "   ———— . . . 409
GRIMES, ELIZABETH . . . 398
GRISWOLD, FREDERICK . . . 211
   "   HARVEY . . . 211
   "   SUSAN 224
GROOM, AARON 239

GROOM, JACOB 287
   "   POLLY A. . . . 260
   "   SALLY A. . . . 337
   "   SARAH 293
   "   WILLIAM . . 249, 260
GROSS, ELIZABETH 164
   "   KITTY 255
GROVER, CATHARINE M. . . 254
GRU, HANNAH 304
GRUB, RACHEL 203
GUDGELL, ELIZABETH . . 326
   "   POLLY 326
GUERDO, EVERETT W. . . . 225
GUERDON, REUBEN . . . 320
GUERRANT, MADALENE . . 356
GUIN, ELIZABETH . . . 362
GUION, LOUIS 123
GULLY, ELIZABETH . . . 412
GUNN, CALVIN 193
   "   CELIA 370
GUNNELL, CATHARINE . . . 307
GUTHRIE, FRANCES A. . . . 148
   "   ROBERT . . . 152, 159
   "   WILLIAM . . . 385
   "   ———— 192

H

HACKNEY, LUCY . . . 348
HADEN, ELIZABETH . . . 269
HAIL, SARAH . . . 377
HALL, A. 352
   "   DORCAS 250
   "   ELIZABETH . . . 285, 402
   "   FANNY 279
   "   HARIETTE 337
   "   JAMES 399
   "   JANE 305
   "   LAVINIA 402
   "   POLLY 264
   "   SALLIE T. 150
   "   SUSAN S. C. 310
   "   SARAH . . 173, 279, 318, 377
   "   SYDNEY 264
   "   WILLIAM . . . 264, 399
   "   WILLIS 306
HAM, JABEZ 265
   "   LUCY 379
   "   STEPHEN 265
HAMILTON, ANDREW . . . 317
   "   ANNA 394
   "   ARCHIBALD . . 346
   "   ELIZABETH . . 351

HAMILTON, FREDERICK . . 290
   "   JAMES . . . 365
   "   JOHN . . . 360
   "   JOHN H. . . . 347
   "   MARY . 165, 305, 313
   "   NANCY . . 301, 406
   "   SARAH . . . 351
   "   ———— . . . 214
HAMLET, SARAH . . . 272
HAMLIN, ELIZABETH . . . 377
   "   EMILY 377
   "   ORVA 377
   "   PERCY A. . . . 377
   "   PIERCY 303
HAMMOND, POLLY . . . 272
   "   THOMAS . . . 192
HAMPTON, MARY . . . 409
HANCE, ADAM 270
HANCOCK, BENJAMIN . . 160
   "   ELIZABETH . 159, 399
   "   F. A. . . . 295
   "   LEONORA . . . 241
   "   NANCY . . . 159
   "   WILLIAM . . . 214
HANFORD, NANCY . . . 298

I

J

K

M

Mc

Q

QUICK, ELIZABETH . . . 278
" JACOB 287
" RHODA 279

QUICK, SALLIE 261
" SARAH 241
" WILLIAM . . . 299

R

RAFFERTY, POLLY . . . 295
RALEY, ALICE 129
RALLSTON, MARGARET . . 308
RAMSEY, ESTHER 310
" HANNAH . . . 355
" INDIA 335
" JANE 269
" JOHN 172
" JONATHON . . 367
" POLLY MEEK . . 155
" SALLY D. M. . . 359
" WILLIAM . . . 183
RANDOLF, ELIZA. . . . 321
" JANE W. . . . 248
" MARY 327
" OBEDIAH . . . 368
" PETER 148
" ROBERT . . . 327
RAINFRO, PAULINA . . . 369
RALLEF, SUSAN 339
RAMER, ELIZABETH . . . 391
RANGE, LOUISA 255
RANKIN, ———— 255
RAPP, ESTHER 309
RATAKIN, ANN ELIZA . . 328
RATCLIFF, ATHA . . . 173
RATEKIN, JOHN . . . 366, 375
RATTSBURN, JOSEPH . . 225
RAWLINGS, ELIZA. . . . 378
" ELIZABETH . . 383
RAY, BENJAMIN D. . . . 409
RAYBORN, MARGARET . . 392
RAYMOND, EVELINE . . . 263
" ———— . . . 182
READ, ALEXANDER . . . 316
" ELIZABETH . . . 302
" MARY 309
" POLLY CHICK . . 316
" ROBERT 309
REDMAN, GEORGE W. . . 184
" MARTHA W. . . 369
REDMON, POLLY 402
REED, MARIA 359
" MARY 256
" PRISCILLA 282
" TOLIVER 407

REED, ZACKARIAH 408
REEDS, GABRIEL 242
" JALEE 348
REID, NATHANIEL 165
RENGO, HENRY 179
RENO, BAYLIS 327
" ELIZABETH 363
" FRANCIS 368
REYNOLDS, ANNA 320
" EDETHA . . . 282
" JOHN 409
" MARTHA . . . 320
" REBECCAH . . . 360
" SARAH . . . 414
" THOMAS . . . 410
" WILEY . . . 405
" WILLIAM . . . 368
RICE, AMANDA 320
" ANNA 288
" HANNAH 389
" MARIA 291
" SALLIE 218
" SCHUYLER . . . 209
" SHELTON 368
" WALTER 168
" WILLIAM B. . . . 288
RICHARDSON, POLLY . . 362
" SARAH . . 379
" ———— . . 359
RICHEY, JOHN 183
RIDDLE, SALLY 351
RIDDEN, SALLY 369
RIDGEWAY, MARTHA . . 404
" MARY . . 375
" NINNIAN . . 369
" WILLIAM . . 314
RIGGS, HANNAH 152
" JONATHON . . . 182
" MARY 294
RILEY, JOHN 367
" MARY 411
RIPPEY, FANNIE 399
" SALLIE 399
RIPLEY, RICHARD . . . 243
RIVES, POLLY 382
ROBBINS, MIRANDA . . . 173

T

Y

Z

GENERAL INDEX

TO

"PIONEER FAMILIES OF MISSOURI"

A

B

C

D

E

F